COMRADES AND COMMISSARS

COMRADES AND COMMISSARS

THE LINCOLN BATTALION
IN THE SPANISH CIVIL WAR

CECIL D. EBY

THE PENNSYLVANIA STATE UNIVERSITY PRESS
UNIVERSITY PARK, PENNSYLVANIA

Library of Congress Cataloging-in-Publication Data

Eby, Cecil D.
Comrades and commissars : the Lincoln Battalion in the
Spanish Civil War / Cecil D. Eby.
        p.   cm.
Includes bibliographical references and index.
ISBN-13: 978-0-271-02910-8 (cloth : alk. paper)
ISBN-10: 0-271-02910-2 (cloth : alk. paper)
1. Spain—History—Civil War, 1936–1939—Participation,
American.
2. Spain. Ejército Popular de la República. Abraham
Lincoln Battalion.
3. Americans—Spain—History—20th century.
I. Title.

DP269.47.A46E39 2006
946.081'373—dc22
2006030171

The Pennsylvania State University Press
is a member of the
Association of American University Presses.

It is the policy of
The Pennsylvania State University Press to use
acid-free paper. This book is printed on Natures Natural,
containing 50% post-consumer waste, and meets
the minimum requirements of American National
Standard for Information Sciences—
Permanence of Paper for Printed Library Material,
ANSI Z39.48–1992.

for CLARE, LILLIAN, *and* SHARON

my MORALE OFFICERS

CONTENTS

Spain in the Spring 1937

Bay of Biscay

Santan

Bur
FRAN
CAPIT

● Salamanca

Mac

Toledo

PORTUGAL

Tagus River

Lisbon ✪

Cordoba ●
Guadalquivir Riv

● Sevilla

Cadiz ●

Mala

ATLANTIC
OCEAN

> *When sorrows come, they come not single spies,*
> *But in battalions.*
> —Hamlet, *IV, v, 78*

> *Non hic Centauros, non Gorgonas, Harpyasque*
> *Ivenias, hominem pagina nostra sapit.*
> *[No centaurs here or gorgons look to find,*
> *My subject is of man and mankind.]*
> —*Robert Burton,* The Anatomy of Melancholy

The Lincoln Battalion numbered about twenty-eight hundred Americans who journeyed to Spain in groups of one hundred or fewer during 1937 and 1938 to join the Spanish Republic in its failed effort to subdue a right-wing coup led by General Francisco Franco. (About seven hundred and fifty died in Spain.)[1] Their exact number will never be known because some early volunteers were killed before they could be counted, and others traveled under aliases or *noms de guerre*, allowing them to be counted twice or not at all. Passage to French ports from New York was paid by the CPUSA (reimbursed by the Spanish Republic), except for a small number of stowaways and men crossing on their own. Once in France they passed into the custody of the CPF (Communist Party of France), which arranged passage to the central base of the International Brigades at Albacete. There the majority went into the newly organized Fifteenth Battalion of the XVth International Brigade, while the rest became medical orderlies, truck drivers, or base personnel. (Later an American artillery unit named the John Brown Battery saw limited action with obsolete German cannon on the Toledo front.)

So entrenched is the folk belief that once upon a time an Abraham Lincoln BRIGADE fought in Spain, that it borders on political sacrilege to report the sad truth that no such military unit ever existed—in Spain or anywhere else. To

---

1. Early in 1938 the commissariat listed and numbered all men currently in the Lincoln Battalion who were members of either the CP or the YCL. In all there were numbers for 2276, of which 1186 were named. Presumably the unoccupied 1090 spaces included men killed, missing in action, deserters, and non-Communists. Among the first arrivals nearly all were Communists. Later, when casualties reached shocking levels, the CPUSA realized that the Party was losing too many stalwarts and began recruiting among "idealists and adventurers"—especially college students—whose loss would be less important.

proclaim otherwise—whether through honest ignorance or intent to deceive—
is entirely false. Back to basics: In the Spanish civil war a brigade consisted of
from four to six battalions. There was, indeed, an Abraham Lincoln BATTAL-
ION, serving with other international battalions—French, Yugoslav, British,
Spanish, and Canadian—in the XVth International BRIGADE, one of several
international brigades, initially separated from regular Spanish brigades, and
administered by the Comintern. The reason why the Lincoln Battalion alone
was magnified into a whole brigade owed nothing to the men themselves (who
were fully occupied with other things, like fighting a war) but to publicists in
the CPUSA back in New York, who decided without permission from the Comintern or the Spanish government that the American commitment to the "War
against Fascism" being waged in Spain would be magically quadrupled in size
by altering a single word. History, as written by addicts of Communism, was
less a record of what really happened than of what ought to have happened. "To
enter into the details of inter-party politics," writes George Orwell, "is like diving into a cesspool."

Nearly forty years ago I wrote a book about American volunteers in the
Spanish Civil War titled *Between the Bullet and the Lie* (from George Orwell's
Homage to Catalonia). After its completion it never crossed my mind to write a
sequel. Enough was enough. But from all directions came heaps of new material: former combatants lodged their papers in university archives (most
notably, Brandeis, Illinois, and Adelphi), while the official records of the Lincoln Battalion, carried to Moscow after the war, were copied by the VALB (Veterans of the Abraham Lincoln Brigade) and archived at New York University.
Moreover, I had over the years corresponded with Spaniards who had read my
book after its translation into Spanish as *Voluntarios norteamericanos en la
guerra española* (1974). Their contributions, while rich and important, had
unfortunately arrived too late for use in my book. The most important of these
was a letter from a Valenciano named Fausto Villar Esteban, who faulted me on
some details about the battle of Segura de Los Baños (my version having relied
on the published testimony of a former Lincoln commander). As it happened,
Fausto Villar Esteban served from October 1937 to April 1938 as a draftee in the
Lincoln Battalion and had written a day-by-day memoir describing what he saw
and felt among the Americans, followed by a meticulous narrative of his two
years in Nationalist prisons after capture at Gandesa. He mailed me a copy with
permission to use it however I liked. His manuscript is a unique source of battalion history because for the first time we see how Spaniards—who were
largely written off as second-echelon comrades even though they eventually
outnumbered the Americans in the battalion—viewed their service in the

International Brigades. Villar denied the claim of CP publicists that native Spaniards eagerly sought to fight with the Internationals. Almost without exception they wanted places in all-Spanish units, where, if captured, they could expect a prison term, not execution on the spot—the usual fate of brigaders taken in battle. Fausto and I exchanged letters for five years until his death in 1996. I arranged for a copy of his manuscript to be archived in the Labadie Collection of the University of Michigan Graduate Library and began to think seriously about writing another book about the Lincoln Battalion. In a real sense, this book is a memorial for Fausto Villar.

Back in the 1960s research in Lincoln history was often a maddening experience, as though falling into a Lewis Carroll rabbit hole. Out there—somewhere in the American republic—were hundreds of veterans who might be interviewed, but how to obtain their names, addresses, phone numbers? After World War II, when the United States embarked on a purge of Communism, Lincoln veterans came under attack because an estimated 80 percent of them—Earl Browder's number—had at one time or another been members of either the YCL (Young Communist League) or the CP, although enthusiasm for the Party sagged after their return from Spain. Regarded as political automatons, they were hounded by what they called the "Federal Bureau of Intimidation" and feared that if they revealed openly and honestly what they knew, it would be construed as ratting on their former comrades and denigrating the nobility of the cause that had drawn them to Spain. As a result, the majority wanted to be left alone.

The obvious place for a researcher to begin was in New York with the executive secretary of VALB (Veterans of the Abraham Lincoln Brigade). He readily arranged meetings with veterans in the vicinity, but without fail he led me to men whose recollections conformed to what might be termed a rigidly canonical version of Lincoln history. Whenever I asked for addresses of veterans who had strayed from the fold—most notably because they had repudiated the CP—I met excuses. They were not available—ill health, no forwarding address, promises of anonymity, and so on. On the other hand, those who adhered to the Party line were usually available for interviews. Certain subjects were tabooed—rumors of wholesale desertions, prison terms for political deviants, jagged relationships with other Internationals, executions of volunteers. Had these things happened or not? Conversations with hard-liners often took this tack:

> "I'm interested in what happened."
> "You ought to be interested in *why* it happened."
> "I know why—but the 'what's' are scarcely known."
> "No need to know about them, if you understand *why*."

Or

"I want to record the experiences of the men in Spain."
"You miss the point—the men were nothing, the cause was
  everything."
"But there is no cause without the men."
"True—but the men were means to the higher end."

To write within the boundaries prescribed by VALB partisans is to enter a narrow space where mushy platitude and rusty propaganda have crowded out most of the air. "Assertion abounds," writes a historian of neutral ground, "but only infrequently is it buttressed by any more authority than an earlier assertion by a like-minded author."* Fortunately, on my own, after combing newspapers of the era, playing hunches, and placing hundreds of telephone calls, I found veterans willing to answer any question I might have.

Despite all the evasions and distortions, I never lost my admiration for these Americans who had shoved rhetoric aside in order to fight for a cause in which they believed, with matériel scavenged from dozens of countries, and in a place as remote for most of them as the moon. Their epitaph might read: "They fought well with what they didn't have." Any attempt to impose unity of thought or action on nearly three thousand men would be patently absurd. Instead, I choose to write a consensus narrative based upon scraps and fragments drawn from oral interviews and written narratives that do seem to say, "This is how it truly was."

ACKNOWLEDGMENTS

My major debt is owed to Peter Potter, former editor in chief and associate director of the Penn State Press, who encouraged and supported this project from the beginning. In the same spirit, I thank my present editor, Cherene Holland, and her able staff for transforming words into a book. Among the library staffs of research universities, I thank Lisa Long and Victor Berch at Brandeis University; Mary Burkee, Gene Rinkel, and Madeline Gibson at the University of Illinois; Gail Malmgren at New York University; and Elaine Gardstein and Gary Cantrell at Adelphi University.

No debts are owed to that corporate behemoth, the University of Michigan, which offered no financial assistance or other contribution, unless the permanent termination of my Internet account, without warning or explication, perversely qualifies as a "help." Fortunately, the flagship of humane letters is still afloat in Ann Arbor, at least in the administration of the Harlan Hatcher Graduate Library. In particular, I thank Julie Herrara in Rare Books and Grace York in Government Documents.

It is a particular pleasure to recall Robin and Sarah Strother King of Luxembourg, who carried me in their van in 2000 as we visited far-flung places in Spain associated with the Lincoln Battalion. James Hopkins of Southern Methodist University and Herbert Romerstein generously shared their copies of documents made in their research in Great Britain and Russia, respectively. Further, I was buoyed by the evaluations of my manuscript by Jim Hopkins and Stanley Payne of the University of Wisconsin. Two veterans of the XV International Brigade Fausto Villar Esteben gave me typed copies of their memoirs of the war—material never seen before except by the authors. The appendix in the book lists the names of other veterans whom I interviewed in person or by phone.

Finally, I acknowledge the spurs employed, in a slow period, by Gerald Linderman, Thomas Collier, and Michael Riordan during our Monday afternoons given over to solving all world problems.

1

GETTING THERE

After six months of war, parades and demonstrations barely ruffled the surface of downtown Barcelona. Whenever bands and cheering crowds occupied the Plaza de Cataluña and lightly shook the surrounding windows with anthems and vivas, only sporadic clerks at the United States consulate abandoned their desks. The reason for these disturbances was ever the same: International volunteers arriving from France or Catalan outfits departing for the front. But on January 6, 1937, Mahlon F. Perkins, the consul general, spotted from his window a sight never seen before in marches and rallies. Up the broad avenue came the Stars and Stripes, and behind it ambled about sixty men in an assortment of 1918 doughboy uniforms. They were lined up in four-front squads with their leader out in front, a .45 automatic strapped to his hip. Perkins watched in puzzlement as the group halted under his window and began singing "The Star-Spangled Banner." They probably sang as badly as they marched, but they knew the words to the second, and even to the third, stanzas.[1] The specter that had haunted the Department of State for the past three months had materialized under Perkins's window. Despite "the most scrupulous policy of nonintervention" in the Spanish cockpit, a policy spelled out by President Franklin D. Roosevelt and underlined, many times, by Secretary of State Cordell Hull, the first group of American volunteers had surreptitiously slipped into Spain.*

A clerk dispatched to screen the paramilitary band returned with the news that they were in Spain to "fight for their principles." Some claimed to be veterans of the World War; others were callow youths barely out of high school. As they marched off, one of them shouted, "We're just the beginning!" Consul Perkins had reason to recall this challenge on the following day when sixteen more Americans appeared, these carrying a blazing red banner marked "AMERICAN

---

*ED. NOTE: Throughout the text and footnotes, asterisks refer the reader to the Notes section (beginning on page 251), where corresponding citations are listed by the page upon which the asterisk appears.

1. A common notion during the 1930s was that if a man could recite the Declaration of Independence by heart or sing any stanza of "The Star-Spangled Banner" beyond the first, he was probably a member of the Communist Party.

BATTALION." A day later the consul counted twenty new arrivals, these carrying a red banner marked "ABRAHAM LINCOLN BATTALION."*

As yet, only a trickle of American volunteers was spilling across the French
frontier. Hopeful that the leak could be plugged and caulked, Perkins cabled
Washington, which on January 20 ordered consular representatives in France to
board each incoming liner and to stamp U.S. passports "NOT VALID FOR
TRAVEL TO SPAIN."* It became evident, however, that bureaucrats brandishing
rubber stamps would not intimidate men prepared to expose their flesh to Fascist bullets. When, for instance, Samuel A. Wiley, the consul at Le Havre, warned
sixty-five suspected volunteers arriving on the *S.S. Paris* that according to a 1909
statute, Americans who fought in a foreign war were liable to fines, prison terms,
and possible loss of citizenship, some of the miscreants laughed disrespectfully
and someone at the rear gave him the Bronx cheer.* Even before these volunteers had disembarked, an anonymous bard commemorated this confrontation:

> "The frontier's closed! You can't get through!"
> Were the words of the U.S. Consul.
> But all of us laughed, because we knew
> He was only flapping his tonsils.*

Powerless to dissuade them, Consul Perkins in Barcelona could do nothing
more than count them as they trooped through the city, singing and laughing
in their sheepskin jackets. These innocents were not privy to information available to Perkins, who had learned that hundreds of French volunteers had
deserted and descended upon Valencia and Barcelona, where they were
demanding sanctuary from their consuls. Earlier, the Republican authorities
had looked the other way when Internationals attempted to flee from Spain,
but recently they had threatened to punish foreign deserters exactly like their
own. So far as Perkins knew, the State Department had not formulated a policy
to cover American volunteers: Should they be accorded diplomatic protection,
or had they forfeited this privilege when they agreed to serve a foreign power?
With remarkable prescience, he summarized his views in a cable to Washington. "In view of the hardships which they will soon undergo, I am apprehensive
that some of them will be calling for assistance in the not distant future. I
should be glad to be informed of the Department's general attitude toward
the question of expatriation and loss of the right of protection of American citizens enlisting in the Loyalist armies."* Secretary Hull's response, on February
1, was unequivocal: protection should not be extended to United States citizens
who fought in Spain. Though the State Department had no power to prevent

Americans from traveling wherever they wanted to go, it had no obligation what-soever to protect those who violated the terms of their passports. Did this mean, Perkins inquired, that American volunteers were *not* to use the consulate as a mailing address? They most certainly were *not*. That was that. In time this pol-icy would bring grief to both disenchanted volunteers and overzealous consuls. By the end of January, three hundred Americans had crossed into Spain.

This hegira, which eventually drew more than thirty thousand volunteers from all over the world—about twenty-eight hundred of them Americans—was inspired by the events of November 1936. The army of General Francisco Franco had pushed into the outer *barrios* of Madrid and seemed on the verge of a final thrust that would carry it into the heart of the city and deal a deathblow to the Second Spanish Republic. Neutral journalists took refuge in their embassies and predicted Madrid was doomed. General Emilio Mola, second-in-command of the besieging army, announced that while four Nationalist columns converged upon the capital from outside, a "Fifth Column" of armed *provocateurs* prepared to strike from within. On November 7, 1936, *Mundo Obrero,* the Communist Party daily of Madrid, printed in red ink these headlines:

ALL OUT TO THE BARRICADES

THE ENEMY IS ACROSS THE RIVER

But in the days that followed, newspapers reported that a phalanx of foreigners had strengthened the trenches and barricades of the city. Forming well-disciplined lines, they buttressed Loyalist units hurling back Nationalist attacks in Carabanchel, the Casa del Campo, and University City. The XIth Interna-tional Brigade (their numbering system began with XI, not I), consisting of vol-unteers recruited by Comintern (Communist International) agencies in a dozen European countries, had come to the aid of Madrid, and despite repeated attempts by the Nationalists to break the defensive ring, the city held.

Fascism, rampant elsewhere in Europe and Asia, seemed blocked at the gates of Madrid. For anti-Fascists everywhere the moment was galvanic, the mood contagious. In the United States the question arose: What could one do to assist the Republic? The answer was simple and the apparatus ready—contribute to the North American Committee to Aid Spanish Democracy.[2] (Not, of course, to

2. The list of sponsors of this committee reads like a "Who's Who of the 1930s": Van Wyck Brooks, Martha Gellhorn, Rockwell Kent, Sinclair Lewis, Archibald MacLeish, Dorothy Parker, Elliot Paul, Elmer Rice, Upton Sinclair—to drop but a few names. It drew its support from old-fashioned liberals of the *Nation–New Republic* persuasion, men and women of goodwill who

the National Spanish Relief Association, created to support Franco's Catholic fiefdom.) Youths chafing for a more active role in defending Spanish liberty could enlist in the International Brigades, provided they had access to the right people in leftist political or trade-union organizations. No mere adventurers— or "romantics" as Party regulars disparagingly called them—need apply; nor, at this stage, were bourgeois hotbloods welcomed. (Only later, after horrific losses, did the Party open recruitment gates for political "unreliables.") At this stage, the ideal recruit was a youngish man with a proved—or at least promising— record in the Communist Party (CPUSA) or Young Communist League (YCL), but, on the other hand, not so promising that his death in Spain would be a major loss to the Party.[3] What the volunteers possessed, beyond ordinary men, was an unusual willingness to sacrifice personal ambition for a political ideal. Many were deceived about what they would find in Spain—and how difficult it would become to return home—but none were shanghaied into going. (The Soviet Union, on the other hand, encouraged five or six hundred Eastern Europeans to join the International Brigades with the implicit understanding that good work in Spain might result in eventual Soviet citizenship. This consideration carried no weight for Americans.) And the volunteers were so ideologically distant from mercenaries that nearly all of them expressed surprise, in Spain, when they learned that they would receive regular military pay—ten pesetas per diem (the average daily wage for a Spanish worker was only three pesetas). By contrast, the dozen American volunteers who flew in the Republican Air Force—none of them members of the International Brigades—received $1,000 per month with bonuses for enemy planes destroyed.

The Comintern provided the unifying structure for the International Brigades, ostensibly a militant wing of the Popular Front movement, which had been organized to draw in anti-Fascists in Western democracies—especially in France and England—as buffers against Nazi Germany. Initially Stalin was lukewarm about intervention in Spain. If Fascists and Republicans cut each others' throats fighting for a moribund "democracy," so much the better. What he did not want was a victory by any radical leftist faction, like the Trotskyists or Anarchists,

---

deplored the rise of Fascism. The State Department reported that less than half of the funds collected by relief groups ever reached Spain. Most effective was the Medical Bureau to Aid Spanish Democracy at 62 percent; the least effective was the American Committee for Spanish Relief at zero percent.*

    3. According to one volunteer, a "red-diaper" Communist, "No one told us that serving in Spain would advance us in the Party. They didn't have to. We all knew it." But this is not to imply that political ambition was always the major reason for fighting in Spain.*

because their revolutionary programs would be sure to alarm the Western Powers and give them second thoughts about supporting the Popular Front. Within the first week of the war, Moscow sent a directive to "preserve at any cost" the Popular Front façade and join the bourgeois government of the Republic. Georgi Dimitrov, who headed the Comintern, applied his rubber stamp but suggested ulterior motives: "We must act in the *guise* of defending the Republic. . . . When our positions have been strengthened, then we can go *further*."* At the Seventh Congress of the Comintern in August he made it clear that the real purpose of the Popular Front was defense of the USSR, but its policy of exporting revolution had been shelved.* It would support the Spanish Republican army, but not the workers' militia, which would be difficult to control because it backed revolutionary policies. In the same month, Alexander Orlov arrived to set up the NKVD apparatus charged with purging revolutionary Marxist opposition.*

In late July 1936, only two weeks after the Franco coup, the Comintern and Profintern met in Prague with Dimitrov in the chair and set aside a thousand million francs in order to form and arm a brigade of five thousand men to fight under their umbrella in Spain, the funds to come from donations from anti-Fascists in the world at large. Volunteers would assemble in Paris, where the Communist Party of France (CPF) would make arrangements for transportation to Spain. Within weeks of the call, the first volunteers began to arrive, eager to join the fight against Fascism, even though the Spanish Republic had not been informed of this unexpected windfall. (A small number of foreigners like George Orwell arrived under the auspices of other left-wing organizations, but only as isolated free agents, not as members of a powerful international bloc like the Communist Party.)[4] Eventually men from fifty-three countries passed through the Maison des Sindicates in the Batignolles quarter on their way to Spain.[5]

Responsibility for organizing the International Brigades from the ground up fell to Luigi Longo (*nom de guerre*—"El Gallo"), a Comintern heavy hitter from

---

4. Many of these early volunteers, mainly Germans and Italians, had come to Barcelona in July for a Workers' Olympiad, a protest against the Berlin Olympics then in progress. They joined whatever paramilitary group recruited them. Their isolation and subsequent persecution by Communists is graphically rendered in Orwell's memoir, *Homage to Catalonia*, which traces his own service with the POUM, a putative Trotskyist centuria and his near death when that party was purged by the Communists in May 1937.

In the fall of 1936 an Italian American anti-Fascist committee based in New York called for three hundred men to join a Garibaldi Column in Spain. Captain Umberto Galleani, a World War veteran, traveled to Spain to make arrangements.* When his efforts came to nothing, the Italian American volunteers already in Spain, including Galleani, had to join the International Brigades.

5. Originally, in-transit volunteers were housed in the Ancien Militaire Hospital, abandoned in 1931, but after France joined the Non-Intervention Pact, they had to be farmed out to small hotels and rooming houses in the quarter.*

Italy destined to become its inspector general.* (In the 1960s he would serve five years as the secretary-general of the Communist Party of Italy [CPI].) In early October, while André Marty, the head of the International Brigades, thrashed out details with the CPF, Longo set off for Spain. His mission was to inform the Republic that the Comintern had sponsored an army and to arrange for a permanent base. At Figueras, a fortress town near the frontier, he found hundreds of volunteers milling about unsupervised and restless. Each train brought new recruits. The local authorities allowed them to camp in the dungeons of the fortress but refused to feed them. In Barcelona the Partido Socialista de Unificación Cataluña (PSUC)—a Communist splinter—offered Longo assistance but only on condition that the men join Catalan units and not continue on to Madrid. Because Barcelona was a hotbed of the quasi-Trotskyist Partido Obrero de Unificación Marxista (POUM) and the Anarchist Confederación Nacional del Trabajo (CNT), this was out of the question. The Comintern had no intention of abetting the regional fragmentation already evident in Spain with formation of autonomous republics in both Catalonia and the Basque Country. Longo raced on to Madrid, which offered him even less. Largo Caballero, the Socialist prime minister, distrusted Communists and shuttled him from office to office in a pointless bureaucratic game. The government seemed riddled with apathy and defeatism even though the sounds of approaching artillery fire clearly charted the advance of Franco's Army of Africa, whose Tercios de Extranjeros (Spanish Foreign Legion) and Fuerza Regulares Indígenos (Moroccans) easily outflanked makeshift roadblocks thrown up by *milicianos* and sent them flooding to the rear. (It was said that the *milicianos* never saw the backs of the Moors until the Internationals arrived.)* The mood of the Republic was characterized by the minister of war, who opined that Madrid, a city of nearly a million inhabitants, was more easily attacked than defended, a ludicrous theory since the highest estimate of Franco's strength stood at fewer than twenty-four thousand men.

By all odds the most disciplined and effective fighting unit in the Republican Army was the so-called Fifth Regiment, recruited by the Communist Party of Spain (CPE). It quickly outgrew its regimental size and by the end of the year contained more than forty thousand men. This regiment had a local base at Albacete and offered it to Longo, who had been informed on October 10th that five hundred volunteers chafed at Figueras, and another five hundred were coming by boat from Marseilles. At 4 a.m. on October 12, Longo reported to the headquarters in Albacete, where a sentinel refused to admit him because his officers never rose until nine. Once aroused, however, they moved efficiently. Two days later the first volunteers arrived by train and on average two hundred more reported every day thereafter. Without the assistance of the Fifth Regiment the International Brigades would have been stillborn.

Longo faced a nearly impossible task. Facilities in Albacete were nearly nonexistent. There was no water for washing, no blankets or mattresses, though the nights were bitterly cold. The first volunteers slept in the *plaza de toros,* huddling together to conserve body heat. They spent all day in lines waiting for food and had to share plate and spoon with two other comrades. By the time a man finished breakfast he joined another line for dinner. Longo's entire autopark consisted of three motorcycles and a couple of autos belonging to individual volunteers. Somehow he had to organize and classify "thousands of men diverse in temperament, customs, attitudes and political orientation."* Adding to his problems was a babel of tongues. At group meetings the national commissars sat according to language, all facing an interpreter. With the keynote speaker and a dozen interpreters all talking at once, the room became a gibbering madhouse.* In this sea of faces it was impossible to identify qualified commanders. After one volunteer pulled from his satchel the uniform of an Albanian colonel, he became a company commander until exposed as a mere tailor from Lyon.* At Albacete the volunteers had no uniforms, no weapons, no evidence that they were soldiers. Finally Madrid sent down piles of surplus Tercio uniforms, but when the volunteers realized their "Fascist" provenance, they refused to wear them and they had to be sent back.*

Longo devised a master plan calling for five hours of military instruction every day, but he admitted this was impossible to achieve. (It included two-and-a-half hours of "political theory" and collective work.) He had to listen to men grousing—"What are we doing here? I came to fight Fascists, not to walk the streets of Albacete." They were not an army but a mob. In Valencia two hundred new arrivals were denied permission to make a triumphal march through the city on the grounds that the nonintervention policy would forbid it, although the real reason was that they looked like a mob of ragged derelicts, not proud liberators.* The worst cases were in the French contingent (15 percent had to be rejected), which included men over fifty and children under sixteen, the sweepings of shelters and orphanages. Judges often gave suspended sentences to defendants who agreed to go to Spain, and TB cases were told that their health would improve under the Spanish sun.* The incidence of drunkards was always higher among the French; apologists blamed it on the daily ration of Spanish wine, which contained 4 percent more alcohol than back home.

Longo installed a draconian police system designed not only to maintain order but also to counteract "sabotage and sedition."* He deplored the attitude held by many volunteers that decisions came from below, not from above. To his amazement, men overruled the decisions of their superiors and insisted on settling difficulties by voting! In his view, "Military discipline differed from democratic discipline."* Any competent military leader would have agreed, but Longo's recipe went further. On October 16—only two days after the first arrivals at the base, he created the commissar system. (As a sop to anti-Communists in the government they were called, at this juncture, "commissars of war" not "political commissars.") Commissars outranked military commanders, who were only "technocrats." While their avowed purpose was to inculcate liberal values, their real purpose was political indoctrination. In his own words—the commissar had to be "an apostle of strong discipline, rigorous, serious, *capable of uncovering the work of enemy spies.*"* One surefire way of identifying spies was to finger anyone who sowed confusion by questioning what they were doing there, encouraging men to transfer into Anarchist or Trotskyist units, or—the paramount crime—talking about "Communist terror" in Spain or the USSR.[6]

By the first of November 1936, André Marty, the commander of the International Brigades, could report to Stalin that the Albacete Base had collected three thousand men—80 percent of them Communists or Socialists.* Earlier he had denounced the Anarchists in Spain, who were appropriating raw materials in factories for their private use; the engineers at the factories dared not intervene, fearing denunciation as Fascists. Marty had a long-term solution to the Anarchist problem: "After victory we will get even with them, all the more so since at that point we will have a strong army."*

Despite this pandemonium, in less than one month Longo cobbled together four battalions, each loosely based on national lines, which became the XIth International Brigade.[7] Beginning on October 22 the battalions were farmed out to different villages for basic military instruction. Then ten days later they received their first weapons—rifles of different makes and calibers, along with some machine guns predating the World War. But this grubstake training program ended abruptly on November 5, when orders arrived to move all available Internationals, with or without training, to Madrid, where the Nationalists were pushing into the southern *barrios.* A day later the government abandoned

---

6. The June 1937 issue of the *Boletín* of political commissars of the International Brigades "urged weeding out deviants and to maintain constant vigilance toward defeatist elements, Trotskyites and deserters."*

7. These were the Commune de Paris (French and Belgian), the Edgar André (German and Austrian), the Garibaldi (Italian), and the Dombrowski (Polish and Hungarian). The numbers XI to XV had originally been reserved for new brigades of the Fifth Regiment, which surrendered them to the International Brigades.

the capital to a Junta of Defense and fled to the safety of Valencia. Leaving the Italian battalion behind as a nucleus for new arrivals, the XIth Brigade, commanded by "General" Emil Kléber (Lazar Stern), a Red Army officer, rushed to the defense of Madrid. To arouse civilian morale, he marched his Internationals along the Gran Via, where crowds hallooed "¡Rusia! Rusia!" Soon the leftist press began to attribute the successful defense of Madrid to the International Brigade. The XIth Brigade fought well and hard, but the worldwide publicity campaign to attribute the successful defense of Madrid to a single unit nettled Spanish commands whose efforts and sacrifice were greater but not publicized. Ultimately Kléber's success backfired, for it led to his being branded as an "adventurer" and, after several later failed operations, to his recall to Moscow and his execution.

Just as the Comintern had organized the International Brigades and set up an International Control Committee in Paris, so the CPUSA founded the Abraham Lincoln Battalion as its contribution to the fight against Fascism shaping up in Spain. The Party had no intention of dipping into its coffers to finance the battalion. Instead, money would be raised through "front" organizations like the North American Committee to Aid Spanish Democracy, whose members in most cases would not know that they were supporting the battalion, much less that the CPUSA was whistling the tune that both of them danced to. It was a well-oiled mechanism: the Party would provide an apparatus for shipping men to Spain and would, in the end, take all the credit, provided there was credit to take. In the name of anti-Fascist fervor, the "sympathizers" picked up the tab.

Because November 1936 was a month of strikes along the New York waterfront and among the garment workers, a large percentage of the first American volunteers came from these trades. Recruitment was a hush-hush affair. A second-generation Communist named Bill Harvey (Horwitz), who worked as a furrier, happened to be talking with his union boss about Spain and burst out with "Boy, would I love to be there!" He forgot about it until a week or so later, when he received a letter in a plain envelope. Inside was an onionskin, without address or signature, which read: "Please appear on the Ninth Floor"—adding a date. The "Ninth Floor" was the headquarters of the Central Committee of the CPUSA on East 13th Street—"an inner sanctum, a holy place." At the appointed time Harvey faced a screening battery of five men. The leader seemed to be Fred Brown (Alpi), a former Italo-Austrian who had attended the Lenin Institute in Moscow (where he worked with Bela Kun, the deposed Hungarian Soviet leader) and who now served as the Comintern's representative to the CPUSA. Brown, a hearty bear of a man with a goatee trimmed in cosmopolitan style, exuded the urbane charm of an old-world aristocrat, which he was not. Beside him sat a dour figure wearing rimless spectacles who peered intently from a prune-face bearing the scars of an ancient acne battleground. This was the military adviser, Captain Allan Johnson (McNeil), a former U.S. Army officer with overseas service (as a payroll officer in the Philippines). Next in line was Charles Krumbein of the Political Committee, a prime mover in the Party. The other two were easily forgettable functionaries—little Osrics with high-sounding titles like "Secretary of the New York Committee of the Communist Party of the United States of America" and the like. They queried Harvey politely, making notes at suitable moments. Then Captain Johnson shot a question at him, "Have you ever fired a rifle?" "I have," Harvey replied, recalling a shooting gallery at Coney Island. A few days later he was thrilled when a message arrived, once again on unsigned onionskin, telling him that he had been accepted.* Morris Mickenberg (Maken) another interviewee, remembered that when he told the committee about his brief service in a Brooklyn unit of the National Guard, the captain leaped up and barked out "Attention! . . . Left Face!" and other commands for the edification of the committee, which promptly approved him. "That demonstrated I had real professional military experience."*

Every night for several weeks the chosen few drilled at the Ukrainian Hall down on East Third Street. Guards at the door told them to keep their mouths shut. During rest periods, Party hammers like Earl Browder, the secretary-general, and Jack Stachel, director of the maritime section, made brief speeches explaining how they were the vanguard of an American working-class army privileged to open their war against World Fascism on the battlefields of Spain. A special treat was the arrival of Ralph Bates, an English novelist and IB commissar, who alone among the visitors had actually been to Spain. Clad in a resplendent Republican uniform (which he surely did not wear on the streets of New York), Bates was a spellbinder. "He looked like he was ten feet tall," recalled one recruit. "He almost made us feel that we were being strafed by a Fiat and bombed by Capronis." The theme of his speech was that the Fascists were cowards and ran away. He told them that in Spain they must not say they were Communists. "From now on," and he winked at them, "you are all just Anti-Fascists." This puzzled some of the regulars. "Why conceal it? We thought we ought to *proclaim* it."*

One night their leaders were introduced, both selected by higher-ups in the Party. Phil Bard, political commissar, would be in charge of the group until they reached Spain and began training, at which time James Harris, military commander, would take over.[8] Bard was a cartoonist for *Young Worker,* the official newspaper of the YCL, a position somehow more suitable for this quiet man in his late twenties than leader of revolutionaries shipping out to war. Pale, thin, and asthmatic, Bard was a pushover for volunteers cast from rougher molds. One of the seamen later complained that the world of Phil Bard was bounded "by a subway ride from the Bronx to Union Square, with an occasional trip to Brooklyn." Not quite true, for Bard had once worked as a CP organizer in the Ohio National Guard. (The Party had censured him when he refused to distribute some antimilitarist leaflets demanding that corporal punishment be abolished in the three-week summer camp, despite his protests that no such punishment existed.) His masterpiece was a five-hundred-square-foot mural at the *Daily Worker* office titled "Capitalism in the USA." (He was against it.)

By contrast, James Harris (Jackson) was a Polish-American seaman rumored to be an ex-Marine sergeant who had fought in China as an adviser to the People's Army.[9] He was solidly built, sandy-haired, unassuming, and almost inarticulate. To the seamen he seemed like a bona fide proletarian—not a bookish Union Square radical. He gave instruction in about-face and parade-arms to the original cadre, mainly seamen like himself, each day leavened by beardless youths from the Bronx YCL eager to learn how to kill Fascists. Out-of-towners began to arrive, largely from Boston and Philadelphia. They were put up at the Sloane YMCA on 34th Street and given $1.50 per diem maintenance allowance. Shortly before Christmas, about a hundred of the most promising men were separated from the others and informed that they would sail in a few days on the *Normandie.* The hall erupted in a melee of thumping, stamping, and cheering. They were divided into ten squads. Absolute secrecy had to be maintained. Men could not communicate with their families or volunteers in other squads, and only squad leaders were permitted to speak with Commissar Bard. And above all, there was to be no drinking! They were issued ten-dollar bills and instructed how to purchase passports. (The Party arranged for men without U.S. birth

8. The political commissar could overrule the military commander when ideological issues took precedent over military decisions. Commissars had been instituted in Soviet armies to counteract real or imagined bourgeois attitudes held by professional military officers. However, one long-term Lincoln veteran defined their role as "thought control agents, intellectual policemen."*

9. Credentials more easily doubted than disproved. Repeated letters to the Military Personnel Records Center, requesting confirmation or repudiation of prior military service claimed by (or—more likely—for) men who fought in Spain, brings nothing more tangible than brochures such as "Records in the National Archives Relating to Confederate Soldiers." A foolish secrecy is a trait apparently shared equally by the hierophants of the U.S. government and the Communist Party of the United States (CPUSA).

certificates to obtain Spanish passports.) They invented fanciful reasons for traveling out of the country—visiting an uncle in South Africa, completing art work in Poland, studying theology in Palestine. Mentioning Spain was an absolute no-no. *Noms de guerre* were common but by no means universal; many young men just wanted to keep parents from finding where they were going.[10]

Following a timetable designed to space them at wide intervals—to throw off Federal "spies"—an "old man in his late thirties" named Akalaitis led different groups to an Army-Navy store under the Third Avenue El, near 14th Street, to purchase fifty dollars' worth of equipment per man from the store owner, a Party sympathizer not unwilling to mix profit with politics. In identical black cardboard suitcases, bound with yellow straps, the recruits packed away a random collection of army surplus—khaki-twill shirts, overseas caps, pants with roll-up puttees, woolen mittens, and fleece-lined jackets. With their own money, some bought sheath knives and even long-tubed gas masks, musty with the smell of dead rubber. (Morris Mickenberg had his first doubts about the "much vaunted efficiency of the Communist Party," when he observed that everybody in his "secret" group carried identical black suitcases.)* Back at the hall they tried on their uniforms, and most threw away their leggings, which unraveled down to the ankles. "I could not imagine myself on the battlefield advancing with rifle in one hand and holding up my leggings with the other."* A few brazen souls went uptown and opened charge accounts at fancy men's stores. "The better the store, the more gullible they were," remembered a ringleader of this raiding party. The theory was that they would worry about paying when they returned, and if they failed to return, how could they be sued? A pair of boots from Abercrombie and Fitch lasted one volunteer the whole war.

They were to sail on December 26. Party chieftains held a clandestine *bon voyage* celebration (sans alcohol) in the Second Avenue Yiddish Theater near CP headquarters a few hours before they embarked. Each man got a parcel containing a carton of Lucky Strikes (favored by the Party because of the "strike" nuance), a Gillette razor, two cakes of Palmolive soap, and a tin—little white stars on a navy blue background—of G. Washington coffee (an early "instant"). They were handed third-class tickets issued by World Tourists, Inc., a Manhattan outfit specializing in trips to the Soviet Union. (No one asked who paid for their passage because everyone knew.) Further, each man received a ten-dollar

10. The proliferation of aliases among the volunteers, for political and idiosyncratic reasons, has made an accurate count of veterans impossible. Many men were recent immigrants—some without final citizenship papers—whose names had not been writ in stone. Others were killed or had deserted before the brigade recorded their names. No exact number of American volunteers can be known, but twenty-eight hundred have been certified.*

bill to cover shipboard expenses—*no drinking!*—including tipping, a repugnant bourgeois affectation but necessary to buttress the fiction that they were just tourists. Before arriving at Le Havre they were to receive fifteen dollars apiece to prove to port authorities they were not vagrants—but this money had to be returned to Commissar Bard as soon as they cleared customs. As a symbol of his authority, James Harris packed away an Army .45 automatic, but no one else was permitted weapons. If they were asked where they were going in France, they should say they were bound for the Paris Exposition. (It apparently occurred to no one that the exposition would not open until that summer.) They signed no agreement or contract about how long they would serve in Spain—an oversight that would plague many of them later.

Like parachutists bailing out of airplanes, they left the theater one by one at regular intervals. Earl Browder, a cigar clamped in his jaws, stood near the door and shook each man's hand. One volunteer recalled his surprise at finding that Browder's hand was soft, warm, a little gummy—not the hand of a working-man. They went off to war on the uptown subway, the nickel coming from their own funds. No family or friends waited at the pier to see these tourists off on their Grand Tour. At the last minute, four men changed their minds, dropping their number to ninety-six.[11] There were no roistering send-offs or political speeches. The men obeyed their instructions—to be as inconspicuous as possible. It was ironic that in order to risk one's life for a noble cause, one had to be careful not to run afoul of the law.*

With the thermometer steady at sixty-two degrees, it was winter-cruise weather as the *Normandie* cast off its lines at 3 p.m. on December 26, 1936, carrying the first group of American volunteers to the Spanish civil war. It was Saturday, the city seemed empty and quiet except for the bells of Trinity Church on Wall Street. Their backgrounds defy generalization. Aboard were a Negro county-fair wrestler and fisherman from Provincetown, a Japanese-American cook from the West Coast, a New York furrier, a *Daily Worker* columnist, an Armenian carpet-salesman, a City College soccer star, a U.S. Army deserter, a Texas redneck, a Russian-American stowaway, and a self-pitying Greenwich Village aesthete who told everyone he expected to die. (Despite propaganda written by Franco's journalists, their ranks included no "members of the old Capone mob.")[12] Yet this summary suggests only where they had come from,

11. The count of this first group is usually given as ninety-six. In Barcelona, Consul Perkins counted seventy-six. Unfortunately, the passenger list compiled by the Department of State at Le Havre is incomplete and does not differentiate between those bound for Spain and other travelers.*

12. A Nationalist pamphlet, published in 1940, characterizes the Lincoln Battalion: "Its armament was excellent; its equipment, perfect; its human material, deplorable. The combatants were Negroes

not what they believed. Far from being the dregs of the lumpenproletariat, these men comprised an activist elite—the sort who had grown up taking by instinct the side of the runt in schoolyard fights. Without exception this first contingent were all members of the CPUSA or the YCL, united in their hatred of Fascism in all its myriad forms—whether resulting from politics, economics, or racism. As a black volunteer in the next shipload put it, "I wanted to go to Ethiopia and fight Mussolini. . . . This ain't Ethiopia, but it'll do."*

Many had been to sea as sailors, but passenger experiences were a novelty. (An exception was a later volunteer, Sam Levinger, a rabbi's son from Ohio, who at the age of fourteen had visited Hitler's Brown House wearing a Boy Scout uniform.) About a third of them were a hard-core group from maritime unions, all fiercely loyal to each other and somewhat condescending to "the snot-noses of Union Square," who got their revolutionary fervor out of books. On board were some of the longshoremen who had torn down the Nazi flag of the *Bremen* while it was docked in New York. In that ruckus they had taken—and shed—blood in the fight against Fascism. A handful or so had acquired some military training in the lazy peacetime army of the National Guard. Douglas Seacord, said to have taught gunnery at West Point, had drilled them in bayonet technique back at the Ukrainian Hall using broomsticks.[13] Joe Gordon (Mendelowitz), a man's man and a Communist's Communist, had learned more about fighting as a youth in the Williamsburg district of Brooklyn than in the U.S. Horse Artillery, from which he had recently deserted after the Party decided he would be more valuable as a soldier in Spain than as an organizer at Fort Meade. The national guardsmen among them consisted of CP infiltrators like Tony DeMaio, a sullen hard-wire from Hartford. A few had taken courses at the Workers' School, downstairs in Party headquarters, on how to organize Communist Party cells in the U.S. armed forces. One graduate, a seaman named Robert Gladnick, had been a mole at Randolph Field in Texas. Though he had never had military training, at least he had an osmotic taste of military environment.[14]

---

from Broadway, Chinese from the ports of New York and Los Angeles, gangsters from Chicago, and militants from the Communist cells of Philadelphia. This battalion also included American Indians. For enlisting, each man was given a large sum of money—some four hundred dollars, at least."*

13. In describing the prewar activities of American volunteers flying under CP colors, the expression "said to have been" is probably more accurate than "was" in most cases. The Party favored propaganda over historical fact. If a comrade's biography contained details that promoted the Party, these would be used; if not, they would be concealed.

14. Before this, Gladnick had propagandized the U.S. Fleet at San Pedro, California. One assignment entailed sneaking copies of an antimilitarist, pro-Communist book titled *Kaiser's Coolies* aboard the USS *Pennsylvania*. On visitors' day he found that the book was already shelved in the ship library stamped, "Property of the US Navy."*

Compared with these warriors, the Jewish college students and intellectuals aboard the *Normandie* were abysmally green sprouts. All had done their stint on picket lines and were up on Party theory, but few had ever fired a rifle. A major reason they gave for volunteering was "to take a crack at Hitler." They had been told—and had read over and over in the *Daily Worker*—that German storm troopers reinforced Franco's army. This racial dimension of the war was lost upon the contingent from Boston, Irishmen like the Flahertys and their friend Paul Burns, a labor writer pushing middle age. For them Fascism was simply a reactionary political movement bent upon destroying the hard-won gains of the working class. It had to be eradicated in Spain before it spread like a virus through the soft-rot of the Western democracies. They were weary—and wary—of ballot boxes and picket lines; they wanted to confront the enemy head-on, with steel. The war in Spain offered a special taste for each palate. Most would have echoed the explanation of one volunteer, "Going was as natural as eating."*

A winter crossing in a Depression year: they pretty well had the boat to themselves. The ex-sailors and longshoremen, having just left the NMU kitchens of the New York waterfront, where they had dined on leftovers from the Fulton and Washington fish markets, reveled in the French cuisine aboard the ship. Defying Bard's strictures against drinking, they put away bottles of wine at meals and argued that teetotalers made lousy soldiers. Moreover, in scouting the ship they discovered that statuesque girls of the Folies Bergères were aboard. Despite Bard's admonition that these girls were bourgeois parasites—hadn't Lenin warned against "drinking from a public cup"?—the seamen stormed second class. More than one among this waterfront crowd had served time in the "Rough Riders Ward"—the VD clinic of the Marine Hospital on Staten Island. A dose was a dose was a dose. They had no money but soon established mutual interests among the Folies girls, many of whom reminisced about ancestors buried in the Communard cemetery. The seamen, if their tales contained even a grain of truth, broke sexual records with the girls on their crossing. Probably this was one of the few times in history when French girls bought drinks for American soldiers.*

Even though it must have been perfectly clear to everyone aboard who they were and where they were going, Commissar Bard continued to behave as though the ship were infiltrated with spies. Whenever the men gathered together in groups of more than five, he dispatched Bobby Pieck, his eighteen-year-old assistant, to whisper commands to disperse. (Pieck was the nephew of Julius Deutsch, once commander of the private Austrian Socialist Army, the Schutzbund.) The men whiled away their hours at poker—playing for matches, not money, because gambling was a capitalist vice—at muscle-building exercises, and in thumbing dog-eared ROTC manuals (which explained how to shoot down an airplane with a rifle). In a crowded, tiny cabin deep in the bowels of the ship, "Robert Raven drove us nuts when he insisted on practicing his close-order drill in the room."* Some joker dreamed up stories to needle Bard. He told him that the French had a 300 percent duty on new shoes: this meant that the four-dollar brogans would be taxed twelve dollars each at Le Havre. "With the ten bucks we got, that puts us two in the hole." Bard ordered the men to break in their shoes "so they will look second-hand when we go through customs." On the next day nearly a hundred men in business suits tramped the decks of the *Normandie* shod in identical army boots. The Folies girls thought it was hilarious.*

Yet halfway across, the purser posted a newsflash for their benefit: Chairman McReynolds of the House Foreign Affairs Committee had declared he would urge the Department of Justice to apply the section of the Criminal Code providing a $3,000 fine or a year in prison for enlistment of Americans in a foreign war.*[15] Bard's face wore a strained "I told you so" expression. To be arrested at Le Havre and extradited would be an ignominious defeat for the International Brigades and the Party. Infantry manuals and other incriminating documents went out of portholes.

At Le Havre, customs officers in pillbox caps winked at the volunteers and passed them through without looking into their identical black suitcases. Some even whispered "Vive la République!" It was New Year's Eve, and the Americans wondered how big a time they could have in Paris on a couple of dollars. To their disappointment, they were scattered to boarding houses and dingy hotels in the port area for two days because earlier arrivals had swamped the facilities of the Paris Control Committee. They pored over American newspapers left behind by the crew of the *Washington,* just sailed—there was the "sit-down" strike in Michigan, where thirty-four thousand workers occupied seven General Motors plants and defied the capitalists to evict them. Later they got an introduction to international trade-unionism when some seamen led them into the red-light district, where "women of all dimensions in fish-net robes and nothing else on"* picked coins off tables with their labia and later showed them that they, too, possessed union cards. Some distributed calling cards like "Mme Rose—Specialties." (In the second shipload of Americans, some men contracted VD and were deported from Spain—which probably saved their lives.) Fifteen

---

15. A month later the State Department invoked a 1907 law according to which American citizens serving as combatants for a foreign power could be fined not more than $1,000 or sentenced for up to three years in prison. At the same time, a House committee introduced a bill to deprive such persons of U.S. citizenship.*

Americans missed the Paris train on January 2. Vahram Kevorkian, a French-speaking Armenian who had once hawked "oriental" rugs of Belgian manufacture to bargain-hunters in Paris, stayed behind to round up the stragglers, while Commissar Bard shepherded the main body to Paris.

There was no hoped-for Paris leave. After a free meal—bad enough to be commented on at the time and good enough to be recalled in the lean months ahead—they were shunted across the city to the Gare de Lyon by an irascible guide whose only English seemed to be "Americans! Shut up!" and boarded #77, the night train to Perpignan, popularly called "le chemin de fer des Brigades International," or, more locally, "The Red Express." (A month later, when French frontier posts closed and volunteers had to reach Spain by hiking over the Pyrenees, railroad routes for volunteers were changed frequently to evade police surveillance.) The third-class compartments were crammed with hundreds of International volunteers: factory workers from Milan, purse-lipped refugees from Germany, cement-jawed Slavs, blonds with rucksacks from the Baltics. For many of them everything they possessed after half a lifetime of labor lay wrapped in small paper parcels held between their knees. The babel of strange languages spilled over onto the platforms outside, where hundreds of cheerful French well-wishers saw them off. It was a heady moment. A foreign volunteer asked Joe Gordon his nationality. "Juif," he replied. Robert Gladnick, a natural polyglot who spoke Russian by birthright and English from American schools, was already conversing in Italian and Polish to the foreign volunteers. As the train pulled from the station men were singing "The International" in a dozen languages. The words were different but the melody and the message were universal. French men and women ran alongside the train to grab their hands, throwing kisses and wishing them luck and victory. The volunteers were the wave of the future, drops in the tide of international unity. When Gordon began to sing the Zionist anthem, "Hatikvah," he was joined by hundreds of voices from all the cars of the train, despite the anti-Zionist plank of the CP. As the train rolled south in the dark, long sausages strung from luggage racks like a line of hanged men wobbled from side to side.*

At daybreak a vast river, the Rhone, appeared out of mist. In the frost-rimed fields, workers in blue jackets and black berets pruned dark vines rising like claws from the red earth. Bonfires of vineyard cuttings lighted the way to Spain. Beyond Valence, they felt the nearness of the Mediterranean as the train glided past honey-colored villas on terraced hillsides and spiky palmettos dotting village squares. Leaning from open windows and basking in the warm sun, volunteers raised the Popular Front fist to bicyclists waiting at crossings as they clattered past. Avignon was a fleeting glimpse of a saw-toothed castle and a broken bridge. Béziers was a working-class town on a steep hill like Wilkes-Barre, where they bought bottles of red wine and huge sandwiches stuffed with an oleaginous substance that looked like raw ham but tasted like raw bacon. Beyond Narbonne the tracks ran across salt flats beside the sea, and a lookout called from the window. "Hey, I see the Pyrenees!" In this region, the populace, accustomed to volunteers and bored by the tangled webs of Spanish politics, seldom bothered to wave back. From the railroad yard at Perpignan a French guide led them into a high-walled enclosure and told them to shut up and keep out of sight. A doctor gave them a short-arm inspection. (One American flunked and was turned back.) They were dirty, tired, and hungry. Some sneaked out and brought back long loaves of bread, but no real food, while others carved their names on trees in the enclosure. "Some day if I am still alive, I'll get back to see if I can find my name on one of those trees."*

After nightfall they were loaded into battered school buses, which bumped for several hours over a rutted road climbing toward a gap in the looming mountains. Beyond the French frontier station, shut down for the night, their headlights illuminated a band of armed men wearing blankets. From a hut hung a red and black banner—the party flag of the Spanish Anarchists. Somebody on the bus shouted, "Viva la República!" but an Anarchist called back, "No, Viva la Revolución Proletaria!"[16] Both gave their official salute, the Anarchists clasping hands overhead as a symbol of brotherhood and unity. A jolt of international solidarity swept through the buses like an electric charge as they lurched across the frontier into Spain. By this time they were sick unto death of "The International," sung on the train countless times in a dozen languages, but they sang it again. None of them knew the national anthem of the Republic which they had crossed an ocean to save.

It was January 3, 1937. Their first massacre was fifty-one days away.

Dropping down off the mountains, they debussed on the parade ground inside the Castillo de San Fernando, a massive fortress, complete with wide moat and six-meter-thick walls, crowning the height of Figueras. Assigned a section of straw within a dark subterranean casemate, they hung their suitcases on saddle hooks jutting from the wall. Hundreds of volunteers milled about the castle—

16. A disagreement that later had sinister repercussions. For the Anarchists the war was an opportunity for social and political revolution; for the Communists it was to preserve the Republic until it could be made into a Soviet satellite. In May 1937 a civil war within the civil war erupted in Barcelona between the rightist Republicans (mainly the PCUS—Communist Party of Catalonia) and the leftists (mainly the Anarchists and Trotskyites).

Germans who had escaped from concentration camps and swum the Rhine, Austrians in ski suits who had skied down from Alpine ranges, and even a few Swiss women with disheveled blond hair who hoped to enlist. The walls were painted with exhortations like "PROLETARIER ALLER LÄNDER, VEREINIGT EUCH!" in a dozen languages. Now safe over the frontier, the Americans could cast off their civvies and don their khaki uniforms. "Our international comrades stared at us in astonishment. We looked so superior. Little did they know. . . . Most of us had never held a gun."* All were keen to know whether more Americans would be coming and whether the United States would supply material aid. To his unruly cohorts, Commissar Bard spelled out the law: breaches in discipline would no longer be tolerated—especially drinking. "We are an army of the People, not an army of drunks!" Putting teeth in Bard's spiel, Harris piped in, "That means all you guys!" In a cavernous room lined with plank tables and lit by two weak lightbulbs, they were served goat chops from a skillet twenty-five feet wide and beans from steaming washtubs. Although there was no water on the table, the men gamely pushed aside the long-necked glass *purones* of wine. An Anarchist officer came over to teach them how to drink. Seizing the flask, he flourished it above his head and poured a thin stream directly into his mouth. The Americans complimented his skill but still refused to drink. The mess officer had glasses and cups brought for them. Again they refused. The puzzled officer rapped the table for attention and delivered a plaintive speech: "American comrades, we Catalans are a poor people. We know our wine is a poor country product. We do not have the fine vineyards of your country. America is a rich country, and we know that the wines of Scranton and Pittsburgh are among the best in the world. This we know. But we beg you not to insult the poor products of Cataluña." Daniel Zorat, Bard's interpreter, tried to explain that the Americans refused to drink on moral grounds, not because they had contempt for Spanish wine, but the long-faced *comandante* shook his head in disbelief. These *extranjeros* lacked respect for Spanish ways. A few days before he had placed under arrest an English leader who spat out a mouthful of oily beans and demanded that his men be served decent food. With mounting irritation he said that in Spain a man who did not drink was not a real man. What were these Americans? Bard found himself in a dilemma: Party discipline required that an order, once given, had to be obeyed, and at the same time he had been warned of the Anarchists' hostility. It was the hard-boiled Harris who cut through the dialectical impasse. Grabbing a *purón*, he shouted, "Okay. Guys. Drink—as guests!" With yells of jubilation, the Americans proved to the Catalans that they were real men.*

It was the custom at Figueras to assemble recent arrivals on the parade ground, and following a few perfunctory words about the dangers lying ahead, to give them the option of returning to France, but it took a very unusual man to turn tail and endure the contempt of his comrades. (Later in the war, when the stream of foreign volunteers was drying up, turning back at Figueras was forbidden.) Once they had entered the fortress, leaving it was problematical. For no stated reason, guards sometimes permitted men to pass through the immense gateway and stroll down to the town center—at other times not. The Americans arrived at a permissive phase. One American remembered that he dawdled behind his group out of curiosity, to visit a Trotskyist recruiting office he had noticed when they arrived in town. He reviled them as political devils incarnate but was burning with curiosity to examine their pitch. He walked up and down past their office, like an adolescent boy in front of a whorehouse, but each time he prepared to duck inside he spotted a shipmate and, fearing denunciation, dared not enter.*

A few days later all the International volunteers marched down to the railroad station, led by the Americans, who were alphabetically first. As they passed through the streets of Figueras, townspeople lined the curbs, calling them "*compañeros*" and bombarding them with almonds. The Americans got a heady draught of revolutionary fervor. The Balkans sang "The International," and the Americans replied with "Solidarity." The streets were festooned with Republican flags and political banners, although stalwarts grimaced when they passed placards marked POUM—reputed to be the hated Trotskyites. They boarded a local train, camouflaged with crazy zigzags of green and yellow paint and most of the windows broken or boarded up, which seated on wooden slabs six men on one side and two on the other. "We got flat wheels on this train," went the old joke.* It moved at a snail's pace, so they could, or so it was said, jump through the windows if the train was strafed. They had already picked up two plagues which remained with them to the end—lice and dysentery.

It was midafternoon when they marched from Barcelona's North Station to the Plaza de Cataluña. At this early stage of the war the city was "a bloody marvelous madhouse." They passed through a great mob yelling "*Hermanos! Hermanos!* Brothers!" Women pulled sticky fists from babies' mouths to make the clenched fist salute of proletarian brotherhood. Men would stop them on the Ramblas to give them a chorus of "The International." Men here and there in immaculate suits wore no ties, to show their commitment to the working class. "It was like being on top of a mountain."* Bill Harvey, a second-generation Communist, found himself crying. "A million people loving us up and we're loving them up too. . . . We're going to make a new world where there'll be no poor and no wise bastards who think they own the whole goddam place. We all own it . . . and we're goin' to fight for it."*

Following this high came their shenanigans under the window of Consul General Mahlon F. Perkins. After they had sung "The Star-Spangled Banner," a band burst forth with "Himno de Riego," the Republican anthem. The Americans began to laugh. The tune sounded to them like one they knew in the States as "Here Comes Barnum and Bailey—the Circus Is Coming to Town." They joined in, laughing and shouting the "Barnum and Bailey" refrain. At the finale, the crowd surged forward to congratulate the Americanos, who alone among the foreigners appreciated their anthem. A guide escorted them to the Lenin Barracks for a banquet. Once inside they discovered it belonged to the POUM. Under pictures of Trotsky, Phil Bard looked ashen, but it was too late to turn back. Yet instead of having their faces kicked in, they received a sumptuous meal served by a friendly band of Trotskyists who didn't seem like bad guys at all.[17] Still, there were complaints, and thereafter International volunteers messed only at the Karl Marx Barracks, an exclusively Communist preserve.

Dawn found them south of Tarragona, the tracks running beside the Mediterranean or sweeping through hamlets—"unreal, like Hollywood villages."* They sang "The International," "La Marseillaise," "Casey Jones," "Over There," and even "The Star-Spangled Banner." On the south-facing slopes almond trees were already in pink blossom. Spaniards working in the fields clenched their right fists and called "Salud!" A lookout at the window shouted, "Hey, guys, I see orange trees!" Thereafter at every station, leather-faced *campesinos* and children with thin arms and legs tossed in oranges as the volunteers threw back cigarettes and loaves of bread. (The major granaries were in the Nationalist zone.) One volunteer, who insisted on paying for his fruit, found himself charged the equivalent of one penny for two dozen. For hours they gorged, tossing the skins and pulp at dozing comrades. In Valencia, capital of the Republic since the government had fled Madrid, they ate in the big *plaza de toros,* across from the station, and emitted mock groans when they saw their dessert—two oranges per man. Bullfight posters flapped in the wind. Since the outbreak of war no bulls worth mention had been fought in Republican Spain because most matadors gravitated to the wealthier Nationalists. Besides, Spaniards of both sides had taken up a different blood sport.

That night the train wound up between the jagged peaks of the coastal *sierras* to the Levantine *meseta,* an arid upland plateau beaten by winter winds that

---

17. When I asked one of Joe's cronies whether they used the suffix "-ite" or "-ist" in referring to followers of Trotsky, he replied, "We always called them *fucking* Trotskyites." He then pounded his fist on a table, as though crushing vermin, and shouted, "POUM? POUM! POUM!"

whistled down from Aragon. They stuffed holes with bundles of clothing and newspapers. (They quickly learned that in Spain it was always either too hot or too cold.) In springless carriages the wooden-slat benches grew harder. Some tried to sleep on the benches; others curled up in the aisles or under the seats. The train halted frequently to clear trees and obstructions from the rails—the work of saboteurs, it was said. At a long viaduct crossing a three-hundred-foot ravine, guards walked ahead examining the rails and signaling the engineer. In the blacked-out train, lit only by a few blue-painted bulbs, four anonymous Americans and two Canadians composed what they hoped would become the "official" marching song of the Lincoln Battalion. The tune was based on a yet-to-be-identified college ditty; the words, a conglomerate of collegiate hoopla and proletarian cliché:

> We march, Americans!
> To defend our working class,
> To uphold democracy
> And mow the Fascists down like grass;
> We're marching to vic-to-ry,
> Our hearts are set, our fists are clenched,
> A cause like ours can't help but win,
> The Fascists' steel will bend like tin.
> We give our word, they shall not pass,
> (shouted) ¡No Pasarán!
> (again) WE GIVE OUR WORD THEY SHALL NOT PASS![*18]

With a few changes here and there—not so many, really—Fordham could have borrowed it for a football rally. The composers sent it to *New Masses,* which published it, of course. Most of the seamen and furriers laughed at it. They preferred "The Caissons Go Rolling Along" and other military chanties from imperialist nations. (After meeting Fascist steel in their first battle, no veteran ever sang the "Marching Song" again, unless sardonically. Strictly political pabulum for the crowds back home.)

At gray dawn they looked through grubby eyes across a tabletop plain with an African cast to it. There were fields where nothing was growing and random villages where nothing was moving. Whenever the train halted at a huddle of

---

18. A defector later claimed that the song originally concluded with the lines "When we get back home once more / We'll do the same thing there." This became a flash point for American rightists, convinced that men had enlisted in the International Brigades to acquire military training that would assist them in overthrowing the U.S. government.

roofs, small boys raced to the platform, not to shower them with oranges and almonds, but to beg tobacco, bread, money. Romantic Spain was behind them. This was the real Spain. Americans had come to reclaim these miserable villages and to liberate these squalid lives. If their hearts were fuller than their pockets, there was nevertheless always something to pass through the window.

At ten o'clock in the morning of January 8, the first American volunteers arrived in Albacete, saffron emporium and headquarters of the International Brigades. A band heavy on percussion welcomed them with its repertoire of United Front anthems, including "The Star-Spangled Banner" and "God Save the King." Pasted on the walls of the railroad station were posters plugging the International Brigades, one featuring a trio of heads—Caucasian, Negroid, and Oriental—wearing French *poilu* helmets of World War vintage. "It looked like a town in a movie—a cowboy movie," recalled one volunteer. They marched behind their band up the short Calle de Alfonso XII (the tabooed monarchist name had not yet been changed), past the blue-tiled pleasure domes of the Gran Hotel in the Plaza de Altozano, and then through the narrow streets of the *barrio chino,* where shack rats with meaty arms leered at them from open windows. (Since Marty's crowd had decided that a "Fifth Column" was lurking in Albacete, each group of new arrivals was paraded ostentatiously through the town.) Suddenly down the street came an awesome file of German volunteers marching with perfect alignment and singing in chorus the "The Song of the United Front" in exact time to their stamping feet.* This was a platoon of Thaelmanns, men of the famous XIth Brigade, among the heroic cadre of Internationals celebrated for saving Madrid in the bitter fighting back in November. Fierce in battle and fanatical about discipline (as the other brigades were not), they carefully tended flowerbeds in their bivouacs. The newcomers continued to the former Guardia Civil barracks near the bullring, which reminded one volunteer of a desert fort in a cheap movie with a courtyard half concrete and half mud where hundreds of men milled about. The whole place stank, for there was no sewer connection, only pits, emptied by IB prisoners who carted away offal in dripping pushcarts.* Inside, twenty volunteers crowded into each room designed for four—two men for each cot, latecomers on the floor.*

Needing more space, the volunteers wanted to bunk in the unoccupied left wing on the ground floor but were hustled out. This was forbidden territory. Although no one told them why, the bloodstains on the walls of the lavatory conveyed a story of mass executions as vividly as any good cave painting spoke of animal slaughter. These first traces of war absorbed the newcomers, who examined them minutely. They aired two theories: either Nationalists had massacred Republican hostages or Republicans had slaughtered Nationalist prisoners.

No one in Albacete wanted to talk about it. The fact was that during the first days of the war 150 members of the Guardia Civil had taken refuge in the barracks with some right-wing civilians and held out for eight days against eight thousand militia until forced to surrender. The officers had been led into the lavatory and executed on the spot, along with some of the civilians.* Six months had passed and the bloody walls remained. There was a shortage of barrack space but not of soap, water, and swabs, but the authorities had no doubt decided that the walls should be left as a reminder of what an anti-Fascist war entailed. On the roof of the building were prison sheds containing civilians suspected of harboring Fascist attitudes. A later arrival among the Americans pulled guard duty up there and reported to the commandant that a prisoner who identified himself as the Count of Chinchón had offered to deposit a hundred thousand pounds sterling in the Bank of England in return for helping him escape. The American was outraged. "I told him that I had come to Spain to fight against the likes of him. I told him to shut up or I would send a bullet through the door and kill him." The commandant laughed: that *loco* had offered him even more money.*

Food awaited men who had not eaten since Valencia, but only after speeches. They lined up in the barracks courtyard, a concrete well ringed with iron balconies like a prison block. Cheers of instant recognition greeted the arrival with Luigi Longo of a walrus-looking Frenchman wearing an enormous beret that "hung down like a soggy black flapjack."* This was André Marty, a member of the executive committee of the Comintern, one of the founding fathers of the International Brigades, and a revolutionary icon. He became a hero in his own time for his leadership of the French Black Sea mutiny in 1919, which had prevented the French navy from supporting the White Russian armies. As a man who had refused to take up arms against the Soviet Union, he found favor with Josef V. Stalin and became not only a dedicated but also a fanatical Communist. In his welcome speech Marty compared the arrivals with the arrival of the Yanks under Pershing twenty years before "to save Europe from barbaric Huns." This ethnic slur did not sit well with some stalwarts, who recalled that the great Lenin himself had denounced the World War as an imperialist conspiracy. "It was a shocker," mused one man. "Were the Thaelmanns, those superb men who had just passed us and who had saved Madrid, nothing but a bunch of *Huns?*"* Nor did their surprise end there. Marty exposed his raw nerve—a paranoid obsession with spies. In his foghorn voice, he warned them to identify and to purge from their ranks all Trotskyites and other "political deviates." This diatribe seemed to pass over the heads of most of those enthralled by the idea of being "Popular Front" warriors, but some of the old guard knew exactly what he meant by "purge." All of Marty's energy served his mistrust—"his spy-disease, that Russian syphilis," wrote Gustav Regler, a revolutionary who knew him well.* (He liked to throw a stranger off guard by nonchalantly asking to see his POUM card.) Later, it would be claimed that Marty always demonstrated more zeal in exterminating imaginary Trotskyites than in prosecuting a war against real Fascists, but he had not yet earned his nickname, "Le Boucher d'Albacete."[19]

On the next morning the men reported to the *plaza de toros* on the edge of town, a structure that looked like it had been squeezed from a confectioner's tube. Here each volunteer was photographed for his *livre militar* and filled out a long questionnaire. Those listing their political party as "Communist" had to change it to "Anti-Fascist" to accord with the Popular Front fiction.[20] Marty chastised French volunteers wearing red bandannas. "You don't wear those things if you're going into battle. You are temporarily not communists, and you don't hang red flags around your neck for Fascist snipers." From a warehouse they received uniforms assembled from hand-me-downs of half a dozen armies—mainly French—though some shirts carried the brass eagle buttons of the U.S. Army. They laughed and cursed as enormous men tried to shoehorn into dwarfish garments while five-footers draped themselves in coats designed for giants. To their disappointment, they received no weapons. Albacete had barely enough for base personnel. The Americans were shamed when volunteers from other countries pointed scornfully at their doughboy uniforms. Why had they come to free Spain from Fascism wearing uniforms of the most capitalistic country in the world? A few sensitive souls stuffed their conspicuous fleece-lined jackets into garbage cans as proof of their international fervor, only to be shocked, on the following day, to see them on the backs of grinning French volunteers.

Officers collected their passports, ostensibly for "safekeeping" at the base, although the real reason was to minimize desertion by making flight from

---

19. In *For Whom the Bell Tolls,* Ernest Hemingway captures the spirit of the man perfectly when Marty refuses to call off the botched offensive because of his belief that spies and traitors were at work. To the CPF he admitted to executions of five hundred volunteers for various crimes, including rebellion and espionage.*

20. Underplaying the role of the Communist Party in the International Brigades served two ends: first, it made it easier to obtain funds and men from bourgeois sources; second, it minimized antagonism against the International Brigades from other groups in Republican Spain. This ploy did not fool the Anarchists, who believed from the beginning that the International Brigades existed to bring Spain into the Soviet orbit after the war. They argued that the Republic had all the manpower it required to wage the war successfully. If the USSR really wanted to help—they were wont to ask—then why doesn't it send more armaments?

Spain nearly impossible. Many of these passports made their way to Soviet military intelligence at The Hague and performed valuable service in Soviet espionage activities in years to come. (The man who killed Trotsky in Mexico City was carrying the passport of a dead North American volunteer.) Some men, smelling a rat, stuffed their passports in shoes and claimed they had been lost. Each man was interrogated about his special qualifications. An American identified as Joe said that in the States he ran speedboats. "Excellent, Comrade," replied his questioner. "You will fit into the infantry."*

For a few days the recruits drilled in the bullring, although French officers using French jargon barked commands that not even the French recruits seemed to understand. During a rest period a Detroit auto-worker smudged a swastika onto his handkerchief and played *matador* to John Lenthier, a Boston actor, who snorted and tore the cloth to shreds amid cheers.* On their time off, the Americans prowled the city, which turned into a sea of mud at the slightest drizzle; they sampled the local *coñac*, which has been described as a blend of equal parts rancid olive oil and low-octane gasoline; and they bought the local specialty, jackknives with handsome mother-of-pearl handless but worthless tin blades. There was little else to do for these city boys, unless one wanted to queue up outside a door in the *barrio chino*—but the female wares, recalled a volunteer, were "pretty awful," particularly after the whores of Le Havre. In Albacete, the IB hierarchy billeted at the Gran Hotel held *droit de seigneur* over every girl with either beauty or spunk. There was even a rumor that André Marty had a private harem in a villa outside town. Nobody seemed to believe it, but they enjoyed thinking about it. Posted in shop windows was a ubiquitous sign reading "NO HAY TABAC," which meant "There's no tobacco," though one American comrade remarked, with deep disgust, "Well, if they make cigarettes out of hay over here, I wouldn't wanta smoke 'em."* They soon learned to hoard butt ends for rerolling later and not to pass a pack around. Some CP zealots believed that the authorities ought to prohibit Internationals from panhandling the new arrivals for cigarettes and from picking up butts off the street, like Bowery bums. The Circulo Mercantil, or Casino, had been requisitioned by a military committee after the local gentry had either been shot or run out of town, but it still featured billiard tables and some fossils of a bygone era—a starved-looking string orchestra in tails.*

Certainly the most depressing place in town was the Plaza de Altozano. The municipal and provincial buildings had been taken over by IB bureaucrats—pouter pigeons in swank uniforms. There were fleeting glimpses of Marty himself, popping in and out of his chauffeured limousine decked with tiny flags. Always hovering about him were his next-in-powers, section heads and *jefes* of something-or-other, bundled up in shaggy coats. These were long-striding fellows with lopes "that made them seem like wolves in sheep's clothing."* If an officer ranked high enough, his wife could join him in Albacete. (Madame Marty was there. Gustav Regler visited her room privately to examine the collection of automatic pistols that she proudly spread out on her bed.) The Gran Hotel might have reminded someone of the Ritz, but a union hall, never. Guards with machine guns stood at the revolving door and turned away those without special passes. In Albacete only one man cast a vote—André Marty, Soviet-nurtured czar and grand marshal. Ironically, he had risen to power in the French Communist Party on a platform of antimilitarism.

The Americans had little time to study the intricacies of rearguard politicking and infighting. During the second week of January they left for their training camp. They were glad to go. Albacete could make a working stiff feel pretty small.

2

MEN OF LA MANCHA

Located fifty-six kilometers northwest of Albacete, Villanueva de la Jara was the most distant of all villages seized by the International Brigades as training camps—so distant, in fact, that it officially belonged in the province of Cuenca, not Albacete. The heaviest industry was a chocolate factory, a delapidated enclosure shut down since the beginning of the war, although the immensity of the fortresslike church suggested that religion had been a major competitor. As their trucks drove into the village, the men caught fleeting glimpses of faces at windows disappearing behind closed blinds. With its unpaved streets, primitive sanitation, and mud-daubed houses it seemed for Americans like something at the end of the world—or beyond. Even the half dozen Americans from the South were appalled by the naked poverty of the place.

The townspeople distrusted, even feared, the Internationals, and with good reason. Before the war they had been little more than serfs of absentee landowners, but now Comintern cadres ruled their lives. Their antagonism had begun when an overflow of French volunteers, most of them "uncontrollables" billeted in the Convent of Santa Clara, had become so unruly and drunken that Marty had to remove them closer to Albacete. Before pulling out they had studded the floors with excrement and defaced the walls with obscenities. It was not the desecration that alienated the villagers, who had looted sacristies at the outset of the war, but rather the anarchic behavior of the French, who had seized wine cellars, propositioned their womenfolk, and brawled in the streets. Therefore, when the Americans climbed out of their municipal-green trucks in the tiny *plaza mayor,* they heard doors banging shut throughout the village. In time, the mayor, flanked by his town-hall clique, and joined by a horde of kids, materialized. Before conducting them to the convent he pointedly proclaimed that he held no political beliefs whatsoever before concluding with "Viva Rusia!"—an allusion which mystified the Americans.[1] (Franco's propagandists

---

1. In 1939, Juan de Dios Perez Alvarillo, mayor of Villanueva de la Jara, was tried, convicted, and executed as a war criminal by the Franco government for the murder of twenty Nationalist sympathizers.

harped on the Russian origin of the International Brigades.) The mayor was evasive about what had happened to the "Fascists" of the village when peasants seized control, but later the Americans heard a fanciful tale about a priest high in the church tower who opened fire on the villagers with a "machine gun," until a local Munchausen scaled the tower (from the outside!) and killed the monster with a knife.*

Santa Clara still bore the traces of French occupation. "Garbage clogged the drains, crap was piled on the floor, the whole place was flooded,"* recalled an American. Cursing their comrades-at-arms, they turned to with switch brooms and slop buckets. They had arrived at dusk—it was after midnight when they finished. When they dug a long latrine trench in the courtyard, somebody claimed the nuns' little bastards must be buried there and the nunnery used as a house of assignation for lascivious monks of the village. "In such manner we titillated each other."* The stone walls of Santa Clara were so thick that men could sunbathe on windowsills with enough room to twist and turn. The building was wonderfully cool during warm days but bitterly cold at night, for blankets were scarce. To wash and shave, men lined up at the courtyard well and pulled up buckets of ice-cold water by hand. (An unconfirmed story, still current in the village, contends that a Fascist doctor was executed for pouring poison in the well.)* Bathing was out of the question. The food was execrable—usually a sort of gristly mule stew and garbanzos—but the men of the Cuban section quickly made friends among villagers willing to barter their edibles for provender filched from the battalion cookhouse.

Having shunted them to the most remote of all the training areas, Albacete largely ignored them. Officially they became the 17th Battalion, XVth (International) Brigade—unofficially (but never ratified by the men), the Abraham Lincoln Battalion.[2] Truckloads of new faces arrived nearly every day, adding to the leaderless confusion. Since Phil Bard had come down with asthma and remained at Albacete as their representative among the French heavies at the base, James Harris assumed command. The original table of organization called for two infantry companies of three sections each, a machine-gun company, a medical section (including a well-trained unit from the Netherlands), a supply and transport department, and a headquarters and military staff. The sections

---

2. No unit in Spain officially named the Abraham Lincoln Brigade ever existed. That fiction was the result of efforts, entirely stateside, to aggrandize the American participation at the expense of the other battalions of the XVth Brigade. Frederika Martin, chief nurse of the American medical unit in Spain—and an unstinting supporter of American volunteers—reported that she was "embarrassed and ashamed" by this grandiose lie to magnify the military role of the CPUSA. In her words, it was "purely propaganda."*

were subdivided into "groups" of about ten men each. From top to bottom in all International units, commissars existed at each level of the hierarchy to oversee political instruction, to write reports about each man in their charge, and to watch with eagle eye for evidence of political "deviationism." (If sexual deviation existed, it was not revealed or discussed.) André Marty decreed that the commissars were "the unshakable rock on which the magnificent IBS were built."*

Because the seamen, including longshoremen, were the most cohesive (and pugnacious) faction, they set themselves off as future machine gunners and christened themselves the Tom Mooney Company.[3] Picking out whomever they wanted and hustling out anyone foisted on them from above, they quickly became a kind of super-company with the best *esprit de corps* in the battalion. But outsiders often resented the Mooneys. "The guys in that company were tough guys," complained one. "You couldn't get in if you weren't hard-core something-or-other."* They got the best military commander in the outfit, a Tennessean named Doug Seacord, a soft-spoken man with a handsome pirate's face, who was rumored to have been a gunnery instructor at West Point. Gathering about him Party stalwarts like Joe Gordon; Douglas Roach, a black wrestler nearly as wide as tall;[4] and Ray Steele, a club-footed seaman who could outrun most men in the battalion, they began training with two rusty Colt machine guns dating back before the World War. Soon they were deep into such gunnery problems as "inverse section fire to secure oblique fire" and insulated by hard work from the bickering and factionalism breaking out in the other companies. Seacord was a superb instructor. Any man unable to strip and reassemble his gun blindfolded was kicked out. The great drawback of their training was the failure of Albacete to send them live ammunition. (Just before they went up to the front a small supply arrived, and each gunner was allowed to fire two rounds.)

Now that Bard was gone, many volunteers wished he were back, for he had been a link, however weak, in the chain leading back to the Party organization in New York. Authority had broken down. Harris labored to set up a training program but could not cope with the anarchy already plaguing his battalion and compounded almost daily with truckloads of new recruits. A power struggle

---

3. Thomas Jeremiah Mooney, a militant working-class leader in San Francisco, was imprisoned on a charge that he had engineered a bomb explosion, which killed ten bystanders, at the Preparedness Day parade in July 1916. Jailed until 1939, Mooney was wooed by the Communists and eventually captivated by them.

4. Seacord was also a black, but so lightly colored that few knew it at the time. He and Roach were inseparable; both had organized fishermen in Provincetown, Cape Cod, where Roach picked up extra money as a circus acrobat.

developed over the vacant post of political commissar with Philip Cooperman (Kuppermann), the pudgy Party secretary, pitted against Marvin Stern, an unpopular college soccer player with a carping voice. Since Cooperman's convention-hall remoteness did not wear well, Stern took over by force of will and proceeded to place Harris under arrest "on charges to be preferred at a later time." Dumbfounded, Harris ordered Stern's arrest for insubordination, only to discover that in the International Brigades a commissar could overrule a commander, because political rectitude outweighed military rank. Part of the trouble stemmed from the age-old feud between trade-union men and Marxist intellectuals—the doers and the thinkers—but Stern's uncompromising Marxism got him into trouble with the Albacete overlords when he alienated the village mayor by arguing that land confiscated from the gentry should be collectivized. (Stalin opposed collectivization in Spain because it might upset his Popular Front masquerade.) In the end a grievance committee mediated. Thereafter, the commissar slot was filled by a cumbersome *troika*—Cooperman, Stern, and Bernard Walsh, a cartographer who had served a short stint in the New York National Guard. Morale in the battalion sank further after the new commissars conspicuously avoided the daily drills and field maneuvers required of lesser lights. Some men talked of deserting the International Brigades and joining the Spanish infantry. In alarm, Comrade Lucien Vidal, Marty's deputy at Albacete, rushed out to upbraid the Americans as "naughty children."* He explained that they were not in a Party meeting at home but in a "Loyalist army" that demanded strict discipline and respect for hierarchies of command. Disobedience would be tantamount to defeatism or Trotskyism. "The men were greatly surprised at the news," but afterward their discipline stiffened.*

In their garbled efforts to forge a chain of command and to fabricate a military unit, the Americans did not suffer alone. Similar problems had plagued the British Battalion at nearby Madrigueras, a huddle of huts twenty miles down the road. One of the earliest company commanders had to be dismissed when he refused to send away the French girl who had followed him from Paris; another of like rank proved so lackluster that he was made the transport officer, even though no battalion transport existed at the time. Military exercises consisted mainly of improvised battle drills in which an officer atop a hill blew his whistle—the signal for his men to "attack," across open country, an entrenched "enemy" that could have wiped them out to a man at four hundred yards. An officer with a rattle simulated enemy machine-gun fire. (There was never an exercise designed to show men how to make an orderly retreat—a disastrous oversight in view of what would shortly occur.) The battalion commander—

rarely seen by the rank and file—was Wilfred McCartney, a paunchy *grand-boulevardier* who, even in Spain, drank nothing other than good champagne and bottled water. Although admired by the officer caste for military competence, he had no rapport with the common element, which (alluding to Harry Pollitt, head of the CPGB) he called "Harry's Bolshies."* A staff officer in the Great War, he had more recently emerged from prison for allegedly giving state secrets to the USSR. In Spain he became so enmeshed in the corridor cliques at Albacete—which were trying to dump him, not because he was ineffectual but because he was not a Communist—that he had little time to supervise the activities at Madrigueras.[5] As deputy he chose Tom Wintringham, a balding radical poet with an Oxford degree, to whip into shape the two British companies whose battlefield debut (though no one could have foreseen it) was less than two weeks away.*

More unruly and divisive than the Americans and having taken no teetotaling pledges, they drank whatever they liked, which was everything. Worse than drink, however, were the disruptive ethnic rivalries among men who had come from the far corners of the British Empire. Wintringham tried to impose some order in this imperial melting pot of Englishmen, Scotsmen, Welshmen, Egyptians, Cypriots, Maltese, Indians, and Irish. While he earned their respect for his military lore—he was a Great War veteran and former military editor of the London *Daily Worker*—his upper-crust speech and mannerisms grated on working-class men, who dubbed him "Bleedin' Lord of the King's Cock Horse." On one occasion, seeking a comrade in the recreation room, he interrupted a BBC broadcast only to be angrily shouted down by a roomful of rank and file, who had the satisfaction of seeing their commander "creep out like a mouse,"* as one of them put it in a letter to chums back home.

Efforts to enforce discipline with confinement failed—because the lockup had an iron stove and was the warmest spot in town. No one saluted, because recognition of rank was "bourgeois" or even "Fascist." In this atmosphere of egalitarianism, an order had to be prefaced with prefaces like "Comrade, as one man to another . . ." Eager to join the anti-Fascist fight, the British railed against political voodoo. Instead of being trained for battle, "we got lectures on Marxism—how many tractors the Soviet Union had produced, how many

---

5. McCartney never made it to the front. On the eve of his departure Peter Kerrigan, his political commissar, shot him in the foot, and he was invalided out of Spain. The shooting was said to have been an "accident" but the CPGB distrusted McCartney because he was not a member. The two men had been drinking and were exchanging pistols when Kerrigan's went off. Considering the ubiquitous presence of sidearms among the IB officers—ever alert for lurking spies and Trotskyites—it is a miracle that more feet and legs were not drilled with holes.

hectares of wheat were growing in the Ukraine." A recruit yelled, "We don't want this bloody rubbish—we need to be taught how to fight, how to take cover, lie doggo. . . . We're not going over the top with a copy of *Das Kapital* in our hands." A commissar stepped up and told him "to shut [his] bleeding gob before someone put a bullet through [his] head."* For machine-gun instruction, Wintringham had twelve old American Colts, which worked well enough when fed factory-loaded belts but not at all when the belts were loaded by hand. (The story got around that the guns had been shipped to Imperialist Russia during the war by way of Murmansk and the belts via Vladivostock only to reunite in Spain.) The most minuscule speck of dirt jammed a gun. The gunners had to spread linen altar cloths from the church whenever the guns were stripped down. "It all seemed to smack of poetic justice."* As a swagger stick Wintringham adopted a steel ramrod—useful in clearing burst cartridges from the breeches of the Colts. By his count these guns averaged 120 shots per hour— a rate of fire slower than that of an ordinary rifle. Gun oil was nonexistent. He tried to borrow some axle grease from local farmers, but they never used it on their big wooden cart wheels. Whenever a motor vehicle strayed into Madrigueras, a Tommy crawled underneath to milk it for transmission oil. Even worse than the Colts were the Chauchauts, French machine guns that never worked at all. Somehow Fred Copeman, a fist-tough ex-seaman in command of the machine-gun company, got hold of a few Lewis guns, and his men became so proficient that they could hit tin lids thrown into the air, but on the day that they were to leave for the front Marty appeared in camp and demanded the guns, which he intended to issue to a French battalion. Having gotten wind of this, Copeman buried the guns and refused to give the location. Marty was enraged but helpless, for the British were urgently needed on the collapsing Jarama front. As an incentive to turn over the guns he gave the British twelve heavy German Maxims, mounted on wheeled carriages in the Russian style, excellent weapons although no one had experience in handling them.*

International solidarity did not sit well with the Britons. Less adaptable to Spain than other nationals, they objected to the food (particularly the use of olive oil rather than lard), clamored incessantly for tea, and adjusted to wine only because their daily ration included no beer. (In Paris they had been stunned when "pasty things," not bacon and eggs, comprised their breakfast fare.) Then they were plagued by the forty-odd Irishmen assigned to their battalion, most of them hardened veterans of the Irish Republican Army, who had drawn beads on English soldiers (and paramilitaries like the Black and Tans) during the Rebellion. Spain reminded them of Ireland—weren't both victims of political tyranny? While they tolerated working-class British volunteers, they loathed the officer caste at Madrigueras, "swell-headed adventurer types with their swagger canes," reeking of rank and privilege.* But their greatest loathing was reserved for "General" Eoin O'Duffy's private army of six hundred Irish-men now serving in Spain on the Franco side. How they longed to meet that band of church-supported reactionaries on the field of battle![6]

As though parodying their national character, the Irish badgered the English by adopting emerald-green berets, despite IB prohibitions against national or sectarian emblems. (Since the International Brigades drew men from more than thirty countries, chauvinism was inevitable.) Battalion officers ignored the berets but cracked down when some of the Irish began speaking Gaelic to one another, and since none of the British censors could read Gaelic, they infuriated the Irish by demanding that letters home be written in English.[7] Frank Ryan, their charismatic leader, understood his men's rancor, but he held to the line that they had come to Spain to fight Fascism, not imperialism. The problem was that Ryan was in such great demand as a speaker and organizer throughout the International Brigades that he was often away, and whenever he was away trouble boiled over. During one absence, McCartney arrested the Irish section leader as an "undesirable" and ordered his deportation from Spain. But the crowning blow came on Bobbie Burns night, January 25, when 150 Britons (70 percent of them Scots) gathered in a *bodega* called the Republican Club to celebrate the "People's Poet." Sardines on bayonets replaced haggis and turnips, while burly men in skirts created a sensation among Spaniards peeking in at the windows.*

It began with poetry recitals and the singing of Scottish songs, progressed quickly to a soused evening of songs and jokes, and ended with obscenities and insults directed at the Irish. "The Irishmen drank like fish. . . . They wouldn't take orders from McCartney. Finally they and the English got drunk and there

---

6. The encounter never came about, although in mid-February they were within miles of each other on the Jarama front. As O'Duffy moved his men up to attack, a Nationalist unit mistook them for Internationals because of their unfamiliar uniforms and fired on them. In the melee two Irish crusaders were killed. Thereafter, the O'Duffyites performed only trench duty, where they lost four more men from artillery fire. A short time later they returned ingloriously to Ireland.

7. Officially the British unit carried the tongue-twisting moniker Saklatvala Battalion, commemorating Shapurji Saklatvala, M.P. from North Battersea, a Communist and leading light in the Indian Nationalist movement. Needless to say, this name was not chosen by the men themselves (few of whom would have heard of him) but picked out by the CP apparatchik in London on the grounds that it would encourage IB enlistment from the huge Indian population in the Empire. (It did not.) The volunteers regarded the name with either indifference or contempt, and it rapidly faded away in favor of the "British Battalion"—ultimately the 57th Battalion in the XVth Brigade. The London clique touted the name "Clement Atlee Battalion," but there was so much opposition among the men, who argued that Atlee was at best a political equivocator on working-class issues—at worst, a traitor—that it, too, was dropped.

was a punch-up," was how Fred Copeman summed up the fracas.* Another account says that a British platoon on guard duty that night arrested nearly the entire Irish detachment. (Later the Irish regaled neophytes with a Blarney tale of how they had forced the British officers to accede to their transfer into the Lincoln Battalion by surrounding headquarters with a ring of machine guns.) In any case, when heads cleared, the Irish called a meeting and voted 26 to 11 in favor of transferring to the Americans up the road. The Comintern ideal—submerging ethnocentrism in a unified political brotherhood—had proved a dismal failure.[8]

That said, it was a godsend to the Americans to be seeded with experienced soldiers rather than their dropouts from the National Guard, and the Irish quickly found themselves appointed as company adjutants and section leaders. Among them were seasoned veterans who had weathered a hard campaign on the Córdoba front in December 1936. On the other hand, a future Lincoln commander worried that their reputation as uncontrollables might poison the Americans. He wrote his wife that the Irish were "a bunch of drunks who spent their time fighting amongst themselves."* Would they fight the Fascists with the same élan? Aware that there were Roman Catholics among them, Lincoln commissars collected and hid all the prayer books of the convent, which the Americans had torn up as toilet paper. Much to their chagrin, however, the Irish had brought their own and were using them for the same purpose.

The Irish formed their own section, named the Connelly Centuria after an Irish martyr, with their own commander and commissar (the latter from Liverpool, unknown to them at the time). Some Boston Irishmen, corralled by the three O'Flaherty brothers—Ed, Charlie, and Frank—eagerly joined them. All told, the Irish were "long on blarney and short on recruits," so they filled their spotty ranks with new faces from Brooklyn or the Bronx, gaelicizing them as O'Greenberg and O'Goldstein. (Villanueva de la Jara became Villanueva O'Hara.)* The Irish were full of military stratagems and opinions, often introduced by "Here's how we used to do it when fighting the Black and Tans . . ." Mike Kelly liked to parody Catholicism in cautionary aphorisms like "Remember, lads, 'tis a mortal skin to cross your own line of fire."* Although to hard-line

8. On his return Ryan was furious at McCartney for exacerbating the national rivalry. He was successful in restoring his section leader but not in convincing the Irish to return. Later when McCartney accidentally shot himself on the eve of his return to England, Ryan wrote, "The bastard wounded himself in the left arm with his own revolver . . . and got the London *Daily Worker* to say he was 'wounded by Fascist rifle-fire near Madrid!'" Consistently Ryan held that Ireland's nearest ally must be the British working class and that the Irish and British must serve side by side in Spain.* Subsequent volunteers from Ireland consented to serve with the British.

Party stalwarts the Irish seemed hopelessly "romantic," they provided some relief in humanizing the Lincolns, who often took themselves far too seriously.

The French-dominated bureaucracy at Albacete only added to the difficulties at Villanueva de la Jara. Directives, whenever they arrived, were written in French and had to be laboriously translated. (Complaints about the language problem netted only a few copies of useless French-Spanish dictionaries, for French-English dictionaries were unavailable.) Since rations for the battalion were scanty and often spoiled, the Lincolns had to forage in the village and purchase supplies with their own money.[9] Cartons of American cigarettes listed on invoices vanished on the road between Albacete and Villanueva, but French truck drivers merely shrugged when cursed or accused. The Americans made some progress in drilling with eight-man squads until Comrade Vidal came up from Albacete for an inspection and explained why they should scrap this backward American system in favor of the French twelve-man squads. He demonstrated a complicated diamond formation of open-field maneuver in which the squad leader hand-signaled groups of three men to advance, much as a conductor batons an orchestra. Though beautiful to watch, the Americans never adopted it.* Vidal went on to warn them that union-hall methods of soliciting opinions from everyone smacked of Anarchism. Proper decisions had to come from specialized cadres at the top—which Communist jargon called "*democratic* centralism" (emphasis added). More welcome was Vidal's spiel about how cowardly the Fascists were in battle. "According to him, they ran away when faced with heavy fire. The boy scouts cheered."* Perhaps the apex of French arrogance came when French Jews told American Jews that their own Yiddish was linguistically rich and pure, while the American version was vulgar. "The French were the scum of the International Brigade," concluded one American echoed by countless others.*

Complaints from Villanueva piled up on Bard's desk at Albacete: Where was their training equipment? What happened to mail from the States? When would overnight leaves be authorized? Why couldn't they be billeted closer to Albacete? But Bard had no weight whatsoever with the IB bosses at the Base. The CPUSA was only a speck in the body politic of a corrupt capitalistic power, and Bard was a nobody in that party. He represented a nation that, as measured by Comintern values, was slightly more important than Albania but considerably less so than Bulgaria. Marty publicly vented his disgust with those "spoiled

---

9. All veterans agreed that the food in the International Brigades was abominable. Part of the problem was that the incompetents and shirkers were shunted into the cookhouse. The best food available to the men came from a local entrepreneur who set up a stand in the square and, for a few centimos, dispensed delicious roasted potatoes garnished with a swipe of garlic and olive oil.

cry-babies," those "arrogant Americans," and warned that unless they stopped whining, he would send them home in disgrace.* Supported by no one and scorned by both his countrymen at Villanueva and the claques at Albacete, Bard agonized in solitude, waiting for the time (not very far off, as events proved) when his asthmatic attacks would send him home. The CPUSA had committed a grave error in not sending a comrade with more grit and better credentials to represent the Lincolns, for they were, at this stage, little more than second-class citizens of the world revolution.

The Americans at Villanueva fought a losing battle with their latest enemy—boredom. The battalion commissariat tried to organize soccer matches, but these became little more than shin-kicking contests. Usually, a game "ended in a draw because everyone played it differently."* Someone had brought an American football to Spain. Games of "tackle" always drew a crowd of village boys, who marveled at the performance without the foggiest notion of the rules. One Sunday the Lincolns marched over to Motilla del Palancar, eight miles distant, to see an amateur bullfight in a crumbling arena that "looked like it was a thousand years old." Fascinated by the starchiness of the spectacle, they were nevertheless a little ashamed of its frivolity. "It proved to be an odd and interesting day," wrote a volunteer, "though some of the boys expressed it as being a rather cruel sport."* (This from a youth who had come all the way from Camden, New Jersey, to kill Fascists.) Most of all, however, the men wanted overnight passes. While the *troika* issued a few for dental work in Albacete, not everyone was lucky enough to have bad teeth. (In requesting leaves, whorehouses in Albacete were called "dental clinics" until the commissars caught on.)* When grumbling over the paucity of leaves reached a flash point, the commissars called a meeting in the church to explain that motor vehicles had to be used for transporting men and supplies to the front, and so on. All old excuses. Finally Dr. William Pike took the pulpit to pour oil on troubled waters. "Comrades," he began," I know you guys want to go to Albacete to get laid. But if you went, you'd get a dose and be unfit for the front. But there's one thing you all can do." He paused, and the men listened eagerly. "You can masturbate."* Some laughs rang out, but when they realized that Doc was serious, there was an uproar of jeering and hooting.

Despite their desire to escape from Villanueva, the Americans were nonetheless successful in winning back the villagers' good will lost by the French. The 17th Battalion hospital, a one-man operation run by Dr. Pike, a graduate from the University of Chicago, was installed in a barn-sized villa on the *plaza mayor* and opened its doors to the civilian population as the first free clinic in Villanueva history.* (Prior to this, a maverick *practicante,* Eugene Fogarty of

British Columbia, who had married a local girl half his age and had applied for Spanish citizenship, had administered his universal nostrum to the local population—aspirin and bed rest.)[10] The battalion movie projector ran three times a day, one show given over to the townspeople, who seemed to enjoy equally well the Soviet classic *The Sailors of Kronstadt* and *How to Operate a Maxim Machine-gun*. Like Spanish youths, the Americans hung out at the *plaza mayor*, where young girls, escorted by their mothers, took their *paseo* every evening. Harry Fisher, a union organizer from New York, invited a girl to a movie. The girl accepted, the mother nodded approval, and on the evening of the date she arrived at the hall with her entire family. They watched the movie—Harry on one end of the aisle and the girl at the other end with the family in between.* The Cubans of the "Antonio Guiterrras Column" (which included half a dozen Puerto Ricans and a Mexican) quickly established rapport with the villagers through a shared language. Their leader, Rudolfo Armas, became the cynosure of admiring eyes as he strolled during the paseo with a young Villanueva girl who had consented to become his wife. They planned to marry as soon as the war was over.

At first the villagers had been frightened of the American blacks, associating them with the ferocious Moors of Franco's armies. Doug Roach changed this overnight when he walked on his hands and performed other acrobatics that captivated the local children. Thereafter they waited devotedly for him at the convent door and tagged at his heels like a pack of puppies. With the ice broken, Americans found candy for the tots and amused themselves teaching them the words of revolutionary songs and listening to them sing:

> On the line, on the line,
> On the peek-it, peek-it line.*

John Lenthier produced a musicale for battalion and villagers alike that featured Jewish truck drivers' songs in Irish brogue, a former Wobbly crooning Joe Hill's "Scissorbill," and a Harlem black chanting Langston Hughes's "Scottsboro," topped off with his rendition of "The Marching Song of the Lincoln Battalion." During their stay at Villanueva only one man, Ray Steele, had to be locked up as

---

10. "Eugenio Fogarte" briefly took up practice at nearby Iniesta, but as a hated International he feared *depurtación* by Franco authorities and fled Spain, leaving his wife and children behind. After World War II the Canadian government notified Jacoba Morena de Fogarty that her husband had been killed in the Far East, and she received a small lump-sum pension. Of the half-dozen marriages of British volunteers to local girls at Madrigueras, the church nullified all after the war save that of one man, who still summers in the locality.*

drunk and disorderly. The Americans so far surpassed the French in establishing rapport with the populace that some of the men slipped away in the evening to split a stray pack of Luckies and savor a simple omelet with a family. Seated on low stools or crouching around an open fire on the floor, they ate from a communal bowl, the single spoon passed around and used only for spreading food on bread. One American never forgot his visit with a local family in a single-room house with a floor of hardened clay. They were joined by other family members who came and went as they pleased—a goat, a scrawny dog, a lamb, and noisy chickens, "none of them inhibited."* Yet the villagers became agitated after hearing nightly gunshots at Santa Clara. A whispered word—*ejecuciones.* But it was only target shooting in the convent chapel.[11]

It was apparent to many of the Americans—particularly Doug Seacord—that the Lincolns were not acquiring the basics of military art. At drill only a few ancient rifles were available, so most men performed the manual of arms with broomsticks or canes. The joke went around that in a real battle sticks and stones might be more lethal than such firearms. They inspected—but did not throw—Spanish concussion grenades, which resembled sardine cans with tails.

The winds of change began to blow in late January, when there appeared two figures destined to lead the battalion out of confusion and into catastrophe—Sam Stember from Philadelphia and Robert Hale Merriman, most recently from the Soviet Union.

Both Stember and Merriman were in their thirties—but at that point their resemblance ended. Sam Stember was a loser. A smaller-than-life figure, he had the sagging mien of someone who had spent his best years behind a beat-up desk in a dingy office, grinding out Party leaflets on a mimeograph machine. To most of the volunteers he seemed like a used-up hack slipping backward after a long uphill climb toward the middle rungs of the Party ladder. He emitted, almost like a body odor, a weariness and dreariness that led the men to nickname him "Last-Chance" Stember. Others called him "The Jello."* It seemed absurd that such a creature had been sent by the New York office as commissar to develop political leadership and to put some snap into the battalion. Yet

11. Thirty years later when I visited Villanueva de la Jara, middle-aged villagers seemed more willing to talk about the French volunteers. "Big drunks—those Frenchmen!" they said laughingly. One of the boys who used to follow Doug Roach had become the mayor's assistant. He said he always assumed the Americans were a trained army waiting to be sent to the front, for he recalled no training program whatever. The Americans stood around smoking. He liked them and always wondered what happened to them in the war. He added that he thought the United States was the hope of the world—but that it should join with the Soviet Union and destroy China.

once upon a time Stember had been something of a Party mover. A veteran of the World War, he became the linchpin of the short-lived Workers' Ex-Service Men's League, an outfit founded by the CP to oppose the American Legion. Probably the zenith of his career occurred in the summer of 1932, when he helped organize the CP contingent of the Bonus March on Washington. City police fingered him as primarily responsible for the rioting, which ended with evicting the Marchers and burning their Hooverville shantytown in the Anacostia Flats.* How his career as a disrupter would prepare him for work with the Lincoln Battalion remained to be seen. At his inaugural ceremony, Marvin Stern of the *troika* asked the men to give the comrade a vote of confidence. A lone voice cried out, "Does it have to be unanimous?" Tony DeMaio, a Hartford tough (soon to gain notoriety as an IB *chekist*), confronted the dissident. "It has to be *unanimous.* You want your goddamn head broken?"* Without further discussion Sam Stember became the political commissar of the battalion.

It was during Stember's tenure that the battalion voted, again "unanimously," to call themselves the "Abraham Lincoln Battalion." More "democratic centralism" at work, because the Central Committee of the CPUSA had chosen the name *before* the *Normandie* cohort had left New York. (In fact, the men themselves had unfurled a Lincoln Battalion banner when they marched through Barcelona back in January!)* To everyone's surprise, Marvin Stern promptly resigned from the commissariat and entered the ranks. While not popular, he was respected for his dedication and energy. Now it appeared that he had been purged in some conspiratorial proceeding behind their backs. He had said that he was keeping a diary and would send it to the New York office. So when he vanished from the battalion a short time later—never to be seen again by the Lincolns—many suspected foul play.[12] In any event, with the arrival of Stember, the word "comic-star" first took root among the Americans as the moniker for any commissar they disliked.

By contrast, Robert Hale Merriman was a winner. If Spain was the last chance for Stember, it offered the first chance for a Californian whose dossier was the best recruiting poster the Lincoln Battalion ever had. Magnetic leader, studious intellectual, university athlete, and dedicated proletarian—it all seemed too good to be true, yet it was. Born in 1906 in Eureka, California, Merriman had grown up in half a dozen logging towns in redwood country. His father was a lumberjack, and his mother a schoolteacher with literary aspirations.

---

12. When some volunteers asked Phil Bard and Steve Nelson—a later battalion commissar and central committeeman of the CP—what had happened to Stern they were harshly reprimanded and told never to bring up that question again.* No answer has ever been forthcoming, although battalion records list him as killed in Spain.

After high school he felled trees and fed pulp in a paper mill. There he had fallen in with an old Irish radical, who forced him to question some of his *laissez-faire* assumptions. Young Merriman became intrigued by the theory that the strong ought to do something for the weak beyond exploiting them, but after he had saved enough to enroll at the University of Nevada, his ambition was still to rise out of his economic class rather than to raise his class up with him. He drove over to Reno in his own Dodge roadster—one month later the stock market crashed.

At the university, Merriman quickly became a campus wheelhorse and beau-ideal of fraternity row. Standing six-feet-two and weighing in at 190 pounds, he was a clean-cut, Anglo-Saxon go-getter. The Depression nipped the college years of classmates, but not Merriman's. He got a job at Penney's (where a lot of his earnings went on discounted clothes), worked part-time in a local funeral parlor, ran the business end of the college newspaper, commanded a company of the ROTC unit for the money ($7.50 per month), and served as house manager of his fraternity, the prestigious Sigma Nu. Campus photographs reveal a well-scrubbed, all-American boy who looks as though he had just stepped out of the pages of *Frank Merriwell at Yale*. "He was very ambitious," recalls a Nevada classmate. "A" grades were easy.*

Yet Merriman had a rebellious streak that made him balk at easy success, traditional canons, and time-worn taboos. Although his professors found him an omnivorous student, he disliked being forced into a mold. On one occasion, when the university tried to force him to take a required course, he refused. The president himself intervened and demanded that he take it. After research in Nevada statutes, Merriman found a forgotten law that supported his right to waive the requirement. (The law was subsequently changed.) Later, in an editorial he denounced compulsory ROTC as incompatible with American democracy, much to the surprise of the military staff, which regarded him as a superior officer, and to the consternation of the president, who made a public speech about "rabble-rousers" on campus but did not have the courage to name Merriman specifically. On graduation day the campus "radical" married Marion Stone, a sorority queen and university cheerleader, and received a commission as second lieutenant in the U.S. Army Reserve.

That fall Merriman found a post as assistant instructor of economics at Berkeley. Conditions in the country were so tight that for a time he had to support his wife's parents. He moonlighted as a polisher at a Ford assembly plant, where he helped publish an illicit union-shop newspaper. When the plant went out on strike and the Cal football team came over as strikebreakers, Merriman led demonstrations demanding that the jocks stay on the gridiron where they belonged. In 1934 he won a Newton Booth Traveling Fellowship for a research project dealing with collective farming in the Soviet Union. When the Spanish civil war broke out, he and Marion were in Russia, where he was completing a thesis on collective farming at the Moscow Institute of Economics.[13] He always said that he had never heard of an American unit until he arrived at Valencia on a Soviet freighter in mid-January 1937. At Albacete, on January 29, he enlisted in the International Brigades and was at once welcomed by the Marty cabal because of his military "experience"—or so they said. Yet there may have been darker reasons for his stellar rise. In the Soviet Union, the *Yezhovshchina*, purges that would ultimately eliminate three-quarters of the Central Committee, was under way, and it is likely that no one at Albacete was quite sure who or what stood behind Merriman. If he was a Kremlin spy, it would be better to treat him with kid gloves. The scuttlebutt in Albacete was that he had come straight from the Frunze Military Academy, until it was replaced by a rumor that he had come straight from the famous Lenin Institute. Neither was true. His only known job in Moscow was innocuous—helping to install a phone system to the United States.* (Also arriving at Albacete at this time was Sterling Rochester, an American black, who had been working at the Lenin Institute on his dream project—the establishment of a separate black republic in the United States.)*

In any event, with Merriman on the scene the days of James Harris were numbered. The problem was how to sack Harris without arousing his followers and thereby adding to the factionalism already ravaging the battalion. For the moment, Merriman was installed as battalion adjutant on the basis of his ROTC training, an appointment that upset no one at Villanueva. (Merriman later told Sandor Voros of the brigade historical section that his instruction was "to beef up" Harris.)[14]

The Lincolns received Robert Merriman with mixed feelings. The intellectuals and student revolutionaries regarded him as one of "their kind"—an efficient

13. The fact that Merriman arrived directly from the USSR convinced most volunteers that the collective-farming story was a cover for his real activities—studies at the Lenin Institute. His wife's memoir, which chronicles his studies meticulously and convincingly, refutes this and emphasizes that he was never a member of the CP. This is borne out by documents in the Moscow archives. When Merriman went off to Spain, he apparently expected to return to Moscow as soon as the war ended, which he thought would be soon.

14. In his book *American Commissar*, Voros, a CP defector, often harshly criticized the Lincoln Battalion leadership. However, Merriman so charmed him that he accepted as gospel everything that Merriman said about the early days in the battalion. Ironically, those Party "stalwarts" who dismiss Voros as a self-apologetic liar nonetheless accept his estimate of the Merriman epic without quibble or question.

(but not ruthless) college man with military training to boot. Yet many of the seamen and old-timers thought they saw ambition written all over him and guessed that the days of Jim Harris, only an ordinary seaman, were numbered. "At first I liked his big, open smile," remembered one man, "until I noticed that he never *stopped* smiling."* With steel-rimmed spectacles slipping down his well-chiseled nose, Merriman called to mind the Hollywood image of a young professor. But when he made his move, he moved fast. First, he took over Harris's lectures on tactics. Next, he relieved him of drafting daily orders. Then came frequent trips to Albacete, officially to argue about promised equipment and to confer with the Base—all ostensibly with the object of "saving" Harris. No one ever recalled a trace of friction between the commander and his adjutant, but some noticed that Commissar Stember began to bypass Harris to confer directly with Merriman. Merriman was taking control of the battalion in increments.

The men were beginning to split down the middle about Harris. The growing pro-Merriman faction groused that Harris had the mentality of a sergeant—a good sergeant, to be sure, but a sergeant nonetheless. Although he seemed to know what he was talking about, he talked so little. They complained that in lectures he would posit some complicated tactical problem, then wheel to ask a recruit, "What would you do in that case?" No matter what the reply, Harris was apt to shake his head and say, "No good. You'd kill off all your men that way." The pro-Harris faction disagreed. They pointed to his experience training Chinese units. He knew what he was doing, although he failed to "inspire those young men with the hero syndrome." A case in point was the afternoon when he turned the convent chapel into a shooting range with targets resting on the altar. No desecration intended—"He wanted us to hear bullets close to our ears and in shattering volume. It worked, too!" To these men Harris was the real McCoy.*

Merriman failed to break down the stateside grievance-committee attitude within the battalion that virtually stifled development as a unified military unit. Too often meetings ended in arguments, and sometimes fights, because each comrade abided by what he thought was the legitimate Party line—and to hell with whoever disagreed. "There wasn't even a semblance of military organization," recorded a volunteer.* The situation worsened when men banded together in secret caucuses; those not included became enraged and organized factions of their own. Finally, Stember banned Party meetings altogether on the grounds that they encouraged wrangling over picayunish details without respect for decisions made from above.

Granted, there now seemed to be more zip in the drilling, gunnery, and lectures, although target practice barely existed because nearly all live ammunition went to the front. Besides, the few Steyr and Ross rifles on hand tended to jam after each shot, and the bolts often had to be knocked loose with a rock. (The men had not been issued rifles of their own.) A few defused Mills bombs were passed around to give them a sense of their heft. Trench mortars did not exist, although a few tired Russian Maxim water-cooled machine guns arrived. To simulate the sound of gunfire, Merriman ran a stock across wooden slats, in the manner of a boy rattling a paling fence. Attacking across open terrain, the Americans always seemed to bunch together rather than to disperse. Parade-ground maneuvers always remained beyond (or beneath) the attention of the Lincolns, who never learned to march in micrometer precision like the German and Slavic volunteers.

One night the enemy bombed Albacete. The war was creeping closer to the Lincoln Battalion. Maneuvering through the sunny hillsides around Villanueva became more serious. Motley groups in khaki field trousers, carrying imaginary weapons, attacked imaginary Fascists. On the skyline, solitary umbrella pines stuck up from the plain like green barrage balloons.

Early in February news filtered down that the Nationalists had launched a new offensive against Madrid, slashing across the Jarama River southeast of the capital in order to cut the Valencia road, the principal artery feeding the nearly surrounded former capital, and to push north to Alcalá de Henares on the Madrid-Zaragoza artery. Originally planned for January 24, it had to be postponed until February 6 because rain and fog had reduced visibility to zero and turned the terrain into slurry. By an odd coincidence the Republic had assembled fifty tanks and one hundred artillery pieces in the same sector for its own offensive on February 5, but the Nationalists struck first, took the major Jarama bridges, and secured a foothold on the plateau east of the river.

Few foreign newspapers ever reached the Americans at Villanueva de la Jara other than the French-Communist *L'humanité*, which few of them could read, along with outdated copies of the *Daily Worker* from time to time. (Newspapers like the *New York Times* were prohibited along with other "Fascist propaganda.") Nevertheless, there were signs that something big was in the wind. Couriers reported that almost overnight the three sister battalions of the XVth Brigade—the Saklatvala (British), the Dimitrov (Yugoslav), and the Sixth of February (French) had vanished from their camps. But at Villanueva nothing happened. New recruits trickled in every day until the battalion numbered more than four hundred. They chafed with impatience. They had come to fight Fascism, not to play at war in a time-warping pueblo.

Finally on February 12, the order came to move—not to the front but to a new camp in the piney woods at Pozorubio, a few miles north of Albacete. The men were enraged, blaming their call-up delay on spiteful anti-Americanism among the Marty clique. At least one man in the battalion rejoiced. Doug Seacord, the machine-gun instructor, knew that they were still too green to be committed to battle. Normally sober and steady, he had begun drinking so heavily that his runner, Bill Harvey, had to cover for him. Even though he had never fought in a battle, as a former professional soldier, Seacord must have guessed what might happen when his untrained battalion went into action led by a former Army sergeant and an ROTC shavetail.

At that very moment, the afternoon of February 12, one other American in Spain was experiencing at first hand what lay ahead for the Lincolns. Joseph Seligman, a nineteen-year-old Swarthmore College student from Louisville, lay with the British among the olive trees at Jarama trying to beat back a massive frontal assault of Moors. A few months previously, at a Swarthmore party, a classmate had toasted, "Here's to the good life," and Seligman corrected him. "No, here's to *life.*" Radicalized by a college art teacher who had convinced herself she was a Soviet spy, Seligman traveled to Spain on his own, crossed the frontier with a fake passport, and in mid-December joined the British Battalion. Wanting to be the first American to see action, he refused transfer into the Lincoln Battalion, which enrolled him posthumously. (He was so little known among the British that their official record spells his surname wrong and fails to list his first name.) For Seligman, life would be neither good nor long. Before the sun set on his first day of battle, he was mortally wounded in the head. (The *Halcyon,* Swarthmore's yearbook, in print before news arrived of his death, reads: "A quiet thoughtful, literary atmosphere allowing many hours of repose . . . would be Joe's ideal habitat.")*

The first American massacre was now only eleven days distant.

3

THE YANKS ARE COMING

In the midmorning of February 15, 1937, a convoy of forty trucks—Chevrolets, Bedfords, Matford, no two exactly alike, bumped into Villanueva de Jara and parked in the *plaza mayor*. Americans drilling on the hillsides immediately returned to town and assembled their field kits, leaving nonessentials behind. A kid from New York carried along a sack of crucifixes he was collecting, and a Texan nicknamed "Peanuts" grinned when he showed his squad leader a knapsack crammed with goobers and almonds. "Best nourishment in the world," he said.* Women from the village came out, tears in their eyes, to see them off. "I think they were genuine tears," a seaman remembered, "even though they never knew us, really."*

Stalked by a brand-new ambulance, the trucks drove past the parish church (lately the battalion garage and gasoline warehouse), crossed the ditch called the Valdemembra River, and turned south on the Albacete road. Because troop movements had to be made at night, to avoid the scrutiny of "spies," they took their time passing across flat country that suggested patches of Nebraska or Oklahoma. The convoy contained about four hundred Lincolns. The original *Normandie* contingent had received less than five weeks of haphazard military training, later arrivals, from the Bronx YCL, less than three days. Most had not yet fired a weapon. Now they were scrambled together to plug a gap in the line where the British had been decimated three days before, but this bad news they learned only later—and piecemeal.

It was dark when the convoy parked in the Albacete *plaza de toros*, the assembly point for all Internationals bound for the front. Someone whispered, "This bullring is where spies, fascists, and traitors are put up against the wall to face a firing squad."* Old-hat to those once housed in Guardia Civil barracks. In the bandstand, floodlit by headlights of the trucks and surrounded by his pistol-packing entourage, stood André Marty. Shaking his fist, his voice echoing raucously over the PA system, he explained that the Republican front along the Jarama River had caved in: once again Internationals must save Madrid from the unholy alliance of the Axis powers aiming to dominate the world. "¡No pasarán!" he shouted. Every American understood that much Spanish. "¡No pasarán!" they thundered back.

Then Peter Kerrigan, the British representative at the Base, delivered a short exhortation. British lads were already hotly engaged with the Fascists and had been cheered that "the Yanks are coming." He urged them to hurl back the enemy as their fathers had rallied against the Huns on the battlefields of France. He had nothing to say about reports reaching Albacete that the British had taken two hundred casualties during their first hours—not days—of battle, had roundly damned their leaders for their catastrophic losses, and had menaced the brigade commander with clubs.* (Conditions at the front were so chaotic that the battalions already engaged had gone without resupply of food and water for two days.)* Phil Bard offered no parting homilies for the Americans. A political nonentity, he had not joined the heavies in the bandstand. Speeches over, Marty departed. Truck lights went off, leaving the plaza lit by a weak bulb swinging in the wind.

In the chill February evening they lined up behind a supply truck and unloaded heavy boxes about the size of coffins. Breaking them open, they found new bolt-action rifles, each wrapped in Mexico City newspapers and oozing Cosmoline. With each came a small cloth bag stuffed with cleaning brushes and small tools but no rags. "Clean them!" came the order. "What with?" came a plaintive voice. "Use your shirttails," barked Seacord. The rifles were Remingtons, some barrels stamped with the czarist double-eagle, others with the Soviet hammer and sickle. The latter were seven centimeters shorter and a few ounces lighter, but their bolts were prone to jam when overheated. (Some rifles were stamped only with "Made in Connecticut.") The men nicknamed their rifles "*Mexicanskis*," and the story passed into local folklore that they had been manufactured in the United States, sent to the czar in 1914, copied by Bolshevik artisans, sold to Mexico for revolutionary work, and then donated to the Spanish Republic. Some had leather slings, the rest only flimsy linen ones.* Each man got a cartridge belt with three leather ammo boxes, 150 cartridges, and a wicked-looking needle bayonet with a triangular blade that could stick a Fascist like a pig but not cut his throat. There was no time to test-fire the rifles, which in many cases lacked locking attachments for the bayonets. Each man also received a metal helmet. Most got the French poilu style of the World War (which proved to be only metallic eggshells when struck by steel or lead). Nothing but war museum stuff. "Wouldn't have kept a doughnut out, but they looked ornamental—the French always liked to dress their men well."* A few lucky men received ugly chamber-pot helmets manufactured in Czechoslovakia from a superb quality of steel.[1]

1. I found specimens of these two types of helmet in a Jarama dugout in 1966, where they had lain head to head for thirty years. The French ones were pitted and corroded, but the Czech ones had only a thin scale of rust and were as sound as ever.

Final orders confirmed James Harris as commander, Robert Merriman as battalion adjutant, and Sam Stember as commissar.[2] As captains they received field glasses, sidearms, and cloth map cases (but no maps).[3] First Company, which included the Irish and Cuban sections, was commanded by John Scott (Inver Marlow), a volatile Englishman of the Byronic school whose outward mien suggested greater familiarity with a West End club than a union hall. (The only known photograph of Scott shows a husky, curly-haired man in Bermuda shorts seated in front of a chessboard.) Yet Scott was devoutly committed to the working-class movement. Outraged by conditions in China and India, he had joined the Communist Party and gone to New York as a columnist for the *Daily Worker.* Then slipping away from his desk without a word to anyone, he joined the first group on the *Normandie.*

Second Company was commanded by Steve Daduk, who had been hanging around Albacete since late fall recovering from a wound. His bragging rights were impressive, for he claimed to have been shot down over Madrid while flying for the Malraux International Squadron during the early months of the war. (On the other hand, some Americans recall his stories of fighting in the Thaelmann Battalion.)[4] He was a peppery redhead of five-feet-six who wore, instead of the regulation uniform, a blue *miliciano* boilersuit with red bandanna round his neck. Sent to Villanueva on a temporary basis to assist in the training program, he stayed on because of his reputed military experience. Some volunteers opined that Daduk's autobiography improved with each telling. He had dozens of horror tales about units caught in the open and wiped out. He instituted nighttime drills for his company—marching, digging, assaulting the village—that wore out his men before sunup and led them to migrate into other companies, when possible. Altogether a "luster-bluster."*

2. Merriman told Voros a strange story about Harris's becoming "unnerved" in the bullring, where he "grabbed rifles out of the men's hands saying he was a rifle inspector" and had to be ordered away by Stember. Harris having disappeared, Merriman became commander. No other eyewitness source mentions this altercation. Three men in the convoy with whom I spoke remember Harris in the bullring when they pulled out and in Chinchon when the trucks stopped. Harris probably grabbed rifles and proclaimed himself as an "inspector" but it is unlikely that he was removed because during the first days at Jarama he was still the commander.

3. This was not unusual. The only maps the British Battalion had at Jarama were made on the spot by the combatants themselves. In fact, these crude sketches provided the division commander with the only maps he had of the terrain. It seemed to have occurred to no one that accurate maps were available at the Cartographical Institute in Madrid. In 1967, I had no difficulty purchasing from the Institute detailed topographical maps dating back to the early 1930s.

4. Daduk's flying career owes more to Comintern publicists than to discoverable fact. In *Airmen without Portfolio* (1997), John Carver Edwards, who wrote the definitive account of American pilots flying for Republican Spain, makes no mention of Daduk at all.

48

Third Company, the pride of the battalion, remained under Douglas Seacord. Though his gunners were intractable and independent, Seacord never had to raise his voice or lose his temper with them. "We behaved like a bunch of anarchists," one gunner said, "but we loved that man."* This company received half a dozen Russian-made, water-cooled 1914 Maxims, guns so heavy that they had to be mounted on wheeled carriages and towed about like toy cannon. Though cumbersome and somewhat inaccurate, they were tough and usually reliable, although spare parts were hard to come by.

At midnight the battalion, numbering 418 men and now officially registered as the 17th International Battalion, boarded canvas-covered five-ton trucks and rolled up the highway toward Madrid, 150 miles to the northwest. (Earlier the British had traveled most of the distance by rail, but that route had been severed by rapid enemy advance.) Of the 450 British who had left Albacete only seven nights before, less than a hundred at that moment remained in their shallow trenches under the olive trees on the Jarama plateau. The Americans had no inkling of this. "No idea where we were going except to put up a defense of Madrid."*

The night was bitter and moonless. Lacking space to sit down, they stood or crouched, supporting one another and cursing the driver whenever their truck whammed a pothole. Before leaving Albacete they were warned that anyone showing a light would be shot on the spot, so drivers flashed on their low beams only when a sixth sense signaled that a curve, or another truck, loomed ahead. Although their destination lay more than a hundred miles distant, officers ordered them not to talk, so that the enemy would not hear them coming! Among the men the greatest fear was that the trucks would overturn and they would be crushed by tons of machinery and comrades-at-arms.* There were no bladder stops: a man in need had to edge through the press to the tailgate and let go. Then he would have to fight his way back to his place, because everyone preferred nearly suffocating at the center to freezing on the edge. Somehow the story got around, and was believed, that an enemy scout plane monitoring their movements followed them all night.* (How anyone could identify an enemy plane at night was never explained.) Once they stopped with all motors off, and some men later swore that they had heard the drone overhead of bombers.*

First light found them, blunted by exhaustion and numbed by a bone-deep cold, at Chinchón, a village perched on a ridge overlooking the lush, green vale of the Tajuña, a small tributary of the Jarama River, which lay just beyond the mountains to the west. Beyond the valley floor rose another ridge, or smallish mountain, topped by a wide plateau dotted with olive trees. This was the extreme southern flank of the battle of Jarama, then raging along a twelve-mile front. Ten days before, the Nationalists had launched their offensive, designed to cut the Madrid-Valencia highway and starve the capital into submission. The main thrust had been halted farther north, nearer the city, so both armies were snaking southward, probing for weaknesses in the enemy line. To block the enemy from the left bank of the river, the bridge at La Marañosa had been mined and a company of the André Marty Battalion assigned to defend it, but on a quiet night, when no sentinels had been posted, Moorish troops crept up and cut the throats of seventy Frenchmen as they slept. When the charges were set off, the bridge merely lifted into the air and fell back like a huge pontoon. By midmorning of February 11 the Nationalists had streamed across the river in force and occupied the high ground sloping down toward the Tajuña valley. The Americans had been hastily collected to assist the British in holding the sector next to the road from San Martín de la Vega to Morata de Tajuña.

The rumble of distant artillery was reverberating across the valley as the Lincolns climbed out of their trucks just beyond Chinchón with orders to test-fire their *Mexicanskis*. Of the four hundred men loading clips with five cartridges and gingerly opening fire upon the limestone walls of a cement quarry, only about fifty had ever used a rifle before.* Although still gummy with Cosmoline, no rifles exploded. Because of their light weight, they kicked like mules and tended to shoot high without the counterbalance of the needle bayonet. The latter had no scabbard but were fixed to the boss of the rifle. They easily fell out and were lost. Though a few summer-camp campaigners of the National Guard complained that the butts were fashioned from wood too soft for smashing Fascist heads, most men were delighted to have their own weapons at long last and eager to use them. Captain Harris told the company officers that they would shortly move up to a third-reserve position. They were safe where they were, but could expect shelling or air attacks when they descended into the Tajuña valley.

In late afternoon the Lincoln trucks wound down the valley road, jammed with vehicles and reinforcements moving up to the line. Overturned and charred vehicles littered the ditches, but in the fields *campesinos* thrashed olive trees with long poles, harvesting the fruit and ignoring mechanical nuisances that interrupted their more important task of producing food and oil. It was hot, and the road became littered with sheep-lined jackets pitched from the trucks. No sooner had the men climbed out of the trucks in Morata than a squadron of enemy bombers (Capronis, it was said) popped over the western ridge. Men in the village began running in all directions, but most Lincolns stood frozen on the highway, looking up slack-jawed, as the first bombs screamed down. Wide of their mark, the bombs exploded in an olive grove

50

outside the village, and before they could return, six *Chatos* (Snub-noses)—Russian I-15 biplanes—pounced on them, sent one plummeting in flames, and drove the others off. Americans joined other Republican soldiers in cheering and pummeling each other, shouting "*¡Nuestros!*" (Ours!).* One Lincoln lying on his back in the road is said to have fired shots at the empty sky.* What a glorious initiation into battle! "A couple of German [brigaders] congratulated us on our sangfroid—not knowing we knew no better."*

Morata, a major road junction of the sector, looked like a Hollywood set for a war movie. Beside the field kitchen in the bombed *plaza mayor,* a disabled Russian tank squatted like a prehistoric toad. The houses looked like rotten teeth—houses without walls, houses without roofs, and in a few places nearly intact roofs without houses. The stork nest on the gable of the town hall had not been disturbed, but the storks had deserted.

Morata was the hub for operations on the plateau. Seven miles north lay Arganda, the original objective of the enemy offensive; five miles east lay Perales de Tajuña, headquarters of the Russian tank battalion (close enough to lend support but far enough away to ensure that their valuable, experimental vehicles would not be captured if the front collapsed). The western road wound up to the battle zone on the plateau, about one mile away. By this time the front was locked into place for the duration of the war, although both sides continued to batter and probe, always hoping for a significant "breakthrough."

Though no one knew it at the time, there had already been major casualties among the Lincolns. The two lead trucks had outrun the rest of the convoy and were bumping along the shell-pitted Arganda road far to the north. Johnny Parks, an American Indian from Philadelphia, in charge of the first truck, had grumbled back at the quarry that the officers were too close-mouthed about their directions. Since none of the drivers had maps, and no military police were posted at road intersections, they had missed a turn and were proceeding down a road held by the enemy. After topping a rise and coasting down a long hill, they spotted soldiers in unfamiliar uniforms flagging them down. Fascists! Too late to turn around, the driver accelerated to break through. Soldiers of the Tercios de Extranjeros opened fire and damaged the steering mechanism of Park's truck, which overturned and was struck by the next truck in the convoy. Stunned and bewildered Americans, half asleep from their long ride, spilled out and tried to take cover under the vehicles or in a roadside ditch. Some fired rifles they barely knew how to load, but they were no match for battle-hawkish legionnaires. Others sought safety by crawling into a culvert and were easily killed when enemy soldiers rolled in grenades. Fifteen Americans and one Canadian were killed in the melee, and one wounded volunteer taken prisoner. In the brief firefight, one legionnaire was also wounded. The legionnaires administered first aid to the prisoner, planning to send him to the hospital in the morning, but at night some Moors from the 2nd Tabor of Melilla, who had come over to scavenge the corpses and wreckage, found the prisoner and cut his throat.[5]

These men vanished as completely as if they had never existed. Had it not been for Dr. William Pike, in the third truck, who sensed something was wrong and ordered his driver to stop while he confirmed directions, the entire Lincoln convoy might have been swallowed up.* Doubtless to minimize the catastrophe, battalion officers told others in the convoy that there was one truck missing. True to form, Commissar Stember tried to cover up the blunder by blaming it on a "Trotskyite spy."* In time, however, the Party made good use of the calamity. If an American demanded the return of his passport, he was likely to be told that it had been "lost" among other papers on the missing truck. Even volunteers arriving in Spain months afterward received the same explanation for missing passports! Not all the men bought this story: "How come," they muttered, "they took our passports into a battle zone rather than keeping them safe at the base?"*

Guided by a close-mouthed Austrian brigader, the Lincolns filed on foot up the dark mountain, now starkly silhouetted against a blood-red sunset that turned the western horizon into a firestorm. Yet the view back into the valley, with its whitewashed farms and mills, white-blossomed pear trees, and feathery poplars lining the Río Tajuña, was incongruously pastoral. Russian tanks clanked down the torn macadam road like threshing machines headed for the barn after a day in the fields. Americans waved at the oil-smeared heads in the open hatches, but the Russians ignored them. The rumble drew sporadic shelling. Watching skittish Americans looking for cover, the guide grinned: "*Das ist der Wein. Das Fleisch kommt noch*"* (loosely translated, "That's just the appetizer"). It was completely dark when he led them up a mule path crossing a narrow-gauge railroad track and over loose stones and briers to a flat-topped knoll. They had no idea where they were and could see nothing. The Austrian explained that the enemy held a ridge on higher ground, a mile or so west.

5. When *Between the Bullet and the Lie,* my book about the Lincoln Battalion, appeared in a Spanish edition, a former sergeant of the Tercios de Extranjeros, Santos Clemente Garcia, sent me a copy of his diary entry for February 16, 1937.* Some years later, Robert Gladnick, a Jarama veteran, to whom I had sent the letter, went over the ground with the sergeant and marked the spot on his map. Presumably the Americans were buried nearby. Nothing marked the place when I visited it in 2000 except a drainage ditch along a barren highway. On November 24, 1937, the *New York Times* erroneously reported that two trucks carrying thirty-five men each and a headquarters car had been cut off. For another account, including the names and home towns of the Americans, see Geiser, *Prisoners of the Good Fight,* 12–13.

Advising them to dig in, he vanished. A few machine-gun bullets whistled overhead.

"Dig in!" shouted the Lincoln officers. With what? In New York some men had received collapsible spades in their kits, but had dumped them long ago. They dropped on their knees and stabbed the rocky ground with bayonets and shoveled dirt with their helmets and bare hands. An officer yelled, "Your life will depend on the best shelter you can dig!"* Bill Harvey had worked as a farmer on a Michigan farm, but this was a tougher job. "It was fear—that cut my lung capacity."* After hours of work his hole was barely visible. Next to him, William White, a powerful black volunteer from Philadelphia, lay comfortably in a foxhole so deep it could have served as his grave. Water froze on this arid hill at night; digging had kept them warm. Harvey tried to get some sleep. He blessed his mother for having made him a windbreaker, cursed Stember for not bringing up shovels, and himself for having thrown away his fleece-lined coat during the hot afternoon.[6] The night brought a near tragic turn when two Spanish soldiers, wanting to say hello to the newcomers, wandered onto the hilltop, and just missed being killed by jittery Americans.

At first light a row of apple trees bordering the mine railroad that looped around their knoll materialized in front of them. To the west rose a much higher ridge, hovering like an ocean wave, irregular and buckled. Enemy trenches were out of sight up there among a thick stand of olives, about a thousand yards off. The road from Morata to San Martín de la Vega twisted between folds of hill directly in front and led up into enemy territory. To their rear the Lincolns had a picture-postcard view of the Tajuña valley, where mules with food and ammunition were being kicked and coaxed up trails to the plateau. Immediately below them was a battered road-mender's shack on the Arganda road with a blue-tiled sign "MADRID 32 km." This served as the brigade field headquarters. In a verdant hollow nearby, smoke drifted from a whitewashed country inn, taken over as the XVth Brigade cookhouse, the discovery of Bob Gladnick, who followed his nose and brought back to his pals fresh bread and a pot of coffee.[7] Enemy spotters immediately exploited their first mistake— digging foxholes on the skyline. At six o'clock a few shells lumbered overhead and exploded harmlessly beyond them. An American voice cried in falsetto,

6. The erratic circle of holes scratched out on the hilltop by the Lincolns was still there when I visited the spot in 1967 and 2000. I infer that in the darkness they were not certain where the enemy was—or how close—and therefore were trying to protect all flanks.

7. The cookhouse had provided a rallying point for waves of deserters after the massacre of the British Battalion on their debut at Jarama. Today the inn has returned and is a major stop on the itinerary of returning veterans of the International Brigades.

"What the hell are they trying to do—kill us?"* But joking vanished when subsequent explosions crept up the hillside toward them. Grabbing bayonets and helmets, they frantically dug deeper. A line of machine-gun tracers now drifted toward them from the western ridge, the bullets cracking overhead like clapping hands.[8] A young seaman named Charles Edwards was handed a pair of binoculars and told to locate the enemy machine gun, but he was pestered by others begging a peep through his glasses. "Keep your heads down!" he snapped. "There's a sniper up there." "What about you?" "Fuck you! I'm the observer," he replied.* The next moment a bullet smashed his head, killing him instantly. Shells exploded about the hilltop. A voice shouted through the dust, "Don't worry, Comrades! They're only 75s," which meant nothing to most of them. "Chelebian just had his head blown off!" shouted Marty Hourihan, a seaman and former teacher from Alabama.* Misak Chelebian, a New York Armenian, died without a groan. Few knew him well. He was remembered as "a sweet old man" (in his late forties), who spoke nearly unintelligible English and had recently lost his wife—or so somebody said. During a lull in the bombardment Stember managed to bring them thirty-five picks and shovels, which they employed lying on their bellies.

Douglas Seacord was cursing mad. They had been posted on a position overlooked by the enemy. Furthermore, he was growing unhappy with Oliver Law, a latecomer to his company who had been appointed his adjutant, a promotion that passed over half a dozen abler men. Law was a Texas black prominent as a CP organizer on the South Side of Chicago. He claimed to have served as a sergeant in the United States Army—the reason given for his promotion. Following the artillery barrage, a flight of bombers came over, so low that the men could see their bomb-bays opening. Glinting objects came down. Law shouted, "It's all right! They're dropping leaflets!"* Seacord shouted back, "Shut up! They're bombs!"[9] As the men gazed up in horror, the bombs wobbled down, seemed to bore in on a horizontal plane, screeched over their heads, and exploded well beyond the knoll. As the bombers banked for a second run, a Cuban section leader ran amuck: whipping out a pistol, he ran up and down the

8. The sound was magnified when bullets struck something, leading to the belief (unconfirmed) that the Nationalists were using explosive bullets. One reason for the panic in the British Battalion during their first day at Jarama was that when a bullet struck a tree or a rock (or a man) it sounded like a rifle being fired nearby. The result was that men often were convinced that the enemy had taken their flanks and they were cut off. For the same reason, in the same battle the opposing Nationalist troops believed that the Internationals were using explosive bullets.*

9. Peter Carroll, usually an apologist for the Lincolns, confirms the leaflets story and adds to it. Law said, "Lookee, Boss, they're dropping leaflets," and "Boss Merriman, them sure was powerful leaflets." According to Carroll, Law was "unabashed" by his exclamations.*

trench lips yelling, "I'll kill the first man who moves!" Before he could precipitate a panic, he was tackled and dragged down. The next day he was gone.* The bombers missed again. No bombs came nearer than 200 meters.*[10] The smoke and dust was mistaken for poison gas; men who had not thrown them away fumbled for their gas masks. After the crisis, the men laughed about "Leaflets" Law and joked about whether in the next bombardment they ought to wear their metal helmets over their balls instead of their heads.

By nightfall two Americans had shot toes off in order to be evacuated,* at least one man had deserted,[11] and half a dozen others lay lightly wounded. The Lincolns called their knoll Suicide Hill.[12] Here they remained for five days subjected to light barrages and sniper fire but sustaining no more fatalities. Meanwhile Harris had a conference with Colonel Copic, the commander of the XVth Brigade, who summarized how he directed the British attack on February 12. According to the translator, Harris enraged Copic with his comment on the colonel's tactics, "That was stupid."*

During the night of February 19 or 20, there occurred the controversial "Moonlight March" of the Lincoln Battalion, an episode that has raised unanswerable questions. The unvarnished facts seemed to be these. On his own authority, Captain Harris assembled the battalion behind Suicide Hill and led them on a march toward enemy lines. After wandering about for a short time, they returned to their point of origin. That same evening Harris was replaced by Merriman. His defenders professed that he wanted to acquaint them with night maneuvers under battlefield conditions. Repeatedly he had dunned into them that frontal assaults against an entrenched enemy were suicidal and that the Communist guerrillas, with whom he had served in China, had abandoned the trench-warfare tactics of the World War in favor of stealthy night attacks. This explanation is supported by the testimony of an interpreter at brigade

10. It was traumatic, for all that. For decades afterward, Bill Harvey was plagued by a recurring nightmare—he was trapped in a New York subway tunnel while bombers roared out of the dark tunnel and bore down on him.*

11. A.R. made good time. He reached the U.S consulate at Valencia on February 23 and applied for sanctuary against arrest and for assistance in returning home. This was denied, although he was sheltered at the consulate for several days. Early in March he left his uniform with the consul and attempted to reach Barcelona dressed as a civilian. His fate is not known. The uniform was returned to Washington as formal evidence to show that Americans were serving in a foreign army and therefore should have their citizenship revoked. (The Valencia consulate kept their wartime reports on Americans in Spain until 1968.)

12. Coincidentally, the British Battalion had dubbed their first defensive position at Jarama Suicide Hill, though with greater justification. It had been attacked and seized by Moors after a fierce firefight that accounted for most of the English and enemy dead. This Suicide Hill was located on the plateau, about two miles west of the American position.

headquarters who heard him say, "I'm not attacking in the daytime," for which Copic denounced him as "a coward—a favorite word of his."*

The pro-Merriman faction embellished the story with lively details. Merriman himself claimed that he was at brigade headquarters when Harris, missing since the convoy left Albacete, "appeared on the scene from nowhere" and told the men that they were moving to a new position. He then led them on a noisy march two kilometers northwest into no-man's-land. Alerted by the ruckus, enemy machine gunners opened fire, and a random shot disabled one man. That they passed over an actual battlefield has been confirmed by a Finnish-American who counted more than thirty dead bodies (not Americans) along the road.* When Stember asked where they were going, Harris replied, "Follow the North Star." About this time Merriman caught up with the column, ordered them to return, and had Harris removed in an ambulance. When men asked the commissars where he was, they were told that he was a habitual drunk. This explanation failed to convince those who knew him well: "Harris was a juicer, but even when juiced he walked ramrod straight."* Months later a rumor spread that Harris had been killed while fighting in the Dombrowski (Polish) Battalion.* Whatever the truth, he did not return, and Robert Merriman now held the reins of the Lincoln Battalion.[13]

Survivors of the British Battalion, in trenches off to the south, could have given some pointers to the Americans about what to expect, but contact between the battalions was prohibited because the British had been so "shredded" in their first battle that brigade staff feared their accounts would destroy Lincoln morale. It did make a grown man's blood run cold to listen to the anecdotes of the British adjutant commander, Fred Copeman, who had a graphic eye for detail. "God, in half an hour two hundred of our blokes were dead. . . . I saw poor old A.W.E. Smith, nearly bloody seventy and said, 'What the hell are you doing there?' and he said, 'I wanted to see some of the action,' and I said, 'You're bloody well seeing it now,' and then there was a little plop and his head fell off. . . . And Davidovitch, funny little fellow. A stretcher-bearer. He said 'Fred, it is butchery, real butchery' and so help me God as he said it his whole guts fell out like bloody giblets. It was odd. He didn't fall down, he just stood there and picked them up in his hands and stuck them back in, saying, 'I've been hit, Fred, I've been hit.'"* Copeman could run on in this vein for an hour—and often did.

---

13. The three major sources for the Harris-insanity theory were not entirely disinterested: Robert Thompson, in later years secretary-general of the CPUSA, who did not arrive at Jarama until several days later; William Wheeler, a New York teamster, subsequently Merriman's closest friend at La Pasionaria Hospital in Murcia; and Merriman himself, who passed on his version to Sandor Voros, the battalion historian, in July 1937.

Because the Lincoln machine guns were superfluous in their third-reserve position, Brigade loaned some of them to the Sixth of February Battalion, which held a vulnerable section of the front lines south of the road to San Martín de la Vega, the center of the XVth Brigade line. Seacord welcomed this chance to test his Maxims. Among crews assigned were two inseparables, Joe Gordon and Bill Harvey. Harvey was ecstatic when Seacord gave him an immense automatic pistol, until he discovered it had a broken hammer. "Wear it," said Seacord, laughing. "It'll look good on your hip."* The crews moved out on the night of February 21, set up their wheeled guns behind walls overlooking a deep ravine, and were told to expect an attack in the morning. These squads were the first units of the Lincoln Battalion to be employed on a firing line.[14]

The sun was already high when the Mooneys heard eerie wailing and chanting coming from behind the opposite hill. One of Harvey's men had been handed a gunnysack filled with hand grenades and wanted to know what to do with them. "They looked so lethal," Harvey remembered. They had never handled one before, and no one wanted to hold one, much less hang it on his belt. Pete Shimrack of New York suggested they bury them so they would not go off if hit by a bullet. Good idea—they hurriedly dug a deep hole. They had a bad moment at midday when two men trying to bring them food were shot and began to scream with pain. Two doughty Frenchmen crawled out and hauled them to safety. On the right two Soviet T-26 tanks began a rapid fire on the enemy positions. Then, to Harvey's astonishment, in front of them a Moorish *tabor* rose from their trenches "in the perfect unison of the Roxy Rockettes" and dashed down the hill toward them.* Their faces and tunics were the color of dirt but some had what looked like white towels around their heads. Without pausing to fire, they plunged straight down, their red-lined cloaks winging out behind them. Harvey's mouth turned to dust. Captain Van den Berghe, a Belgian officer of the Sixth of February, passed down the word not to fire until he gave the command. As though ordered to fix bayonets, the Franco-Belge pulled out and lit foul-smelling cigars, which the Americans interpreted as a pretentious gesture of Gaelic nonchalance performed to impress them. Squatting on his hams and smoking a stogie, Van den Berghe watched the Moors with the calm absorption of someone who had paid good money for a ringside seat.

14. Harvey jotted the names of his squad on a crude sketch of the position: [Vahram] Kavorkian, [Peter] Shimrak, [Joseph] Cuban, [Steve] Tsermanges, Maendidis, [Nick] Skepastiotis, Wagulevich, and [Joseph] Tannenhaus. (Those without a first name do not appear on VALB rosters; probably they were killed at Jarama or deserted.) Ethnically it was typical of the Lincoln roster at this time—a far cry from the "old American stock" that recruiters and fund-raisers back in the States praised when they discussed the national origins of the Lincoln Battalion.

Everyone else along the line fidgeted. The running figures had nearly reached the trough between the hills when Van den Berghe sprang to his feet and shouted something. As though a switch had been pulled, the Franco-Belge loosed a stunning volley. The Moors in front looked as though they had tripped over a wire. Harvey pulled the trigger of his Maxim. It fired one shot and jammed: "It curled up like a one-shot penis."[15] When the remaining Moors began surging upward toward them, the Franco-Belge picked up sticks of dynamite, lit the fuses with their cigars, and flung them down the slope. Within ten minutes it was all over, except for sniping at Moorish bodies that still writhed or twitched. When the Lincoln gunners returned to Suicide Hill, they tried not to strut.

The malfunction of Harvey's gun soon was repeated in other Maxim squads. Purchased from armory boneyards, many guns were troublemakers and had to be sent back for repair. Some squad leaders begged for permission to dismantle and reassemble them for another go, but most of the Mooney guns went back on the eve of their first battle.

Late in the afternoon of February 21, the Lincoln Battalion moved from Suicide Hill to the front line to relieve the battle-torn Dimitrov Battalion. The Republican command had resolved to probe the enemy lines at half a dozen places simultaneously to find a soft spot, and the Lincolns were to deliver a frontal attack in the sector just north of the San Martín road. For five days they had peered at the spooky olive groves of the upper plateau, hoping in vain to catch a glimpse of invisible snipers hidden by trees so far away that they resembled silver-green smoke puffs. At dusk the battalion moved out in single file, a long straggling line with Captain Merriman out in front. He had no guide, no doubt expecting to be met somewhere along the road and directed into reserve trenches.

Posted at a protected curve on the San Martín road stood a London soldier, Jason Gurney. Badly shaken by the decimation of the British Battalion, he had been assigned light duties with the staff as a mapmaker. He was startled to see what he thought were about five hundred men dressed in doughboy uniforms "like costumes belonging to the days of silent films," proceeding straight toward the enemy lines, which lay ahead around the curve. Gurney rushed at them shouting, to be met by "a tall, bespectacled character like a schoolmaster, draped in pistols, binoculars, and all the panoply of war." Merriman was indignant at this ragamuffin who had burst out of nowhere and interfered with "the script he had prepared for himself." Had Fate not placed Gurney at that spot at

---

15. With the Maxims the problem usually lay in the belts. Many of the machine-loaded belts held cartridges of slightly different gauges. When hand-loaded, the Maxim was a dependable but not precisely accurate gun. The others issued to the Internationals—Colts and Chauchats purchased by profiteers at armory boneyards—were of museum value only and soon disappeared.

that particular moment, the Lincoln Battalion would surely have blundered into the Fascist lines.*

Subdued and serious, the Lincolns filed into sandbagged ditches on the plateau. After nightfall this became an eerie place. Shells had split olive trees into nightmarish shapes. Undamaged trees were festooned with olives, which rained down whenever a burst of enemy machine-gun fire raked the grove from higher ground. Sentries unnerved everybody when they got off random shots, convinced they had seen caped Moors flitting through the grove. Assigned trenches too shallow to stand up in, the Americans had to crawl and stoop like infants or old men and yearned to dash across the four-hundred yard gap between the lines to meet the Fascists in a head-on fair fight. Their morale was high. Ever since Villanueva de la Jara, Comintern experts had saturated them with tales of how the Fascists would throw down their weapons and run away. Why not? Fascists had no messianic ideology to inspire them like the Lincolns, who had been told so many times that the International Brigades were "shock troops" that they believed it.

In the growing darkness thirty men in a machine-gun section at the rear lost contact with the men in front and missed the entrance to the trenches. In cutting cross-country they found a line of trenches from which came voices babbling in a foreign language. Moors! As though one man, they hit the dirt and began crawling back the way they had come. Suddenly "as if a curtain were being raised on a Broadway show," a round of applause broke the silence. Dim forms were sitting on their trench parapets pointing at them and laughing uproariously as they continued to applaud. The Americans had blundered into the trenches of the Sixth of February Battalion, which held the Lincoln right flank. They crept back to the road where Lieutenant Seacord was looking for his lost sheep.*

Early in the morning of February 23, Merriman went over the attack plan with his company commanders and section leaders. An hour before sunset, Russian tanks would push up through the grove toward the enemy positions. While these knocked out strongpoints, the Lincolns would seize the enemy trenches, from which a harrowing fire would be laid down against enemy terrain south of the San Martín road. Any man in decent shape should be able to cover four hundred yards in a few minutes. About this time Daduk's frontline composure wobbled. He babbled that Americans were being used as cannon fodder and were being sent into a death trap—which explained why officers were in such short supply in the International Brigades. He then denounced Harris, claiming that he had been sent by the Soviet Union to spy on Merriman. Such mad talk, on the verge of their initiation into battle, fluttered waves of panic through his company. Merriman and Stember, after confirmation from

Brigade, cashiered him at once and appointed as commander Eugene Morse, a one-time New York cabbie with a brief stint in the U.S. Army. (In 1934, after completing a special course at the Workers' School run by the CP in New York, Royce had attempted to plant a Communist cell in a Louisiana Army base, but after this flopped he returned to driving a cab.)* Daduk, hospitalized in Albacete, was quietly discharged because of "complications from an old wound."* Within six weeks, resurrected as a war hero, he returned to the States to promote the Lincoln Battalion in a coast-to-coast fund drive.*

In their shallow ditches the men fitted, unfitted, and refitted their bayonets. Out of earshot, Merriman and Seacord stood together, apparently arguing. Merriman was listening with professorial tolerance, from time to time wiping his glasses, while Seacord was leaning forward, his body tight and his face angry. It made the men uncomfortable to see their officers quarreling—but probably not as uncomfortable as they would have been if they had known what it was about. It was the classic contrast between the man of mind and the man of action. At such times it was better to listen to the battalion comic, Paul Burns, a pudgy labor writer in the Boston crowd. "Thunderclap" Burns was proud of his Vandyke beard, and he enjoyed misquoting poets. "A tree that may in summer wear," he would begin, intoning like W. C. Fields, "a nest of Maxims in her hair. Tsk. tsk"* Over on the left Bill Harvey debated with his crew where to set up his gun, hoping that he could get it to work. As he stepped into the open, a sniper bullet flattened him "like a sledge hammer blow," lodging in his neck, next to his spine. He was paralyzed but felt no pain. His crew pulled him to safety, and someone said, "Poor Bill. He's dead." He tried to tell them that he was alive— and not to bury him—but could not utter a word. When they put him on a litter, he found his voice and said in a barely audible whisper, "Long . . . live . . . Third . . . International." He lived—but never fought again.*[16]

Exactly on schedule, two Soviet tanks clanked up the San Martín road in the gloaming and spun into the olive grove in front of the Lincolns. Their 45 mm cannon and Dichterev machine guns began hammering the enemy parapets. The Americans went over not as a collective wave but by sections, the Cubans and Irish out in front. Cursing and yelling, the others climbed out of their ditch and raced into the grove. Kneeling from time to time to fire a round at distant piles of red dirt—they saw nobody—the Lincolns abandoned half-learned squad maneuvers in favor of some post-pioneer instinct to fight from tree to

16. In 1967 Bill Harvey (then William Herrick) and I visited the Jarama battleground. We found the exact spot where he had been setting up his Maxim and was shot, three decades earlier. Because no doctor ever dared to remove it, the bullet remained in his neck.

tree. It was easier than anyone could have imagined, for the enemy at the moment was too busy fighting off the tanks to bother with clusters of unarmored humanity seeping through the grove. But there was too much sidewinding, bunching, backtracking. The Americans pecked at, but did not seriously engage, the enemy.

All at once everything seemed to go wrong. There was an explosion and a geyser of liquid fire shot up as one of the tanks burst into flames. An instant later there came such a storm of machine-gun bullets that it seemed to "dig up the battlefield like some gigantic machine."* Riflemen advancing behind the tank "split like wild rabbits in every direction."* The grove was illuminated by a garish light, dazzling to the oncoming men. While the sister tank scuttled back to the safety of the road, the Lincolns swept forward, around the burning vehicle. They must have been perfect targets—those behind the bonfire were floodlit, those ahead were silhouettes. As bullets from a now aroused enemy lashed the grove, many Lincolns took refuge behind trees. Those in the advance found that the grove ended and ahead of them, sloping slightly upward, lay a vineyard, naked and open, perhaps two hundred yards wide. No cover existed in that wide emptiness other than gnarled grapevines protruding from the earth clay like hundreds of arthritic hands. Small groups gamely ventured across.

Deployed next to the San Martín road, the Cuban section advanced, led by their charismatic leader, Rudolfo de Armas, who raised a clenched fist high in the air and signaled his men forward. Hit in the leg, he stooped to check the wound when he was hit again in the head and jaw. He was probably dead before he hit the ground. Men were falling everywhere as enemy bullets harrowed the red clay. Some fled back to the safety of the olive trees; others, trapped in the open, tried to shrivel to bug size behind grape stumps and tossed pitiful handfuls of dirt in front of them to hide from enemy gunners.

Probably a majority remained hopelessly dispersed and failed to regain their units. A section leader named Jeremiah DeWit wandered with his men across the San Martín road four times without finding anyone to tell him where to go. He blundered ahead in the darkness and bumped into a Moorish machine gunner who opened fire at point-blank range. Those trying to flee ran into the fire of the Dimitrovs, who mistook them for an enemy assault force. Trapped between the Moors and the Dimitrovs, for three hours the American group endured a massive crossfire that killed six of them. DeWit finally wormed back, his nerves gone. He gave his command to an assistant and went to a first-aid station led by two Dutch medics (one of whom was also in the throes of nervous breakdown). Three days later, from Dr. Pike's hospital, he filed a report about the battle and then mysteriously vanished. (Because his name figures in scraps of battlefield communiqués but is not found in any "official" roster of the Lincoln Battalion, he must have either deserted or been executed.)*

A few feet out, Lieutenant John Scott tried to rally his company after its momentum had vanished. He shouted, "Continue the advance!" and fell with three slugs in his body. Still alive, he passed on his command to William Henry, a Belfast worker, who lay down beside him and began scooping dirt in front of their heads. Other men frantically tried to scratch holes to salvation. Enemy machine gunners raked the vineyard, concentrating their fire wherever they heard stricken cries, "First aid!" Men pinned down learned not to fire back, for the tiny spurt of flame from the rifle muzzle attracted a massive counterfire. The attack was dead. The activities of Merriman are sketchy. We know that when he ordered the charge, "his own men refused to follow him." He drew his pistol and forced them ahead, but once "in no-man's-land the men disappeared."*

Joe Gordon found Scott lying on his belly where he had fallen in the vineyard. No one had tried to evacuate him. When Gordon promised to get help, Scott said weakly, "Don't. It's a waste of time." "What the hell do you mean, 'waste of time'?" barked Gordon. "You're a human being, ain't you, and besides you're Captain Scott, see, and besides Joe Strysand will never talk to you again if you died." Scott managed a weak smile: Strysand was his runner and closest friend. Gordon crawled over to the road and sprinted back to the first-aid station. "Captain Scott's wounded! He's dying! Where's a stretcher? Hurry up!" The medics were French and Dutch who understood no English; besides, Gordon spoke in a wet lisp that not even his best friends always understood. When he tried the sign language and his twelve words of Spanish, the medics became nervous. They assumed he had gone crazy. Minutes later an interpreter came in and wrung Gordon's story from him. They collected two first-aid men and filed up the road to retrieve Scott.

Because their stretcher was gleaming white, they drew fire as they moved across the vineyard. One medic dug into the ground and refused to move until the interpreter pulled out a pistol and threatened to shoot him. Scott groaned slightly when they pulled him onto the stretcher. "He couldn't groan any harder if he wanted to—he was so weak." Paul Burns and a volunteer named Shapiro helped to carry him to the road, but as they climbed down an embankment a burst of machine-gun fire wounded all of them except Gordon, who again had to return to the rear for help. "What a hell of a situation," he said afterward. "You go after one wounded man and now look at the mess!"* At the first-aid station he begged help from Cooperman, the Party secretary, who wanted no part of it and relayed Gordon to battalion headquarters, where Merriman, beset with problems, sent him back to Cooperman.

Failing to find an ambulance driver willing to drive up the road, Gordon collected four Lincolns and set out again. Halfway up they found Burns and a Cuban dragging Scott, a yard at a time. When Scott reached the station, he was still breathing. Going back to assist Gordon, Ralph Greenleaf was killed instantly when a bullet punctured his helmet as easily as cardboard. Farther on, they found Shapiro, whose loud groaning attracted enemy fire as they carried him back to the road. He had a smashed ankle and his foot wobbled like a pendulum. "What a night!" said Gordon. "Killing can be a pleasure compared with saving a life." But everyone was sure that Scott would live. Joe Strysand threw his arms around Gordon's neck and kissed him. Bloody and exhausted, Gordon staggered over to his machine-gun section. A short time later, word came down that Scott had bled to death.*

It was nearly midnight before the Americans snaked back to their ditches. Some never received the order to retire and found themselves alone on the battlefield at dawn with the rest of the battalion hundreds of yards to the rear. Although individual volunteers combed the grove looking for particular missing comrades, there was little systematic effort to recover the wounded. Almost all cohesiveness and organization had broken down. Ignoring regulations, commands, and threats, the men broke up ammunition boxes and built fires in the trenches to brew helmetfuls of G. Washington Coffee. Few squads bothered to post sentries. "If the Fascists had counterattacked," confessed a section leader, "they'd have walked right through us."*

By daylight most of the cries and groans from the battleground had ceased: there was nothing out there but scattered bodies. Stronger than pity was the secret thought—"better him than me." Enemy snipers hammered at the American trenches. For the first time, the Lincolns were able to see the enemy, all of them Moors, who showed their contempt by walking—not running—across the open gaps in their trench line. "Seeing them was like confronting an abstraction," said an American.* Joe Gordon stood up to take a look and was hit by a bullet, which entered his left eye and came out behind his ear, but he walked under his own power to the dressing station. No food came up till midday, when tubs of cold coffee and pots of rice sludge passed down the trench from man to man. Robert Taylor, a section leader from Boston, and his WPA friend, Bob Norwood of Brewer, Maine, eagerly ladled themselves cups of coffee. Norwood's bent head fleetingly passed in front of an open space in the sandbags. "I've got mine," Norwood said, "this is my last cup." A bullet whined through the opening, clubbing him across the trench, splashing his brains into the pot. Taylor jumped back in horror, threw his cup away, and retched.* This scene was nearly repeated in Marty Hourihan's section. A runner stood up to spoon rice into his mess kit and was struck in the face by a sniper bullet. Blood splattered the trench wall and the hungry men. Looking down at his plate, one of them wailed, "The dirty son of a bitch! He got blood on my pudding!" but he scraped off the red part and devoured the rest.*

News from the line was bad. Rudolfo Armas, leader of the centuria of Cubans who had fled Machado's regime, was a major loss. Commissar Stember was reported missing—but not missed. Of the "exactly 373 men" Merriman listed in his report, twenty were dead and forty wounded.*[17] For what purpose? The men could not say. "Upstairs they called it a probe. To us it was a shaft," said one.* At division or brigade level, sixty men amounted to nothing, but among the groundlings these sixty men were comrades of flesh and bone. The world was not changed. That patch of vineyard laced with interlocking machine-gun fire was still there. They had met the Fascist steel, and it had not bent like tin, as their song had promised. The dressing station behind the lines was packed with wounded. Bill Harvey reported, "They screamed in German, English, French, Serbian, Hungarian. I screamed in New York Gutter, my very own tongue."* The dominant mood in the battalion was one of anger and frustration rather than fear and dejection. The men built sniper boxes and fired at the Moors crossing open spaces. (By the end of the day the enemy no longer walked across—they ran.) But the volunteers were haunted by a feeling, still very much undefined, that their first attack had failed because the leadership had not known, or had failed to explain, exactly what they were to do and how to do it.

Perhaps more chilling than their actual losses was the thought of what these might have been, had they been forced to attack in daylight and been turned into hapless targets in no-man's-land. One thing they knew: to defeat Fascism would take much more time and be much more difficult than they had originally supposed. At Villanueva, Yale Stuart (Skolnik), former lifeguard at the CP spa, Camp Unity, had fretted that the war might end before they got a crack at the Fascists. That no longer figured among their present worries.

In his military diary Colonel Copic reported that the Franco-Belge and the Dimitrovs failed to advance, and the English nudged ahead sixty meters after nightfall. The American effort was not of enough significance for him to record anything at all. For the Lincolns, the skirmish of February 23 took the bloom off the rose, but the men themselves were not wholly demoralized. Not yet.

---

17. This may have been the only battle in the history of the Lincoln Battalion where the losses were overestimated. Brigade was very disappointed with this initial performance of the Americans, and it may have been politic for Merriman to inflate the casualty count to support his claim that the men had made a "supreme effort."

4

THE JARAMA MASSACRE

The newly formed "B" Division, comprising the XIth (German) and XVth International Brigades, was commanded by General Janos Gal (Galicz), the most mysterious—and by all odds the most incompetent—of the International general officers in Spain. He spoke German with a Slavic accent and Russian with a German accent. Apparently he thrived on this aura of mystery, encouraging it whenever he could. During the World War he had served as a common soldier in the Austro-Hungarian Army until captured by the Russians. In the POW camp he received a crash course in Marxism and at the end of the war joined the Red Army and climbed upward. He participated in Bela Kun's brief soviet republic in Hungary until its collapse, when he fled back to the USSR. Packed off to Spain, Gal commanded the XVth Brigade in the opening days of the Jarama battle. Promoted to a divisional general, he possessed strict views of how generals should treat their inferiors, views based upon how, over the previous twenty years, generals had treated him. Any Balkan potentate might have envied him for his slavish staff. It was not uncommon for him to receive minor functionaries while lounging on a couch. His staff saluted their general—and one another—incessantly, and they spoke only when their general spoke to them. (Gal forbade conversation at table—among his forebears in the Hungarian peasantry food was devoured, not talked over.) He was an unmagnetic, quick-stepping little man whose boots had the highest gloss ever seen at Jarama. Probably the only first-rate thing about him was his tailor.[1]

At this stage in the battle for Madrid, it should have been evident to the worthies in both armies that with the Nationalist failure to seize the Valencia road and starve the city into submission, the Jarama offensive had reached a

---

1. There are no favorable treatments of Gal in any of the literature of the Spanish civil war. Even his fellow commanders seem to have despised—or ignored—him. Herbert L. Matthews of the *New York Times*, who knew them all, described Gal as "a Hungarian fighting for the Comintern rather than Spain." Ernest Hemingway claimed that conditions in Gal's sector were "deplorable," and that "he should have been shot." He was—but only later, when he returned to the USSR.

stalemate.[2] As a defensive operation, Jarama had been a Republican success—the Nationalists had been stopped. But Gal was an insecure man, a foreigner in the Red Army during a period in Soviet history when outsiders were increasingly unwelcome. Doubtless he reasoned that the Comintern would be more impressed by a stunning offensive, brilliantly conceived and executed, than by bulldog defense. Even though each side had thrown up a nearly impregnable system of frontline and reserve trenches zigzagging nearly twenty miles to the east of Madrid, Gal pored over charts and reports, searching for a magic key. Always he came back to Hill 693, called Pingarrón, the highest point in the plateau between the Jarama and the Tajuña rivers. During the first days of the battle a *tabor* of Moors had seized and fortified it. Gal resolved to get it back, as a first step in hurling the enemy back across the Jarama River. It mattered little to him that the International Brigades were plagued by desertions,[3] that the men were exhausted and demoralized, and that he lacked adequate artillery, tanks, and planes to support his attack. For Gal, Pingarrón had become, in Herbert Matthews's phrase, "a fetish of position."[*] He vowed that it must be taken "at all costs" by an overwhelming surge of sheer manpower.

One rung below General Gal stood Lieutenant Colonel Vladimir Copic, the XVth Brigade commander, a thick-set Croatian with sausage fingers and cleft chin who arrived on each frontline visit festooned with a network of straps, belts, and other harnesses supporting map case, pistol case, binocular case, and other paraphernalia of battle. Like Gal he had been a conscript in the Austro-Hungarian Army, captured by the Russians during the Great War, and "liberated" through volunteer service in the Red Army. Returning to Croatia after the war, he published a radical newspaper, took a seat in the Yugoslav parliament, and spent five years in prison for political conspiracy. Exiled to the Soviet Union, he volunteered for Spain along with other superfluous foreigners hoping to earn permanent citizenship. When Gal was assembling his XVth Brigade, Copic arrived at Albacete and joined the Dimitrov (Slavic) Battalion, where Gal

2. There were four major offensives against Madrid, and all of them stalled. The first, in November 1936, crossed the Manzanares River and penetrated into the western edge of the city. The second, in December, swung farther west between the Guadarrama Mountains and the western suburbs. The third, in February 1937, comprised Jarama. The fourth, in March following, conducted primarily by Mussolini's army, struck from the northeast along the Guadalajara road. After these failures Franco shifted his theater of operations to the north. Madrid was never taken by assault.

3. By the end of that February, the French consul at Valencia had supervised the evacuation of four hundred French deserters aboard French warships. The Spanish authorities made no attempt to impede this evacuation—they probably even encouraged it because of growing enmity between the Internationals and the Republican troops. However, when the French closed their frontier on March 3, the Republicans seized sixty more deserters at Valencia and shipped them back to the IB prison in Albacete.

found him and elevated him to XVth Brigade commissar. (In time the International Brigades became a family affair for the Copics; Vladimir's brother Milan ran Camp Lukács, the IB prison outside Albacete and later become commandant of the infamous Casteldefels prison near Barcelona.) Copic had all the qualifications for success as a commissar: he understood the political verities, he had experience writing propaganda, and he knew how to conceal contempt for his commanding general. Indeed, he did so well that after Gal went up to division, Copic inherited the XVth Brigade. In this role he cultivated the thorny pathway to political salvation by not questioning the decisions of his superiors and by passing the buck whenever conditions required it—which was often. Such was the man destined to be the brigade commander of the Americans for the next eighteen months—a man with an apparently uncanny talent for often being lightly wounded or on leave whenever disaster struck.

As its part in the Pingarrón offensive, the XVth Brigade would attack at its extreme right flank, just south of the San Martín road. Since the other battalions of the XVth Brigade—the Dimitrovs, the Sixth of February, and the British—had already been decimated in the fighting of the past two weeks, it fell to the Lincolns to make a major diversionary move while Gal's main attack with the 24th and 69th Brigades (both Spanish) developed toward Pingarrón, a flattish summit about a mile to the southwest. Gal and Copic let it be known that they were displeased with the Americans, in part because of their poor performance on February 23, and in part because, like the British, they tolerated debate and demanded explanations. Gal had no intention of explaining anything to anyone—except, of course, to those writing reports to the Kremlin. And certainly a sycophant like Copic, never inclined to deviationism of any sort, concurred in his general's master plan.

While Gal and Copic powwowed in the valley, Captain Merriman labored to reorganize his battalion on the plateau. Desperate for someone with military experience to assist him, he pulled Seacord from the Tom Mooney Company as battalion adjutant. This helped him regain some support lost for the jumble of the February 23 attack. Although many men muttered that Merriman was just a "college-boy," they universally admired Seacord. Officers were coming and going so quickly that the rank and file began to lose track of them. (Who filled all the company commander slots vacated during the week before the next battle still remains a puzzle.) The few days they had to prepare for a second attack were so frenzied and the attack itself so catastrophic, that recollections of details beyond those of one's own squad were largely blotted out by time and trauma. In effect, the parade ground apparatus of distinct companies all but melted away as the Americans fragmented into small clans of armed men beginning to take to heart some of the mutinous rumblings among the French and English—always blamed by commissars as the poison of "Trotskyite wreckers." It was demoralizing for the Americans to hear that the French bragged about self-inflicted wounds that took them out of the front lines.[4]

Meanwhile, on February 26, the Lincolns moved one kilometer south, crossing the San Martín road, where they dug on their knees all night.* Here the ground was uneven: the Nationalist and Republican trenches writhed and bulged toward each other, following contours of the land. Ahead of them a shell-wrecked olive grove extended into no-man's-land perhaps fifty yards. Beyond lay a forbidding dip about two hundred yards wide containing stunted vines. On the far slope, faintly visible through torn olive trees lay mounds of fresh dirt marking the enemy trenches. The British, who had once occupied this position, vacated it eagerly, and the Americans soon discovered why. Not only was it raked by head-on fire from the enemy trenches, but also it was battered by angle fire from machine-gun nests on both higher ground to the south, toward Pingarrón, and to the north, along the San Martín road. Yet the British had been asked only to hold it, not to press an attack from it.[5]

As they psyched themselves up for battle, the Lincolns flooded the home folks with letters. Apparently, personal forebodings were out; political razzmatazz was in. The war in Spain as relayed by section leader Robert Taylor sounds like a page out of Baron Munchausen. He wrote a chum in Boston about the bombardment back on Suicide Hill. "We were shelled for five hours steadily, but after the 2nd hour we started a card game and every time we heard a close one coming we thumbed our nose." While it is certain that Taylor never saw an enemy soldier during the befuddled attack on the twenty-third, a letter home parroted the Popular Front line: "Most of them [the enemy] are Germans or Italians and if they want to quit they find an officer ready to shoot them." Dazzled by his nonexistent Spanish comrades, he wrote, "Some of the Spanish kids of 16 or 17 years run out, climb on top of a tank and heave a grenade into the peep hole." He said that he eagerly awaited the next battle and promised to "give those Fascists a good dose of American Hell." Agitprop all

---

4. A Detroit volunteer told me that he saw a Frenchman stick his hand above a parapet and hold it there until a bullet penetrated the palm. He then strained his credibility when he said that the Frenchman flourished his wound in the faces of his companions, who became so enraged at his easy evasion of battle that they bayoneted him.*

5. Perhaps the major blunder of the Jarama offensive occurred after the British had been routed on their first day of battle, for the Nationalists, had they pressed their attack, could have walked through this sector nearly unmolested and secured the heights commanding the Tajuña valley. Their failure to do so resulted in a permanent stalemate on this front.

the way. The letter, snatched up by a left-wing book publisher a few months later, showed how easy it all was.*

A day or so before the attack, sixty-five new American faces arrived from Albacete, many of them still in the street clothes they had worn aboard the *S.S. Paris.* (The New York committee no longer provided volunteers with fifty dollars' worth of surplus uniforms.) Some wore Ked sneakers they had brought from the States. Many were YCL members from the Bronx. They had been in Spain just six days and went up to the front immediately. Trucks carried them up from Morata to battalion headquarters, a dugout on a lee slope, where "a tall, lanky man with glasses" (Merriman) welcomed them. From stacks of rifles each recruit picked up a Russian rifle and 150 rounds of ammunition.* They were impressed but bewildered—few of these city boys had ever handled firearms of any kind. Before they climbed up to the trenches, a one-week veteran named Robert Gladnick gave them an hour's crash course in taking a rifle apart, cleaning it, and putting it back together. How to fire it? Don't worry about that now. They would learn that when they climbed the hill and fired a round at distant enemy trenches. ("Hold it tight against your shoulder or it'll break your arm.") These new men "didn't know a butt from a barrel," wrote a veteran.* One youth mistook a trench mortar for a stove pipe.

That night it snowed, and the newcomers slept in the open for the first time in their lives. In the morning they tramped down to battalion headquarters for further lessons. A Greek-American armorer named Steve Tsermengas juggled a defused grenade and explained how to pull the ring to activate the firing pin.[6] Then in a rocky gully they crouched behind boulders while each man pitched a live grenade into the gulch—accomplished without casualties. Then Tsermengas gave them five grenades apiece and sent them back up to the trenches prepared for war. Commissars always promised recruits a "concentrated" training course before meeting the enemy. As one volunteer lamented, "I'll say it was concentrated all right—concentrated into one day."*

Unable to obtain maps for his officers, Merriman had pencil sketches drawn from the battalion chart, a cartographic antique that marked elevations not by contour lines but by brown hatching resembling centipedes. Yet this was vastly better than the Michelin road maps used by many of the first Republican commanders at Jarama. Because there were seventeen different makes, models, and calibers of firearms used in the battalion, Merriman kept on his headquarters

---

6. Most grenades used by the Republicans at Jarama were of the sardine-can type, without a fragmentizing exterior like the "pineapple" or Mills bomb. They were more likely to wound than kill an enemy unless at close quarters.

table a wooden plank with a labeled specimen of every cartridge taped to it.[7] Boxes of miscellaneous cartridges had to be dumped out and sorted by size and type. Among the machine guns these ranged from 7 mm for the 1914 Hotchkiss and 7.62 mm for the Maxim 1910, through 7.65 mm for the 1915 Chauchat (later called by a small-arms expert "one of the most poorly constructed weapons ever developed"). The variations were even greater for rifles and pistols. No more than four machine guns were "operational," which is to say that they functioned some of the time. But the terrain was very poor for placing the guns, cut up as it was by ravines. Thus the most dependable Maxims were placed closely together on a hillock beside the road. These guns might be able to spray the enemy trenches in the manner of a fireman with a hose, but they would not be able to establish a crossfire or converge upon a single point from two directions.

On February 26, Captain Merriman went down to the bucolic retreat beside the Tajuña River, where Gal had installed his dacha. Surrounded by charts, telephones, and Napoleonic protocol, the general explained the role of the Lincoln Battalion in the gathering battle. Precisely at 7:00 a.m., Republican aircraft would bomb and strafe the enemy lines, followed by an artillery barrage. Then a company of tanks would grind down the enemy barbed wire to clear a swath for the American advance. Just north of the San Martín road the 24th Brigade would go over the top from its position a few hundred yards to the rear of the Lincolns (from ditches where the Americans had launched their ill-fated February 23 attack). After the Spaniards had drawn up even with the Americans, Captain Merriman would lead his men swiftly ahead and seize the enemy trenches. Once this objective was attained, reinforcements would be hurled into the gaping salient. Farther to the south, Spanish units would seize the summit of Pingarrón, forcing the Fascists to fall back across the Jarama River. On paper, Gal's war-college plan accounted for everything except the obvious—specific instructions on what to do if the promised airplanes, artillery, tanks, and Spanish ground support failed to materialize. To deliver this attack the Lincoln Battalion numbered about four hundred men.

On this day Commissar Stember briefly appeared in the trenches for a pep talk. He said it would be easy—nothing to worry about. Artillery would soften the enemy, and tanks would precede the assault. For the new arrivals Stember was a novelty: "We seldom saw him; he spent most of his time in the comfort and safety

---

7. On their first day in battle the machine-gun company of the British unit discovered too late that their Maxim belts had been fitted with cartridges designed for a Maxim of a later model and were useless. The truck dispatched to bring up the proper ammunition overturned, killing a man. Eventually the ammunition had to be brought up by manpower.

of the cookhouse."* For these last few days he had been preoccupied with morale-building tasks like bringing coffee up to the line and organizing groceries.*

The dawn of February 27 revealed an overcast sky, with the low ceiling of imminent rain. The men breakfasted on three cups of tepid coffee and a thick hunk of bread. Clamped on their heads were their brown French helmets with cowlick crests, and on their *Mexicanskis* were long needle bayonets, said to be feared by the Moors. It was a bronchitic day—damp and cold. Some men wore greatcoats or fleece-lined jackets, but the newest arrivals had strapped knapsacks and blanket rolls to their shoulders as if planning to camp out in enemy trenches at the day's end. Peering through firing apertures, they looked slightly uphill into a blank and silent void, motionless except for wisps of fog drifting across no-man's-land. From time to time a machine gun chattered briefly, sounding a little like an outboard motor with a pitted muffler.

On a lee slope behind the line Captain Merriman briefed his officers. The plan called for an intricate maneuver in narrow trenches. At the hour of attack, First Company, which held the right flank nearest to the San Martín road, would go over first, while one section of Second Company would slide over to occupy the trenches vacated by the First and to serve as a reserve. Second Company would go over ten minutes later, and the Tom Mooney Company would remain behind with their machine guns until the others established a front.* In concluding, Merriman spoke of discipline and timing, and as always, he spoke well. To the leader of the reconnaissance squad he said, "You go over last. Shoot anyone who fails to precede you." A few men glanced briefly at one another, lifted their eyebrows, but made no comment. Then, as though he were playing the lead in *What Price Glory?* Merriman said, "We will now synchronize our watches."[8] A couple of men fumbled at their wrists; others pulled out dollar Ingersolls and began winding stems.*

Zero hour came and went. Nothing happened. No doubt Merriman shook his watch, but there was still no sound of shell, tank, or plane. Half an hour later, sporadic rifle fire broke out north of the San Martín road in the vicinity of the 24th Brigade, delegated to lead the attack. The Lincolns opened fire through their sandbagged apertures and only drew upon themselves a devastating reply. Within minutes the Moors had obtained dominance of fire, and bullets began slashing open the battalion sandbags. The Americans huddled and waited.

---

8. The Spanish civil war was probably the first major war in history in which the combatants adopted mannerisms and even codes of behavior from motion pictures. Literature of the war is loaded with allusions to men undergoing moments of *déjà vu*, the source being "just like in the movies."

Time wore on, and the mist burned off. A Republican battery fired a few salvos, some shells falling into the British sector farther south. It was assumed that this was the signal for the massive barrage, but the 75s abruptly quit.

On the field telephone—connected only that morning—Merriman called Colonel Copic about the air and tank support and learned there would be a brief delay. The voice on the phone inquired whether he had laid down an aviation signal on the road. A what? Merriman said no one had told him anything about an aviation signal. With mounting impatience, the voice explained that a large white T must be laid down so the pilots would know where to lay their bombs—or rather where *not* to lay them. A simple task at night, but extremely hazardous now, for the road was under heavy fire. Dutifully Merriman assembled an assortment of underwear, shirts, and towels pinned together to form a T. The two men who "volunteered" to place it on the bullet-swept road were universal favorites, both of them battalion runners: Joe Strysand, a thirty-year-old organizer in the New York teachers' union,[9] and Bobby Pieck, once Phil Bard's assistant on the *Normandie*. They dashed out with their signal, which looked like dirty laundry on a clothesline, and succeeded in placing it before both were chopped down. No one dared to retrieve the bodies, one of which smoldered from an incendiary slug. Apparently the signal merely tipped off the enemy that the main push would come near the San Martín road, for their fire intensified in that sector.

A short time later, two Soviet tanks lumbered up from Morata, fired a few .45 mm rounds from the road cut, then backed out of the battle. Were more tanks coming up, or were these two the extent of their armored support? No one knew. Encouraged by their appearance, the Spanish brigade north of the road advanced a few yards, then fell back virtually in rout. Lieutenant Colonel Hans Klaus, a former Imperial German officer who now served as Copic's chief of staff, was inspecting the Lincoln trenches at this time, and Merriman asked him for advice. Klaus thought he should not move out until the Spaniards came abreast across the road, but he had no authority to countermand an order from Brigade. However, a short time later Copic rang up Merriman and accused the Americans of cowardice. Why had Merriman not sent his men into the attack? He said that the Spanish brigade had already advanced seven hundred yards and were being cut to pieces because the Americans refused to move to their support. Merriman was flabbergasted at this fantastic lie. He told Copic that the Spanish had already retreated to their original line.

---

9. An organizer in a teachers' union should not necessarily be confused with a teacher. By trade Strysand was an agent for theater tickets, but had gone bankrupt during the Depression. He was a graduate of the Hebrew Orphan Asylum of New York but never attended college.

"Don't contradict me!" bawled Copic. "Move your men out!" He gave the Lincoln Battalion ten minutes to come up to the position, confirmed by his headquarters map, where the Spanish were said to be. Reluctant to expose his men without support, Merriman contested Copic's order, warning that his battalion would be wiped out. Copic rang off abruptly, and dispatched two staff officers by motorcycle with orders to remove Merriman from command if he refused to attack. Two Englishmen, Commissar D. F. Springhall and Lieutenant Clifford Wattis, raced up a mountain path and reached the communication trench just as three Republican planes dipped over the lines and dropped a light packet of bombs far beyond the enemy positions. According to one volunteer they were not *La Gloriosa*—Russian fighters figuring prominently in the leftist press—but "some sort of hangovers from Hell's angels of the World War."* (They came and went so rapidly that many Americans never saw them at all.) The staff commissars learned that Merriman had already requested covering fire from the British Battalion on his left. All the Tom Mooney machine guns broke down after firing a belt or two except for one on a hilltop far to the rear. Some could be fired only as single-shots—slower than a rifle. Enemy bullets were ricocheting off their armored shields with great slamming clangs.

Doubtless Springhall was appalled at the prospect of attacking under such conditions, but he had no authority to call it off. Disobeying an order in Marty's army was prima facie "evidence" of Fascism or—worse—Trotskyism. (On the Córdoba front, a few months earlier, a French brigade commander who failed to advance had been summarily executed by Marty's order.) Merriman met them with a grim smile. He was peeling off his field glasses and preparing to lead the attack in person. Impressed by his example, the two Britons resolved to follow it. By this time enemy fire was pulverizing the Lincoln sandbags. It sounded like "the heavy pounding of a riveting machine."* It was about high noon.

At the whistles, Americans on the right flank climbed up the trench wall, some dashing forward with animal yells, while others peeped cautiously toward the enemy lines. Merriman walked up and down the parapet waving the men out and shouting. Lieutenant Wattis, soon to become a legend in Spain as a hawk in battle, strode through the trench, tapping malingerers on the shoulder with his swagger stick and allegedly prodding armpits with his revolver. One of the newcomers, a boy in muddy tennis shoes, slipped back with his forehead against the trench wall as though sleeping or crying. A companion shook him, until he saw a stream of red ooze pouring from under his helmet and filling his collar. Yet few men were hit as they clambered out of the trench. The enemy fire fell off, if anything. For about thirty seconds, Nationalist officers allowed the

Americans to emerge from their burrows so that they could be butchered in the open. Then they let go.

The sudden volley caught Merriman in the act of raising his arm to wave the men forward. He was knocked back into the trench by a bullet that broke his left shoulder in five places. As he turned to look at Merriman, Springhall was struck by a bullet that carried away his upper teeth from ear to ear. Seacord had fallen heir to the Lincoln command, but he never learned of this honor, for along with dozens of others in the advance he and two companions were killed at the same time.[10] It was said that only Ray Steele's Maxim worked at all, and only a short time before breaking down.* (Martin Hourihan, a future Lincoln commander denied that *any* machine gun worked.)* Since Oscar Hunter and Doug Roach, two blacks in the Mooney Company, were never able to operate their Maxim, they stayed in their hole gamely loading and firing two rifles belonging to men killed.*

Among the February 25th arrivals was David Smith, who had been sent to the Irish section. When told of the impending attack, two Irishmen, veterans of the fiasco on the twenty-third, took him aside and "in no uncertain terms said, 'This will be a fuck-up. If you want to live, just do as we do.'" When the firing began, the Irish rose out of their trench, advanced only a few yards, and began digging shallow foxholes. They had no support. Men were "dropping all around." They returned to their home trench. Looking about him, Smith saw that the British made only a token attack, while the Dimitrovs, the most experienced battalion of them all, seemed to ignore the order altogether. Moreover, to Smith it appeared that the Lincolns who had taken part in the attack on the twenty-third "just went through the gesture," while the recent arrivals suffered tremendous casualties.*

Four men running side by side fell to the ground the instant the enemy volley lashed the hollow. A seaman just behind was impressed by their training-manual responses, until he crawled up and found them all dead.* By this time bullets were spewing up tiny geysers of earth all around him, and he hunkered down behind a pile of his dead companions—all of them YCL members from the Bronx. Not far away, a lone American wandered about unharmed, squinting at the enemy trenches as though undecided whether to run forward or backward. Behind one tree a Lincoln "veteran" of the attack on the twenty-third instructed a new arrival in how to load and fire a rifle. Neither had ever handled a rifle back in the States.

---

10. A few weeks later a letter arrived for Seacord from "Celia," written on the day of the massacre. In it she describes how, while on her way home from a Cagney movie, she saw the moon over East River and thought of him. She closed the letter with, "It's getting late so goodbye, my love, and take good care of yourself, Your, Celia."*

Some section leaders had the foresight to recognize the catastrophe for what it was. In Second Company, Ed Flaherty, one of three Boston brothers at Jarama, flatly countermanded a Wattis order for a carrier to go over the top with boxes of ammunition. What were the men out there going to do with more bullets? "Who the hell are you to give orders to my troops?" demanded Flaherty. When Wattis said that he was from brigade headquarters, Flaherty told him to "go to hell back there" and then shouted to surviving men to hide behind trees and rocks until nightfall.*

Bob Taylor, a Detroit section-leader, recalled reaching the hollow close to the enemy line, where he saw a network of red stripes hovering above the ground like surveyor's strings. Although he had never before seen such a phenomenon, he realized that these were tracers of an interlocking crossfire from enemy machine guns on the flanks. Men who did not know what it was were plunging into it and dropping in swarms. He dispatched a runner to instruct the Lincoln gunners to concentrate their fire on the enemy flanks, but the runner was laced from head to foot before he could rise to his feet, and seconds later Taylor himself was knocked unconscious by a mortar explosion that wrapped his helmet so tightly around his ears that it had to be hacksawed off.* Some Britons found him wandering in a daze and got him back to safety. In two battles Taylor's section had been reduced from forty-two men to ten.*

Another man reported that he got about fifty yards into the vineyard before he was hit. "I thought someone had kicked me in the leg. Went down surprised and plenty sore. Got up again only to flop once more." He found some shelter and waited for a stretcher-bearer. None came through that awful fire. He lay there all day, took three more wounds, and crawled back at night.* Elsewhere, men tumbled down, convinced they had been hit, only to find that they had tripped over vine-claws.

According to plan, Second Company, now led by Arturo Corona, a Cuban, rose out of their trench and dashed forward to get even with First. A few hesitant men hunkered in the trench until Corona stood on the parapet and forced them out with his pistol. But faced with the lashing fire, he called off the attack. By this time it was as difficult to retreat as to advance, but an order came (presumably from Wattis) to resume the attack. It was out of the question. Corona slipped back into the trench, where he learned that through seniority—or just happenstance—he now commanded the battalion. Commissar Stember, who had not budged from his cubbyhole down at the cookhouse, now busied himself by ordering coffee and cognac to be sent up for the men (with the proviso that they crawl back to the trench to get it). He told Corona that Wattis had taken command and had ordered the men to resume the attack. Corona promptly countermanded it and passed word that men out in front should try to steal back after dark.*

Further advance was impossible. Those men farther back gathered some protection from olive trunks and opened fire against the enemy trench line. One rifleman found, however, that whenever he lowered his head to sight down the barrel, his hunching shoulder tipped his helmet over his eyes, spoiling the shot. Another man heard a deafening explosion, "as if my head has been lifted off my shoulders. Have I been hit? I don't feel anything but a complete numbness in my head." Looking back he saw a prone volunteer who had discharged his gun with the barrel next to his ear and had nearly shot a man in front who was glaring back at him.* Within minutes the attack had been crushed. Before being evacuated to a dressing station, Merriman had tried to pass his command to Philip Cooperman, the Party secretary, who recoiled as though handed a rattlesnake. An experienced political toady, he knew the pitfalls of complicity with disaster. The men out in front could advance or retreat, shoot or be shot, but he wanted no part in it. On his way to an ambulance, Merriman insisted on being carried to brigade headquarters, but Colonel Copic refused to talk with him, saying that he was too weak to be permitted to speak.

All this while the Americans out front were being slaughtered. Those pinned down could not tell the quick from the dead. One volunteer recalled feeling as though he were play-acting: the director would soon say, "All right, let's try that scene again." Then nearby some man cried out, "Oh!" less in pain than in surprise. "Is that man hurt?" he heard himself ask. Back came an emotionless reply, "He's dead." Out in front a body caught fire. It smelled like burning hair.*

Enemy snipers picked over the field. Trapped men lay as immobile as they could. One flicked up small handfuls of dirt in front of his head, hoping to build a wall between himself and a bullet. Another recalled, "I had convulsions. My bowels let go. I was scared." Dutch stretcher-bearers were shot down whenever they attempted to drag in the wounded. Much later it was reported that a lone American, Milton Rappoport, reached the enemy wire, where he was gunned down and lay for days like a spattered statue with an unexploded grenade clutched in his hand. This tale became very popular—at least among anti-Fascists back in the States. "Just more Party bull shit," said a survivor sixty years later, "nobody—but nobody—got near that wire."*

Dr. Pike had expected the worst and gave Stelio Toplianos, his head medic, a large ammunition box full of first-aid supplies, including sixty-two bandages. "Topy," or "Pappy," was a thirty-seven-year-old Greek-American from New York who weighed less than 140 pounds and had been classified as too old and too small to serve as a rifleman, although he had been toughened as an amateur boxer and a three-year veteran of the National Guard. For a few minutes it was quiet when the men went over the top, but minutes later bullets "hit every foot of ground." Smashing into trees, they sounded like someone was "cracking a thousand nuts." He quickly used up his supply of bandages on a line of men in the trench, then replenishing his stock he crawled out in no-man's-land seven times locating casualties. He brought back four or five men on his shoulders, pulling in the last one by a rope because he was too exhausted to lift him. When unable to dress wounds because of a bullet in his hand, he continued to search for casualties between the lines. "One comrade actually was smoking—another must have had 250 bullets in him." Finally exhausted, he gave his blanket to a wounded comrade and remained all night at his first-aid post, unable to sleep in the cold rain with a ballooning hand. At daylight he ventured out again to see if anyone out there was alive. He saw two men trying to crawl back, but the enemy opened fire and killed them. For a whole day he remained on duty until Dr. Pike sent him to the hospital for a month because of exposure, flu, and an infected hand. Later he returned to his comrades at Jarama.*

In the middle of the afternoon it rained. As visibility dropped, men ventured to crawl back and to pull in the nearest wounded. A narrow and steep goat path was the major communication trench leading down to the dressing station, and it soon became clogged with men bleeding, vomiting, coughing, raving, and dying. Men fell out of stretchers and piled up at the bottom. Too exhausted to drag the dead from the upper passageways, the living ground them underfoot. Seriously wounded men drowned in pools of mud, water, and blood. There was no food, no medicine, no doctors.* A youth wailed over and over, "They killed my buddy—they killed my buddy!" Coated with Jarama muck, the lucky ones leaned against the trench wall gasping like beached whales. Out front among the vines and under the olive trees their unlucky comrades lay "with [a] curious ruffled look, like dead birds." Bob Gladnick later described what he saw— "some sort of stage setting created by a Hollywood mad genius" as the living and the dead were piled on top of one another in the narrow trench and gazed about "with puppy-like eyes."* The light faded quickly, and the ditch blackened. The walking wounded continued to trickle to the rear, slithering down off the plateau in the darkness. There were not enough able men to move the stretcher cases. The best they could do was to crawl under blankets with them to give them some warmth against the freezing rain. (Since there was no concerted effort to move the wounded until dawn, the worse cases usually died.) Adding to the mayhem, Wattis showed up and, in front of the grungy survivors, lambasted Corona, "You are a coward because you retreated. . . . You didn't have the guts to complain to me. . . . I think you are yellow." Supported by Stember, whose nerve was returning, Corona told Wattis to leave the trenches. Wattis left for Brigade with a parting shot. "I am already doing so because I belong with men—not with you."*[11]

At that moment the Lincoln Battalion consisted of about eighty effectives. All the others were killed, wounded, or missing.[12] Although total casualties in other battalions of the XVth Brigade had been even higher, these had occurred over a period of weeks, not hours. (For the Jarama campaign British casualties stood at five out of every six men, the Thaelmann at four out of five, the Dimitrov at seven out of eight.) In their blind rage, the men lashed out at Merriman as the author of their misery.

Merriman, however, knew exactly who had been responsible. Two days later, from a hospital bed, he scribbled two messages on his 1931 calendar pad. The first went to the men of the battalion complimenting them for "their splendid bravery . . . in the face of such heavy fire." His second message, addressed to his successor—whoever that might be—indicted Colonel Copic as an incompetent leader, if not an outright liar. Merriman explained that the original plan called for the Lincolns to cover the left flank of the 24th Brigade, which was on their right flank.

> Ten o'clock was set to go but the 24th did not move. . . . We all waited. After communicating several times with the 24th, they promised to move forward very soon. . . . Even Colonel Hans Klaus gave me the order to advance the battalion, hoping to encourage the Spanish. Our

11. Although listed as a Lincoln volunteer, none of the "official" studies of the battalion mention Corona by name, and the only evidence that he was a short-term commander comes from a transcript of the Wattis trial on March 13. Corona himself seems to have been disgusted with the Lincolns, for a few weeks later he used his Spanish background to attach himself to the Communist division of El Campesino and served there until the end of the war as a major. After the war he is said to have opposed both Batista and Castro.

12. Voros (*American Commissar*, 362) says 153 killed out of 377 on that day alone. Rolfe (*Lincoln Battalion*, 57) says of 500, 127 killed and nearly 200 wounded. Landis (*Abraham Lincoln Brigade*, 90) says of 450, 127 killed and there were only 60 left in the trenches. Colodny (*Struggle for Madrid*, 92) estimates 250 dead and wounded out of 450. By contrast, the British lost 19 dead and 5 wounded (Graham, *Battle of Jarama*, 66). The battalion records were dispersed at the end of the war. Record-keeping was slipshod at best, and their "statistics" are rarely accurate. Herbert L. Matthews of the *New York Times* was told that 127 men had been killed and 175 wounded during the February 27 attack, figures subsequently canonized by repetition. The "official" history of the battalion uses Matthews's figure for the number of dead, adds twenty-five more wounded, and estimates a hundred effectives holding the line. Robert Gladnick, a survivor, estimates that eighty Lincolns were in the trenches on the morning after the attack.

men advanced under impossible conditions and did it without a murmur. Later by telephone I talked with our Brigade Commander Kopick [*sic*] who told me that the Americans had been a disgrace because they had not advanced at ten o'clock. [He] said that the 24th advanced 700 meters. This was not the case. He claimed that it was their second line which we observed on our right. I went to check on this and at the time the order came through to place a white mark on the *most advanced* point of each Battalion and found the mark of the 24th about 100 meters behind our position.

To blame the Americans for failure of the attack was an intolerable injustice. "If this policy is carried on it is because someone wants to find a scapegoat to cover up his own mistakes."* That "someone" was a bitter paregoric compounded roughly of two parts sheer Gal to one part mere Copic.

In his private diary, not published until 1971, Copic blamed Gal for the catastrophe. According to Copic, Gal told him that the 24th had advanced and demanded that Copic force the American battalion to move out "immediately and occupy at all cost the positions of the enemy."*

It was nearly daylight before gunnysacks of goat chops and demijohns of *coñac* came up from the cookhouse. The sun came out on an icy cold morning. If the enemy had attacked at that moment, they could have paraded through the Lincoln sector behind a marching band. Bill Wheeler, a section leader, recalled that the rifles were "a mess—full of mud,"* while others were "bent out of shape from firing."* On all sides the dead lay "in peculiar unnatural positions. One lies facing the sun, with his fist clenched in an antifascist salute. Strange waxed features. Like broken dolls."* Brigade political officers arrived and tried to persuade the men to return to their trenches. "I will never forget the worried frown of a French political commissar running from group to group with a flowing poncho over his shoulders, pleading with the men to go back."* This was Captain Van den Berghe, a Belgian dispatched by Copic as temporary commander with orders to make the Americans clear their trenches of the dead.[13] Digging graves was out of the question. Instead, days later, they dragged the torn bodies to an unexposed spur, piled them into stacks, and set fire to them. Later they piled rocks and earth on top of them to form a collective grave. Smashed

13. Some have claimed this captain was Lajos Rajk, in later years the Hungarian minister of the interior until he was executed about 1950 for suspected Titoism. But this sounds as shaky as the story circulating in Villanueva de la Jara that Tito addressed the Americans at their convent. (Tito, incidentally, also served in the International Brigades, but as a liaison officer in the Paris office.)

helmets were stacked on top of this limestone cairn.[14] If the bodies were ever counted or identified, no reliable record has survived. Later a Franco-Belge "labor battalion," consisting of brigaders serving sentences for desertion and drunkenness, went out every night until March 10 and brought back more cadavers, but not all were found. (Many North Americans killed on the twenty-seventh were, and remain, "unknown soldiers" because their names exist on archival scraps but not on "official" rosters prepared by the VALB.)

Merriman later described his first dressing station, which overflowed with dead, dying, and wounded.[15] "It was a butcher shop. People died on stretchers in the yard. I had to sit up. . . . Went to operating room. Pulling bullets out of a man who had become an animal. Several doctors operating on stomach exploring for bullets while others died. Question of taking those who had a chance at all."* There were limited or no painkillers and wounded men reacted ferociously to the undressing of their wounds. At this place a Detroiter who had been pitched into a pile of known dead and dying revived from a concussion and roused the attention of an orderly about to wheelbarrow him off.*

The next step was a three-hour ride—"Nightmare of a ride. Lost our way," recorded Merriman—over a rutted road that killed some—and tortured all—to the brand-new American facility at El Romeral, fifty miles to the south.* Here a unit under Dr. Edward Barsky, which had arrived only a few days before, was settling into a school building. They had found an unwired, unplumbed, unpainted, and unpartitioned building, but within hours, on orders of the village mayor, scores of local workers turned the raw structure into a field hospital. Mildred Rackley, a New York nurse, reported that on their third day forty patients arrived—probably from the battle on the twenty-third. Six kilometers of road were so rutted and potholed that the staff feared that jolting ambulances would kill badly wounded men. When told of this, the village mayor prohibited all peasants from going into the fields so that they could carry baskets of stone and earth to fill the holes. They had barely finished when the next sixty

14. To my great surprise, in 1967 I found this cairn virtually untouched. Underneath the upper layer of large stones was a great pile of bones and skulls. Unexploded artillery shells littered the plateau and French metal helmets lay scattered in trenches. But when I returned to the site in 1983, these relics had disappeared and there were few signs that a battle had been fought there. The olive orchard had become a favorite weekend picnic ground for Madrid families. During another visit in 2000, I found the only clear evidence of a bygone battle in this sector was an eroding reserve trench—more like a ditch—backed up on the cliff edge above the cookhouse.

15. This was located at Villarejo de Salvanés, a microscopic settlement a dozen miles from Morata. In a bar three tabletops served as operating tables, and benches tied in pairs as beds.

wounded arrived from the battle on the twenty-seventh, many of them shot through the head. When the lights went dead during an operation, Dr. Barsky performed "works of art" with eight flashlights.*

The glut of wounded men completely overwhelmed the medical staff and their facilities. Nurses worked without shifts and opened their own veins for transfusions. A young nurse recalled how she "cut through the clothing of boys I had danced with on our way to Spain."* The extent of American casualties at Jarama is best told by statistics from Romeral—ninety-two patients from the fight on the twenty-third and two hundred from the fight on the twenty-seventh.* Complicated cases—like Merriman's broken shoulder—required "another bad trip" to Alcázar de San Juan, where he cabled his wife in Moscow, "Wounded. Come at once."* He had no idea where he would be other than somewhere in Spain. She would have to find him.

On dead ground behind the trenches of Jarama a bonfire of ammo boxes became the locus for men nearly incoherent in their grief and outrage. Here the wounded were assembled to await evacuation along steep trails, now greasy from traffic and rain, which led down to the cookhouse. Captain Van den Berghe found it impossible to get the survivors to do anything except cluster around the bonfire. Fortified with *coñac,* they were changing from a leaden lethargic mass into an angry, mutinous mob. Groups of Lincolns began slipping away, stunned by what they had endured. By the time they had slid down to the cookhouse, they had become a formidable horde, many still with rifles, cursing, railing, muttering. Someone angrily shouted, "On to France!" But as an indeterminate number fled down the highway to Morata de Tajuña, a squadron of XVth Brigade cavalry blocked their way with lances and automatic rifles. The main function of these horsemen was to range through the territory behind the lines, rounding up deserters and stragglers. When they galloped forward with lances pointed, the Lincolns threw down their rifles—those who still retained them—and were herded back to the purlieus administered by Colonel Copic. Most of these horsemen were White Russian émigrés from France who had joined the International Brigades to earn the privilege of returning to their motherland. On their way back Robert Gladnick, a Russian-American, struck up a conversation with the Cossack *Ataman*, who had driven a taxicab for seventeen years in Paris and was astonished to find a countryman among the Americanskis.*

Colonel Copic immediately improvised a tribunal to punish the Americans for "cowardice and desertion in the face of the enemy." (Smaller groups of Americans succeeded in avoiding the Cossacks and fled six to eight miles before being turned back.)[16] The kangaroo court took place in a high-vaulted cave, one of the numerous *bodegas* that honeycomb the hillsides of the Tajuña wine country. His staff included Lieutenant Colonel Hans Klaus, the chief of operations, who served as prosecutor.[17] It is alleged that Copic asked for the death penalty for every tenth man, the rest to be relegated to a "labor battalion"—a penal gang of the unworthy and the unfit who were forced at gunpoint to dig trenches in no-man's-land or to lead suicide attacks. George Aitken, the brigade commissar, looking back on the trial years later, spoke sympathetically about the American grievances: "They were thrown straight into it, and they had enormous casualties. . . . *For a time there was trouble in the American battalion over it*—they felt they'd been thrown into a hopeless fight" (my italics).* (As a founding member of the CPGB and former manager of the London *Daily Worker,* Aitken had the most authoritative Party voice on the bench. He reported that higher-ups wanted executions but he refused on grounds that it would be "catastrophic for enlistments.")* The eight defendants had no counsel other than one of their own number, who tried to follow the heavy-duty German of the prosecutor's diatribe, which included a verbose discussion of the labor movement in Germany and its role in the proletarian revolution. Since the proceedings had to be translated on the spot into French, Spanish, and English for the tribunal, the trial promised to be a long one, though the verdict was never in question. Meanwhile, the prisoners had discovered that their wine cellar truly contained wine, and using helmets as basins made good use of a bad time. Within a short time few of them had any understanding of the proceedings and cared even less.

This judicial body was suddenly interrupted when General "Pahlev," commander of the Soviet tank corps in Spain, entered with his entourage and

16. The number of deserters among the Lincolns is not known. One survivor claims that more than three-quarters of the survivors were involved in the "mutiny." Five Americans, still in uniform, did storm the American consulate in Valencia, where asylum was denied.* (The French consul reported four hundred deserters.) Probably some men assumed to have been killed in the battle were actually deserters who managed to escape from Spain. As might be expected, the "official" accounts of the Lincoln Battalion did not admit that there had ever been a mutiny until well into the 1980s, when the hegemonic cadre of the VALB recognized that too much evidence existed to deny it any longer.

17. The mysterious Colonel Klaus had served in the Imperial German Army during the Great War and afterward allied himself to various left-wing movements. After fleeing from Hitler and being closely watched by police in France, he arrived in Spain during the first weeks of the war and served as a bombardier in a converted mail plane—dropping his bombs by hand from a hole in the fuselage. In January 1937 he became chief of staff of the XVth Brigade under Gal, then Copic.* Although his knowledge of revolutionary theory was said to be encyclopedic, as an officer he was without charisma.

demanded to know what was going on. A Cossack officer had informed him that the brigade had placed a Russian-born American on trial. The tribunal bolted out of their chairs, and Copic explained that the Americans were being court-martialed for desertion. This effrontery infuriated the general, for Red Army officers regarded Internationals as the sweepings of the Comintern. That a rag like Copic had dared to place a "Russian" on trial touched Pahlev to the quick. He seized Copic by the tunic, called him a jackal, kicked over the table in front of Klaus, and shouted *"Von! Von!"* (Out! Out!). Thus ended the trial. Though he had no authority over—and probably less interest in—the Lincoln Battalion as such, his elitist contempt for Copic and his foreign flunkies, along with his fury that they would dare to place on trial a fellow Russian, may have saved some Americans from summary execution.*[18]

The mutineers then filed back to the plateau, where they were arrested all over again and assigned to a labor battalion digging trenches in no-man's-land.* Commissar Stember tried to reassert his authority—even to the point of punctuating his threats by waving his pistol in the air—but the men just glared and cursed him to his face. They openly swore that they would never go into battle again or obey the orders of yes-men like Stember and Merriman (now dubbed "Captain Murderman").[19] A succession of commissars—English, French, and German—visited the Lincolns to pontificate about grand strategy and noble sacrifice, but their speeches sounded like what they were—rationalizations, excuses, lies.[20]

Later in the day, Captain Van den Berghe took inventory of the American battalion—on hand were 180 men, 140 rifles, and 35,000 rounds of ammunition.* His reorganized battalion consisted of only two companies—the machine gunners under Liam Tumilson (a Belfast Irishman) and an infantry segment, with Robert Gladnick, Robert Wolk, and Ed Flaherty as section leaders. (No battalion commander was named, because no one was willing to accept the

---

18. Two weeks later Robert Gladnick accepted the general's invitation to join the Russian tank corps, where he served the remainder of the war, crossing paths with the Lincolns only at the battles of Brunete and Fuentes de Ebro.

19. It is unreasonable to blame Merriman for the fiasco of February 27. Nothing in his ROTC training at the University of Nevada could have prepared him for the military problems and chicanery he encountered at Jarama.

20. The level of political development among the men of the Lincoln Battalion was probably higher than that of any other American military group in history. The political commissar system originated in peasant armies as a mean of indoctrinating illiterates with the reasons for fighting (and of supervising military officers whose loyalty might be suspect). When Americans balked at the system of what many of them called "comic-stars," they were quarreling with means, not ends. They were not peasant cannon fodder but men who, while agreeing with the objectives of the anti-Fascist struggle, had keen noses for sniffing out hypocrisy and prevarication.

job.)* Since the Americans were in no condition to hold the line, the Franco-Belge Battalion—others say the Rákosi (Hungarians)—took over the trenches, allowing the Lincolns to withdraw for "rest and reorganization." Copic assumed that the French would be more soldierly, but their pride at relieving the Americans quickly tarnished, as he recorded in his diary. "They [the French] abandon their positions several times. There are cases of self-mutilation in the battalion. Their officers are not at the level of their duties." Unable to control them, the French commander finally agreed that his battalion be entirely reorganized with most of the men transferred into other units.*

For the crucial date of February 27–28, Copic jotted nothing at all in his diary, no doubt waiting to see where the finger of responsibility might point before he committed himself on paper. On the day following he did visit the Lincoln trenches and recorded, "The morale of the Americans is very depressed." (An unidentified American was closer to the mark, "If we had suffered another hour more all of us on this side would be in hell.")* But Copic pooh-poohed the complaint that the battalion had lost half its men. "Actually the battalion lost 60 to 70 men, some dead, some wounded. Most had scattered." In other words, they had *deserted*—but he lacked the courage to use that word. For Copic morale and discipline were symbiotic attitudes. On a more positive note he did establish a bathhouse in Morata and assigned a truck to ferry the survivors. Since the English had held up better than the Americans, they got the first turn. Unfortunately the driver overturned the truck into a ditch, spilling out the men, many of them "seriously hurt," wrote the colonel.

On March 1, Lincoln survivors gathered under a cliff behind the lines and in a rump parliament selected a slate of new officers. Although opposed by the brigade officers, who "tried every trick in the book to stop the meeting,"* they settled on Arthur Madden, a steelworker from Gary, Indiana, as co-commissar to neutralize Stember. As commander they insisted upon being led into the next battle by one of their own, even though after canvassing everyone present, they found no one qualified to lead. The stormy forum lasted for half a day before they picked a compromise candidate, Martin Hourihan, a former seaman (purser's section) who had had a brief stint (as a clerk) in the U.S. Army. He could serve as Captain Van den Berghe's adjutant while learning the ropes.* Outrage displaced fear as the reigning mood of the battalion. They voted to petition Brigade for their immediate removal from frontline service (with some men returning home); two weeks of military training under real officers rather than "self-elected amateurs"; courts-martial of those responsible for sending untrained men into battle; and permission to contact the central committee of the CPUSA (called by one skeptic "like nothing so much as a child crying for its mother").* Five men carried the petition to Colonel Copic, who passed it on as evidence of American insubordination and mutiny.

Dr. John Simon, a medical officer who had joined the Lincolns at Villanueva but had not been present at the massacre, attended this meeting and recorded his impressions: "I've never heard anything like it. Boys were crying because they didn't know how to use their rifles. The machine gunner broke into tears as he explained how the guns wouldn't work. . . . One soldier explained how a boy went over the top with full equipment—and died. Another built a mud wall between himself and our trenches—he didn't know which side the fascists were on. Another tried to dig a hole with the muzzle of his gun. The fascists cut down the trees with their machine guns, then killed our men hiding behind them." On the day following, Simon had to post a guard over a comrade "who tried to hang himself because ordered to the front tomorrow."²¹ For mental cases, Simon's medical supplies were limited to doling out potassium bromide as a tranquilizer and phenobarbital for those with seizures.*

During their three-day rest they thrashed over and over the events of February 27, raising the question that no one in the hierarchy cared, or dared, to answer: Why had not the suicidal attack been called off when it was obvious that success was impossible? No weight of propaganda could counterbalance their intimate awareness that more than a hundred comrades had died in vain. If the attack proved anything it demonstrated the abject incompetence of the officers who had planned and pressed the massacre, officers who now begged them to respond to shibboleths like "discipline" and "courage." Moreover, they began to question the legal assumptions underpinning their act of volunteering to serve in the International Brigades. They had taken no oath to uphold the Spanish government or vow to defend its flag. (After all, the International Brigades were extraterritorial, wholly separate from the regular Republican Army, and they always fought to retain their autonomy.) Dissidents proclaimed that a volunteer who wished to terminate his service should be allowed to do so: having come to Spain on his own free will, he thereby had the right to depart whenever he pleased. If he "deserted," what, on legal grounds, had he deserted from?

Voicing complaints openly and noisily was wholly natural for men accustomed to open hearings at union grievance committees. Their truculence often

---

21. This was Andrew Royce, an Iowan who on February 27 had been in charge of a section because of service in the peacetime U.S. Army—presumably as a CP organizer. Half the men he led over the top were killed. He deserted and was declared berserk. Thereafter he remained in the autopark until the base was cleaned out after the great retreats of March 1938, when he was forced into the line again, but during a bombardment had to be held down. Sent to the rear permanently, he returned home with the Lincolns in early 1939.*

astonished volunteers from countries where complaints about the status quo were likely to be put down by force. It was this residue of democratic zeal among the Americans, working from bottom to top rather than the other way around, that so outraged the Albacete clique, many of whom argued that Americans should be fed piecemeal into other units as needed rather than constitute a separate battalion of troublemakers.

Now that the battle was over, Stember reappeared from the cookhouse to represent the authority of the Party and to place blame for the catastrophe squarely on the failure of the men to acquire true discipline—by which he really meant "obedience." On hearing that Hourihan, a Party nonentity, now commanded the battlion with Madden as co-commissar, he threatened them, "This means war!" To which a volunteer snatched up a rifle and said, "Get the shit out of here or we'll show you a war!"* Rebuffed in the flesh, Stember lost no time in locating a mimeograph machine and churning out a cautionary leaflet designed to silence those who dared question authority or complained:

> Those who challenge the military or political authority of Company, Battalion or Brigade commanders are self-seekers who are no less guilty *than the deserters who have been sentenced to hard labor in the Labor Battalion at a recent trial.* (emphasis added)*

This is an important document, coming as it does from the senior battalion commissar, for it confirms what has been unflaggingly denied for seven decades—that the Americans did mutiny at Jarama, that they were tried, and that they were punished with transfer to a labor battalion.

Alluding to the recent mutiny and no doubt worried that this might somehow highlight his own role in the disaster, Stember continued.

> In the American Battalion, such a committee flared up recently and for a short time demoralized the battalion until finally order and discipline was reestablished. But these traitorous elements are waiting for still further opportunities. . . . Our slogan must be, no traitors in our midst, absolute discipline, one unified, single command.

This screed he sent up to Brigade, which—responding with unusual dispatch—published it a few days later in the official newsletter.* The Lincolns merely scoffed at the leaflet—so much "ass paper."

The Americans were fortunate that weak reeds like Copic and Stember were in charge, and not André Marty, who would have concluded that their mutterings were tantamount to Fascism—or worse, Trotskyism. Marty and Longo had already created a special prison camp outside Albacete for political deviants, and his method of handling dissent was draconian. On one occasion, having learned that some Franco-Belge had broken into a wine cellar and emerged hopelessly drunk, he ordered their commissar "to shoot a few in the presence of others" and "tie the others to trees in the heat of the day."* For Marty the Americans were the worst of the lot—they were "spoiled capitalists" and "proletarian millionaires." And in the end, the Comintern directorate closed ranks by not allowing volunteers to "de-volunteer," on grounds that this would have shouted to the world that the Popular Front against Fascism had no teeth. In the succeeding months, open discussion began to erode. As in any army, men continued to complain—but they were more likely to look over their shoulder to see who was listening.

As co-commissar-elect, Madden set out to assess blame for the massacre, but in view of the dictatorial structure of the Comintern brigades, this effort was doomed. Since Merriman was long gone, Copic was deaf to their complaints, and Gal in his riverside spa was as remote as God or Stalin, the Americans sought a more accessible scapegoat. For a time the rumor mill featured as resident villain Lieutenant Colonel Hans Klaus—after all, hadn't he served as Prussian officer in the German army during the World War? "Sure, look at his uniform, how immaculate, see how tall and stern he stands! He's got to be a Nazi."* But finally they settled upon Lieutenant Clifford Wattis, the Briton who had forced men over the top at pistol point. Madden, an experienced CP organizer, harvested accounts from men incensed by the dastardly "comrade" and then demanded that Wattis be tried. Doubtless relieved that the eye of the storm had moved elsewhere, Copic agreed to a public hearing at brigade headquarters on March 13. He appointed as head of an ad hoc "Juridical Commission" Captain Vladimir Stefanovic, the brigade *chef du controle des cadres*. (A personal evaluation sent to Moscow at the end of the war noted that Stefanovic had been "in charge of counterespionage in which he is very skilled.")* Immediately he vetoed Madden's request for twenty witnesses, knocking it down to four. (Brigade held a trump card, concealed from the Lincolns, which could be played if Madden pushed too hard, for on February 24, the day after the first attack, he had shown the white feather. In a letter to Merriman he requested immediate transfer to the auto-park because he had "many years experience as a truck driver."* Had this been publicized, his reputation would have plummeted to the level of a Stember.)

The tribunal met in Copic's headquarters, a villa well removed from the stench of battle. From the rank and file of the brigade came three judges—one each from the American, British, and Dimitrov battalions)—with a fourth from brigade headquarters. George Aitken, the brigade commissar and member of the Central Committee of the CPGB served as "political expert." Copic and Stember were conspicuously absent. As mouthpiece of the dissidents, Madden charged Wattis with responsibility for an unnecessary number of losses on the days of attack, but his specific accusations seemed mere peccadilloes: ordering men to carry ammunition to the men in no-man's-land, although the pouches of both quick and dead were found to contain nearly 150 cartridges; giving Brigade false information concerning the number of dead and wounded; going to bed at four in the morning and leaving no instructions about outposts, guards, or cleaning weapons. Although the loaded-gun episode had been dropped from the formal indictment, it cropped up repeatedly in the transcript. Unfortunately for Madden's case, his four witnesses turned into sheep under Wattis's withering cross-examination, probably because they were having second thoughts about bringing charges against a staff officer. What was gained by winning a theoretical point if one ended up in a labor battalion for some trumped-up charge? Phil Cooperman, long since exposed as a Party yo-yo, in answering Wattis's question about what kind of pistol he had seen, replied, "a big one." Bernard Walsh, touted as a military expert because of brief service in the U.S. Army, fared little better. When he explained that during the attack he had been posted as an observer on the far left flank, Wattis asked him, "What battalion was on our left flank?" Walsh replied, "Either the Franco-Belge or the Dimitrovs—I'm not sure." Feigning great surprise, Wattis quipped, "So the battalion observer does not know who was on his flank?" More damning for the prosecution, none of the witnesses were willing to admit under oath that they had actually seen the revolver, and as prosecutor, Madden himself was not allowed to testify. In his final speech Wattis lashed out at the Americans. The trial had proved only one thing—"Then and now the morale of the American battalion is bad." He said that casualties among the English, the Dimitrovs, and the Franco-Belge had always been greater, but in those battalions the survivors did not attempt to place responsibility upon individuals who did their duty. "I came to Spain to fight fascists and I thought [this] brought all the other comrades, but it seems that I was wrong," he said. "These men [the Americans] are fighting amongst themselves."* The judges found Wattis guilty of minor charges and recommended that he serve in a battalion as an ordinary soldier. To this Wattis agreed provided he did not have to serve with the Lincolns. But in their final report the judges waffled when they promised "an opportunity to make further investigations." None followed. Wattis retained his rank.

For the Americans there was no closure on the massacre they had endured. Learning of their continued demoralization, General Gal himself came up to the cookhouse to answer questions about the battle. Speaking in Russian, with translations into Spanish and English, he spoke of grand strategy and outlined positions on a map tacked to the wall. When asked why there had been no tanks and little artillery, "he said he did not know but would look into it." When asked about the huge number of casualties, "he said he was sorry to lose so many valiant soldiers but war is not a life-saving institution and casualties were to be expected."* Few Americans were consoled. One veteran, many years later, said of Jarama, "There seemed to be no command, no communication, no contact. . . . After that I ended up in a state of absolute terror. I was also terrified of being terrified."* Perhaps even worse was the fear that nothing would be corrected because those in command had covered up what had happened. Thirty years later, Charles Nusser, a loyal Communist, spoke of the massacre and its aftermath as an "attempt to shut up the whole business."*

Even as the Lincoln Battalion recovered from the shocks of February 23 and 27, more Americans were pouring out of liners docking at Le Havre and Cherbourg. A contingent from the *Île de France,* the first to climb the Pyrenees to reach Spain after France closed the frontier, was delayed for ten days at Figueras because Albacete felt compelled to conceal the tragedy from the newcomers. With them was Captain Allan Johnson, the military adviser of the Central Committee, who had been briefed on what not to tell the men about the massacres. In the dungeon of the Castillo he called a meeting and spoke of the Jarama battle. The Americans had "stopped the Fascists dead in their tracks. . . . Only one American was killed and only four were wounded." The men cheered long and loud. Then Johnson added that the Americans had named themselves the Lincoln Battalion. More cheers. (He did not explain that the Central Committee in New York had chosen the name—the volunteers in Spain had nothing to do with it.) Finally, when he told them that they would leave in the morning for their training base, the dungeon reverberated with roars of enthusiasm.* On this high note, Johnson encouraged the newcomers to surrender their passports to IB officials for "safekeeping."

The American attack on February 27 was the last gasp of a major offensive that had raged across the Jarama hillsides and left an estimated 10,000 casualties on each side (2,800 of them in the International Brigades).* In effect, the battle had ended two weeks before, when the British Battalion stopped the Nationalist thrust against Morata. The British had given the Nationalist armies pause. They had held long enough to allow Republican Communist troops under Enrique Lister to anchor the extreme left flank. Although they had been decimated, there had been a reason for their losses. It is difficult to rationalize such a role for the Americans. Pingarrón was never taken, and the trenches attacked by the Lincoln Battalion remained in enemy hands until the end of the war. For the Americans the wounds of that brutal initiation never completely healed. Never again would American volunteers accept with unwavering trust the decisions of rear-echelon commanders, for they had learned that these notables, despite their glittering assurances, knew as little about waging a real war as they did.

5

WAITING ... WAITING

Commissar Stember and Party hard-wires distrusted the new Lincoln commander, a political maverick so defiant of the Party line that at times he seemed not even to know what it was. Captain Martin Hourihan, a lean, toothy, boyish-looking man of thirty-two came from a pious, middle-class Roman Catholic family in Tonawanda, New York. While his mother hoped that he would enter the priesthood like her deceased older brother, he hung out with the football crowd at St. Agnes High, not with the choirboys. At fifteen he ran away to the West Coast, where he joined the IWW to obtain a seaman's ticket. Then after several trips on the San Francisco–New York run, at seventeen he joined the U.S. cavalry, where he served six years until dishonorably discharged in Texas for "radical tendencies"—writing bulletins criticizing the camp.[1] In 1932 he married an Alabama woman, but the marriage collapsed when, according to "official" sources, he participated in the Anniston textile strike of 1933 and, on returning home, tried to organize sharecroppers on his father-in-law's farm. Drifting to New Orleans, he worked in the purser's department of several ships in the Gulf trade until beached by a massive maritime strike along the Eastern seaboard in 1936. Joining picketers in Philadelphia, he was arrested after a fight with scabs and spent twenty days in jail. On the day after his release he went to New York and volunteered to drive an ambulance in Spain. When informed that the Party needed riflemen, he joined the pre-Lincoln group and arrived in Villanueva de la Jara just two weeks before being rushed up to Jarama.

---

1. In my 1966 interview Hourihan said nothing about a dishonorable discharge but claimed his mother bought him out of the army. Unfortunately it is nearly impossible to explain the disparities in "official" accounts of Hourihan's life—or, indeed, of many other Lincoln veterans. The reason is that for the Communist Party propaganda was more important than fact—it was not so much *what* happened as what *ought to have* happened. At least three "official" biographical packets exist for Hourihan—including one filed in the Moscow archive among the XVth Brigade papers.* Most erroneously claim that he graduated in engineering from Alabama Polytechnic Institute (now Auburn University). He did not, although after a short course at Troy State he obtained a teaching post in rural Greenlaw County. (Only long after the war, in 1959, did he receive his bachelor's degree from Huntingdon College, Alabama.)

Since neither Union Square revolutionaries nor urban industrial workers blended easily with recruits from Alabama—unless they were black—Hourihan had no command until his squad leader was killed on February 23. In the attack four days later he led the same group but managed somehow to bring them all back alive.[2] He had no illusions about his experience as a military leader and welcomed the tutelage of Captain Van den Berghe, several times a guardian angel during Lincoln troubles. Unfortunately, the Belgian became immobilized by a rheumatic attack on March 8, which pitched Hourihan into the snakepit of full command.

Looking over his men, Hourihan saw not the much-vaunted International "shock troops" making heroic copy in left-wing newsrooms of the world, but a poorly armed and badly trained civilian mob, quite literally "in shock" and eager to hang up their helmets and go home. They numbered only 121 men—78 in the infantry company and 43 in the Mooneys—and drastically needed time to plug gaps and to rebuild morale. (His own count of men killed in all the Jarama fighting stood at 119.) Above all, they needed protection from Balkan butchers like Gal and Copic, who defined a good soldier as a man who obeyed commands as unquestioningly as a lead ox. Hourihan had no faith in miracles. "One time I read the Bible. It was just a book."* The slaughter of February 27 had nothing to do with courage or cowardice, and everything to do with the gap between amateurish IB commanders, who had not realized the Jarama battle was over, and trained enemy officers, who had.

Even though a committee of Lincolns chose him as their commander, the men remained surly and suspicious. They accused the steering committee of arranging cushy staff jobs for themselves, which was glaringly evident in some cases. Dr. William Pike pestered Hourihan to replace shallow stinking ditches—little better than latrines—with well-drained trenches and dry dugouts, but officers trying to collect digging parties were told—"Go fuck yourself!"* The doctor did succeed in commandeering twenty-eight "shell-shocked" men who had been sentenced to hard labor for hiding in a wine cellar during the February 27 attack. With them he turned a goat path into "Pike's Pike"—a road for ambulances.* Yet the task of rebuilding morale was not entirely hopeless. Hourihan knew that the Party had to support him lest the battalion collapse again into chaos, and he could depend on a solid phalanx of officers like Paul Burns, an avuncular Boston journalist who rallied his men

---

2. Years later, when Hourihan quit the Party and was being denounced in the leftist press as "an enemy of the working-class," he was criticized for *not* having lost men during the February 27 attack—proof for them that he had been more interested in saving lives (including his own) than in exterminating Fascists.*

during both attacks, and Liam Tumilson of Belfast, who took command of the Mooneys after Seacord's death.[3] Ed Flaherty, one of three Boston brothers, took over Hourihan's First Company, although for the first month Hourihan had to run the company until Flaherty learned the job.

For days, enmity between the XIVth and XVth Brigades had been festering. The Franco-Belge slipped into the Lincoln trenches and stole anything they could lay their hands on, especially blankets, cigarettes, and booze. Americans sneered that the French were "thieving drunks"; the French jeered that the Americans were "spoiled cowards." (The French also disliked the Spaniards, calling them "Penguins" because they were short and fat.)[*] The two brigades shared stables for their cavalry squadrons at a farm near Morata, where the French displayed their superiority in horse-stealing, assisted by a veterinarian so adept at disguising a horse that not even its owner could identify it. Later, as mechanized transport replaced horses, the French were masters. Not even removing the ignition or four wheels forestalled a theft. In one week they stole seven trucks and four automobiles, including the personal limousine of the 19th Corps political commissar.[*] The only recourse a victimized unit had was to send out men to steal them back.

Hourihan had no tolerance for interbrigade thievery. He drove the French out of his sector at pistol point and established sentries on both flanks to keep them away. When complaints came from Albacete about his chauvinism, Hourihan retorted, "They're not Internationals. They're bums."[*4] He had a point, for the commander of a troop of French cavalry estimated that 50 percent of his men had served prison terms at home, although he declared that they were "at heart not bad men—just uncontrollable when drunk."[*5] The commander of the Sixth of February Battalion openly boasted that discipline

---

3. William Tumilson came from a working-class Protestant family but changed his name to the Gaelic Liam when he became aware of British oppression. One evening, an ex-Black and Tan, supposing Tumilson was Orange to the core, boasted about his paramilitary exploits in County Cork. Tumilson pitched him over the Lagan Bridge into the river. He recounted that tale without a smile. "Never asked him if he could swim, but it seems he could as he was seen again—but not in Belfast."[*] He had served as a machine gunner with the French earlier in the war, but when posted to the British Battalion, he resigned with the other Irish and joined the Lincolns at Villanueva de la Jara.

4. Copic's diary is full of notes about the French. The April 10 entry is typical. "At night 35 men came from Albacete, mostly French. All were immensely drunk and made a scandal in the pueblo. All the pueblo pushed for their evacuation. The drunks wanted to shoot the non-drunks who agreed to the decision of the tribunal." Or this from April 30: "Most of the Franco Belge Battalion wander drunken through the town and cause enormous scandals. Their CO and Commissar have lost control of them."

5. The criminal element was higher among the French than among other nationalities. After all, Spain was close by for anyone wishing to avoid the gendarmerie, and it was said that French judges sometimes offered a choice—jail or Spain.

had improved after he had three troublemakers shot.* When Brigade ignored Hourihan's requests to be briefed on developments elsewhere along the front, he dispatched his Cuban volunteers to infiltrate Spanish units north and south to find out what was going on. His spies learned that both sides had settled into a holding phase.

Adding to Hourihan's annoyance was the bitter feuding between Stember and Madden, constantly countermanding each other's orders and dragging in Hourihan as arbiter. Like most Lincolns, he regarded Stember as a coward unfit for commissar,[6] but he had come to despise Madden as a shirker and rabble-rouser cankered with "the venom of a man . . . who'd rather stay in the trenches than go over the top."* By the first of April both were gone: Stember had disappeared into the byways of Party activity in the States—including recruitment speeches—and Madden had wrangled himself an appointment to the officer's school at Pozorubio and thereafter busied himself with intraparty affairs. (Toward the end of the war Madden would resurface briefly with the Lincolns, with pathetic results.)

At times it seemed that Captain Hourihan had written his own catechism for the Americans in Spain, but he made it clear to the powers above that the Lincoln Battalion would not be crucified a second time on a cross of "international solidarity." Far less malleable than Merriman, he was an effective interim commander in a period when the Americans desperately needed assurance that someone with backbone stood between them and the despotism of the Copic-Gal claque.

In the afternoon of March 14 the front suddenly erupted again as Moors, proceeded by Fiat tanks, stormed the trenches south of the XVth Brigade, an episode recorded in brigade lore as "the Battle of Dead Mule Trench."[7] That sector was lightly held by skittish *quintos* (conscripts) of the La Pasionaria Battalion, who panicked and fled. The contagion spread to the next sector, occupied by the British Battalion, where a never-identified officer, who had been lecturing men on the importance of holding the line at all costs, abruptly yelled, "Follow me in formation!" and led a flight to the rear.* At this moment the brigade brass was in conference with Copic at headquarters, so the line was held mainly by unofficered men, many of them among the despised "demoralized elements" of the labor battalion. They dropped picks and shovels, grabbed

6. A later commissar delivered the final verdict on Sam Stember: "'Old Man' Stember thought that the job of a commissar was to provide coffee after a battle!"*

7. Thirty years later, I located the site by the perfectly articulated skeleton of a male in the trench.

rifles, and began blazing at the Moors sweeping into the trenches on their left flank. The attack had come so suddenly that no one had time for the luxury of fear. Shouting absurd, euphoric slogans like "Don't fire till you see the whites of their eyes!" and "No pasarán!" they peppered the Moors while Soviet 9½-ton tanks armed with 45 mm cannon easily routed the lightly armed Fiats. (Russian tankers scorned Fiats as patrol cars and called their drivers the "riot police.") Although the enemy seized a chunk of Republican trench, their main body was rolled back, leaving a two-hundred-yard gap in possession of the Moors, who could neither advance nor retreat. In this confused fight Tumilson, a much-admired Irish commander of the Mooneys, stepped in front of a loophole and was killed instantly by a sniper shot through the back of his head.* Later that day Dr. John Simon wrote in his diary that he was now wearing the belt knife that had belonged to Tumilson. "Now nothing belongs to him. His forehead felt like pulp."*

Within minutes Captain Jock Cunningham, the ferocious, bushy-browed commander of the British, came dashing up the hill shouting, "You bloody Yanks! Goddamn you—we won't leave you in the lurch!"* Jock had been a boxing champion of the Argyll and Sutherland Highlanders in Jamaica back in 1920 before serving a brief prison term for mutiny. He loved a good fight. Close behind came his adjutant, Fred Copeman, a gigantic seaman (and a ringleader in the Invergordon Mutiny of the Royal Navy in 1931) who had been known to pick up skulkers by the seat of their pants and hurl them in the general direction of the enemy. Grabbing handfuls of Mills bombs, a mixed force of Americans and British stormed down the length of trench, flushing out Moors in fine style. One man would toss a grenade into a blind corner of the trench zigzag, and the others would quail-shoot the Moors who tried to scramble out. The enemy ran out of grenades in the nearly subterranean fighting and never caught on that their opponents were only a patched-up raiding party, and not a full battalion. The counterattack ended when Cunningham found the trench blocked by a dead mule and scrambled up on the parapet in full view of the enemy, where he caught a machine-gun burst that somersaulted him into the trench, his chest and arms spurting blood like a pump. Copeman dragged him back a hundred yards to where the "La Pasionarias," partially rallied, were throwing up a cross-ditch. Lieutenant Wattis, a crack shot, found a high point and began picking off Moors. A French commissar joined him, and they shouted "Bravo!" and "Encore!" to each other until a shot went through the Frenchman's eye and "smashed half his face" all over a curious American who had crawled up to watch the show. Wattis had to pull the body back into a trench because the American, sickened and in shock, could not function.*

The brigade dug cross ditches to prevent further enemy penetration but failed to retake the lost trench. Casualties among the Americans were light, and the encounter lifted the spirits of nearly everyone, especially the former deserters in the labor battalion, who were at once metamorphosed from "cowards" into "heroes." For the first time in Spain the Americans could look out into no-man's-land and see mounds of the enemy dead, not their own. Spaniards of "La Pasionaria" came over to thank them personally. Moors continued to occupy a segment of the lost trenches, forming an enemy salient in the Republican line, but they failed to break through.

One Lincoln became the most lionized American casualty of the war. As the fighting surged back and forth in a trench, a wounded Canadian handed Robert Raven a grenade, warning him that the pin had been pulled. From the hospital at Villa Paz, Raven dictated a letter to Philip Cooperman, the Party secretary, that tells what happened next:

> Suddenly we ran into four soldiers whom we thought our own, but their helmets and clothes proved them to be fascists. They tried to capture us. We tore away and ran back thirty meters and grabbed some grenades. My Canadian comrade opened the lever of his grenade and handed it to me, which he should not have done. However, I crawled up towards the fascists under cover and was about to toss the grenade when there was a terrific concussion in front of me and I felt my face torn off. Naturally, I dropped the grenade [which] exploded at my feet filling my legs with shrapnel. My comrades must have retreated again and I kept crawling blindly, dragging my body through those trenches calling "Comrade, Comrade."*

Disfigured from head to foot and permanently blinded, his agony came to be dreaded by medical assistants, one of whom recalled that if they pulled back his bedclothes and a sheet brushed his foot, Raven would scream, "My toes! My toes! Damn you!"* The point was that those toes had been amputated, but as a doctor told a distinguished visitor, "He doesn't know that." "I wonder if he'll ever know it," asked Ernest Hemingway. "Oh, sure he will. He's going to get well."* (The story sounded phony to Hemingway until Cunningham, whom he admired, confirmed it.) Not only did Raven get well, he also became one of the best fund-raisers the Lincoln Battalion ever had. Crowds in Madison Square Garden wildly shouted, "No pasarán!" as Raven (with the fraudulent rank of "lieutenant" bestowed by Party propagandists) rose eyeless to address them.*

Who but a stone-heart could say no to a man who had given not only his blood but also his eyes to the Spanish Republic?[8]

After this narrow escape the Lincolns showed more willingness to improve and extend their trenches. In his diary Copic wrote that an American told him that it would have been better from the beginning if, instead of making attacks in the open, they had dug their way forward in this "pacific manner."*

March was very bad. "Always it rained," wrote one volunteer. "The mud clogged our rifles. The rain came down. The icy wind from the Guadarramas froze us in our trenches."* It was never cold enough to freeze the ankle-deep mud and never warm enough to bake it hard. Since their cartridges were refills, easily spoiled by moisture, men blew their noses between their fingers and saved handkerchiefs for wiping down their ammunition and rifle bolts. From the cookhouse half a mile below, two men lugged up pails of ersatz coffee. Cold coffee wasn't much better than no coffee at all, and it was always cold. Mud, mixed with feces and urine, invaded their food, their tobacco, their blankets. It was weeks before fortification officers taught them how to prepare decent dugouts; before this, they stood day and night in open ditches without duck-boards. Tin helmets shed rain but refrigerated sinuses. The easiest way to get warm was to work up a sweat with pick and shovel, and the easiest way to catch pneumonia was to cool off afterward. In the lush Tajuña valley, which lay behind them like a picture postcard labeled "Sunny Spain," apple blossoms came and went, but the highlands were swept by icy winds. Morale dropped lower than the thermometer.

The worst duty, performed by labor battalions, was retrieving bodies from the killing grounds of February 23 and 27. Doctor Simon attended one such expedition under cover of darkness only ten days after the fighting. The odor was overwhelming, and the bodies were "schrecklich schwer" to carry. Four men crawled over the sandbags, stretchers were passed across, and a patrol waited behind the parapet to give the stretcher-bearers covering fire. In time a man crawled over the parapet dragging the front handles of the stretcher and quickly "the whole thing is in the trench, stinking body and all." The bearers

---

8. Raven told Hemingway, "It was quite a bad fight, you know, but we beat them and then someone threw this grenade at me." At first, Hemingway, often a shrewd judge of character, did not believe the story because "it was the sort of way everyone would like to have been wounded. But I wanted him to think I believed it." But Captain Cunningham, whom Hemingway admired, confirmed the story, and Hemingway wrote a syndicated dispatch about Raven. The VALB arranged what became a tumultuous marriage for Raven and set him up in a New York florist business.

manhandled the stretcher through narrow trenches, clearing the way by shouting "Toden!" After the papers and other belongings were removed, the body was buried under a growing cairn of rocks.*

March also brought winds of change. For reasons that remain unclear, Oliver Law was given command of the machine-gun company.[9] Many complained that the staff had bypassed men better qualified. They objected to Law, not because he was black (this might have stood in his favor, if anything, for racial tolerance was a key principle of the battalion), but because many who knew him well regarded him as ignorant and ineffective.[10] "He was too authoritarian and incompetent," wrote one of his gunners. "He had a slow way about him. One would think he was one of those slow, lazy slaves from down South."* Even other blacks addressed him mockingly as "Comrade Law." Two of them, Douglas Roach and Oscar Hunter—both fervent Party loyalists—staged a mock protest parade in the trenches carrying signs saying "EQUAL RIGHTS FOR WHITES." Roach was universally admired in the battalion, while Hunter laughingly characterized himself as "the only Negro in the world who can neither sing nor dance."* They voiced the obvious—that the Party wished to boast that a black man was leading a predominantly white unit in Spain. But with the crippling memory of the massacre still fresh, the Lincolns wanted leaders they could trust—not ideological cartoons. Trouble brewed almost at once. At a morning inspection Law ordered Pat Stephens, a Canadian gunner, to remove two sandbags to improve the field of fire. Stephens objected, arguing that the opening would expose the gunner to enemy sniper fire, but Law overruled him. That same day a Cuban named Perez was shot dead through the opening. Ray Steele and Jim Katz, both veteran gunners, filed a charge of incompetence against Law, and a board of inquiry, headed by Hourihan, met to consider the accusations. Specifically Law was charged with causing the death of Comrade Perez, nepotism—promoting cronies to safer posts at headquarters—and with salting away caches of extra food for himself. The board, packed with commissars and hard-line Party men, overruled Hourihan and exonerated Law. In addressing the court, Law denounced Steele and Katz as "undisciplined troublemakers,"* and the court warned the witnesses against future bad behavior. The verdict further alienated neutrals in the battalion and intensified hard feeling between the

9. Battalion publicists later wrote that during the February 27 attack, only the machine gun of Oliver Law remained in operation throughout the day, pounding the Fascist lines. However, in a conversation with me in 1967, Hourihan categorically denied that Law was anywhere near a machine gun on that day although he would not tell me where he was.*

10. On the *Queen Mary*, when Canute Frankson was assigned a corner table to himself "like a despised stepchild," Dan Hutner, a white volunteer, joined him as a protest.*

commissariat and the lower ranks. Steele, characterized as a "Huckleberry Finn character" by a rifleman, was just the sort of gunner you wanted in the tough fight, even though when off duty he often had to be jailed for brawling.

More problems lay ahead for Oliver Law as disgruntlement among the rank and file got out of hand. Battalion spies reported a spate of covert meetings in which "bad elements" incited men to desert and to show their contempt for officers and staff. The Virgil Morris case crystallized this movement. As head of a section (equivalent to a platoon) during the February battles, this thirty-one-year-old rangy longshoreman with four years in the U.S. Army had proved his mettle as leader, but he resisted the encroaching caste system during the long trench vigil. For overstaying a short leave he was transferred to a labor battalion. When asked by a group of men how he liked it, he scoffed at the punishment and replied that being in the Labor Company was a damned sight better than being on the line. A spy reported this to Law, who arranged a tribunal of commissars to hear the case. He told Morris, "It is not an honor being in the Labor Company. Men came thousands of miles to be an honor to the people who sent them and not a disgrace." To this Morris replied, "At least in the Labor Company you are treated like white men." On the following day Hourihan was drawn into the contretemps. Far from being contrite, Morris launched into an attack upon the leadership. He told them that he did not blame anyone for overstaying a leave or for not coming back at all. "The next time I get a chance I would not come back myself. The leadership stay away from the front. If that's the way the leaders do it, then we should stay away." This ended his useful service in Spain. Morris was sent under guard to Albacete and sentenced to serve two months at Camp Lukács, the IB prison near Chinchilla. Thoroughly enraged at the International Brigades, he turned into a recidivist deserter and served three more prison terms. During a return to Camp Lukács, he grabbed the rifle of a guard and called on the men to "kill" their officers. A judicial commission accused him of spying, adding that he maintained contact with the U.S. military attaché. He escaped one more time and nearly made it across the French frontier. Miraculously he escaped execution, probably because of his notoriety as a folk rebel.*

There seemed to be no stopping Oliver Law's rise to stardom. The vacant post of adjutant-commander of the battalion had to be filled, and a ukase came down from New York that the appointment must go to Law. While his record claimed that he had served six years in the 24th Infantry, it did not explain what he did there. Was he a mess boy? It did not matter. At that time the CPUSA was conducting a nationwide campaign to attract more blacks into the Party, particularly among farm laborers in the South. Party publicists pointed out that in 1935 Law helped organize a rally for Ethiopia in South Chicago, which drew ten thousand people (and perhaps more important, two thousand police). Here was a prime candidate for the Party hierarchy. (On this issue Abe Smordin, a Lincoln volunteer, recalled how the Party conducted its membership drives during the 1930s. "We would grab anybody who attended two meetings—one if you were black.")* On a platform of racial equality the CPUSA had run James Ford, a black, for vice-president of the United States in 1936. While Hourihan and a large body of men opposed Law's appointment, it had passed beyond their control. A black man appointed second-in-command of a predominantly white American military unit—Party publicists made the most of it. The *Daily Worker* published a long skit titled "Oliver Law, Hero of Jarama Front," which singled him out among six blacks in the battalion as paramount in leadership and gallantry. Along with his army career it listed, as evidence of his proletarian commitment, six weeks in a Bluffton, Ohio, cement plant and driving a Yellow Cab in Chicago.*[11]

On March 19, Brigade Commissar George Aitken welcomed a draft of 110 young peasants from the byways of rural Murcia who had arrived as reinforcements. "We are the anti-Fascists of the XVth Brigade," he shouted. "We are styled 'The Brigade that does not retreat.' Together we will crush the enemy of Spain and of the whole human race!"* It sounded like a tall order, and the conscripts failed to cheer. As members of the newly organized 24th (International) Battalion, the new *quintos* marked a major milestone in the history of the XVth Brigade, though no one thought much about it at the time. The dilution of the "international" character of the Comintern Army had begun, painful evidence that the manpower reservoir of Internationals was drying up. Creation of an all-Spanish 24th Battalion marked the first step, soon to be followed by adding Spanish companies to foreign battalions, then by the placing of Spanish platoons into foreign companies, and finally by the disappearance of foreigners altogether. All this still under the rubric of "International," fathered by Georgi Dimitrov, and approved (less enthusiastically) by Josef Stalin.

The Lincolns inspected the *quintos* as if they belonged to a different phylum. These boys were reluctant dragoons, not eager volunteers—political blank slates. Most were illiterate. Among them was a sprinkling of old men, like their leader Captain Martínez, a fifty-year-old career officer whose pistol dragged his belt down under his belly. They carried cheap guitars, slung over their shoulders, and

11. To vote for the Communist candidates was to absolve oneself from the taint of "racism."* Since James Ford was booked for a visit to the Lincoln Battalion in April, the Party was especially eager to install Law as a figurehead. Unfortunately his press clippings are so conflicting that there is reason to doubt many of them.

wore ropes of garlic around their necks. Even their physiques were different—their bodies were smaller than the Americans', but their callused hands were larger and red, like bruised beets. Dr. Simon examined them and concluded their physical development was comparable to that of American children or adolescents. It was folly to send them to war, for emotionally they were "ridiculously helpless and childish."* Considering their years in abject poverty, it was little wonder that they found the food slopped out by Lincoln cooks "luxurious."

For them the war was a mysterious unpleasantness to be endured, not an ideological arena in which good was pitted against evil. No one, least of all themselves, expected them to become future "shock troops." Generally they consorted together, but did what they were told—so long as it was not digging trenches, which like all Spanish soldiers they avoided. But they taught the Americans how to make watertight *chabolas,* huts of branches, mud, and grass, which soon sprouted like mushrooms in the dead ground behind the trenches. They skillfully incorporated tree roots into their shelters whereas the Americans up to that time had used olive trees only as places to relieve themselves while protected from enemy fire. Dr. Pike was at first mystified why the Murcians did not succumb to dysentery, which plagued the foreigners, until he observed the braided strands of garlic that festooned their dugouts. But his attempt to convince foreigners to take up garlic chewing met storms of protest, particularly among the British. "Bacteria which had no effect on most Spanish bodies ran riot through [our] intestines," wrote a British commissar.* Yet those rare Americans who took pains to know the *quintos* found them staunch comrades, friendly and resourceful. Pat Stephens found a boon companion in Juan Abed, who invited him to visit his farm after the war. He promised big watermelons and a beautiful sister he could sleep with. Everybody laughed. When a Spaniard asked if he would allow Patricio to sleep with his own wife, Abed said, "I have no wife. But I will let him sleep with Franco's wife." More laughter.*

Later in March a van appeared in the courtyard of the cookhouse. Lettered on the outside was "COMISARIA POLÍTICA—PASAREMOS!" Inside were supplies of reading matter—Party pamphlets and throwaways, for the most part—and a mimeograph machine for printing a frontline newspaper. Tacked over the editor's stick-leg table were two pin-ups, one of Dolores Ibarruri ("La Pasionaria"), mother superior of the Spanish Communist Party, and Josef Stalin—both fully clothed.* Their newspaper, *Our Fight,* contained two mimeographed pages chronicling successful industrial strikes in the States, soccer scores from England, and strident appeals for discipline and unity. As a concession to the increasing number of Spaniards being inducted into the brigade, there was a one-shot insert urging volunteers to "Learn Spain [*sic*]" with lists of

Spanish verbs (without conjugations).* In vain, Soviet advisers lamented to Moscow that the Internationals held themselves aloof from Spaniards in their outfits, refused to learn Spanish, and promoted Spaniards only under duress.* Jason Gurney, who served with both the Americans and the British, noted that few of his comrades knew much of anything about the country they had pledged to save from Fascism and rarely made friends beyond their own circle. As a matter of fact, many volunteers blamed Spain and Spaniards for their litany of woes. Gurney stood almost alone in offering the *quintos* English lessons. More often than not, Americans taught them only obscenities.

Always *Our Fight* railed against the mushrooming grievance committees that were "were making demands in the Brigade as if they were fomenting demands against the Capitalist class."* (Good Communists adhered to an odd doctrine they called "*democratic* socialism," in which democracy came from the top down, not from the bottom up.) "Comrades, let us not grumble," began an editorial. "Let us carry on. Can we use a rest? Yes! But it must not be as a result of committees, but when our comrades in the BRIGADE can get it for us."* More milk from the Party teat.

Despite the editor's boast that *Our Fight* was "striking a blow at the Fascist enemy," for the Lincolns it made more noise than sense. If it was ludicrous to read that "Toscanini, famous conductor of the New York Philharmonic orchestra, has spit in Mussolini's face by refusing to attend the 70th anniversary of La Scala," it was rotten when a sanctimonious prop-editor wrote, "Olive trees symbolize peace because men are buried under them."* However, sometimes Party jargon became unintentionally comic as when Doc Pike, alarmed by unburied excrement in the trenches, attempted to convert latrine digging into an exalted proof of proletarian fervor: "Upon this foundation of collective effort, a superstructure of individual care can be created, resulting in healthier bodies, saner minds, working together for the good that brought us together, the overthrow of Fascism, the triumph of democracy."* Pike was a stickler for digging latrines and waged his own lost war to keep them clean. He became incensed by a Cuban who had missed the hole. "Don't you know where to shit?" "Yes, but it's too late now," said the culprit, buttoning up and walking away. Pike tried sarcasm, "The next time you have to go, let me know and I'll show you where." "OK, Doc, what you can do now is show me how to put the stuff back into my ass," replied the Cuban, strolling off chuckling.*12 Dysentery

---

12. When Doctor Simon first observed that excrement lay everywhere unburied, he reminded himself that Hebrews carried spades for this purpose in military campaigns. But he too, through fatigue and indifference, adopted the prevailing habit of just kicking some dirt over it.*

was no laughing matter; like lice, it was egalitarian in making no distinction between officers and ordinary mortals. The British were especially susceptible because of their addiction to tea, which they made in metal helmets with unboiled water. Although the April 10, 1937, issue of *Our Fight* denied the existence of typhoid among the Internationals, a special ward was established in a Murcia hospital to treat typhoid cases.* Even fifty years later a British veteran complained that he still suffered from diarrhea first contracted in the trenches of Jarama.*

From *Our Fight* the volunteers learned that there now existed in the United States an outfit called Friends of the Abraham Lincoln "Brigade." On their own authority Party hierophants in New York had elevated their battered, undermanned little battalion to full-fledged brigade status, thereby shunting aside the other three battalions of the XVth Brigade, all of them senior in service and performance! News of the FALB (Friends of the Abraham Lincoln Brigade) provided a field day for a New York wag named Morris Mickenberg, who solemnly announced that a new organization FONIC (Friends of the Non-Intervention Committee) was now signing up Jarama vets. It argued that the CPUSA had tried to intervene in Spain, but since it had failed, it was time to go home. The commissars waxed wroth, but fearing Mickenberg's quirky humor, which the men enjoyed, they did nothing for the moment except to put his name on their black list of deviationists. (Their revenge would come later.)

Weary of the treacle of propaganda oozing from each issue of *Our Fight,* the rank and file got up an opposition newspaper consisting of snippets and fragments tacked to a bulletin board just behind their trench. This, the first in a series of "wall newspapers," was called the *Daily Mañana,* edited by "Manual Labor," and featured "All the fits that news can print." A zany publication, it owed more to Harpo Marx than to Karl. There was a column written by General Nuisance, who predicted that "the war will be over as soon as we win," and there were news bulletins like "Flash! We see where the government has ordered the devaluation of the Franco." It poked fun at the machine gunner who had taken a bite of Spanish bread that demolished his bridge, and the volunteer who had written his mother that the boat bringing him to Spain had docked at Albacete.*

This was when "comic-star" became a generic term for any commissar disliked by the volunteers.

April was benign. "The vines in No-man's-land sprouted green. Suddenly we realized we were sweeping the dirt out our trenches instead of bailing out water. Spring had come to Jarama."* On the shell-pitted slopes at Jarama, spiky plants put out dainty yellow and purple blossoms, which when crushed smelled like Vick's Salve. Dead-looking olive trees, splintered by shot and shell, sprouted long green shoots. An agricultural student from Farmingdale, Long Island, set out hand-lettered signs along his trench: "CARE FOR THE GRAPES—THEY SUFFER WHEN YOU HIT THEM."* Trenches became streets and avenues named for Communist deities like Marx, Lenin, and Stalin, although these names were soon changed to those of places back home like Broadway and Union Square. Even private domains were sprouting up along the trench line, staked off by signs like "JOE'S PLACE—PASS AT YOUR OWN RISK." Another read "KEEP OUT! PROPERTY OF CHARLIE THE SNIPER." Charlie Regan, a middle-aged Irish-American, kept a careful tally of every Fascist he shot—or might have shot. He squinted and fired at an enemy too far away and too deeply entrenched to be seen at all and hollered in triumph, "Just got one!" When pressed for details, he backed off a little. "Well, if I had one o' those Zeiss telescopic sights, it'd be a cinch. Then I could count their lice and rats. The way it is, they're a little far off for me—my eyes are sore, strainin' at 'em. A Zeiss sight."*

Harry Fisher and three other Americans on guard duty early one morning labored over an ideological conundrum. They had spotted, in plain view, a "lousy fascist with pants down, taking a shit." One comrade took aim but was rebuked by a comrade. "How the hell can you shoot a guy taking a shit in such innocence?" A third suggested, "Let's be democratic, just like at union meeting. Let's take a vote." They passed out slips of paper as ballots—a cross meant shoot him, a circle meant no. Opening the slips they found circles. Later they agonized over their decision—suppose he had been the sniper killing our comrades? For all that, how could you bring yourself "to shoot a guy with his pants down? It just doesn't seem like a fair fight."*

The earth was greening, and wounded men returned daily from hospitals. They were Rip Van Winkles peering into strange faces. Even the terrain of the February 27 massacre looked different—trenches had replaced ditches and dugouts seemed · luxurious. Some refused to speak about the February battles; others buttonholed newcomers and wanted to speak of nothing else. Very few had a clear picture of what had happened—it seemed as far away as Gettysburg or Thermopylae.

As Franco softened his hold on Madrid, General Gal eagerly planned another attack. Chagrined by his previous failures to take Pingarrón—and no doubt nervous about how these appeared to the Kremlin—he cobbled together a plan that would "drive the Fascists across the [Jarama] river in a scissor-like maneuver."* Gal was the sort of commander more willing to lose a hundred men in an advance than ten in a retreat.

The plan was to deploy three international brigades: the XIIth (Garibaldis), the XIIIth (Dombrowskis), and the XVth, assisted by the Spanish 66th Brigade, which included the undependable La Pasionaria Battalion. On April 5 an aerial bombardment at 0630 would be followed by an artillery barrage at 0635. At precisely 0700, twenty tanks would lead the Garibaldis and Dombrowskis across about a hundred meters of no-man's-land into the Fascist trenches. The XVth would provide massive covering fire until the enemy trenches were breached. Then the Lincolns would go over the top under covering fire from the remaining battalions. It sounded wonderful. Whether Gal actually believed this offensive would reach the Jarama River, which lay four kilometers away, is beside the point. Hourihan expected the worst. Having experienced how commanding officers resorted to buck-passing and outright lying to cover up their incompetence, he protected himself from charges of misconduct by assigning two battalion observers to chronicle each stage of the attack—minute by minute! The result was a three-page, single-spaced document—by all odds the most detailed account of the Lincolns in action ever compiled.*

So much for the plan. Here is what happened. The airplanes arrived at 0630, dropped a single load of bombs, and disappeared. Their only impact was to tip off the enemy about an attack. The XVth laid a massive covering fire as the first wave of Garibaldis seized Dead Mule Trench, but the second wave did not move. The Dombrowskis never rose from their trenches, and among the Pasionarias only half a dozen men popped out of their trench and immediately went to ground like prairie dogs. When the tanks arrived an hour later, the enemy had recovered from shock and begun to shell the Republican lines. One tank got stuck in a shell hole, and caught on fire as its three crewmen bailed out; the others skittishly fired a few shots and backed off. The drivers complained that they had to identify themselves by waving red flags when they came under fire from Republican gunners. By noon the Lincolns had fired more than fifty-three thousand rounds and were down to twenty-five rounds per man. Minutes later Copic ordered the Lincolns over the top to relieve the Garibaldis, trapped between the lines. Gal had hounded Copic to push out his brigade, asserting that three more tanks were on their way and claiming that the Pasionarias had reached the enemy trenches. Hourihan found himself where Merriman had been on the day of the massacre. The Pasionarias had not moved. He asked for a delay to replenish his ammunition and to coordinate with the tanks.

Incensed, Copic shouted into the telephone, "You're cowards! You don't perform your duties! You're not aggressive enough!" (In his notes Hourihan wrote, "This is the second time Copic called the Americans 'cowards.' The first time was on the 27th of February.") Men covering the Lincoln flanks with two

"Shau-shaus" (the notorious French Chauchot machine guns) had plenty of ammunition, but it was the wrong caliber. Not that it really mattered—these antiques usually jammed after firing a few shots. The British would normally have supplied covering fire except that their ammunition was nearly gone.

At 1305 the entire Lincoln Battalion, without the promised tanks, went over the top except for a section left as reserve. The left flank, which found some cover from a knoll, got within forty meters of the enemy parapets while the right flank flopped soon after leaving the trench. Hourihan told the men to dig in as best they could. Five minutes later Copic ordered them to continue their advance. Hourihan refused. Copic then ordered the British to leave their trenches and relieve the pressure on the Lincolns. The British commander declined on grounds that their ammunition was used up. Fresh supplies were sent up at 1700, when Copic repeated his demand that they attack. The British refused. Under cover of darkness the Lincolns crawled back.* Despite the vast amount of steel and lead that had whizzed about them all day, their casualties amounted to only five killed and one wounded. Compared with their previous attacks across no-man's-land, April 5 was a victory of sorts. They had not been slaughtered because their battalion commander had the brains to detect a foolish order and the courage not to follow it.

In his diary Colonel Copic laid the blame on General Gal: "During these operations the Division commander spoke several times about [our] occupation of the enemy positions and also about the advance of the Pasionaria Battalion, but these cases did not correspond to the truth."* He owed the Americans an apology for calling them "cowards," but there is no evidence that he made it. Thereafter, the lines ossified until the end of the war.

In March they had bailed out and drained trenches; in April they swept out fine, red dust that covered everything, like velveteen. The back slopes at Jarama resembled Hoovervilles, but they were home. Like groundhogs, the men had dug subterranean chambers containing sleeping alcoves and chiseled staircases in the red clay. Some dugouts had corrugated iron roofs camouflaged by olive branches and sod. A New York Irishman grinned at Herbert Matthews of the *Times* and cracked, "We ain't going to pay any rent after this war. We'll just build dugouts in Battery Park."* A few carpenters, perfectionists who scorned iron as a heat conductor, erected clapboard doghouses with plank flooring. At battalion headquarters, cool and hidden like a bootleg coal mine, a typist pounded the keys with two index fingers while a wind-up Victrola played "Night and Day."* Every morning between nine and nine-fifteen an enemy battery shelled the San Martín road. "Our alarm clock," explained a veteran. "You can set your watch by it." Although they deplored the morning fusillade from the enemy trenches exactly when rations came up in the morning, they solved that discomfort by learning when the enemy rations arrived and pummeling them at the same time. Eventually both sides ceased the morning duel and breakfasted in peace. Unlike the Nationalists, the Internationals had no mortars, a fearsome weapon that could drop a projectile into a trench like a high lob with a basketball. An English mechanic, working with a steel tube and brass valves, managed to fashion a homemade aerial torpedo mortar that could throw explosive cans far out into no-man's-land. On the third day, however, it blew up, lightly wounding the inventor and his chums.*

Along the trench line sentries posted every twenty yards kept watch while their buddies lay in hives scraped out of the trench wall, snoozing, reading, or writing hundreds of letters.* At times the men seemed to live only to write them and to wait for them. Whimsical, boasting, ironical letters chronicled the inner dimensions of men along a "dead" front, or as Ed Flaherty put it, "as quiet as a Sunday afternoon in Machiasport, Maine."*

Dear Joe—It felt like the millennium when I heard a bunch of schoolkids singing the "International" and to see little tots of two or three raise their clenched fists in salute. It will be a grand place to live when we finish what the fascists started, and I'm almost convinced I shall remain here.

Dear Dave—After the war is won we will gladly supply you with fascist helmets that you can use for flower pots and an armored tank or so to use for collecting dues or transporting MacCallum's Scotch Whiskey. . . .

Dear Mr. Editor—These murderers are not satisfied with the use of bullets. They use dum-dums. And recently they have perfected a new brain child of the civilized scientists from Heidelberg University—an exploding bullet! You remember my passport was stamped "Not valid for Spain." Well, the bullet cut my passport in half. . . .

Dear Hattie—When a heavy bomb explodes nearby it almost raises you from the ground and you feel as though your guts were being sucked clean out. . . . One fellow was creased between his stump and artificial leg. The poor horrified *medico* almost fainted when the leg came off in his hand.

Dear Marge—The unpicked olives age in the trees and drop to the ground, literally covering it. The juice is wine-like purple when the olives rot. In the past we have learned lots about olives from the most intimate associations, lying among them or on the ground until we were all over purple-red color. It makes you feel something like a salad.

By May, Ping-Pong and baseball had replaced sniping and grenade throwing at Jarama. The prevailing idea was no longer to shoot the enemy but to induce him to desert. Each side battered the other with megaphones advising men to shoot their officers and cross over. The Internationals guffawed at these invitations, but the broadcasts set off a flurry of desertions among Spanish-born troops of both sides. A few Cubans did desert to the Nationalists about this time—blamed on defective political instruction—but no Americans went over to the enemy. Nationalist prisoners were a great disappointment. They did not look like "Fascists"—only wretched conscripts eager to escape war and indistinguishable from Spanish Republicans except for their khaki overalls. (One of them, probably to curry humane treatment, reported that the February 27 attack had nearly succeeded—clearly impossible.) The Republicans drowned out their enemy when they brought up a public-address system so vast that it had to be transported by two trucks, the first containing electrical equipment and a bulletproof room for the announcer and the second supporting the speaker, an apparatus twenty feet long and six feet wide at the mouth. "I could hardly believe my eyes," remembered an American. "It was a street corner speaker's nightmare." This demonic contraption frayed the nerves of friend and foe alike as it blared forth endless surrender harangues, interspersed with recordings of "Ave Maria" so loud that the individual words were lost in the ear-splitting decibels. The consensus was that "it would do pretty well for Union Square gatherings," but its presence came to be a torment for the Americans. Fortunately for the announcer, his cabin was bulletproof.* If you couldn't kill your enemy on this dormant front, you could at least annoy him.

Meanwhile they waited. They were bored, they complained. They became obsessed with cigarettes. The first two questions that Lincolns asked American visitors were "How are the strikes coming?" followed with "How about a cigarette?" They griped that Anarchists and Trotskyites back in Barcelona were pirating their American brands, and that French were helping themselves to the rest. (By far the most popular brand was Lucky Strike, probably because of the talismanic impact of the name, although good proletarians pretended to prefer Twenty Grand because they were union made.) Men begged folks back home to put a few cigarettes in each letter. Spanish cigarettes were insufferable. The loose, black grains that came in paper "pillow slips" were supposed to be rerolled but usually crumbled into dust in the making. The tailor-made Spanish types were dubbed "antitanks" because of their lung-piercing potency. Veterans descended upon new men and lectured on the merits of sharing, but greenhorns quickly learned the efficacy of hogging. Even the brigade hierarchs suffered. An American whose eye had fastened on Copic's cigar tagged him, but when the colonel neared the end of his smoke, he borrowed a pin so that he could inhale a few more puffs.*

Desertion began to assume epidemic proportions. In his diary Copic complained that men were wandering to Morata without permission, and some went on foot to Aranjuez and Chinchón. Desertions in the Franco-Belge companies ranged as high as seven per day, and they shrugged off punishment. Gnawed by the feeling that they would never return home, men began to desert in small groups. Some Britons stole a truck and made it as far as Barcelona.* Overstaying a Madrid leave by a few hours meant court-martial. At one such trial the British commander was amazed to hear the president of the Military Court demanding—but not obtaining—the death penalty.* Some of the worst cases were sent to the noncom school at Pozorubio, not because they deserved promotion but because it was a painless way to get rid of troublemakers. As discipline eroded, the political commissariat seemed to go berserk. Furious that wine was arriving into the line mysteriously, they concluded that it was being sent by Fascists to undermine morale—a clear case of sabotage. Again they demanded the death penalty for those responsible.* Hysteria ran its course; no executions were carried out at this time. Perhaps the greatest change was that in the pre-Jarama days if a volunteer became unmanageable he would be warned that unless he shaped up he would never be allowed to go to the front, whereas now an incorrigible sequestered in rear billets knew that unless he reformed he might end up at the front—and possibly in a labor battalion, where life was cheap.*

The strain of minimal existence in fetid holes with nothing to do or look forward to had shattered rational patterns of behavior. A case in point was an epidemic of typhus that swept across the Jarama encampments. Medical officers were frustrated when three companies of Franco-Belge, for reasons they could not explain, formed a solid phalanx against inoculation. The food was execrable—tasteless and monotonous. To pay for special rations not issued by the Republican army, paymasters docked three pesetas from every man's daily stipend, but where was the evidence of this? Certainly not in the stew ladled out from iron washtubs. Bindle stiffs riding the rails back in the States ate better stuff than this "mule meat" occasionally fortified by a slurry of beans or lentils.

"The flavor [of the meat] wasn't so bad," remembered a veteran. "It was the texture. I could never swallow a piece of it, no matter how small. The more you'd chew it, the bigger it would get, until your mouth felt like it was full of rubber bands." Part of the problem came from relegating battalion washouts to the cookhouse, where their worthlessness was apparent in every meal. "Them left-handed half-wits in the kitchen," groused one man. "They don't know piss from boilin' water. Like the other day, we got half a sheep sent up, prime meat, and damned if they didn't leave it lay in the sun till it got up and walked off with the maggots in it. I saw that, too. And a cook runnin' after it with a lasso."*

During their long trench vigil, which lasted from March through June, the Lincoln Battalion left the line for a rest only once. At the end of April they boarded trucks. "We didn't know where we were going and we didn't care, as long as it was away from the Jarama Front."* Only later did they learn that they were to march in a May Day parade at Alcalá de Henares, auto-park of the "Serbian" tank battalion. (Because of the "Non-Intervention" farce, Soviet tankists tried to pass as Serbians, not Russians.) Trucks dropped the men in the dusty arcades of the *plaza mayor*. They were billeted in an icy church, the first roofed building many of them had entered in over two months, but they erupted in anger when the Alcalá commander refused to issue them mattresses because they were not attached to his command.* The Lincolns fanned out in all directions and scoured the city for booze. Hourihan made no attempt to restrain them—they had earned a binge. He and the battalion officers bedded down in a *fonda* where they dumped their lice-infested clothes and luxuriated in showers of cold water with real soap and slept on beds with clean sheets.

The next morning, when Hourihan and staff went over to the *plaza mayor* they witnessed a scene that recalled "the aftermath of a bubonic plague." Men were lying on the sidewalks or propped up against the walls, half-dressed, some lying in pools of their own vomit. "Practically the entire Battalion was blind, paralytic drunk."* Some men still on their feet were rummaging through the crypt of the church, prying up burial stones over long-dead ecclesiastics and searching for valuables. One Lincoln digger wore a bishop's mitre on his head. Hourihan, a lapsed Catholic, restored order and posted a guard. Yet the Americans were angels when compared with a battalion of the Franco-Belge XIVth, who "wandered drunken through the town and caused enormous scandals"—presumably assaulting women—after their officers lost all control of them.*

Despite their condition, a remnant of the Lincolns made a creditable showing the next afternoon at the parade under banners that read "PASAREMOS" ("We shall pass"), a new Republican slogan replacing the old "NO PASARÁN"

("They won't pass").[13] The high point of the celebration was a review in an open field. "Men with mud of Jarama still in their ears, men with their behinds sticking out of their pants," stood at attention while dapper officers cantered past on horses that looked recently dry-cleaned. After speeches in a language few of them understood, they marched back to their barracks-church, only to be told, "Assemble at six. Full pack. We're moving out tonight." Their destination—the old trenches at Jarama.[14] Hourihan feared a mutiny when he told them, but they only grumbled. Said one, "Jarama's home. A hell of a lot more comfortable than this joint. Not so draughty."*

Back in their old trenches, they found one major change. In their brief absence, French units of the XIVth Brigade, who had relieved them, had turned their area into a fetid pigsty. In navigating their trenches they had to run a gauntlet of feces, and found their dugouts littered with rotting food, broken bottles, and empty food tins. However, there was one benefit, "Our beefing was amplified beyond Copic and the Brigade staff; we could now curse the French, which made a pleasant change."*

So they waited, wrote more letters, sniped at an invisible enemy, played more Ping-Pong. Nothingness became a major enemy. "It was static warfare so much," wrote a volunteer, "that you began to wonder what was taking place."* Competent and ambitious men like Oscar Hunter found life especially irksome. After recovering from a wound he became commissar at the auto-park, where his most demanding job was passing out condoms on payday (accompanied with a canned lecture on VD) or using a Mack truck to pick up deserters intercepted at the French frontier.*

In lighter moments they made up songs:

Oh, the Lincoln boys fought at Jarama
They made the Fascisti cry "Mama."
They held down the line
For months at a time
And for sport they would play with a bomb-a*

13. Both derived from General Henri Pétain's rallying cry against the German offensive toward Paris in 1916, *"Ils ne passeront pas."*

14. One theory to explain the Lincolns' unexpected return to Jarama holds that Spanish troops were pulled from the line to suppress the so-called Trotskyist (POUMist) insurrection in Barcelona. Commissars used the occasion to whip up hatred of the POUM. Robert Minor spoke to the men for two hours on the events in Barcelona, arguing that the Trotskyites were on the Fascist payroll. Such hatred paid dividends. As Jerry Warren (Weinberg), a Lincoln volunteer, wrote bitterly, "Soldiers giving their lives at the front and those 100 percent revolutionaries, our Trotskyite friends, organize a revolt in the rear. If I ever see a Trotskyite at the front, I'll sure as hell shoot him."*

Rotting in this bywater of the war, an English volunteer spoke for all of them, "Unable to wash . . . we dug dirt from our eyes, nose and mouth, accepted the myriad flies which swarmed everywhere, especially in the discard trench we used as a latrine."* June unraveled slowly. To this period belongs "The Valley of Jarama," a ballad composed by Alex McDade of Glasgow for the whole XVth Brigade, but more or less monopolized by the Lincolns as their own anthem. Sung to the tune of "The Red River Valley," and popularized in the States by Pete Seeger, it spoke not of the horror of fighting but of the boredom of endless waiting.

> There's a valley in Spain called Jarama
> That's a place that we all know so well,
> For 'tis there that we wasted our manhood,
> And most of our old age as well.

> From this valley they tell us we're leaving,
> But don't hasten to bid us adieu,
> For e'en though we make our departures
> We'll be back in an hour or two.

> Oh, we're proud of our British [Lincoln] Battalion,
> And the marathon record it's made,
> Please do us this little favor,
> And take this last word to brigade:

> "You will never be happy with strangers,
> They would not understand you as we,
> So remember the Jarama Valley
> And the old men who wait patiently."

Colonel Copic snorted with contempt when he heard the song: Americans were such babies. Speaking of "loss of manhood."* Yet the song remains as the most haunting, and wistful, ballad sung by American volunteers in the Spanish civil war.

6

TOURISTS AND TRIPPERS

Having no stomach for publicizing his Jarama debacles, General Gal cordoned off the XVth Brigade and banned journalists from the sector. Yet he failed to silence the cries and complaints of wounded men in Interbrigade hospitals, where Anglo-American newsmen heard how the Lincoln Battalion had lost over half its men in its maiden battle. Journalists descending on Morata with demands to visit the trenches were told that the plateau was off-limits to visitors because it was bracketed with artillery fire. When Herbert L. Matthews of the *New York Times* expressed his willingness to incur this risk, Gal turned tough: it was not that he personally cared what happened to capitalist war correspondents, but he feared their movements might draw fire upon soldiers. He added that when the front "stabilized," journalists would be allowed in.

Party cards carried more weight with Gal than press credentials. After a ten-day cooling off, scribblers from the crypto-propaganda media of the Left went in. One of the earliest was James Hawthorne of *New Masses,* who arrived on March 9. He wrote with enthusiasm of the good food, courageous dead, and the "*symboliste*" landscape. After examining unkempt survivors in trash-infested trenches, he wrote about "the decor of Hell" and peered through a loophole at gashed olive trees and lumpish corpses. When the divisional and brigade staffs lavished praise on the heroism of the Americans, Hawthorne sucked it all in. A Hungarian surgeon spoke of a Negro with a bullet in his stomach who could still manage a "wide smile." "And they are all like that." No less a personage than General Gal himself remarked, "The Americans covered themselves with glory. They are good soldiers." He went on to observe that American bodies retrieved from no-man's-land were found with their fists clenched in the Popular Front salute! No doubt dead Americans gave Gal less trouble than living ones. In his story for *New Masses,* Hawthorne said nothing about massacre or mutiny.*

James Hawthorne was inspired by what he found at Jarama, but not sufficiently moved to enlist. (As Hemingway says somewhere, "Paper bleeds but little.") However acceptable such ludicrous propaganda was to the stay-at-homes who read *New Masses* and dreamed of killing Fascists in Spain, the Lincoln survivors were enraged when they read his story. Having little taste for romance, they found nothing glorious about the bloated corpses scattered along the far slope. And months later, when another reporter from New Masses turned up in the trenches, they protested that they were "sore about being described as the tin-Jesuses of the proletariat." Outrageous lies that transformed useless battles into military victories damaged morale; "it made us wonder about the honesty and political reliability of party leaders."*

Next in line among leftist tourists came a celebrated proletarian poet from England. Stephen Spender had been issued a CPGB card by Harry Pollitt, the secretary-general, who persuaded him to go and then sweetened the journey by giving him an expense account. Before parting, Pollitt said playfully, "Go and get killed, comrade. We need a Byron in the movement." At Jarama, led by Major George Nathan, a cane-twirling Englishman of brigade staff, and followed by a skittish Indian writer, Spender climbed up mule paths to the plateau where stray bullets whipped overhead "like shrieking starlings." As they entered the communication trench, the elegant, battle-loving Nathan coolly advised them to stoop low because they had attracted enemy snipers. Then, amused by their crestfallen faces, he added jovially, "We make a point of not allowing our front-line visitors to be killed." Bent nearly double, the six-foot Spender and the five-foot Indian filed down the trench like Mutt and Jeff, while Major Nathan breezily pointed out the sights. At one point the Indian stopped Spender to intone oratorically, as though gestating a poem, "I can see Death's great question-mark hovering between the trenches." The metaphor annoyed Spender, who felt the environs better suited for dialectical materialism than grotesque personification. A machine gunner invited him to fire a burst at the enemy trenches. Though reluctant to do so, the men flocking around seemed so disappointed by the pacifism of England's best-known radical poet that he finally closed his eyes and fired a few rounds, "positively praying that I might not by any chance hit an Arab." Out in no-man's-land, unrecovered bodies lay in inert clusters like "ungathered wax fruit."*

The most distressing event of Spender's visit was his conversation with a forlorn eighteen-year-old English boy from a Liberal family, who guided him back down the valley. The youth said he had run off from school because he had been told that the Spanish Republic was synonymous with liberalism. Now he was bitterly disillusioned because the International Brigades were run by Communists. When Spender pointed out that the defense of the Republic was nonetheless a liberal cause, the boy replied, "I don't know about that. All I see are the Communist bosses of the brigade." Startled by this confession, Spender promised to see if he could arrange for his companion to be shifted to a noncombatant position, but the boy lamented, "No, my life is to walk up the ridge here every day till I am killed." (Six weeks later, Spender learned that the boy's prophecy had come true.) Although the British Party had sent Spender to Spain to write in support of the war against Fascism, he had a personal mission. He intended to locate Tony Hyndman, a former lover, who, distraught because Spender had abandoned homosexual liaisons for marriage, had run off to join the British Battalion. (Suspecting what might happen, Spender had given him thirty one-pound notes in case he wanted to return.) Though a peacetime Guardsman, Hyndman had no grit for war. After the battalion's bloody initiation at Jarama, he had escaped to Valencia in search of a ship to Britain until captured and sent back to the front as a prisoner in a labor battalion. As an "expendable" during the March 15 fracas, he was wounded in the head and sent under guard to Albacete and charged with Trotskyism. Threatened with execution, he begged for a chance to reform, and his case was placed on hold. Spender got permission to visit him. The minute they were alone, Hyndman blurted out, "You must get me out of here!" He blamed Spender for encouraging him to adopt causes he did not believe in. Now he feared that he would be sent back to a labor battalion, where dissidents and troublemakers were likely to be shot—whether by friend or enemy made no difference to the CP.[1] All his anti-Fascist enthusiasm had vanished. He said that he was now a pacifist and added that he was useless as a soldier because he had developed an ulcer. Awash in guilt, Spender appealed to the British commissariat, which countered that if Hyndman were released, it would set off a stampede among other Britons. In the end, the Party, fearing adverse publicity from Spender, discharged Hyndman for medical reasons, even though the ulcer story was clearly a dodge. It was a narrow squeak. Once back in England both men dropped out of the Party. Later when Spender wrote in a *New Statesman* column that all recruits should be informed, in advance, that the Communists controlled the International Brigades, he was rebuked by a Party man who argued that the ends justified the means. For the poet such prevarication was as bone-chilling as the matter-of-fact tone of Milan Copic (Colonel Copic's younger brother), head jailer at the IB prison, who mockingly told him, "We are always happy when our friends are sent to [detention] camps. It is so good for their education." It was a rough object lesson for Spender that the noble idealism of Communism had an "indifference to awkward facts."

---

1. Hyndman's fear was not fanciful, for undesirables in the International Brigades were often eliminated in this way. He had come to Spain with Bert Overton, also a former Guardsman, who had commanded a company at Jarama. When Overton panicked on the first day and led his company out of battle, the right flank collapsed and the battalion was nearly destroyed. Overton was court-martialed and placed in a labor battalion, and was subsequently killed at Brunete in July.

Political disenchantment more quickly devastated Spender's friend, the poet W. H. Auden, who announced in December 1936 that he would soon join the International Brigades.[2] After changing his mind in favor of driving an ambulance, he arrived in Barcelona a month later, only to be shocked by the sight of burned-out and looted churches and by information that ten bishops and thousands of priests had been murdered by Republican supporters. After nosing about Valencia for a few weeks, he abruptly decamped for London. However, Faber in May 1937 published his poem "Spain," a pamphlet of five pages, which included the lines

> To-day the deliberate increase in the chances of death,
> The conscious acceptance of guilt in the necessary murder.

This apparent endorsement of political murder aroused such a storm of protest that he amended them three years later.

> To-day the *inevitable* increase in the chances of death;
> The conscious acceptance of guilt in the *fact of murder.*
> (My italics)

(Even this was unacceptable in certain quarters because of its confession that the Spain Left had actually murdered people.) Thereafter, Auden rigorously fended off questions about what he did and saw in Spain. His wartime visit remains the least documented episode of his life. In 1955 came his final verdict on the Spanish civil war: "Nobody I know who went to Spain during the Civil War who was not a dyed-in-the wool stalinist [*sic*] came back with his illusions intact."*

As George Orwell put it, "So much of left-wing thought is a kind of playing with fire by people who don't even know that fire is hot."*

Late in March, Captain Hourihan began to issue twenty-four-hour passes for Madrid. It was about time, for the men were becoming sex-crazy. "Lord," moaned one. "It's been so long now I'm afraid I'll never get the wrinkles out. . . . Major problem is how to keep from going 'fruit' altogether. Already the boys are beginning to ogle each other."* Abstinence was all the more

---

2. That the Spanish civil war nurtured a host of writers and intellectuals owes much to the activities of Willi Muenzenberg, the Comintern agent who coined and publicized the slogan, "We must organize the intellectuals." By contrast, the Nationalist cause attracted few supporters among Western intellectuals.*

maddening because Doc Pike had handed out condoms by the gross as far back as Villanueva, but there was no use for them except as waterproof tobacco pouches and rifle muzzle covers. The first group left in an empty munitions truck amid the cheering of the men left behind, who seemed nearly as jubilant as those who went. For a few pesetas per day, they could bunk down in a luxury hotel controlled by the Catering Workers' Union and try to soak off grime and lice in a hot tub. Food in Madrid was scarce, but with ration chits they could eat in style at the Hotel Gran Via—"usually mule-meat and chick-peas but the wine was excellent."* Cafés displayed collectivist signs like "Comrades, do not damage the furniture, it belongs to you" and "Comrades, do not kick the waiter. He is also a man."* Always the lure of what one might find in the city was greater than what was there. Cigarettes had disappeared from shops long since, the food was as bad as that at the front, and the liquor "tasted like varnish remover laced with vanilla extract." (Lieutenant Robert Taylor once claimed he found three bottles of Johnny Walker Red, but few men accepted this tale as gospel.)* Worst of all, the sexual mores of Spanish girls were so impeccable that they would have earned hosannas from any vigilant Mother Superior, for despite a thin veneer of liberalism, their core was *catolicisma española*. "Every time you go out with one of them," griped one volunteer, "she holds a wedding ring on one hand and her mama in the other."* The sleeker class of prostitutes, whose blonde hair was turning black at the roots because peroxide was commandeered for hospital use, had left the public domain for private arrangements. "Black widows" abounded, but most Americans objected to liaisons with women older than their mothers. Besides, prostitution was regarded by many zealots as a degenerate relic of capitalism—as apparently deflowering virgins was not. Those brigaders willing to conflate pleasure with politics favored a whorehouse decorated with huge pictures of Marx, Stalin, and Lenin, despite its being the lair of a few "monsters."*

Madrid was a city in which revolution and reaction coexisted in a cockeyed truce. In the hand of the equestrian statue of Charles IV in the *plaza mayor* hung a red and black Anarchist flag. Women queued up in front of bakeries to be told what they already knew—that there was no bread that day; but a few doors away smart shops featured Schiaparelli perfume and silver fox furs. The Popular Front greased its wheels with capitalist money. Movie houses showed Greta Garbo in *Anna Karenina,* the Marx Brothers in *A Night at the Opera,* and Al Jolson in *Casino de Paris.* For those seeking political edification, there was always Charlie Chaplin's *Modern Times,* a satire on assembly-line industrialism, which had the longest run of its history at the Capitol on the Gran Via, which had a gaping shell hole in the ceiling covered with a tarp to keep the light out.

Less than two miles distant, enemy batteries on Mount Garibitas fired shells down this avenue—dubbed Shell Alley—every afternoon at the exact minute the feature let out. (The theater manager could have changed the schedule, but it would have done no good, for the Nationalists also subscribed to the morning newspapers.)

Like the *madrileños*, visiting Lincolns learned to hug the comparative safety of the south side of the Gran Via or to infiltrate rapidly into the narrow maze of back streets leading to the Puerta del Sol. One Jarama veteran marveled at the sangfroid of a Spaniard who leaned against a wall during a barrage while picking his teeth with total absorption. And it was a favorite trick of veteran journalists, like Ernest Hemingway, to frighten the wits out of newcomers by taking them on a stroll down the comparatively safe lee side of the Gran Via just as the Garibitas batteries opened fire. Visiting the front line was easy—only twenty-minutes away by tram. Taking the subway, however, was not recommended because the final stop was on the Nationalist side of the lines. The best ringside seat for viewing the battle—Parque del Oueste, but keep your head down. Weather preference for touring reversed because of air raids. Rainy days good—sunny days bad.* Foreigners placed Spanish chauffeurs high on their list of hazards. After a memorable drive on mountain roads, Steve Nelson wrote, "Perhaps to save his tires he kept the truck on two wheels much of the time."*

As a center of tourism, wartime Madrid had lost its stars. The paintings in the Prado had been packed up for safekeeping and the façade boarded up. The famous Sybil and Neptune fountains were buried under a deep layer of bricks and sandbags. Republican snipers fired with impunity from the windows of the National Palace, which overlooked enemy trenches in the Casa del Campo, since the monarchist officers in Franco's forces did not like to deface a venerable Bourbon shrine. The Retiro Gardens, having been converted to an artillery park, was no longer a place to get away from it all. In the zoo, the carnivores were dead or were starving by degrees. (It is said that when the elephant died, strange cuts of meat appeared in the butcher stalls of Madrid—though this story is also told of Barcelona.) Fancy hotels like the Ritz and the Palace had been converted into hospitals—especially appropriate since their chalk-white façades had always suggested rich men's sanatoria. Under the gilt and crystal chandeliers of regal dining rooms stretched rows of white cots filled with unshaven men, and on the walls hung multicolored posters with slogans like "BEAT FASCISM BY LEARNING HOW TO READ AND WRITE." Many an International volunteer eager for the destruction of the capitalist system came to Spain only to die at the Ritz.

Evenings in Madrid were better. An Anarchist committee had taken over Chicotes Bar off the Gran Via. In this wild cabaret anything could happen. Like the time a drunken *miliciano* amused himself by shooting guests with a Flit can filled with lavender water, until he was shot dead by a soldier with a real pistol and dragged out by his heels, his fingers still locked around the Flit can.* Then there was the time Milly, an American employee at the censor bureau, a dowdy girl with piano legs and cement-sack breasts, got drunk and put on a striptease pantomime called "The Widow of General Mola," commemorating Franco's second-in-command, who had recently died in an airplane crash. (General Mola was the patron devil of Madrid, best known for coining the term "Fifth Column.")* For the Americans, the nearby Miami Bar was a bit of home in old Madrid. A record player scratched out "You Are My Lucky Star," and the fresco on the wall featured languid boys and girls surfing in a blue sea as a yacht heeled down in a faded blue background.*

Lincolns on leave received a welcome at the Hotel Florida on Plaza del Callao, headquarters of Anglo-American journalists and official visitors, all of whom were on the lookout for interviewees who might save them a jolting— and perilous—trip out to Morata. Ignoring Don Cristobál, the prissy reception clerk who pored over his stamp collection trying to forget how low his hotel had sunk, the Lincolns camped out in overstuffed chairs in the lobby under a travel poster that read "VISIT CUBA." The interior consisted of a deep well with stairs and balconies rising four floors, obliterating privacy about goings-on between rooms. To save electricity, the elevator was sealed off for the duration. It was at the Florida that the Lincolns rubbed shoulders with everybody who was anybody in Republican Spain. John Dos Passos stayed there while commuting to nearby villages to study collective farming. Professor J.B.S. Haldane the British gas-warfare expert and well-known Cambridge geneticist, always came and went with his "Tommy" tin hat, his gas mask, and a leather jacket unbuttonable around his middle girth. Herbert L. Matthews of the *New York Times*, whom the pros touted as the best war correspondent in Spain, had a room at the Florida. His road companion, Sefton Delmer of the *Daily Mail*, rented two rooms, a sunny large one on the front exposed to shell-fire, and a dank but safe hole on the back, which he used for sleeping. He had bought up a cache of Chateau Yquem 1904 looted from the wine cellars of the National Palace—labels signed with date of entry into royal cellars—date of exit blank.* A few doors away was Claud Cockburn of the London *Daily Worker*, a prolific word-slinger who had once written, on Party order, a book about Spain in seven days. Cockburn had never visited the Soviet Union and had no intention of ever going there, because as he put it, "I am not interested in watching revolutions; my job is *making* them." Among the "influx of shits" catalogued by Martha Gellhorn was Errol Flynn, who breezed into the Florida one April day, announced he had come to fight Fascism—as "a sort of correspondent"—and breezed out the next while his press releases claimed he had been wounded on the Madrid front.* Gellhorn was not impressed by the hero of *Captain Blood,* "who looks like white fire on the screen, but is only very very average off."*

But the innermost circle of privilege and patronage at the Hotel Florida was presided over by Ernest Hemingway, who cabled dispatches to the North American Newspaper Alliance at a dollar per word. Regular members of his *tertulia* included Martha Gellhorn (his third wife-to-be), Herbert L. Matthews, and Sidney Franklin, a bullfighter from Brooklyn, New York. Visiting Lincolns soaked in his tub. (It was said that the Florida was the only hotel in Madrid that still had hot water.) Hemingway had no use for *políticos* or "comic-stars." As he once told Joe North of the New York *Daily Worker,* "I like the Communists when they're soldiers; when they're priests, I hate them. Yes, priests, the commissars who hand down the papal bulls. . . . That air of authority your leaders wear, like cassocks."* North objected to Hemingway's "murky ideas of Bukharin" and argued that Communists made good soldiers because they had political conviction, but Hemingway was not having it. "Conviction with the capital C. Fatherland with a capital F. Goddamn the capital letters." Shadow-boxing around the room, he went on, "I keep trim that way, to fight the communists. I suppose you stay fit memorizing a chapter of *Das Kapital,*" as he mockingly made the sign of a cross. On another occasion he told North, "Listen, Comrade Stalin, we've [the NANA] filed more good stuff in one day than the *Worker* has printed in two years."* High on his list of unspeakables were André Marty and General Gal—further down was Colonel Copic, who "ran his brigade like a badly administered pig-sty" or "an old woman with locomotor ataxia trying to be a blocking back against the New York Giants."*

Most of all, Hemingway personally admired those who fought without political commitments of any sort—American fliers like Frank Tinker, who shot down Nationalist planes for fifteen hundred dollars per month (plus bonuses), and Harold "Whitey" Dahl, who sought his advice about the dollar value of a "Van Dick" painting he had pilfered from some *castillo.* The only contact the Lincolns ever had in Spain with the American pilots came through crap games on the floor of Hemingway's room. Tinker was aghast when he learned the Lincolns made only ten pesetas a day. So little money for being shot at? Moreover, Arkansan to the bone, he was miffed by the designation "Lincoln" Battalion. "Why not a Jeff Davis Battalion?" he asked.

For all that, Hemingway's dispatches from Madrid sparkled with graphic details. He described the flight of an artillery shell as beginning with a "heavy coughing grunt" from a green pine-studded hillside, followed by a rushing sound like "ripping a bale of silk," and ending with a final "crash of dust and granite."* Tanks he characterized as "deadly intelligent beetles." He often visited the Jarama trenches in one of his two private cars and, unlike Spender, eagerly joined the Lincolns in the frontline trench where he fired a few rounds at the enemy from a machine gun (which the men did not appreciate because its tattoo usually unleashed a lethal volley in return). On one such visit he met Major Allan Johnson, who greeted him in a "spooky "way: "My name is not Johnson. I am from the American General Staff." (The first part was true—his name was McNeil—the rest was a lie, and Hemingway knew it.)* Yet he respected Hourihan, who became a lifelong friend and a guest in Cuba after the war.

Perhaps irritated by the demoralization of the Americans at Jarama, Hemingway preferred the businesslike German volunteers of the XIth Brigade, a unit that always took the heaviest casualties yet managed, like a blooded fighter with great heart, to bore in once again. On one occasion he raged when some Americans picked the lock of his *armoire* and filched two jars of marmalade he had brought from France. His anger stemmed less from stinginess than from his "solder-complex," as Josephine Herbst described it. He had dipped into his own pockets to donate an ambulance to the Republic, but someone who stole from a friend was a thief, not a soldier. The cynicism of Hemingway's faithful squire, Sidney Franklin, depressed the Lincolns. He enjoyed telling everyone how he had decided to come to Spain. One day Ernest had rung him up and said, "Lo, kid, want to go to the war in Spain?" and Franklin had quipped, "Sure, Pop. Which side we on?"* Since almost all of his *matador* pals had sided with Franco, Republican publicists made much of Franklin, apolitical though he was. At the Florida, Franklin rattled away that sex was no more important than a glass of water—"take it or leave it." And when he declaimed that nobody cared about anything, deep down, except money and security, a Lincoln whispered to Josephine Herbst that it was untrue: "What they want is happiness, and something to believe in."

The girls at the Florida were a remarkable collection. Lolita of the round, innocent face was the mistress of a counterintelligence officer; whenever they quarreled—which was often—he locked her up for a few days. Carminea, a buxom Amazon with black eyes, wore a towering, spangled comb in her hair, Andalusian style, and claimed to be the prewar women's wrestling champion of Spain. (Hemingway called them the "hors de combat.") Whenever the vice squad broke into her room at five in the morning, she always had the same excuse—she was keeping in shape for the return of peace. The two most popular girls were Farida and Fatima, Moorish sisters, both suspected of fifth column activities. When Málaga fell to Franco's army, Fatima announced, "*We* have taken Málaga!" After they had been carried off to jail for a spell, Dr. Hewlett Johnson, dean of Canterbury, took their room. A group of Anglo-American volunteers, led by a Scotsman, saw the "Red Dean" enter the room in his shorts and assumed he was a client. When he failed to emerge, the Scotsman reeled up to the door and battered it with his fists, "Come oot, yer old bastard! Ye've been mair ane twenty minutes in there! Yer time's oop. Come oot!"

Since all the girls at the Florida regularly donated blood to the Red Cross, some volunteers opined that this certified to their purity in other areas—a scientific fallacy, as they learned.* The indefatigable Dr. William Pike regularly came to the Florida to examine the whores for disease. Whenever he arrived they would shout, "Aqui viene Capitan Fucking!" One girl followed him into the toilet to see exactly how a condom worked.*

Because the Florida took a stray shell now and then, it was a poor place for sleeping. One morning ten Americans stretched out in the lobby were jarred awake at six o'clock. Unable to return to sleep, they began to sing and woke up the paying guests, for the acoustics of the place were marvelous. In the middle of "Sewanee River," a shell struck the building, sending the elevator cables crashing to the basement as Don Cristóbal wailed, "They're trying to ruin my business!" Herbert Matthews came down and asked the Jarama veterans how Madrid bombardments compared with those at the front. "This is much worse!" exclaimed one man. Another chimed in, "Out at the front we know what they are trying to hit and how to avoid it, but here we feel trapped like rats." "Yeah," broke in a farmer from the Midwest, "we came here to have a good time, and now look at us. We can't even get out of the hotel."*

Disappointing as Madrid often was, many volunteers overstayed their leaves and ended up in the labor battalion at Jarama. The brief passes were so prized that Captain Hourihan punished anyone who failed to return on time. There was mounting pressure, throughout the International Brigades, for home leaves, but this was vetoed by the commissariat. They argued that the Spanish authorities would not allow it (patently false because the political cadres of the International Brigades left and reentered Spain at will). Besides, there was now in the government a growing anxiety about the autonomy of the International Brigades, because of their Comintern affiliation. The real reason for denying home leaves was the fear that once the men—whether French, British, or American—reached home they would never come back again, and this massive defection would endanger the Popular Front concept of a war to the death against Fascism

By early April, General Gal began to permit journalists friendly to the Republic, though officially neutral, to visit the Jarama sector. One of the first arrivals was

Herbert Matthews, who found the Lincoln headquarters in a little house not far from the main square of Morata, "where there was even a grinning Negro from down south to greet us and there was good fellowship and excellent meals."* Later, when he was leaving the trench and waved good-bye, a Lincoln shouted, "That ain't the way to do it! Here's the way!" and raised a clenched fist in a vigorous salute.*

Among the brood of journalists appeared three American women, who ranged across the political spectrum from right-center to left-center: Virginia Cowles of the London *Sunday Times*, Martha Gellhorn of *Collier's*, and Josephine Herbst, a freelance.

In mid-March a tall blonde in Saks Fifth Avenue slacks with a green chiffon scarf on her head strode through the American trenches, collecting a gaping entourage in her wake. Martha Gellhorn blithely explained that she had come down to Morata in a Ford station wagon "camouflaged in such a way that you could see it ten miles off."* Since the front was quiet, men were sunbathing on the lee slopes. She talked with Hourihan, "a lean slow-talking boy who had been a schoolteacher in Alabama," and she asked others if they ever got homesick. Edward Flaherty of Boston said he never did, because he had brought two of his brothers with him. The trenches reminded her of the rubbish-strewn ditches in empty city blocks where slum children played. She did not mention the smell.

In Morata, flies swarmed over the soldiers and trucks in the littered *plaza mayor*. The field hospital, a white farmhouse covered with vines and invaded by bees, lay seven kilometers away. Here Miss Gellhorn found two doctors pouring peroxide on the shoulder of a wounded youth. The liquid foamed on a long shrapnel wound that resembled soil erosion, "ridged and jagged and eaten in." Although his stomach quivered with pain, he did not cry out. The place reeked of ether and sweat. All the serious cases had been evacuated to hospitals in Murcia. There were incongruities: an English nurse wearing long ribbon bandages to keep her hair out of her eyes looked like an illustration from *Alice in Wonderland*, and in one bed a French soldier was wearing an artificial leather flying cap exactly like those in vogue among American schoolboys. Yet everyone seemed "desperately tired." She saw little romance and no glory at Jarama.

Always she was more comfortable in describing urban scenes like—"streetcars with people sticking like ivy on steps and bumpers of trams" and "hotel lobbies like Des Moines with wicker chairs and signs promising to press clothes immediately" or "a desk clerk praising Mallorca and recommending a hotel there." She supported the Republican cause but was not blind to its defects. On returning home she described the war as "a carnival of treachery on both sides."*

By contrast, nothing at first seemed to go right for Virginia Cowles, despite her famous interview with Mussolini on the conclusion of his Abyssinian war. A cloud of suspicion attached to her when she arrived in Madrid wearing a hat (emblem of patrician privilege) and carrying a suitcase with red and yellow stripes (the Nationalist colors). Worse, her sponsor, the London *Sunday Times*, stood far to the right on the war. With her stylish black clothes and "shoes with very high heels" she proved to be an incongruity when climbing through the debris of bombed buildings or crossing streets pocked with shell-holes. J.B.S. Haldane escorted her to the front lines on the edge of Madrid. The pudgy professor wore breeches too tight and a tin hat with broken chin strap he had used in the World War—the only tin hat she saw in Spain. In gutted city blocks she found bisected flats high in the air, like stage sets with tables set for dinner, chairs pulled up, and doors banging back and forth in the wind. They filed down narrow trenches where men fired through sandbag openings. A Spanish soldier handed her his rifle—does she want to take a shot at the Fascists? She declined but did look through a periscope at enemy lines fifty yards away—a jumble of stones and grass. In between were three twisted bodies—"Los muertos nuestros," said a boy softly. Haldane asked her how she liked it and bridled at her, "Not much." He reminded her that in the Great War women had not been allowed within six miles of the front and told her that she should be "grateful for the privilege."*

A few days later, quite by chance, she stumbled upon a major journalistic scoop when, half-lost with her interpreter in the Tajuña sector, she wandered into General Gal's riverside dacha. Taken under guard to the general, he adamantly refused to allow her to visit the American trenches. With sullen green eyes, Gal viewed her upper-class mannerisms, her stylish clothes, and her *Times* press card with undisguised loathing. To make matters worse Miss Cowles asked suspicious questions, such as "Have many Fascist planes been over here?" and "Do you think the enemy will make another drive soon?" It was as though Gal had been introduced to Mata Hari in the flesh. Breaking off a spray of roses from his garden, he handed them to her, saying curtly, "You can write your story from the garden. No one will know the difference, and here is a souvenir to remind you of your adventures at the front." She abandoned hope of interviewing the men of the Anglo-American brigade.

Much to her surprise, a week later in Madrid, she received an invitation to lunch with Gal at his headquarters. His staff car carried her out to Morata. It was raining, and orderlies ran about the mess room collecting rain water from the leaking roof. By wartime standards the lunch was lavish—partridges, vegetables, bread, butter, and strawberries—but it was a solemn rite. No one dared to speak. After lunch Gal spoke to her though his interpreter, David Jarett (Zorat), a New York City court translator. "I may take you to the front this afternoon, but first you will have to remove those gold bracelets you are wearing. The enemy would be sure to spot them." His staff laughed uproariously. His testosterone courtship continued. Looking at her black suede shoes, he added, "You are too soft. You would get tired and want somebody to carry you."

They drove up the dark mountain to the plateau after the rain had stopped. The road was lined with tanks squatting, half-hidden, among dripping olive trees. Over the crest distant artillery flashed like lightning. When shells burst near by, Miss Cowles wanted to run, but thinking how this would only confirm Gal's theory about her, she struggled to control her fear. At the top stretched deep, muddy trenches that twisted beyond her vision through fields of red clay. Soldiers fired shots through sandbagged openings. They had no overcoats. Their soaked clothes hung on them like loose layers of skin. The general passed down the line, patting riflemen on the back and shaking hands with officers. Asked how he enjoyed the front, an American Negro, just up from training camp, replied, "Ah appreciates de glory, suh, but to tell de truth, ah was pufficly satisfied in de rear." Although the men played out light comedy roles for their visitor, she could see that their faces were lined and worn and their bodies ravaged by colds and dysentery. To Miss Cowles they lacked the swagger of legionnaires fighting for the joy of adventure: they were idealists but down-and-outs, few suited for war. One weary American told her, "You might suggest to the General we get a vacation. Not that we have any kick about the neighborhood, but the view is getting monotonous." They knew, of course, that Gal was keeping them in the line to teach them "discipline"' and to punish them for their failure during the attack on the twenty-seventh.

Returning to Gal's bucolic *finca* in the valley, Miss Cowles learned that she was to be kept there, virtually a captive, for three days so that she might understand, as Gal phrased it, "what we are fighting for." Presumably he had more tangible goals in mind as well. She was assigned a room not distant from the general's and issued two filthy blankets, toothpaste, a comb, and eau de Cologne—the basic tools of a woman of pleasure. After dinner Gal noisily broke open a bottle of champagne and emptied its contents into thick glass tumblers, which he passed around the table. Then he toasted his guest, "Here's to the bourgeoisie! May we cut their throats and live as they do." He seemed put down when she raised her tumbler mockingly. "I suppose in your bourgeois world you were taught that Bolsheviks were lacking in culture," he went on to say. "It is untrue. We often drink champagne in Moscow." At this point a young officer broke in with a remark that convulsed the whole table. Jarrett translated for her, "He says champagne is good but vodka is quicker."

A husky blond Russian proudly showed her a snapshot featuring a woman with thick black curls in a knee-length skirt lying on a rug with a rose dangling from her mouth. Miss Cowles thought at first that it must be a joke—possibly some burlesque of a "degenerate" Hollywood vamp of two decades before. But the young Russian was deadly serious; he proudly announced it was a picture of his wife. After examining the photo with the mien of a connoisseur of such things, General Gal said that the Soviet Union need never be ashamed of its womenfolk. The youth blushed with pleasure. Afterward they sat in the garden while a soldier serenaded them with Russian love songs. An orderly material-ized out of the gloom, reporting that the Fascists up on the hill wanted to bor-row some books and magazines. Gal forbade it. He explained that during the day literature was often exchanged under a white flag in no-man's-land, even though the emissaries often wound up hurling obscenities at each other. Fear-ing Fascist trickery, he prohibited these exchanges at night.

During the day General Gal allowed Miss Cowles to poke around headquar-ters and the village. At night he worked earnestly both to convert and to seduce her, taking a certain glee in recounting bits of his autobiography. Once he con-fessed that heretofore he had considered it sinful even to speak to the bour-geoisie, but that now he had decided that she had been misled by her back-ground and education. Speaking of his life before the Revolution, he said bitterly, "I used to live like an animal. Now I live like a human being." Then, in almost the same breath, he boasted of his special privileges, such as the private automobile at his disposal whenever he visited Moscow—never aware of ideo-logical contradictions. He regarded it as inconceivable that anyone truly exposed to Communism would not embrace it, and it was beyond his ken that any other economic system had merit. When he saw that his arguments made no impression upon Miss Cowles, he did not despair. "Read the works of Lenin—all thirty-seven volumes," he said. "When you are well instructed, join the Party. You will be useful as an undercover agent."

When her three days expired, a staff car arrived to carry her back to Madrid. Gal invited her to return whenever she liked. Then he added roguishly, "You won't return, but you will boast to your friends that a Red Army general took a fancy to you." The attraction was one-sided. Beneath the crust of poorly assim-ilated Marxism lay the crudeness of a simple-minded peasant who had climbed above his station. Gal was a child-man spooked by garbled tales of capitalist ogres and bourgeois bogeymen. It was not, as the American volunteers thought, that he was malicious or stupid, rather it was just that he was incredibly provincial and abysmally ignorant. Miss Cowles never saw him again. A few months later he was summoned to the Soviet Union, where the authorities first took his automobile from him—and then his life.

Of the journalists who visited the Lincolns during the spring of 1937, by all odds Josephine Herbst was their favorite. Josie was a true revolutionist, fondly remembering rallies of the Wobblies back in Iowa as a schoolgirl and having traveled on her own in the Soviet Union. (She liked the people but was troubled by the purges.) She had arrived in Madrid carrying a heavy knapsack and battered typewriter, even though "it didn't seem to me that the typewriter held a ghost of a chance against the new weapons."* She settled down among the *tertulia* Hemingway at the Hotel Florida, but was soon annoyed by the superficial cliques of highly paid correspondents in cutthroat competition with one another. Unlike the others, all day-trippers to Jarama, she took a room over the café in Morata de Tajuña. On her first trip to the front, she was dropped off at the battalion cookhouse, where she found in the courtyard only a cat sitting under a wooden rake and a few hens scratching through a wet hayrick. Inside were two Americans in cinnamon-colored uniforms sitting around a bone-white table, peeling potatoes. When she explained who she was, they nodded without interest, so she helped them peel, and all of them discussed the weather. Soon a heavy-duty truck came by and carried her up to the plateau. The driver explained that the road had been recently regraded so they could carry up supplies without being seen by the Fascists. As they neared the top, stray bullets zipped overhead and brought down a light rain of olive leaves. Birds had deserted the place. The Lincoln headquarters consisted of a deep pit furnished with a bare table, a telephone stand, a cot, a first-aid cabinet, and copies of *Mañana*. Men popped out of holes like badgers to gaze at the "female" in tan tweed suit and brown woolen topcoat. A near-sighted Ohioan who had rubbed his bread with a stalk of garlic, edged through the pack shouting, "Hey, who'll introduce me to the bitch."* Visiting the Spanish company she asked a *quinto* if he was learning English. "*Sí, sí,*" he said proudly. "Fuck you." She congratulated him on his accent. He beamed.*

Josie felt that the Jarama soldiers lacked a "heroic scale."* The best exuded resignation, the worst only masochism or apprehension. When she asked about newspaper reports of the "victories" she had read about, they jeered. One volunteer mentioned with loathing a newspaper story about a Cuban baseball pitcher among the Lincolns who reportedly had thrown grenades like baseballs at the enemy trenches. The truth was that he had never been close enough to a Fascist to hurl anything, except obscenities. Why, they demanded to know, had no reporter written the truth—that, for example, out of the sixty-four Cubans originally mustered into the battalion only twelve remained?* Even more irritating than fallacious news stories were letters from the United States, which egged them on "like the cries of cheerleaders roaring away to enhance a game they were not playing." They were sick and tired of the lies.

She loosened tongues. Not that they talked about the war, or regaled her with ghoulish accounts of corpses, that conversational staple among Hemingway's crowd in Madrid. Rather, they tried to penetrate the hopelessly complex labyrinth of responsibility for the ghastly horror of February 27. Merriman was now openly called "Murderman." Though there were few enough who could remember him, they praised Seacord, who possessed such authority that he never had to raise his voice when giving an order. But what they seemed to like best was to talk about dreams, reveries, vivid images of home. Jarama was an interlude between two realities. Despite their gloominess, she was cheered by the thought that these soldiers "were not only fighting *against* an enemy but also *for* something beyond." Poor morale was pandemic at Jarama, and the Lincolns had no monopoly on it, although the commissariat routinely denied it. If anything, the British seemed even more dispirited than the Americans. An outbreak of typhoid swept the trenches, but despite pleas and then threats by Dr. Pike, many Britons refused inoculation. They argued that they had been promised relief from the front and that they were "striking" to obtain what the bosses had promised. Moreover, as one of them piteously told Miss Herbst, if the Moors attacked while their arms were immobilized by serum, they would not have a chance. Whenever you fight Moors, he added, "you always keep a bullet for yourself." She concluded that the men at Jarama were very innocent and very young. If they were gloomy, it was because they believed—with reason—that conditions were apt to get worse before they got better. They had been badly seared by a brutal initiation into a wholly useless battle and by a sequence of events that were incomprehensible. Who could really blame them for feeling a little sorry for themselves?

By contrast men of the XIth Brigade (largely German) seemed animated and joyful rather than morose and self-pitying. The men put on a gala for her, featuring an accordion solo with comic asides, a hilarious clown with flour-whitened face and pink skirt over his uniform, a rapt Hungarian violinist, and a Romanian troupe singing "Who's Afraid of the Big Bad Wolf." They had known tyranny and suffering in their native countries but had not been broken by it. Their rollicking *Bruderschaft* reminded her of IWW camps back in Sioux City when she was a young girl.

Although Republican Spain proved to be more accessible for casual visitors than Franco's satrapy, the Nationalists were no slouch when it came to wartime tourism. In May 1938 Charles S. Bay, the U.S. consul at Seville, was invited to Burgos to open negotiations for purchasing forty American school buses for an unusual purpose—to inaugurate a series of "battlefield tours" commencing in June. An influx of international visitors was anticipated (no Communists need apply), for as the newly appointed director of tourism put it, "It is not often that a country at war invites tourist travel."* Indeed, it was not. When Dorothy Parker applied for permission to visit Republican Spain, a State Department functionary advised her that she would "have much more fun on the Franco side."*

The projected tour inspired an ironic note from Thomas Wolfe that General Franco had not only taken great care in preserving old ruins but "has even shown remarkable ingenuity in the creation of new ones." He went on to say, "I should like, if opportunity presents itself, to visit the various craters and ruined masonries throughout the town of Barcelona, paying particular attention to the subway entrance where a bomb exploded, and where one hundred and twenty-six men, women, and children were killed in one economical gesture. . . . I should like to pay a visit of devotion and respect to the Chapel . . . where General Franco's wife and daughter go to offer prayers for the success of the Defender of the Faith." Wolfe never got to Spain, but his anti-Fascist sentiments were duly noted in Munich, where he was beaten up by Nazis in a *Bierstube.**

In July the first such tour of battlefields in northern Spain got under way—nine days for four hundred pesetas per diem, guide and tips included. (The brochure conveyed more than it intended with its addendum: "Unlike new journalists, the tourists will not be fingerprinted or photographed at Irun."* Moreover, undeveloped film must not be taken out of Spain. Evening dress not necessary but bathing suit recommended. Tops required for men.)*

For well-heeled trippers the war in Spain would be sanitized. The "real" war lay elsewhere, like that described by the vignettes of a North American volunteer jotted down during his own tour of wartime Madrid:

> You see a shell hit a queue of women standing in line to buy soap.
> A part of one woman's torso is driven against a stone wall
> so that blood is driven into the stone with such force
> that sandblasting later fails to clean it.*

and

You see a 9-inch shell hit a street car filled with workers.
After the flash and the roar and the dust has settled,
the car is on its side. Two people are alive,
but they would be better dead,
and the others need to be removed with shovels.
A dog has nosed up to the wrecked car and sniffs
in the dust of the blasted granite
As the next shell comes screaming in a descending rush,
the dog goes rushing up the street
with a four-foot piece of intestine trailing from its jaws.
He was hungry, as everyone else is in Madrid.*

7

THE TORRENTS OF SPRING

With jubilation, the New York *Daily Worker* broke the news that Americans were fighting in Spain despite prohibitions imposed by reactionaries in the U.S. government. Even reading between the lines of this Communist Party newspaper, one found only chronicles of glory and never hints of catastrophe. Readers were told that in its first battle the Lincoln Battalion of the famous International Brigades had advanced "almost half a mile" into territory disputed not only by the mercenaries of General Franco but also by the bullies of Mussolini and the butchers of Hitler. Other newspapers in the United States agreed that the presence of Americans fighting in Republican Spain made sensational copy, although their stories rarely reached the exuberance of the *Worker,* where columnists did not have to limit themselves to the bare bones of fact.[1] Even Party hard-liners like Milton Wolff, last commander of the Lincolns, faulted the stories of Joe North, the *Daily Worker* reporter, because he "unfailingly underestimated casualties. Defeats were minor adjustments in the line." And even more reprehensible, "He believed everything he wrote in the *Daily Worker.*"* Another journalist in Spain put it more scathingly. Writers of the *Worker* ilk reminded him of "whores at a block party—they had just as much right to be there as anybody else—after all, it was their own block giving the party—trying to erase the stamp WHORE by rubbing up to respectable housewives."*

In publicizing the Lincoln Battalion, the CPUSA was engaged in a successful—even brilliant—shell game which consisted of taking credit for a wildly popular cause without taking responsibility for a venture illegal and, in the end, disastrous. Even as he denied that the Party recruited for Spain or that the Comintern directed the International Brigades, Earl Browder, secretary-general of the CPUSA, reported that 60 percent of the American volunteers were Communists. (This percentage was, of course, understated in order to elicit support

1. Vincent Sheean, correspondent for the *Herald Tribune,* touring the front with Joe North of the *Daily Worker,* was at first astonished that his fellow reporter took little interest in military operations or in verifying information until he realized that no matter what happened, the *Worker* reported the Party line.

from anti-Fascists of all creeds.)[2] Browder's strategy was to proclaim that Republican Spain was being defended by men of good will who earnestly believed in democracy. It just happened that the majority of these activists were Communists. This policy accorded with the Popular Front strategy laid down by the Seventh World Congress in 1935, by which the goal of world revolution would be temporarily shelved in favor of a coalition in which the Party would cooperate with all political parties—no matter how odious—which opposed Fascism. The American public tacitly favored the Spanish Republic, so long as it did not have to be inconvenienced by active participation in its defense. At the same time, elevated by the high-sounding expression "neutrality," the public opposed lifting the arms embargo, without which the Spanish Republic had to die.[3] However muddy this attitude may appear in hindsight, there was nothing inconsistent about it at the time: Americans distrusted Fascism and exalted democracy, but they did not distrust the one or favor the other enough to abandon their neutrality. The Popular Front policy delighted them, because it suggested the other great political bugaboo, Communism, seemed to be teetering toward a democratic pole.

Nevertheless, as Earl Browder well knew, no fund drive in the United States would get anywhere at all if it urged heartland Americans to support freedom fighters in Spain by mailing checks to the Communist cell of their choice. The machinery had to operate noiselessly at levels hidden from the naked eye. As we have seen, there already existed the North American Committee to Aid Democratic Spain,[4] which in its heyday employed twenty-five people full-time in its national office and had branches in 131 American cities. Membership consisted primarily of liberal, not necessarily radical, men and women who supported the Republic with heart and pocketbook and who probably hoped that their dona-

2. Among the Jarama group, 90 percent or more were Communists. But this percentage decreased steadily as casualty lists demonstrated that the Party was losing too many stalwarts. The result was that large numbers of "Liberals" from other parties, enthralled by the publicity of a "war against Fascism," were encouraged to join the Lincoln Battalion. The year 1937 marked the floodtide of enlistments; by 1938 there was only a trickle.*

3. According to a public-opinion poll of December 1938, 76 percent of Americans favored the Republicans over the Nationalists, yet 79 percent favored retention of the arms embargo to both sides. Early in 1937 a join resolution prohibiting shipment of arms to either side in Spain passed the Senate by a vote of 81 to 0, and the House by 406 to 1.* (The only congressman to vote against it was John T. Bernard, Farm-Labor from Minnesota, who later toured the Republic and visited the Lincoln Battalion.)

4. Not to be confused with the granddaddy of them all, the North American Committee for the Defense of Democratic Spain, an earlier, short-lived organization, allegedly initiated by a Spanish Republican delegation, which collected $100,000 in seven weeks.

tions purchased woolen mittens and condensed milk for Spanish orphans. They probably would not have believed, if they had been told (which they were not), that their money was administered by the CPUSA. As a matter of record, in some cities—Milwaukee, to mention only one—the executive director of the Committee and the recruiter at the CP headquarters turned out to be the same man.[5] The North American Committee to Aid Democratic Spain and the CPUSA headquarters functioned as clearinghouses for dozens of subsidiary organizations such as the Ben Leider Memorial Fund, which collected donations to bring back the body of a Jewish flier shot down near Madrid in the spring of 1937,[6] and the Lawyers' Committee on American Relations with Spain, a group whose real purpose was to find loopholes in the law through which military aid could be funneled to Spain. Hundreds of thousands of pamphlets and leaflets were disseminated through this network. It sponsored and distributed films, some of excellent quality, such as *Heart of Spain, Spain in Flames, Madrid Document,* and *The Spanish Earth* (produced and directed by Joris Ivens with script by Ernest Hemingway).

Funds were raised through dances, bazaars, rallies, fairs, auctions, picnics, shooting matches, and tag days. A dinner of the League of American Writers, chaired by Malcolm Cowley, cleared $1,650 and concluded with the auction of an autographed manuscript by Theodore Dreiser, guest speaker. Advertisements like the following appeared in left-of-center periodicals:

HEAR THE VOICE OF THE LINCOLN BRIGADE

BROADCAST DIRECT FROM MADRID

(Arranged by Friends of the Brigade, Political leader of the Brigade, John Dos Passos, Josephine Herbst, Joris Ivens, Sidney Franklin, Father Leocadio Lobo and others.)

5. At times this duality of roles approximated Restoration comedy. In Milwaukee, a would-be recruit was turned away at the Committee office by Mr. X, who advised him *sotto voce* to try the Party headquarters a few blocks away. Arriving here, the recruit found Mr. X, here known as Comrade Y, who asked a few perfunctory questions about politics and accepted him as a prospective rifleman in the Lincoln Battalion. Comrade Y then sent him to the Committee office, where Mr. X reappeared to provide the recruit with application forms designating him as a "social worker."

6. Ben Leider, a former reporter for the *New York Post,* was said to be the only American pilot who flew for the Republic because of political convictions rather than money. (What he did with his fifteen hundred dollar per month is not known.) His body was exhumed from the Air Force cemetery at Colmenar Viejo and returned to New York in August 1938. A funeral procession of two thousand marched from Times Square to Carnegie Hall, where services were held prior to burial at Mount Hebron Cemetery in Flushing. Although Leider had no connection whatsoever with either the International Brigades or the Lincoln Battalion, his guard of honor consisted of 125 Lincoln veterans repatriated because of wounds or Party influence.*

MECCA TEMPLE
April 24 at 8:00 p.m.
Admission 30c and 25c
(This ad is good for 20% reduction on price of your ticket.)*

One could attend a "Barricades Barbecue" in a warehouse on West 17th Street to dance and listen to Leadbelly, or a "Lincoln Birthday Party" featuring Lillian Hellman, or a "Farewell Dinner to Ludwig Renn (Baron Veith von Golzenau)" at the Claridge Hotel. For those less politically intense, there were many opportunities to help the boys in Spain and to have a good time, too. This playbill might have fetched even Liberty Leaguers or American Legionnaires.

MOONLIGHT CRUISE
July 23
FEATURING
Dick Carroll and his International Swing Band
and
The "No Pasarán" singers
"Every ticket sold helps buy smokes for our boys in Spain."*

(At the exact time of this patriotic outing, the "boys in Spain" were being cut to pieces by the Nationalist counteroffensive at Brunete, after seventeen harrowing days in the line.)

Never before (or again—as events proved) had the CPUSA sponsored such an array of programs enlisting so many supporters or enjoyed so much snowballing publicity. Ironically, the crusade against Fascism in Spain drew bourgeois souls who would have recoiled in horror from political tags like "dictatorship of the proletariat." And since the Party had lost 20 percent of its following during the four years between 1932 and 1936—their vote for the U.S. presidency plummeting from 102,991 to 80,159—the war in Spain came as a public relations godsend. The leadership was shrewd enough to know, however, that sympathy for the good fight in Spain was not tantamount to affection for the USSR. Rather, Americans were responding to a historical nostalgia for that bygone era when thirteen fragile colonies struggled for self-determination against an autocratic "oppressor." Party propaganda cleverly exploited this tenuous parallel. Under the slogan "Communism Is Twentieth-Century Americanism," cartoonists depicted battle-hardened titans of the Lincoln Battalion marching behind the fife and drum of the "Spirit of '76." Americans were at last redeeming long-overdue debts to Lafayette, Kosciusko, and von Steuben. The *Daily*

Worker featured a Washington on horseback standing above massed ranks of an entrenched People's Army with the caption "Our famous Continentals would recognize in their defiant cry to the foreign invader and fascist tyrant the living spirit of '76—'They shall not pass!'"*

Party hacks ransacked American history to show how the International Brigades were "the Lafayettes of the modern industrial age" or the "Paul Reveres waking the drowsy world to the midnight threat of Fascism." (Eventually the Veterans of the Lincoln Brigade adopted the Liberty Bell as its logo.) Where did General Francisco Franco fit into this diorama? With George III and Benedict Arnold, of course. In Madison Square Garden, Earl Browder worked over his audience as he explained how the Communist Party "revered the spirit of the frontier, the covered wagon, Buffalo Bill, Casey Jones and other heroic figures in our nation's copybook past." Who, in the present age, most resembled Jefferson? Lenin, obviously. And no doubt there were many Americans who cringed as Browder proclaimed on Washington's birthday, "We love our country with the same burning love which Lenin had for Russia."* Fortuitously, some very unproletarian researcher had discovered that during the Civil War Abraham Lincoln had thanked Karl Marx for writing in support of the Union. Now these two great populists marched side by side in Spain. All in all, after the Great Depression, the Spanish civil war was the best recruitment gimmick the CPUSA had ever had.

Viewed in the chill light of realpolitik, the strategy of the Communist Party was ingenious. Such was the manipulative skill of Earl Browder and other "sages of Twelfth Street" that win or lose in Spain, the Party stood to gain. If the Republic won, the victory belonged to the USSR, for having repudiated the hypocrisy of nonintervention. On the other hand, if the Nationalists won, the defeat could be blamed on the effete democracies that had refused to assist the Republic. And in either case, the Communists did not have to ante up anything, for the costs were being borne by the other members of the Popular Front.

Although the USSR gathered laurels for standing alone among major powers in supplying the Republic with aircraft, tanks, artillery, machine guns, rifles, technical advisers, and other military hardware, after the war came the revelation that all of this was paid for—at shockingly inflated prices—by the Spanish Republic. Back in October 1936, when it appeared that Franco's army would take Madrid, Largo Caballero, the prime minister, agreed that the Spanish gold reserves—fifth-largest in the world and amounting to 510 tons and valued at $518,000,000—would be sent to Russia for "safekeeping." In a spirit of solidarity the USSR pledged to discount prices (most Republicans believe they were free), but once the gold was in hand the discounts were eliminated or reduced.

In Paris banks, rubles were converted to dollars and then into pesetas, dripping substantial hidden profits along the way. Among the totally useless arms sent were thirteen thousand single-shot Vetterli rifles dating from 1868 and seven hundred machine guns (St. Etiennes and Chauchats) withdrawn from the Western Front in 1914. The Republic also had to pay all expenses for Soviet advisers (including holiday and leave time) as well as the costs of shipping, renovating, and repairing all equipment sent from the Soviet Union. The unspent residue remained in the USSR.*

By the spring of 1937, the CPUSA was prepared to cut loose from the sheltering lee of the North American Committee to Aid Democratic Spain, which had become too large for exclusively Party control and which now clamored for objectives of a "relief" organization like the International Red Cross. To channel funds directly into the Lincoln Battalion and to have undisputed control over these funds, the Party chartered a new organization calling itself the Friends of the Abraham Lincoln Brigade (FALB). The name was a lie twice over. It evoked nonviolence (as in "Society of Friends") and elevated the Lincolns from mere battalion to brigade status to inflate the participation and prestige of Americans in Spain. (At this time the Lincolns were only one of six battalions in the XVth International Brigade.) No matter—in America the fiction carried more weight than the fact.[7]

The FALB took charge of the recruitment, transportation, and rehabilitation of American volunteers. Under its auspices, a small group of veterans carefully screened by Party hierophants—no malcontents need apply—were repatriated from Spain and toured the country, speaking at union halls, at universities, at fashionable soirees—wherever there was an audience eager to listen and willing to pay. Fresh recruits for the Lincoln Battalion were never publicly sought, but if a likely youth cornered a speaker privately, he might obtain a street address or a telephone number where contact could be made. In the beginning applicants outnumbered the slots available because to be accepted in the battalion was an honor likely to turn a young man's head, but this changed dramatically in 1938 when news of defeats and accounts of appalling conditions filtered back from Spain.

Back in the United States, officers of federal, state, and municipal agencies donned cloak-and-dagger costumes to root out pockets of "Red Army" recruitment and

---

7. Subsequently, Lincoln veterans, who knew better, accepted the fiction when they joined the Veterans of the Abraham Lincoln *Brigade* (VALB). If any of them ever tried to change the name back to "Battalion," the event has not been recorded in their magazine.

support in mainstream and backwater America with nearly psychotic vigilance. Acting on a tip from a Minneapolis bricklayer who defected from a group of Lincoln recruits in Paris, the sheriff of Sullivan County, New York, collected a posse and beat the bushes between Fallsburgh and Woodridge seeking a "Spanish Camp" where recruits allegedly took military training. When he uncovered a small farm owned by a former employee of the North American Committee, the sheriff was exultant, until he noted that the "secret camp" was overlooked by a large resort hotel.* Out in Detroit, Sergeant Maciosek of the "Red Squad" reported that the Communist Party "quota" for Michigan called for five hundred recruits. (Had this been true, Michigan alone would have accounted for more than one-sixth of all Americans who ever fought in Spain!) But when the House Un-American Activities Committee (HUAC) later put him on the stand, the sergeant was able to submit the names of only twenty-two men known to be in Spain. At times the Red hunt got rough. Police in Detroit broke into the house of the FALB executive secretary and carried off his files. Eleven people were jailed in Milan Prison on charges of having recruited for a foreign power, although authorities had to drop pending charges after five days. Among the "incriminating" evidence never returned to the local secretary were a CP card (Spanish Branch) and a broken pistol (donated to the Lincoln Battalion by a Lansing schoolteacher). An inventory of similar absurdities would fill a large book worth neither writing nor reading.

To support the Republic at this time in any activist role was to be associated willy-nilly with one or more jerry-built offshoots of the Comintern. For most American activists the primary objective was to subvert or repeal the nonintervention policy of the government at least to the extent of allowing the Republic to purchase arms. Protest letters to congressmen might as well have been directed to the Dead Letter Office because Washington lay entrenched behind the slogan "Scrupulous Non-intervention in Spain." While Liberals stood aside, Communists rode in the bandwagons, whipping up massive rallies and parades where wounded veterans (in tailored uniforms furnished by the FALB) led euphoric crowds singing "The Star-Spangled Banner" beneath gigantic portraits of Abraham Lincoln and George Washington. (One wonders whether jobbers in the photographic trades rented the same portraits to the German-American Bund when they held their sing-alongs in the same halls and in the same streets.)

Jealous of the Communist success in cornering the market in Spanish aid, the American Socialist Party called for a "Eugene V. Debs Column" to fight in Spain. They managed to stage a kickoff march down Fifth Avenue before vanishing into oblivion. The pacifist wing of the Party expressed outrage that

Debs's name would be used in abetting militarism, in much the same way that a Quaker group might have protested naming an outfit "the Jesus Christ Artillerists." It was alleged that only five would-be members of the Debs Column reached Paris, where they were stranded with neither the funds nor the know-how to cross into Spain. The recruits either drifted home or, swallowing their pride, enlisted in the Lincoln Battalion. The Communists were, of course, exultant at the ignominious performance of their bitter rivals for the proletarian vote. It might be noted that when Norman Thomas, the Socialist leader, visited Spain in the spring of 1937, he did not seek out the Lincolns at Jarama or pay his respects to the Marty faction at Albacete.

Efforts by the Roman Catholic Church to enlist support for Franco's Spain came to little more than exerting enough political pressure to prevent Washington from lifting the arms embargo. Over the longer run this probably had greater influence upon the final outcome of the war than any other single effort in the United States, for in 1939 at a cabinet meeting, President Roosevelt stated that the embargo "had been a grave mistake" because it "controverted old American principles and invalidated established international law."* Otherwise, attempts to arouse popular support for Franco ended in failure.[8] Despite the anticlericism of the Spanish Left, whose slaughter of priests and burning of churches during the first months of the war alienated most Americans, a poll nevertheless revealed that forty-eight percent of Roman Catholics in the United States favored the Republic. The American Committee for Spanish [Nationalist] Relief, sponsored by the Church, folded before it had collected thirty thousand dollars—all of which had to be used for administrative expenses.

Behind the fanfare and trumpery, however, the Central Committee of the CPUSA was alarmed by the Jarama disaster. An exposé revealing the existence of mutinies, labor battalions, and massacres would be disastrous for Party unity and credibility. The error, as they now saw it, was in sending over volunteers bereft of experienced Party leadership. Beginning in March, they began to seed drafts of lower-echelon "expendable" foot soldiers with prestigious Party officers. Robert Minor, a white-haired former *Daily Worker* cartoonist, became the American representative to the International Control Committee, just one

---

8. At least one American, Guy Castle of Oxon Hill, Maryland, volunteered to serve in Franco's Foreign Legion. After being wounded and refused a discharge, he tried to swim from La Linea to Gibraltar but was captured and sentenced to be executed for desertion. Through appeals by his mother and the British consul at Gibraltar (the U.S. consul having refused aid), Castle was released in March 1938. Subsequently a reporter in Washington, he had "nothing but praise" for the reckless daring of his fellow legionnaires.

rung beneath the Comintern in directing the International Brigades.[9] Another prominent Party leader, Steve Nelson, went over to fill the slot vacated by Sam Stember, while William Lawrence took Phil Bard's old post as the American representative at the Albacete base. Allan Johnson (McNeil), reputed to be a former officer of the Fifteenth and Twenty-Seventh Infantries of the U.S. Army, became commandant of a new training camp reserved for Anglo-Americans at Tarazona de la Mancha, near Albacete.[10] Trailing this galaxy were lesser luminaries like Joe Dallet, an organizer from Youngstown who had once run for mayor on the CP ticket; David Doran, a national officer of the YCL; and Sandor Voros, erstwhile cadet in the Austro-Hungarian Army and more recently a political writer for Earl Browder.

But next to Minor, the heaviest hitter the Party sent to Spain during this doleful spring was Harry Haywood, a thirty-eight-year-old black, whose kudos included service in the army during the World War, studies at the Lenin Institute in Moscow, and membership in the Politburo of the CPUSA. Furthermore, he came at a time when the Party was desperately trying to recruit among the African American population, North and South. After Party bagmen like Stember and Madden, Haywood looked almost too good to be true—a black Robert Merriman—and rumor had it that he would become a star among commissars, not just a comic-star. It remained to be seen what he could do, and unfortunately no one in Spain knew that the Central Committee of the CPUSA had twice tabled his application, for unstated reasons.[11] Whatever his limitations, self-effacement was not one of them. Even before reaching Spain, Haywood met harassment. Since the frontier was closed, he had to join a hundred other volunteers in fording a river and in climbing a rough path over the Pyrenees. To avoid gendarmes they moved at top speed, and he had difficulty breathing. When he finally fell to the ground gasping, a file-closer stuck a pistol in his side and said, "Get up, you bastard, you volunteered, it's too late to change your

9. His most famous cartoon featured a gigantic hulk of a man, all muscles but without a head, being examined by an exultant army doctor, who had found the "perfect soldier." This antiwar cartoon, of course, predated the Party's enthusiasm for the war in Spain.

10. Johnson was slated to replace Hourihan as military commander of the Lincolns. He came up to Jarama in March and helped with trench fortifications for a short time. Very unpopular among the men, Johnson then took command of the American training camp at Tarazona de la Mancha, where rookies were erroneously told that he had been "wounded" after frontline "service" at Jarama.

11. Probably the Committee knew about Haywood's reputation as a womanizer in Russia, where he spent long periods at Yalta. According to his own account, students there regarded him as "an insatiable womanizer" and infuriated him by plastering on a wall a cartoon captioned "Comrade Haywood doing Practical work in a Crimean Rest Home," which featured him surrounded by a dozen pretty Russian girls.*

mind!" Comrades intervened, asserting that he was no shirker but "an important anti-Fascist leader." One of the guides, an old man, installed him in a hut
for the night, dashed back down the mountain, and brought up wine and
cheese to fuel the new commissar into Spain.*

A Dodge touring car awaited Haywood in Albacete along with a personal
chauffeur who served as his batman during his six months in Spain. He conferred briefly with Marty, Longo, and others of the supreme commissariat before
setting off to inspect Jarama with Bill Lawrence, also newly arrived. Albacete was
rife with stories, accurate and exaggerated, about the American disasters up at
Jarama—"much worse than we had expected"—with responsibility laid
squarely on Gal and Copic. Haywood's dander was up, and he prepared himself
for a knockdown with the XVth Brigade commander. But on entering Copic's
villa at Morata, he found that Copic was none other than "Sako," an old Lenin
School acquaintance, who embraced him warmly. Their camaraderie rapidly
dissipated. Copic privately explained why the Pingarrón attack had been necessary but had failed because the Americans had been "pampered by easy living in
the States and unprepared for the rigors of battle." Everyone took a drubbing
that day, he said—"the Americans were nothing special." "I grew angry—this
account amounted to a disparagement of the American effort and a complete
denial that the command was in error."* Moving up to the trenches, he greeted
Oliver Law, an old comrade from their battles with the Red Squad of Chicago,
and listened to a swarm of bitter complaints about the brutal incompetence of
both Gal and Copic. The men were particularly angered because, unlike other
battalions of the brigade, they had served three months on the line without a rest
period. Haywood returned to Albacete and demanded the removal of Copic, on
grounds that he had lost the confidence of the Americans.*

One can well visualize the fury of the base commissariat on receiving this
demand from a Comintern nobody barely over the frontier into Spain, and par-
roting the complaints of a battalion of spoiled Americans. Marty refused to see
him, but Vidal, his adjutant, promised "relief," which he defined not as rest
behind the lines but as issuing the Lincolns new weapons so that they could
prove their mettle in battle. As a sop to Haywood, Albacete appointed him
political commissar of a regiment (not yet in existence) with the rank of lieutenant colonel. The new commissar promptly left on a sartorial expedition to
Valencia to purchase an appropriate uniform. He arrived in time to hear a La
Pasionaria diatribe detailing the crimes of Trotskyists. Lowering her voice ominously at the end, she asked a packed auditorium: "What are you going to do
with such people?" Pandemonium broke out—"Kill 'em! Shoot 'em!" After the
hubbub died down, the mob passed a unanimous resolution supporting her

and the Central Committee of the Spanish Communist Party. Deeply moved, Haywood concluded that the real future for him lay in Valencia, not Jarama. Thereafter, the rank and file in the Lincoln Battalion saw their head commissar only rarely. It was just as well. He soon disgraced himself during a visit to the trenches. The men gawked in amazement at this splendid apparition arrayed in a spanking new tunic with polished brass buttons striding in expensive leather boots and twirling a swagger stick. When a sudden burst of gunfire passed well above their heads, Haywood threw himself into the muck of the trench. After he dirtied himself a second time, Haywood acquired a permanent place in the comic folklore of the Lincoln Battalion.*

Contrasting with Haywood's sartorial elegance, Steve Nelson (Mesarosh), the new Lincoln commissar, always wore what the men wore—a mismatched uniform and stained French helmet. The man sent by the nomenklatura of New York to put some teeth into the Lincolns would have been overlooked in a crowd. He was a small man of thirty-four with thinning hair and a button nose. Athough his voice was gentle and always controlled, it carried authority. A natural-born psychologist, he towered above the natural-born fools found too often in the Lincoln hierarchy. Even though he demonstrated an uncanny ability to inspire loyalty, he did not require admiration to gratify his ego. His magnetism had nothing to do with credentials, appearance, or military experience, for most of the men by this time were unimpressed by rank and soured on politicians. Beyond having read a single book by B. H. Liddell Hart, he admitted he knew nothing of battle or war. Although dedicated to the principles of the Communist Party, Nelson seemed to know more about human nature than the fine print in *Das Kapital*. (He may have witnessed some fighting while an observer with the Chinese Communists in 1933, his first assignment after completing his course at the Lenin School.)

The first time Steve Nelson ever pondered a sociopolitical question was as an eleven-year-old in Chaglich, Croatia.[12] A few weeks after the assassination at Sarajevo, he had to drive his father and four neighbors, in a peasant cart, to the district mobilization camp, where he never forgot the sight of hundreds of sad-faced peasants milling about in a barbed-wire pen. From Chaglich, great throngs of apathetic men departed for war—broken handfuls drifted back. If a war had to be fought, workers should band together and destroy the exploiting classes—not each other.*

12. In conformity with the CP emphasis on the "native son" origins of the Lincoln Battalion, Party publicists moved Nelson's birthplace from Croatia to Steelton, Pennsylvania. As in so many historical "facts," what was true counted for less than what would best serve the Party.

In 1919, Nelson immigrated to the United States and found work in a Pittsburgh slaughterhouse, where he worked eleven hours a day. In winter the jabbing contrasts in temperature between freezer and smokehouse broke the health of strong men. Then one icy day he heard that the owner wintered in Florida. Most of his fellow workers accepted this fact complacently—the way of the system. Nelson pondered the dilemma. The men worked, the boss did not—yet he prospered, they did not. Seeking an answer, he joined the Socialist Labor Party, but annoyed by the do-nothing forensics of this working-class debating society, he left it for the Communist Party in 1928. He attended the Lenin Institute in Moscow, briefly traveled in China, and on his return rose rapidly in the CPUSA. He was not a conventioneer. He could make a rousing speech and disappear from the platform before anyone quite realized he was gone. He had come to Spain with the Joe Dallet entourage and even though he far outranked Dallet in the Party hierarchy, he deliberately melted into the mass to preserve his anonymity.

Nelson found the men at Jarama still demoralized by the February massacre. Their idea of a useful task was constructing a stone and cement monument to commemorate their dead comrades rather than deepening and draining their trenches, which in some places would have barely sufficed for a platoon of dwarves. Major Johnson employed military maxims like "What is taken with the rifle must be held with the spade" without visible impact, for he sounded too much like Sam Stember. By contrast, Nelson believed in the efficacy of persuasion—men would do things his way but without quite realizing it. As he watched a Lincoln deepening his dugout, he remarked to bystanders, "There is a fine comrade!" Someone asked why he said that. Without taking his eyes off the man with the shovel, Nelson explained the importance of strong fortifications. The digger had probably not intended to take out more than a few shovelsful, but under the intent gaze of the others, he worked up an honest sweat. A voice in the crowd said, "What's so special about that guy? Hell, I can dig better'n that." Soon all of them, including Nelson, were heaving dirt.* (Sixty years later, those trenches were still there.)

Nelson had the sticky job of requesting from General Gal that the Lincolns be relieved from the line. Clad in oversize ski pants tied at the ankle with twine, a rusty brown shirt, and a shapeless brown beret covering his balding head, Nelson went down to Gal's dacha, where even orderlies and chauffeurs wore steam-pressed uniforms. Gal sat behind a massive desk, coldly eyeing Nelson as though inspecting a creature from an inferior phylum. On the wall behind him was a life-size portrait of himself in the uniform, garnished with epaulettes, of a Spanish Republican general. "The whole thing floored me," Nelson later remarked. When he said that he wanted to speak "man-to-man," Gal cut him down. "*I* am commander of this division. *You* are in that division." Nelson said that he represented the men of the Lincoln Battalion. Gal interrupted. "There are no delegations!" Nelson plunged ahead, explaining that his men thought their commanders had let them down: in a People's Army; if leaders proved inadequate, they could be removed. Gal then became "very upset." He unleashed a storm of abuse upon the Americans, accusing them of "imperialist" contamination—the customary Marty line. Nelson listened, in his earnest manner, to this diatribe until a moment of relative calm, when he proposed that the newly formed Washington Battalion replace the Lincoln in the trenches. Gal swung to the defensive, arguing that he could not spare the gasoline. Nelson countered by saying this excuse was senseless. Gal shouted, "You are talking to a *general!*" Nothing came of this meeting, but Nelson had at least showed Gal that henceforth American commissars would stand up for the rights of their men. The worms had turned.*

The Jarama debacle was such a closely guarded secret that not even a Party regular like Sandor Voros had any inkling of it. Though a seasoned writer of propaganda he had been taken in by glorious accounts of a Lincoln victory. Therefore, when a Central Committeeman in New York briefed him on the eve of his departure for Spain, he listened in stunned surprise: "The Party is in trouble, Voros. All that stuff you've been reading about the heroic Lincoln Brigade in the *Daily Worker* is crap. If the truth comes out and the enemies of the Party pick it up, we're going to have a scandal. The truth is that the Lincoln Brigade mutinied the first day it was sent into action and had to be driven at pistol point into attack. The comrades in Spain are completely demoralized. They want to come home and many of them are deserting."* Since no one in the Party really knew how many Americans there were in Spain, where they were, or whether they were living or dead, Voros had the job of setting up an archive and historical commission.[13] If the Republic won the war, he would stay in Spain and help restructure the Party there; if it lost, he would go to the USSR. As sweetener and accolade, he received a silk ribbon with instructions to sew it into the lining of his coat, an innocuous-looking scrap of silk that identified him as a bona fide Comintern agent. His father was not impressed. When told where his son was going, he exploded, "Bums fighting bums. I can smell a bum from a mile. Hitler

---

13. "History" needs to be redefined in this context. For the CP it did not mean assessment and description of what had occurred during a given period of time, but rather what the Party would decree *should* have happened. Because Voros collected data on all aspects of the IB operations (including matters tabooed by the CP), his memoir has been excoriated by Party hard-wires.

and Stalin, they both smell the same to me." Choking back tears, Voros senior went on, "You are my eldest son! Stay away from those bums. . . . You're disgracing the family." It took months for Sandor Voros to discover what the old man meant.

The Paris roundhouse for trafficking in international volunteers was the Maison des Syndicats, a trade-union hall not far from the Metro stop "Place du Combat" in the heart of the "Red" arrondissements. Behind a high wall on the rue Mathurin-Moreau, lines of dingy offices overlooked a cobblestone courtyard that was either muddy or dusty, depending on the weather. Taking orders from the Comintern, the CPF administered the underground network that dispatched volunteers to Spain across a frontier officially closed since February 1937. It was Top Secret and hush-hush—even though the French authorities knew all about it.

Mrs. Charlotte Haldane, wife of J.B.S. Haldane, escorted a group of British volunteers to Paris that spring. For the Haldanes, the Spanish fight was a family affair. She had already agreed to allow her underage son to enlist in the International Brigades, while her husband, a World War veteran, had gone ahead to observe, based in a Madrid hotel, trench conditions at Jarama.[14] He had a gas-mask fetish. His stepson could serve in Spain provided he carried one, and he convinced the CPGB that all British volunteers had to be equipped with them, only to be bitterly disappointed when none could be found for sale in England. Because of her fluency in French, his wife was a godsend to the Place du Combat cadre, who begged her to remain. She left an invaluable inside account of the entire transit operation.*

Behind an unmarked door she found the office of "Jack" and "Eric" (their surnames never used), the Americans in charge of Anglo-American drafts. Because names and addresses could fall into the hands of the wrong people, they carried the entire personnel directory in their heads. "Police spies," Jack reported, "were thicker'n rats in a sewer."* If a volunteer was caught, it could mean jail and deportation. Although the early volunteers had crossed into Spain cheering and singing, rightists in the government had changed all that. Obedient to the terms of the Non-Intervention Agreement, France closed the frontier, forcing volunteers to hike by night over the Pyrenees or slip across in

14. Mrs. Haldane wrote of the incongruity when her tweedy husband decked himself out in a leather motorcycle jacket and rushed off to wartorn Madrid "like Hemingway and other left-wing intellectuals who were having a lot of fun and frivolity and pseudo-military excitement in that heroic city." Her admiration was reserved for true proletarian-warriors like Jock Cunningham or Fred Copeman, the latter "a working-class aristocrat with the temperament of an autocrat and a touch of the good old peppery Indian army Colonel."*

small boats. Bottlenecked in Paris during the spring of 1937 because of an internecine civil war in Barcelona between the Communists and POUMists, several hundred Americans and Canadians were scattered about in lofts, boarding-houses, and private homes of the Batignolles quarter. Some men in transit to Spain had to be diverted and placed in alpine hotels until the fighting ended. (After a week of street fighting, the Communists won, arranged for the POUMist leader Andreas Nin to "disappear," and virtually purged Spain of Trotskyist heretics.)[15]

"Jack" was a Marxist missionary named Arnold Reid (Reisky), a New York Jew of twenty-six who quit the University of Wisconsin to organize for the Party in Mexico and Cuba. Married to a Cuban schoolteacher, he spoke Spanish fluently and had a deep affection for Hispanic culture. The Central Committee sent him to Paris to unravel the red tape slowing the traffic in volunteers. It was a formidable task. Between January and September 1937 nearly every liner from the United States to Cherbourg or Le Havre disgorged American volunteers, who overflowed the meager facilities at the Maison. These vessels ranged from luxury craft like the *Normandie* and *Queen Mary* to clunkers like the *President Harding* and *Lafayette*.[16] On instructions from the Department of State, U.S. consuls boarded each incoming ship in France and made an inventory of every American suspected of being a Spanish volunteer. The Americans elaborated as their destinations such howlers as "religious studies in Poland" and "tourist" (with ten dollars in his pocket). Harry Fisher said he had come for "skiing in the Alps." "Sure it's not in the Pyrenees?" quipped the consul.*

Adding to Jack's problem, the French officials at the Maison contemptuously charged that the Americans were "lousy with money," that they were, in effect, capitalists and "proletarian millionaires." (At the same time, with provoking inconsistency, they regarded the German and Italian volunteers as poverty-stricken lumpenproles bound for Spain to escape prisons and firing squads in their own countries.) After threats that he would carry charges of chauvinism to the Comintern, Reid obtained their grudging cooperation, but with his *permis de séjour* long expired, he was weary of dodging down back alleys one step ahead of the gendarmes, tired of picayunish infighting with

---

15. George Orwell's *Homage to Catalonia* is the classic account of this civil-war-within-the-civil-war. The author, a wounded POUMist, by chance found himself in Barcelona during the fighting and barely escaped to France with his life. Ironically, he had planned to join the International Brigades because he thought them more "dedicated" to the fight against Fascism.

16. The liners most often utilized were the *Mauritania* (nine crossings), the *Harding* (eight), and the *Berengaria* (eight). The number of volunteers ranged from 101 aboard the *Paris* (arriving February 6) to 5 aboard the *Washington* (September 1). After May 1937 it was rare for a vessel to carry more than 5 volunteers.*

Party hacks, and frustrated by his shepherd's role in herding volunteers to Spain. Paris was muck and mire—Communist bureaucracy at its worst. "Eric," his assistant, was a Harvard man in his late twenties whose real name was DeWitt Parker. An aesthete as well as a Marxist, he was as much at home in the Latin Quarter as in the rue Mathurin-Moreau. He was openhearted, intelligent, dedicated. His French was so good and his wit so keen that he became a great favorite among the plainclothesmen and gendarmes who snooped around the Maison. Like Reid, he begged Party leaders to send him to Spain, but he was always held back because the Paris operation took priority. (Their wish came true some months later, with tragic results, as we shall see.)

Nearly every boat train brought fresh volunteers into Paris, most of them eager for a last spree before going to war. These made a beeline to the back-to-back brothels along Boulevard Jean Jaures, where girls in pairs sat under signs reading

15 FRANCS, EVERYTHING INCLUDED

SOLDIERS ON LEAVE FROM ALGIERS, 12 FRANCS

(The diary of a former Philadelphia insurance agent recounts that in Paris, after a hesitant start, in four days he "got laid" three times.)*

William Sennett of Illinois told his girl back home that in Paris he actually saw a man walking out of a pissoir buttoning his fly and at the Folies Bergères a woman "with only a small patch in the lower region and her breasts completely exposed" gyrating on stage with three men.* To circumvent the dangers of brawling, drinking, and whoring, any of which might shut down the whole *rite de passage,* Reid confiscated their money, doling out a few francs every day for cigarettes and a couple of beers. VD was the greatest menace because in Spain it brought a trip to jail, not to the front line. Mrs. Haldane agreed to speak to the volunteers on sexual hygiene. At the Maison, in a room packed with Anglo-American volunteers, she offered spellbinding lectures with horrific pictures illustrating the ravages of advanced syphilis. Many Britons were shocked—not by the subject but by the fact that a bona fide English lady (with the accent to prove it) not only knew about these things but spoke of them so clinically. "However advanced their political views, their morals were puritan."*

This is not to say that fleshpots were the sole preoccupation of the Americans in Paris. Passionate revolutionaries with a historical bent made a pilgrimage to the wall in the Père-Lachaise Cemetery, where 147 Communards were slaughtered by reactionaries in 1871. The Paris Exposition drew others like Paul Sigel, who described to his girl at home the Russian Pavilion, a marble building eighty feet high topped with a worker and woman, the man with fist clenched as though reaching across to smash the eagle on the German Pavilion. He reported that the crowd booed the German icon but cheered the Soviet statuary.*

Because suitcases packed with extra clothes could not be carried over Pyreneean goat trails, men left them at the hall, with assurances they would be there on their return. Each volunteer received a blue beret on the theory that this would help to gallicize his unmistakably American appearance. They carried only a clean shirt, a bar of soap, a toothbrush, and shaving gear. Reid gave the leader of each group a specially marked cigarette to be recognized by the French contact man at the railroad station, who would put them on the train. (On one occasion the leader forgot his instructions and smoked it.)*

Not least among the worries of Reid and Parker was Albert Wallach, a Detroit volunteer. On the boat he had ruptured himself at calisthenics. When the French CP refused to admit him to one of their hospitals, Reid dispatched him to the expensive Anglo-American Hospital at Neuilly. After six weeks and an operation to boot, after Wallach's bill dwarfed Reid's small budget, he ordered Wallach to climb out of a window and flee for sanctuary in a friendly boardinghouse. Gendarmes ransacked his room but he had crawled into a wardrobe and was overlooked. Eventually Reid was able to smuggle him to Marseilles.[17]

By late spring a trickle of men from Spain, wounded and ragged for the most part, began to show up at the Maison. Discharged from the International Brigades, they waited for a chance to work their passage back to the States. Since Reid had no money to buy them clothes, Charlotte wanted to break open suitcases belonging to men bound for Spain, but was blocked by Reid and the French commissars, because it violated the sanctity of personal property. When Charlotte went over their heads and prevailed, men returning from Spain helped themselves to piles of clothing spread out on the floor. From time to time these tatterdemalions, the visionary gleam long gone from their eyes, overlapped recruits bound for Spain. Such encounters rarely raised the morale of the newcomers. There was a laconic exchange between a new volunteer and a veteran whose rigid leather glove obviously covered an artificial hand, or no hand at all. "You guys just get back?" asked the vet. "No, we're just going." "Oh," replied the vet, "more suckers."*

17. Wallach's bad luck was just beginning. He was aboard the *Ciudad de Barcelona* when it was torpedoed off the coast of Catalonia. He fought in the Lincoln Battalion until the pell-mell retreats during the spring of 1938, when he went to pieces and deserted. Returned to the line in a labor battalion, he deserted again. His luck seemed to turn. He hid aboard the *Oregon,* a merchant ship moored in Barcelona. Just before the vessel sailed for New York, Wallach went ashore on an unknown errand and fell into the hands of Tony DeMaio, an IB policeman. In the IB prison at Casteldefels, on the Tarragon road, he was dropped into an empty cistern. Fellow prisoners heard his groans but he was never seen again.*

When the CPF demanded that men bound for Spain surrender their passports at the Maison, Jack openly fought the policy because he anticipated the problems lying ahead when Americans tried to return home, especially those of foreign birth. On the other hand, French volunteers and those from Fascist countries made no objection—the former because they wanted to avoid identification by their own police and the latter to prevent retaliation against their families at home. He may have known that the passports would be turned over to the NKVD for use in espionage. In any case, he balked at confiscating them. Tipped off about Reid's disobedience, IB officers in Spain made two more attempts to collect them—at Figueras and at Albacete, just before the men went up to the front—and usually succeeded after explaining that if a volunteer ever had to apply for a new passport, he would be coached what to say and not say about his activities in Europe. Or, in the words of a disenchanted New Yorker, "The Party method—first to steal your passport, then advise on how to perjure yourself."* (The British had no such problem because most came to Paris on special passes dubbed "dirty weekend tickets," which required no passport.)

After complaints from the CPF about Reid reached Bob Minor in Valencia, he was transferred to Spain with the assurance that he would work with the CPE in matters dealing with American volunteers. Once in Valencia, however, Reid realized something was wrong when he was sent up to the XVth Brigade like any member of the rank and file awaiting assignment. According to a confidential report, he arrived "in a rather demoralized state. Considered himself a cadre that should be saved. Wanted to go to the artillery where it would be safer. Had fear of the front." He was sent as a minor commissar to the Spanish battalion. Deeply alarmed, he prepared a long political autobiography, concluding with "Never has the Party taken disciplinary measures against me. Never have I ever endured long jail sentences [as an organizer in Latin America], although detained several times." It came to nothing. Although evaluated as "the best commissar in the Brigade," he remained with the Spaniards until he was killed some months later on the Ebro front.* Charlotte Haldane, who had fallen in love with him, frantically tried to trace him, without success. Bill Rust, a key figure in the CPGB, told her that he had been shot in either the chest or back. "He was sold down the river by his own Party, Charlotte," and he added the name of Bob Minor.*

Since none of the Americans—not even Bob Minor, the top Party man in Spain—rated either submarine or private plane to ferry top-priority personnel—the volunteers had to wait their turn to slip aboard a fishing boat or to follow a guide over the Pyrenees. In May the backlog was so great that the Control Committee put five hundred men (most of them from other countries) aboard the *Ciudad de Barcelona* at Marseilles. Twenty miles north of Barcelona, an Italian submarine torpedoed the vessel, carrying an unknown number—including seven Americans—to their deaths. (Lifeboats locked in their davits could not be freed.) For weeks the fishermen of Malgrat salvaged unidentified bodies from a thick beach scum of oil, hemp, and lumber. An opaque curtain immediately dropped over the *Barcelona* disaster.

The survivors were warned not to talk about the disaster and were rushed south to Valencia, where Sandor Voros, who met them there quite by accident, saw a scoop for publicizing a "Fascist-atrocity" story in American newspapers. He collected the names and hometowns of forty-three Americans known to have been aboard and in his mind's eye saw the headlines—"LOCAL BOY TORPEDOED BY FASCIST SUBMARINE." He rushed off to Bob Minor and demanded a typewriter. But Minor became "livid with anger." Snatching the notes from Voros, he shouted, "What are you trying to do—demoralize the people back home?"* Eventually the steamship company admitted that the vessel had been torpedoed but declared that it had carried no passengers—only a cargo of fish, bread, and vegetables for hungry Spain.*

A group of thirteen Americans and five Canadians led by Steve Nelson became legendary heroes even before their arrival in Spain.* Trying to cross the frontier in *Sans Pareil,* a tiny fishing boat with a one-lung engine, they were boarded by a French patrol vessel and towed back to Port Vendres. As a high-ranking Communist, Nelson had to be concealed. Carrying a passport issued to "Joseph Fleischinger" (an uncle), he slipped quietly into the ranks as Joe Dallet, a Youngstown organizer, took command. Before they docked he distributed all incriminating documents among the men and ordered them to chew them into paste. (One man outdid the order by swallowing his ration.) At dockside each man swore that he was only a tourist, answers that enraged port authorities, who knew that not even crazy Americans toured Europe lying in the bilge of a fishing boat, their clothes saturated with an ooze of motor oil, saltwater, and fish krawm. As the police herded them off to the provincial prison at Perpignan, villagers and captives turned the procession into a victory march, shouting "Vive la République!" and "Vive le front populaire!"*

The French police speedily learned that these were not ordinary prisoners. On the bus ride to the prison, an American picked the lock of his handcuffs and politely handed them back to his guard at journey's end. When the prison doctor attempted to inoculate them against smallpox, the Americans rebelled, "You can't shoot your Hitler germs into us!" Once locked inside, they transformed the prison into a bedlam of noise, pounding on the door of their cell, and demanding immediate penal reforms. A turnkey burst into their cell, cursing them in French, but drew back intimidated when Dallet cursed him back in French, English, and Yiddish. Alarmed that this mood of insurrection might spread to the other prisoners, the warden transferred them to a separate wing and gave them carbolic acid to disinfect their cell and quicklime for the trough latrine. They adhered to their tourist story and refused to respond to any questions without Dallet on hand. Meanwhile, Popular Front groups in Perpignan rallied to their support and sent in baskets of food. Newsmen swarmed down to see for themselves whether the French government would enforce the Non-Intervention Agreement or free the prisoners. The warden exclaimed, "Nothing like this has ever before happened in Perpignan prison. Nothing!" A U.S. vice consul came from Marseilles to confiscate their passports, but the French authorities refused to surrender them on grounds that they comprised part of the permanent records of the case. Although the Department of State ordered its consul to arrest these men and arrange for deportation, it could do nothing because no funds existed for expenses of escort, transportation, and maintenance. Despite all the hubbub, no one fingered "Joseph Fleischinger."

Because the crowds clamoring for the release of the captives threatened domestic security, the trial was moved to Ceret, a narcoleptic village in the foothills of the Pyrenees, eighteen miles south of Perpignan. When advised that six months would be automatically added to their sentences for contempt of court unless they abandoned their tourist pose, Dallet agreed to drop it. Personally, he was delighted by the opportunity to publicize the determination of International volunteers to overcome barriers thrown up by the Non-Intervention Agreement. With the help of an attorney from Béziers supplied by the Comité d'Entre Aide Franco-Espagnol, Dallet set about his task with the instinct of a natural showman.

Underneath the do-or-die, hard-crust manner of Joe Dallet lay soft, bourgeois fat. Unlike the men with him, he had not been born in poverty and raised on revolution. Class war had not been bred in his bones but donned like a new suit. His father did not work in a sweatshop—he ran one.

Born in Cleveland in 1907, Joseph Dallet Jr. grew up in Woodmere, Long Island, a parvenu suburb of New York. As the only son he was the center of adoring eyes of mother and sisters. At Lawrence High School he took the right courses, read the right books, and entertained opinions as far right as an American education would allow. He became infatuated with modern poetry and advanced to intermediate Chopin on the piano. Joseph Dallet Sr., a silk manufacturer, was a first-generation American Jew with expectations that his heir-apparent might become something wholly different—a first-generation Wasp perhaps? He enrolled his son at Dartmouth in 1923 (at the age of sixteen), but the rah-rah atmosphere of Hanover quickly alienated him.

Perhaps in self-defense, he championed proletarian ideas and a classless society, ideas that probably did not shock his classmates as much as mystify them. (At Harvard this heretical radicalism would have found an outlet, but at Dartmouth it passed as merely odd.) Dallet was scorned, laughed at, and—worst of all—ignored. On weekends he drove down to New York in his canary-yellow roadster to confer with labor leaders—or so he claimed. Yet when he was dropped from Dartmouth in the middle of his sophomore year, he took a job with Massachusetts Mutual Life. In 1928 he made the grand tour of Europe in the grand style and seemed to have had little working-class fervor. As he later told Steve Nelson, "Waiters were just flunkeys. That they were human beings, that they had wives and families and problems, that they were alive and worth knowing—it just never occurred to me."* The Crash of Twenty-nine brought Communism to him with the rush of a religious conversion.

A Dartmouth dropout and a rich man's son would have made good agitprop for the Party, but Dallet disliked having his shameful background aired. Plunging into organizing for the Sheet and Metal Workers Industrial Union in McKeesport, Pittsburgh, and Youngstown, he ruthlessly tried to purge lingering traces of his bourgeois upbringing. His language became so ungrammatical and his manners so coarse that genuine proletarians, unlettered men with natural dignity, thought he went too far. Sometimes his speeches were so rabidly partisan that they wondered whether he might be having a secret joke at their expense. They need not have worried. Apparently Dallet was convinced that real proletarians behaved this way. Just as he concealed his wealthy family, so he concealed his Jewish background. To John Gates, who later became the highest-ranking American in Spain, he was transparent. "'Dallet' [dalet] means the letter 'D' in Hebrew. Of course he would never admit to being Jewish. He made every effort to conceal his Jewishness and to keep people from seeing it."*

In domestic matters he drew the line. He married Catherine Puening, daughter of an internationally known engineer, not a pipe fitter. Reared in Europe, her first language was German, and she was well connected. (Her mother was related to Queen Victoria and was once engaged to Wilhelm Keitel, who was hanged in 1946 for war crimes.) After random studies at the Sorbonne, Kitty was married to a maverick Boston musician until an annulment in 1932. Ten days later, she went to a New York party to meet a Communist—"Most of us had never met a real live Communist"—and married Joe Dallet six weeks later. Her application for CP membership was turned down but she was allowed to join the YCL after an apprenticeship grinding out Party throwaways on a mimeograph machine and hawking the *Daily Worker* in Youngstown. The couple lived—ironically on relief checks—in a rundown boardinghouse while Joe ran for mayor of Youngstown on the CP ticket. Down the hallway lived John Gates, a future brigade commissar in Spain, and Arvo Halberg (better known as Gus Hall), later chief of the CPUSA. Since they were too poor to have a stove, the four of them ate in cheap working-men's cafés. Kitty endured two and a half years of poverty before abandoning Joe to join her father in England. Dallet blamed it on her bourgeois upbringing, but neither wished to make a final break. When she heard that Joe had volunteered for Spain, she met the boat at Cherbourg, and they had a week in Paris on her money with Steve Nelson tagging along. With their marriage rekindled, they vowed somehow to rendezvous in Spain. On the last day she bought both men warm shirts, gloves, and socks, and afterward mailed Joe a snapshot every week.*

At the Ceret trial in faraway France, Dallet blossomed like a sinister plant, and his letters to Kitty mirror a bruised personality craving adoration from his wife, from his courtroom mob, from his men. Of the trial he wrote: "We go in chains. . . . Everyone stares and we raise our right fists in salute and more than half of them return the salute. It's swell. My picture was in the Perpignan *Independent* today, taken as I came out of jail, fist raised." Then a few days later: "The lawyer tells me the papers are full of it, and he volunteered to send you a copy. Did he ever send you that picture of me? The photographer yesterday also sent you a picture of yesterday's demonstration." High purpose and revolutionary dedication vanished amid the popping of flashbulbs as Joe Dallet clenched his fist for photographers. He needed this sort of ego gratification. In a quieter mood, he confided to his wife, "Some day you and I must travel this land together and hire a small sailing boat and sail along the coast." Here was the true voice—a Woodmere yachtsman, not a McKeesport working stiff.

Throughout the trial Dallet led, and his men followed. This was his finest hour: if Dartmouth had taught him anything, it was how to needle the bourgeoisie. When more volunteers, picked up in the Pyrenees, were brought to Perpignan, Dallet organized a "jail soviet," which won them privileges unheard of in French prisons. He set up classes in Marxist theory and in Spanish, and he orchestrated thunderous songathons that thrilled the crowds milling about outside, craning to catch a glimpse of *les voluntaires*. With informers, scabs, and weaklings Dallet took a dictatorial line. Among the prisoners were some foreign volunteers who had suffered police torture in Italy and seemed ready "to confess to anything the authorities demanded." When Dallet learned that a badly frightened Italian told police that he had volunteered because the CP promised him ten thousand francs—a confession so preposterous that even the public prosecutor threw it out—he moved quickly. In front of the other men he denounced and insulted the informer. Proudly he recounted the aftermath to his wife: "He hung his head and was too scared to speak. We all threatened him and I was surprised how well I could curse in French. I found out yesterday that when they got him back to jail they beat him up and completely ostracized him." Yet this same Joe Dallet sat down at the piano in the home of the Ceret police inspector to play Chopin from memory and thereby demonstrate that Communists were men of culture. The reporters loved it. Once more flashbulbs popped. Afterward Dallet begged Nelson, the only American witness, not to tell the guys about it, for he did not want to be mistaken for a "bloody bourgeois intellectual."

The Ceret trial resulted in a pyrrhic victory for the prosecution. The Non-Intervention Agreement was legally intact because the captives were found guilty of border violations. But the sentence mocked the verdict: they were given twenty-day jail terms, with credit for fifteen days already served. The judge warned that unless they left France immediately, he would have them deported, to which Dallet replied, "Then deport us to Spain!"* Before their release, Dallet ordered his men to decorate the cell with so many slogans and hammer-and-sickle emblems that the wall would have to be whitewashed after they had gone. It was good college-boy fun. Their exit from prison was triumphant. "Crowds gather around us in the streets," he wrote Kitty. "We are the idols of the YCL and the Pioneers." People "begged" him to come back and promised "to turn their places inside out" if his wife would join him there. (He did not mention that three Americans got drunk at a Popular Front dance, disgraced themselves, and were packed off to the States as "disruptive elements.")

The only route to Spain now was up. They climbed to a pass in the Pyrenees by creek beds and mule paths, skirting border patrols at night. Beams of searchlights from French border police swept the mountain. For seven hours they climbed this cruel ladder behind a Spanish guide who whispered, "*Camaradas, ¡Adelante! ¡Adelante!*" as he prodded them on. The worst moment came when the stars faded and the cold sky turned blue-gray with coming dawn. Border guards could now spot them. Dallet described to Kitty their passage: "The last peak was a 5000-foot climb over loose and jagged rock, through thick stiff underbrush. And we had to race against sunrise to get over without being seen. I carried a 165 pound guy practically by myself that whole climb. Christ! When we crossed the line we almost cried for happiness. Some people did cry, and I had a hell of a job restraining myself." In the Dallet canon, tough guys never cried—and somehow they knew the exact weight of the weakling they had to carry. (For the record, the guides used only three passes through the Pyrenees, all of them about the same elevation, just slightly over six thousand feet.)

Concluding his letter, a surge of testosterone strength swept through Joe Dallet: "It was a most interesting trip—and so successful I could holler for joy and if you were here, I'd crush the breath out of you." Dartmouth man, Youngstown hero, Perpignan martyr—one sees Joe Dallet standing erect at dawn in the snowy wastes of the Pyrenees among the exhausted shapes of weaker men. A Soviet artist might have done much with this vignette. From such an eminence there was nowhere to go except down. And one must picture Joe Dallet at this moment in order to appreciate just how far down he would eventually sink.

8

THE WASHINGTON BATTALION

Throughout the spring of 1937 fresh American recruits flooded into Spain through the Paris–Perpignan conduit on waves of optimism, for this was a happy period when readers of CP newssheets like the *Daily Worker* trumpeted stories predicting imminent Republican victory. If a man expected to fight in this grand purge of Fascism from a tainted world, he should act quickly in order not to miss the triumphal finale. Recruits from other countries fell off dramatically during this period—even from neighboring France—but transatlantic liners continued to disgorge Americans at Cherbourg and Le Havre. Sometimes U.S. consuls recorded the age and occupation of each newcomer. (Walter O'Kane of Dixon, Illinois, at eighteen was the youngest; Frank Ferrero, unemployed and homeless, the oldest at fifty-two.) Predominantly working class, their numbers swelled with men from nearly all vocations—attorneys, dentists, writers, teachers, engineers, salesmen, florists, college professors. About half a dozen were licensed pilots hoping to earn $1,000 per month by flying for the Republic but choosing to serve in the International Brigades when pilot quotas filled. A small number walked down the gangplank, changed their minds, and returned home immediately. (They were lucky—once in Spain no one could turn back.) A Nebraska bricklayer vanished in France, and when his money ran out, he told a consul that he had joined the volunteers only to get a free trip to Europe. A tubercular case never completed the trip, for he died aboard ship and was buried at sea.

Because Villanueva de la Jara had been closed, American volunteers now trained at the former British camp in Madrigueras, described by a volunteer as "narrow dirt streets set down a thousand years ago and forgotten."* They cleaned out a derelict warehouse as a barracks, while an overflow spilled out into a cinema with a large gallery. In both places the latrines were so disgusting that men preferred the fields. The village was crammed with foreigners—mixed units and subunits of brigaders awaiting reassignment, or banished from Albacete as undesirables. Discipline seemed not to exist, for they roamed the streets like stray dogs. Worst among them were gangs of drunken Frenchmen, whose disparaging yarns about how the International Brigades were just cannon fodder, coupled with their reckless drinking and brawling, spread doubt and defeatism among idealistic newcomers. Nighttime was a bedlam with loud-speakers blaring "The International" and other patriotic uplift.

"Training," wrote a volunteer, "never demanding, got easier as it got hotter." When he voiced concern that they were receiving no instruction in military arts, he was told "our discipline would show itself superior to the fear-inspired disciples of other armies, certainly to that of Franco."* What little training they received came from men with prior service in the American or Canadian armies, like Bill Hallowell, a forty-year-old Canadian professional soldier with a short fuse. When recruits fell out of step, he would unload his thesaurus of martial argot and obscenities. None of the men had led sheltered lives, but they took umbrage when, after an afternoon of mistakes, he told them, in disgust, "The whole bunch of you are nothing but a bunch of bloody cunts." They reported this to their acting commissar, who said, "What the hell are you beef-ing about? This is an army. Hallowell has been a soldier all his life and this is the only language he knows. Do you expect him to call you a bunch of bloody com-rades? Get used to it. The fascists will do much more than throw cuss words at you." In short order they began to curse Hallowell back. He just smiled—the kids were becoming real soldiers.* Hallowell was better than nothing—but not by much. He taught them the manual of arms and the rudiments of close-order drill, but no one could pretend that this was serious preparation for twentieth-century warfare. This first draft at Madrigueras went to the firing range only once, where they were allowed five shots at a distant target. Later drafts learned marksmanship only through sighting cards on a target. Despite their inexperi-ence, dollops of them were sent as replacements to Jarama, where apparently they could receive on-the-job-training.

When news reached New York that the Madrigueras training camp was a dis-aster, the Politburo sent over Mirko Markovicz to organize a new American bat-talion and to whip them into shape. A thirty-year-old Montenegrin Serb, Markovicz had impressive Stalinist credentials. Active in the Yugoslavian CP since 1924, he had studied in Moscow at the Communist University for National Minorities of the West, taken a doctorate in economics (Marxist curriculum), completed a cram course at the Soviet Military Academy, and emerged as a colonel and commissar in the Red Army. In 1935 the Kremlin sent him to the United States to organize the Yugoslav section of the CPUSA. (To his later regret he failed to take out final citizenship papers.) On April 24 at Madrigueras he found about a hundred Americans mixed up with other nationals in a hodge-podge of formations. He was stunned by their independent attitude—notably their absence of respect for who he was and what he represented. Months later, in an interview for the brigade historical commission, he lampooned the typical American volunteer—"We're volunteers. If we want to accept orders and discipline, it's O.K. but if we don't like an order, we don't have to carry it out. We have the right to decide what to obey and what to reject."* A fresh recruit from the States told him, without apology, "The trouble with this army is that the leadership is too sectarian. . . . If they weren't so sectarian, they would know the men don't care for so much discipline." Good Communists did not talk, or even think, like this. It reeked of Anarchism—and Markovicz resolved to stamp it out.

Unlike Copic and Gal, who regarded the Americans as spoiled children of capitalism, he diagnosed the real problem. They had to be separated from the moral miasma around them. "Discipline was bad in Madrigueras," he wrote. "There were a lot of drunkards among the men, especially among the French. The Americans were comparatively the best behaved and disciplined . . . expecting a strict army routine. When they saw the laxity and looseness prevailing, they too quickly fell in with the prevailing conditions." To escape contamination, he petitioned for an exclusively North American camp in a different location. This was denied on grounds of expense, but Albacete did authorize him to form a tentative second American battalion and to add to it the dozen or so North Americans drifting in nearly every day.

The new battalion, not yet named but consisting of three companies, came into official existence on April 30, 1937. It spent May Day on a *subbotnik*— digging a canal to supply Madrigueras with fresh water. On the day following, the men decorated the theater with banners and after patriotic speeches held an entertainment and dance for the villagers. "There were plenty of girls and we had a good time till after midnight," recorded John Koblick.* For the first time, doors in the village opened wide for the Americans, who gave candy to the children and were soon sharing meals of beans and eggs with families and recovering from their surprise that the family burro passed back and forth through the kitchen from its own room in the tiny mud-brick house. "You will never leave their house hungry, even if it means they have too little," wrote a Lincoln.* They joined the nightly *paseos* in the village *plaza,* holding hands with young girls but always trailed by watchful parents. To their surprise they learned that villagers thought that President Roosevelt had sent them to make war against the Fascists, and they surprised the villagers in turn by describing the poverty, unemployment, and homelessness in Depression America. One woman, disturbed that an American wore glasses and worried that perhaps he could not shoot well, offered him a large knife to use against the hated enemy.*

On the day after the dance, Markovicz instituted a rigorous schedule for the Americans—reveille at 0530, lights out at 2100, with seven and a half hours of training in between. When fifty men, who had been in camp for two months, protested against "more training" and demanded to be sent to the front, Markovicz obliged. On May 12, James W. Ford, Communist vice-presidential candidate in 1936, and Robert Minor came to town and received an enthusiastic welcome from the Americans, who used this festive occasion to argue about a suitable name for the new battalion.[1] Minor stumped for George Washington, but the men voted overwhelmingly for Tom Mooney, at that time serving a life term in Alcatraz for an alleged bombing incident in 1918. Minor, aware of the precarious morale issues in the battalion, wisely did not dampen their enthusiasm, for he knew that the Politburo of the CPUSA would never accept their nomination. After all, wealthy parlor pinks would be spooked by an association with a notorious radical like Mooney. Sure enough, some weeks later a telegram arrived from New York congratulating officers and soldiers for "choosing" the name George Washington Battalion. Like Lincoln, Washington entered the Spanish war not as a volunteer, but as draftee.[2]

After heated arguments with Albacete, Markovicz succeeded in establishing a new Anglo-American training camp at Tarazona de la Mancha, twenty miles northwest of Albacete. A former convent with vine-embossed courtyard served as their barracks, inspiring a Welsh volunteer to write his parents: "Dear Comrades, We go to church twice a day. We eat there. . . . The church was built in 1520 and this is the first time it's been put to decent use."* The British slept on the floor but the Americans collected wood and built two-tier bunks and made straw ticks for comfort. ("They could not accept hardships like the British," bragged a Scotsman.)* To avoid gouging by private vendors, the Americans opened their own wine shop and canteen. Well stocked from the United States, it opened to tremendous business, and for a short time welcomed comrades from the Spanish and British battalions. However, international brotherhood took a skid when non-Americans were told to keep away—not enough to go round.*

1. Minor and Ford also visited the trenches at Jarama. Minor spoke to the men in dead ground just behind the trench. Since he was hard of hearing, he was oblivious to bullets whizzing just over his head. When he made an emphatic point, he raised his hand above his head with a finger pointing skyward. The men stared at his finger "transfixed," expecting a bullet to remove it. When they applauded, the enemy thought they were preparing an attack and began rapid machine-gun fire. In turn, this made the Americans think the enemy was attacking them, and they rushed back into the trenches. Finding a rifle somewhere, Minor joined them.*

2. While other IB units customarily took names of political radicals—Dimitrov, Rákosi, Thaelmann, Marty, and so on—the American Party continued to flaunt its slogan "Communism Is Twentieth-century Americanism" and ransacked schoolboy history in search of proto-American Radicals like Tom Paine and Patrick Henry. The single exception was the early Tom Mooney machine-gun company, which continued to use this moniker until the end.

Architecturally, Tarazona was a stone or two upscale from Madrigueras. In the town center, blanched wooden balconies adorned with flowers hung precariously over a dilapidated but picturesque *plaza mayor,* and a *bodega* called Sloppy Joe's served good rabbit stew. If a man drank too much, he cooled off in a little stone hut up the hill near the cemetery. Except for rotten booze, money could buy only hazelnuts or a slab of marmalade. "With soap, you could buy anything."* The pursuit of tobacco was relentless. Unless a man hid it, he was likely to share his cigarette with a dozen moochers. In the plaza a hand-cranked barrel organ endlessly played "Popeye the Sailor Man" and "The Music Goes Round and Round." (The organ grinder in Albacete had more political zip because his instrument played "The International.") About the only diversion in Tarazona was a semimonthly delousing with vinegar and alcohol—it stung—followed by a hot shower from a peripatetic water truck. (The British, more accustomed to insect infestation, just wrote home for anti-lice salve.) Training began in earnest. Recruits, who eventually reached five hundred, now rose before dawn and marched to their mess hall in the local cinema. Covering one wall was a large sign, "DO NOT WASTE BREAD. IT HELPS OUR ENEMY"— unnecessary, as it proved, for there was little enough to waste. At eight sharp they formed in the *plaza* to salute the red-gold-mauve flag of the Republic. Then followed instruction in close-order drill, infiltration, fortification, camouflage, riflery, first aid, and topography—or reasonable facsimiles thereof. Once a day they attended Spanish lessons in the parish church, where the townspeople had hung a streamer across the nave, "LONG LIVE THE SOVIET UNION, BEST FRIEND OF THE SPANISH PEOPLE." (Men complained that this banner bypassed the American contribution. Where were the dead Russkies in this war?) They now took apart and put together rifles and machine guns and practiced throwing dummy grenades. Unfortunately, they had no live ammunition, and some months later the rifles were replaced with wooden mock-ups.*

The Americans found Markovicz a strange fish—overbearing and unpredictable. His English was so atrocious that his men—no fussy grammarians themselves—found it difficult not to laugh whenever he barked an order. A Stalinist to the core, he invoked Lenin to dun into their capitalist brains that poker was a form of theft, he threw a recruit into the stockade for "undermining the war effort" because he insulted the food, and he was not above using his fist to italicize an order.* Having come to distrust military amateurs, the men came to respect, with reservations, the no-nonsense professionalism of Markovicz.

Captain Allan Johnson (McNeil), who earlier had served as the "military expert" on the screening committee at CP headquarters in New York, took over the training program at Tarazona. He was a man of about forty with a face like wilted lettuce. His uniform never varied: heavily starched American army issue, except for brown beret and engineering boots laced up to his knees. Among the recruits at Tarazona the story circulated, encouraged by Johnson, that he was a World War vet, a graduate of the U.S. War College, and a former captain in the U.S. Army. In his office hung an American flag with a yellow hammer and sickle sewn across the stripes. "The flag of the future," he said. "Someday you'll see this in the United States, too."*

To say that Johnson was "in charge" of the training camp bends the truth to the breaking point, for the volunteers did not see much of him. He made flying trips up to the Jarama front, where he periodically held the title "chief of operations," and to Albacete with requests for paraphernalia, usually ignored. Visits to the front supplied him with patriotic grist, which he fed to recruits. He told how Bob Raven had lost both his eyes when a grenade exploded at his feet, yet his spirit was so untouched that he recited propaganda slogans to nurses while being prepared for surgery. "At least that was what we were told," recalled a skeptical recruit. When news reached Johnson that some men were complaining about conditions at the camp, he called them together, wrinkled his brow, and rebuked them, "If you complain here, what will you do when you get to the front? Here you have mattresses and a roof over your heads to protect you from the rain, while at the front the men are sleeping in the trenches in the mud and freezing cold?" The men felt like coddled sissies. "All of us were silent with shame." Of course, no one thought to ask where Johnson slept when he went to Jarama.*

Up at Jarama the veterans had little use for Johnson. Hourihan immediately spotted him as a phony. Johnson was on hand briefly during the April 4 attack, and when a few Lincolns got pinned down about thirty yards from an enemy trench, Johnson ordered them to dig in and fortify. This was madness—the stranded men would be trapped when the enemy trenched around them and shot them like starved rats popping out of their hole. Hourihan countermanded the order of his "chief of operations." One veteran spoke volumes when he later wrote of Johnson, "He never spent any time with the boys in the trenches."*

The first flush of enthusiasm marking the early period in Spain began to dissipate. Officers demanded salutes, and within the networks of Albacete they ate special food at special tables. (While Merriman continued to eat with the rank and file, he insisted on the salute.) Class distinctions were anathema for Anglo-Americans, and in place of "No pasarán!" at rallies, one began to hear "No fucking *pan* [bread]!" while retaining the clenched fist.* They delighted in an anonymous poem, "The Albacete Generals."

> On the front of Albacete
> Meet the generals of the rear,
> Oh! They fight the grandest battles
> Though the shells they never hear . . .
> See them strolling in the evening
> To the grogshops for their wine,
> For they are the brave defenders
> Of the Albacete line.

Johnson's favorite military maxim, "What is captured by the gun must be held by the spade," became a Lincoln joke, skeptics muttering that they never saw *him* dig with anything except his spoon.* Often he helped himself to chocolates and cigarettes from a cache sent by the FALB for all the Americans. On one of his sorties to the storeroom, Jack Corrigan, the guard, stopped him and asked for his permit from the *intendencia*. Johnson announced that as commander of the camp he needed no permit and headed toward the cigarettes. "Hold it right there!" said Corrigan, leveling his (empty) rifle at him. Johnson was astounded. This was mutiny—a soldier could be shot for less! "Put down that rifle or I'll have you arrested!" But when he saw the look on Corrigan's face he changed his mind, left in a huff, but preferred no charges. "Jack sure had a lot of guts,"* went the consensus. But Corrigan brushed it off. Back in New York he had become a folk hero when he defied a platoon of flatfeet by climbing the Eternal Light flagpole at Madison Square Park to raise a "Free Ernst Thaelmann" banner. Compared to that, Captain Johnson was a pushover.* (Corrigan disappeared during the great rout in Aragon a year later—abandoned by his men as he heroically covered their flight.)*

Among his efforts to inculcate discipline, Captain Johnson issued an order that Americans must salute the Spanish flag in the town plaza. This rankled men who refused to salute anybody or anything, and certainly not a foreign flag. Outraged, Johnson held a meeting and warned that those refusing would be arrested. "How close to the flag must we be before it becomes necessary to salute?" quizzed an American. Thirty feet. "But how will we know when we are within thirty feet?" Johnson said that a circle would be painted thirty feet from the flagpole. "Inside the circle, you will salute!" Thereafter the men amused themselves by almost stepping on the line, going into elaborate contortions as though nearly falling off a cliff, or pretending they were drunk but never drunk enough to step on the line.* Johnson was so consumed with strict obedience to orders that he lectured new recruits on how they would be punished for lack of discipline even before they had been there long enough to do anything wrong!*

Ghosts from the past came and went. One of them was Sam Stember, awaiting orders to return home, who continued to blame the failures at Jarama on lack of discipline. The recruits were not fooled. They had heard how he hid in the cookhouse during the attack on the twenty-seventh and afterward emerged from his burrow to call the survivors "a bunch of babies." "That son of a bitch, Stember," wrote a recruit. "If he ever comes back here, we'll shoot him."* (Back in the States, Stember shared the stage on fund drives with wounded vets who "showed tremendous heroism" and with nary a word about "babies.")*

Dave Mates, the Washington Battalion commissar, newly imported from New York, had a reputation as a Party organizer and agitator, having served during the worst years of the Depression as city secretary of the Unemployed Councils of Chicago. The *Tribune* had once branded him "the most dangerous Anarchist since the Haymarket Riots." (To call Mates an Anarchist missed the point by a country mile.) No one ever quite figured out why the CPUSA had sent him, or what he was supposed to do—least of all Mates himself. Taking advantage of his rank, he failed to turn out for morning parade at 0615 until Markovicz set him right about his obligations as a commissar. Thereafter, "Mates joined the morning formation, usually arriving late and completing his dressing while there."* His confidential Party file says it all—"seemed to do very little. Thoroughly disliked by everyone and in disrepute."* He was never more than a ventriloquist's dummy for senior officers. To top it off, he was accused of taking money to arrange transfers for volunteers.*

In May Robert Merriman joined the Tarazona staff from La Pasionaria Hospital in Murcia. With his arm in a wing cast he was a poor advertisement for war, but as ever he exuded competence and optimism. The recruits knew that he was sometimes called "Murderman," but at Tarazona he gained their respect because he did not gloss over what had happened at Jarama—even though he withheld demoralizing statistics. He admitted that in both attacks the Lincolns failed to gain ground, but he credited them with helping to block the Nationalist attack on Madrid. (He would later command a third North American unit being formed at Tarazona, the Mackenzie-Papineau Battalion.)

With Merriman now and then appeared his wife, Marion, who had raced from Moscow after learning that he had been wounded. She had the distinction of being the only female officially enrolled in the Lincoln Battalion—she wore culottes instead of trousers and agreed never to request service at the front.

Smart and attractive, she took a room at the Hotel Regina in Albacete and busied herself trying to untangle the Gordian knot of personnel records trailing after the Americans.[3] Steve Nelson had outlined the problem when he arrived in Spain: the base did not know how many Americans had arrived, how many were dead or wounded, or where they were. "There's no record. They are scattered from hell to breakfast."[*4] One of Marion's first tasks was trying to verify deaths of Americans to satisfy insurance companies requiring evidence.[*] Among the Lincolns she quickly became a kind of amalgam of virgin queen and den mother. The men she liked, but not the Party functionaries. Colonel Copic, already in her doghouse for his homicidal orders at Jarama, "didn't walk, he strutted. He didn't smile, he gloated." Philip Cooperman, Party secretary of the Lincolns, was "plump and perspiring, a clown with pom-poms."[*]

Bob joined her on weekends, and they encouraged those in Albacete to gather in their room for conversation and tea cakes—even when Bob was out of town. Marion knew how to neutralize romantic advances without giving offense. Once when an ideologue made a convoluted pitch about the duties of communal sharing, which included sex, she replied that such sharing was out of bounds. If she slept with him, she said, then to be fair she had to sleep with two thousand of his comrades—but "just wasn't up to it."[*] Although the Americans respected her "hands-off" demeanor, other brigaders—especially among the Comintern Yugoslavs—saw her as a creature to be conquered. Markovicz made repeated attempts, even to the extent of intercepting Bob's private mail hoping to find cause to make Marion jealous. These having failed, he sent a staff officer to explain how very important he was. She was amused by this Miles Standish strategy, but Bob was not, although he buried his anger to preserve order. Sometime later, when Base received a report that two English women visiting the Marcia hospitals were encouraging Americans to desert, Marion agreed to go down with "two pleasant Slav officers" to investigate. They remained overnight at the hospital. During the night one of the officers sneaked into her room, clamped his

---

3. Although the VALB has published a roster of the Americans who fought in Spain, these will always be incomplete. Repeatedly I find documents—especially those pertaining to the Jarama period—that contain names of men never accounted for in the VALB archive. Even rosters that the XVth Brigade prepared in Spain listing the names of all Americans then living (about March 1938) who had membership in the CP or YCL include names not recognized by the official VALB list. In many instances passports, which would have certified their presence in Spain, vanished when sent to the USSR for use in espionage work.

4. The personnel of the Lincoln Battalion were in worse shape than the personnel records, for Nelson found the demoralization and anarchy of the Jarama survivors worse than anything he had imagined: "They even had a rump meeting to elect officers. The political commissar couldn't handle the situation."[*]

hand over her mouth, and raped her. When he had finished, she was able to kick him off and spent hours sobbing and scrubbing herself in a cold-water tub. The next day the rapist was arrogant and proprietary on the long drive back to Albacete. She never told Bob, fearing that he might kill the man. For the next month she was petrified that she might be pregnant and resolved to have an abortion (illegal in Spain). She never divulged the man's name.*

Despite Hourihan's insistence that the Washingtons be sent up at once to relieve the abnormally long trench vigil of the Lincolns, Bob Minor refused. He envisioned a spanking new battalion that when ready for the front would be the best-trained unit in the International Brigades. Besides, better that the new men be kept in political quarantine from contamination by the "demoralized elements" of the Lincoln Battalion, just as in February the Lincolns had been kept away from the badly mauled Britons. In effect, except for commissars and staff, the Lincolns had almost no contact with the Washingtons. To their chagrin and anger Lincolns found themselves treated as pariahs whenever they tried to visit friends or relatives at the Tarazona camp. On one such occasion, three wounded Jarama vets—Joe Gordon, Bill Harvey, and Doug Roach—hitched a ride to Tarazona to visit Gordon's brother. At the barracks door a commissar turned them away, "No Lincoln bastards are coming in here to demoralize *our* men." They bulled past the comic-star and raised a commotion. Leo Gordon was in there, and they demanded to see him. Joe Dallet intercepted them and made them promise they would not discuss Jarama. In the mess hall they had to sit off to one side. Bob Minor made a speech, and in his rolling Texas drawl made disparaging remarks about Moors as "those *black* men from Africa." Roach, a black, was on his feet like a shot, glowering at Minor. Gordon, his eye socket swathed in a bandage, and Harvey, his neck in a giraffian cast, had to pull him back. The three then stamped out, while Minor, who was hard of hearing, continued his harangue.*

The training program at Tarazona suffered from the near absence of military professionals. Unlike countries of Europe, the United States had no peacetime conscription, and there were few World War vets aroused by Spain. (Any cause sympathetic to World Communism horrified the American Legion.) The Central Committee sent out feelers to find and enlist experienced Army officers willing to serve in Spain. The trick, however, lay in locating candidates with both military experience and political commitment. However, in February a godsend, who claimed to be a disaffected former U.S. Marine Corps officer named Vincent Usera, walked into Party headquarters in New York and said he wanted to go to Spain. Suspecting a trap or a government stooge, the Central

Committee assigned two trusted organizers to squire him around and to pick his mind. One of these, Saul Wellman, a truck driver from Camden, delivered his report. After two weeks' observation, Usera's credentials shone like pure gold. Apparently he had joined the Corps in 1926, at the age of seventeen, served three months on a gunboat in China with the Yangtze River patrol, and earned a commission in Nicaragua during the Sandino "revolution." The Guardia Nacional arranged for him to train recruits in guerrilla warfare. Usera described one incident where he took a platoon of Guardia into the mountains and unexpectedly encountered "all of Sandino's army." He led his men in a three-day retreat through twenty miles of jungle, constantly under fire and carrying all their wounded. For this he received a captain's commission in the Guardia Nacional and served as the U.S. liaison officer to the Nicaraguan president's staff. In 1930 he went on to the Basic School at Philadelphia Navy Yard, where he trained to become an instructor of Marine officers. Transferred to Newport after six months, he moved easily in that social milieu. Women said he reminded them of Errol Flynn and responded accordingly.*

Usera's career in the Marine Corps ended abruptly—or so he said—when he became involved "in a personal way" with the wife of "somebody who had more influence than I did." Whether discharged honorably or dishonorably he did not say. For the next two years, under the wing of a "Mrs. Vanderbilt" in Newport, he did something in "show-business"—without spelling out the particulars. When this failed, he moved to Washington and opened an insurance brokerage, but after four years he "became convinced that he was no business-man." After a "Progressive" acquaintance informed him in February 1937 that Americans were fighting in Spain, Usera left for New York. While he seemed to be a political naïf, the Party recognized how valuable he might be in their training program. For several weeks he drilled recruits in New York under the watchful eyes of two Party spies, both of whom recommended him for service in Spain. Party surveillance did not end there, however, for all three shared a stateroom on the *Queen Mary*. In Paris the trio palled together in cafés like long-lost companions—not comrades—during a delay of several weeks when transportation to Spain was suspended because of the revolution-within-the-revolution that gripped Barcelona in May.*

On arriving at Tarazona, Usera expressed "shock at the shape of things." It was no training camp at all, as he understood it. He later reported that Markovicz had "good military knowledge" but was handicapped as leader because of his inadequate English. The existing program consisted of a brief morning conference of officers—always supervised by political commissars—who were then turned loose on their own. Each commander was wholly responsible for whatever instruction he deemed suitable, and there was never a checkup on what he had done. With the exception of a class in communication taught by Leonard Lamb, a New York teacher (later a Lincoln commander), there were no orientation lectures for all the officers. In field maneuvers the men had no knowledge of how to deploy against an enemy—for them scouting was the same as attacking, since both consisted of taking a few paces and flopping to the ground. While they learned how to take apart rifles or machine guns blindfolded, they barely knew how to fire them. (The Washingtons went to the rifle range only once during Usera's tenure and fired only three rounds.) Markovicz considered marksmanship unnecessary because the European system emphasized laying down a thick blanket of fire rather than pinpointing specific targets like the British and Americans. Noncoms received no special training other than suggestions, or commands, or curses from their company commanders. Although a new officers' school, conducted primarily by Soviet officers, had mushroomed in the piney woods at nearby Pozorubio, there were no clear criteria for selecting candidates. Usera had his work cut out for him. There must have been times when he yearned to be back in the Marines or the Nicaraguan army. One such day was May 25, when the Washingtons conducted their first field maneuver, which "went very well," Markovicz wrote in his journal, "except that the scouts got lost."*

The men realized at once that Usera was a bona fide professional with no tolerance for shenanigans, such as demanding a vote for anything they disliked, and they learned that there was more to this military trade than close-order drill as taught by Bill Hallowell. From his first assignment, roving through units with suggestions *en passant*, he graduated to command of a section and finally to full command of Third Company, which included many raw and reluctant Spanish recruits. Usera never seemed to comprehend why able-bodied Americans had come to fight for a rickrack country that paid a slave's wage, and the American commissariat asked themselves that same question about Usera. Hard-liners sniffed for telltale signs that he was an ONI (Office of Naval Intelligence) agent sent to spy on them. He was their top-hole mercenary—but who paid him? "P.W." (Paul Wendorf), a commissar assigned to file a confidential report on Usera, spelled out the major problem: "He readily admits that before coming to Spain he had had no connection with nor knowledge of the labor movement."* In sum, he was—or pretended to be—a total political ignoramus, but at least without taint of Fascism or Trotskyism.

As an instructor Usera soon outclassed both Johnson and Merriman and moved into the post of chief training officer, the second-highest military (as opposed to political) position at Tarazona. "P.W." reported, "[He] visits the companies training in the field every day, observes their development carefully, and steps into situations which he sees need correction." On top of this he spoke fluent Spanish—which none of the other leaders did—and the story got around that he came from a wealthy Puerto Rican family. The men liked but were never close to him. He told stories about how pirate bands in China. opened fire on patrol boats precisely at three in the afternoon, while the marines lay down behind sheets of boilerplate and returned fire for a few minutes. He said it was all perfectly harmless. Yet some Washingtons weaned on cruel stories of Great Power exploitation of Chinese "coolies" in China were not amused. In general, the rank and file respected Usera's competence, but he always remained a *rara avis* to them. To Party hard-wires, Usera was an "adventurer," a pejorative term for one who fights with them without commitment to any cause except his own private gratification.

Throughout the International Brigades, political factionalism intensified after an insurrection broke out in May, when major parties within the shaky Popular Front coalition in Barcelona fortified buildings and opened fire on one another. The upshot was that the Communists, who presumably had engineered the conflict, obtained greater power in the government and began openly to purge the Trotskyites and to undermine the Anarchists.[5] Although no Internationals took part in the Barcelona fighting, the event strengthened the influence of the CP in the Republican government in general and the army in particular.

After the Barcelona insurrection the whole character of the International Brigades began to change. One heard less about "liberty" and more about "discipline." The clenched-fist gesture of solidarity gave way to the traditional military salute, anathema for working-class purists who had fought upper-class privilege all their lives. The fiction that a commissar was a "delegate" of the men began to fade. Increasingly, men looked upon their commissars not as appointed delegates but as, in the words of a disaffected volunteer, "a thought control agent, an intellectual policeman."* Power was a pollutant, and it corrupted men who, under normal circumstances, might have scorned it. Even in everyday routine, the changes became conspicuous. The gap between officers and ordinary "comrades" was widening rapidly. Officers now received better food, served by waiters

---

5. Orwell returned to Barcelona in late April, after having fought in the POUM militia in Aragon. Like most front-line soldiers, he was unprepared for the pressure building up against the Trotskyists. Caught in the middle of the street fighting, he was forced to flee across the frontier to escape capture and execution. Ironically, he had been taking steps to enlist in the International Brigades at the time the purge began because he regarded the Communist units as more disciplined. His *Homage to Catalonia* is a definitive account of the conflict and its repercussions.

in private rooms. They no longer picked out a uniform by rummaging through a pile of junked garments in a warehouse but sped off in private cars to patronize gentlemen's tailors in Valencia and Madrid. Even Merriman succumbed to the uniform craze, although he still ate with the men. While he demanded salutes as tokens of respect, he corrected recruits who called him "Sir"—for him as inappropriate in a People's Army as the Fascistic "señor."*

Within the International Brigades, discipline and obedience became the measure of all things. Desertion, disobedience, drunkenness, and even grumbling became political crimes. Because the International Brigades were virtually independent of the Spanish government, individual volunteers found themselves at the mercy of their commissars, without recourse to the Ministry of War. Draconian punishments were meted out, with no reasonable relationship to the actual offense.

Among the first to discover the hardening mood of the Party, on June 15 Zygmund Piasecki of Toledo, fueled by *coñac* in the Albacete station, hopped aboard Locomotive 870 and throttled for Valencia. (Other reports in his file conflict with this: one suggesting that he failed to get out of the station, but "other engines could have been crushed," and another saying only "supposedly he pulled the whistle in a train while drunk in Albacete station.")* In any case, tried and convicted of "espionage" (not drunkenness and disorderly conduct) he received a death sentence, later commuted to twenty years in prison at hard labor.[6]

For propagandists in the CP, the nearly maniacal purge of putative Trotskyists in the late spring of 1937 displaced the "war against Fascism." Andreas Nin, the head of the POUM, was kidnapped and assassinated by an unidentified gang—believed to be a German hit squad from the International Brigades—and his party banned from the government. And back in the United States, the *Daily Worker* warned against the Trotskyist heresy by publishing articles detailing where individuals and cells of the enemy had been eliminated like infestations of termites. At the height of the Moscow Trials, for example, Earl Browder, secretary-general of the CPUSA, published in *Pravda* a multipage screed targeting a worldwide conspiracy of Trotskyist heresies and singling out, among a host of others, "the head of this gang of bandits in the USA . . . the notorious swindler Max Eastman."*

The nucleus of Camp Lukács, the IB prison, was a farmhouse on a windswept plain, surrounded by jerry-built huts and pens, six miles outside

---

6. Piasecki remained in prison until April 1939, five months after the American volunteers had been repatriated. As the Nationalist armies were converging upon Valencia, Woodruff W. Wallner, the U.S. consul, appealed to the authorities, which relented at the last moment, and allowed him to flee to France.

Albacete near the Chinchilla road. As early as May 1937, it housed two hundred brigaders, most of them French. Normally a prisoner was detained without a specific charge. Every night names were called and the men taken away, those remaining never learning whether they had been shot, returned to the front, or released. (A favorite punishment was to put a prisoner into a labor battalion and send him to dig trenches within reach of enemy fire. A report of "death in battle" usually collected donations from friends and relatives at home.) Some men were impounded at Camp Lukács for months without trial. As regularly as a clock, a Polish-American prisoner pounded his cell door every night, shouting, "Copic [Milan the warden], you low type, get fucked by the Pope and shit in the milk of your mother! *Let us out!*"* The volunteers, who despised the brigade police as much as they did any right-wing goon squad back in the States, made up a song about them to the tune, "I'm Popeye the Sailor Man":

> I'm BP the fighting man, pop-pop
> I'm BP the fighting man, whack-whack.
>> My muscles all ripple,
>> When I hit a cripple.
> I'm BP the fighting man, pop pop.

It was never sung in Camp Lukács, of course.

No army survives very long without discipline, and discipline not based upon moral or physical force is worthless. The real issue, however, was whether witch-hunting was an efficacious instrument in building unity, or was, in the long run, destructive of the unity it attempted to build. Drunks, deserters, malingerers, and thieves had to be punished, but when they were punished in the name of some ambiguous heresy like "Trotskyism," the leaders undermined their own credibility and exacerbated the symptoms of collective demoralization. An officer of the Lincoln Battalion, in later years, spoke of the purges in this way: "In February the enemy was Franco—that's why I went to Spain; by June it was Trotsky—that's what I never understood."*

Power altered personalities beyond recognition. Symptomatic of malignant charges seeping into the once-holy cause of ridding the world of Fascism in all its guises was the case of Ralph Bates, an English writer attached to the International Brigades as a commissar-at-large. He once bragged to Stephen Spender that he had persuaded a young deserter to return to battle, even though he had secretly arranged for him to be sent to a post where he would certainly be killed. Then he added, "I have just had a message to say that he is dead. Of course, I am a little upset . . . but I did right." Spender was horrified, not because this revelation was true, but because he knew it was false. Bates did not have sufficient authority to make his victim shine his boots, much less to arrange for his execution. It was the fabrication of a literary man who had tasted power, perhaps for the first time in his life, and wanted another writer to envy him. This same intellectual stood before a Writers' Congress in Madrid, while the battle of Brunete raged outside, and announced, to an assembly of international writers, "You will notice that I am dressed as a private, but really I have the rank corresponding to that of general."* War spawned weird behavior. The insidious way that power infected ordinary souls explained why Spender characterized his visit to the International Brigades as "frightening."

The ranks of the George Washington Battalion were quickly filled, and subsequent volunteers were assigned to a third battalion commanded by Robert Merriman and commissared by Joe Dallet. What to call this third North American unit resulted in a prolonged hassle between advocates of "Tom Paine," "Tom Mooney," and "Patrick Henry." (Nobody knew anything about the political ideology of Patrick Henry, but his slogan, "Give me liberty, or give me death!" was a grabber.) The stalemate ended after a group of Canadians protested that their countrymen had fought in the Lincoln Battalion from the beginning and were now mustered into the Washington, but had been unrecognized. Although Merriman treated protesters like quirky children because "the people of Europe don't know much about Canada," he gave in when the Americans unanimously agreed with the Canadians.*

The third North American unit became the Mackenzie-Papineau Battalion, named for William Lyon Mackenzie (1795–1861) and Louis-Joseph Papineau (1786–1871), leaders of the independence movement in Canada. The original plan called for all Canadians to join the Mac-Paps, but this did not prove feasible. Americans always outnumbered Canadians, even in the Canadian battalion.

Meanwhile, Markovicz was obtaining recognition for his battalion, which on June 4, 1937, was officially incorporated as the 19th Battalion of the XVth Brigade. The rank and file got wind that they would soon be moving up to the front, and their morale soared. The air was electric. They were especially eager to meet their older brother, the Lincoln Battalion. At morning parade Markovicz habitually greeted his men with a snappy military salute followed by, "Salud, Comrades!" to which the men usually mumbled something and halfheartedly swung an arm. But on June 9 when he greeted them, to his great surprise the entire battalion saluted and roared back, "Salud!" At that moment both commander and soldiers felt they had been transfigured into real soldiers. On June 11 he ordered the battalion to assemble with full equipment for a night maneuver. Suddenly a tandem of personnel trucks pulled into the plaza and parked with engines throbbing. Only then did Markovicz spring his surprise. His night maneuver was a hoax—they were bound for the front! With whoops and yells five hundred men swarmed aboard. The whole loading took less than half an hour—too fast for good-byes to the Mac-Paps, poor devils obliged to remain behind for more training. Awakened by the trucks, some Mac-Paps came out to watch the departure of their comrades to the front. Where these were bound, they did not know, but by the time dawn lighted the little plaza, the Washingtons were gone.

With thirty men each in twenty-man trucks, the exhausted Washingtons bailed out at Tarancón for breakfast after a sixteen-hour run. Their field kitchen had broken down somewhere on the road—and stayed there for days. A surly unit of Anarchists who occupied the town had never heard of them, denied them access to their food stores, and refused to refuel the trucks until Markovicz took the gas at gunpoint. Three hours later they disembarked at Tailmer, their destination five miles east of Morata. No one expected them there either. The town was jammed with soldiers and refugees from Fascist territory, the village stores had no food for sale, and the men bivouacked in an open field while the staff found an empty stable. Here they learned with disappointment that they would not join the Lincolns at all because after four months on the front lines, they had just been relieved and sent for a rest to Albares, a village farther up the Tajuña River.

Other disappointments awaited the Washingtons. Their mission was to relieve the Dimitrov Battalion occupying tents outside Morata. At the site they found that the Yugoslavs had stripped the camp of everything portable, including tents, cookstoves, and all weapons except sixty-one battered and dirty rifles. Markovicz was incensed at such "uncomradely behavior"—all the more so because the malefactors were fellow Yugoslavs. Here was his battalion, in a reserve position, less than a mile from the front trenches, yet without the means to fire a shot in their own defense, much less to plug a gap in the line. Their sole armament consisted of one Maxim machine gun (nicknamed Mother Bloor) and two light guns stolen from somewhere. Markovicz stalked off to complain to Copic, who passed the buck: "The division commander is accustomed to intervene in Brigade interior matters."* Undaunted, Markovicz obtained an audience with General Gal, who explained that the blame lay squarely with the Socialist government of Largo Caballero, which distrusted the Communist orientation of the International Brigades, but he did scrounge 190 rifles from the auxiliary services—like *transmisiones* and *intendencia,* which did not use them. These relics arrived in terrible condition and required a day of cleaning and repair. Somehow the Washingtons acquired tents and established a canvas city in an olive grove outside Morata, where they remained for the next two weeks.*

In the distance the Washingtons heard booming guns but never occupied the old Lincoln trenches, now held by the 24th (Spanish) Battalion. Despite the regnant policy to keep them in tight psychic quarantine from the Lincolns, the cordon sprung leaks. Occasional Lincolns who wandered into camp found themselves besieged by battle virgins with one overriding question—"What is it really like up there?" Having been saturated with accounts of Lincoln victories, Lincoln heroism, and Lincoln bullet-biting, the Washingtons were prepared to pay homage to their older brothers but instead heard demoralizing accounts by veterans like Irving Chocheles of New York, who spoke of the February battles. "It's been hell. I've seen men dead . . . cut to pieces . . . badly wounded with their guts hanging out, some with their heads practically blown off." He was interrupted by the objections of a prickly newcomer, who reminded him that casualties were few and the Lincolns had achieved a tremendous victory. "Bull!" replied Chocheles, "We had the shit knocked out of us!" He appeared upset and paused.

> We were told to go over the top screaming and yelling, and thought that would surely scare the hell out of the fascists. . . . When the order came to attack we were like a bunch of boy scouts, the good guys chasing the bad guys. In seconds we were chopped down. . . . We went over the top screaming and yelling at the top of our lungs. It didn't scare the fascists. Oh, the screaming continued for a long time, but it was from the wounded stretched out in no-man's-land. . . . It was just plain slaughter.*

The newcomers had been warned about Trotskyist talk. Could Chocheles be lying? Hadn't they pored over a recent issue of the *Daily Worker*, which, in a two-page extravaganza, claimed that the Americans and Cubans had "held the entire line under withering fire" with a loss of only twelve dead and twenty wounded? Was Stember on target when he faulted the Lincolns for "lack of discipline" and scoffed that they were "babies"? They craved more access to Lincolns to confirm or to deny Chocheles's unsettling confession. It was always more comforting for a recruit to hear the blasé pitch of an ex-soldier: "It ain't bad. It ain't bad at all—you get used to it. You never see the enemy; you shoot and shoot and you never see 'em. It ain't bad at all."*

Meanwhile, Markovicz used the lull for training stretcher-bearers, ammunition carriers, and the kitchen force. News came from Brigade that his battalion would attack with tanks—an exciting prospect. Morale remained high, despite a tropical storm that blew down the tents and turned the olive grove into a sea of mud where men could neither lie nor sit for two days. The enemy used this springtime *tormenta* to launch a surprise attack, and the Washingtons had orders to stand by. It looked like the real thing but came to nothing. "The spirit of the men was excellent despite their being soaking wet," wrote their commander. Only when drafting three men from each company for kitchen duty did Markovicz meet heated resistance, "The men picked complained bitterly and wanted to know why they were discriminated against—they considered this work as some sort of punishment and lower in dignity than being a fighting soldier." Only a passing phase, Markovicz observed a month later, "Once the battles started, the situation changed. Plenty of men volunteered then and asked to be transferred to the kitchen."*

A mutiny did occur, but only within the officer caste, not the rank and file. With Harry Haywood as spearhead, the top-ranking American Communists demanded that Copic be relieved as commander of the XVth Brigade because he had lost his men's confidence. The mutineers, who included Nelson, Johnson, Hourihan, and Mates, sought to form a new brigade led by Americans. Merriman, who had suffered more than any other under Copic's tenure, refused to join them. The British had no affection for a martinet like Copic, but they interpreted this move as a signal that the Americans planned to take control of the brigade because of their numerical and financial superiority. Men who, like George Aitken, brigade commissar; Major George Nathan, chief of operations; and Major "Jock" Cunningham, the commander of the British Battalion, had distinguished themselves as outstanding leaders from the first hours of the Jarama fighting had no intention of yielding to Johnny-come-latelies. Markovicz refused to join the conspiracy, making it clear that he flew the flag of the Comintern, not the CPUSA. On learning that his own commissar had joined the mutineers, he gave Mates a tongue-lashing and forced a retraction. Copic's headquarters became the setting for the final act of this palace coup when Haywood entered to deliver his ultimatum. Copic's diary for June 18 records the exchange.

> H. tells me that as a delegate of the Party it is his duty to tell me that the men have no confidence in the CO of the Brigade and want to replace me. That if this lack of confidence is justified or not is another question and he does not want to explore it but says it has to be considered and taken into account as the opinion of the mass. H. has already in previous discourses in the battalion incited against the CO. I told him that he could communicate his views to the Division CO but if he tried

173

again to organize factional meetings in the battalion against the command, he would be arrested and sent to Albacete.*

Further humiliation lay ahead for hapless Harry Haywood, who had alienated the rank and file by his arrogance and cowardice, Nelson and the American commissars by his ostentation and uselessness, and now the Comintern clique by his defiance of Party discipline.

On top of this, only two weeks before the opening guns at Brunete, General Gal began to restructure the troubled XVth Brigade. His new table of organization called for two regiments: the first composed of the Dimitrovs, the Sixth of February, and the 24th battalions under the command of Miklos Szalway, a rugged Yugoslav always called by his moniker, "Chapaiev"; the second composed of the Lincoln, Washington, and British battalions under Major Jock Cunningham, whose rally of the British during the first days at Jarama had saved the Republican left flank from collapse. Although Cunningham despised him, Harry Haywood became his regimental commissar. When Martin Hourihan was kicked upstairs as regimental adjutant, the Lincoln command went up for grabs—but not for long. As many veterans feared, Oliver Law took over the battalion.

In an unusual obeisance to camaraderie among his inferiors, General Gal held a banquet for his staff and the six battalion commanders and commissars at his riverside dacha. Having been briefed on the aborted mutiny, he poured healing glasses of vodka on troubled waters, outlined his expectations for the coming offensive, and received from his retainers toasts to his health and continued success. He explained his 15th Division would also include the XIIIth Brigade, the Dombrowski, which was on the way from a hard campaign in the South. The camaraderie ended with an abrupt explosion of epithets in Russian and Hungarian. The general had just discovered that Lieutenant Colonel Hans Klaus, Copic's second in command, had—for reasons never explained—boycotted the banquet. Gal dispatched a messenger with an order for him to present himself at once. Markovicz recorded the embarrassing finale: "Throughout the banquet Klaus was put on the spot, General Gal berating him both directly and indirectly."

Of all this internecine squabbling the volunteers fortunately knew nothing. At 1900 on June 30 their life brightened when an order came down to collect field gear and await transportation to the front.[7] For two weeks they had lived

---

7. This equipment, which weighed 20–25 kilos, consisted of rifle, 200 rounds of ammunition, canteen, blanket, one or two hand grenades, gas mask, musette bag, knapsack, mess kit, pick and shovel, and steel helmet.

under canvas, hearing only the occasional boom of distant cannon. When told they would soon be in action with the legendary Lincolns, the men "yelled with delight and jumped around with the agility of deers [sic]," and topped off the evening "singing revolutionary songs."* Repeatedly, officials had dunned into them that they were the "best trained battalion in the International Brigades." Now they would prove that they upheld the IB tradition as a "bataillon de choc."

9

STALEMATE AT BRUNETE

On June 13, 1937, the Lincolns finally left the trenches at Jarama.* Somebody counted it up—they had been 116 days in the line, and despite the shaky math this number entered the canon.*¹ Trucks carried them to Albares, a time-forgotten village of three hundred souls tucked away in the hill country north of Morata de Tajuña. From the highway, a hundred stone steps wound up to the packed-earth *plaza mayor*, where they put the church to good use—kitchen in one corner, ammo depot in the other, and sleeping quarters in the center. The women of the town stitched mattress covers from flour sacks, and the men stuffed them with clean straw. What luxury after trenches. Pockets bulging with nearly four months' pay, nine men made a beeline for the only *bodega* in town. No whiskey—no *coñac*, only a vat of *anis,* a licorish-tasting distillate as clear as mountain water and as potent as grain alcohol. "Sissy stuff!" declared their ringleader. "Gimme a liter." Fifteen minutes later they had taken the *bodega* apart and were converging on the town itself before Paul Burns and a squad from First Company clubbed them to the ground. The townspeople were alarmed, probably less by the drunkenness than the violence of the ad hoc military police. Worried about public relations, Nelson assembled the battalion in the plaza and sentenced the hangdog nine to five days in the brig—a stone shed near the convent, built to house tools but more often used as a *pissoir*. The leader, a revolutionary of twenty years' standing, is said to have wept with shame.*

Early the next morning Nelson was awakened by a delegation of villagers, hats in hand. "More trouble," thought Nelson, wondering what his men had done now. But the village spokesman explained, with great courtesy: "We think you know better than we how to run the army . . . but we all felt sorry for the man who cried and the other men you put in jail. They were so long in the trenches and they did no harm to anybody. . . . And so, *señores,* in the name of the people of our village, we ask you, we beg you, not to be too hard on those

---

1. An Irish volunteer claimed that the date of departure was June 17, while a Finnish-American, whose notes are very precise says it was June 12, after 100 days.*

pobres."* Nelson released the prisoners at once, and a few days later the whole battalion turned out to help harvest the barley crop. (Lamed and blistered by cutting grain with short sickles, they wasted such prodigious amounts that the villagers had to beg the *señores* not to trouble themselves again with the menial chores of a poor *pueblo.*)

The straightest arrow into a Spanish heart lies through his *niños.* When Dr. William Pike removed a sliver of glass from the eye of a small boy whose father was too poor to pay for a Madrid specialist, Albares belonged to the men of the Lincoln Battalion.[2] Later Nelson held a fiesta for the townspeople in a poplar grove below the village. Doug Roach quickly won over the children with some old carnival acts. Hunching down under the belly of a burro he lifted it over his head to cries of the youngsters' *"¡Olé!"** This was a travel-poster interlude. "The clean air and the scent of sweet clover was all around us. I think in my old age I would not mind retiring there," wrote a veteran.*

For the first ten days the men did nothing—and they did it well. There were a few two-day passes to Madrid issued by Oliver Law, who took over as acting commander when Hourihan and Nelson went on leave. Law announced a special treat—General Gal had agreed to come to Albares to speak to them about the Jarama campaign and promised to answer questions after his speech. With great fanfare the general arrived with his heavy-leather bodyguard and met the men in the village church. The debacle of February 27 was paramount in everybody's mind. He explained that the attack had been carefully planned but failed because the Lincolns had not understood the importance of strict obedience to orders. They had failed to attack according to basic infantry tactics. In conclusion he promised that during their rest at Albares they would receive intensive drill in battlefield technique. When angry-looking men rose to ask questions, Law quickly closed the session, claiming "the lateness of the hour." As a consequence of the visit, Law instituted a training regimen consisting of useless practice in the manual of arms and close-order drill. There was also one hike of several kilometers in route formation with the men in gas masks.*

They filled in the rest of their weeks at Albares dozing during the heat of midday among sacks of flour at a mill in the valley. The women of the village sat in groups shaking the bright-orange stamens of the crocus flowers to harvest. There were communal shower baths from a special water truck, with collapsible

---

2. In 1967, when I visited Albares, a millworker affectionately recalled an American Negro—clearly Douglas Roach—who rode children on his back and whose pockets were always loaded with candy for them. "He was the kindest man I have ever known." When asked whether the Americans were good men or bad, a fellow worker replied, "They were all good men. There were no bad men in *el batallón Lincoln.*"

nozzles protruding from the tank like fragile legs of a gigantic insect. There was tooth pulling and filling by the brigade dentist, who had a lab mounted in the van of a Matford truck. This became a popular spectator sport, always drawing an appreciative crowd of villagers and soldiers alike. (The story is told that Ed Hodge, a Kentuckian, known as the laziest man in the battalion, had most of his teeth pulled when he fell asleep in the chair.) When Nelson returned from his leave, he arranged a series of intercompany baseball games (won by the seamen) and swimming contests (lost by the seamen). The British at neighboring Mondéjar had a surprise one evening when twenty peasants mounted on burros invaded the village, waved sickles—as political icons or tools of trade?—and challenged the *extranjeros* to a *fútbol* match. This opportunity for the Britons to shine in front of the local girls faded when the young Spaniards overwhelmed them within the opening minutes.

A draft of about a hundred fresh men came up from Tarazona, half of them Canadians, creating four companies instead of three.* Though word trickled down that a big Republican offensive was in the offing, it was too hot for much training. Besides, weren't they battle-seasoned vets? They closely followed the news from the States via the *Daily Worker*. Police had shot down unarmed strikers at Republic Steel in South Chicago. At Lansing a mob of reactionary students at Michigan State nearly drowned eight CIO organizers in Cedar Creek. Troops had to be marshaled in Youngstown to subdue strikers. Jean Harlow was dead, and in her obituary was this astonishing item—"For years she worked toward the unionization of the motion picture industry." The *Worker* continued to caricature public enemies like Franco, Hitler, Mussolini, Trotsky, and Henry V-8 (Henry Ford). At Albares there were the usual complaints about the exasperating virginity of the local sex goddesses, who never seemed to stir out-of-doors unless guarded by one or two chaperones. "It ain't Lolly's grandma bothers me," lamented an American. "I don't mind her taggin' along. Only I do wish they'd leave the goddam burro at home once in a while!"* Once there was a dance in the village square with the brigade propaganda truck playing American records, but "the girls always kept a few inches apart."* The only man who had any luck with the village girls was Ray Steele, the clubfooted machine gunner, who looked like a Teutonic warrior out of Wagner. He made great progress and became "engaged" to a local beauty from the neighboring village of Almoguerra.*

When Hourihan moved up as Cunningham's regimental adjutant, Oliver Law took command of the Lincolns. This was a major coup for Party propagandists, who proclaimed that he was the first black in American history to command a predominantly white battalion. Fred Copeman, the British commander, expressed surprise at "a bloodie darkie in charge of a Yankee Battalion.

I didn't think they had any time with them."* Although many Lincolns, recalling his near court-martial at Jarama on a charge of incompetence shuddered at the prospect of being led into battle by Law, they kept their mouths shut. To object would be interpreted as blatant racism. Since Jews numbered about fifty percent among the Americans, no one wanted to insert a racist card in the deck. They had enough problems without that.[3]

Oliver Law was born on a Texas cotton farm, circa 1904. The official line held that he had served in the U.S. Army for six years and after the World War made his way to Chicago. He was a man of many parts—meat packer, a failed café-owner, slumlord, and militant in the black movement of the South Side. The reasons for his rise to prominence in the Party are unaccountable, apart from the campaign to recruit leadership among the black population. (Even Steve Nelson admitted, long after the war, that the choice of Law resulted from the Party's need to recruit within the black population.)* "Why Law?" Jarama veterans asked. If the Party insisted upon a black commander, there were several better candidates at hand. "Law was not a Negro as I thought of Negroes," recalled a New York furrier, a close friend of Doug Roach. "Law was an illiterate, southern darkie. The kind you picture with a watermelon." Thirty years later Oscar Hunter, a black volunteer, said of Law—"A tragic character. I took him over there; over there he took me over. The guys running the battalion made him a figurehead."* Although the "official history" of the Lincoln Battalion credits Law's machine gun with fine work during the February 27 attack, this has been disputed by some survivors. In response to my question, Hourihan, a man always reluctant to criticize fellow veterans, flatly denied that any machine gun assisted them on that morning "and most certainly not Law's."* Another survivor reported that when he crawled back late at night to bring food up to the line he found Law in the cookhouse, where he and others were hiding behind gigantic wine vats.*

3. At least eighty-three American blacks served in the International Brigades and about twenty were killed.* Antagonism toward Oliver Law resulted from doubts about him as a person and as a leader, not from his race. In all fairness, it must be emphasized that the American battalions in Spain were decades ahead of comparable units of the U.S. Army in matters of racial tolerance.

Spasms of anti-Semitism and racism flared up occasionally in the British Battalion, which had no blacks at all and only a minuscule number of Jews. A Briton who used the word "Yid" went to trial, where the issue was resolved with an apology. Among the British, snobbism was a greater problem because the upper-crust accent was anathema to most men of the working classes. Furthermore, chauvinism surfaced when Americans began to outnumber the British and to dominate command appointments in the brigade. For example, Malcolm Dunbar, an outstanding English officer from an upper-class background, held John Gates, a respected American commissar, in contempt not because of leadership failures but because he "couldn't stand this tailor Jewish boy from New York."*

Even though Law was a hapless victim, a puppet manipulated on strings being pulled by puppeteers elsewhere, authority did not sit gracefully on his shoulders. He seemed to have, remembered another veteran, "this big chip on his shoulder that he was daring you to knock off." Yet whenever a newsman appeared in the neighborhood, Law was trotted out to deliver a set speech: "We are here to show that Negroes know how to fight Fascists" or "The Spanish people have the same aim as the Negro people—we are both fighting for our national independence."*

The summer idyll of the Lincoln Battalion ended on the evening of July 1, when a dispatch rider brought orders for the battalion to stand by. At four in the morning a bugler assembled them in the village square to board the trucks. They waited all day beside their equipment because Law, fearing drunks out of control, refused to allow them to leave the square. This afforded plenty of time for the familiar chant: "The Goddamn XVth Brigade—can't it do *anything* right?" They sat in the square till eight in the morning of the following day when the trucks finally arrived and Albares said good-bye to its *americanos del norte.* . . . The first major offensive of the Republican Army was on.

Wheeling its army around Madrid on a wide arc to the north and west, the Republican command concentrated fifty thousand men out of sight in the pine barrens and craggy foothills of the Guadarrama Mountains, fifteen miles east of the city. The offensive called for a surprise thrust southward through the lightly garrisoned Guadarrama valley to the village of Brunete, a major crossroads eight miles from the jumping-off point, to be followed by a swing to the southeast to seize the Estremadura highway, which supplied the Nationalist armies at the southern edge of Madrid. Communist cadres of the Republican Army, along with four of the five International Brigades, had been assigned the major roles in the offensive and promised to benefit enormously in prestige if the offensive suc-ceeded.[4] Concomitant with this, another force from Madrid would fall upon the rear of the Nationalists retreating from Madrid, and then fusing with the Brunete valley force would trap the enemy in gigantic pincers. The offensive had a twofold purpose: to force the enemy to lift its siege of the capital, and to divert troops from Franco's ongoing campaign in the industry-rich Basque Country.

While the Republic had proved its tenacity in defense, it had never initiated a successful offensive against a major Nationalist army. Just two months before,

---

4. Prime Minister Largo Caballero (Socialist) favored an offensive in Estremadura, which was weakly held by the enemy, in order to cut Nationalist Spain in two. For obscure reasons, the Soviet military mission refused artillery, tank, and aircraft support for this offensive, without which it could not hope to succeed.

it had botched a poorly planned and miserably executed attack across the Guadarrama Mountains toward Segovia, which had been repulsed with horrendous losses, including decimation of the XIVth (French) Brigade.[5] The new plan counted upon surprise and rapidity of movement to break the enemy positions. If these were lost, there would be jarring counterattacks by a desperate enemy bottled up in its narrow salient south of Madrid. The specific assignment of General Gal's newly created 15th Division, which included the XIIIth (Slavic) and XVth brigades, was to descend into the Guadarrama valley, seize the village of Villanueva de la Cañada, and then, veering east, secure Romanillas Heights (better known as Mosquito Ridge). Because this ridge commanded the entire Guadarrama valley, a failure to seize and fortify it would mean that the enemy could blanket the valley floor with artillery fire.

The Republican troops moved to their attack positions in high spirits. To avoid observation, they filed at night through the deep ilex forests of El Pardo, once the hunting lodge of the Bourbon kings (and in later years the private seat of General Franco), and climbed the Guadarrama foothills. Revolutionary songs surged back and forth along a ten-mile stream of men toiling toward the mountains. And at night sometimes a thousand men, representing thirty nationalities, would sit listening to the folk songs of a dozen Welsh miners.* Truckers drove with blue headlights to avoid revealing a mass movement of vehicles. Ignoring the prohibition, some Anarchist drivers kept lights on full and refused to cut them off until the British commander passed down the line of trucks shooting out the bulbs.* Yet by dawn this immense body of men and machines lay hidden and invisible to enemy observation planes. Several times the Nationalists had spotted dust on the El Escorial road, but they assumed it came from nothing more than reinforcements for mountain garrisons. The offensive took them by surprise.

The assembly point for the Anglo-American regiment was the five-kilometer stone, eight miles south of Torrelodones. Because guides lost their way and the roads were logjammed with men and vehicles, all battalions arrived late after exhausting night marches through woody hill country in total darkness The Washingtons, who reached the site first, eagerly awaited their first official encounter with the famous Lincolns, who straggled in two days later. Copic reported there had been "chaos on the road," climaxed by hours at Loeches, when stalled traffic could move neither forward nor backward.* One American truck was lost en route, and the driver of another (Harry Saksonsky) was killed

5. This offensive subsequently became the setting for Ernest Hemingway's *For Whom the Bell Tolls*, which enraged the militant Left for its portrait of André Marty as paranoid incompetent.

in a collision. The Lincolns arrived exhausted and bitter—seventy men crowded into each truck. Drivers complained that officers had been their biggest problem because they had insisted on riding in the cabs, which had room for only one passenger.*

Lieutenant Phil Detro of the Washingtons (a future Lincoln commander) recalled how they reacted to the news that the Lincolns were coming in. "[We] all ran out to the road to get a glimpse of these much-sung heroes we had heard and read so much about." It was a letdown. "[We] found a group of men tired, war weary, disgusted, sullen, who were grumbling about everything: 'Why do we have to walk with so many trucks on the road—everybody else is riding but we have to walk, etc."* The Washingtons had expected to be awed by seasoned Jarama soldiers, not this seedy bunch of petty complainers. By contrast, one newcomer remembered that waiting for the order to go into battle was "like waiting for Christmas." Christmas it was not, but it was the Fourth of July, which they celebrated with a double ration of Hershey bars and packs of Lucky Strikes sent by the FALB. Fireworks were strictly forbidden, and the promised beer failed to arrive. (The International Brigades ignored the American holiday, although in New York Earl Browder used the occasion to deliver a speech "Communism Is the Americanism of the 20th Century.")*

After an all-night march they camped near Valdemorillo at an Edenic mountaintop *finca*, the agricultural toy of some absentee "Fascists"—or at least capitalists. A swimming pool, filled with green slime, lay next to an ancient chicken house. Among the pines and junipers, Jarama vets, haunted by their agoraphobia and obsessed with defense, carefully stacked up field stones as protective shields beside their blanket rolls, a practice that mystified the Washingtons. The afternoon was blazing hot, but the night was crisp and clear, cooled by winds from the mountains. It was like sleeping in an observatory. They nicknamed this farm "The Pearly Gates." Bob Taylor of Detroit thought he sniffed gin somewhere, but it proved to be only trampled juniper.*

Battle orders arrived at 2:30 a.m. on July 6. Captain Law's hands shook as he passed the note to Steve Nelson.* Within half an hour the two American battalions were moving downhill to their takeoff points—knolls overlooking the Brunete valley floor. In this straggling, dust-blinding march, the Lincolns lost an hour. As soon as the sky lightened, Republican artillery split the profound mountain silence and the echoes of explosions reverberated from the valley floor.

For their first hour, the Americans were only spectators in the battle, which was spread out below them like a model on a tabletop. "It was like a day at the cinema."* Major Nathan, chief of operations, lifted his cane and saluted Steve Nelson, "Steve, old boy. Our chaps stop here for a bit. Have a look down below.

Pretty sight, eh?"* To the south the full length of the Guadarrama valley lay open in prismatic clarity. Tanks wallowed across the flattish, treeless plain ahead of dark specks marking the first wave of infantry. Four miles south lay a white village, Villanueva de la Cañada, threaded by the arrow-straight road to Brunete, four miles farther south. Paralleling this black ribbon of macadam, three miles farther east, ran the Guadarrama River and on the far hilltop Mosquito Ridge, flecked with trees. Republican airplanes were unloading bombs upon the garrisoned enemy villages. Farther to the southwest, greasy black smoke billowed up from a knocked-out munitions dump at Quijorna. The mounting sun quenched the mountain breeze. A searing furnace heat rose from the valley floor. Even before descending to the plain, they had emptied their canteens.

Even as they watched the developing battle, things began to go wrong. The tanks and infantry surrounding Villanueva failed to take it. Inexplicably they collected together like filings at a magnet and veered off to the east. The original orders had spelled out that the XVth Brigade would not move to the valley floor until Villanueva had fallen. Now General Gal had to countermand it. Instead of proceeding directly to Mosquito Ridge, the brigade had to assist in securing the town, the major supply artery for the campaign. The Dimitrovs plunged down the long slope to the sun-scorched plain, followed by the Washingtons and the British. Held in reserve, the Lincolns had a short reprieve.*

The valley, which from above had seemed undulating with wheat fields, turned out to be pimpled with hillocks and gouged by *barrancas,* rain-water gullies. Although there was better cover than anyone had expected, the broken topography encouraged men to disperse. Watercourses marked in blue lines on charts were bone-dry. Already men suffered from thirst, and water tanks failed to come up from the rear. ("Guadarrama" is an Arabic word meaning "river of sand"—an obscure etymological point unfortunately overlooked or ignored.) Men were passing out with heat exhaustion even before they came within bullet range of Villanueva, their trail littered with throwaways—blankets, gas masks, musette bags, and food tins. The village lay on the crest of a slight slope, and the houses were so low that machine gunners in the church tower had a wonderful 360-degree field of fire.[6] Four hundred yards out, as the XVth Brigade advanced through knee-high wheat, these gunners stopped the attack cold and forced

---

6. According to Robert Gladnick, at that time a technician in the Fifth (Soviet) Tank Battalion, there was also a German officer with a 37 mm antitank gun in the tower. This gun knocked out more than a dozen Soviet tanks and deflected the initial attack. After the battle, Gladnick found the German officer being interrogated and asked whether he would be shot. The Soviet colonel said, "That Fritz is going to the Soviet Union ahead of me. He will teach us all about German antitank tactics, and after that we will exchange him for some of our men that Franco has."*

those in the advance to use their helmets to rake out burrows in ground "so hard you couldn't make a dent in it." The Americans bunched up in a *barranca* forty feet wide. This haven of safety became packed with Americans who refused to move forward. Some British stragglers joined them until Captain Copeman, with curses and fists, herded them back into the main body, which moved cross-country to block a possible escape route to the south, along the Brunete road.* In the open, they were spotted by machine gunners in the village tower who easily picked off twenty Britons in ten minutes. The men had to dig in—or failing that, to remain immobile—and wait for dusk. They could not equalize the fire against them because their machine-gun company with the heavy Maxims had lagged far behind in the logjam of men and vehicles. Not that it would have mattered. In the hundred-degree heat, without adequate water supply, the barrels of the Maxims would have burned out after firing a few rounds. The only water in the battalion came from two Britons who crawled back and forth to a creek bed with what they could carry in their gas-mask tins.* The fields of dry grass and wheat stubble caught on fire, raising greater fears for disabled men. Since the attack had stalled, Copic ordered the Lincoln into the valley. Law led his men into a protective *barranca*, which appeared to lead toward the town, but eventually veered off and ended in a shallow ditch. Here they halted, lacking good cover, unable to move forward or backward. When "Pappy" Toplianos arrived and prepared to pull back a wounded man, Law forbade it. "You'll get killed and expose us."*

Shortly after noon, Hourihan came down with orders for the Anglo-American commanders to rush the town. He learned that Law had failed to reconnoiter the terrain in front, and now his men were trapped in their hole, bewildered and angry.[7] According to one Lincoln officer, their commander was crouching on the ground in fear. "Law was cowardly at Brunete. He was completely inexperienced."* Hourihan denounced Law in front of the men and ordered him to report to Brigade.[8] Then he personally led the Lincoln vanguard out of the cul-de-sac to an assault position west of town. Here slugs from the church tower dropped him with a smashed thigh bone. While he was being carried away on a stretcher, other bullets "grazed his ear, his prick and nuts."*

7. As it happened, the Nationalists had fortified Villanueva in May and were worried that this ravine might be used in attacking the village. Among the work detail attempting to fortify the ravine was Frank Thomas, an Englishman serving in the Spanish Foreign Legion, who reported that the task was beyond the resources of the engineers and had to be abandoned. Defense of the village had to depend on an antitank gun and machine guns in the church tower.

8. In an autobiography Hourihan prepared for the XVth Brigade records, he referred to himself in third person: "He was wounded on the first day of the Brunete offensive when stepping out of his role as Brigade staff officer he led the Lincoln battalion into attack."*

Thus ended his military service in Spain (and left him a cripple for life). Since Vincent Usera, Law's adjutant, had mysteriously vanished, Steve Nelson took command of the Lincolns, which by this time had broken up into small pockets firing sporadically from the *barrancas*. From somewhere off to the east came reports from the metronomic firing of the Thaelmann Battalion—a "load-aim-fire" pattern like a Guards Regiment at Waterloo.

Valuable time was lost, and the XVth Brigade foundered in a frustrating eddy of the battle, the main currents having swept past Villanueva hours ago. From his hilltop perch Copic reported to Division that artillery fire was missing concrete pillboxes altogether and only playing havoc with the houses, but General Gal denied this. The lethal church tower remained as a monument to Gal's stubbornness. Nelson resolved to sit tight and clean out the enemy garrison in the morning. The men had no water, no food, and were running out of ammunition. The dust and glare had reduced their eyes to powdered slits.

It was nearly sundown when runners from Brigade again demanded that Villanueva be stormed immediately. Battalion commanders were blamed for disrupting the timetable of the offensive—an unreasonable buck-passing since the original plan called for no activity whatever by the XVth Brigade at the village. "What the hell!" exclaimed Nelson's assistant when he read the order. "We're doing all right. We'll get into a mess if we try anything. The guys are tired."* But Nelson gamely readied Paul Burns's First Company. Heavy firing and anti-Fascist yells broke out on the opposite side of town. It was the Dimitrovs—who "never go back," wrote an awed Briton,* assisted by a fresh Spanish brigade, who bored into the village. The enemy garrison fled into private houses, while the attackers converged so rapidly that they briefly exchanged shots in the darkening alleys near the main square. Prodded by this stimulus, a few Americans pressed through wisps of barbed wire and over the sandbags of the Nationalist front line, although Paul Wendorf, a reliable eyewitness, wrote that most of them slept all night outside and did not enter until morning.*

Squeezed from the town center, a band of Falangists of the Bandera of Faith seized a dozen villagers as hostages and pressed down the Brunete road in the gloaming. A hundred yards outside town they ran head-on into the British Battalion coming up from the south. Mistaking them for civilians, a Briton commanded them to halt. Seconds later he was killed by a grenade. Then, as the screaming hostages scattered into the fields, the Falangists fired machine guns into clusters of the British. For ten minutes the firing was ferocious in the growing darkness, until the Falangists had been wiped out to a man. Several women were killed when bullets detonated impact grenades carried by the enemy. A British company commander leaned down to help a wounded Falangist, who shot him through the heart. The surprise attack from behind the skirts of women, combined with the loss of a popular comrade, enraged the British. They swarmed into Villanueva, now garishly lit by burning buildings and red explosions, slaughtering those sweepings of the enemy holed up in hayricks and cattle sheds. Fearing a cold-blooded massacre, Captain Fred Copeman ordered his men out of town and allowed other battalions to clear out the enemy pockets. They had moved so rapidly that they nearly collided with the Dimitrovs, who entered from the other end and had to be identified by their anti-Fascist shouts. They silenced the guns in the church tower by tossing in straw and setting it on fire. The Fascist machine gunners died screaming.*

By sunup on July 7, Villanueva was a gutted, silent husk. The Americans were exhausted but for the first time in Spain they had participated in a successful assault of an entrenched enemy. They dozed in shady corners, munched red-pepper sausages captured from enemy stores, and peeked through crannies in the barns on the edge of town where the prisoners had been penned overnight. The prisoners were disappointing: nothing at all like the Fascists depicted in *Daily Worker* cartoons, only wretched creatures—unkempt, dirty, terribly frightened. They crouched in corners expecting to be shot, as their officers had warned them. When interrogated, all eagerly insisted they were ardent Communists. By midmorning, contradictory orders came down from Brigade: hold the village until relieved—march south to join the major attack near Brunete—move southeast to Mosquito Ridge, a strategic high point in the sector. Only later did the men learn that Brigade was feuding with Division about the balls-up of the day before. General Gal was blaming Jock Cunningham, the military commander of the XVth, for the delay—or to put it more accurately, Gal was blaming Copic who passed the blame on to Cunningham. By the time the XVth Brigade finally got under way, it was early afternoon.

The offensive was already doomed, although no one knew it at the time. On the day before, Frank Graham, a British scout for Cunningham, mounted on a scrounged horse, had ridden to the summit of Mosquito Ridge and found the place unoccupied.* But since then the Nationalists had emplaced artillery batteries behind the ridge and had begun to shell the village. Mosquito Ridge was becoming a fortress.

The men pushed eastward toward the Guadarrama River, three miles away, crossing open country where they were visible at great distances. Troops of cavalry ranged the wheat fields to their rear, prodding stragglers forward. Out in front the Washington Battalion marched in a tight parade-ground formation, despite warnings from Lincoln vets that they should disperse. Four heavy bombers—identified later as Italian Capronis—swooped over and drew a few rifle shots from the groundlings. A great mistake—for without the shots the pilots might have mistaken them for friendlies. They banked, roared back, and unloaded. While Markovicz and staff puzzled over a map, men were opening food tins or relieving themselves beside the road. A nearby Briton recorded what he saw: "We looked across at the Washington Battalion. Suddenly there was a bang and a huge pile of smoke and there were only thirty-two of them left. They were massacred in seconds."*⁹ Seeing that the Americans were entirely exposed and arrow-looking things were coming down, Captain Copeman of the British Battalion thought "God help them!" just before ground-shuddering explosions. "We passed on, making our way between huge craters, round the edges of which the bodies of dozens of Americans were still smoldering. They had turned a curious black."* After this initiation into air power, the Washingtons went to the opposite extreme, fanning out and losing contact with each other. "We were just individuals running wildly without orders."*

At the end of the second day of the offensive, the XVth Brigade had failed to reach the river. After the blockage at Villanueva had been cleared, so many different units had poured through the gap that the entire chain of command had become snarled. That night, strays from the Franco-Belge Battalion plundered the Anglo-American camps: "Hell of a row like a football match. They fired rifles, lit lights and pinched our stuff."*

In the morning of July 8, tanks came up unannounced and led the Americans down a steep slope to the river. (A Detroiter remembered his fear of being run over by a tank that clanked a few feet behind him at full throttle.)* With "blood-curdling yells," the men splashed across the Guadarrama River—at three feet deep only a "crick" for the Western guys—and pushed through the canebrake and poplars on the far bank. "A lovely spot for a picnic," recorded a volunteer. "Tree-lined river, cool waters, shady trees, rolling hills all around."* Another was moved artistically by the sight of "three soldiers plastered against the embankment, profiled in bas-relief like a Greek frieze."*

About a mile and a half ahead lay the long summit of Mosquito Ridge. The terrain ahead went up "like a Goddamn roller-coaster."* It warped through scattered ilex trees, looking exactly like what it was—the private hunting preserve of the duke of Alba. Pheasants whirred from the undergrowth, and frightened rabbits bobbed ahead of them. "The first hundred yards was like a jolly affair,"* and how encouraging to turn over dead enemy officers and see gaping wounds in their backs.* Near Casa de Mange, a white farmhouse, four cows grazed quietly, oblivious to all the commotion until they tumbled over with

9. Thirty-two left of an uncounted group—not of the entire Washington Battalion.

their legs up. "It was tragic to see poor innocent beasts killed like that," lamented a Briton.*

Invisible snipers infested the parklike enclosure and fired a few rounds to slow the advance before melting to the rear. With the enemy at last in sight, the Americans behaved more like hunters than soldiers. Instead of sweeping around these ambuscades, they poured out of canebrakes, in the path of the tanks shouting, "Fascists! Let's get 'em!" A group of Americans flushed some Nationalists from their cover and sent them dashing up the hill. "It was a fox hunt," recalled a veteran.* The enemy dropped their rifles, mess kits, and blankets. While some Americans steadied their *Mexicanskis* on one knee for potshots, others shouted "¡*Adelante!*" and raced after them. This was how Fascists were supposed to behave in battle. But the retreat was deliberate, not headlong. Wallace Burton, said to be a veteran of the French Foreign Legion, explained that those mysterious white cloths hanging on tree branches were range markers—indispensable information for machine gunners and mortar men preparing a surprise.*

On all sides the slope was flecked with figures running or crawling. Other than upward, it was impossible to know where to go. "Confusion—didn't know just what orders were," an anonymous American jotted in his diary.* Harold Smith, a Washington section leader, hesitated when out of nowhere came Markowicz waving a big machine pistol around his head and cursing him for stopping. "I tried to explain and asked for orders, and all he did was wave that pistol round his head and yell, 'On to Madrid.' Anyway he pointed in a general direction. So I waved my pistol around my head and yelled 'Adelante' and all the guys followed."* The lucky ones found a *barranca* that offered cover until several hundred yards from the crest.

Avoiding heavy fire by picking dead ground, they worked up the hill and joined Lieutenant Philip Detro, a lanky company commander from Texas, who was digging in around the roots of a big ilex tree several hundred yards from Mosquito. Here and there, soldiers were snailing up toward "that big black hill."[10] The attack, said a survivor, was "chaotic"—pitting human will and bone against a mesh barrier of shrapnel and lead. "It was terrible up there," he remembered. "I had all the fear symptoms—palpitations of the heart, bulged eyes, and pissed pants."* This was the high-water mark—literally—of the Americans at Brunete. Detro ordered his men to fire at the ridge with rifles and a

---

10. Suburbia is rapidly encroaching on Mesquite Ridge, which in 2000 was the site of a transmission antenna. The Americans had to approach it across open ground and through scattered ilex trees and would have been visible for miles. Today the top is scarred with trench lines. By contrast, the ridge to the west shows no signs of the former battle and suggests that the Americans might have been able to envelop and flank the Nationalist position.

pan-fed Dichterev machine gun. To advance farther would be tantamount to collective suicide. He sent Smith back to Markovicz for instructions. Markovicz, who was trying to collect his scattered ranks, said Detro should hold on until the tanks came up. "Until the tanks came up"—that phrase was always good for a sardonic laugh. Meanwhile, eight of the fifteen Americans under the brow of Mosquito Hill had been killed. Most of the others were dead or dying, including two brothers, Joe and Sam Stone. Evacuation of the wounded was out of the question—too many and under fire, which was getting heavier by the minute.

The first Russian tank to pop over a hillock at their rear exploded from a direct hit by an antitank gun. Troops bunched up in *barrancas* a few hundred yards from the crest watched tanks fire off their stock of 45 mm shells before scuttling to the rear. The infantry had outrun their lines of communication and supply long ago. Officers had difficulty positioning themselves on their charts—one *barranca* was like any other, and few were charted. Even the hospital tents lay two or three miles to the rear, which meant that many "light" wounds proved fatal. The heat was suffocating—as though oxygen had been sucked from the air. By late afternoon men dispatched to the river with empty canteens found it bone-dry. For a day or so one could dig a hole in the riverbed to draw a pool of dirty water, but even this source quickly dried up. They had no water for the water-cooled Maxims so men under fire had to crouch down and urinate in the tank, one penis at a time. "All hell would be breaking over your head and you'd be afraid to pull it out in case it got shot off."* Orders came from Division to seize Mosquito "at all costs." Through the night the Republican commanders worked to collect their splintered units in order to make a final attack in the morning. Meanwhile, the Nationalists threw every spare man into the trenches being scraped out along the ridge.

The morning of July 9 dawned hotter than any before. Taking advantage of the deep gulches winding upward, troops farther down the slope inched forward. Somehow Oliver Law was back in command of the Lincolns, although Captain Van den Berghe, their reliable mentor from Jarama days, had been assigned to help him. Twice the Belgian warned Law about likely spots for ambush, but each time Law ordered squads forward and saw them cut to pieces. Men began to lag behind or fan out to the flanks. The woods provided opportunities for lagging behind to avoid combat. (Captain Fred Copeman later estimated that the British lost a hundred men in this fashion, and doubtless the figures for the other battalions, if known, would have been comparable.) Yet bands of stalwarts fought up toward Mosquito Ridge at a rate of a few yards per hour. Battalion and company cohesion disappeared. Mosquito Ridge came under piecemeal attack by armed bands of brave or ignorant men who lacked proper briefing, preparation, support.

After advancing perhaps a hundred yards, Oliver Law's group ran into another ambush. There was a rattle of gunfire on all sides. Law, about twenty yards ahead of the group, shouted, "We got them on the run. We can chase them off that hill."* Neil Wesson of Detroit, who was spotting targets for a machine gunner, described what happened next: "We were looking for an enemy M.G. who was hitting us and the gunner yelled to Law who had binoculars, to see if he could spot the S.O.B. Law, who was lying on his stomach, got to this knees to see better and found the S.O.B. Just as he pointed for us the enemy slugs got him and he slumped down. We found the S.O.B. and got him. Then when we turned around somebody had Law and they were moving him."* Law went down with a bullet in the belly. He died within a few hours. There are two irreconcilable accounts of what followed, one that claims he was shot by one of his men, disturbed by his poor leadership—Law had already led his men into several ambushes—and the other in complete denial of this. Because both versions have been sworn to, "the truth" depends on whom one prefers to believe.[11] In so much of Spanish civil war history, truth took second place to politics.

For four more days the XVth Brigade held to its line scratched out below Mosquito Ridge. With each passing hour the Nationalists became stronger. Mortars stalked the *barrancas* with fearsome accuracy; high-velocity shells tumbled ilex trees on top of men dug in among the roots. Enemy pilots in light planes—The Messerschmitt 109 made its debut in battle—flew with impunity above them and unloaded boxes of grenades upon clusters of men in the woods. "Their planes were coming over so low you could almost see the pilot's eyes." The XVth Brigade had no antiaircraft guns, so as the planes flew leisurely figure-eights above them, men lay on their backs in the open and fired at them with rifles. "It was ridiculous."* Casualties from these makeshift bombs were low—what mattered was the terror of being helpless. Major casualties came from overwhelming machine-gun fire. At night, Moors above them barked and howled like jackals. It was chilling, like songs of death. An American group calling themselves "the Convulsionaries" went through its repertoire of noisier songs to block the yelping above them.

Even with the front strangled, Gal continued to send up attack orders like a lunatic pushing toy soldiers in a sandbox. Repeatedly he promised joint operations with tanks, but invariably the tanks were late, or did not appear at all, much to

11. Interestingly, Law garners only half a sentence in Rolfe's "official" history of 1939—an erroneous "Oliver Law was killed in the attack on Villanueva de la Cañada," which does not mention his race. Not so in Carroll's "official" history fifty-five years later, *The Odyssey of the Abraham Lincoln Brigade,* where Oliver Law occupies five pages of text along with seven more footnotes. The reasons for this surge in prominence needs no commentary from me.

the relief of the infantry. Even when tanks came up, they refused to advance, well aware of the potency and accuracy of the antitank guns on Mosquito. In his frustration Colonel Copic tried to stop a tank from turning back by threatening to shoot the officer, but with hatches slammed shut, the tank waddled off to the rear.

Hounded by Corps, Gal sent down plans for a do-or-die assault on July 11. Artillery and aerial bombers would pound the summit at 1100, and the XVth Brigade, supported by the XVIth Brigade (Spanish), would rush to the top. Fortunately for the men involved, the order did not reach brigade headquarters until 1140, requiring cancellation. Undeterred, Gal changed the time of attack to 1230. Completely fed up with Gal's barrage of impossible commands, Markovicz sent him a note: "The situation of the battalion is difficult. Impossible to advance. Field without cover and covered by Fascist fire. We lack means to fortify. We cannot carry munitions or water. A danger that the enemy will shift to the offensive, in the right wing, in front of us. This can happen at any time and I am unable with my force to do much about it."*

Gal changed the time to 1630, with the Dimitrovs as spear point. The tanks arrived on schedule but did not fan out for a strike, and the Dimitrovs stayed within their perimeter. "The tanks have much fear of advancing and the men also," Copic wrote in his operations diary.

The offensive had failed, and the Republicans desperately scratched out defensive lines. Gal ordered his division to begin fortifying strong points under Mosquito. He blamed the failure on "insufficient activity of the command"—that is to say, on others, not himself. Although ordered to dig, the men were too exhausted after four nights without sleep. When a volunteer exclaimed, "We are just digging our own graves," the others were too weary to do anything but curse him.*

Beneath the crest of Mosquito the men had no thought of victory, for the terrain ahead of and behind them was raked by snipers, machine guns, and aviation. They worried because relief parties trying to bring up sacks of food and ammunition were annihilated as they came down an exposed hillside. "[We] could see them coming down the hillside, like flies on a wall, and laid bets on whether they could get through."* Water was foul, and diarrhea so bad that men slit their trousers to save time.

As the tide of battle turned, the enemy responded immediately with counterattacks. Nelson, worried about an armored attack, brought up two antitank guns and concealed them from observation planes. Their commander was Lieutenant Malcolm Dunbar, reputedly an English squire from Trinity College, Cambridge. (Actually he was a Scotsman from the University of London.) Dunbar was a strikingly handsome officer, with great sense of style, but the

American officers never knew what to make of him, because he never revealed his political opinions and was once overheard talking with his adjutant about Socratic dialogues.* He watched coolly as eight tanks and a battalion of Moors came down Mosquito Ridge. He held his fire until the tanks came within five hundred yards. Seconds after his command, the lead tank burst into flame, and the second revolved like a paralyzed insect. The others scurried back up the hill. The Moors came on, bounding downhill with fantastically long strides. Ray Steele, the head Lincoln machine gunner shouted, "Give 'em twenty-five more yards. Keep your shirts on." When they were a hundred yards off, Steele's Maxim opened with his trademark, a clattering "shave-and-a-haircut, two-bits." The other Mooney guns joined and halted the Moors on a red dime. Given an open field, Maxims had an incredible killing power. (At Jarama an English gunner turned his gun over to his assistant because he could no longer endure seeing the havoc it wrought upon ranks of attacking Moors.) In the melee Dunbar went down with a wound and left for the hospital. Always the cool Hollywood Englishman, he sat smoking a cigarette in a long holder while having his wound dressed.

When telephone lines opened, Colonel Klaus reported to Nelson that Vincent Usera was at brigade headquarters saying that the Lincolns had been smashed and asking for reinforcements. "We're not in a safe position," Usera said. "No frontline position is safe!" Nelson bellowed. "You get the hell back here!" On his return, "cheery and crisp" Usera coolly said he was ready to command the Lincolns, but the men were not having it. Usera tried to take charge. "You'd be a helluva guy to give orders. We haven't seen you the whole fucking day!" exclaimed Carl Bradley of the staff. Usera drew himself up, "Am I not the adjutant of the battalion?" "No, you're not," broke in Nelson. "Report to Brigade. Leave your pistol here." After writing a note declaring he was at their disposal, Usera gave a smart parade-ground salute and faded away.* (Sent back to Tarazona, he resumed his duties as Number Two Training Officer—with continued plaudits for his efficiency—and eventually returned to the States. Miraculously, he escaped prison and execution.)[12]

As though Nelson had not had enough problems, Harry Haywood pushed into his command post and accused Colonel Cunningham and Major Nathan

---

12. During World War II, Usera attained the rank of major in the U.S. Army and was decorated for service in Europe. Two IB vets encountered him in later years. According to Milton Wolff, the last Lincoln commander, Usera told him that he had been sent to Spain by the U.S. Army to observe and report.* Even forty years after the war in Spain, Nelson and others of the Party hierarchy racked their brains trying to find out why Usera had come to Spain. (VALB folklore sometimes elevated him to the rank of general in World War II.)

of conspiracy and discrimination.* It all began with Nathan's behavior a few days before. As he passed Haywood on a march, he "snarled out of the side of his mouth, 'You'll get yours!'" Haywood asked for an explanation, but the major moved on without looking back.* Later that day Colonel Cunningham unfolded a "military [topographical] map" and asked if he could read it. When Haywood admitted that he could not, Cunningham abruptly folded it up and turned away in disgust, "apparently having confirmed some derogatory judgment of me." The last straw had just occurred. Haywood had spent the night trying to relocate some rolling kitchens, and when he returned to the regimental command post, it had been buffeted by a devastating barrage. Dead bodies blocked the dugout entrance, and men jammed the interior. Cunningham was yelling something on the phone. When he hung up, he shouted to Haywood, "Where the hell have you been?" "Rounding up the kitchens; you knew that," Haywood replied. "Fuck the kitchens!" came the retort, "You should have been here!" When Haywood protested, Jock unleashed his crowning insult, "Aw, fuck off. You're no good anyway. You're scared now." Haywood lunged at the colonel but was restrained and told to carry his problem to Brigade. Useless advice, because he had already complained to Copic, whom he believed (with probable cause) had spread poison among the staff. (In his diary Copic wrote only that Haywood had been "drunk and grumbled he had been offended.") He then descended the food chain to Nelson, who was expected to ignore the battle raging around them in order to settle a private feud. Ever respectful toward a member of the American Politburo, he suggested that Haywood withdraw from the brigade and seek satisfaction at a less critical time. After a few weeks visiting Americans in the hospital, Haywood sailed for home at the request of Earl Browder, secretary-general of the CPUSA. Browder arranged for his removal from the Politburo, and in a report to Moscow assessed his role in Spain as "exceedingly bad, characterized by factionalism, drunkenness, and irresponsibility," adding that he had not been disciplined because he was a Negro.* Before leaving Madrid, Haywood did join Langston Hughes and other blacks in a "Negro Peoples' Broadcast" to the United States but he was so drunk and incoherent that Edwin Rolfe, the director, had to write his speech (and never forgot his encounter with "an idiot, a degenerate, lazy, ostentatious bastard").*

Fighting, or even moving, in the heat of the day under a broiling sun became a torment none ever forgot. The sun was so intense that it caused a kind of snow blindness in which the color of objects was molten white. The dry grass crinkled under foot. Trees turned into dust balls. Down at the riverbed, long dry, water details dug desperately. At a depth of ten feet enough water seeped through the sand to form a shallow pool, but it tasted like uncooked chowder of rotten fish. In one such waterhole stood a corpse. A Detroit volunteer remembered, "We drank the slime at the bottom of the hole without dragging out the stiff—we never even thought about dragging it out."* Dr. Harold Robbins, in saner times a Hollywood physician, filled a gasoline truck with disinfected well water. Fearing another outfit might hijack the precious liquid, he drove it to the front himself. On the way an enemy plane dropped a bomb that blew out the rear end of the vehicle. The water poured out upon the ground and disappeared like a drop of ink on a blotter. Dr. Robbins lay slumped over the steering wheel, dead of a concussion without a mark on his body.* The most dependable source of water came in the horse-drawn wagon of Joseph May, at sixty-three the oldest British volunteer, who guarded every precious drop like a junkyard dog. He had no awe of rank or its privileges. Once when he caught Colonel Copic urinating near his wagon, he shouted, "You dirty basket! How dare you? Don't you know better?" Facing this outraged Cockney, whose great bald head was italicized with a handlebar moustache, Copic apologized.*

Conditions among the British worsened. They had been ordered to lead the column and to occupy the southernmost flank in the Mosquito Ridge attack. Without artillery support and too remote to be adequately supplied, they took such a buffeting that only 185 men of the 600 who went into battle remained. Captain Fred Copeman, usually sturdy as an oak, seemed to be cracking up. His men watched aghast when he pulled out his pistol and roamed about, threatening anybody in his way and muttering gibberish to himself. The death of Charlie Goodfellow, his adjutant and best friend, had unhinged him. "His bloody brains are in my lap. His head is off. He has only got his neck."* (W. H. Auden had written about poets, in their enthusiasm for an anti-Fascist war, "Exploding like bombs." Auden, only briefly in Spain, never met Goodfellow, an industrial worker, not a poet.)

Wally Tapsell, the Cockney commissar of the British Battalion, proposed to lead a delegation to General Gal and demand relief on grounds that "in a people's army there is no place for a general who ignores the men under his command as individuals." George Aitkin, brigade commissar, agreed to accompany him. Hours later Aitken returned alone, reporting that Gal had rebuked Wally when he blamed other battalions for failing to support them. In a seething rage Wally then told Gal he was "not fit to command a troop of Brownies, let alone a People's Army."* He was immediately arrested for gross insubordination and threatened with execution. This pitched Copeman over the edge. He stormed off to confront Gal, leaving orders that if he failed to return within two hours, the machine-gun company should be sent to rescue him. Somehow the difficulty was resolved. Tapsell was released, but after the battle Tapsell and Copeman (along with Jock Cunningham and George Aitken) were all sent home to answer charges by the CP for incompetence and defeatism.

A full-blown mutiny, witnessed by a visiting French officer, erupted in the XIIIth Brigade, which had been acting in concert with the XVth during the campaign. Cut to pieces in a ferocious Nationalist counterattack, the Slavs of the XIIIth were finally relieved by units of *marineros* from Valencia, who within an hour broke and fled to the rear. Once more the XIIIth was ordered to plug the gap. Krieger, an Italian Communist who had served as brigade commander for only a few days and was only a name to his men, assembled his officers and explained that they had to return to the trenches they had just left. One officer objected: "I won't go! It is unfair to expect us always to plug gaps left by others. I would rather lose my bars than give an order like that." Krieger became furious, "Where do you think you are? In an office? In a factory? I order you to go immediately to lead out your battalion. After the battle I will judge your case." "I won't go!" resounded the officer. Krieger struck him with his fist. "Arrest this man." Not just a few soldiers but hundreds of soldiers stood within earshot. "You want us to return to the front? Never!" they shouted with one voice as Krieger pulled out this pistol and faced the storm alone. He singled out a soldier in the ranks. "You will not fight?" "No." "One, two, three! Your last word?" The soldier nodded, and Krieger shot him in the head. The men exploded, and brigade officers had to form a cordon to avert a lynching. Like a burst dam, men flooded to the rear, grouped themselves together on the highway, and began a march toward Madrid. Companies of *Asaltos,* the Republican police force, blocked them on the road and disarmed them. By order of the Madrid Government (not Albacete) the XIIIth Brigade was dissolved, its men assimilated into other International Brigades, and its equipment cannibalized by other units.*

Chaos spread like cancer throughout the Republican Army. Spanish conscripts tried to flee through the British position and had to be shooed back into place with grenades. "I don't think I should say much about that," a shamed Briton told an interviewer forty years later, implying more than he said.* As things fell apart, Jock Cunningham, always a cool hand in battle, began to lose control. When an overworked German doctor at the field hospital refused to evacuate men because he was too busy, Jock raged, "If you don't get these men out, I'll fucking well shoot you!" The men were promptly moved.* On another occasion, when a Spaniard on his staff began moaning "Mucho malo!" Cunningham lifted him off the ground, "booted him in the arse," and sent him spinning, "I'll mucho malo you, you bastard."*[13] During the ebb and flow of this pandemonium, the brigade antitank section, unable to remove a gun, got El Campesino's men to pull it away, but they refused to give it back. A Russian stormed in from Brigade to demand an explanation for the missing gun from Hugh Slater, a British journalist who had replaced Dunbar. He accused Slater of cowardice for losing the gun, stuck a pistol in his belly, and told him to get it back. Slater's runner neutralized the situation when he stuck *his* pistol in the Russian's belly and routed him out. The Briton spoke no Russian, but the Russian got the message.*

About July 14 the Lincoln and Washington battalions pulled back into a grove west of the Guadarrama River for a rest. The hygiene truck came up with showers and underwear.* Yet rest was precarious, for enemy planes continued to scatter bombs at random. Within the two battalions losses in killed and wounded approached four hundred out of close to eight hundred just eight days before. With sixteen killed in one day, perhaps the kitchen staff had suffered most, for they had to carry up sacks of food across open terrain neatly registered by enemy gunners, while telltale smoke from stoves served as targets for ranging bombers.* At this time the two American battalions were fused with Markovicz as commander and Nelson as commissar. Although officially named the Lincoln-Washington Battalion, in common parlance "Washington" soon faded away. Copic had been evacuated to Madrid with a light wound, leaving Colonel Klaus as brigade commander—and also as major scapegoat if conditions worsened—as they did.[14] (Ominously, Klaus vanishes from brigade records after this battle, except for "transferred elsewhere," which could mean anything.)*

In the evening of July 16, word came down that the enemy was breaking through at Villanueva del Pardillo, a village located six miles north that anchored the Republican left flank. Division sent the Americans to help hold the town. Henceforth orders would emphasize "holding," not "taking." As the verb changed, so did the battle of Brunete.

13. Cunningham, a fighter not a thinker, never recovered from Brunete. Recalled to Britain, he blamed Harry Pollitt, the CPGB secretary, for sending young men to Spain to be slaughtered. Thereafter, Pollitt never talked with him without a bodyguard. Cunningham continued to denounce the Party and "died a bloody tramp, picking up fag-ends. No one knew when he died, no one cried for him. He'd a pauper's bloody funeral."*

14. In his retrospective operations diary, Copic reversed his usual condemnation of the Americans. "The American Battalion [*sic*] has conducted itself very well. In the moment of retreat and panic of other units, it has been the battalion which retreated according to order." Granted, he may have wished to neutralize criticism for the Haywood affair.

No transport. So they marched all night through the riverbed in ankle-deep sand, which sifted into shoes and turned shoes and socks into sandpaper. Some men tied their shoes around their necks and tried to walk barefoot, but the sand packed into open blisters. Whenever the head of the column stopped, those behind staggered into one another and fell asleep. Officers moved up and down the line kicking and cuffing them awake. The Mooneys had to dismantle their Maxims and carry them on their backs. Ray Steele, now company adjutant, and Doug Roach "organized" a horse from somewhere and piled on the guns and ammo cans. Nelson bawled him out. "Don't you know this is no way to act in a Republican army—stealing horses?" Steele said, "O.K., Comrade Steve, we won't do it anymore."* The lecture over, Nelson urged them forward, horse included.

At sunrise they crawled out of the riverbed and entered a reserve trench half a kilometer from the Pardillo front, where they received, to their great surprise, hard-boiled eggs. "The first—and last—taste of chicken food I had in dear old Spain," remembered one volunteer.* It was a day of miracles. Next came what seemed, in retrospect, like a collective hallucination. Leaning against a rattle-trap ambulance parked off the Cañada-Pardillo road was the driver, an attractive, bobbed-hair American girl who smiled as they filed past. As the first woman they had seen in over two weeks, they were too much in awe even to whistle. This was Evelyn Hutchins Rahman of Snohomish County, Washington, a legendary chauffeur whose brother and husband also served in the American medical unit. Having learned that Spaniards "drive by the horn," she had installed on her flimsy vehicle a monstrous noisemaker guaranteed to blast any truck from her path.*

Half a mile from Pardillo the Americans entered a deep *barranca* lying in a hollow below the town. Forests were now far behind: this was open country of pinched mesquite and parched barley. The men had no clear idea of where they were or what they were doing. A rumor passed through that they were on a guerrilla expedition, to take the enemy from the rear.[15]

Throughout most of the day they lay in their *barranca,* too exhausted to dig in. Arguments flared up and died in the suffocating heat. John Cookson, a Ph.D. candidate in physics from the University of Wisconsin, expounded in his nasal twang his *idée fixe,* a dam across the Strait of Gibraltar that would supply all Europe with power. He went on to say that Lenin's *Materialism and Empiro-Criticism* bore directly upon this problem.* Somebody asked a New York

---

15. Sense of time and place became muddled after Mosquito Ridge. Heat prostration and physical exhaustion induced "nightmarish wanderings" and "dreamlike sequences." In retrospect, it became nearly impossible to reconstruct a chronology of events unless a volunteer had written something down, and few did. No mail came or went during this period.

schoolteacher what he thought of Granville Hicks's writing. The teacher eyed his questioner as though he had lost all his marbles and replied, "That's a dumb thing to ask." A Chicago volunteer boasted that what they needed were a couple of really tough *hombres* like Al Capone: he'd show the Fascists a thing or two. But a Brooklyn volunteer contested this. "Capone was only a big stiff who got his break with prohibition and was a yellow rat who'd have turned tail here in half an hour." Others limply agreed or told them to shut up. In the heat, everybody felt punchy and drained.*

Suddenly a shell exploded a hundred yards away. In their hollow they felt safe, but they quit talking. High above hovered a tiny speck. A World War vet yelled, "Look out, Comrades. It's an observation plane!" Everyone ducked, but the plane flew away. Half an hour later there was a noise overhead like threshing machines. "Get down! Bombers!" men shouted. Seconds later the bombers unloaded over the *barranca* as deftly as dropping pebbles into a well. The procumbent Americans clawed downward, but it felt as though the ground were pushing them upward into the lethal, open air. "I was hugging the earth, pressing into it with my hands, my feet, my face . . . but the ground was pushing you up higher. I felt I was perched up high and knew that they could spot me for miles. You knew there was a shaft pointing to the small of your back and the bomb would hit you right there and blow you into a million pieces."* Bunched up, they were in a death trap.

The earth shook with volcanic upheaval. There was an impression of being hurled high into the air: "We had a helluva time just staying on the ground. We had to hold on to the grass to keep from rising." White-hot shards of shrapnel whizzed trough the ravine and set fire to the grass. Black smoke billowed from the pit, and from the pit came the smell of cordite. "During the bombing I was praying, 'Oh, God, let this pass, Oh, God,' when [Edgar] McQuarrie's body was thrown upon mine."* When the planes had droned away, Nelson crawled out and ran along the lip of the ditch with sinking heart. He assumed his men had been annihilated. Heads popped up and looked about. Apparently lifeless bodies rose up. All were as black as coal heavers. "You sat up, you looked around—your whole section, the whole company, everybody alive, not a single one hurt."* (This was not strictly true—but only three were killed and five wounded by a bomb ten feet away.)* Nelson called it "the miracle of the war." The dead were not bloody—shrapnel had gouged holes like biscuit cutters in thick dough.

Republican soldiers on the higher ground around Pardillo had had a bird's-eye view of the bombardment. When they saw nearly the whole battalion crowding out of the ravine and running uphill toward them, they broke into exuberant cheers and met the Americans with wineskins. Minutes later, Moors attacked the village, and the Americans assisted in beating them back. Some of the enemy hid behind a pockmarked house between the lines until a tank shell brought down the walls. The Lincoln-Washington machine guns then chopped them down as they fled back to their line. In their exuberance at the kill, the gunners dashed out to harvest victory trophies—mainly Moorish hats and badges. For this they received blistering reprimands because by abandoning their guns they had endangered the entire defensive line.*

For the next three days the reconstituted Lincoln Battalion occupied trenches little bigger than ditches around the once-whitewashed village of Pardillo. This was a comparatively placid byway of battle. Nationalist counterattacks focused on Brunete, far to the south. In this sector it was the sniper who did damage.

On July 20 orders came to return to their old positions under Mosquito Ridge. Once again they slogged through sand dunes down by the river in total darkness. At dawn, while they were sleeping in canebrakes beside the river, bands of panicked Spaniards rushed past, shouting that the front had broken. With three tanks the Lincolns disputed the enemy at the riverbank, although all were "nearly collapsing with heat and exhaustion," while many men were unable to walk because their feet were raw.* Retaking lost positions was now out of the question. An order to attack Mosquito once more "created an unbridled fury in the men!" reported a Finnish-American officer.* A bright spot was the discovery of a food kitchen abandoned by the XIIIth Brigade. Stripping their mules of ammunition, they loaded up with ham, bread, and coffee, and when Markovicz ordered them to replace the food with munitions, they absolutely refused. In this tense standoff, Markovicz had to back down.* It was about this time that a contingent of Spanish naval infantry took to their heels, and Colonel Klaus ordered Markovicz to plug the gap. Seeing that his battalion would have to cross terrain under murderous fire, Markovicz refused. "This can't be done. I am against it." When Nelson as brigade commissar insisted they obey, Markovicz said that back home he would hold Nelson responsible for whatever happened to the Americans. Klaus relieved Markovicz on the spot, ordered him to report to Gal, and gave Nelson the battalion. Fortunately for the Lincolns, Klaus had second thoughts and canceled the attack.*[16]

For the next two days, the Americans tried to form a defensive line always to discover that the Spanish units on their flanks had melted away. They had a

---

16. Some accounts allude to his release because of "illness," the "official history" does not mention his removal at all, but Nelson himself has confessed that it occurred for the reason given here. Markovicz then transferred into a Slavic brigade and served out the war with distinction. On returning to the United States early in 1939, he was held on Ellis Island for failure to establish his citizenship, but eventually made his way to California and defected from the Party.

moment of satisfaction picking off Moors, who scattered in all directions after an artillery shell blew up the Casa de Mange.* On the southern horizon black smoke hung a thousand feet over the village of Brunete. Through black fumes and ocher dust the sun turned into a "bloodred ball." Black diagonal crosses on the rudders of Nationalist aircraft dominated the air. Airplanes dropped incendiaries; parched grass and brush burned like tinder and forced them back into the open country toward Villanueva de la Cañada.

As the Republican front collapsed, the high command resolved to fortify Villanueva de la Cañada, and in the evening of July 25 the Lincolns were relieved from the line. Scattered about as they were, many groups never received the order and had to form small bands for protection in case they strayed into enemy pockets.* Good news came for Ray Steele, their best gunner. He was to report to the officers' school at Pozorubio, and Nelson arranged for him to stop over at Albares to see his *novia*. Too happy for caution, Steele stood tall and wandered about saying good-bye when he was hit in the heart by a sniper bullet.

In moonlight they filed through a macabre pile of stones, which threw up silhouettes like those unearthed by archaeologists' shovels. A battered tile plaque identified the place as "VIL–NUEVA DE LA –AÑ—." Just eighteen days earlier they had dropped down from cool hillsides to seize this village. Of the eight hundred Americans who had come down, only three hundred went back up.[17]

Daylight caught them on the open road winding into the foothills near Valdemorillo. With thousands of others they toiled upward, passing thousands of others on the way down—fresh meat for the Brunete cauldron. "Those fresh shaved faces," recalled an American. "We must have looked like the House of David, or a line of bums using rifles as crutches." What the veterans most feared now came into view. A dozen Junkers (some say Capronis) droned up the long valley, following the ribbon of highway. Antiaircraft batteries began popping from the higher hills to the west. Panic-driven soldiers scattered into ditches and *barrancas*. Suddenly, the lead bomber exploded softly in a brief effulgence of orange flame and black smoke. Debris drifted down "like falling leaves—bits of metal, fabric, and men." The other trimotors swerved like startled birds and dropped their bombs on empty fields. Thousands of soldiers on the hillsides burst into frenzied cheers at this million-to-one shot of some anonymous Republican gunner.*

Back at "the Pearly Gates," about ten kilometers behind the front line, a cool mountain brook trickled into a dammed pond. Around it poplars grew so close

---

17. In "American Volunteers in the Spanish War," Adolph Ross lists (by name and home town), sixty-three American who were killed or died of wounds at Brunete. The number of wounded, while unknown, may be reasonably estimated at four times that number.

that they blocked the sun. The grass, deliciously fragrant, grew a foot high. What remained of the Lincoln-Washingtons bivouacked in green shade beside the first running water they had seen since the Guadarrama River had run dry. Far, far below them the battle of Brunete gasped to a spasmodic inconclusion. Nelson told them they were out of it for good. When they clamored for food, he tried to shame them with a story of Lenin's suffering. True enough, wrote an embittered American, "But you cannot manufacture enthusiasm. . . . In the I.B. the big events don't come off—only death, heat, and exhaustion."*

On their second night at "the Pearly Gates" Nelson summoned the battalion to a meeting in the grove. He had bad news. Republican divisions at Quijorna, eight miles to the south, had been surrounded. The XVth Brigade was the nearest support. They had to go back. Out of the darkness came a wailing cry, "For Chr' sake, Steve, you're not going to tell us to go back!"* Nelson tried to explain to men he could not see, "If the lines break you are not going to be able to stay here. . . . We will either be driven out of here or we will die here. We don't have a chance except to go back." Not even Nelson dared tell them that at a brigade meeting the British (37 men left out of 360), the Dimitrovs (93 out of 450), the 24th (125 out of 400), and the Sixth of February (88 out of 360) had refused to return to battle.

Nelson expected catcalls and curses, but a lone voice said, "You're right." The men moved off to collect their equipment and then followed Nelson through the whitewashed gates of the farm. On the highway a dispatch rider intercepted them and passed Nelson a written order, "The Spanish comrades have extricated themselves and the situation is in hand. The XVth Brigade will remain in camp." No one cheered. It was like a reprieve from a death sentence. Some veterans later said that the supreme moment of their service in Spain came at the moment when they agreed to return to the battle.*[18]

But the Americans were out of it. After several days' rest they moved twenty kilometers farther to the rear until the third of August, when trucks began picking them up for the welcome return to Albares. Those serving in the brigade auto-park (the teamster unit) were not so lucky. Refused permission to leave the battle sector with the infantry, they held a meeting and voted to go back to Albares or Albacete. This had to be granted to prevent further mutinies, but the ringleaders were later denounced as "traitors and Fascists."*

18. While this moment has been historicized by frequent repetition, an earlier version exists that relates that the men were in the process of voting whether to return when the counterorder arrived. Even this may be questioned, in view of the demoralization of the survivors. After the battle, many Americans besieged Albacete demanding repatriation on the grounds that they had served six months. Moreover, five deserters seeking a way home checked in at the U.S. consulate in Barcelona. For every one who reached Barcelona, how many others were apprehended on the road?

A major loss for the brigade was the death of Major George Nathan, killed by a random bomb from a Junker as the XVth was withdrawing from the battle. Spiffy and regimental to the end, during lulls in the battle he entertained visitors at lunch under shaded oak trees, offering them sliced tomato salad and fruit jam, served on a table carefully laid by his batman, whom he kissed and fondled openly.* His funeral drew a distinguished crowd, for he was admired by Soviet "observers" for his "cool arrogance under fire," even though he had been refused membershp in the Communist Party because of his sexual orientation.

The grueling battle at Brunete had ended, not with a bang but a whimper. Like so many other battles in Spain, both sides claimed the victory, although the Nationalists mustered the strongest arguments. After all, the boasted Republican offensive had not broken their siege of Madrid, nor had it prevented the fall of the Basque Country. The Republic, on the other hand, calculated that it had "liberated" seventy-five square kilometers of territory—even though this was a territory without industry, depopulated, and with only subsistence agriculture. It cost the Republic twenty-five thousand casualties, 80 percent of its armored force, and one-third of its aircraft, whereas the Nationalist casualties amounted to only seventeen thousand.* The outcome of the battle had no strategic importance whatever. Neither side launched a further offensive in this sector, and the lines that existed at the end of the battle, like those at Jarama, remained fixed until the end of the war. For the Americans, perhaps the greatest achievement of the battle was the recall to the Soviet Union of General Gal to answer charges of military incompetence and eventually to be swallowed up in the purges. For the brigaders this was not much—but it was something.

10

THE ROAD TO ZARAGOZA

After more than a year of war, nothing of much consequence had transpired on the Aragon front, a sector of fortified villages and sandbagged high points extending southward from Huesca and Zaragoza to Belchite and Teruel. Many months before, Anarchist militia with histrionic names like the "Iron Column" and the "Battalion of Death" had left Valencia and Barcelona amid shouts of "On to Zaragoza!" But bombast rather than bombs characterized war on this blighted upland plateau, a moonlike place of empty spaces and scraggly vegetation. The front in Aragon was so sparsely garrisoned that in some sectors it could not really be said to exist at all. Once both sides had thrown up roadblocks and built bunkers on the higher hilltops, they found little else to do. The terrain itself fostered a do-nothing, defensive mentality. Where it was not gouged by serpentine canyons, extinct tributaries of the Ebro River, it was pressed flat by the weight of some prehistoric sea. Nearly anything that stirred in this treeless region could be spotted by an enemy miles away—so why stir at all? Aragon had become a kind of peaceable kingdom. An American who served with the Anarchist militia complained that "all they did was argue and fight among themselves to find out how their revolution was supposed to come about." Instead of uniforms, the more affluent among them wore leather jackets garnished with red and black kerchiefs.*

Among war correspondents, the Aragon front had its own folklore. George Orwell, who served with the militia in this region, called this front "a comic opera with an occasional death."* Troops were said to be so bored by inactivity that their commanders tried to bolster sagging morale by spreading false rumors that a battle was in the offing. It was bruited as fact (and probably was) that Fascists and Anarchists competed in soccer games between the lines, heavily attended by soldiers from each side.* Another British volunteer on this front recounted that his Spanish commander each evening "lined up his platoon on top of a parapet and had us sing three verses of the 'International.'" To which he appended, "Surprisingly our casualties were light."* Catalan militia— primarily Anarchists—harbored the illusion that they were performing acts of belligerence when they engaged in rifle duels with an enemy entrenched out of sight, half a mile away. Barcelona newspapers published aerial views of Zaragoza "under attack by Republican aviation." (But the same prewar picture postcards were old stock at every kiosk in the city.) Among the apocrypha of the Aragon front is the story of a Madrid general inspecting a field hospital. "How many cases have you treated in the past six months?" he asked the chief surgeon. "One, my general." "Ah," mused the general, "he fell out of bed, I suppose."* More reliable, though no less revealing, is the recollection of Sefton Delmer, an English journalist visiting an Anarchist headquarters, who asked to look over the sector map and was jeeringly told, "A map? We don't go in for maps here. We leave that stuff to the fascists and the reactionary military."*

Through this backwash the Republican Army of the East under General Sebastian Pozas planned to send eighty thousand men in a massive assault upon Zaragoza. The theory was that Franco would be forced to stall his offensive against Santander in the north in order to shore up the Aragon front. Moreover, there were other considerations less pragmatic than symbolic. Zaragoza was a holy city once visited by the Virgin Mary (on January 2, A.D. 40, to be precise). Her shrine, known as Nuestra Señora del Pilar, had been consecrated by none other than Santiago (Saint James) himself, who, among his other duties, served as patron saint of the Spanish infantry. Were it to fall into the hands of the godless hosts of the Republic, the ramifications would be dire for Nationalist morale. To take it, Pozas planned a rapid sweep up both sides of the Ebro River, his main attack temporarily bypassing fortified places like Quinto, Belchite, and Fuentes de Ebro, which could be strangled at leisure. Unable to depend on the Anarchist militia who occupied the region (unquestioning obedience to orders was anathema to most Anarchists, who also hated Communists), Pozas called for the best troops of the Madrid sector, which included segments of the mainly Communist "Fifth Regiment," fierce enemies of the Fascists and Anarchists alike. The offensive was scheduled to begin on August 22, less than a month after the last salvos of Brunete. While at Brunete one-fifth of the attacking force had been Internationals, in Aragon the fraction dropped to one-twentieth or less.*

No one could have foreseen that, in the end, Aragon would prove to be the region that decided the war.

Back at Albares and nearby villages, the XVth Brigade again reshuffled its table of organization. The dual-regiment system disappeared. Since the Sixth of February had been reduced to a bare company, it was absorbed into the French-speaking XIVth Brigade. Thus were left four battalions: the Lincoln-Washington (henceforth known as the Lincoln), the British, the Dimitrov, and the 24th (which was entirely Spanish). The British had been so badly mauled at Brunete that the four highest-rankers—Jock Cunningham, Fred Copeman, George Aitken (brigade commissar), and Wally Tapsell (battalion commissar)—went off to London to answer charges of misfeasance by the CPGB. Cunningham, who had been hailed as the "British Lenin" in the London *Daily Worker* just a few weeks before, was accused of ill-defined "Fascist tendencies" and "temporary insanity." Although his men admired him as an outstanding fighter, the CPGB made him the scapegoat for disciplinary problems in the British Battalion, and he never returned to Spain. Among other things, after Brunete he opposed tighter Communist control in the International Brigades (prima facie evidence for the Albacete crowd of his "insanity"). Copeman and Tapsell later returned to Spain, but without their former influence. Now that the guns of Brunete were silent, Lieutenant Colonel Copic, miraculously recovered from his wound, emerged from the hospital to resume command of the XVth. Steve Nelson was promoted to brigade commissar, and Robert Merriman returned on August 11 as brigade chief of staff. At Albares there was talk about an intensive retraining program, but it proved nearly impossible to pry the men away from soaking in the river, and the commissars dared not push them too hard—especially in view of out-and-out mutinies among the Internationals at Brunete.

Perhaps to disguise the connection between the Comintern and the International Brigades, the Albacete faction appointed Hans Amlie, a Socialist, as new commander of the Lincoln Battalion. Just as Oliver Law had been their civil-rights plank, so Amlie became their Popular Front centerpiece. He was about forty years old with a lined Baltic face and spiky, graying hair. He had grown up in Binford, North Dakota, a microscopic crossroads, where his father was a prosperous wheat farmer who dabbled in unsuccessful inventions. Politically he was a late bloom of the Populist movement that swept the upper Midwest during the LaFollette era. After attending school at nearby Cooperstown, Amlie joined the U.S. Army and fought in the World War. After his discharge, he drifted west and worked as a miner and prospector. His outrage at conditions in mining towns and the owners' role in the "Ludlow Massacre" placed him squarely on the workers' side of picket lines. As he told Herbert L. Matthews of the *New York Times,* "They sent men down to work where silicosis was inevitable. Two years' work, one year of dying, and no compensation—that was their career. I've always fought for them, and so I lost job after job, for the owners got to know me."* During the 1930s he took part in strikes up and down the Pacific Coast, but always as an independent. When friends drifted off to join the Lincoln Battalion, Amlie hung back, distrusting the Communist orientation of the International Brigades.

But when the Socialists organized their own ill-starred Eugene Debs Column, he joined them and was slated to become their commander. But this paper organization died a-borning—only a handful of volunteers ever reaching Spain. Amlie and half a dozen others hung around Paris waiting for nothing before joining the Lincolns to protest against Socialist apathy.

At Tarazona de la Mancha, Amlie helped train the George Washington Battalion, and when they attacked Villanueva de la Cañada, he commanded First Company. After his men were pinned down by fire from the church tower, he tried to lead them into a *barranca* but was hit in the hip by a shot that paralyzed him from the waist down. Before he was pulled to safety, his knapsack was punctured by fourteen bullets. After discharge from the hospital at the Ritz Hotel, he turned up at Albares, his face pale and drawn, and was at once elevated to Lincoln commander.

It was no coincidence that the older brother of this new Lincoln commander was the Honorable Thomas R. Amlie, former Republican congressman of Wisconsin.[1] Not unexpectedly, Party publicists and fund-raisers trumpeted the family connection. Could the Lincoln Battalion be branded as a Communist-front organization when it was commanded by a Socialist? Poor Amlie, let down by the Socialists and now manipulated by the Communists. Probably he sensed that he was being used as an expendable publicity resource but acquiesced because he believed he could assist, in some modest way, the cause of the Republic, in which he sincerely believed. Having come prepared to give his life, Amlie did not scruple at the use of his name. He was an earnest, simple, almost saintly man, for whom the war in Spain was truly a crusade. Dedicated to his men, he was incapable of ruthlessness or cruelty. Stooped and haggard, his outward features seemed to mirror the person inside. But unfortunately, he lacked the common touch.

Amlie's first order of business was to obtain extra spectacles for each man obliged to wear them, for, as he wrote his brother, he feared their glasses might get broken in battle and they would become functionally blind. Always he worried about his men, a solicitude rarely returned. His Midwestern accent and rural values seemed alien to East Coast Jews, some of whom complained that he was "anti-Semitic" (probably because he was oblivious to ethnic diversity). Moreover, the men poked fun at his amorous behavior. He was planning to marry Milly Bennett, a tough-talking, voluptuous American newswoman in

---

1. Thomas R. Amlie had been appointed to fill a death vacancy in the House of Representatives between 1931 and 1933. Subsequently he ran for the Senate as a third-party candidate without success. Convinced that capitalism had failed and that Communism was "dialectics adrift," he hoped to find middle ground with his American Commonwealth Political Federation, a farmer-labor bloc.

Madrid, who, unknown to him, bedded down with volunteers she met on the dance floor. (The scuttlebutt in the battalion was that she had been engaged to three of them, each killed in battle—a good story but untrue.) It was Milly who performed the striptease "General Mola's Widow" in the Miami Café mentioned in Chapter 6. Milly Bennett was "one of the boys," who liked to regale her audiences with raunchy stories like the one about a Lincoln veteran who had one testicle shot off and haggled with a whore about a fifty percent discount. Before the war she had been a friend of Bob and Marion Merriman in Moscow, and their friendship continued in Spain, though Marion stood like an attentive watchdog over her husband. (She expressed gratitude that Bob was too serous for dancing because in that activity Milly could drive men wild.) In order to marry Amlie, Milly had to shake herself loose from a marriage to a Russian ballet dancer acquired during her years as a Moscow journalist. She enjoyed arguing with Bob about his faith in the New Russia, which she dubbed "the second coming of Christ with a hammer and sickle in one hand and a bottle of vodka in the other."* The Merrimans were amused by the incongruity of her new courtship. She got nowhere with Amlie in political discussions. Whenever boxed into a political corner, his usual riposte was, "Shut up or I'll smack you in the tits."* Although peculiar, Amlie was popular among his men, although the Party minions faulted him for "rank-and-file tendencies"* and privately called him "The Hick."*

As ballast for Captain Amlie, whose Socialism did not sit well with the Party heavies, the new Lincoln commissar was John Quigley Robinson, a Belfast-born seaman forty years old, who had been instrumental in the recent CP takeover of the Deep Sea Division of the New York waterfront. Robinson was a little man who walked with a rolling gait and whose brogue came out of the corner of his mouth. Whereas Nelson wooed dissidents with the demeanor of a fatherly man listening attentively to the trite mumblings of others, Robinson floored them with his bluntness. His profanity was rich and metaphorical; his delivery deadpan. No spectator ever forgot his confrontation with an unruly seaman, who hulked above him and brandished a big fist under the little commissar's nose. According to the story, the seaman finished his diatribe with a string of oaths, spat at Robinson's feet for emphasis, and snarled, "What do you gotta say to that?" Looking him up and down for a moment, Robinson drawled, "I think you're full of it." Onlookers gathered round to break up a fight but the complainant seemed less bellicose. "So what?" he finally bawled out. Still looking him up and down, Robinson retorted, "So, go fuck yourself." The seaman reflected on this before replying, "Well, if that's the way *you* look at it, it's O.K. with me." The men called their commissar "Popeye," but not to his face.

Publicly, he was always "Robbie."* He had no military experience whatsoever, but that ran true to form in the Lincoln Battalion.

After Brunete the effectiveness and prestige of the International Brigades had plummeted. In his report to Moscow on August 19, Luigi Longo, inspector general of the International Brigades, compiled a casualty list for each of the brigades involved. The XVth sustained the heaviest losses. Into that battle went 2,144 men; out came 865, a loss of nearly sixty percent. To this figure he had to add 735 wounded and 165 who "disappeared."* More upsetting was the report of Vital Gayman, head of Albacete Base, who complained that the Internationals were consistently sent into the worst sectors of a battle. He feared that the XIIIth might be permanently unable to fight. "This brigade is not destroyed, it has been murdered." Furthermore, he lamented that the British Battalion "has fallen victim to a wave of collective desertions which has begun to affect the American battalion." More troubling, "even officers are contributing to this demoralization."* An indeterminate number of Anglo-American deserters were imprisoned in Camp Lukács, the penal colony near Albacete, and subjected to a "reeducation" regimen. More specifically, records show that sixty demoralized Britons, most of whom had performed six months of service in Spain and expected to be sent home, were held there in September while authorities debated whether they deserved punishment or rehabilitation. Apparently neither worked, for the British base commissar reported that he "received a very rough reception" on the "several times" he went down to reason with them.* They felt trapped because of a recent government edict that all Internationals would remain in the army until the final defeat of Fascism. They were no longer volunteers: they were conscripts.

Dilution of foreigners in the International Brigades continued as Spanish recruits filled vacancies among the rank and file, although few foreign officers spoke Spanish. One entire Spanish company was now integrated into each of the four battalions of the XVth, despite ill-feeling among both language groups. Anglo-Americans groused that Spaniards were prone to flee to the rear and to desert. Certainly there was less *esprit* among Spanish recruits in the International Brigades than in regular Republican units, and with good reason. When captured, Internationals were often executed on the spot and Spaniards serving with them, even though they had been drafted, were in danger of the same fate because their captors would conclude they were "Reds." Moreover, many Anglo-Americans regarded the Spaniards unfairly as second-class soldiers and ignoramuses simply because in crises they failed to understand commands in English. (Illiteracy was so endemic among the rural recruits that classes in reading and

Colonel Vladimir Copic (Yugoslav), commander of the XV International Brigade, poses with Captain Gabriel Fort (Franco-Belge), commander of the Sixth of February Battalion in the trenches at Jarama.

Captain Robert Hale Merriman, commander of the Lincoln Battalion at Jarama, was commissioned as second lieutenant in the U.S. Army reserve after completing the ROTC course at the University of Nevada. He came to Spain directly from the USSR, where he had been studying collective farming.

The high-water mark for the Americans at Brunete, just below the crest of Mosquito Ridge.

Ernest Hemingway, Hugh Slater, an Englishman commanding the XV Brigade anti-tank unit, and Herbert Matthews, correspondent of the New York Times. Hemingway went to Spain four times during the war.

Four unsung and unidentified Lincolns following the Quinto assault. The ski-pants, tunics, and Remington "Mexicanski" rifles were standard issue. The carefully wound puttees and military bearing of the volunteer at right bespeaks a probable veteran of the world war.

Colonel Stephen Fuqua, the American military attaché in Republican Spain, reviewed the Lincoln Battalion after the battle at Quinto. With him are Dave Doran, a fledgling commissar at the time, and Captain Hans Amlie, commander of the Lincoln Battalion.

The Belchite clock tower as it appeared in 1967, thirty years after General Walter's division razed the town in September 1937. The town was never rebuilt. (In 2000, the battered tower still remained, but all the townspeople had vanished.)

Captains Philip Leighton Detro,--and Leonard Lamb. Unable to obtain a commission in the Republican Air Force, Detro joined the Lincolns and served as battalion commander at Fuentes and at Teruel, where he was killed by a sniper. Lamb was a New York social worker who took over the battalion several times on a temporary basis. Wounded several times, he survived the war.

The son of a Long Island manufacturer and a Dartmouth College dropout, Joseph Dallet was a CP organizer in Ohio before serving in Spain as commissar of the Canadian battalion. Resented for his authoritarian behavior, he was killed at Fuentes de Ebro. His widow married Robert Oppenheimer.

The supreme CP power brokers in Spain converged at Fuentes de Ebro: Major Merriman, Earl Browder, general secretary of the CPUSA, Colonel Copic, Robert Minor, the CPUSA representative in Spain, and Commissar Doran.

Saul Wellman, commissar of the Mac-Paps; Robert Thompson, commander of that battalion at Fuentes; and Dave Doran, commissar of the XV Brigade. Doran disappeared in Spain; the others served in World War II, where Thompson earned the Distinguished Service Cross for heroism at Buna, in the South Pacific.

General "Walter" (Karol Swierczewski), Polish commander of the 35th Division, inspects the rifles of a Spanish unit. By 1938, he had concluded that most Spanish brigades were more soldierly than their international counterparts. Best known as "Geneal Kolz" in Hemingway's *For Whom the Bell Tolls*, he survived the war, but became a victim of political assassination in Poland.

A Lincoln soldier at Argente preparing for the Teruel campaign, where the temperature often sank below zero degrees.

The Lincolns hold the trenches near Celadas, north of Teruel. The enemy attacked across the open Concud plain, visible in the distance.

Joe Bianca, a seaman voted "the best soldier" in the Lincoln Battalion for valor as a machine gunner during the long retreat in March 1938. He was killed on Hill 666 near Gandesa.

Milton Wolff, at the age of twenty-two the youngest commander of the Lincoln Battalion. With a voice compared to a "Brooklyn cabby at a Dodger's game, "El Lobo" (Spanish for "wolf") gained respect from Spaniards on both sides of the war.

Internationals captured by the Nationalists in April 1938 and forced to give the Fascist salute—one reluctantly—before boarding trains for the POW prison near Burgos.

An unidentified American prisoner arriving at San Pedro prison in April 1938.

International prisoners of war photographed at San Pedro prison.

The trial of a deserter after the demoralizing retreat of the XV Brigade in March 1938. The number of executions is unknown.

Executed for desertion after the calamitous retreats of March 1938, Paul White had compiled a good record in the New York maritime union and in Spain until he broke. He deserted to see his wife and baby in New York.

In July 1938, Republican soldiers attacked the Nationalists across the Ebro River by rowboats and by wading in the last major Republican offensive of the war.

The Lincoln command hierarchy prior to the Ebro campaign. Aaron Lopoff, company commander, Milton Wolff, battalion commander, James Watt, battalion commissar, and Joe Brandt, the special CPUSA overlord.

Commissar John Gates (Sol Regenstreif), the highest-ranking American in the XV Brigade at the end of the war. Disliked by the men for his authoritarian personality, he was respected for his personal courage and dedication to the cause. He served a prison term in Atlanta during the Joseph McCarthy purge, but later he denounced world communism.

"Doc" John Simon, called "the fabulous" by the Lincolns, who debated whether he was extraordinarily brave or just plain foolhardy. He was not an M.D., but a combination of "pharmacist, intern, male nurse, and "what-have-you."

Alvah Bessie, author of the memoir *Men in Battle*, at the age of thirty-two one of the old-timers among the Lincolns. After the war, he served a prison term for refusing to cooperate with the Dies Committee and on his release was blacklisted like others of the "Hollywood Ten."

writing Spanish began to be organized for Spaniards in the brigade.) Reports of Soviet advisers consistently decried the failure of the International Brigades to integrate Spaniards into their leadership cadres. Promotions for them came slowly or not at all, and rarely at staff level. Even rations of cigarettes and chocolates favored the foreigners. Resentment of their second-class status smoldered—all the worse because the Republic was committed to abolish class distinctions. Little wonder Spaniards deserted. Unlike the Internationals, they had places to go.

After Brunete the IB commissariat made a noisy effort to purge Albacete of "rear-line bureaucrats" and other hangers-on by sending them immediately to the front while combat veterans with six months' service assumed their administrative jobs. The rotation intended to defuse the bitterness of men who clamored that their time had expired. By mid-August, Brunete veterans were showing telltale symptoms of battle fatigue—they were "tired, weary, and nervous," recorded a member of Merriman's staff.* But the rotation scheme failed. Many combat veterans, convinced they had already done their part, hung around cafés in Albacete rather than join the ranks of pencil pushers, whom they despised. Besides, authorities determined that combat soldiers usually made poor clerks, and vice versa.

About 120 North Americans (including Canadians) who had served six months congregated in Albacete to demand repatriation. Bill Lawrence, the American base commissar, uncertain whether they would be allowed to go home, tried to discourage them by processing only five to fifteen papers per week, and placed them in a unit he called the "Veterans' Company," where they served on KP or loafed in offices. With nothing to do their morale skidded to zero. When nearly unmanageable, they were sent to Tarazona and agreed to work on a wood-chopping project. This fell through because Captain Johnson, the camp commander, could not provide enough trucks to carry them to the logging site, which lay seven kilometers distant, and the men refused to go on foot.[2] As they continued to grumble and sulk, Johnson, whom they thoroughly disliked, employed his litany "lack of discipline," which they cursed or ignored. When the repatriation carrot was withdrawn in mid-November, except for

---

2. At this time Johnson, like a fanatical Puritan, was trying to purge another nest of vice and disobedience among the Americans. To his dismay he had learned that during the Brunete campaign, nurses at "Villa Paz," the American hospital near Saelices, were "going beyond the call of duty in giving favors to wounded men, so creating something of a minor scandal."* A scandal? Surely not for the nurses, for one of them reported that before leaving New York "they gave us four packs of prophylactics. The doctor said it was to care for our emotional life, that we were going away from our sweethearts and husbands."

those seriously wounded, the Veterans' Company disbanded, and malcontents went back to active duty in the brigade.* Three of the most vocal troublemakers were sent to Tarazona, where an unnamed commissar denounced them at a public meeting as traitors and saboteurs—without specific charges. They disappeared. "I presumed they had been shot," recorded a newly arrived American.*

When, in the evening of August 18, Major Merriman received orders to transport the XVth Brigade to the Aragon front, he discovered that 197 Americans were in Madrid, swallowed up in boardinghouses, *pensiones,* and whorehouses from Retiro Park to the Puerta del Sol. Requisitioning trucks from the IB autopark, he delegated Paul White, a former official in the Seamen's Union, to ferret out the absentees.* Meanwhile he loaded the staff contingent onto trucks and got under way to Valencia, where they were to board a troop train for Aragon. Assisting White, Edwin Rolfe (Fishback), a leftist poet who edited the brigade newssheet, the *Volunteer for Liberty,* found himself speeding down empty streets at four in the morning, pounding on doors of darkened hotels, demanding guest books from grumpy concierges, and rousing volunteers from all manner of nocturnal lairs. Within six hours White and Rolfe achieved the near-impossible: they had collected full rations (sardines and bread) along with all but five of the absentees. By late afternoon a truck convoy got rolling for Valencia to rendezvous with other units of the XVth Brigade.

Valencia proved to be a city of no trains, no food, no munitions, no billets. Copic stormed about the ministries but nobody knew anything—or wanted to know anything. (The glory days of the International Brigades were long past—increasingly requests to the Republican Army for support were met with indifference, and even hostility.) In desperation he ordered the men to bivouac in the bullring, but an armed guard refused them entry. After another fruitless mission Copic ordered the gate bashed in, and for two days the men camped inside while they loaded two trains. Spanish workers peevishly demanded their rights to time off and overtime as guaranteed by the Republic and refused to load stocks of heavy equipment, including 486 machine guns and 400 rifles. Then after two top brass "borrowed" Merriman's staff car and took off for Aragon, even Merriman's solidarity seemed bruised, "Damned dirty trick if you ask me."* Markovicz surfaced as a tag-along, grumping about losing the command of the Lincoln Battalion and hoping to regain command of something, but because of his refusal to support that suicidal order at Brunete, he had become an unclean thing in the XVth Brigade. (Later when his application for repatriation to the USSR was denied, he eventually found a slot as chief of staff in the 129th International Brigade, a new unit formed around the old Dimitrov Battalion.)*

A few days later the XVth Brigade detrained at La Puebla del Hijar, a ramshackle assortment of dried brick huts on the Zaragoza-Barcelona railroad, the assembly point for troops assigned to sweep up to Zaragoza along the south bank of the Ebro. From here they marched to Azaila, the last village within Republican lines, a wretched place on an escarpment that looked as though it had been constructed, then abandoned, by cliff swallows. To the west stretched a colorless dust bowl, without shrub or tree. Mikhail Koltzov, the *Pravda* correspondent, described the region: "Not a tree, not a bush, nothing except heat. No water." Sleep was impossible—"suffocating in tents but enormous mosquitoes outside." He mused, "Is it possible that we are not in Africa, or Central Asia, but in Western Europe, only three hours from Paris?"*

From the flaking church tower at Azaila, staff officers focused their binoculars on the church tower at Quinto, seventeen kilometers distant. They had been given three days to seize the place. Nowhere ahead was there sign of human creature or human habitation other than a deserted road-mender's shack located at what seemed an infinite distance. To their right the Ebro, a snaking green ribbon, scored a path through russet canyons to the sea.

Steve Nelson went forward with his staff to the most advanced Republican post, where the outgoing Anarchist commander, wearing a black and red ascot, supervised the withdrawal of his men. Making no comment on conditions at the front, he saluted the Internationals with icy formality and strolled off to the touring bus that would carry him and his troops back to Barcelona. Lashed to the roof of the bus were mattresses, suitcases, two wine kegs, a wind-up phonograph, and a tennis set—paraphernalia that aroused scornful commentaries from Americans (who found it convenient to forget that at Jarama their field equipment included Ping-Pong tables, checkers, softballs, and a wind-up phonograph). Open in plain view, emblazoned with a gigantic red cross, lay the field hospital, which had obtained a "pledge" from Franco that it would never be bombed. Merriman discovered that during the six past months it had received only two wounded men, yet had been fully staffed and equipped. "The whole damned front is that way," he lamented.*

Returning to Azaila, Nelson stopped at a tiny farm tucked away in an irrigated ravine and offered to buy the farmer's entire stock of green vegetables. The old peasant, tight-lipped and suspicious, outlined his terms—strictly cash and carry. But he pushed away Nelson's wad of Republican pesetas with contempt. "You call *that* money?" he asked. Merely paper trash issued by the

Republic. Crops were real—politics and paper were tricks. Looking west toward Fascist-held territory, the old Spaniard articulated his own political philosophy. "There has been no fighting here—all has been peaceful. And now it's going to change. Why couldn't you let us alone? Fight your own war at Madrid. The Fascists let us alone, and we let them alone."* He himself had witnessed a soccer match between Republican and Nationalist teams without any trouble. "They cheered us, quite politely, when their team lost the game." Nelson left in disgust. This peasant was lucky he was not in the International Brigades, where men had been shot for less. In the minds of Party stalwarts, the Aragonese *peons* obviously needed strong doses of "re-education."

In the predawn hours of August 24, 1937, the long-awaited Aragon offensive got under way as armored units quickly battered through enemy roadblocks along a front forty miles wide and plunged westward toward Zaragoza. The XVth Brigade had orders to move by truck to a knoll three kilometers from Quinto, which had been bypassed by the vanguard. Merriman's diary summarized his morning's work: "Trucks never came. I rode motorcycle, tried to borrow trucks from 11th Brigade. Great traffic jam—lines of artillery—tanks, etc. Great confusion. . . . A more discouraging night I have never spent. Everything late and daylight found us in old location."* Realizing that if his men had to hike to Quinto on foot they would be too exhausted to make an attack, he stationed armed guards on the highway with orders to stop and search every passing truck. Those containing only cargo were hijacked, their contents jettisoned beside the road, and boarded by combatants. This was a "ticklish business," recalled a sentinel, because some Anarchist drivers balked at taking orders from "Communists." But by dawn the entire brigade was in its assigned position outside Quinto, every man fresh and ready for the attack.*

Quinto lay upon a long slope between arid high plateau, "barren as a desert," and irrigated valley, "which looked like the biblical Promised Land," wrote a volunteer. Three kilometers south rose Purburell Hill, a fortified ridge that beetled over the Barcelona-Zaragoza highway and railroad running along the south bank of the Ebro. While the British feigned an attack on the face of Purburell, where the incline approximated 45 degrees, the other battalions slipped through gullies to a protected area one kilometer above the cemetery wall on the far western edge of Quinto.

Behind eight light tanks, the Lincolns infiltrated across the dust-whipped highland, moving downhill toward their first objective, a line of shallow trenches and barbed wire strung around the whitewashed cemetery enclosure. Except for the blunt tower of the parish church, the village itself lay almost out of sight in bottom land. Framed against a vivid blue sky, the Americans came under waspish small-arms fire from the cemetery and church tower. Captain Amlie quickly pulled them back. The defenders of Quinto numbered about twelve hundred, most of them underage Requetés and Falange with little or no experience in battle.[3] The Nationalists deployed a 70 mm antitank gun to block any armored attack along the single long street of Quinto, although their heavier pieces were useless now that the Internationals were virtually on top of them.* The attack stalled while nine French 75s laid an opening barrage on the village. Meanwhile, the Dimitrovs moved northwest of the village to cut off any Nationalists attempting to escape toward Zaragoza.

In mid-afternoon half a dozen eight-ton Soviet tanks moved up to the plateau and clanked through the American lines, their 45 mm guns peppering the enemy strongpoints, anthill cones strewn about the down-slope, and grinding up the barbed-wire barriers. Having no antitank weapons up here, the Nationalist line collapsed. With the Dimitrovs leading the charge on the left, exultant Americans, some of whom had shaved their heads like Mohawks, dashed forward on the right with war whoops. Resistance was short-lived. Those Nationalists not in rabbit flight toward the village cowered in their holes with hands over their heads. For several minutes the scene resembled a footrace. Even after the Lincolns had swept through the flattened wire, enemy soldiers were popping out of their barrows and bounding away in all directions. The ground lay strewn with enemy helmets and rifles. Since the Lincolns had no protective headgear, Frank Bonetti stopped long enough to pick up a metal helmet, brushed off a colony of flies, but found inside "half a man's skull." So much for protection.* The tanks continued as far as the municipal dump, a multitiered escarpment hanging over the western precincts of Quinto, from which they bounced shells off the church tower looming above them. As at Villanueva de la Cañada, the parish church was the most heavily fortified place in town. The tanks could advance no farther, for the arabesque alleyways of Quinto were death traps for vehicles. Ferreting out the enemy snipers was the job of foot soldiers. Thus far Quinto had been more a lark than a military operation. The number of American dead could have been counted on two hands with fingers left over—if that much. Captain Amlie pulled his men back to the cemetery enclosure for the night, reserving the next morning for a mop-up of the village.

3. The Requetés consisted of Carlist paramilitary units drawn from all classes of Basque society. The Falange was an extreme nationalist movement of Fascist inspiration, primarily from the middle and upper classes. Franco successfully employed both organizations in his eclectic movement without allowing their respective fanaticisms to endanger his overall control. In time the Requetés became, along with the Spanish Foreign Legion and Moorish units, the most effective fighting units in his army.

The Nationalists had had a bad day, but their night was a disaster. Somehow their munitions dump caught fire and went off like a gigantic fireworks display, the big stuff last. In the Purburell sector an IB patrol found and smashed the pipeline that supplied the hilltop fortress with water. Since the enemy up there had been dormant during the day, Colonel Copic concluded the place was lightly held and ordered the British and the 24th to attack in the morning with only rifles and grenades. He gave them a pep talk that few Britons ever forgot: "There are only thirteen men on that hill. Go ahead and take the hill."* The morning was dead quiet when the British, under Captain Peter Daly, a veteran of IRA battles in Ireland, began clawing up the forty-degree slope. Suddenly the hilltop came alive with gunners. Daly dropped with a mortal wound, and the rest of the battalion might have been massacred if the enemy above had not tipped their hand by firing prematurely. The British, by this time nearly halfway to the top, tried to dig holes in the plum-pudding soil as grenades tumbled down the slope. The enemy even rolled down boulders, which accelerated to fantastic speeds. Those who could, crawled back—the others played possum and waited for darkness. The British were furious with Copic and Merriman, who promised to soften "Purple Hill" as soon as the other battalions mopped up Quinto.

Meanwhile, the Nationalist garrison in the town consolidated their force in order to make a last stand at the church, the railroad station, and some fortified houses in the lower town. At daybreak the Mooney machine guns and an anti-tank gun rattled the bell tower, raking out a hole twice the size of the great west window, allowing the rifle companies to slip into the lower town and begin a long peekaboo search for snipers in the houses. They knew nothing about house-to-house tactics other than mimicking scenes from movies. One American dashed into a doorway and staggered back outside with a bayonet gash in his leg. An enemy soldier inside had tried to pin him against the wall. Thereafter, they bombed every house and watched oaken doors cartwheel down cobblestone streets. A Lincoln section leader watched one of his new men lob a Mills bomb through an open window, but no explosion followed. "Did you pull the pin all the way out?" The recruit replied, "Pin? What pin d-ya mean?"* Unlike the telescopic impersonality of Brunete or Jarama, the fight at Quinto was a confrontation against a tangible enemy. Flaring up and down, the fighting raged through squalid alleys flanked by one-story adobe huts and stables. The defenders took advantage of interconnecting cellars under the houses to make subterranean maneuvers within the town. This the Lincolns discouraged by tossing grenades and containers of nitroglycerine into cellars, flushing out terrified women and crying children but gathering no prisoners.

A major firefight broke out around a valuable prize abandoned in the town square—a water truck supplying the village garrison. While the Lincolns pushed the enemy back, Dave Doran, one of Nelson's green junior commissars, climbed aboard and drove it out of town to the brigade kitchen, where its contents reappeared in the evening stew. It was somehow appropriate that Doran, an Albany tough, should first draw attention to himself in Spain by heisting a truck, but this was only the prologue to a series of dramatic spectacles staged by Doran on his rapid climb upward in the chain of command.

Although the main street lay directly under the church on the cliff, the Lincolns were protected from snipers in the tower by the walls of the houses. On the other hand, it was impossible to attack the church from their position. A frustrated American took careful aim and fired a shot at the bell in the tower. When it gave forth a "cheerful clink," immediately everyone took a shot at the bell. "The Fascists must have supposed us crazy."*

Although the brigade antitank guns continued to carom one-inch shells off the thick walls of the church, the enemy inside fought with the desperation of trapped animals, mainly recruits whose resistance had been fortified by lurid stories, recounted by their officers, of how *los internacionales* tortured their prisoners. They mounted barricades in the windows, located ten feet off the ground, and fired at anything that moved outside. Machine gunners remained in the belfry, although by this time the British antitank guns had turned it into a rotten cheese. Finally, a group of tough Dimitrovs battered down the west door with an immense beam and opened fire into the murky interior.* They obtained a foothold in the vestibule, where they came under fire from the baptismal font and the high altar. By this time the hard core of the defenders had ascended into the organ loft, from which they dropped grenades into the nave. Then began a Sisyphean labor to smoke them out. Bundles of straw were tossed inside, and grenades pitched in to ignite them, but this took a long time because the grenades just blew the straw to smithereens. A brigade report claims they rolled a drum of gasoline into church, which "finished the job."*

Nelson led a group completely around the church by hugging the walls, but five Lincolns were shot when they stepped back a few feet to shoot at the windows. An interpreter yelled to the defenders, offering them fair treatment if they surrendered. It worked. Some fifty-seven soldiers—most of them eighteen or nineteen years old—managed to squirm through a drainage hole barely a foot and a half wide.* Fearing execution, they tried to cover all bases by crying, "¡Viva la República! ¡Viva el gobierno! ¡Viva Rusia!" Some Americans were flattered at being mistaken for Russians—others were annoyed. "Hey, we're Americans!" one shouted. A prisoner said, "Someday I hope to prove to you that I am a good union worker and also loyal to Spain."* In gratitude for being taken alive, the captives ran to their liberators with open arms. Harry Eaton recoiled, "I can't embrace a Fascist! But their white exhausted faces looked so eagerly at us, what could we do? It was beautiful. We mingled—but not with the officers."* Not entirely beautiful, for some of the enemy soldiers were shot while attempting to surrender. According to Milton Wolff, later the battalion commander, "No one spoke of the prisoners who had been executed. It was as though it had never happened."* The bulk of their officers remained inside the church and had to be stalked through the gothic half-light and gunned down one by one. By mid-afternoon, after the Dimitrovs had dislodged the last snipers by heaving cans of gasoline into their nests, the village had been officially secured. Yet Purburell still held out.

That night Britons captured an enemy sergeant and platoon that had come down for river water. They divulged startling information—the Purburell garrison seethed with over five hundred men, not the thirteen reported by staff. The defenders outnumbered the attackers, but they had no water. In time, they would have to give up without firing a shot, but the brigade was falling behind the timetable for the Zaragoza push. At dawn the three battalion antitank guns unlimbered on adjacent hills and pounded the trenches surrounding the knoll with one hundred shells. When they ceased firing at nine o'clock, the British gingerly edged forward under their new commander, Paddy O'Daire, another IRA veteran. They were barely under way when a dozen Nationalist bombers came from Zaragoza and unloaded. The British cringed—they were in the open—but the bombs fell on top of Purburell. Black smoke purled over the summit. Along the crest handkerchiefs waved on bayonets. "The fascists on top thought the planes were ours."* As the Britons surged upward, the white streamers vanished, and a rattle of rifle fire came down from the top. (It was later learned that soldiers trying to surrender were forced to resume the battle by their officers, who shot those who had hung out white pennants.)

The antitank battery again pummeled the elongated line of trenches rimming the edge of the plateau. White flags again fluttered along the crest. The XVth Brigade hurried up, pushed aside the wire, and jumped into the trenches. The first ones on top saw Nationalist recruits throwing their rifles far down the slope so their officers could not force them to continue fighting. For two days they had been without water. Ignoring the bayonets of the feared Internationals, they swirled around them, pointing to tongues and croaking, "Agua! Agua!" Brigaders who had scaled the hill, enraged at the false surrender, now poured water down the cracked throats of men they had sworn to kill to the last man.* The POWs fought among themselves for the canteens.* The "Fascist" prisoners proved a great disappointment—"looking more like candidates for a Boy Scout camp than real soldiers, and extremely happy to be safely in our hands."* The accidental bombing, coupled with the high-velocity shelling from antitank guns, had turned the plateau into a butcher shop, with "pieces of meat everywhere, lying around, covered with dust and dirt."* The enemy officers had run through their shallow trench to their headquarters bunker at the northeastern promontory of Purburell Hill. None surrendered. One of the last ones to be hunted down and destroyed was a White Russian officer who brandished his pistol and screamed in Russian, "Red pigs! Red pigs!" As a group of Americans approached him, he placed his pistol against his temple and blew out his brains. From his body they took a Cyrillic Bible and a czarist sword.*⁴ The brigade took several hundred prisoners from Purburell. Ordered to point out officers among them who had donned coveralls to avoid detection, the privates complied, and seventeen officers were lined up for execution.*

According to a British doctor at division headquarters, General Walter (Karol Swierczewsksi) put his pistol to the heads of some captive officers, shouted, "Za Dubois!" and pulled the trigger. (Dubois, a popular French officer, had been killed by a sniper.)* Then the general ordered a group of prisoners to be shot. Dragooned to serve on the firing squad, William F. McCarthy of Brooklyn fired his rifle—loaded with dumdum bullets—a foot above their heads, "Making certain that thanks to God—I would not shoot someone in cold blood."* Apparently others of the squad felt the same way, for commissars had to deliver the coup de grâce to a surprising number of men surviving the squad's volley. One youth received only a superficial wound in the leg. Some Americans, upset by these cold-blooded murders, tried to arrange his removal to a hospital, but before this could be done, a volunteer identified only as "Crazy O'Leary" stepped up and shot him in the head.* (The Lincoln Battalion roster lists no one named O'Leary.) Since most Lincolns regarded the executions as a shameful blot in their history, they hung a veil of secrecy over the

---

4. Although contemporary accounts of the Purburell battle referred to concrete bunkers and "revolving gun turrets with overhead cover" designed by German engineers, my careful search of the abandoned hilltop in 2000 found no concrete bunkers, only shallow and hastily dug trenches. In view of the inaccessibility of the hilltop, it seems unlikely that all such traces would be obliterated. For the record there were no German engineers assigned to Aragon defenses. The wonder is why the XVth Brigade found it necessary to charge up the steep hillside at all, because they had already cut the water supply and the besieged were trapped. Besides, the trenches were situated at the eastern end of a long mesa butting on to a plateau to the west at the same elevation.

event and saw to it that the names of the firing squad were never divulged.[5] One American witness, who knew them all personally, wrote, "I intentionally forgot them."* (Nelson's own account of the Quinto battle contains no mention at all of executions.)

Quinto had fallen in three days, and at a cost of about thirty men in the brigade killed, by all odds the most spectacular victory in which the Americans had a role.[6] Most of the enemy prisoners, however, turned out to be pathetic conscripts happy to be out of the war and indistinguishable from the conscripts in their own companies. At first hand the Americans learned that pinning hate-labels like "Fascists" on such political naïfs was patently absurd.[7]

Awaiting their next assignment, they had a three-day rest close to Piña station, a few miles up the line toward Zaragoza. They luxuriated in a muddy irrigation ditch, waged ferocious combat on mosquitoes, and stayed under cover when Nationalist bombers flew over. "We were very happy at our recent victory at Quinto and felt that nothing could stop us now."*

In the larger picture, on the day Quinto fell, Nationalist reinforcements from the Madrid front arrived in Zaragoza on trains so packed that some soldiers suffocated to death in the cars. At the same time, artillery and aircraft (but no men) were detached from Franco's offensive in the north and sped to Aragon. Santander had fallen, and those Republicans not captured in the city were fleeing westward into Asturias. Meanwhile, General Pozas's offensive had stalled twelve miles short of Zaragoza at a place along the river called Fuentes de Ebro. The enemy also held on to a mountain chain extending southward from the Ebro to the western edge of the Belchite plain. Having occupied hundreds of square miles of scorched wasteland, the Republic now seemed unable to maintain its momentum of attack. And with each passing hour the Nationalists massed enormous firepower behind an increasingly formidable line. In Republican circles there was now as much talk of repelling counterattacks as taking Zaragoza.

5. An unnamed junior commissar wrote a bitter two-page account of executions at Quinto which claimed that "S.N." (Steve Nelson?) was responsible for some of them. "I do not want to be part of the setup here. My heart is against so much that it represents. I saw the bodies of twenty officers, their heads cut open, riddled with bullets. Such a savage bloody execution after such a beautiful victory."*

6. Nationalist historians have largely ignored the Quinto affair as a skirmish without military significance. It is not mentioned in Martínez Bande's definitive work on the Aragon offensive, *La Gran Ofensiva sobre Zaragoza*.

7. In 2000, when I asked an eighty-year-old retired worker in Caspe why he had fought on the Nationalist side, his mime spoke volumes. He just shrugged, grimaced, and drew an imaginary knife across his throat.

A major trouble spot had developed at Belchite, a fortified town eighteen miles southwest of Quinto. The place had no military significance whatever because the Republican offensive had already bypassed it and penetrated a dozen miles farther west. If left alone, its garrison would expire from starvation, but, like Purburell at Quinto, the Republican commanders insisted on taking it. Therefore, General Walter's 35th Division, consisting of the XIth (German) and XVth brigades, rushed from the Ebro to assist Spanish units already in place. Belchite was regarded as such an "easy" objective that Indalecio Prieto y Tuero, the minister of war, planned a victory fiesta within the city walls for journalists and other dignitaries as soon as the enemy had been rooted out. A Nationalist force of about a thousand men defended the place under conditions of siege. After their ring of concrete bunkers was smashed, they fortified the churches, factories, and outer houses of the town and refused to surrender. (They had nothing heavier than machine guns and small arms because their armorers had evacuated the artillery pieces to prevent their capture.) Egging them on, Nationalist radio alluded to Belchite as a second Alcázar[8] and cited past history to recount how Belchite had once successfully weathered a siege by the great Napoleon. On the other hand, the Republicans, embarrassed by the existence of an enemy pocket—however irrelevant—deep inside newly gained territory, repeatedly broadcast that Belchite was on the verge of surrender. Newspapers made Belchite sound as though the outcome of the war would be determined by its fate—the Nationalists demanding that history be repeated and the Republicans that it would be rewritten.

On September 1 the XVth Brigade marched south across a wide empty plain along a road as straight as a tightrope. From behind mountains to the west came the rumble of artillery. Men scanned the sky for signs of Fascist airplanes, for there was no cover in this open plain, but they marched unmolested, except for the heat. Even the wind was hot, like the exhaust of an engine. They passed through Codo, a hamlet populated only by cadavers of Nationalist soldiers picked over by magpies. On a commanding knoll stood a chapel encircled with fourteen pillars. The place had been loopholed and sandbagged with machine-gun posts between the pillars. "The modern way of fighting for Christianity," penned a foot soldier sarcastically, "turn the churches into fortresses, and then blame us 'Reds' for smashing them up in order to get the garrison out. . . . Every time it is the same story; the Church is the Fascist key-fortress."* Scattered

---

8. During the summer of 1936 a Nationalist force had been besieged in the Alcázar, a military school in Toledo, for seventy days until relieved by a column of Franco's army. See Cecil Eby, *The Siege of the Alcázar* (New York: Random House, 1965).

about were leaflets dropped by Nationalist planes—Carlist propaganda featuring Christ with a bloody face, flanked by photographs of his present disciples, General Franco, his face distorted by a smile, and General Mola, peering in his froglike way from behind thick eyeglasses.

A mile north of Belchite they entered an olive grove jammed with camions, tanks, and bivouacked troops, which had wasted the past week assaulting the town unsuccessfully. Modesto's wing of the Army of the East had driven the Nationalists back into town from concrete bunkers and well-constructed trenches at high points around the city, but despite a major attack by twenty tanks from five directions, accompanied by an aerial bombardment and a three-hour artillery barrage, the Nationalist garrison withdrew into its outer perimeter and held. Modesto's troops were now packing up to join the major phase of the grand offensive closer to Zaragoza—already far behind schedule—leaving the task of taking the town to General Walter's 35th Division, assisted by one Spanish brigade.

A major crossroads in Aragon, Belchite had already been attacked eighteen times by Republicans—mostly by lackluster Anarchist units. The original garrison numbered 2,273, but these included posts in outlying areas. Within the city itself the official count was 534 soldiers along with about 2,200 civilians who had not evacuated before the circle closed. The *comandancia* had a wireless radio connection with Zaragoza, which promised that a relief column was on its way. (It was stopped twelve miles northwest of Belchite, mainly by the British Battalion.) The mayor reported drastic shortages of water, munitions, food, and medicine. Republicans had blown up the irrigation canal, which had supplied the city with potable water, and the garrison had to stack their unburied dead under floors of houses crammed with people of all ages.* The stench was insupportable. Nationalist bombers dropped munitions, food, and medical supplies, but most of it fell into Republican hands.

In General Walter's plan, the Americans were to attack the city from the northwest, across a slight ascent over terraces supported by rock walls. Through olive trees they could glimpse two church towers silhouetted above the town: San Agustín—mistakenly called a cathedral by the press—with a chimney-shaped belfry guarding the northern approach, and San Rafael, with a cone-topped tower commanding the eastern sector. The Lincolns occupied the most advanced Republican "trench," a shallow drainage ditch four hundred yards from the first houses of the town. Complicating problems of attack, defenders had opened irrigation valves and turned the environs into a flood plain. Any tank attack would have to proceed along one of the exposed roads. While the Dimitrovs swung off to the northwest, Amlie pushed the Lincolns into the olive grove. The British Battalion had been dispatched to the mountains west of Belchite to look for an enemy relief column, while the 24th (Spanish) Battalion went on standby reserve. The Lincolns infiltrated across a succession of artichoke and cabbage gardens lying between the olive grove and the town, taking advantage of terrace walls. In the growing twilight, some Lincolns reached ditches within a hundred yards of San Agustín and dueled with snipers in the belfry. This was a great mistake, for their ditch was too shallow for sitting or standing, and houses ringed the town with the compactness of a solid wall. Every window harbored a sniper. Within minutes a harrowing fire beat down on them, forcing them to play dead in their ditch.

As casualties mounted, Captain Amlie tried to recall his men. Meanwhile Commissar Robinson heard his field telephone ringing. On the line was the voice of John Cookson, his sergeant of *transmisiones,* who wondered how the telephone sounded. "It works fine," said Robinson. "Where are you guys?" "In Belchite," replied Cookson, in his matter-of-fact Cobb, Wisconsin, twang. "Belchite!" Robinson shouted, "Get the hell out of there—you're surrounded!" Cookson lost no time in returning to the battalion, although he brought all his precious apparatus and wire with him. It would take the Lincoln Battalion three days to fight their way to the place where Cookson had placed his call.

Many Americans never received the order to withdraw. Daylight of September 2 found them pinned down in shallow ditches by a lashing hail of fire from San Agustín and the houses along the northern perimeter of the town. Unable to move forward or backward, they played dead and waited for the torrent to subside. Only the Jarama vets among them—no more than a handful—could remember having seen such textbook patterns of interlocking machine-gun fire. A couple of men who bolted to the rear were cut down among the artichokes and cabbages.

When Amlie notified brigade headquarters that large numbers of his men were trapped, Major Merriman ordered him to advance the battalion and to seize the church and surrounding houses. Amlie was stunned by this command to lead his men into a certain death trap. He refused to obey the order. Merriman began shouting through the phone, "You've got to, you hear! You go or face court-martial!" (The words of a man with a short memory—had he forgotten that infamous suicidal order of February 27?) The major promised artillery support, a promise fulfilled a short time later when shells began exploding, not in the town but upon Lincoln positions. They were only poorly aimed 75s, but no one complained of boredom. (It is not clear whether the shelling resulted from an intention to force the Americans forward or merely from errors in gunnery.) More effective was a sheltering barrage against the houses and church laid down by the three 47 mm guns of the brigade antitank battery commanded by Hugh Slater, an English gadfly and writer.[9] Slater was very proud of his guns: at a distance of a mile he claimed he could put a shell through an individual window, and during the first two days he poured twenty-seven hundred shells into the town.* But while he could badger snipers in Belchite, it was up to the Lincolns to pry them loose.

Meanwhile Amlie pushed his men across half a dozen terraces to within two hundred yards of San Agustín. In between lay an open field. By this time he had lost two company commanders and enough men to make him hope they were only wounded. No one doubted that to cross that last field meant certain death. Again Merriman rang up and demanded that he assault the church, the key to the defense of the town. Turning to his staff, Amlie groaned, "What am I going to do? Court-martial at the front means *execution!*" The solution was simple, rejoined one man, "You order us to go and we'll refuse. Then you tell them to come down here and we'll follow *them!*"* Robinson knew nothing about warfare, but he had a keen nose for a trap. He endorsed Amlie: if Brigade intended to bring out the firing squads, they had better arrange one for him too. Steve Nelson came over to oil the troubled waters and found the usually phlegmatic Amlie, leaning against a wall with a bloody bandage around his head, simmering with outrage. "What the hell is the matter with you guys?" he snarled. "That town's bristling with machine guns, thick as hair on a dog's back, and you want to send infantry against them! You want to slaughter the whole damn battalion?"* Copic entered the fray. Nelson had told him that the battalion wouldn't attack because they had not received their morning coffee.* When Division demanded to know why the Americans were not advancing, Copic, daring not to mention the coffee incident, accused Amlie of "sabotage." He instructed a courier to tell Amlie that "if he doesn't move I'll have him shot, the S.O.B."*

Nelson clearly saw that the men lying in the shallow ditch would be picked off "like ducks in a pond." The battalion had to go forward. To the right of the Lincoln headquarters lay an olive factory, a long, low building. Nelson observed that despite the bodies of Republican soldiers strewn about the factory perimeter, no muzzle flashes came from those windows. Collecting a small group, he slithered down the road to it, and peeked in through a hole smashed by shellfire. Inexplicably the place had been abandoned. Nelson passed down the word

---

9. Slater had come to Spain as correspondent for a Communist news agency and joined the International Brigades. His real name was Humphrey Slater, but he adopted Hugh because it sounded less upper class. His gunners admired his efficiency but were unhappy with his snobbish mannerisms. Slater was not the sort to roughhouse with his men. After the war his novel *The Heretics* (1947), part of which was based upon his experience in Spain, attacked Communist orthodoxy.

and within a few minutes Lincoln gunners occupied the place, which ran up to the first houses of Belchite. Setting up a Dichterev at a window, Lincoln gunners engaged the Nationalist snipers in the belfry, less than fifty yards away. Nelson had discovered the vulnerable underbelly of Belchite. Dozens of men could be massed here, under cover, to press their attack upon the town.[10]

For two days the Lincolns dueled with snipers without making significant inroads into the town. Despite the support by Slater's pinpoint-accurate antitank guns, each time the Americans tried to advance, snipers popped up like dragon's teeth and drove them back. For a time the men, led personally by Major Merriman, labored to advance by knocking down connecting walls, but the results were unsatisfactory. (In the 1920s, Belchite house-owners had been introduced to Portland cement—a brand known as "Samson," whose metal decals were nailed above doors—which was nearly impervious to pickaxes wielded by hand.) The Republican command seemed unable to coordinate massive assaults: units attacked piecemeal without covering fire and were easily stopped. Whenever heavy artillery reduced a strongpoint, another sprang up. Tankers learned the hard way that narrow streets mounded with rubble were impervious to tank attack, because knocking houses down just created defensive positions for the enemy. An officer in the Spanish battalion reported, "Our artillery has fired upon our positions, killing four and gravely wounding three, which has demoralized our forces," but he gamely added, "We maintain our positions. I await orders."*

Provisioned by airdrops, the defenders read about their heroic defense in Zaragoza newspapers and fought on. Their airplanes dropped leaflets promising that the relief columns were converging on the city. They threw up barricades of cobblestones and mattresses along every alleyway leading toward the center of the city and fought with the desperation of men who accepted as gospel what their officers told them about how Internationals massacre prisoners. The presence of many wives and children in the garrison complement intensified their determination to resist. To discourage flight and desertion, officers compelled some units to fight barefoot. Their leaders urged them on with the cry, "Die like men today—not like rabbits tomorrow!" The mayor's final radio message to Franco was widely circulated in Spain as an exemplum for schoolchildren: "If before you arrive, death arrives, we welcome it! We will resist until we die. Long live Spain! Long live the Army!"

10. According to an account of the battle written by Emanuel Lanzer, a Lincoln machine gunner, only a few weeks after the event, it was the Dimitrovs, not the Americans, who first occupied the factory.* Since no Dimitrovs have been on hand to contradict them, Lincoln historians often appropriated Dimitrov military accomplishments as their own. In their reports Russian advisers like Kléber and Walter consistently allude to the superior fighting élan of the Dimitrovs.

Finally on September 5, the thirteenth day of the siege, six Republican tanks broke into Belchite. Prisoners had already charted the town and pinpointed enemy barricades and lines of communication. Bombing parties then proceeded to destroy every house on the route to the Nationalist *comandancia,* a five-story concrete building in the *plaza mayor.* An antitank gun, wheeled up to the city gate fronting the Plaza de Goya, fired point-blank up the long Calle Mayor, the only straight street in the town. By late afternoon tanks and artillery had converted the nearby houses into rubble, and two waves of the Lincolns converged on San Agustín, one from the factory and the other across the artichoke fields. They broke into the rear of the church and at the west portal set up a Dichterev to beat off a counterattack. Even with the church occupied, a lone sniper held out in the belfry for another twenty-four hours. He may have been the sniper who shot Nelson in the thigh a short time later, when, in a careless moment, he walked past a window in the olive factory. Nelson's career in Spain was over.

Throughout the remaining daylight hours of the fifth, the battle for the central district wavered back and forth. At a corner some Lincolns built a barricade out of full grain sacks, and Ephraim Bartlett, a barrel-chested Colorado miner, picked them up one by one and carrying them like shields advanced them toward enemy fire. Nearby lay old Charlie Regan—the famous "'Charlie the Sniper" of Jarama days—with a crushed left arm that had to be amputated. (Meeting Nelson in the hospital, Regan gave the clenched fist salute and said, "I still got this one!" He died in the hospital without ever getting a Zeiss scope for his *Mexicanski.*) They named this place "Dead Man's Point" to commemorate him.* On a wall near the barricade hung a hand-lettered sign that read "FORBIDDEN TO PLAY HANDBALL HERE," the owner doubtless sensitive to noise and vibration.*

The Lincolns registered their disgust with what seemed like inadequate tactics employed to invest a heavily fortified town. As the enemy snipers continued to take their toll, men hedged orders to move. If one found a snug corner or wall not sprayed with machine-gun fire, he was a fool to move on. When everything else seemed doomed to fail, someone at headquarters suggested that they hitch an antitank gun to a truck and crash through a barricade, allowing the riflemen to flood into the breach. On hearing earnest discussion of this tactic, reported a Canadian, "We all wrote our letters." About this time Walter briefly retired the XVth Brigade because they would not advance and were "dedicating themselves to pillage."*

During the night Belchite burned with a ghastly realism "no Hollywood film could ever give."* Tongues of flame reflected off the black pall of smoke hanging above the dying town. Spectators a mile away smelled the stench of putrescent, roasting carrion. At eight o'clock about five hundred Nationalists, including civilian families, collected at the city hall and vowed to break out at any cost. They hoped to find the relief column somewhere northwest of town. Stumbling over one another in the gathering darkness, they rushed down an alley leading north but ran into a devastating fire from the 24th Battalion and retreated to the city hall. Two more attempts next to the parish church also failed. Finally at ten o'clock they tried again. Lieutenant Pete Nielsen recalled the break-out. His men had fallen asleep, and he was standing in a doorway near the barrier, listening to the speeches and music booming from the Republican *altavox,* when grenades exploded in the alley. Guards across the way retreated quickly and Nielsen feared he had been cut off. But the enemy party, which included families as well as men in dresses, rushed past him and reached the grove north of town.* About two hundred fugitives were reported to have reached the Nationalist lines. Many of these escaped through an underground network as complicated as a prairie-dog town. Others used the tunnels to pop up behind brigaders.

On the morning of September 6, with ultimate victory no longer in doubt, Republicans bombed their way through smoking houses. Major Merriman led bombing parties across rooftops, dropping grenades into chimneys and courtyards—just to be sure. Merriman made each man assigned to a bomb party hold out his hand. If it shook, it meant he was rattled, and he was left behind.* A red blanket or scrap of clothing was hung from the window of each secured house. Carl Geiser, an assistant commissar who had left Ohio State University for Spain, and Ralph Thornton, a Pittsburgh black, found a civilian hiding in a garret with a rifle in his hands. Terrified, the man shouted, "Please don't shoot! I have seven children" Geyser felt the gun barrel. It was hot. He turned the sniper over to some Spaniards, who identified him as a Falangist who had organized a squad that tortured and executed Republican sympathizers. He was turned over to the local militia, which shot him, probably in the middle of his monologue about seven children.*

San Rafael, the cone-steepled parish church on the eastern edge of town, had become the nerve center of the resistance, other pockets of fighting being little more important than twitching ganglia. It had been converted into a hospital-fort containing several hundred wounded men, most of them armed. No one relished the prospect of storming that place. It would be a death trap—for both sides.

While the military commanders worked out a plan, Dave Doran, the upstart commissar who had hijacked a water truck at Quinto, stole their show. He wrote out a short speech and brought a propaganda truck to within a block of the church. An interpreter translated it and read it over the loudspeaker. Doran did not promise pie in the sky; he had a single theme—quit or die: "Come over to us and live. . . . We have you surrounded. . . . Our guns are trained on you this minute, to blow you to a million pieces at the first streak of dawn. Drop your arms and come over the barricades one by one. . . . All who come over will live. . . . If you don't come over, you will all die. There is no escape. If you don't come over you will all be killed in the morning."*[11] The loudspeaker voice, as booming as the voice of God, suddenly shut off. It was growing dark. The snout of an antitank gun peeping around a corner italicized the message. Then, in the gloom, a lone figure crawled out from the church. He was wounded and begged for a doctor. Doran collared him and ordered him back inside to fetch his companions. The soldier crawled back and for half an hour nothing happened. Then all at once rifles clattered on the cobblestones and the street next to the church was filled with shouts of "Viva la República!" as the maimed, the crippled, and their able-bodied comrades poured out of the church. Five terrified nuns crept out from the hospital. They expected to be raped and killed, so when Dr. Mark Strauss met them with bandages and medicine, they burst into tears.* When told that the victors were Americans, prisoners thought that meant that the United States had entered the war on the Communist side.* After fourteen bitter days the siege of Belchite ended. There are guarded allusions to the execution of prisoners of officer rank. Lieutenant Hernandez, who led one of the Spanish companies of the XVth, wrote, "Every one of the officers met his fate," by which he did not mean prison terms.*

Even though General Pozas received a congratulatory message from the minister of war on the "ardent valor and magnificent enthusiasm" of the Army of the East, the general was not so sanguine.[12] Zaragoza had not fallen, and he outlined the reasons in his official report: too little time to prepare for the offensive, slowness in seizing intermediate objectives, a dry and waterless terrain, "natural" fortifications at Quinto and Belchite (particularly the latter), and the poorly trained and inefficient reinforcements from Madrid.* Pozas's disparagement of the Madrid troops (the outgrowth of the famous Communist "Fifth Regiment" that, along with the Internationals, had fought Franco to a standstill at Madrid in the fall of 1936) reflected the burgeoning fear of old-line

11. Nationalist accounts allude to the huge mobile *altavoz*, which alternated soft music with patriotic songs and choric renderings of "The International." Whenever they heard the Bolshevik anthem, the Nationalists attempted to drown it out with their national song "Cara el Sol" (Face the Sun) and "Himno de la Legion." While they disparage Doran's effort as the work of "some commissar or militiaman with intellectual pretensions," they nowhere mention the mass surrender of soldiers within the church.*

12. In the same telegram one finds this astonishing observation: "This felicitation is from the Spanish government to the Spanish general and for an army totally Spanish." For Minister Prieto the participation of Walter's 35th Division of two International brigades conveniently did not exist.*

officers that Communist units like those of Modesto and Lister—both "fighting generals" highly regarded by their men—were taking control of the Army. The remarks of Lister on the campaign were more substantive. Quinto and Belchite should have been bypassed, and the troops wasted in picking these pimples should have been engaged in the real fights on the edge of Zaragoza. It was Brunete all over again. If Villanueva de la Cañada had been bypassed, Mosquito Ridge would probably have been taken, forcing Franco to lift his siege of Madrid. "What good to us were Quinto and Belchite—above all the latter, where we wasted all our reserves?" queried Lister. "And for nothing. There we used up several divisions for days while between Quinto and Belchite there was a gap of thirty kilometers with very few enemy."*

Exhausted, the Americans reflected indifference to the "victory." Every sixth man was *hors de combat* (twenty-three killed and sixty wounded). So great was the fear of an epidemic in the town that the dead were dragged into the *plaza mayor,* soaked with gasoline, stacked, and burned. In other locations details dug holes and threw in the remains of humans, pigs, and goats.* When the order came for the Lincolns to bivouac in the olive grove north of town, Carl Geiser spoke for all when he said, "Belchite—the stinkingest town I was ever in." Leonard Lamb, who took command of the Lincolns after Amlie was relieved, bitterly criticized the leadership which had made them "storm that stupid, stupid town against tremendous odds and many of our people killed because it had been announced—by the War Ministry—that Belchite had been captured."* As they filed out, the Lincolns passed a wall advertisement, illuminated by the smoky light of the funeral pyre, which read ZETSO-EXTERMINATOR. Whether Zetso was the name of a man or a brand, they never found out. Either way, it was appropriate. Among the olive trees the men built cane lean-tos as protection against the orange dust, stirred by endless motor caravans crossing the plain and trapped by eyebrows and hair.

Prieto's plan for a victory banquet within the walls of Belchite had drawn carloads of journalists, but it had to be canceled because safe walls were in short supply and feasting in surgical masks was out of the question. A few journalists—very few—covering their noses and gagging, edged into the carnopolis but retreated quickly. Ernest Hemingway, Martha Gellhorn, and Herbert L. Matthews arrived to inspect Belchite and found a town so totally ruined that often one could not tell where the streets had been. People were digging under piles of mortar, bricks, and beams pulling out corpses. Mule carcasses, cooking pots, framed lithographs, sewing machines—all covered with flies—made a surreal collage. Belchite was less town than nasty smell.[13] The visitors dropped in on the Lincoln Battalion and wrote dispatches featuring Merriman, who outlined the campaign for them "as carefully as if we were his freshman class in economics back in California." His men told how he had bombed his way forward, and although wounded six times by grenade splinters, had refused to have his wounds dressed until the cathedral [sic] was taken. A more mundane report came from a freckled redhead from Brooklyn, who said, "You ought to of seen us at Belchite. Boy! The marines got nothing on us." Even Hemingway, always skeptical about post facto battle reports, wrote that their accounts seemed to be "the sort you never know whether to classify as hysterical or the ultimate in bravery." But he reported that "since I had seen them last spring, they have become soldiers. The romantics have pulled out, the cowards have gone home along with the badly wounded. . . . Those left are tough with blackened matter-of-fact faces, and, after seven months they know their trade."* Gone was the strain of defeatist self-pity that marked the Jarama period. But missing, too, were most of the faces of that faraway time only seven months ago.[14] To Martha Gellhorn the men seemed very unwarlike and very American with "voices that you'd hear at a baseball game, in the subway, on any campus."*

Someone had to be blamed for the delay in taking Belchite, so Captain Amlie and Commissar Robinson became convenient scapegoats. Amlie, who had been lightly wounded, received an indefinite hospital leave while his repatriation papers were being prepared at Albacete. For a few weeks he hung about the battalion, a brooding Lazarus-figure, hoping to be of help but shunned like leper. Finally he was packed off to his fiancée in Valencia, and shipped home. The Party was able to wring a few more drops from him before discarding him altogether. ("Too old but will be useful in propaganda," a commissar wrote to Moscow.)* Back in the States, he traveled as a fund-raiser and outraged many of his former cohorts by harsh criticism of the do-nothing attitude of the American Socialist Party toward Spain. After this, oblivion.[15] Removing Robinson

13. The destruction of Belchite was so enormous that in the 1940s an entirely new town was constructed one mile west of the ruins. Except for clearing the rubble from the streets, Old Belchite was supposed to be left as it was on the day the armies moved out. In 2000 it was still an uninhabited ghost town, though the ruins are slightly more ruinous than when I first saw them thirty years ago. The ravages of the war are more striking here than in any other place in contemporary Spain.

14. Robert Merriman become the working model for Robert Jordan, the American guerrilla in Hemingway's For Whom the Bell Tolls. General Walter appears as Golz, and André Marty appears as André Marty. The military episode treated in the novel is the failed offensive against La Granja, in the Sierra Guadarrama, in May 1937, just before Brunete. The only International unit in this offensive was the XIVth (French) Brigade.

15. During World War II, Amlie managed a War Food Administration camp in California housing seven thousand itinerant workers. Then after the war he continued to run the camp for

THE ROAD TO ZARAGOZA

was much simpler: he was "recalled" at the request of the New York Party. Carrying secret papers prepared by Nelson, he went home by way of a detour to Moscow, where he had a gala time and spent three weeks reporting on the Americans' performance in Spain.*

The Aragon offensive had become another Republican disaster. Its two main objectives had failed—Zaragoza had not fallen, and the campaign had not diverted Franco from his campaign in the north. With the fall of Bilbao and Santander, 65 percent of the industrial production of Spain passed to the Nationalists, along with most of its mineral resources, 400 cannon, and 150 aircraft. One-quarter of the Republican Army—150,000 men—had been cut off or captured. Henceforth, the Republic would ride an ebbing tide culminating in a complete Franco victory.*

For the Americans, Quinto and Belchite stood out as victories—and in an existential sense they were. For the first time they had attacked and taken strongly fortified positions. Granted, they were opposed by raw, expendable recruits and not the Moors and Tercios de Extranjeros of previous battles, but at least they had achieved specific objectives. The men had no way of knowing how inconsequential their two victories were. In their reports to the Kremlin both Walter and Kléber understood this. The offensive had been botched from the first hours by awkward progress forward and by confused signals between commands. While the Republican armies had demonstrated skill and determination in defense, all of its offensives had ended in failure.

The high points in the history of the International Brigades were long over, and the decline was felt from top to bottom. Russian observers like Kléber, who had personally led the march of the fledgling XIth Brigade down the avenues of Madrid just a year before, recognized that the days of glory had ended. From saviors, the Internationals had become intruders, and were increasingly unwelcome. Prieto, the minister of war, made no secret of his distrust of Soviet participation and his dislike of Russian advisers, and General Miaja, Republican supreme commander of the Madrid sector, openly used insulting language when forced to confer with them. Indeed, Russian advisers reported that in some high circles the Internationals were being blamed for the Republican

---

private growers. The septic tank clogged regularly and had to be cleaned by lowering a man to free the drainage pipe from within. Since this job was dangerous, Amlie always insisted upon doing it himself. In 1950 he was asphyxiated by sewer gas before his men could pull him to safety. With him died a workman, also overcome, who had climbed down the rope to save him. By this time Milly Bennett had moved on.*

failures in battle, for—so went the argument—if the Internationals, along with their sponsor the USSR, were to leave Spain, the Germans and Italians would pull out as well. Even worse, some Republicans now actually accepted the lie promulgated by Nationalist propaganda—to wit, that the Germans and Italians intervened in the war only *after* the Russians had arrived!

Meanwhile, the battalion spent September in a series of frustrating moves back and forth along the Aragon front, bivouacking near wretched villages of consequence only to census takers and cartographers. Among the Lincolns the rumor spread that the fighting was over until the spring campaigns, and this seemed strengthened when newspapers tellingly began to refer to the "Belchite Offensive"—not the "Zaragoza Offensive." Half a loaf was better than none. Unfortunately, soothsayers among the Lincolns were dead wrong. High Command, not content to let sleeping dogs lie, was planning to loose the dogs of war one more time. The Aragon tragedy would have a final act, and North Americans were destined to be among its principal players.

]]

FUENTES DE EBRO

Life insurance rates for American volunteers in Spain, if such policies had been available, would not have been cheap. As we have seen, the Lincoln Battalion had lost most of its men in its first battle, and the Washington Battalion had ceased to exist as a separate entity after two weeks in the line at Brunete. These were not extraordinary losses—probably they were on the light side, when compared with those suffered by the XIth Brigade, which had been horribly decimated in every battle. No doubt the Comintern dismissed the casualties as the price Popular Frontists had to pay for joining the holy crusade against Fascism—at bargain rates from their point of view, considering that none of the dead or wounded were Russians. As news of repeated disasters filtered back to Albacete, the inquiry into the causes of failure brought forth "the usual suspects"—accusations of "sabotage" by Trotskyists and other Fifth Columnists. Ludicrous as this might seem, it was no more ridiculous than explanations reiterated by American Party functionaries at the Base like Bob Minor and Bill Lawrence, who insisted that failures on the battlefield were the result of poor discipline and lackadaisical attitudes. The men themselves—not their leaders at the front—were the culprits.

Trying to fill the gaps in the Lincoln Battalion with untrained replacements was like stuffing putty into rat holes. Henceforth (at least among the North Americans, who were the only Internationals still coming to Spain), new men would be held in training at Tarazona de la Mancha until they had completed a rigorous training program. This underlay the organization of the third North American contingent, which became the Mackenzie-Papineau Battalion—or the Mac-Paps. The germinal idea was exactly the same that underpinned the Washington Battalion: the Mac-Paps would become a band of exemplars who would arrive at the front superbly trained, supplied, and officered. (With a monumental ignorance of basic human nature, the Albacetians theorized that the newcomers would be a model of discipline and efficiency around which the so-called "veteran" battalions, rotten with defeatism, could rally.) To their credit, they lamented the slaughter of their countrymen, but they confused cause with result:

demoralization and desertion were pandemic among the Lincolns not because of individual besottedness, but because of external factors that the arrival of a battalion from the gates of Heaven could not change. The men themselves did not doubt that the Republic deserved to win the war—but the Nationalists dominated the air and had superior firepower, and were growing stronger every day. Moreover, there was a growing suspicion among the rank and file that enemy commanders might be better than their own. So far as the men in the front lines were concerned, military placebos were so much snake oil.

On the surface at least, the training camp at Tarazona de la Mancha was supposed to tick like a well-oiled clock as it absorbed young crusaders from the States and Canada. Veterans of Jarama and Brunete who arrived there after being discharged from hospitals or the IB prison at Camp Lukács wandered through an unfamiliar world. The ugly little town bustled with an air of supervised activity, half war college and half boys' camp. The master plan called for intensive classes in just about everything—map reading, armaments, transmissions, sniping, fortifications, Spanish history, first aid. The old tribal methods of selecting chiefs had given way to bureaucratic channels for appointing officers, most of whom possessed certificates of achievement from the new officers' training school at nearby Pozorubio, where a few Soviet advisers beefed up the faculty.[1]

Agitprop aside, the quality of instruction at Pozorubio remained as dismal as the camp itself, a dozen primitive cabins constructed out of untrimmed pine logs laid like corncribs and chinked with handfuls of clay. Leonard Lamb, a future acting commander of the Lincolns, spoke of "meaningless classes conducted in seven languages, and English was not one of them."* While the Soviet advisers smoked Lucky Strikes, their Comintern students got Gaulois. When Saul Wellman, an American buoyed by pep talks about international solidarity, asked his instructor for an American cigarette, the Russian took a deep drag and blew smoke into Wellman's eyes with the quip, "Enjoy the smoke."* In any case, the days when a volunteer was handed a rifle and allowed to fire five rounds at a hillside on the eve of his first battle belonged to the past, and no one regretted their passing. But most of the returned veterans disliked what they found, even if they secretly admitted that the changes might be necessary. Gone was the easy camaraderie of the early days, and they wondered whether all the saluting, displaying badges of rank, and tailor-made uniforms were really as important as the commissars professed to believe. Steve Nelson had not known

1. Some of the Soviet "generals" had little faith in the training operations at Tarazona and Pozorubio. Much to the anger of André Marty, Kléber organized his own school behind the front line outside Madrid and admitted only battle-seasoned men. This and other acts of independence from the Albacete orbit eventually led to Kléber's ostracism and recall to the Soviet Union in 1938.

the front of his helmet from the back—but he had been the best commander the Americans had ever had. Now, instead of Nelson, they had Joe Dallet.

Complaints against Joe Dallet became a daily chorus among the men at Tarazona. The high gloss of the Ceret trial had worn off quickly. Adjectives followed him like a swarm of flies. He was cocksure, dictatorial, megalomanic, boy-scoutish—and no end of unprintable. With sleeves rolled up nearly to his armpits, a big .45 dangling from his Sam Browne belt (originally buckled on him by Robert Merriman in a quasi-knighthood ceremony), and a big Stalin-style pipe clamped in his jaws, Joe Dallet was the monarch of all he surveyed in two-bit Tarazona. In the name of "Party discipline" he supported the segregation of officers from the rank and file at mess. If a man neglected to salute him, he could count upon a string of insults at best or a cooling-off in the brig at worst. But with Dallet it was not so much what he did as how he did it that pissed off the men. He wore the proprietary air of an overseer inspecting a gang of migratory wretches doing piecework in his grove. They sensed that his authority came not from inner strength but from the delegated power of the Party. He was a warden, not a leader.

Dallet thrived in Spain. To Kitty, his estranged wife, he confided that he had acquired "a pretty good tan from drilling without a shirt," that the battalion had "sung popular songs, smoked, and joked" while being massacred on February 27, and that "one sector of the front is *only* 90 miles west" (my emphasis). And he shared his experience of how he played war while on the shooting range: "Man, what a feeling of power you have when entrenched behind a heavy machine gun! You know how I always enjoyed gangster movies for the sound of the machine guns. Then you can imagine my joy at finally being on the business end of one."* Nearly every line he wrote and every move he made seemed somehow calculated to impress someone—his wife, his superiors, his men. He boasted about his accommodations at Tarazona, where he lived "like a real bureaucrat" in a big room all to himself. Between the lines the message was unmistakable—a nobody in Youngstown had become a big shot in Spain. Obscurely Dallet understood this change within himself and stood armed with rationalizations. As he wrote Kitty: "You probably have noticed that since I left Paris I have lost some of the rank-and-filest tendencies that I had there and before leaving the States. However, the situation does not permit having them and it's a question of jumping in wherever you can do the most good, no matter what your personal inclination might be." What this really meant was that the "rank and file" had become pawns in his maneuvers along king row.

No one detected the change in Joe Dallet more quickly than the men in the Mac-Paps. They were mystified by his mercurial behavior—bullyragging and threatening one moment and fawning and apologizing the next. His tantrums may have derived from his upbringing as a spoiled child, alien to most of the men. Whenever his followers failed to gratify his need to be worshipped, Dallet could become ruthless and irrational. No one ever doubted that he drove himself harder than the men he commanded, but often his instructional devices smacked of nursery games. He instituted, for example, a military game patterned on the spelling bee, in which recruits competed for prizes by answering such theoretical questions as How many bullets does a Maxim fire per minute? How many seconds elapse between pulling the pin of a Mills bomb and its explosion? How many machine guns are necessary to set up a crossfire? He encouraged galas and was delighted by the table decoration at a party held by the machine-gun company, as conveyed to Kitty: "Tables and walls decorated with slogans, and in the center of a square of tables, freshly cleaned and beautifully draped in red, was their pride and joy, their love, their machine gun." As proof that one was a "right guy," Dallet insisted that every man participate in the horseshoe-pitching tournament he whipped up, and he demonstrated the right stuff by advancing to the semifinals himself. (One wonders whether he was a natural horseshoe jock or whether his competitors sensed his *need* to win.) It was a moot point whether Tarazona was patterned on Fort Leavenworth or Camp Unity. (And some recruits, organizers in the National Guard, knew both places well.) In a letter he alluded to his superiors promising a "cleaning out" of Anarchists in the camp and noted that he was supervising a "trial of deserters" with hints that a few of these had been executed.*

Late in May, Kitty began to apply pressure to join him in Spain. After all, André Marty and Bob Merriman had their wives with them, and Marion Merriman had become an official member of the International Brigades. But at this stage Dallet still retained enough egalitarian scruples (or fear of disapproval) to veto the idea: "It's this way—the boys up in the front lines are naturally prey to all the rumors that at the base the officers are eating, drinking, smoking, etc., that they have their wives or other women, etc., etc. Actually the boys up front get better food, they get first crack at cigarettes, etc., but we must lean over almost backward to deprive them of any excuse for the above stories." But Joe did not lean over backward very long. In mid-July—reports circulating in the camp about the killing fields at Brunete—he lost his squeamishness about exercising the prerogatives of power. Eagerly he wrote Kitty: "Wonderful news. You can come. Get in touch with Jack [Arnold Reid] in Paris, for whom I enclose a note, and he will put you through." Part of this change stemmed from a hardening of opposition toward him by men of his battalion. A grievance committee, supported by many officers and minor commissars, wanted to depose him.

Deeply shaken, Dallet sought the advice of Steve Nelson. He wanted to submit his resignation, but doubtless Nelson reassured him. Although his veneer was as tough as ever, Dallet was inwardly bruised. His men were repudiating him; he needed Kitty to buttress a sagging ego. Into his letters came a sober, even morbid tone. A visit to Madrid prompted this comment: "There was no bombing at all except for some three shells that landed many kilometers way. I don't want to be bombarded at all, but if it *must* happen, I hope it happens while I am there." It was as though he were courting the violence of battle as a way to prove to his men how wrong they were about him. He must have known that some were openly betting that he would turn yellow at the first sound of an enemy gun. Dallet knew that the motto of a good commissar was "first to advance, last to retreat." But he did not know what he would do when battle became a fact rather than a theoretical abstraction. Would he advance or turn tail and run?

The time soon came for him to test himself. Three days after the fall of Belchite, in early September, the Mac-Paps entrained for Aragon. Kitty, delayed in Paris with an appendectomy, never reached Spain, so Dallet went to war very much alone. He sent this retrospect to his wife: "All the dirty work you did for years, cranking leaflets, passing them out in snow and sun, visiting contacts, etc. was not in vain. Everything we worked for, for years, is coming true in steel."*

In their reports to Moscow at this time, key Russian advisers reflected waning confidence in the whole International Brigade experiment. They agreed that the Republic had been saved four times by timely International intervention—in November at the gates of Madrid, in January at Las Pozas, in February at Jarama, in March at Guadalajara (where the Italian XIIth Brigade humiliated the Italian thrust at Madrid). In each case the Republic had proved its mettle in defensive operations, but each of its offensives had failed. General Walter reported that the Internationals had performed miserably at Brunete, where on July 26 there was "great panic and flight" in the XIIth and XIIIth Brigades. (He opined that the XIth and XVth were spared this humiliation probably because they had been withdrawn for a rest a few days previously.) Because of refusal to obey orders and desertions en masse, the XIIIth had been temporarily disbanded, and its arms and supplies "vulturized" by regular Spanish brigades. Up to this time the complaint was always heard among the Internationals that in tight situations Spanish units were likely to cut and run, thereby forcing the foreigners to save the day. But Walter, who commanded the 45th Division at Brunete, and Kléber, commander of the 35th, both reported that the Spanish brigades held up better and achieved more than the much-vaunted International brigades in their divisions. Both Russian commanders fumed about the foreigners' patronizing idea, accepted as gospel, that Spaniards as soldiers were "cowards." The truth was, they explained to Moscow, that the International Brigades were now worn out—demoralized by too many battles and too much punishment during their months in Spain. Once upon a time these men had boasted of being "shock troops," but now they grumbled that they were nothing more than cannon fodder.*

After Brunete the Albacete hierarchs, who had always demanded severe punishment for any hint of demoralization or defeatism, found themselves suddenly inundated with deserters from the front flooding back to the Base. (It seemed like an odd place to seek refuge, in view of Marty's growing reputation as "The Butcher of Albacete," but perhaps in the mind of badly shocked men it was a familiar place, the nearest thing to "home" these men had found in Spain.) By the end of July brigade police had rounded up four thousand of them, from all nations, and incarcerated them at Camp Lukács, the notorious IB prison.[2] The base commander later reported to Moscow that 80 percent of these defeatists had been reeducated and returned to the front "as good anti-Fascist soldiers," which was obviously a whopping lie. (More interesting—the report fails to say what happened to the remaining 20 percent *not* returned to the front!) Uncounted numbers ranged through the villages and country of La Mancha, many of them still armed, leaving behind a legacy of looting, drinking, and terror among villagers until tracked down and subdued by brigade security officers.*

After Brunete the Spaniards in the International Brigades outnumbered the foreigners, so "International" had become a misnomer. For example, Germans in the famous XIth Brigade amounted to only two hundred men, or about 10 percent of the whole. In the XIIth the proportions were the same, and the brigade commander made a case that the time had arrived to disband the unit and to arrange for the veterans to seek asylum in France. (Returning to Fascist Italy was out of the question.) Foreigners in the XIIIth—Slavs and French— numbered even fewer. Half of the XIVth were still French, but it was no secret that authorities in France were dumping jailbirds, drunks, and vagrants into Spain, where they were sucked into the International Brigades. Only in the XVth did the "foreign" contingent (English, Canadian, American, and a few

2. The NKVD had arrived in Spain with a team under Alexander Orlov in the fall of 1936 and taken root at Alcalá de Henares. Their security organization, the SIM (Servicio de Intelligentsia Militar) infiltrated and eventually took control of the military police agencies of the Republic. Copic's brother was warden of Camp Lukács. His American understudy, Tony DeMaio, a charter member of the Lincoln Battalion, specialized in ferreting out defeatism and alleged sabotage in the XVth Brigade. During much of the war he roamed the streets near the American consulate in Barcelona, tracking down deserters who were seeking help to escape from Spain.

Cubans) approach 50 percent, but their dilution increased rapidly after the Aragon offensive.

The heyday of British enlistment was long past. They were having such difficulty attracting recruits that Albacete aired the possibility of merging the British and the Americans into a single battalion, but the reaction among the Britons was so vociferous that proponents dared not proceed. Morale was precarious enough, and too much national rivalry existed in the brigade. After Brunete the balance of power in the XVth Brigade shifted dramatically in favor of the Americans, who achieved numerical superiority and began to dominate the brigade staff. "They yap too much and they've got too much money," Fred Copeman complained about them, while Sam Wild, the new British commander, could barely conceal his dislike of the Americans.* Like Copeman, Wild had been a mutineer in the Royal Navy, where he became "anti-Queen, anti-King, anti-ruling class, anti-officer, a typical Irishman, against everything." A splendid soldier, like Cunningham and Copeman, Wild was no diplomat.* Among other things the British reproached the Americans for saluting red banners, for it showed disrespect toward their own country.* Even in the United States recruiters had to fish in the pool of inexperienced idealists among the college crowd (originally disparaged as "romantics" or "adventurers") because their deaths would not damage the Party.

Within the Republican cabinet, the shaky coalition between Socialists, Anarchists, and Communists began to shatter. Prieto, minister of war and a member of the Right Socialists, was alarmed by the proliferation of Communists in high posts within the Army, for he believed that they intended to seize power if the Republic won. For him the Soviet imperium was as noxious as the Franco insurgency. When the Republic had had its back to the wall a year earlier, he had courted Marty out of necessity, but now that he had mobilized a national army of half a million Spaniards, the shoe was on the other foot and he began to kick as hard as he dared. The most effective units of the army were still under Communist control—units led by Lister, Modesto, and El Campesino; the International Brigades under control of the Comintern; and the notorious SIM (Servicio de Investigación Militar), a secret imperium that worked within the army to ferret out "defeatism." As early as June 1937, Prieto moved to break down political activism within the armed services. As a first step, he prohibited Party propaganda of all kinds in the army and forbade officers from proselytizing among civilian populations. Next he turned upon the International Brigades to bring them under government control. His Estatuto de las Brigadas Internacionales, a decree promulgated on September 23, 1937, dissolved the autonomy of the International Brigades by placing them firmly within the Republican Army. This meant that the International Brigades fell under the authority of the Foreigners' Bureau of the Ministry of War, which had been created in 1920 to incorporate non-Spaniards into the African Legion. In effect the International Brigades had become the Republican counterparts to Franco's despised foreign legion. This statute was so offensive to the ideals of the International Brigades that some brigades were on the brink of mutiny.*

According to Prieto's ukase, the International Brigades henceforth would consist of equal parts of foreign and Spanish volunteers. Half of all promotions beyond the rank of sergeant would be made by the Ministry, the other half by Albacete. The International Brigades would continue to train foreign volunteers, but once these men reached their brigades, the Ministry would decide how and where they would be used. Uniforms would be identical, except that the Internationals were permitted a special emblem (a three-pointed star slightly fatter than the Mercedes trademark) on the right side of their jackets or shirts. Theoretically, the Albacete base would be reduced to a processing center, a clearinghouse for gifts and mail from abroad, and an archive for the records of the foreign volunteers. In order to curtail the swelling power of the SIM, all personnel in the International Brigades would be subject to the regular Code of Military Justice. There were compensations. Internationals were now accorded the same privileges and rights as those in the Regular Army with respect to pensions, death benefits, and domestic leaves. Any volunteer with a year of service and a clean record would be issued a certificate, if requested, entitling him to eventual Spanish citizenship (contingent, of course, upon a Republican victory).[3] Although the publication of Prieto's plan was not tantamount to its implementation (the Marty faction fought it tooth and claw), the government emphasized that while it would tolerate the presence of "anti-Fascist" foreigners, it would not accept their meddling in political affairs.

For all its mistakes, Brunete had shown that the Republic had the wherewithal to mount an offensive rather than remain in a purely defensive posture. And the hope grew that the Western democracies might be ready to intervene in Spain if the Republic could just gain a decisive victory somewhere and be assured that Spain would not become a Soviet puppet regime. Since the decree no longer tolerated political officers in the Republican Army, there was a further

---

3. The offer of citizenship was especially attractive to men unable to return to Fascist countries. Few Americans expressed interest in remaining in Spain except for several blacks attracted by the promise of living in what they conceived to be a nonracist society.

objection to the decree within the IB higher-ups because it abolished the rank and pay (and special uniforms) of commissars, who previously held the same rank and pay as military commanders.*

Nothing in the statute congratulated or thanked the International Brigades for their service and sacrifice in the war, and signs of this ingratitude became immediately apparent. Prieto had allowed General Miaja, commander of the Madrid sector, to disband the XIIIth Brigade on the charges of cowardice, sedition, and desertion. Adding insult to injury, Miaja confiscated the armaments, vehicles, and supplies of the XIIIth and gave them to units of the Republican army. On another occasion, Colonel Vicente Rojo, his chief of operations, after arranging for the artillery batteries of an International brigade to be returned to armories for overhauling and repair, refused to give them back. As the crowning blow, it was not uncommon to hear highly placed Republicans now blaming the Russians for failures in the war effort, arguing that their presence discouraged the participation of non-Communist coalitions of the Popular Front. Fact had become so warped that ordinary people and soldiers in the ranks echoed diatribes of Nationalist Radio, which proclaimed that Hitler and Mussolini had joined Franco to save Spain *after* Stalin had intervened. In the months ahead the International Brigades would continue to provide news copy for foreign journalists, but not headlines.

As might have been expected during this feverish period of the Moscow trials, the Albacete operations came in for detailed cross-examination. What the official reports proved was that the entire IB organization was being suffocated by a bloated bureaucracy safely harbored beyond the dangers of enemy fire. A head count taken in August 1937 found that Internationals in frontline units numbered 9,041 against 3,349 ensconced at Albacete.* Breaking the numbers down further, of those stationed at Albacete 37 percent were on permanent assignment to the General Staff, 23 percent were classified as guards, police, and chauffeurs, and only 39 percent were in camps being trained for the frontline service. (The report is not clear, but the latter figure may even have included those incarcerated at Camp Lukács.) After complaints came down from the Comintern, Albacete undertook some measures to cut the fat. All officers on duty at the base had to report to Headquarters for personal interviews before they could continue drawing their salaries. It was then discovered that seventy of them had no duties at all and were unable to explain why they had been commissioned as officers. Top Secret reports from professional soldiers among the Soviet advisers like Kléber and Walter conveyed in letters to the Kremlin their disgust at the incompetence and featherbedding of the Albacete clique.* Walter told a fellow Soviet officer that the only way to deal with an envoy from Marty's camp was to send him on his way with a kick in the pants. Kléber tried to implement constructive changes, bit by bit. One target was the garbled IB postal system. All incoming mail came to the Madrid post office, but instead of being sent directly to units at the front, it had to be transshipped to Albacete, where it was sorted and censored by a huge staff under one colonel and two lieutenant colonels. Cleansed of suspicious and subversive matter, it then returned to the Madrid post office for distribution. Since the transit took anywhere from fourteen to eighty days and was a waste of both personnel and petrol, Kléber argued that the central IB post office should be moved to Madrid. He failed to reckon with the vehemence of the Albacete faction, which protested that a Red Army adviser had no business meddling in Comintern procedures. In the end nothing was done after one lieutenant colonel had been dropped from the postal roster.

Soviet commanders also exposed an epidemic of corruption within individual brigades. Walter revealed that in making head counts the brigades kept two sets of books—one for Albacete, the other for Division. The trick was to inflate the Albacete reports so that more funds, transport, and supplies could be obtained, but to deflate the Division reports so that when an attack failed, the commanders could blame it upon a paucity of men.[4] General Walter, after a surprise inspection of the XVth Brigade, reported that the miscounting of the Albacete report amounted to 923 men, or nearly double the complement of a battalion. These men probably once existed but had been scattered by hospitalization, reassignment to other IB services (the propaganda department, located in Madrid, was much sought after), and desertions. By inflating the number of men in a brigade, the commander could also partially conceal the shocking disparity between the percentage of Spaniards in the brigade versus the percentage of those on the staff. After the Ebro campaign, for example, 75 percent of the XVth Brigade consisted of Spaniards, but they comprised only 14 percent of brigade staff. (The discrepancy was even greater in other brigades, the Germans of the XIth being the worst offenders.) Increasingly, native Spaniards tried to avoid assignment to the International Brigades. It was bad enough to feel like a second-class citizen in your own country, but added to that was the danger of

---

4. In the International Brigades each man had three pesetas per month deducted from his wages. This was placed in a slush fund allowing special purchases of foodstuffs from private vendors and distributed to the men at the front. Obviously, everything was to be gained by inflating the personnel strength of a brigade. The same was true with cigarette rations. This special levy for the Internationals caused bitterness among the Spanish battalions serving with the Internationals, for they did not receive the additional foodstuffs and the foreigners rarely shared.

being executed on the spot if captured, which happened all too frequently. Walter found other deplorable conditions during his inspection of the Americans. He told Moscow that he had been shocked by the condition of their rifles. Peering down bores he saw rust and corrosion that recalled to his mind a seventeenth-century musket barrel that had been dug out of the rubble at Belchite. Ninety-five percent of their rifles lacked bayonets and cleaning rods were long gone. (By contrast, in a nearby Spanish brigade all rifles had been cleaned and fitted with bayonets.) Discipline was so lax among the Americans that their camp reminded Walter of the "cozy atmosphere of a Quaker society."* Altogether the International Brigades by late fall of 1937 were a ragtag lot. Yet on them would fall the burden of making a final desperate attack to punch a hole in the enemy line and reactivate the dead Zaragoza offensive.

For five weeks after the fall of Belchite, the XVth Brigade milled around Aragon. Camions shuttled men, armaments, and supplies from one mud-daubed village to another in a series of bewildering moves that disoriented all of them, including their leaders. On one occasion they prepared for an offensive near Huesca—a battle zone that had been a virtual death trap for other International Brigades—fortunately called off on account of rain, and the desertion of a lieutenant colonel said to have given the plans for the attack to the enemy.* Logistics, however, had never been better: for the first time the Lincolns moved rapidly and comfortably in motorized convoys.[5] Even though they went in circles, they traveled in style. (Some wag among them called this rigmarole "maneuvering to confuse the enemy.") Toward the end of September, the XVth went into reserve in the mountains north of Zaragoza. It was almost luxury to be under canvas. One night a motion-picture van arrived. On the flickering screen set up among olive trees, the XVth Brigade watched themselves taking Belchite for Paramount Pictures.

As chill winds, harbingers of autumn, swept down from the Pyrenees, applications for release and repatriation by six-month veterans continued to pile up at brigade headquarters and at Albacete, but there were only two ways to obtain a discharge—uselessness (bad wounds) or clout (Party pull). A group of twenty-five disgruntled Americans left Aragon without permission and turned up in the office of Bill Lawrence in Albacete, where they claimed their six-month "contracts" (nothing on paper, of course) had expired and warranted

5. Regular Spanish units were less fortunate. It was now customary for the International Brigades to conceal the number of vehicles they had. The XIth, for instance, listed thirty-eight in its motor pool, but General Walter found out the number was actually ninety-four! By contrast, a Spanish brigade nearby had no vehicles at all, not even an ambulance for 2,760 men.*

repatriation. They were court-martialed and escorted back to Aragon under guard.[6] A smaller number, including Paul White, who had an outstanding record in Spain, stole an ambulance and took off in the general direction of France. White had a change of heart and loitered in Catalonia until picked up by brigade police and sent back for trial. Dave Doran, who had taken Steve Nelson's place as brigade commissar, demanded they be shot. Loath to assume this responsibility on his own, he called a meeting of battalion and company commissars and demanded their unanimous approval. But the commissars used a lingering vestige of union-hall democracy to vote down Doran's recommendations. The deserters received sentences of hard labor and eventually rejoined the brigade. Doran, more Stalinist than parliamentarian, was unhappy with the verdict. With his arrival as supreme political czar, the XVth Brigade entered a despotic phase.

Short, husky Dave Doran (Dransky) had grown up as the tough kid on his block, a tenement dead-end in Albany. While pussies like Joe Dallet studied how to pass as working class, Doran was the real McCoy. His father had emigrated from Russia in 1907 to the Lower East Side of New York, where he worked as cigar maker and photographer's handyman. Hating the ghetto, he moved upriver to Albany in 1910, the year his second son was born. Before he was out of short pants, Dave was hawking the *Albany Times* on street corners and delivering groceries for the A&P. While his father babbled about the glories of the Old Country (with no effort to return there), the son learned how to fend for himself in the New. He was good with his fists and accurate with a rock. Nobody called him David except his mother. At sixteen he dropped out of school and later claimed that his only pleasant memories of Albany High were of geography class and Joseph Conrad.*

Doran shipped out of New York on a tanker owned by Morgan Line, a company said to be so rough on seamen that experienced men tried to avoid it. His family got no letters and heard no news until one day when he turned up in Albany with a broken nose and jaw, fruits of shore leave in Sweden. The jaw never healed properly, and his twisted face froze into a scowl. At sea he read a lot—especially Ibsen, Sinclair, and Galsworthy. But Conrad was his favorite. Like Lord Jim, Dave Doran seemed to be waiting for a supreme test.

---

6. According to three witnesses who later fled to Barcelona and sought refuge at the U.S. consulate, these men were executed. The witnesses were terrified: they tried to make a deal with the consul whereby they would set forth the names of recruiters in the United States in return for safe passage to the French frontier. The offer was declined, and they were subsequently picked up by brigade policemen, led by the notorious Tony DeMaio, and returned to the line. One of them, Albert Wallach, was imprisoned in DeMaio's prison camp at Casteldefels and was never seen again.

Scurvy put him on the beach in 1929. For a time he worked as an apprentice to his uncle, a New York paperhanger and sign painter. In his free time he hung around the Hungarian Workers Club on 59th and First Avenue, where he met some Wobblies. The turning point, or so his later publicists claimed, came in 1930, when he found his landlord evicting a family. Although he barely knew the victims, he demanded that they be permitted to remain. When the slumlord whined, "What do you expect of me—charity?" Doran replied, "Not charity—justice!" Two months later he joined the YCL.

The League sent him South to build membership among the unemployed, particularly among Negroes, regarded as an impossible task because few of his prospects had sufficient political experience to comprehend trade unionism, much less Communism. He arrived in Chattanooga on a freight with a total budget, for personal maintenance and operations, of three dollars a week. Probably no one at YCL headquarters expected to see him again. For a year he kept on the move, doggedly sniffing for potential strikes and riots, the breeding ground for recruits. In Scottsboro, Alabama, he was beaten up for protesting the innocence of the black boys accused of having raped a white woman. During the Gastonia textile strike, he built a membership roll from zero to two hundred in three months—or so his later publicists claimed. He was a master of CP shenanigans. Police dragged him off the steps of Charlotte City Hall for alternating quotations from the Declaration of Independence with a petition demanding unemployment relief. He worked with other groups in the Black Belt trying to organize a Soviet Negro Republic, even as he remarked to a fellow recruiter, "Do anything you want, just be sure to get plenty of publicity."

Soon Gil Green and other leaders of the YCL realized that Doran was too valuable to be thrown away in the South, which was a notorious wasteland for Party recruitment. By 1933 he had been recalled to organize the real stuff—steelworkers in Allegheny County, Pennsylvania. In the Pittsburgh area, "Red Squads" among the police ruthlessly warred with "agitators," and Doran went underground, regularly changing his name and residence. Before he was twenty-five, he was a member of the Central Committee of the YCL. Bored by the picayunish details of his job, he repeatedly asked permission to go to Spain but was rejected on grounds that he was married and was too important for the Party. But after the fiasco at Jarama, he was sent over to bolster party discipline among demoralized elements.

Letters from Doran to his wife from Spain were about as perfunctory as Party throwaways. From Tarazona he wrote: "Trying hard to be a good soldier and fill some Fascist bellies with lead. Feel certain that I can more than hold my own when we meet the bastards out there. The tough training has really hardened and toughened me. Just what a guy needs after being a functionary of the League a number of years."* In three pistol-shot sentences he used the words "hard" and "tough" twice each, and these words reflected the core of his worldview. Unlike Dallet, with whom he worked at the Tarazona camp, Doran had not been polluted with a bourgeois prose style. He talked mean because he was mean. A machine gun was an implement for filling "Fascist bellies with lead," not a literary symbol. And for Doran a clenched fist had less to do with Popular Front solidarity than with hitting something. Issues, like colors, were either black or white. Probably in his single-dimensioned view of the war, Franco's armies were really composed of Fascist mercenaries, financed by obese capitalists, and commanded by Gestapo degenerates. Shades of gray seemed lost on Doran.

Going into battle at Quinto as one of Nelson's juniors, Doran found that the firing line was not the picket line. In battle, something more was required than collecting scrawls on a petition or nailing a placard to a pole. It is significant that his golden moment during the battle came when he hijacked the water truck and drove it into the American lines—exactly what a dead-end kid could be expected to do. Although he must have been proud of his exploit (which later got raves from left-wing publicists), he did not mention it in the letter written shortly afterward to his wife: "The thing I like best is that I have gone into action against the enemy and have had ample opportunity to work under rather sharp and direct fire. Always did want to test myself and am not entirely disappointed with myself." "To test oneself"—Joseph Conrad had said it all before.

After Nelson's wound at Belchite and Doran's stunt with the loudspeaker at the parish church (his speech was later called "the heavy artillery of the science of politics"), Doran assumed the post of XVth Brigade commissar. He had done well indeed. Within four months of his arrival in Spain, he had become the highest-ranking American in the International Brigades, for as political adviser to Copic he held a rank equivalent to lieutenant colonel. He was only twenty-six. What no one knew at this time—and how they would have shuddered had they known—was that Doran's ambition was to assume *military* command of the brigade. That moment would arrive in time, but in September 1937 it was still in the future. For the moment he had to be content with nearly absolute political power. Men had followed Nelson because they believed in him;[7] they would obey Doran because they feared him. Most of the draconian measures, the persecutions, and the executions carried out in the XVth Brigade, belong to the Doran period.

7. During the Quinto-Belchite fighting, the cry "Don't let 'em get Steve" passed down the line. When they learned that he had been wounded, the men were appalled, but when word came that his wound was not life-threatening, they cursed him roundly—for not staying in a safe place behind the lines.

In mid-September there was a parade outside the XVth campground at Aza-ila to bid farewell to the Dimitrov Battalion and to welcome the Mac-Paps. Every honest volunteer had to admit that the Dimitrovs had been "our crack battalion." At Jarama and Brunete they were sometimes so far ahead of the other battalions that they were, in effect, between the lines. They had served for so long as the backbone and sinew of the brigade that the others felt an empti-ness, as though a vital organ or nerve had removed, as the gaunt, gallant Slavs formed a pathetically thin line and marched away to join the 129th Brigade, a mixed International unit including Czech and Bulgarian battalions. Unfortu-nately for the XVth, Colonel Copic did not go with them.[8]

As the Mac-Paps marched up to take their place, a Briton shouted in falsetto, "Aren't they just darlin'?" They did appear too sleek, too natty, too young—more like cadets than soldiers. The old-timers were visibly cynical about the fighting potential of this "best trained battalion of the International Brigades" and wondered how long it would take for the gloss to wear off. Dallet glowed "fresh and clean," while his battalion "looked down at us, scurvy, filthy, demor-alized bastards because we ain't singing the International every hour on the hour."* In turn, the Mac-Paps were shocked at their first sight of the Lincoln Battalion: "thin to the point of emaciation, bloodshot, pus-running eyes, facial bones sticking out, brusque to the point of rudeness." Their conversation bor-dered on sedition. "They complained, cursing the staff, the lack of food, and wondering when the people back home were going to force their governments to lift the blockade."* On the first night that they camped together, some Lincolns, tortured by the Mac-Paps bugler, stole his bugle, stamped it flat, and flung it back.* So there! Aragon was no parade ground. And at the first staff meeting, Doran, whose enmity toward Dallet seemed to be instinctive, ground him down at every opportunity. Aragon was no summer camp. The aura of special privilege quickly tarnished in the dust, lice, dysentery, and pleurisy of Aragon.

Even as the Mac-Paps psyched themselves for their first battlefield trial, rumblings against Joe Dallet swelled to mutinous proportions. Just before the attack, Dave Doran reported to the American representative at Albacete that "a percentage of the men openly declare that dissatisfaction with Joe and there is some talk of removal. . . . We are definitely against a removal and will not toler-ate the suggestion of one." The solution might lie in a regimen to teach him

8. General Walter had "borrowed" the Dimitrovs from Kléber and then refused to give them back. He repeatedly reported to Moscow that they had been mainly responsible for the successes at Quinto and Belchite. Copic was, of course, despised by Walter and Kléber both, who were profes-sional soldiers, not political mannikins.

"how to act self-critically and to involve the men in suggestions and improvements and changes of political work," although he confessed it was "rather a late date to change the situation prevailing in that battalion. At some future time it might be necessary to move Dallet to a less important position."*

On October 10, the XVth Brigade bivouacked around the cemetery overlooking the old battleground at Quinto. In the moonlight the shattered houses shone like jagged silhouettes of icebergs. The village was so depopulated that a newcomer remarked that "the cemetery was the liveliest place in town." Even though the sky buzzed with airplanes, mostly enemy, and sounds came to them of a massive artillery barrage upriver, no one quite believed the rumors of reopening the Zaragoza offensive. Carl Geiser, the new Lincoln commissar, set up headquarters in a vacant house and planned to settle down comfortably. No sooner had he flopped on his first mattress since training camp than a runner barged in. The brigade was moving up to the front immediately.

Leonard Lamb, slated to succeed Amlie as Lincoln commander, was in the hospital after shooting himself in the foot while cleaning a captured pistol.[9] So the command went to Philip Leighton Detro, one of the most unlikely Americans ever to fight in Spain. This lanky, six-foot-four Texan seemed to take few things seriously, least of all himself. He liked to say that he had originally come to Spain to collect fifteen hundred dollars a month as a flier and that he had crossed the frontier on April Fool's Day. While other politicos like Joe Dallet tried to eradicate all lingering traces of bourgeois upbringing, Detro openly talked of his wasp heritage (probably exaggerating it for dramatic effect). Among pious proletarians, he was a blasphemer. Not only did he flaunt Texas attitudes—strapping his pistol low and tied to his thigh with a leather thong as though fast on the draw and miming the "level stare" like the hero of a Zane Grey novel—but he claimed to be a spiritual Mississippian.* While in training at Tarazona, he was suspected, at various times, of being a romantic, a nincompoop, or a spy. Way back when, or so he spun his yarn, the Detros had been wealthy Mississippi planters at a time when wealth in Mississippi meant "slave owner." One of his mother's kinfolk had been a general in the Civil War—"on the Confederate side, of course." ("Of course," echoed comrades from the Bronx.) When Reconstruction brought misery, poverty, and "nigra problems,"

9. A native of Cleveland, Leonard Lamb graduated from CCNY and NYU and served as a social worker in the Emergency Relief Bureau of New York City prior to going to Spain. Wounded several times he always returned quickly to the battalion and served loyally until the Lincolns left for home.

the Detros moved on to Conroe, Texas, to grow up with the country. But times were bad, and the Detros were always genteel-poor. His mother took a job teaching school. After graduation from Davy Crockett High School in 1928, he began to work his way through Rice Institute but quit after a year to ship out of Gulf ports on a tanker. In 1932, while on shore leave in Germany, he heard Hitler deliver a speech, and in the street brawl that followed, Detro lost a shirt sleeve. Politics was not the issue: "I didn't like getting pushed around."*

Aboard ship, Detro began to fancy himself as a writer. In 1934 he quit the Merchant Marine and enrolled at the University of Missouri in the journalism program. He joined Alpha Tau Omega, a fraternity for Southern gentlemen, and took flying lessons at Columbia Field. Classmates felt he was "a restless, soldier-of-fortune type." In one semester he completed third-year Spanish and flunked creative writing. At year's end he was "excused from the university" for having accumulated seventy-seven overcuts in his classes—something of a local record. For a year he worked in New York for a writers' syndicate.

When Detro heard that the Republic was recruiting fliers at fancy prices, he submitted an application to the Spanish consul but learned he had not logged enough hours. He then tried to join the Lincoln Battalion, but the Party turned him down, probably as a poor political risk. But after the Jarama fiasco he was accepted because of his National Guard and ROTC experience, limited as this was. On the boat going over, when another volunteer asked him what he thought of the Spanish situation, the gangly Texas drawled, "Back where I come from, they think Spain is too far away to affect the price of cotton." He enjoyed the role of political dummy, like the time he said he thought the "class struggle" had to do with getting from class to class at the University of Missouri.[10]

At Tarazona he commanded a squad. At Brunete he took over Amlie's company and led them up Mosquito Ridge, where he was lightly wounded while tending to a dysentery attack. He missed Quinto but was released from hospital in time to lead a Belchite bombing party. He was never a fashion plate like Merriman or Doran. While other officers were turning up in tailored uniforms, Detro invariably wore a faded beret and a turtleneck sweater several sizes too large for his thin chest. He had grown a mustache, barely visible except in certain angles of light. In manner he affected an ironically chipper style, favoring phrases like

10. One cannot rule out the possibility that Detro pretended to be more apolitical than he really was in order to conform to the Popular Front image projected by the International Brigades. John Gates, who became the highest-ranking commissar among the Americans in Spain, in 1968 told me that Detro had actually been a Party organizer among Texas farm workers. I was able to confirm that he had studied at Missouri and Rice.

"m'boy" and "right-o" in the tradition of Hollywood Englishmen. At twenty-six he was the youngest commander the Lincoln Battalion had yet had. While the men liked his brio, "for him the word 'comrade' did not come easily."*

Late in the afternoon of October 12, as the men climbed into trucks, General Walter called a meeting of the 45th Division commanders to explain the new Zaragoza push. At dawn the XVth would assault Fuentes de Ebro from trenches about a kilometer distant, opening a gap for reserve units to rush through. The British were to deploy on the far right, next to the river, and attack across irrigated vegetable fields, the Lincolns would hold the center and advance along the Zaragoza highway, and the Mac-Paps, on the far left flank, would cross a barren plain cut with a few *barrancas*. A routine plan? Not at all. Walter played his trump card. Fuentes de Ebro had been so heavily garrisoned and fortified during the past six weeks that it was assumed to be impregnable to conventional infantry attack. Therefore, several companies of the 24th (Spanish Battalion) would mount on top of forty-three Soviet BT5 tanks, which would then hedgehop the Republican trenches, sweep across a mile of no-man's-land, and crush down the enemy wire and barricades.[11] As soon as the tanks broke into the town, the Spaniards would jump down and attack the outer defenses from the rear, like a guerrilla force, while the Anglo-Americans moved against the place frontally. In field maneuvers during the past summer, the French Army had parachuted infantry behind "enemy" lines, and the surprise tactic was reported to have been a great success. Since the Spaniards had no air transport fleet, the Russian tank commander, Colonel Kondratayev, decided to imitate the French, carrying the troops on tanks, not airplanes. If it worked, the colonel might revolutionize modern warfare. If it failed? *C'est la guerre.*

What the master planner failed to take into account was that, except for the narrow roadway, the ground between the lines was scored by terraces and gouged by irrigation ditches, none of which showed clearly on his charts. (Experts claimed that tanks with Christie suspension could jump twice their length.) The 24th had received no training in this maneuver, much less in how to ride a tank into a hotly contested battle. The operation was conceived in such haste that the officers had only a few hours to reconnoiter the terrain and prepare their men for battle. Walter regretted that tactical details would have to be

11. Though there is no evidence for it, it is likely that the XVth Brigade leaders, most of whom were Anglo-Americans who had acquired a keen sense for sniffing disasters-in-the-making foisted the tank-taxi idea on the Spanish battalion, which had little clout at Brigade. Few of the newest Spanish recruits had ever seen a tank before, much less ridden on one. Perhaps the brigade staff even thought the youngsters might get a kick out of it.

worked out after the brigade moved into position—that is to say, in utter darkness between nightfall and daybreak. There was not even time to provide company commanders with maps indicating enemy strongpoints. Doubtless the officers would be able to discover these places for themselves—after the attack had begun. Perhaps by a kind of military Braille? (A major blunder lay ahead because the Soviet advisers had mistaken green on their Spanish maps for steppes rather than irrigated, and near-swamp, terrain.)*

To make matters worse, the tank regiment did not receive their orders until 2300 of the night before the attack. To avoid detection by enemy aircraft, they had to take rough and circuitous routes amounting to thirty to forty kilometers that jarred bogies and other mechanical equipment out of alignment. Nothing serious—but no time for even minor adjustments. Only on their arrival were the tankers told they would carry infantry "riders." They objected—there were few handholds on their tanks—but were overruled. The Spaniards would be protected by sandbags—if these were not dislodged. The tank commanders had no time to reconnoiter the ground or to locate enemy strongpoints. But probably they had time to remember that at Villanueva de la Cañada a single German 47 mm gun in the church tower had knocked out twelve of their machines.

As though there weren't enough problems on the eve of battle, Commissar Doran called a special meeting of the brigade commissariat to discuss whether Dallet should be removed from his post. From sundown until two in the morning more than a dozen men discussed, grilled, and analyzed Joe Dallet. The charges ranged from Party heresy—he was a romantic, a totalitarian, a bourgeois—to picayune beefs—his breaking up card games, browbeating a sick man for malingering, even hoarding tobacco for his Stalinesque pipe.* Outside the barn, if the commissars had paid attention, they would have heard the noise of trucks and men moving along the highway toward Fuentes, but the war outside absorbed them less than the kangaroo court inside. On hand as hanging judge was Robert Minor, the Comintern representative among the Americans in Spain. After nearly eight hours of denunciation and dissection, Dallet begged for permission to resign. This was refused, for reasons unknown.[12] It is alleged that Dallet's only defender was Saul Wellman, his assistant commissar, a young truck driver from Elizabeth, New Jersey. While the others flayed Dallet alive, Wellman tried to defend him. (At one point Wellman burst into tears.) By the time this stormy session ended, most of the brigade had long since vanished

12. The ostensible reason, of course, was that his dismissal on the eve of battle would have had a terrible effect upon the Mac-Paps—hardly convincing since the men loathed Dallet. It is sometimes conjectured that Dallet, perhaps influenced by his wife, was "back-sliding" from the Party.

from Quinto, and the commissars had to hustle to catch up. As events would show, their time would have been better spent in planning a complicated attack rather than in purging a comrade.

It was nearly dawn when Dallet reached the Mac-Paps. Although the attack was only hours away, he scratched out a letter to Kitty:

> Kitty Darling: I've been a louse about writing but there was no sure way to reach you and anyway we've been on the jump. Now we're waiting for the convoy—by the time you get this we'll be in action. We are in shape and will do our best. Writing this by flashlight. I hope that by the time we get out of the lines you'll be in the country to spend a few days leave with me.
>
> Until we meet—
>
> Joe

What Dave Doran wrote his wife—if anything—is not recorded.

Behind the Republican lines, just southeast of Fuentes de Ebro, a two-mile stretch of vehicles jammed the road, meaning that most attackers had a long walk with full equipment even before they attained their jumping-off positions. The British, first in line, entered their assigned section of trench in the dark without disturbing the enemy. But the Lincolns, next in line, were spotted in the first rays of dawn and set off a chain reaction of small-arms fire. Ricocheting bullets sparkled against the flint of the highway. Finally came the Mac-Paps, who were etched against the skyline as they moved over a crest and baptized into the rituals of the Spanish civil war with the blood of a dozen men before they reached their attack trench. Within minutes the "best trained battalion" had turned into a "mad jumble of wildly running men, running any god-damned direction to get out of the way of the fire," recalled a survivor.* Never popular among the men, Captain Robert Thompson did attract admiring glances that morning as he stood exposed on the parapet of a trench directing his men into their positions.[13] Those scrambling forward ran headlong into twisted coils of barbed wire that the enemy had strung up when this was their defensive line. Thus the battle for Fuentes commenced with a bizarre scene— Mac-Paps burrowing under or daintily picking their way through wire to reach

---

13. The Mac-Paps were disappointed when Merriman was pulled upstairs to staff and Thompson took the battalion. "We got in command a young man nobody seemed to like. He looked young and inexperienced, and he seemed to be studying papers half the time, as if he had to follow directions."*

their takeoff trenches, which proved to be skimpy and shallow ditches used by their predecessors as latrines. In this hubbub the machine gunners abandoned their Maxims and later had to be ordered back to fetch them. Some Mac-Paps dutifully opened fire on the "enemy," which proved to be the Lincoln Battalion on their right.* A "surprise" attack was now out of the question.

Since the tanks, scheduled to appear at dawn, failed to show, high noon became the zero hour. Through faulty reconnaissance they had been spread out so far to the flanks that it took most of the morning to work back to the center. It was nearly noon before they had been refueled, picked up their "riders," and massed behind the Republican line. An artillery barrage, planned to synchronize with the armored attack, had quit hours before. (Two of the batteries were manned by inexperienced gunners using guns captured—with inadequate shells—from the enemy only two weeks earlier.) Training binoculars on the enemy trenches located on the edge of Fuentes, brigade observers had watched with satisfaction as distant antlike creatures fled into the town upon the opening barrage and later with dismay as the same antlike figures dashed back into their trenches when the barrage ceased. Captain Robert Thompson, a twenty-three-year-old Oregonian who commanded the Mac-Paps, had been wounded in the February 27 fiasco at Jarama. As the present battle got under way, he must have had a rush of *déjà vu.* (All that was needed to complete the scenario was for General Gal to be released from his Russian prison and recalled to command.)

Bill Neure, a much-admired German-American who commanded First Company, held a conference. "His face lit like a Christmas tree," Al Amery recalled. "He said, 'We attack at noon!' as if to say 'The celebration begins at noon.'"* Amery, who had spent twelve years in the U.S. Army and U.S. Navy, shuddered. "Attack at noon? I'd never heard of anybody attacking at noon before, and with a hot fire coming over our trenches?" Neure dismissed them with final instructions, "Just follow the tanks."

Precisely at noon about fifty Republican light bombers, two-wingers moving like lazy dragonflies, banked in a long half-circle and unloaded sticks of bombs on the enemy lines, blotted out entirely by clouds of smoke and dust. ("The most Republican planes I ever saw in the air at one time all through the war.")* This was the signal for the tank attack. But it was nearly two o'clock before the BT5s fired their first salvo and swept forward in a wide formation. Although instructed to move at a walking pace to allow the infantry to follow them closely, the tanks took off "like express trains." They were driving ahead at twenty-five miles per hour or more when they churned through the hip-deep trenches of the brigade. The foundations of the earth seemed to shake. In some cases the ground not only shook but caved in, crushing brigaders under the steel treads. Crouched behind sandbags and hanging on for dear life were the riders of the 24th Battalion—between five to twelve men per tank (sources vary)—mostly Valenciano farm boys more accustomed to donkey than to horse power. As they passed over, some of them gamely managed a clenched-fist salute. Others, their brains perhaps addled by the jarring ride, opened fire on the Anglo-Americans, mistaking them for the enemy.

The thundering passage of the tanks through the trenches created confusion and, in some instances, hysteria. One squad of Spanish *quintos* newly inducted into the Lincoln Second Company assumed that the monstrous machines belonged to a Nationalist column attacking them from the rear and opened fire on the riders—fortunately they were bad shots. Another one threw down his rifle and attempted to surrender to an onrushing tank; he barely escaped being crushed by the treads.

Many of the tank drivers wholly lost their sense of direction. Not only did they fail to smash the wire in front of the left wing of the Mac-Pap position, but they moved parallel to the trench in a westward direction rather than toward the enemy line to the north. Al Amery, a section leader, got his men over the top, but finding their progress blocked by the wire, he sensibly led them west looking for a gap. He found none. Enemy fire was increasing—rounds were zinging as they struck the wire—and the tanks were long gone. His company commissar joined them and asked, "What now?" Amery was equally bewildered, "Jesus! I don't know. We were supposed to follow the tanks, but I don't know where they went."* Bill Neure, hit when he led their charge outside the trench, was dying, so Amery ordered the remnant back into the trench, where they commenced sporadic fire against enemy parapets barely visible at seven hundred meters. While everybody was cursing the madness of running that distance through enemy fire, a youngster named Andy missed the point, "I could do it because I don't smoke, but you guys couldn't make it."

The riders on the tanks were not making it either. Few survived the toboggan ride across no-man's-land, for they were picked off, bounced off, or jumped off long before they reached the enemy lines. At the first barrier, a four-foot rise from one terrace to another, the tanks milled about like a swarm of crazed beetles, not daring to stop because antitank shells punctured their hides like so much cardboard. The jolt in crossing the barrier shook off another layer of riders. Those tanks closer to the river entered a quagmire of waterlogged sweet-potato fields and tall cane crisscrossed with irrigation ditches. They could not move forward, but at least they were hidden in the canebrakes. Most of the British infantry in this sector wisely decided to go to ground, ignoring a Czech staff officer screaming, "Advance!"*

For a brief period in the Mac-Pap sector north of the highway, there was a dim possibility of success. According to Alferez Antonio Duarte, a Nationalist lieutenant in the first trench line, the tank attack came as a complete surprise. First came a mysterious thundering noise from behind a distant hill, followed by the awesome sight of tanks bursting through several breaks in the Republican line and forming a column that "seemed endless." On a front more than a kilometer long, the Nationalists had only three light antitank guns and no heavy artillery at all. When the leading tank got within a hundred meters of the first Nationalist trench, it displayed a red signal flag. Nine tanks surged forward to break through, while the others lined up and maintained rapid cannon fire on the trenches. The lieutenant went on to describe the attack, "About half the tanks were surmounted by bags of sand behind which soldiers crouched. Those not brought down by our machine guns were brought down by hand grenades as soon as the tanks came within good range. Very few of them [the tanks] managed to reach our trench. Their crews were quickly killed or captured. Many of the attackers got out from those rolling 'strongboxes' as soon as they were within range of our grenades and ran away."[14] Tanks burst into flames, and their crews were shot as they climbed out of their hatches. Here and there isolated Spaniards who had survived the ride cowered behind broken tanks, unable to move forward or back.

Since the tanks had no radios, it had to be every man-jack for himself. Duarte explained that the tanks had lost their sense of planned attack and wheeled about trying to dodge spots of heavy resistance. "We stopped them by throwing cans of sulphur and gasoline into their caterpillar treads and into their ventilators." A few tanks succeeded in passing over the trenches and entering the town. The Republican staff had assumed that if this happened the whole defensive line would collapse as trenches emptied in panic. Nothing of the sort occurred. "Some [tanks] passed through our line and we left them to reserves in ravines behind our trenches. Soon I saw two burning tanks coming from the village along the highway, retreating. . . . We then brought back half of our men in the rear to complete the destruction of tanks trying to retreat. We captured sixteen." Although two tanks penetrated into the village, they stalled in narrow

14. Alferez Antonio Duarte gave this report to General H. J. Reilley, U.S.A., who was an observer watching the developing battle from a Nationalist command post. Reilley published his full report in the January 28, 1939, issue of *L'Illustration* (Paris). A typed copy of his report is on file in the U.S. Military History Institute, Carlisle Barracks, Pennsylvania. General Monasterio, commander in chief of the Nationalist cavalry, told Reilley that the war would be over had it not been for the superiority of the cannon mounted in the Soviet tanks. By contrast the German tanks were armed only with machine guns and "were as helpless as the soldier dressed in a leather doublet against a horseman protected by his armor."

streets and were set on fire by rear-echelon rabble including quartermasters and cooks.* Meanwhile, the surviving tanks fired their guns until they were out of ammunition (probably wasting shots in order to fall back as quickly as possible) and then tried to withdraw. Those that made it back to the Republican lines were employed at night like farm tractors trying to recover those embedded in the bog. In all, eighteen tanks of the forty-eight were lost and one-third of their crews killed or wounded.[15]

What all this amounted to was that the armored attack proceeded without any infantry support. As it happened, the home trenches were situated on a slight hump in the floodplain, which meant that attackers were exposed as soon as their heads popped over the skyline. Their first cover, the walls of a terrace, lay several hundred yards ahead. They walked into an enfilading fire that was "simply shocking." Over on the right, beside the railroad, the British were stopped cold within minutes after both their commander and commissar were killed.[16] In the center, Captain Detro led the Lincolns forward to the first terrace under spotty cover of oily smoke from burning tanks. Seeing that further attack was useless, he ordered his men to dig in and wait for the counterattack he expected would soon follow.

Off to the left, the Mac-Paps paid an enormous price for their naive élan. Too inexperienced to comprehend that the attack had been botched, they advanced against a lashing fire with the mechanical precision of actors in a sham battle—"kneel, fire, rise, advance." "This training was useless," complained a survivor, "only we didn't know it at the time." Men were falling like cornstalks, but they seemed to believe that this was how battles were supposed to be fought. "Immediately we ran into a murderous fire and the men started to drop all around. In less than ten minutes our company strength was reduced by half. There was no cover," remembered a Mac-Pap.*

First Company stalled when its commander fell, and Thompson picked Joe Dallet as operational commander to get them moving again.* With his pipe clamped tightly in his mouth and automatic pistol flourished in his hand, he

15. As might be expected, some of the T-26s, which were superior to anything that the Germans had, were hauled away to workshops, where German engineers studied them carefully and carried their reports back to Berlin. During World War II the Russians successfully operated with infantry on their hulls supported by others close behind, but they had learned not to race across rough country at thirty miles an hour. The figures forty-three engaged and eighteen lost are from General Walter's report.

16. The commander, Captain Harold Fry, once a sergeant of His Majesty's Brigade of Guards, had commanded a machine-gun company in the first action of the British at Jarama. Captured by Moors on the second day, he miraculously escaped torture and execution and even more miraculously was exchanged and returned to England. Fry ran out of miracles at Fuentes de Ebro.

walked defiantly into the storm like a soldier in a Soviet poster. He had often preened with his automatic, which he called his "side cannon." (As he had written Kitty, "You don't need ammunition, for the other guy sees it pointing at him and runs.") Picking his way around the harvest of writhing and motionless bodies, every one of whom he knew by name (he made a point of that), he overtook the company and sauntered past them. Was it true, what some men have said, that he walked like a man dazed, drugged, or dead? Did he perhaps wonder whether the bullet that would kill him would come from the front or the back? He was hit in the groin and was trying to crawl back unaided when machine-gun bullets "blasted the life out of him."* For Joe Dallet everything had at last "come true in steel."

Within half an hour the Mac-Paps were following the example of other battalions "less well trained"; they were falling back to their lines or attempting to scoop out holes in the open plain. "The ground in Aragon is hard," remembered one man, "and a tin dinner plate a poor shovel—but a machine-gun is a good persuader."* Some of them advanced about eight hundred meters to a deep ravine opposite the major enemy trench. The British and the Lincolns, wiser or more cautious, were out of sight behind them.* Over the high-pitched racket of small-arms fire, they could hear the boilerlike explosions of disabled tanks. Five men caught in the open took refuge in a shallow hole that might have held two, with crowding. They lay stacked like a club sandwich. The bottom man was nearly squashed by the weight of flesh on top of him but he did not complain.

At nightfall men pinned down in the plain began to crawl back to their lines. The wounded were dragged in and the dead counted. Although publicists later claimed that the Republican lines had been pushed forward several hundred yards, the men knew that the battle had achieved nothing. The only relevant statistics for this death rattle of the Aragon campaign dealt with casualties, which amounted to about four hundred killed or wounded in the XVth Brigade. It was astonishing that so many men had been killed or wounded to so little purpose. Most of the casualties had been hit by small-arms fire, for the Nationalists had weeks before moved their artillery from what they considered a "dead front." (After all, the experienced divisions of General Enrique Lister had been stopped cold at Fuentes six weeks earlier.) Almost all the principal officers of the Mac-Paps had fallen: Captain Robert Thompson was near collapse "from a prolonged fever" and returned to the States, Dallet was dead, one company commander had been killed outright, another fatally wounded, and a third badly wounded.[17]

17. Ross lists the names of thirty-one Americans killed at Fuentes de Ebro, but the total wounded is not known. Thompson later tried to return to Spain but was stopped in France.

At La Puebla de Hijar the medical staff had to convert a railway warehouse into a hospital for five thousand men administered by thirty doctors and nurses. Since the railroad had been destroyed, large-scale and rapid evacuation to the rear was out of the question. In "that pitiful shed of horrors," wounded Anglo-Americans begged for water and morphine while Russian tankers were promptly transported to Barcelona by air.[18]

Among the officer caste, postmortems proved to be long and testy. In a meeting at Lecera called by the chief commissar of the Army of the East, the speakers did not agree on much of anything, except that someone else was responsible. When the Spanish officer demanded to know why the attack had failed, Doran took the stand and delivered "some sort of diatribe."* The Spaniard said he had asked for a report, not a speech, and ordered him to sit down. When he refused, two guards forced him into his chair. Meanwhile Saul Wellman tried to explain that the machine guns were too far away to cover the attack.* Of course, when the rank and file asked why the balls-up, they got the time-worn explanation—"sabotage"—and were discouraged from more probing. The Moscow purges were then in high gear, and Russian advisers wondered how the news of the disaster would be received in Moscow—less because of the loss of human lives than the valuable tanks. They took the line that despite their advice, the Spanish command had insisted on the tank attack, and they had been overruled—despite the fact that Soviet advisers always overruled Republican requests for tanks, artillery, and aviation with the tenacity of misers! No one seemed willing to criticize the foolish tank attack, because that was purely a Soviet brainstorm.

In his diary Copic explained why the attack had failed. The terrain was unknown, and the International Brigades had had no time for even minimal reconnaissance. The neighboring Republican brigades offered no information about enemy numbers or their specific fortifications and strongpoints. Moreover, it was "strange" that the 120nd and 143rd Republican Brigades received no orders to advance or to assist once the attack had begun. It appeared that the Republican units, which had botched their own attempts to take Fuentes de Ebro a month before, wanted the vaunted Internationals to be humiliated. The XVth suffered 120 wounded and more than 100 deaths, most of them in the tank-riders of the 24th (Spanish) Battalion, which also counted 126 missing. But

18. The Republic prided itself on having instituted an up-to-date hospital system for the Aragon offensive. The master plan called for well-equipped hospital trains to follow the troops closely so that wounded men could receive topnotch surgical assistance and be immediately evacuated to Barcelona. There was only one problem: two months of fighting had uprooted much of the railway track, which had not been replaced.

Copic did praise the Mac-Paps "for good results when considering that this was their first comeback experience."*

Other errors, overlooked by the officers, were graphically recorded by the rank and file. Since the foot soldiers had never been taught how to cross open terrain en masse, they had to pick their way over the intervening terrain and became easy targets for the enemy. And why, asked antitank gunners, had officers prevented them from knocking out enemy machine-gun nests? Little wonder that a rumor circulated among them that the battle had not intended to be serious—only an exercise to get them used to attacking under fire!*

Material in the Moscow archives rarely mentions Fuentes de Ebro, as though it never happened at all. Stalin was obviously displeased. The USSR sent only twenty-five more tanks to Spain—bringing their grand total to 331—but only because their transit had already been arranged.* Fuentes de Ebro proved to be "the swan song of the Soviet tank force in Spain."[19] Of greatest importance for the Soviets was the discovery that their tanks, although superior in firepower to anything that the Germans or Italians could field against them, were woefully deficient in armor. In subsequent Spanish battles the Soviet tanks were employed as mobile artillery dodging back and forth from concealed entrenchments but never attacking in massed formations.

So ended what General Enrique Lister called "one of the most stupid operations of the war."* Perhaps the most telling icon of the battle was this blue sign on a road-mender's hut used by enemy snipers:

FUENTES DE EBRO	1 km
ZARAGOZA	23 km

That said it all—an appropriate epitaph for another dead offensive.

For the next ten days the XVth occupied and deepened trenches facing Fuentes de Ebro. Nationalists fired desultorily at well-concealed Republicans, while Republicans sniped at invisible Nationalists. Milton Wolff lamented that he fired his Maxim machine gun without ever having a human being as target. "All the time we were there I never saw one of 'em and I don't think anyone else ever did."* Although noncombatants arrived in spiffy uniforms, festooned with

19. To retrieve disabled tanks, three days later General Walter launched another attack using tanks and the Sixth Republican Brigade under a heavy blanket of artillery fire. The tanks left too early, advanced fifty meters, and retired. In the end, most of the disabled tanks were salvaged (and studied carefully) by the enemy.

Sam Browne belts, map cases, and binoculars, machine gunners like Wolff had to telescope their hands when trying to spot an enemy target.

The major activity was retrieving battered tanks strewn like junked automobiles about no-man's-land. Those tanks abandoned near Fuentes de Ebro ended in machine shops where they were disassembled and analyzed by German engineers. (Although the armor was unexceptional, the armament of these Soviet tanks was nearly double anything in production in either Germany or Italy.) When the Mac-Paps were finally withdrawn from the field, their new commander, a Canadian named Edward Cecil-Smith, tried to buck them up with a speech explaining that recent operations had been "well-planned and successful." A few sycophants remained until the end of the harangue—the others walked away. Replacements arriving at this slack season found that a favorite subject of conversation was the death of Joe Dallet. "The general opinion was that Joe had guts."* He had proved that much. Even Dave Doran served up a funeral oration commemorating his heroic death on the field of battle. Nearly every one had words of praise for Joe Dallet—now that he was dead. More memorably perhaps, some lucky comrade confiscated his big and much-prized can of Prince Albert tobacco.*[20]

20. During the 1960s a section of the Dartmouth College library was dedicated to the memory of Joseph Dallet and $5,000 raised for the project.*

12

TERUEL—THE BIG CHILL

When, on October 25, 1937, the XVth Brigade retired downriver to lick their wounds in a reserve position at Quinto, they were joined by a straggly mob of five hundred Spanish boys, most of them teenagers, sent up from Valencia province to fill holes. The "official history" of the Lincoln "Brigade" calls them "volunteers" who had evaded the draft when their sector lay under Anarchist control but who had stepped forward eagerly as soon as the Communists assumed command. The truth is otherwise. They were all bottom-of-the-barrel conscripts, for the most part illiterate farm workers with about as much political knowledge, or interest, as a peasant in the Mekong Delta thirty years later. They served in the Republican army for one reason only—their home districts were in the Republican zone and they had been dragooned. Moreover, they expressed great surprise—even shock—when they learned that they had become members of the XVth Brigade: surprise because they believed only *extranjeros*, not Spaniards, served in the International Brigades, and shock because if taken prisoner they could expect to be executed on the spot, the alleged fate for any International captured by the enemy.[1]

They were conscripts hungry and tired with the hang-dog exhaustion of refugees too long on the road. They had been dropped off the train near Hijar and forced to walk the twenty kilometers to Quinto. They had no luggage van. Most carried their paraphernalia in wooden boxes or cheap cardboard suitcases. The sun was hot, and soon the ditches became a trail of discarded boxes, scraps of clothing, and personal junk. A few clever ones, like Fausto Villar Esteban, a furniture maker who had been briefed on military lore by a friend, carried his gear in a burlap bread sack slung comfortably over his shoulder. Unlike the others, he was literate and recorded his experiences meticulously in a diary. On their march a convoy of tanks and trucks, bound for the rear, passed them,

1. This same source adds that "many asked to fight with the Americans of the International Brigade."* Among these Spaniards was Fausto Villar of Valencia, who sent me a hundred-page typescript recounting his six months with the Lincoln Battalion. This unique memoir serves as a major counterweight to the political propaganda of that period that lards so many "official" histories.

the soldiers jubilant and crying, "Belchite is ours. Zaragoza will be yours." This reminder of what lay ahead left the new draftees "frozen in our tracks."*

It was dark when they reached Quinto and a guide led them up to the cemetery plateau where a Cuban lieutenant waited for them. He mounted a pile of stones, told them he was a Jarama veteran, and welcomed them to the XVth International Brigade, "the Brigade which no one leaves except feet first and covered in glory." His audience was not inspired—they were alarmed. "We were, every one of us, dumbfounded." Until proper billets could be prepared, they had to sleep on the ground where they were. He arranged for each man to receive a cup of coffee and a few *churros* (dough strips fried in grease), then departed. It was cold, and it was spooky. The *Moncayo*, a bitter winter wind, blew down from the Pyrenees, and they sat stranded without blankets or cover other than the sweat-soaked clothes they had worn all day. Villar, with two companions, found a shell hole, and they slept on top of one another, shifting when the top man got too cold. The pale light of dawn brought into view the tumbledown walls of the Quinto cemetery, studded with shell holes and littered with the remnants of broken coffins, yawning to reveal their dead.

After a light breakfast of black coffee, marmalade, and bread, four lieutenants—Spanish, not Internationals—arrived to teach the rudiments of close-order drill to hundreds of gangly youths stepping over or around funereal debris. The officer asked for volunteers to form a machine-gun company. Most volunteered, less because of enthusiasm for killing "Fascists" than the prospect of riding in a vehicle rather than marching all day on foot. The hopefuls lined up, and the officer passed down the line studying each man grimly. Those not acceptable were pushed out of the line. When dismissed, the recruits made a beeline to stake claims on abandoned sheep-cotes on the plateau, for they had come to realize that future comforts depended more on individual ingenuity than on collective cooperation. It was the gospel according to Darwin, not Marx—though none would have put it that way. The roofs had fallen in, but the walls at least offered some protection against wind. While washing their tin plates and faces in the Ebro, someone found anise roots along the riverbanks. Word of the discovery spread like wildfire, and the recruits dug frantically for something to assuage their hunger.

There was no further drill in the afternoon, for the brigade seemed to have forgotten them. Except for a few Spanish officers, they had not seen or talked with any of the Internationals, who were billeted in the village. But they did catch sight of their commander, Colonel Copic, elegantly mounted on a fine horse like a lord of the manor. Villar told a companion, "It strikes me as odd that in a civil war such as ours, where our officers are simple men from the ranks of the common people, we should be seeing Copic stroll around with such swagger, handling his charger with the elegant composure of an aristocrat." His less political companion only laughed, saying that the elite are the elite everywhere, even in a People's Army, and that "there is no way around it."

At night a cloudburst filled their pens with water and dawn found them chilled to the bone, wet, miserable, and forgotten. Gathering scraps of lumber from smashed coffins in the cemetery, they made fires and huddled around the flames. Picks and spades arrived with orders to erect some shacks from planks of wood salvaged from coffins. Then two trucks arrived with army issue clothing—underwear, shirts, trousers, socks, boots, and balaclavas. They shed their wet rags cheerfully—"now we look like soldiers." A few days later they received long-barreled Remington rifles with triangular Russian bayonets, and two Russian advisers brought a Maxim machine gun, mounted on a wheeled carriage, looking like a miniature cannon. The recruits learn how to fieldstrip, clean, and reassemble their rifles and the names of each part. The glory day came when they first fired their rifles. Whenever a Spaniard missed the target altogether, the instructors growled something in Russian, and the interpreter laughed but did not translate. Yet the Russians passed as a jolly team who did not take their work too seriously, and in the end the Spaniards mastered two essential words, *tovarishch* and *robot*.

One day the recruits were ordered to clean their rifles and to tidy up their uniforms for a celebration. They marched through the streets of Quinto to a field outside of town, where a group of VIPs awaited them. The rumor was that American senators were on hand, and they had to make a good impression so that the United States would send aid to the Republic. While a demolition team exploded some grenades in a ruined house, the recruits jogged past with fixed bayonets as movie cameramen filmed the show. Later they were told that the footage would be circulated in the United States as a documentary showing how the Lincoln Battalion captured a fortified city in Spain. Except for a group of Americans in charge of the grenade explosions, the only "Americans" in the film were Spanish recruits. In fact, this was the first contact they had had with Americans of the Lincoln Battalion, who did not fraternize with them.

No American senators stood among the glitterati, but on hand was the U.S. military attaché, Colonel Stephen O. Fuqua, who allowed himself to be photographed with Amlie, Doran, and others of the brigade. Fuqua's visit in no way represented either an official or unofficial recognition of the American battalion by the United States—Cordell Hull would have been apoplectic at the idea, although his ambassador in Spain, Claude Bowers, would have welcomed it—but photographs were widely circulated by Party publicists at home to hint at such recognition.[2] The colonel, after tours of the battlegrounds at Quinto, Belchite, and Fuentes de Ebro, expressed "admiration for these troops."* It was never clear who invited Fuqua or why he had accepted the invitation. Some said that Major Allan Johnson of the Tarazona base had served with him during the World War; others claimed that it was Amlie who had been his old comrade-at-arms. No doubt the presence of Amlie (brother of a former congressman) and Merriman (college football star and ROTC officer) gave a certain cachet to the Lincoln Battalion, which Doran, hovering on the outer fringe during the festivities, could not provide. Ironically, although the CPUSA touted the presence of Fuqua among its Comintern cohort, the visitation only fueled André Marty's paranoid fancies. Was there some sort of collusion between an American military spy and the leaders of the American battalion? Captain Merriman came under a cloud. After all, he had never joined the Communist Party and he held a reserve lieutenancy in the U.S. Army. Moreover, Fuqua gave him "small presents," such as the leather sleeveless jacket he had supposedly worn during the World War.* Thereafter, as Moscow records show, Marty considered him a questionable character who had to be watched closely for signals of deviationism. Unimpressed by all the folderol, the men in the ranks referred to Colonel Fuqua simply as "Colonel Fucker."

Except for daily drills and rations of food, the brigade hierarchy seemed to have forgotten the green recruits camped out by the cemetery, for there was no ceremony to integrate them into the brigade. Among themselves they muttered angrily about their treatment. They knew that they would be used to fill gaps in the four battalions and hoped against hope that they could join their own countrymen in the 24th Battalion. Their living conditions worsened when an autumn rainstorm flooded the ramshackle huts hacked together with coffin scraps. Permission then came to occupy empty concrete bunkers on the edge of the plateau. A few opportunists claiming Communist affiliation wrangled appointments as commissars and commenced a series of indoctrination exercises. Villar recorded that the new commissar of his squad had earlier bragged how much money he made as a recruiter for the Valencia orchestra by pocketing 30 percent of the first month's wage of each musician he enrolled. Villar pondered: was this the new Communism, or just the worst sort of old-style capitalism?

2. The newsreels have not been located, but at Brandeis University there is a large collection of photographs commemorating the visit. Edwin Rolfe, who wrote the first "official" history (*The Lincoln Battalion*), included one captioned in such a way that an unwary viewer might suspect that Fuqua is not the portly figure in civilian garb but the uniformed officer (Amlie) behind him.

On October 31 the brigade received two days' ration of bread and some small cans of Russian potted meat and climbed aboard a cattle train in La Puebla de Hijar. Their destination, the rest villages of the Tajuña valley. The Spanish recruits hooted with joy as the train moved toward Valencia, even though they grumbled that their temporary leader, Lieutenant Gomez, reserved the roomy brake compartment for himself and his woman. They stopped in Valencia long enough for Villar to snatch a few kisses from his *novia* and hugs from his mother before the train lumbered up to the bleak Castilian upland. At Tembleque trucks ferried them to rest villages: brigade headquarters at Ambite, Lincolns at Albares, British at Mondéjar, Mac-Paps at Pezuela de las Torres, and the 24th Battalion at an unreported site. The new recruits were dropped off at Olmeda de Cebolla, a full day's journey north, where they were held in a kind of political limbo until authorities could sort out where they should go. Eventually they were split into four equal groups and trucked to their new battalions.

Like all the new recruits, Villar had hoped for assignment to the 24th Battalion, but found himself assigned to the Americans at Albares. Scrawny and undersized from generations of privation, the *quintos* felt intimidated by the sheer size of the Lincolns. "They are like mastodons beside us. We feel like children alongside grown-ups, for tall and strapping appears to be the norm among them." Because most of the higher ranks had hustled off to Madrid, Dave Reiss, captain of the machine-gun company, as acting commander made a short welcoming speech to 125 new faces. A commissar followed him with "the usual stuff one gets from all political commissars." Villar liked the easygoing manner of the Americans, symptomatic in the way that they dispensed food. Cooks placed great pots of stew on large canvas tarps spread upon the ground, and each man lined up and took as little or as much as he liked. Accustomed to bad food doled out in starveling portions, the recruits feasted on three courses topped off with a sugared rice pudding. To fill their bellies they no longer had to filch extra hunks of bread and hide them in their shirts. At mess there was only one inflexible rule—woe unto you if you failed to eat what you took, for nothing could be thrown away. The newcomers gawked when they saw officers lining up with their men—first come, first served. In spiffy uniforms they chatted and joked with all ranks. Such informality did not exist among Spanish soldiers. Despite his sense of loneliness and inferiority, Villar admired the naturalness and equality displayed by the Americans.

For the third time the Lincolns took up billets around the Albares mill and settled down for reorganization and "reeducation." Assessing their role in the Aragon fighting, where American dead numbered eighty-one, they felt that Quinto had been lucky, Belchite grueling, and Fuentes de Ebro calamitous.

Applications for repatriation from men with the magic plus-six months' service piled up in Albacete—all rejected. To let a few men go would open floodgates. The men bitterly complained that top Communists came and went to the States as they liked.

Marion Merriman joined Bob at Ambite on November 17 for a second honeymoon. They occupied the mill house on the island, which evoked for her a tiny feudal fortress, complete with moat and carved ceiling in their bedroom. She found him despondent about the campaign coming up and feared the worst when, out of the blue, he told her she must return home and raise funds for the Republic. On their last evening together he gave her two small diaries as though they were a last will and testament. Then she was horrified when he wrung from her a promise that if he never returned home, she would marry again. It was unthinkable, but he insisted. On the morning she left, she looked out of the rear window of the car and saw Bob walking toward his headquarters. "He never looked back. I cried silently as we drove away through the trees."*

Meanwhile, key figures in the International Brigade hierarchy were at that moment in Albacete deliberating on the fate of Colonel Copic, who was blamed for the Fuentes fiasco. Hoping for Merriman's support, the colonel gave his chief of staff a gold watch, ostensibly for his leadership at Quinto and Belchite. (He apologized for failing to have it engraved with suitable inscription but said he had been unable to find an engraver. Marion said it was a cheap watch.) Despite his warnings that looting would not be tolerated in his command, Copic had stashed away a private hoard of valuables that he distributed for personal favors. Merriman was disgusted, for Copic continued to lambaste Americans as "crybabies" and he was "mainly concerned with his own standing among his superiors." Merriman reluctantly wrote a supportive letter, and in the end Copic escaped a recall to Moscow.

Since Copic remained in Albacete repairing political fences, the task of rebuilding the brigade fell upon Doran, who shouldered it eagerly. In just two months the YCL leader from Albany had vaulted from raw junior commissar to a post that was, in effect, the political dictatorship of the XVth Brigade. It appears that he expected to create, through rigorous Party discipline, an elite corps out of the skeptics and malcontents about him. His objectives may have been laudable, but his methods were misguided. Doran sought simple political solutions to complex military problems. What his men needed were better weapons, capable officers, and coordinated staff work. What they got were lectures on "discipline" and warnings that deserters and "Trotskyites" would be shot. He overlooked the highly individualist nature of his men and the obvious fact that a majority of them knew more about war than he did. They were not

Turks or Bulgars locked in a tradition of unquestioning obedience to officers. Of the Doran period, a University of Michigan student observed, "Like most Americans I could not accept the know-it-all, party-line dogmatisms of the Polit-Commissar system, which had originated in armies of illiterate peasants."* Others recorded their antipathy toward the double-think, the half-truths, the blatant lies. How they yearned sometimes to hear the truth—even if it struck them dead—rather than the endless reams of Marxoid propaganda. Yet they were caught in a vicious circle: the more they sloughed off Doran's political indoctrination, the more he heaped it on them. Paradoxically, the goal of "education" as Doran conceived it seemed to require the nearly total collapse of intelligence. He demanded that the mind of a good soldier become a *tabula rasa,* upon which he could write his own script.

Too much time at Albares went to exorcizing political demons. Rallies, pep talks, and mimeographed directives exhorted the brigade to win the war by learning how to salute, improving dress, studying Spanish, and obeying officers. An article in *Our Fight,* the weekly news sheet, explained that a salute was not pukka-colonel nonsense: "A salute is the military way of saying hello. A salute is not undemocratic. . . . A salute is a sign that a comrade who has been an egocentric individualist in private life, has adjusted himself to the collective way of getting things done. . . . A salute is proof that our Brigade is on its way from being a collection of well-meaning amateurs to a precise instrument for eliminating Fascists."* The Winter Palace had not been stormed by workers punctilious about salutes. The American volunteers felt that saluting defiled the egalitarian promise of the International Brigades, and they resisted it with cold determination, even by craning one's neck in passageways to avoid seeing an officer. Moreover, the recent emphasis upon proper uniform impressed only the popinjays of the brigade. Better was the example of Peter Daly, an admired IRA man who commanded the British at Quinto and was killed on Purburell. In the morning Daly always looked like an officer at first light and a hunger marcher by nightfall. Among the Americans, Captain Detro refused to surrender his sloppy turtleneck sweater, even after Doran returned from Madrid in a resplendent tailored outfit. He was a sight—stiffly wired garrison hat, silk-lined opera cape, knee-top boots, and cavalry spurs. (He dared to wear the spurs only once, but the cape remained.) At Albares Doran launched a "re-education program" consisting of interminable lectures on discipline. He marched back and forth in front of his audience, now and then "pausing to admire himself in the glass panes."* In his publicity photo at this time he looms as a Byronic figure standing alone on a mountain peak, for the camera lens had been placed about on a level with his shins and aimed upward almost vertically.

In December 1937 one of the last British volunteers arrived in Figueras, where a Spanish officer tossed his passport into a drawer full of them and said, "We've got dozens . ,. all phonies. We have an office that turns out twenty a day."* He then handed Laurie Lee a bag of prophylactics, a 100-peseta note, and a forage cap with tassel, and added, "You are now in the Republican Army."* The newcomer observed that his new comrades were all "ill-clad, crop-haired, and sunken-cheeked . . . the skimmed milk of the middle-Thirties."* Their training included an attack upon a hilltop defended by men beating oil drums to simulate machine-gun fire—"taken without loss"—and antitank exercises in which a man pushed a pram covered with an oilcloth around a square while its attackers threw bottles and bricks at it, amid howls and curses from the "tanker" whenever a missile hit him. On the railway platform at Albacete in the biting winter cold, a small brass band greeted the arrivals by pointing instruments at them like a firing squad and blowing "a succession of tubercular blasts."* When one new volunteer changed his mind and whined that he wanted to go home, the leader kicked him back into line. The city looked nothing like a poster of Sunny Spain, but a "whipped northern slum," where men wrapped to the throat sat in damp cafés drinking acorn coffee and rolling cigarettes of dried oak leaves.* The training base at Tarazona de la Mancha consisted of snow-daubed hovels evoking "Siberian dejection," where the overriding impression was of bitter cold. Brigaders ransacked churches for burnable kindling and cut down century-old olive trees for firewood, cut up bunk beds and fed them into the barracks stove, and would have burned a thousand-year relic for five minutes of warmth. They marched "[making] a noise to keep warm, our clenched fists closing on nothing." In a church Harry Pollitt, head of the CPGB, down for a visit, warmed them with a rousing speech as he explained how they would not only smash Franco, Hitler, and Mussolini but also the whole world for the working class. Britons swarmed about him, plucking at his sleeve, begging to be sent home, while Pollitt backed through the door, his eyes searching for escape, "Sorry, lads . . . I can't do owt about that."*

More than ever, replacements for the International Brigades came from apathetic Spanish conscripts, and their assimilation remained an insurmountable problem. Few Americans bothered to learn Spanish, beyond a few insults or obscenities like *cojones* and *maricón*. Unable and even unwilling to communicate with each other, the two groups clustered in their own linguistic pockets. At Albares, responding to pressure from Albacete, Doran urged each American to "adopt" a Spanish recruit and to live, eat, and train with him, but the Spaniards resisted this faux camaraderie as thoroughly as did the Americans. Compulsory Spanish classes had been abandoned long before. Indeed, most

Americans remained as monolingual as the company commander who, when asked for the time by an Albares native, replied, "It's una o'clocka." In a confidential report for the Kremlin, General Kléber declared that it was easier to find a Spaniard who spoke German—or even Polish—than a brigader who knew even rudimentary Spanish.* Even Villar, who worked closely with the battalion staff as an observer, never entirely understood what the Americans were talking about, beyond picking up simple nouns and verbs. Yet to somebody's credit the brigade did set up classrooms to eliminate illiteracy among the Spanish conscripts, many of whom had never attended school. Back home, wrote an American, an illiterate was "someone who didn't read the *Daily Worker*. These [guys] could not read anything."* Villar himself became an eager teacher of the *analfabetos*, although it was an overtime task.

As a morale prop, Doran pressed the historical commission of the brigade to complete, in time for Christmas, an illustrated yearbook called *Book of the XV Brigade*. This consisted of a sanitized account of battles by politically canonized participants (no hint of the Jarama mutiny or the Camp Lukács penal colony), abundant photographs, and dozens of biographical sketches (often fictionalized). Doran submitted to the editors a list of men who were to be "played up." On the top were Merriman, Nelson, Copic, and Doran, while Harris and Stember had become nonpersons. "All of this was press agent stuff," Sandor Voros, one of the editors, confessed years later.* The book contained a cheerful and uplifting record of events from Jarama to Fuentes de Ebro and was said to have been appreciated by the men—or at least by those who found their name or picture in it.

Meanwhile, the *Volunteer for Liberty,* house organ of the Anglo-American section of the International Brigades, printed whipsaw bits of humor calculated to raise morale by lowering the boom on the "Fascists." There was, for example, the cartoon featuring two Spanish charwomen: "Funny stink in Room 402, isn't there, Conchita?" "Oh, that's the room Franco slept in one night six years ago." Hitler-Goebbels jokes were a favorite—Hitler, motoring in the country, runs over a pig. He dispatches Goebbels to inform the farmer and is puzzled when his minister returns, loaded down with fruit and vegetables. "What did you tell him?" Hitler asks. "Hardly anything," replies Goebbels. "I just said, 'Heil Hitler! I have the swine run over and killed.'" While the *Volunteer for Liberty* contained detailed accounts of the twentieth anniversary of the Russian Revolution, minor polar expeditions by Soviet scientists, and obscure archaeological discoveries in the valley of the Don, American holidays like the Fourth of July or Thanksgiving passed without mention. (Worse, there were no baseball scores.) And of course, there was always room on its pages for Marty's denunciations of Anarchists and Trotskyists—"scum stealing arms for the front."

As they settled into their rest camps around Albares, the XVth Brigade took a body count of all personnel within its purview, which, in view of the losses soon to come and the mere trickle of replacements coming in from Britain and North America, freezes the personnel statistics of the brigade at their zenith. Dated December 1, 1937, the total membership of the brigade stood at 2,479. (The battalions had recently been renumbered):

57th	(British)	414	(16.7%)
58th	(Lincoln)	413	(16.6%)
59th	(Spanish)	460	(18.5%)
60th	(Mac-Paps)	506	(20.4%)
Total		1793	(72.3%)[3]

The remainder consisted of the 247 members of the *estado mayor* (brigade staff) (9.9 percent)—some of whom were combatants; 139 engineers (5.6 percent); and the 105 personnel assigned to the auto-park (4.2 percent). Included in the residue were the armorers, the communications section, the quartermaster section, the antitank battery, and the 195 individuals assigned to medical services (7.8 percent).* These figures do not account for the universal practice of inflating rosters with nonexistent (or deceased) men so that the unit could demand increased rations, armament (especially automatic weapons), vehicles, and quartermaster stores from limited supplies. (The drawback to exaggerating numbers was that in battle situations more would be expected of larger units.)

The same report enumerated the total number of past and present Americans in the XVth Brigade as 2,471, of whom 295 had been killed or missing (11.9 percent) and 139 had been repatriated. Of the 2,037 Americans on another roster, 1,252 were native-born (50.6 percent), 1,035 foreign-born (41.9 percent), 110 Latino (4.4 percent), and 74 "Negro Americans" (2.9 percent). (For reasons known only to themselves, the compilers did not regard black Americans as "native-born.")

Recruiters for the Lincoln Battalion in the United States, along with Party propagandists, continued to be instructed to ignore or deny accusations that the battalion was under Party affiliation. On their questionnaires filled out at Albacete, the volunteers—often reluctantly—had to list their party as "Anti-Fascist," although no such party existed. In view of this cover-up, political statistics collected in December 1937 were especially important. Of the 2,471

---

3. This tabulation by battalion does not take into account that both the Lincolns and the English had a full company each composed of Spaniards, that Americans were serving with the Mac-Paps, and that Canadians had served among the Lincolns as far back as Brunete. Through habit, the Spanish battalion continued to be called the 24th except in official documents.

Americans in the XVth Brigade, 1,385 were members of the Communist Party (56.0 percent), while 460 were in the YCL (18.5 percent). Among the remainder there were 17 Socialists (00.06 percent), 8 in "splinter" parties (00.03 percent), and 601 who listed themselves as "No Party" (24.3 percent).

These reports went to Moscow but were not available to the public.*

Perhaps Doran's stellar coup was his kidnapping of Clement Atlee and a group of British Labor Party MPs. They had been visiting battle sectors of Spain but had refused an invitation to inspect the British Battalion at Mondéjar, fearing this might be construed as an endorsement of an illegal organization. On December 6, Doran staged his seizure. A XVth Brigade automobile and chauffeur waited outside Atlee's hotel in Madrid until the worthies appeared. Saluting smartly, the chauffeur explained that his car was at their disposal, courtesy of the Republic. Once inside, they were whisked out to Mondéjar (a few miles west of Albares), where the British Battalion was lined up along the road in the winterish gloom.* Just before the limousine with its Union Jack arrived, some jokester released Segundo, the dwarfish village idiot, wearing a mock-corporal uniform with battle stripes running the full length of his arm and riding a bicycle designed for a six-footer.* Segundo led the dignitaries into the village passing the British at attention singing "God Save the King." Under these circumstances the captives could hardly insist on returning to Madrid immediately. In the upper rooms of a mill beside the Tajuña, Atlee was feted by Doran and company, who told him that henceforth First Company of the British Battalion would be known as "the Major Atlee Company." Warming to this flattery, Atlee confessed that the Non-Intervention Agreement was a farce. When Miss Ellen Wilkinson, one of the MPs, asked Doran about his duties as a brigade commissar, Doran thought a minute, "Well, I could have any of these men shot."* At the end of the fiesta they sang "The International" under a red flag, Major Atlee gamely pretending to join in—he did not know the words. A torchlight procession escorted the delegates back to their automobile. Before he departed, Atlee gave the clenched-fist salute but mauled the Republican shibboleth as he shouted, "¡No pasaremos!" (We shall not pass!).*[4]

---

4. In England the CPGB released a photograph of Atlee giving the Communist salute, rich fare for Tory hecklers. He had to insist that he was not a Red and that the salute was "used by all supporters of the Republic—Liberals, Socialists, Communists, or Anarchists."* (It is unimaginable that any Anarchist would ever sing "The International" or use the clenched-fist salute.) A recent history of the Lincoln "Brigade" has this to say: "That Atlee accepted this signal honor is indicative of the healthy orientation of the British Labor Party of that day."* In fact, although the Atlee visit was a coup for the CPGB, most of the British brigaders considered him a questionable Labourite.

A week later the XVth Brigade was ordered to move out. They had no idea where they were bound, but climbed aboard trucks and shouted to familiar village faces, "We'll be back!" The folk of the Tajuña valley rest villages had learned to look upon the goings and comings of the Anglo-Americans as if they were migratory fowl. A season would pass, a battle would be won or lost, and the *extranjeros* would reappear in their villages as regular as the seasons. This time they were wrong. They never came back.

The convoy of trucks bounced eastward on the Valencia road, deeply potholed after a year and a half of wartime use without peacetime repairs. At Motilla del Palancar a road sign at the crossroads read "VILLANUEVA DE LA JARA— 14 km," meaningless to all but a handful on the trucks. Somewhere they boarded a train and stopped briefly at Albacete. The men wanted to get off and hoard food and drink, but armed guards prevented it, as though they were prisoners who, if allowed to go free, might never come back. In the purple twilight the train rolled past little hamlets with blue-tiled church domes and dropped down to the coastal plain through groves of carob, olive, and orange. Overnight they slept in the *plaza de toros*. "In Spain," one man remembered, "they always bedded us down in the bullrings and shot us from the church towers."* The next morning they boarded another train fitted with two machine guns welded together and mounted on the carriage roofs as antiaircraft guns. It was sunny and warm as they crossed the greensward of the Levantine *huerta*, where oranges hung ripe on trees. Once upon a time laborers had bombarded their coaches with fruit, but nowadays it was rare for them to wave. On this trip the Anglo-Americans had to invade orchards and "organize" oranges for themselves. A Briton liberated a melon, but as the train pulled out and gained speed he had to dash after it. Men hanging from windows cheered him on, but he had to throw his melon aside and sprint. Since the coal mines of Spain were now in the Nationalist zone, the train poked upward from one woodpile to the next. As it ascended the coastal mountains, men jumped off, sauntered cross-country, and met the locomotive at summits with plenty of time to spare. (Commissars did not worry about desertions—in this barren region, where could a man go?)

From Caspe, a town perched above the Ebro, they moved south by trucks across an uninhabited region of wind-etched monadnocks to Alcañiz. (Four months later, they would retrace their steps along this road under very different circumstances.) In the mountains the climate changed radically. In this coldest winter of a generation, lacerating gusts from the Pyrenees could knock a man off his feet and slice him like a knife. In open trucks they moved along back roads through obscure villages. In the bitter cold men huddled around improvised braziers in the truck bay—large garbage cans crammed with hot coals—and whenever the trucks stopped, they bailed out and ran up and down the road flailing themselves.* Those recalling the desert heat of the Brunete campaign could hardly believe they were in the same country.

Deep in the hill country of the Maestrazgo, a remote region of Spain, they garrisoned a succession of stone-and-rubble hamlets. The Lincolns drew Agua Vivas, a village so hopelessly poor that some houses had no windows at all. Compared with Agua Vivas, Albares had been a bustling metropolis. Here it was often impossible to differentiate between shanties and sheds, except that the latter were warmer—at least when the animals were inside. The Mac-Paps were quartered nearby in Mas de las Matas, which they translated ominously (and erroneously) as "More of the Killed." (Matas was only a mountain stream.) On a bitterly cold night, the Mac-Paps were jarred awake by a disturbance. They flew to their rifles and crowded the windows. Houses were lit up and townspeople were banging dishpans, yelling and chanting something. A Christmas celebration? Finally somebody figured out the words—"Teruel ha caído!" The Republican Army had taken Teruel. The townspeople embraced the brigaders and drew them into their shanties for cups of wine. Everywhere it was "Viva la República Española!" Surely the fortunes of war had changed. Teruel, sixty miles southwest, had been surrounded and cut off from Nationalist Spain with the enemy garrison trapped inside. Moreover, since the Ministry of War wanted an exclusively Spanish victory to prove its coming of age both at home and abroad, it occurred without Internationals. Morale in the Republic reached its peak: for the first time the Republicans had seized a provincial capital in a military campaign. (And they would never take another, as subsequent events proved.) To celebrate the victory, the Mac-Paps took up a collection, bought a pig, and invited the local population to a cookout. They collected the pig blood in basins and boiled it with onions.* The local girls fueled a few dreams, but nothing more.

The battle developing in subzero temperatures at Teruel was, for the moment, only a remote irrelevance for the men of the brigade quartered three mountain chains away. As Christmas approached they received food packages sent by the FALB—grab bags of incongruities: cans of orange juice, bottles of olive oil (greeted with hooting and booing), cartons of toilet paper (newsprint was rumored to cause piles, though the problems plaguing the Lincolns ran in the opposite direction). Still there were also cartons of cherished Lucky Strikes and Hershey bars. When the brigade quartermaster produced some bottles of champagne and hogsheads of vile *coñac,* they threw a Christmas party, passing out candy bars to the children of Agua Vivas, who had never heard of Santa

Claus, never seen a candy bar, never received a gift from a stranger. Over at the medical unit there was an upscale celebration featuring grain alcohol and American nurses. Only officers need apply.

On December 29, 1937, when the Nationalists unleashed a ferocious counteroffensive to regain Teruel, the Republic reneged on its promise not to deploy the International Brigades. On December 31, the XVth Brigade was ordered to move up immediately to buttress the right flank in the Sierra Palomera, an arid chain running due north from Teruel. Phil Detro held on to the Lincoln command, even though racked by some obscure illness that had converted him into a walking skeleton. Since Carl Geiser had been wounded at Fuentes de Ebro, his place as battalion commissar fell to Fred Keller, a twenty-three-year-old often described as "a young altar boy from Brooklyn." Lincoln folklore records that Keller had been an elevator operator at the FALB office in New York. Conversations with riders had aroused his curiosity about Spain. Like Geiser, he was forthright and popular, although some Party stalwarts opined that "his political level of comprehension was at rock bottom." It is alleged that on one occasion when Doran sent him two well-connected politicos with instructions to put them to useful work, Keller handed them some posters and said, "OK, fellas, here's a political job for you. Go mix some paste and hang up these posters around town."[5]

The Mac-Paps, who had suffered most heavily at Fuentes de Ebro, had been reorganized. Captain Robert Thompson, said to be ill with fever, left for the States, his place taken by Edward Cecil-Smith of Canada, a pudgy little man with a toothbrush mustache who "looked like a beefy college professor in uniform," but had been a journalist and a sergeant in the Canadian Army.* From the XIth Brigade the Mac-Paps had the good luck to obtain a detachment of Finnish-Canadians, widely admired as tough campaigners and machine-gun experts. Dallet's friend, Saul Wellman a New Jersey truck driver, became the Mac-Pap commissar. The big three on brigade staff continued to be Copic, Doran, and Merriman. Men began to bet it was just a matter of time before Merriman took over the XVth Brigade.

To reach the Teruel front in winter required a major battle against Nature. The mean altitude was always over three thousand feet, snow drifted three feet deep

5. Keller proved to be very useful to the Popular Front image because liberal journalists like Ernest Hemingway and Herbert L. Matthews depended upon him for material—some of doubtful accuracy. But a few months later Keller left the battalion to attend a special cadres school, after which he was assigned duties never publicly discussed. Late in 1939 he was subpoenaed to testify before the House Un-American Activities Committee, where he repeatedly denied that he had been a "political commissar" of the Lincoln Battalion—only a "war commissar."

on the roads, and the temperature dipped as low as eighteen below zero. (Centigrade readings always made it seem colder.) The tanks, troop carriers, supply trucks, ambulances, and staff cars clogged the roads and jammed each hamlet and road junction, where only the curses and threats of the brigade staff got them moving again. At a pass of the Sagunto road, a surprise snow pinned hundreds of cars and trucks for two days in a serpentine column ten miles long.* In places, roads tumbled down mountainsides carrying vehicles to the bottom in toboggan rides. Many of the drivers from Valencia and Barcelona had never seen snow before, much less driven in it. On hairpin curves in the Sierra de San Just, a first skid was often the last. Stalled vehicles, after being stripped of wheels and salvageable parts, had to be shoved into chasms to make way for hundreds of others behind them. The waste was shocking but unavoidable. Ingenious drivers patched their vehicles with barbed wire, scraps of string, leather belts, and chewing gum. The wake of the convoy, recalled an American, was littered with "cigarette butts, brandy bottles, and the stink of hot oil and frozen sweat in the deep tire tracks." Yet veteran campaigners professed gratitude for the unbearable weather, which grounded enemy aviation.

At nightfall they unloaded in a rocky field of deepening snow outside a village called Argente. A few miles west lay the Sierra Palomera, a sawtooth chain of barren mountains leading down to Teruel, twenty-five miles away. The front was somewhere beyond those mountains, but the Republican lines were being eroded steadily. Because enemy planes methodically bombed villages behind the front, the Lincolns, already half-numb in the cold wind, were instructed to sleep in the open fields. By the following morning one man in every ten was down with frostbite or "Teruel fever"—a rheumatic ague. It was New Year's Day, 1938.

Nothing happened. The front did not collapse. It froze. After three days of hiding behind lee walls in Argente, trying to escape the bitter winds raging across the valley, the Lincolns moved farther south to the vicinity of Cuevas Labradas, ten miles north of Teruel. (Because of the cold, they dubbed it "Caves of Labrador.") Already the brigade medical unit had established a hospital in an unheated summer house and was treating casualties from other Republican units. The doctors worked by candlelight and with pocket flashlights taped to their heads, and they sterilized their instruments on a kitchen stove. They bedded down patients in their mud- and blood-caked uniforms, for there were no changes of clothes or even blankets. Shell-shocked cases lay next to the stove along with the limb and head cases. It was a rule of thumb that if a man wounded in the head survived the grinding ambulance ride to the hospital, he would not die. Abdominal wounds, however, were usually fatal because of internal hemorrhaging caused by jarring and bucking of the ambulances. Stocked against an outer wall, corpses froze—and that was a godsend. The view from the balcony of the villa was as sharp as a steel engraving—ice-glazed poplars lined the brook-sized Alfambra River like fine dead-flower arrangements.

The amenities of Cuevas Labradas were not enjoyed by the rank and file of the Lincoln Battalion, which bivouacked in the tunnel of an uncompleted railroad. This railroad had everything that a railroad ought to have—graded embankment, station houses, watchmen's huts, dozens of tunnels, everything except rails, ties, and locomotives. (The men called it "the Great Teruel Line.") The tunnel, slightly curved inside, seemed at first to be a God-given barracks and air-raid shelter for the brigade *estado mayor,* until they learned, to their dismay, that the battering winds, instead of roaring over the ridge, took a shortcut through the tunnel. Then when they built fires inside, the floor turned into slush, and icicles dropped like sheets of broken glass. Frostbite was legion. The men had not been warned that in this climate wet feet or sweat could be as lethal as an enemy bullet.[6]

There were other hazards, as Villar and a Spanish officer discovered. On a sunny afternoon they left the tunnel at Peralejos and slid down to the river, where they had a wash and a shave in a poplar grove. While they were trimming their mustaches, a Messerschmitt 109, possibly attracted by their shaving mirrors, burst out of nowhere and machine-gunned them at treetop level. The plane made several passes, but the Spaniards were able to dodge behind trees until the plane made a final pass, dropped some grenades, and soared way. Some Lincolns, who had watched the attack from the tunnel mouth gave them a furious tongue-lashing, claiming that the enemy had discovered where they were holed up and would return at squadron strength to strafe the tunnel. It would be as easy as shooting fish in a barrel. They dared not insult the lieutenant, but Villar was reviled as a "Spanish son of a bitch" until his companion pulled rank and overwhelmed the Americans with his own repertoire of English profanity.

After only one night in the tunnel, Captain Detro led his men up sinuous mule-paths into the Sierra Palomera, a rocky wilderness of unidentifiable stubble and uncharted *barrancas,* where they dug in on the lip of a ridge looking down on Celadas, a distant village boasting a fine Renaissance church ringed by squalid huts. Rough country, all the rougher for men issued canvas shoes when hobnail boots ran out.* The Nationalists were using the place as a staging area for their counteroffensive against the Alfambra River line. From their eyrie, a mile or more away, the Americans could observe the movements of trucks and

6. This railroad to nowhere has never been finished. Today those tunnels not blocked by landfill house agricultural machinery.

men in the village. At this stage of the battle, the front was little more than isolated groups of men trying to fortify widely spaced strongpoints. The Lincolns dug as deeply as they could in frozen ground laced over bedrock and piled up cairns of rock as illusory protection against both wind and lead. They swore that urine crystallized almost as soon as it struck the ground. In their folklore, this position became "the North Pole."

On their second day above Celadas, the Lincolns watched as an enemy force tried to storm Republican positions on similar ridges to the south. The advancing troops were visible as moving specks crossing the open valley while their artillery and bombers pounded the ridge. This advance lay beyond the range of rifle and machine-gun fire, and their antitank guns had not been pulled up to their remote mountain ridge. They could do nothing but watch helplessly and hope against hope that their flank would not be rolled up. The attack was apparently beaten off but resumed the next day. Clusters of the enemy managed to infiltrate through some dead ground between the Lincolns and their comrades to the south. Detro dispatched First Company to plug the gap. After a short firefight at long range, the enemy troops backed down into the valley again.

In the days that followed, massive Nationalist counterstrokes probed the twenty-mile front running north out of Teruel, while the Republicans tried to hold the ground seized during the opening day of the campaign. The Republicans had taken Teruel with manpower—the Nationalists meant to retake it with firepower. Firepower meant incessant waves of Junkers and Capronis. It meant artillery barrages touted as having a "95-percent killing zone." It meant incendiary bombs over the front until virtually every inflammable object burned. It meant, on clear days, fighter planes skywriting the Falange emblem—yoke and arrows—with white smoke against a blue sky. Shellbursts in the chalky foothills geysered powdered stone and white snow and were beautiful to look at—from a distance. "The snow rose in the air like a dirty ghost, and hung there spiky billowing, before collapsing into the ground again."* Shrapnel hissed angrily as it burrowed into the snow. Thawed mud oozed up from fresh bomb-craters and froze again. Bomb-torn telephone and power lines drooped across hillsides like towropes at a ski resort.

The Americans helplessly endured this highly tooled "mechanized doom," to use Hemingway's famous phrase. They passed the time trying to count the enemy planes. "Never saw more than eighty-four Fascist planes overhead at any one time, but of course I couldn't see beyond my ridge."* They examined the ignition panel of a downed Fiat and bitterly noted that the writing was in Italian. When incoming planes strafed them, they dug into the numbing earth, placing their backs toward the sky through some atavistic instinct—erroneous, of course—that backs might be more impervious to bullets than chests. They carried their wounded and bad cases of frozen feet through snow-drifted *barrancas* to the hospitals that had sprung up overnight, like sinister mushrooms, in the wide canyon of the Alfambra River. But the greatest agony was the dehumanizing pounding they had to endure. Men could do nothing but huddle in their holes while they waited to be torn to pieces by a shrieking universe. What made the bombardments at Tereul so terrifying was the enemy's employment of time-fused shells, which exploded, not on hitting an earthly target, but overhead, firing thousands of lethal shards in all directions. Dodging this kind of shell was impossible. Worse, enemy aircraft pinpointed Republican advanced units and called in artillery barrages on their exact position. The only recourse was to trek back down the slopes until out of range.

After six days in the Sierra Palomera, the Americans were relieved, twenty men hospitalized with frostbite. The temperature had risen, and they slogged through thawed muck back to the railroad tunnel near Cuevas Labradas. There they devoured a tub of mule stew, their first hot meal since Agua Vivas. And for breakfast they had the standard Teruel fare—oranges roasted over hot coals. (A local boulevardier dubbed this dish *orange flambé*.) Though casualties had not been high, Celadas seemed worse than Brunete, and Brunete had been bad beyond imagining. Yet the battle was not over.

Teruel, famous for its mules and its Mudéjar architecture, sits on a high knoll above the confluence of the Turia and Alfambra rivers and is surrounded by an array of scraggy gorges, tooth-shaped peaks, and twisted ridges. West of town, however, the Calatayud highway runs up a slight gradient to a palm-flat plain around the village of Concud, three miles out. The Nationalists used Concud as a staging base for their counteroffensive against Teruel, pushing their armies downhill on both sides of the highway, supported by a huge railway gun on an armored train.

On January 14, the XVth Brigade joined the defense of the city, marching by night down the Alfambra gorge. The British were posted in the cemetery of Santa Barbara, a promontory high above the Alfambra that overlooked the Concud plain. They barricaded their Maxims and dug in two antitank guns behind broken marble tombstones and soberly watched thousands of headlights on the Calatayud road, where the enemy assembled men and matériel.

The Mac-Paps held a precarious spur leading up to a furiously contested peak known as La Muela (the Tooth), the key point in the fighting west of the Alfambra. For certain companies of the Canadians, it was hold tight or die, for at their backs was a seventy-foot cliff hanging over the river valley. The Lincolns and the

24th Battalion were strung out across the Calatayud road, on lower ground that was within a few yards of the city limits on the west. Particularly vulnerable to sniper shots, which came from the long slope facing them, they set up a firing line in outlying huts, the *manicomio* (insane asylum), and among trench pits inherited from troops they had relieved. Their left flank was anchored by a flat-topped ridge where the Republicans had massed its artillery batteries. Behind them loomed the broken towers and smashed walls of old Teruel.

An arriving American nurse described the Lincoln position on the ruinous western edge of the city: "What a wreck; not all the buildings down . . . but not a one that hadn't suffered from shell fire; soldiers everywhere, camping, camping over little fires built beween bricks placed on the floors of shops; mud everywhere, counters bashed in, goods everywhere as though a volcano had broken out among 'em. . . . An arched aqueduct leading into the town with one of the arches blown up and hanging in the air."*

For the first three days it was a sniper's war. But for the Lincolns, the creature comforts, after Celadas, were considerable. They slept in demolished houses and stables, and had hot stew and hot coffee (ersatz) from the cookhouse near at hand. From a full larder cooks baked many pies—steaming hot. They broke into abandoned shops and replenished wardrobes with outlandish costumes. Fred Keller, Lincoln commissar, outfitted himself with striped morning trousers tucked into black riding boots, a sheep-lined greatcoat and a black sombrero. A prewar sign nearby—"DODGE REPARACIONES"—evoked home.

When Lieutenant Bill Titus's company occupied a convent in the city, the nuns were terrified until Keller calmed the Mother Superior with his gift of gab. When some men cursed the Catholic Church for its record of repression in Spain, Titus disagreed. A college man and idealist from Grand Rapids, he pitched in and defended those millions of Catholics throughout the world, most of them workers or peasants.*

Villar and his billet companion, a New York interpreter named Alfred Litween, settled into a ruined library. On a table were a pile of books and wads of hundred-peseta notes issued in Burgos, the Nationalist capital. While the Americans helped themselves to the money, Villar settled down with a book published in the Franco zone dealing with the Nationalist march on Madrid. Litween studied his companion carefully and examined the book. Some days later Villar was summoned to headquarters, where a tribunal headed by Captain Lamb interrogated him about his reading. Didn't he realize he was reading a book about a Fascist victory written by a Fascist officer? Villar pleaded no motive beyond intellectual curiosity, and Lieutenant James Cody, his mentor, turned the affair into a joke by congratulating him for taking a book rather than the money. "What are we to do with you? Are we to have you shot or promoted for honesty? Here, take your book but once you've finished it, put it back where you found it. Then you can let us know what conclusions you have drawn from it." The inquiry was over. But Villar had been singed by this inquisition, as he noted in his diary: "Here in the International Brigades, others have been shot for less." He was especially upset because he had been betrayed by his closest companion, who had rifled through his pack, examined the book, and turned it over to the authorities. Litween's apology spoke volumes about priorities in the International Brigades: "I was afraid that you might be one of the many spies with whom this unit is riddled. I am really sorry." "Many spies" was a refrain increasingly heard in the Republican armies.*

On January 17 the Nationalists attacked across a wide front from El Muletón to La Muela in an effort to break across the Alfambra River. The XIth Brigade was decimated and routed on El Muletón, and the Mac-Paps were pinned against the edge of a gorge as the enemy came on, not in skirmish lines but in columns. The antitank battery and the British machine gunners in the cemetery behind the Mac-Paps fired over their heads and halted the attack. But the Canadians were subjected to such a heavy artillery barrage that it filed down the lip of their trenches to a depth of six feet in some places. Clouds of chalk dust settled on the defenders, turning their hair white and jamming guns, which were cleaned and fired and jammed again. The situation became impossible when enemy fire converged on their positions from their entire front. During this pounding, forty Spanish boys in Second Company threw down their rifles in terror and raced to the fancied security of the enemy lines. Nilo Makela's machine gunners opened fire on them without result, although other gunners refused to fire.* A runner went back to beg for reinforcements, found none, but scrounged a typist who had never been in combat. "We needed a couple of hundred men, not a clerk who was petrified with fear even before he got close to the hill," recounted the runner, who made it back, but the typist disappeared.*

Although enemy artillery also shelled the Lincolns on the edge of Teruel, the men there had better protection in huts and buildings and their casualties were lighter. Unlike prior battles, Teruel was a blocking action. It became almost as routine as dawdling over morning coffee, picking up one's rifle, and walking downtown to work. A hut and the men in it might be splintered by a shell or a man's head taken off by a sniper bullet, but for the predominantly city-bred Lincolns these hazards were preferable to the vast, agoraphobic emptiness of Brunete or Aragon. A lone replacement, fresh from Tarazona, unable to find his countrymen, burrowed in with some friendly Spanish conscripts. They gave him a Winchester rifle and some cartridge clips, "Your comrades have gone away. . . . At least you can shoot yourself."*

Captain Detro wandered about on the verge of collapse. His long frame had worn down to skin and bones, and his fine irony soured to sarcasm. Instead of crawling through the too-shallow ditch across the Calatayud road, he defied snipers by loping across in plain view, "moving gracefully, blue beret rakish over one eye." He hated to stoop. At one such crossing a sniper bagged him. When Joe Bianca rescued him and upbraided him for carelessness, Detro replied, "I'm sorry, sir." At the dressing station they found a pinhole shot causing a compound fracture in the right femur, a bad but not usually a fatal wound.* Yet six weeks later he died in a Murcia hospital. An uncooperative patient, he refused to have his leg amputated. (The cause of his death was variously reported as gangrene, malaria, pneumonia, along with "defeatism and fatalism." There was also talk of a romance with an American nurse.)* His adjutant, Leonard Lamb, a New York social worker, took command of the battalion.[7]

The Nationalist onslaught against Teruel in mid-January seemed unrelenting. The Lincolns counted eighty casualties, many of them from frostbite—and the Mac-Paps a hundred and fifty. World War vets, who had pooh-poohed comparisons between the Spanish civil war and the "Big War," had to admit that the artillery barrages here were the worst they had ever endured. Whole city-blocks had been leveled, and streets had disappeared under mounds of broken stones, splintered wood, and crumbling plaster. The men were worn down. Whatever semblance of military bearing they once had had been filed away by three weeks of battle. An American runner arrived at General Walter's headquarters with a message. En route he had bloodied his face in a motorcycle crash, he had not bathed or shaved since Agua Vivas, and he chewed a thick cud of tobacco. Shoving over a pile of maps on the general's table, he perched himself on the edge and delivered his message. The general, having failed to stare him down, remarked archly. "You Americans—very odd people."*

During a lull in the fighting, Mrs. Charlotte Haldane arrived for a tour of the front and was honored for her work in the Paris office with a party held in Colonel Copic's candlelit bunker, buried deep under a church. She had come

---

7. Lamb, a twenty-seven-year-old Cleveland native, commanded the Lincolns briefly after Amlie was relieved. After Belchite he was wounded while inspecting a captured Italian pistol that exploded in his face, at which time Detro took command. For reasons unknown—though doubtless political—Lamb never became a permanent commander, though he compiled an outstanding battle record in Spain.

down to Spain as guide and interpreter for Paul and Eslanda Robeson.[8] British volunteers briefed her that Copic had a "reputation of carefully avoiding the front line." They had a fine dinner with excellent wine, followed by singing. "I sing, even at the front," Copic proudly told his visitors. He had a deep baritone and fancied himself an opera singer. His soirees customarily opened with revolutionary anthems and gradually shifted over to bawdy songs as the night wore on. The entertainment was interrupted when a soldier brought the colonel a heavy silver salver taken from a private house nearby. Copic explained that all valuables were held in custody by his staff in order to avert looting. "Looters," he added menacingly, "are shot on the spot." A week later, in the Barcelona quarters of the Communist Party, Mrs. Haldane was interviewing La Pasionaria when a gift package arrived for the "Red Virgin" containing the same salver that Mrs. Haldane had seen in Copic's bunker under Teruel. She did not reveal its provenance.*

On February 3, the XVth Brigade withdrew from Teruel after five weeks on the line and marched down the Valencia road. As far as the eye could see, there were wrecked, blackened tanks, strafed trucks, demolished staff cars, and piles of house rubble. Yet the road was crammed with vehicles still pumping men, munitions, and optimism into the seven-week battle. Good money chased the bad—for the Nationalists retook the city on February 22.

At Escandón Pass twenty kilometers southeast of Teruel, the brigade boarded an ailing freight train bound for Sagunto, the first stop on their way back to their rest villages in the Tajuña valley. On one uphill grade the men looked out of the windows and saw that they were slipping backward. They were ordered outside to help the wheezing, wood-burning locomotive up an incline. A few kilometers farther on, the train broke down. Doran and Merriman herded the men across stony upland meadows to a hollow deemed safe from the often-bombed railroad. As they huddled together in the cold, Doran told them that a famous visitor from the States had come to see them. Having heard that Paul Robeson was in Spain, the men perked up. A figure heavily wrapped in a black-leather coat stepped in front of them. To everyone's surprise, it turned out to be Earl Browder, secretary-general of the CPUSA.

---

8. Robeson came to Spain after first dropping his son off in Moscow to be properly educated. On his tour he sang "Ol' Man River," "Lonesome River," and "Fatherland" before enthusiastic crowds of Americans at Benicasim (the Interbrigade hospital on the coast), Albacete, and Tarazona de la Mancha. Robeson was the only American entertainer to visit the volunteers during the course of the war. (But he did not sing in the trenches of Teruel, as the left-wing press reported.) Before he left Spain, an American commissar gave him and his wife a highly romanticized account of Oliver Law.

They listened respectfully while Browder spoke of recent labor victories—real or imagined—of his hope that President Roosevelt would soon permit arms shipments to the Republic, and of his conviction that Spain would be the tomb of Fascism. Having proclaimed these pleasantries, Browder then dilated on conditions in the battalion relayed to him by Minor and Doran, mainly about the "demoralized elements" in both North American battalions. He warned that men with "unhealthy attitudes" such as grumbling would be sent home in disgrace. A ripple of laughter greeted his reprimand, followed by some throaty cheers. "Save me the first boat!" shouted someone. "I'm grumbling, I'm grumbling—when do I go home?"* piped in another. At first, the men had thought that Browder might be spoofing them, but when they saw from his expression that he was deadly in earnest, they began to hoot and catcall. The leader of the American Communist Party no longer spoke the same language as the volunteers it had recruited. Earl Browder did not address them a second time.

While waiting at a railroad siding in Valencia, the XVth received orders to return to Teruel. The Nationalists had broken the Alfambra line, and the whole Republican front was collapsing. The Lincolns felt a sense of bitter outrage at the recall and took out their venom on a tun of brandy in a flatcar. When the train commander protested, Commissar Keller explained that because water froze in a minute or two up at Teruel, the machine gunners had only collected antifreeze for their guns. Thus fortified, the Lincolns entrained for the North Pole once again. If the Lincolns frothed in rage, they were nevertheless more fortunate than the Mac-Paps, whose train never got down for a thawing-out in Valencia at all.

To divert enemy forces from Teruel, the Republican command planned a series of daggerlike thrusts against isolated outposts far to the north. The XVth drew Segura de los Baños, a remote hill village sixty miles north of Teruel where they would make a surprise night attack upon scattered outposts in the Sierra Pedigrossa. Once these had been overrun, the path would be open for a sweep down the mountain valley to Vivel del Río, five miles south, a key road junction on the Zaragoza-Teruel highway.

How the brigade got from Escandón Pass to Segura de los Baños or how many days it took, no one knew until Villar's diary came to light. He reported that trucks carried them to Mora de Rubielos, Alcalá de la Selva, Aliaga, Ejulve, Alcorisa, Andorra (not the country), Oliete, Muniesa, and finally to Cortés de Aragón, where they arrived in a snowstorm and bedded down in some "reasonably intact" sheep pens. They had crossed three mountain ranges, dodged bulges in the front, and traversed an alpine wasteland seldom visited by outsiders. All the villages—when there were villages—looked alike, even though it required imagination to call them villages at all. At a distance they resembled rock piles, until on closer view one could pick out an elephantine church (in a style that might have been called post-neolithic), which dwarfed the houses exactly as a Marxist artist would have designed a poster to illustrate clerical oppression. Altogether it was a pitiless region more hospitable to sheep and goats than to human beings. The climate was harsh: winter sunshine could be blotted out by a blinding blizzard within minutes.

Segura de los Baños lay in a ravine below two sharp peaks crowned with ruined castle towers, between which ran the Belchite road. Two miles to the west rose the ridges of the Sierra Pedigrossa, held by the enemy. In between a trickle of ice and water called Río Martín cut a fallow valley. Throughout most of the war the belligerents had gazed at one another through binoculars, neither eager to venture onto the exposed valley. This stasis was about to change. The plan called for the Lincolns and Mac-Paps to push across the valley to the Sierra Pedigrossa, while the British and 24th were to move down the valley toward Vivel, a major road junction.

Morale had never been worse. The attack had been hurriedly patched together without regard for logistics. Since food supplies had never been ordered—or had been lost en route—the men tried to supplement iron rations by foraging like a medieval army. But the peasants had even less to eat.[9] Morale took a further dip when Copic arrived with two leather-jacketed Russian advisers, a telltale sign of trouble coming. With Litween as interpreter, he explained that the brigade would dislodge the enemy outposts in front, then proceed behind enemy lines for seventy kilometers, through a series of mountain paths, and finally attack the main Zaragoza-Teruel road. This would cut the main supply line feeding the Nationalist offensive against Teruel. Copic promised they would have tank and artillery cover in accomplishing their task. Reserve units were standing by to mop up isolated outposts. He concluded by assuring them that the rest of Walter's 35th Division would also be engaged, although the "place of honor" belonged to the XVth Brigade. The men were ordered to empty their knapsacks and pack in enough munitions and iron rations to last for three days. Ahead were seventy kilometers of nearly trackless wilderness garnished with only a few serpentine mountain roads. One wonders whether Copic and his advisers really believed this outlandish plan would work or whether they concocted it only because they were ordered by higher authorities to "do something or other."

9. On the thirtieth anniversary of the arrival of the Lincolns in Segura de los Baños I joined a long line of villagers engaged in their most important activity of the day—waiting in a snowstorm for the bakery to open. (Quite delicious bread, by the way.)

For two days the XVth lay hidden in stony huts of the village, unable to build fires because the smoke might give them away. They argued about what Segura de los Baños meant—the consensus favored "safe water," but a minority preferred "where they keep all the bathtubs under lock and key."* Then, on the night of February 16, as snow flurries lashed the frozen valley, they moved out in single file to attack. The Mac-Paps were ordered to seize Mount Atalaya, the highest promontory; the Lincolns, a crest farther south. In the darkness they crossed paths with other Republican units bound for other crests, other hills. "Little men—little ghosts," recalled an American, "none of them ever seen again."*

After five confusing hours of maneuvering through empty terrain, the Mac-Paps reached the lower slopes of Mount Atalaya just before sunrise and crept upward without being observed. They cut through the enemy wire and charged upward behind a chorus of yells and grenade bursts, quickly overrunning the fortified sheepcotes of a panicked enemy. But this sudden eruption of alarms, shots, and curses on Atalaya only served to alert other outposts along the mountains. These bowled grenades and fired nervously into the valley. The Lincoln machine-gun company, now commanded by Dave Reiss of Paterson, New Jersey, had strayed and failed to arrive at the foot of their ridge until daylight. Reiss, a pacifist before Spain, was heard pleading, "¡Camaradas, camaradas, somos hermanos!" followed by, "Surrender, you bastards!"*

While the Mooney guns hosed the upper regions, Third Company under William Titus fanned out to attack from the rear. Beaten back four times, they lay trapped on the hillside. Unable to retaliate, Titus began to lose his idealism and self-control as he called the enemy "vermin, inhuman gorillas, liars, apes."* Finally he led a rush on the enemy parapets. With two grenades in his hand, he hurdled the wire and was killed immediately. As though horrified by what they had done—and fearing the consequences—the enemy surrendered minutes later, after the triggermen had been killed. Titus had always been a stickler for "iron-clad discipline," and had exhorted his men to be leaders in the fight for world revolution back in the States.* On a third hilltop the resistance proved more stubborn—the enemy managing even to launch a short-lived counterattack—but losses were light. In all, seven Americans were killed during the Segura fight.*

After Lieutenant Milton Wolff, a towering New Yorker and close friend of Titus, had taken hold of the enemy commander and "booted his ass down the side of the hill in full view of his troops," the Lincolns found themselves the sole proprietors of a barren hillside strewn with rusty tins, a few Fiat machine guns, a small group of petrified enemy conscripts, and a large hoard of tinned octopus. This was victory.

The prisoners came down the mountain and were escorted to the rear with their hands on their heads. The enemy commander, a thick-set captain of middle age, and two lieutenants who had not had time to swap uniforms and disappear in the mass, confronted the brigade staff. News had just arrived down the hill that Titus had been killed, and the Nationalist officers, having already been manhandled by Wolff, stood "wide-eyed with terror," waiting to be shot. Lieutenant Jim Cody, through Litween as interpreter, interrogated the prisoners, passing information to Captain Lamb and Commissar Doran. Nearby, the Lincolns watched, waiting for the verdict. To their surprise, when Lamb signaled that the interrogation was over, he saluted the prisoners smartly and ordered them to the rear with the others.

Because of the enemy's dogged resistance, the whole operation was thrown off schedule. Positions supposed to have been neutralized by noon were not taken until sundown. Among the staff grew a sense that "all our plans have come to nothing." Cody argued that those in the rear were "toying with the lives of the Brigaders" and warned that they could expect a massive counterattack in the morning. To no one's surprise, Copic, never seen during the attack, was true to form. His promise of armored and air support was just hot air. (Artillery had been used, but the shots ranged mainly on the Americans or, when corrected, into a valley on the other side.)* The objective for the staff was now to withdraw the brigade without bringing down on them Martyesque charges of cowardice or treason.

Cody's dire predictions rang true. The next morning the enemy counterattacked, while their officers detonated grenades at the heels of laggards to keep them moving. They nearly broke through, but the British and Spanish battalions came up from reserve and stiffened the line. Further advance by the XVth was clearly impossible. In the afternoon six Junkers made a bombing run, but they targeted only concentrations of men in the rear. The Lincolns took some bitter pleasure in hearing that brigade headquarters had to flee pell-mell across the countryside. On February 19, the brigade withdrew on foot to Cortés de Aragón, where at nightfall trucks ferried them through Montalban and Mezquita de Jarque to Aliaga, for their first hot meal in three days.

The XVth had been lucky when stalemated at Segura de los Baños because only fifteen kilometers away camped the entire Italian Army Corps of the CTV (Cuerpo de Tropos Voluntarios)—50,000 men, 60 batteries of artillery, and 250 tanks—a force being assembled for Franco's next offensive, a lightning thrust through Aragon to the sea.

The overriding impression one has of Segura de los Baños is that no one had much stake or interest in the battle then—or now. (Nationalist military historians seem to have ignored it altogether.) Perhaps the most telltale account of the battle is recorded in an "official" history of the British Battalion: "In the course of the day, three heavy and two light guns fired over 40,000 rounds, and not a round was wasted. The fire of the other guns with the infantry companies was no less deadly and efficient. All rounds were fired at carefully observed objectives. The objective had been secured, but at the cost of two British lives."* If battles were evaluated by the incompetence of their strategists and the uselessness of their results, then Segura de los Baños might figure prominently in the history of war.

13

RETREAT FROM BELCHITE

By early March both sides claimed Teruel as a victory—the Republicans because they had captured the city in December, the Nationalists because they had retaken it in February. After seventy days of bitter fighting, the lines had been stabilized about where they had been before the battle began. Under such circumstances, twenty-five thousand corpses could be resurrected as statistics to support whatever definition of victory danced in the brains of the analyst, to the tune of his political anthem. Yet if the cairn of rubble and bone marking the site of Teruel offered no positive endorsement of human sanity, the battle itself had two results: the military resources of the Republic were temporarily exhausted, and the Nationalist forces were concentrated in a restricted sector of Aragon. The struggle for Madrid became ancient history. Within twenty days of retaking Teruel, the armies of General Franco, mobilized in one sector, launched an offensive that, as events proved, was the most decisive and crucial of the war—a lightning stroke that cut the Republic in two.

After being pulled from Segura de los Baños and trudging cross-country through time-forgotten pueblos like Montalban and Mezquita de Jarque to Aliaga, the XVth anticipated a long rest back at Albares. In a sunny grove at Mora de Rubielos, a Rube Goldberg shower truck awaited them with plenty of hot water. After filing through the jets, they got handfuls of delousing cream and worn but very clean clothes. (Within twenty-four hours the lice were back.) Now that battle was far behind them, the Spanish recruits became as frisky as colts and congratulated themselves on their good luck. Overjoyed to be alive, they talked about how they had never lived so well before: food "as good and as generous as in the best hotel of the world," wrote Villar, entranced by chocolates and caramels in the morning, clothing of the softest possible quality (even pure woolen socks—a luxury), and because of battle casualties, a daily ration of two and sometimes three packs of cigarettes per day. American tobacco, too—Lucky Strikes. This was wealth. Although treated as second-class citizens within the brigade hierarchy, nevertheless they towered above Spaniards in the regular army.

While they waited at El Puerto de Escandón for their train, disconcerting news arrived—the Nationalists had just seized Teruel, and they might be thrown into a new campaign to retake the city. Instead of boarding a train, they climbed back into trucks and retraced their route. Or was it going to be Zaragoza again? No one told them anything. Trucks ferried them up to Hijar, on the Zaragoza-Barcelona railway line, where they bivouacked around the town. "The hounds of spring were on winter's traces," as thin blades of wheat pushed through pebbly soil, and pear trees blossomed in irritated valley bottoms. The nights were cold, but no longer did their rifles seize up, as they had at Celadas and Teruel.

This aura of peace was so intoxicating that most of the ranking officers wrote out passes for themselves and went on leave. Colonel Copic's wife had come from Prague, so he joined her in Barcelona. Doran left for a sinus operation. The acting Lincoln commander, Lenny Lamb, went on hospital leave, while his commissar Fred Keller reported to a Special Cadres School for advanced (political) training. Other officers went off for "dental appointments," which often had nothing to do with teeth but in the case of Milton Wolff it did. Thus it was that as the Nationalists, just beyond the western horizon, prepared for their biggest offensive of the war, the XVth Brigade fell apart. Major Merriman seemed to be in charge, although now and then a Russian *sovietnik* named "Nikolai" came down from Walter's 35th Division headquarters to look in. No leaves for the rank and file, who were left behind to harvest the gathering whirlwind.

Several hundred replacements came up from Tarazona de la Mancha, mainly Spaniards, but seeded with some green Americans. The Americans had left the training camp on Lincoln's birthday amid cries of "See ya in Zaragoza!" In charge of them was DeWitt Parker, the Ivy League intellectual who had at last been permitted to escape his tedious liaison post in Paris. Although innocent of battle, he was at once installed as the Lincoln commissar. Frail and thoughtful, he seemed beyond his depth when put against tough guys like Doran, but the men came to appreciate his nonautocratic regimen. Temporary command of the battalion fell to Lieutenant David Reiss, of New Jersey, a figure so lackluster that few men afterward could remember much about him except that he was an "older man" with a fringe of black hair framing a bald scalp and that he was "slow in speech, quick to anger."* He had "fizzled out" at Fuentes de Ebro as commander of the machine-gun company, inexplicably turning inward and behaving mechanically. Both Reiss and Parker had been picked merely to keep the shop open until the battle merchants returned.

On March 6, 1938, the brigade marched twelve miles west to Belchite, where old-timers pointed out to rookies the principal landmarks of the city that they had captured exactly half a year before—Nelson's factory, Dead Man's Point, Doran's church. Grotesquely picturesque, Belchite was a rubbish pile of crumbled brick, charred wood, and dangling wires. After half a year it still stank of the dead. Brass plaques above doorways advertised houses insured against fire by a Zaragoza agency. (One wonders whether this included damage by gunfire.) The ruins were overrun with stray cats and some old people with no other place to go, scuttling creatures clad in black who camped out in crannies among the ruins. Avoiding the wrecked houses where winds banged doors and rattled blinds, the Lincolns spread out in the olive grove north of town. Olive branches no longer meant peace, but they did at least provide a screen against enemy airplanes. Meanwhile, the other battalions moved into the arid hill country to the south—the British to Lecera at fifteen kilometers away, and the Mac-Paps to Letux at eight.

On March 3 General Pozas notified his division commanders that "all signs suggest an enemy attack upon our lines"* without detailing where and when, but Merriman's information was that the XVth occupied a third or fourth line. If the enemy moved, there should be plenty of time to respond. The front, stabilized about nineteen kilometers west, had been dormant since October.

At six-thirty in the morning of March 9, three separate Nationalist armies numbering over a hundred and fifty thousand effectives swept like an uncontrollable forest fire over the Republican defensive line, consisting of poorly coordinated segments of the Republican Fifth Army, stretching fifty miles between Vivel del Río and the Ebro River. The northernmost wing comprised the superb Army of Morocco, predominantly Moors and Tercios de Extranjeros, led by General Juan de Yagüe and supported by forty-seven artillery batteries and squadrons of the German Condor Legion. Two of his best divisions, the 5th Navarre and the 150th Mixed (Tercios de Extranjeros, Moors, and Falange) would converge on Belchite from two directions; and when the Reds had been rooted out, the Navarres would proceed through Azaila and Escatrón to seize Caspe, a major railroad depot on the Barcelona line. Meanwhile to their south, the Africans would move along the Hijar road to Alcañiz, a Republican supply depot. Farther to the south, Mussolini's CVT would cut cross-country to Alcañiz, catching in a pincer whatever was left of the Republican armies near Belchite. The timetable of General Yagüe was as fixed as that of any well-run railroad—Belchite in two days, Hijar in four. His plan called for the liberation of Belchite ("our martyred city," as it was beatified in the Nationalist press) by columns advancing not from one direction, but from three. The main thrust would come down the road from Fuendetodos—the birthplace of Goya— twelve miles due west of Belchite. Other columns would sweep to the south through Azuara and Lecura, while the rest would approach from Mediana to the northwest of Belchite. All this while the XVth Brigade, which idly waited for the long-promised rest village, lay languidly across the path of this juggernaut. Their nearest support was the XIth Brigade in the denuded country halfway to Quinto, but they were not fit for battle, having been terribly mauled in defending El Muletón ridge at Teruel.

With large numbers of their officers and commissars on leave, the men of the XVth, many convalescing from wounds at Teruel, had no incentive to train. They did not fortify, they did nothing except lounge under olive branches. Things were so quiet that Villar resumed his literacy classes for the Spaniards of the brigade. He had made good progress in teaching them to read and write simple things, and shared their childish delight as they proudly showed him letters destined for home, written by their own hands in chicken scrawls. On the morning of March 9, his class was disrupted by the crump of artillery fire off to the west and the roar of approaching air squadrons. Streams of bombers and fighters flew unopposed except for occasional twin puffs from Republican double-barrel French guns.* The bombers ignored the camps in the groves as targets somehow unworthy of attention but moved back and forth "as if their only interest is in shocking and above all, striking fear into us." At least one formation contained one hundred and twenty planes. As the leading aircraft disappeared over the eastern horizon, an equal number of planes hove into sight to the west. On the ground it was so peaceful that the paymaster set up his table under a tree and counted out monthly stipends. Delayed by his classes, Villar arrived after the paymaster had packed up. His most pressing worry—how was he to get through a whole month without any pocket money?*

A few bombs fell on Belchite, but the pilots had no specific targets. Harry Fisher, a Lincoln communications man, stood with friends watching three planes circling the city a mile away, when they saw something none had ever seen before. The leading plane peeled off and dived straight down. Thinking it had been hit, the Lincolns cheered. But just above the ground the plane dropped a light bomb, pulled out of the dive, and soared up again. The others performed the same strange maneuver. Only later did Fisher realize that he had witnessed one of the first uses in battle of a new aerial tactic—dive-bombing by experimental Stukas.*

At three in the morning of March 10, runners jabbed the Lincolns awake. The enemy had broken through near Fuendetodos. An order sent hours before had not been received: "Proceed to area to block the enemy. Create a line of defense. Proceed immediately."* Merriman was bawling out Dave Reiss. "You're supposed to be on a hill two miles from here. I sent a runner [to you] at ten last night. Why the hell are you still here?" Usually in full control of his emotions, Merriman was in bad temper, unshaven, and disheveled. The men were alarmed—no one had seen Merriman like this before. Reiss meekly tried to explain he had never received the order, then roused his men and got them on the road. Someone ordered them to fix bayonets—a ludicrous order because few men had bayonets to fix. It was still dark, very quiet, and "the fear so strong it was like a nightmare," remembered one American.*

They trailed west along the Fuendetodos road in columns of four, bucking waves of refugees ballooned with sacks, all hurrying east as though sucked by a huge magnet. Up front, Reiss ran on about his part in antiwar demonstrations at home. "I was a pacifist, and in a way I still am," he said. "Yet here I am, commanding an American battalion, most of them antiwar demonstrators, taking on the most experienced fighting force in the world. Crazy!"* He posted no scouts ahead or on the flanks because he had been told that they were going up to relieve Republican naval infantry, who held trenches "somewhere" far ahead. On the road they began to meet scattered groups of infantry falling to the rear. Since they did not seem panicked, Reiss assumed that they had been properly relieved by fresh troops.

As the sky lightened, they passed a steep hillock on the left surmounted by El Santuario del Pueyo, a bulbous pseudo-Byzantine hermitage, three miles west of Belchite. Reiss had been informed that the place had been seeded with antitank guns and was a reserve line. On low hills ahead scouts spotted troop movements, and Reiss ordered them ahead without halting his column. About half the Lincolns had passed the hermitage when machine guns opened fire from an ambush ahead, cutting down the vanguard. The Americans were so surprised that at first they thought friendlies must be shooting at them by mistake. But as the firing continued, the ranks split apart, men racing pell-mell uphill toward the rocky crest of El Pueyo, abandoning their wounded on the road.

Reiss was exasperated at what he found along the crest—frightened scraps of the naval infantry unit they were supposed to relieve miles farther west. They lay in shallow trenches and had no stomach for engaging the enemy in force. More unforgivable, they had watched the Lincolns filing below them, but had not bothered to send a runner to inform them of their withdrawal. Worse, the Americans found none of the antitank guns they had been promised. Reiss sent out a few patrols to the ridges rising above them on the south and west, but these were driven back. He dispatched Paul MacEachron, formerly a sophomore at Oberlin College, with his rifle squad to find the enemy. MacEachron apparently succeeded, for he was never heard from again. (Later they learned he had been captured and executed.)

It was a solitary eyrie they held. Ahead, to the west, the Fuendetodos road ran straight as a shot across an empty, colorless plain until it bumped into low mountain ridges three miles ahead; behind, the same plain reached back to the olive groves girdling Belchite. Had it not been for foothills rising three hundred feet above them on their south, the hermitage knoll would have been a formidable position. But, as usual, the Nationalists had seized this higher ground and began to pour down small-arms fire like sheets of pelting rain. Joe Bianca, a fearless New York seaman with a great handle-bar mustache, set up his Maxim on the far left flank and began to answer the enemy fire.

By midmorning, after twenty Junkers unloaded on Belchite, the Lincolns were buzzed, bombed, and strafed by enemy planes—bombers, and swift fighters like the Messerschmitt 109s—which swirled around the hermitage like enraged wasps. Men counted a hundred planes in the sector at one time, and some swore that they passed over them at head-level.* They even attacked a member of the brigade staff who, hearing the racket around the hermitage, had wandered out from Belchite to see the show. Even though he was alone on the plain, hardly worth the attention, three planes made two strafing passes at him. By this time flat-trajectory shells were exploding on the Lincoln hilltop. Except for Bianca's gun, the Americans failed to return the fire. Men squatted in holes and clutched rifles—some with bayonets still fixed. Resistance, where it existed at all, consisted of mere companies or sections dug in along the piney mountains farther to the southwest trying to hold back the enemy while their ammunition dwindled and their flanks were overrun.

Within three hours of the opening guns, the entire Republican front had caved in with troops streaming to the rear—less like a panic than an irresistible flood rolling ever eastward like water from a rotten dam. In the mob were *quintos* clutching fiber suitcases next to artillerists carrying the firing locks of abandoned field guns. When stopped on the road by military police, the fugitives gave out the same story—they had been ordered to fall back to a new defensive line at Belchite. Who issued the order none could say. The Lincoln headquarters in the Belchite ramparts knew nothing of such an order. In almost all cases, high-ranking officers were not among the retreating soldiers. Whether they had deserted to the enemy (the prevailing theory among the commissars), had been abandoned by their men, or had been shot for trying to stop the retreat was anyone's guess. Over at Letux, Major Edward Cecil-Smith with his Mac-Paps tried to hold back throngs of Republican troops at gunpoint, but those in the rear fanned out and slipped around the armed patrols like crazed ants bypassing a pebble in their path.

Faced with this inundation, contact between headquarters and the field units at the front all but vanished. (The Lincolns received no orders at all until eighteen hours after the front had collapsed.) Telephone messages between division and brigade headquarters broke off abruptly when Division moved without notifying Brigade. As the enemy pressed forward with *blitzkrieg* efficiency, Major Merriman rode back and forth in an armored truck between widely separated fragments of the XVth Brigade, seeking a pattern in the breakthrough. But the enemy seemed to be everywhere—and all at once.

After setting up his command post in a deep culvert behind the hermitage, Reiss sent out runners, who, if they arrived anywhere, failed to report back. Yale Stuart of headquarters staff found that all the Lincoln observers on the left flank had deserted. He immediately saw the reason—the western road was "covered with hundreds of trucks, tanks, and artillery batteries unlimbering and firing." He raced back to the hermitage with the news. The telephone connection to Belchite was dead. Harry Fisher and his crew went out to repair the line, but the artillery barrage cut it faster than they could repair it. At about ten in the morning, Merriman arrived to reassure them: the Mac-Paps held the left flank solidly and the British occupied a reserve post in the olive grove behind them.* Before departing, Merriman promised that the British would come up during the next lull in the barrage. But no lull occurred.

A short time later, an enemy armored column appeared on the Fuendetodos road and edged warily upon the hermitage. Men shouted, "Tanks!" and ran back to the culvert, where they clustered around Reiss and two Russian advisers. Others, without orders, lit out for Belchite on foot. Everywhere Lincolns were breaking from the line, plunging down the hill in a mad rush toward Belchite. It took an uncommonly brave man—or an ignorant one—to hold while his fellow soldiers deserted left and right. Third Company, isolated behind intervening ridges on the left flank, learned of the disaster only after a wounded man scrambled back with the bitter news that even the first-aid station had pulled out. As twenty tanks groped the valley below, they hightailed it to the rear. The gun crew of Joe Bianca, which alone had been clattering since sunup, got off, but many at remote outposts never knew of the withdrawal. They formed, by accident rather than by intent, last-ditch pockets of resistance, covering the flight of their comrades until overwhelmed. Survivors would later rhapsodize about the heroism of these men whom they had abandoned in panic.

The plain became speckled with figures running, stumbling, and in some cases crawling toward Belchite, while enemy tanks on high ground shell-sniped them, and the black shadows of airplanes descended like hawks. Like drowning men, they tore off and threw away bulky items—blanket rolls, ammunition belts, mess kits, rifles, machine guns. "On all sides," remembered a survivor, "men were retreating, looking straight ahead and not seeing anything." Those following the highway were pursued by ricocheting machine-gun slugs and shells that bounced off the macadam surface with great slamming clangs. Those reaching the olive grove endured shellfire that tore entire trees from the ground and shook down thousands of olives in a purple rain. There was no accounting for the behavior of individual men. Staggering through geysering shell-bursts, a team of eight men carried a stretcher bearing a comrade whose foot had nearly been blown off—shock was his only sedative—because they doggedly refused to abandon a job promised and begun.

While Reiss and his cohorts stood at the mouth of the culvert debating, a projectile zeroed in on top of them, one of those thousand-to-one shots.[1] When the dust cleared, Commissar Parker lay on his back with his brains spilling out of the right side of his head. "A portion of his face had disappeared." The body parts of two runners lay scattered about, and others were seriously wounded.* Reiss had been flung to one side like a rag doll, his stomach torn open. Some men carried a wounded lieutenant from First Company into Villar's open trench as though bringing him a precious gift, then immediately ran off toward Belchite. Villar found a huge shard of iron embedded so deeply under the officer's left nipple that it had stanched the flow of blood. In broken Spanish the American moaned, "Quiero hablar con americano." But the Americans were gone, and he had to die alone. Villar wanted to stay with him, but his mentor, Jim Cody, rushed over, drew his pistol, and ordered him to come at once to help carry Reiss to a dressing station. Four men, led by Vernon Selby, a West Point dropout, arranged Reiss on a blanket. His eyes were already glassy, and intestines oozed from his belly. These litter-bearers were the last members of the battalion to evacuate the hilltop. As they stumbled with their dying commander after the other Lincolns, "hot-footing it in disarray back toward Belchite," two German planes peeled off and strafed them, forcing them to take cover at an outcrop below the hill. Here they discovered that Reiss was dead. They closed his eyes, tossed the blanket over him and argued about what they should do. It was every man for himself. While the others squatted behind the outcrop, Villar made a mad dash across the plain toward the olive grove. The

---

1. The command post has been variously designated a culvert, a cave, a tunnel, and a gully. Probably it was an open passageway leading to a back door of El Santuario del Pueyo, today altered by reconstruction. Since it was on the eastern side of the building, sheltered from the main thrust of the enemy attack, the missile must have been an aerial bomb.

enemy planes wheeled for another strike. For them it must have been a sport like flushing a rabbit into the open. Villar zigzagged and dived to the ground as bullets spewed the ground around him—but he made it.[2] The sky as far as Belchite and beyond was filled with planes raking the troops with their machine guns and hand-dropping grenades wherever men clustered together.

Peter Kemp, an upper-class Englishman serving as a lieutenant in Franco's Tercios de Extranjeros, described the assault tactics of the Nationalist army. As soon as motorized infantry, screened by armor two hundred yards in front (each company had six old German tanks armed with two machine guns and two Russian T-26s captured at Fuentes de Ebro)—met strong resistance, they halted and called in support from bombers and artillery. Lieutenant Kemp watched the attack on El Santuario del Pueyo. A squadron of silver Junkers dropped bombs on the hill, which erupted like a volcano in reddish-brown smoke blanketing the church. Immediately afterward came a ninety-minute barrage from artillery on the heights to the south. "It seemed impossible that anyone could be left alive on that hill." The legionnaires raced to the top without receiving a shot in reply. Up there were only the ruins of the church, tangles of barbed wire, and corpses identified as Internationals. Assigned to examine unopened mailbags, Kemp found it "tragic" to read letters from loved ones like a Brooklyn girl who wrote: "The radio is on. They are playing the Seventh Symphony. You know how that music brings us together. Please, oh please, come back to me soon."*

The British Battalion lay low in the woods, having no desire to publicize their presence to the planes buzzing the grove. They had broken camp at Letux and moved here to prevent further ambush of the Americans. El Pueyo was by this time swarming with enemy tanks and troops, each column brandishing, as though on parade, the yellow and red flag of monarchist Spain. Minutes later, the British, aware they were flanked, staged an orderly withdrawal from the grove, falling back in alternating echelons. In a shallow trench on the western edge of Belchite, a lone American with a Dichterev machine gun blocked the enemy advance temporarily. Villar joined him briefly until his rifle jammed. The American nodded and waved him back. This anonymous hero was either captured or killed—probably both.

---

2. Harry Fisher witnessed Villar's miraculous escape, although he did not know who he was until he read Villar's memoir sixty years later. He recounted how the Spaniard fell to the ground several times and believed him dead, only to see him rising up to continue his mad race against the airplanes. The other three stretcher-bearers also made their way to safety, although Selby had been badly wounded and was later imprisoned as a deserter when he turned up—lacking a pass—at a Barcelona hospital.

As Villar entered the brigade command post, a concrete bunker on the western lip of the city, he found Merriman standing beside his motorcar. With his high-top engineer boots laced to the knee, riding breeches, and gold-braided cap, he exemplified for Villar the "imperturbable hero" holding his ground while mortar rounds exploded around him. Later inside the bunker, Fausto studied his mentor Cody and Merriman as they pored over maps. Pointing to the phone, Cody exclaimed, "Nothing." Americans came in from time to time to collect the few remaining crates of munitions, but there was no food. Merriman passed along orders to hold the line until nightfall, to use their ammunition niggardly, and to fight with fixed bayonets if they had to. He promised to establish a new line in the morning.

Soon Merriman and Cody began to gesticulate and swear. Merriman said they must fall back to Hijar or "wherever each man can reach." That jolted Villar. It was like yelling, "Run for your lives!" If Merriman thought it was hopeless, what should *they* think? One minute the staff stood gaping—the next minute they had vanished, in a mad rush eastward through the rubble of Belchite.

Dodging random shots from enemy soldiers, Villar tried to follow them, but fell into a trench with leg cramps and total exhaustion. "I think to myself that this time it is the end for me, for the slightest movement causes me great agony." Luckily two Spanish lieutenants recognized him as a battalion observer and pulled him up to the roadway. He could not walk, so they wrapped his arms around their shoulders and half walked, half swung him along a mass of terrified men "racing like madmen for the rear guard." They escaped in the nick of time, for Belchite had sprung a leak. Like water, Moorish soldiers were flooding in from north and south and firing at anything that moved. (On this day General Yagüe reported his extraordinary advance of forty kilometers and the liberation of Belchite at 4:30 p.m.)*

That night beyond the city, the lieutenants flagged down a truck loaded with wounded, which dropped them at Caspe, well beyond the enemy advance. After two more hitches they reached Tarragona the following night, where the officers treated Villar to a meal in a fancy hotel. Convinced that all was lost and the war over, and knowing that as officers in the International Brigades they faced certain execution if captured by the enemy and possible execution if picked up by Republican police in Barcelona, one lieutenant resolved to find a ship in Valencia bound for Africa. That suited Villar who was hell-bent to find refuge with his mother and *novia* in his home city.

Back in Belchite there was only sporadic resistance. A mixed group of Spaniards and Internationals (mainly British) set up guns in trenches above the stagnant pond serving as town reservoir and in the windows of Nelson's old factory. The British used some armor-piercing machine-gun slugs that gave the German-made tanks pause. But by early afternoon a *bandería* of Moors infiltrated the town, and the wild scramble resumed. Men got lost in the olive grove, wandered in circles, and were seized by enemy patrols. The main line of escape lay along the Azaila road, due east. Frank Rogers hitched a ride on a truck filled with wounded, "thirty men stacked on top of each other—sweating, cursing, angry."* Earlier, General Walter had called for all forces to reorganize at a mid-point on the Lecera road, but when Merriman drove down there, he found the highway already segmented by enemy patrols. At one roadblock his car was ambushed, and he escaped only because of the breakneck daring of his driver, who churned cross-country to safety.

Lieutenant William Carroll, the Lincoln armorer, at his munitions dump south of Belchite, shipped off as much ammunition as his few trucks and cars could hold. Carroll himself guarded the remainder until an enemy tank nosed around a building and swung its gun for a shot. "That brought the battle of Belchite to an abrupt end for me. I crossed the river and headed for the rear."* Several kilometers later he found his assistants patiently waiting for orders. "When I told them they were now holding the front, they got off their asses in a hurry." After he overtook the munitions trucks, his men blew the bridge over a dry wash and vanished before the first enemy patrols arrived. Carroll's report proves that there was no shortage of ammunition at Belchite—the problem lay in delivering it. On one occasion drivers of three armored cars loaded with small-arms ammunition stopped and argued about directions. One wanted to go right, the other left, and the third wanted to check in at brigade headquarters for new instructions. All this while time-fused shells burst overhead. They fled in different directions without delivering their cargoes.

The British evacuated Belchite last.* Ninety of them, led by Sam "Moscow" Wild, a tough ex-sailor, picked up fugitives from other battalions and formed them into a rear guard for the fugitives on the Azaila road.[3] Outflanked at one point, Wild ordered his men "to march silently" and led them on a forced march at night to Vinaceite, which had been evacuated by the populace.* After

---

3. Sam Wild, like his predecessor Fred Copeman, had taken part in the Invergordon mutiny of the Royal Navy (protesting a pay cut) in 1931. At Jarama, on the second day, when the British Battalion began to break, Wild's Lewis-gun section was the last to withdraw, prompting Copeman's remark to two British army vets, "Thank God we've got a Navy." Later Copeman became critical of Wild when he heard that his old mate was executing British volunteers. Wild was notorious in the brigade for his brawling (he liked to break up fights among his men by challenging them both, one at a time), his drinking, and his dislike of both Spanish nationals and Americans in command. His men were afraid of him but conceded that he was wholly without fear and completely dedicated to the cause.

sundown it turned very cold. The British found bake ovens still warm, though not hot enough to cook bread, so they ate the raw dough and climbed into the ovens for a cozy sleep. The Lincolns, however, who had borne the brunt of the attack and lost their command structure within the opening hours, were in collective shock. With some exceptions, they wanted to get away and made no bones about it. Panicked fugitives reported having personally seen ditches full of brigaders who had surrendered to the Moors and been shot and castrated— but not in that exact order. (These stories were probably accurate, because forty-one Americans are known to have been killed *after* being taken prisoner during this period, most of them by the feared Moors.)* The Azaila road became jammed with thousands of fugitives from other Republican outfits, jabbering in a babel of tongues. Groups of officers clustered by the road argued vociferously—some said that they must stop and fight, others that they could do nothing. In places where all self-control broke down, stragglers climbed on top of ambulances; and when there was no more room, they pulled out the wounded and piled into the van. The fugitives escaped extermination only because the pursuers were now as exhausted as the pursued. Back in Belchite, some wounded Internationals lying in an extemporized prison received cigarettes and first aid from an Argentine doctor serving with the Nationalists, "All these men are wildly cursing their command, their chiefs, and the whole atmosphere of governmental Spain." Whether they were executed he does not say— but it was likely.*

Farther along, on a hilltop near Azaila, Harry Fisher was astonished by the sight of thousands of small bonfires in the fields on three sides of them. Enemy soldiers, confident that they would not be attacked, were nonchalantly building fires to warm themselves and cook their food. "It looked like a tremendous picnic." It was ominous, but Fisher was too used up to care. He dropped on the spot and slept three hours. At two in the morning (March 11), they were roused up and told to move quickly. Scouts had found a small hole in the enemy encirclement. No smoking—no talking. Some men went through the ring on stretchers, others on the backs of comrades, the only sounds being the groans of the badly wounded. Like docile cattle being herded through a gate, they passed through a double gauntlet of soldiers with machine guns positioned beside the road, protecting their passage. Farther to the north, the XIth brigade, the doughty Thaelmanns, had been cut to pieces, with survivors fleeing in all directions.

Meanwhile, the Mac-Paps were fighting their own war, cut off entirely from the main body of the brigade and without any knowledge of where to go. Through major blunders on the division staff, they had been ordered to advance, not retreat, from Letux when the front was collapsing on the morning of March 10. With the 24th Battalion they reached the village of Azuara, six kilometers west of Letux in the morning, where they endured shelling, bombing, and strafing throughout the day. Shells tore apart the barn that had housed the men and shredded paymaster funds and battalion records, which drifted about like confetti—"tiny bits as if a maniac had torn them to shreds."* Major Merriman came up briefly and pulled out the 24th Battalion (for undisclosed activities), but ordered the Mac-Paps to hold west of the Camaras River. By mid-afternoon all Republican forces had fled east of the river except the Mac-Paps. They were joined by a lieutenant colonel of the 95th Brigade (Spanish), who explained that three entire brigades had disappeared on their right flank because they were about to be cut off. The colonel had salvaged a battalion and vowed they would stay as long as the Mac-Paps did, but his men had other ideas, for they were fording the river and melting to the rear. Significantly, most had thrown away rifles and carried suitcases and bedrolls as if they were preparing for a long trip. "Although he [the colonel] shot four or five of them, he was unable to stop the retreat."* By nightfall only the colonel and half a dozen officers of the 95th Brigade remained. Cecil-Smith gave them a machine gun and posted them on the right flank, but by morning all had vanished, including the colonel. Since no orders came from Merriman during the night, Cecil-Smith pulled his men back across the river and sited twenty-eight of them in the red cliff face along the eastern bank to cover the bridge. With them were some orphaned Republican naval infantry. The major then hustled off to General Walter's headquarters to obtain explicit instructions. Walter ordered him to bring his battalion to the halfway point on the Lecera-Belchite road.

When the major returned to his battalion at daybreak of March 11, he found that enemy artillery was already pounding the cliff face with high-velocity shells. The naval infantrymen had vanished during the night as though by magic. Hastily gathering up his men, Cecil-Smith evacuated the town. Two machine-gun crews in a high rock face were never informed of the withdrawal, for it proved impossible to reach them, and shouts could not be heard above the racket of the battle, compounded by echoes against the cliff wall. This group, under Lieutenant Leo Gordon (brother of Joe Gordon, of Jarama fame) covered the retreat of the others. Those not killed in the fight were executed when captured except for one man, inexplicably saved by an enemy officer.*

In open march formation, the Mac-Paps passed over several hills already occupied by enemy troops, but these, doubtless mistaking them for their own, did not molest them. Instead of leading his battalion to the assigned point of rendezvous, Cecil-Smith reported directly to Lecera, because, as he later wrote,

"It was evident that considerable changes had taken place in our front-line since the night before"—surely the classic understatement of this noncampaign. His premonition was sound, for the Lecera-Belchite highway had been cut even before Walter had issued the order. The Mac-Paps verged on total exhaustion: they had dug all night and had marched twelve miles since sunup. At Lecera they got a two-hour rest before entering the line again.

The motley group of Mac-Paps collecting at Lecera still remained feisty. When the enemy arrived on the outskirts of town during the afternoon of March 11, they met a brisk fire covering an orderly Republican retreat eastward to Albalate del Arzobispo, where a defensive line was said to be established along the Río Martín. Had it not been for incredibly stupid staff work, Lecera might have held out longer. Within fifteen minutes, the Mac-Paps received three contradictory orders, which would have required them to be in three different places simultaneously. In the end, they took up a hillside position south of Lecera and assisted in beating off a tank and infantry assault. But in the midst of this fight, another staff officer arrived and, producing a neatly annotated map, claimed that the Mac-Paps were firing on the XIIIth Brigade, not the enemy. This was absolutely false, as the major knew, but he had to withdraw his men and watch the enemy take the town. Nor did he have the acerbic pleasure of "I told you so," because the headquarters officer had long since moved on to assist other units in arranging "an orderly withdrawal." (The word "retreat" was not used by staff.)

Mac-Paps provided the rear guard for the eleven-mile hike eastward to Albalate. Not a man among them had thrown away his rifle. They even managed to salvage the brigade water truck when a bullet punctured the radiator: Bill Chega straddled the hood and kept the radiator full with a hose connected to the enormous tank. It "looked like a wounded elephant limping in."* But somewhere on the night march they lost other paraphernalia—like General Walter. Many days later he reappeared. "Maybe he went to Barcelona to look for Copic," suggested one disgusted volunteer. (Actually Walter narrowly escaped capture near Alcañiz when his black Chevrolet encountered a road block placed by the 23 di Marzo Division of the Italian CTV.) Merriman was rumored to have been missing, maybe killed. Then beside the Albalate road, a Lincoln spotted a tall figure—"tall, smiling Bob Merriman. . . . When I saw him I felt so happy I almost forgot we were retreating. . . . I felt as if I were approaching someone risen from the dead. I threw my arms around his neck and kissed him."*

Peter Kemp, the British officer with the Tercios de Extranjeros, was appalled by the murder of IB prisoners. During the first day of the campaign his unit caught up with a tank section that had blasted a dozen Internationals (presumably Mac-Paps) out of some ruined shepherd huts. A tank crew climbed out of their turret and began loading rifles. As Kemp approached, shots rang out and the prisoners slumped to the ground. "My God!" Kemp exclaimed to a Spanish companion, feeling sick, "What do they think they're doing?" His companion gave him a grim look and replied, "They're International Brigades."* By contrast, Spanish prisoners received cigarettes from their captors, not bullets. A few days later Kemp's bandera overran a smashed trench of the Thaelmann Battalion. "Germans, expected no mercy and received none. I felt disgusted as I watched the legionaries probe among the fallen, shooting the wounded as they lay gasping for water. . . . I had not come to Spain for this."* Asking for an explanation, he was told by his Spanish companion, "Whether they know it or not, they are simply the tools of the communists and have come to Spain to destroy our country! What do they care about the ruin they have made here? Why should we bother about their lives when we catch them: It will take years to put right the harm they have done in Spain. . . . We never wanted our country to become a battleground for foreign powers. . . . If you were taken prisoner by the Reds? You would be lucky if they only shot you!" (Years later Kemp put this question to a former captain of the British Battalion, who confirmed that if captured he most certainly would have been shot.)* Legionnaires accepted as gospel that the war would have ended in November 1936 if the Internationals had not arrived to reinforce Madrid. A few days later Kemp endured "the most horrible day of my life." After interrogating a British prisoner, he urged his commanding colonel to spare the man's life. Contemptuous of compassion for a hated Red, the colonel ordered Kemp himself to execute him and assigned two legionaries to shoot Kemp if he failed to carry out the order. Once out of the colonel's sight the legionaries obligingly shot the prisoner for him.*

Yet within the pandemonium of escape and flight, heroism mushroomed in unlikely places. Take the case of Joe Dedent, a skinny Italian-American truck driver from Waynesburg, Ohio. He had been pulled out of the auto-park unit in a last-minute attempt to reinforce the Lincolns, and had been with them only four days. No one ever knew him well enough to record why he had come to Spain—in fact, few men even knew his name. While his section was falling back from a three-sided enemy attack, a Canadian named Johnson was hit in the head and lay in the open. The section leader told the stretcher-bearers to stay put—it would be suicide to attempt a rescue in that crossfire. Without a word to anybody and without bothering to unsling his rifle, Dedent vanished. Minutes later he carried Johnson in for the stretcher-bearers. "I got wounded in the ankle, so I'll have to go, too," he said. He limped away, his rifle still slung over his shoulder. "Hey!" he yelled to a Spaniard leading a burro to the rear. "Cama-rada, es possible?" Somebody shouted, "Leave your rifle, for Christ sake. If they catch you with a rifle they'll shoot you." "Don't worry," Dedent yelled back. "They'll never catch me as long as I *got* a rifle." He rode off on the tiny animal, his feet almost touching the ground but his rifle still over his shoulder.* (Dedent survived the war, but as an illegal Italian immigrant he was denied reentry to the United States and returned to his family at Pisa. Johnson died in the ambulance.)

By the morning of March 12, dozens of Anglo-Americans found themselves scrambled among Republican units halfheartedly digging holes along the east bank of the Río Martín between Hijar and Albalate del Argobispo. A retreat once begun is difficult to stop. Men who had been buffeted for three days had lost confidence in themselves and their officers. Squads assigned to defend hilltops doubted that anyone else would hold—why should they? In these marathon retreats the brave and obedient soldiers became victims, for they covered the get-away of others unwilling to defend themselves. And the reservoir of sacrificial lambs was running dry. Runaways from Spanish units were stopped at gunpoint and herded back toward the front, although most had thrown away their rifles and just hunkered down in ditches or behind stone walls. A Mac-Pap guarded a bunch of them—"Spanish kids . . . with eyes like balloons. They just stood there as if paralyzed, staring at me. I held my rifle in one hand and stared back." After an hour a staff officer said, "We can't take care of them." He waved at them, "Vayan! Vayan al frente." They scattered, not to the front, but to the rear.*

Albalate, the focal point of a defensive line, lay in a trough of eroded hollows easily approached by the Nationalists but difficult to defend, even with the sup-port of a complement of Soviet tanks. And as soon as the first enemy skirmishers appeared, at dawn on March 12, the Republican line folded up as panicked men surged north toward Hijar, where the staff promised a new fortified line. Trucks, ambulances, and staff cars raced through, or ran down, stragglers, occupants leaning out of windows shouting, "The Fascists are behind us!" The tanks pulled out without firing a shot. Men on foot were knocked down and run over, wounded men were left behind, machine guns abandoned. Even the Mac-Paps, who thus far had held together, broke apart among the avalanche of fugitives bent solely upon escape. Al Amery, a devout Communist who had served two hitches in the U.S. Army and one in the Navy, was appalled by the pandemo-nium. "Trucks loaded with men passed by with other men trying to get aboard being pushed off. Communists? Jesus! It sickened me. Tanks went by, loaded with men and other men trying to get on. My section disappeared. . . . Back to a bunch of animals in a panic." Even the "official" report of Major Cecil-Smith spoke of the pandemonium: "A panic developed on the highway. Tanks, trucks, ambulances and our cavalry tore through the infantry. Drivers and occupants leaned out and shouted that the fascists were on their heels. The infantry was thrown into confusion and many units lost cohesion. We lost contact with one of the companies of the battalion as other units crowded between us." Avoiding capture was on everyone's mind. At a rest-stop Amery asked a friend, "I wonder what they'd do with us if they captured us." "We're known to be Communists," came the reply. They digested this slowly. Then the friend brightly said, "Jesus! This'll be something to tell your grandchildren about!" After a pause, Amery said, "Yeah." Two days later Amery and his companion formed "a battalion of two," threw away their rifles, and followed the railroad to Barcelona, where they stowawayed on a French ship and escaped to Marseilles.*

Before the column reached Hijar, Moorish cavalry cut the road. "We were taken completely by surprise. They came at us swinging their swords and were gone just as some of us started to fire."* When Major Cecil-Smith called for his Maxims to clear the roadblock, he learned that the guns had been put aboard a truck for safekeeping, but the truck, identified later as belonging to the Rákosi Battalion, was nowhere to be found. The retreating mob surged cross-country five miles to the Hijar-Alcañiz highway, the main route east. Here they mingled with other groups, including a number of Lincolns, who had evacuated Hijar. Once again, while the best men braced themselves to slow down the enemy advance, the worst fled east toward Alcañiz, twenty miles away. Ahead the long road rose and fell and rose again.

For the moment, however, the Nationalists were too preoccupied with mopping up pockets of resistance in their newly won territory to pursue the fugitives diligently. This gave a remnant of the International Brigades, which included fragments of the XIth, time to regroup on a crest three miles east of Hijar, a fine defensive position because they could not be attacked frontally. Their shallow rifle pits overlooked hairpin turns of a road dropping down to an open plain, which the enemy had to cross. But frontal attacks were not their major worry. When Lieutenant Milton Wolff returned from his medical leave, he noted that the men were digging foxholes "in a most peculiar fashion. . . . Facing not only the front but the flanks and rear as well."*⁴ About this time Doran reappeared, resplendent in new uniform. He found that about 75 percent of the battalion was missing, along with nearly all the heavier weapons

---

4. For Wolff's full report and retrospective on the Lincoln Battalion during its retreats to Caspe and then to Gandesa, see Moscow file 545/3/503, dated April 22, 1938.

from Maxims to mortars. His immediate contribution was an order that henceforth any man who threw away his weapon or abandoned an assigned position would be shot. The reaction of haggard men to this edict can be imagined.

In the hills east of Hijar on March 13, the front was deceptively quiet, as though the enemy planned no further advance. (General Yagüe had outrun his support; on this day his Army of Morocco reported only two men wounded.) But the next morning, when enemy cavalry appeared on both flanks, all units retreated toward Alcañiz. (Without offering evidence, "official" historians blamed the retreat on POUM officers in the 13th Corps who had deserted to the enemy.)* What no one knew was that Italians of the CTV were about to converge upon Alcañiz from the southwest. Once again the XVth Brigade was marching into the jaws of a trap.

The twenty-mile hike to Alcañiz on March 14 was rough going for exhausted men deep in the pathology of defeat. The road dipped and rose. From the top of one treeless hill one could see only identical hills cresting like waves on the surface of a disturbed sea. It was perfect country for cavalry, which could approach unseen to within a few hundred yards of the road teeming with men and vehicles. Except for clumps of spiky gorse and occasional locust trees fringing the highway, there was no protection whatever. While Doran and Merriman zoomed ahead in divisional staff cars, the men straggled down the lonely road, nervously scanning the hillsides and western skies for signs of danger. The most reliable men, most of them hard-core Party stalwarts, scouted on both flanks, but never in sufficient depth. Before departing, Merriman told one of his commissars, *sotto voce,* "There is nothing between us and the Fascists except those scouts."* Once again the Mac-Paps held the rear guard—doubtless their reward for having held together better than the other battalions—but even they straggled badly, the stronger men outpacing the weaker by nearly a mile. Seizing an ambulance for a staff car, Major Cecil-Smith drove back and forth, urging laggards to speed up and the pacers to slow down. General Walter forged far ahead in his black Chevrolet. One thing was crystal clear—no one wanted to be last.

Three miles from Alcañiz, Major Cecil-Smith's ambulance rounded a curve and found a Fiat tank squatting on the road fifty yards ahead. Beside it, a crew in blue uniforms were setting up a machine gun. The CTV had cut the road! The two groups studied one another. "Venga aquí!" called a tall, blond blueshirt. "Espero un momento!" shouted the major, nudging the driver to floor it. The reflexes of the driver were quicker than those of the tankers. He hit the accelerator, and the ambulance spun off the highway to the north and careened down a cart road, billowing dust and pebbles. Bullets from the tank were whizzing overhead just as they saw that they were in a cul-de-sac. A small factory reared up; beyond was a shallow lake ringed with reeds and duck blinds. They abandoned the ambulance and dodged behind the factory. "It felt like bullets were trying to turn the corner," remembered the doctor. The only way out was by foot to dunelike ridges half a mile north. The major shouted, "Direction Alcañiz! Every man for himself!" and took the lead. A medic was shot while debating which way to run. The others raced for the hill and escaped. Separated from the others, the doctor got lost, passed camps of Moors dancing and yelling and drumming, and found Alcañiz already occupied by young Requetés. Continuing cross-country and fed by peasants, he finally met friendlies at Maella.* Some hours earlier, General Walter had encountered the Italians but reached Alcañiz after a cross-country detour.[5]

Up and down the long line of retreat, Nationalist patrols began to seize pieces of the highway and to open fire upon the retreating Republicans, by this time a scramble of units and nationalities. To their consternation, shells began to fall among them from both north and south. Like a wave shaken in a taut rope, a spasm swept through the long column. They had not been told that the Italians were coming up from the south, and they did not know at that time that the enemy roadblocks were insignificant. The cry "Fascists!" triggered a collective reflex that ejected them northward in a pell-mell flight. A few officers fired shots above the heads of their men in a vain effort to stop them, but by and large they joined, and even led, the stampede. Moorish cavalry ranged the sector, making saber attacks on isolated groups and vanishing as quickly as they came. The Messerschmitts strafed incessantly, at times so close to the ground that brigaders could distinguish pilots' helmets and goggles—"their guns sparking and cracking like bundles of firecrackers in Coney Island on the fourth of July." One's instinct was to hide and huddle like prey with hawks overhead and not to fire back, although a British Columbian was credited with downing a plane with a lucky shot.* Gerry Delaney, a Canadian, rode toward Alcañiz on a broken-down mare abandoned by a cavalry detachment. Lagging far behind, and unaware that the road had been cut, he rode his "skeleton-ribbed and razor-backed mare" to within three hundred yards of a Nationalist column marching along the highway. When he saw a limousine flying the yellow and red flag of Franco, he urged his "unwilling mount up the terraces as fast as its rheumatic legs could take it."

5. Major Cecil-Smith was justly furious with the brigade staff for allowing this new trap to be sprung upon them, after having escaped so many others during his retreat from Azuara. In his official report he wrote, "From what I have heard since, Brigade Staff was in a position to know of this [enemy roadblock] fairly early, but failed to notify our battalion of the fact."

He hid in a *barranca* until dark, managing to keep the mare quiet, and got back to the Mac-Paps after a five-day cross-country trek.*

Sandor Voros, quickly outrun by the others, found a haven beside a Soviet tank. The Russian observer was scanning the hillsides to the south with binoculars. Suddenly he cursed and shouted orders down to the driver. On a far ridge six horsemen appeared. Voros expected to see the gun barrel swing around to the target and estimated that one shell might bag them all, but the tank shifted around and began to scurry to the rear. Terrified that he would be left out there alone, Voros tried to climb aboard, but the Russian threatened to shoot him. "I am a comrade!" Voros hollered, while the Russian hammered at his fingers with a pistol butt until he let go and dropped into the road. The tank soon disappeared, as did the enemy cavalry, perhaps as alarmed as the tankers.*

Alcañiz, a picture-postcard town on a crag, was moated on three sides by a loop in the Guadalupe River. Its defensive potency had been known since the Middle Ages but largely ignored by the Republican command, which evacuated the place with only token resistance by machine gunners from the Templar's castle on the peak. Just five days before, Alcañiz had been a backwater supply depot some forty miles behind the front; now the CTV and the Army of Morocco had converged on it and were breaking into the western *barrios*. The only escape routes—north to Caspe or east to Gandesa—were clogged with men and vehicles. Heads craned skyward, watching for bombers that could have obliterated this dense, helpless mass. Miraculously none appeared, although an American caught in the logjam recalled that a flock of birds, mistaken for distant planes, stampeded men into roadside ditches.* Throughout this bedlam of strangled motion and this cacophony of tongues, the bells of the collegiate church tolled incessantly, their clangor spreading the alarm of a doomed town to civilians and soldiers already frantic in their efforts to escape from it. Gilbert "Danny" Shannon of Spokane staged a one-man sit-down strike. He said he had not come to Spain to run from Fascists and refused to retreat one more step. Collecting ammunition and tobacco from his comrades, he built a small stone parapet facing the enemy. Ten minutes later his chums heard the sound of intense small-arms fire along the road, followed by silence.* To everyone's surprise, he rejoined them several days later.*

The XVth, which had regrouped temporarily in the hills behind Hijar, now pulled apart once more. Some followed the mob toward Gandesa, forty miles east, while others crossed the Sierra de Vizcuerno toward Caspe, eighteen miles north. Many veterans remembered their earlier truck ride across this desolate, horse-opera landscape back in December when they had gone up to Teruel. It was a forbidding and forgotten country encrusted with red granite boulders, some as large as houses. They had another race against time, for they had to reach Caspe ahead of the enemy, which was presumed to be converging on the city along the Ebro road. (This proved to be the 5th Navarre Division.) Orders filtered down that Caspe, a railroad center surrounded by defensible cliffs and crags, had to hold until fortified lines could be thrown up farther east as a last dike to halt the Nationalist surge toward the sea. In the absence of Copic, Commissar Doran obtained authority—or took it—to employ all Internationals who could be rounded up in the sector. The Albany gang-scrapper at once plunged into the work of mobilizing his ragtag army to stop the vanguard of the 5th Navarre Division.[6] He set every man and vehicle passing into the Caspe perimeter to work. The human material was none of the best. Few retained weapons, most had even lost blankets. One fugitive staggered into town with his trouser legs ripped off: whenever he walked, his scrotum bobbed like a broken spring. Few had eaten a decent meal in six days. Any of them might have served as a model for a Party poster labeled, "Arise, ye wretched of the earth." To feed them, Doran broke into the food stores of the brigade staff mess, a hoard jealously guarded by Colonel Copic. To clothe them, he sent Commissar Voros to demand equipment from the "yellow bastards" at the brigade *intendencia*. Voros found the quartermaster readily enough, but when he demanded 150 blankets, trousers, tunics, boots, and canteens, the officer in charge absolutely refused to supply them without a written order from Doran. In vain, Voros argued that he was Doran's personal envoy. Nor was the storekeeper moved by Voros's sarcasm: "Put a Communist in charge of a load of goods and you get a Capitalist!" Finally Voros delivered an ultimatum: "If those blankets aren't there by ten o'clock, I'll be back again, *but for you!*" Doran's talk about having men shot paid off. The gear arrived on time.*

Probably fewer than three hundred men of the XVth Brigade rallied at Caspe. A greater number of fugitives fled cross-country, halfway to Maella, where MPs halted them at gunpoint. For the past week all of them had lived in a collapsing, malignant universe—when they tried to fight, they had been overwhelmed; when they tried to retreat, they had been hounded to earth. Now Doran lectured and threatened the Caspe group. He spoke of massed waves of

6. There is much confusion concerning the defense of Caspe, which brigade publicists considered as a kind of Alamo, although Spanish historians, when they allude to it at all, attribute the defense to a Lieutenant-Colonel Reyes, a Spanish officer assigned command a few days before the Internationals arrived. Doran commanded no more than five hundred men, scraped together from the XVth Brigade and remnants of the XIth Brigade (Thaelmann), which had been encircled at Vinaceite, and a portion of the XIVth (French) dispatched from the east. As usual, historians of Comintern persuasion ignored the role of Spanish units in the Caspe fight.

fighter planes promised by the Soviet Union and of artillery promised by France. The men heard these things and knew that they were lies, but in the chill dawn of Aragon as the Fascists closed in upon them again they wanted to believe Doran because there was nothing else left to believe. Doran's discourse was stuffed with so much excremental imagery that, considering what they thought about the enemy, about themselves, and about Doran, it had a kind of vulgar eloquence. Even his mad-dog threats to execute deserters struck them as vaguely comforting, for the turned flank had been the bane of their long retreat. Moreover, even those who hated Doran most passionately perhaps wanted to remain with him to the bitter end to prove to themselves that he was the lesser man. Doran-haters must have vented their rage thus: "If that little bastard can take it, so can I. But if he runs out on me, I'll follow him wherever he goes and kill him with my bare hands." For whatever reasons, they rose from the dead and formed a line.

A barnyard maxim holds that a cock fights best on his own dung hill. Caspe had become Doran's.

From the barren highlands southwest of Caspe, the ground slopes gradually down, yielding to olive groves that carpet the plain around the town. Just behind the cubical houses lies the Guadalupe River, which joins the Ebro a mile farther north. The black line of the Zaragoza-Barcelona railroad crosses the river on a high trestle on the northern edge of town and disappears in the warty countryside to the east. The pivots of defense were two hilltops commanding lines of the enemy approach. On the western edge, in the path of the advancing Navarrese division, Reservoir Hill commanded the railroad station and the Ebro River road. On the eastern edge, Castle Hill, a steep cliff crowned with a modern castellated structure, overlooked the river. Advancing skirmishers of the enemy, preceded by tanks, quickly pressed back the Republicans from exterior lines to these dominating positions, but by midmorning of March 15 the defense had stiffened.

The fight for Reservoir Hill continued all day. It was defended by Captain Niilo Makella, a leathery Finn from Canada, who in better times had led the Mac-Pap machine-gun company. With him were perhaps two hundred men, a mixed group of Americans, Canadians, and British. They had obtained a few Maxims lacking carriages, which, when fired, bucked and cavorted. The gunners, most of them Finnish-Americans from Michigan and Canada known in the brigade as "the eight wonders of the world," set up their guns on rock supports and repeatedly beat back enemy skirmishers. To their right rear, a British group under Sam Wild barricaded themselves in the railroad station and broke up enemy attacks trying to infiltrate Caspe through the railway cut. Their major escape route from the town lay across the railroad trestle spanning the river. Doran placed a heavy guard there with orders to fire upon any Republicans attempting to abandon the city by that route. There was plenty of ammunition: the castle contained enough munitions to blow up the whole town.

The commander of the 5th Navarre Division expected the town to fall without too much trouble. He sent in skirmishers. When these were beaten back, he sent in companies with scarcely better results. Finally he hurled whole battalions into the attack. (Some of their historians later claimed the impossible— that five International Brigades held Caspe.)* With a fury goaded by frustration, they shelled, bombed, and strafed Reservoir Hill throughout the afternoon. Outgunned, outmanned, and nearly cut off from the town, Makella withdrew at dusk. While he was standing on a knoll directing the fallback, a tank shell exploded at his feet, tumbling him down an embankment. He bled to death on a hospital train.

Although Reservoir Hill had been defended with remarkable élan and dogged courage, Doran was in no mood for plaudits. He had not ordered the hill evacuated and demanded it be recaptured before dawn. Major Cecil-Smith, who had just arrived in Caspe after a twenty-four-hour trek through the mountains, was assigned to lead the attack. He collected a scruffy force, variously estimated at somewhere between one and two hundred men, some of them unarmed skulkers and *inutiles* scavenged up by Doran's praetorian guards. Three tanks lined up to shell the hill while the attackers climbed the slope. They had two light machine guns but no grenades. Three companies belonging to the XIVth (French) Brigade, just arrived in Caspe, were instructed to assist them, but they refused to budge because, as Cecil-Smith wrote in his report, "their captain adjutant had gone back to town."

For three hours the force worked up the slope of Reservoir Hill by the light of a full moon, while a tank shelled the summit. "All we could really do," recalled one attacker, "was to throw rocks and yell at them."* The covering fire from the tanks was noisily effective, even though many shells exploded among the attackers. The Rákosi Battalion was ordered to make a flank attack, but it never showed. Yet the ragtag attackers not only occupied the hill but captured thirty prisoners, ten mules, three Fiat machine guns, and a range finder. What is even more remarkable, at five in the morning the enemy division west of town received an emergency alert and was ordered to stand by to repel a Republican counterattack.

Meanwhile, Internationals and Nationalists hunted each other in the western *barrios* of the city. Greenish explosions flickered at odd corners as they

tossed grenades at real or imagined enemies. At one point an enemy patrol captured Captain Sam Wild, but as a guard rifled his pockets, he kicked him in the
shins and got away. Near brigade headquarters, in the center of town, a small
group with Captain Milton Wolff walked up to a tank, assuming it to be
friendly. The gunner stuck his head out of the turret, gave the Loyalist salute,
and asked in bad Spanish, "What part of Spain—you?" Wolff replied, "Salamanca," and moved in for a closer look. The tank seemed unfamiliar, much
smaller than the Russian type. He yelled for his men to take cover. A string of
curses—presumably Italian—followed as the gunner slammed down his hatch
and opened fire at point-blank range. Wolff scrambled to safety, but apparently
about a dozen of his men were caught in the road. Some playing possum survived. The next day Harry Fisher found an old New York ycl companion, Lou
Cohen, whom he had not seen in four years. It was not a happy reunion, for
Cohen sat traumatized, staring at the ground. He had been with Wolff's group
during the tank massacre, and explained what had happened. When the tank
opened fire, most of the men were together. Some fell pretending to be dead,
but the wounded were screaming. "The tank stopped firing, and then began
moving straight for the bodies in the street. Some men were able to run away,
but the tank rolled over the others, the dead, and the wounded who couldn't get
away. I heard the crunching of their bones. I smelled their blood. Finally the
tank left." Cohen was sobbing with his face buried in his hands. "I can still hear
the bones cracking, and still smell the blood." Fisher tried to console him, but
Cohen was in shock. The next day Cohen died in a counterattack upon an
unknown hill somewhere on Doran's map.* (Doran disputed Wolff's story,
maintaining that the tanks were Russian.)*

At first light, when it became evident that only a tiny group of Republicans
held Reservoir Hill, the Nationalists pressed forward rapidly. The Internationals were able to hold it only a few hours. When Cecil-Smith found enemy fire
battering him from the rear, he dispatched a runner to Doran, requesting permission to retire. Receiving no reply and observing that the XIVth Brigade,
which had been assigned to guard roads and checkpoints, had vanished, he
ordered a retreat on his own authority along the railroad track. Before reaching
the bridge, he received a message ordering him back. He could not have obeyed
it had he wanted to: "I had lost control of the men."

By midday of March 16, the Internationals had been driven into the northern quarter of Caspe and lost control of the bridge, the railway station, and a
plateresco convent. At a ready-made position in a railway cut, they tried to hold
back the enemy despite what an old Jarama hand called "the most intensive fire
we ever experienced." The entire rim of Reservoir Hill, now fortified by the

enemy, crackled, boomed, and spluttered like a fireworks display. Doran seemed enthralled. He watched the battle from Castle Hill, a higher promontory on the other side of town, coming and going along a steep pathway used to reenact the Stations of the Cross at Easter time. As the battle raged under him, he turned to an assistant commissar and said, "Just look at *my* battle."*

Toward dusk Doran authorized the evacuation of Caspe via the railroad trestle. Many men who had fought well never received the order and were never seen again. Many were one-time deserters and "demoralized elements" whom Doran had armed and sent into battle instead of executing them on the spot. By letting them die at Caspe, Doran gave them an opportunity to salvage their honor, even though no publicists or apologists left any record of their names.

Those who survived were demonic in their fury. Several days later an American who rejoined them in a rest camp recorded his shock at their appearance. They resembled "wild animals, their fierce eyes gleaming with a kind of battle stare that cut through you like wolves in human form. A kind of ferocity lurked in their unwashed bodies and ragged clothes as I have never seen before. And whether they sprawled on the ground, leaned against a tree, stood still, or walked, they never relaxed. Thin, haggard and drawn, they always seemed on the verge of bursting into action."*

In the mellowing perspective of later years, many Lincoln veterans echoed what the publicists said—that the defense of Caspe stood as their sublime moment of their war. A handful had assisted in staunching the advance of a Nationalist division. If militarily it amounted to little, existentially it was everything—nothing less than a surprise punch from a runt knocked about by a bully for fifteen rounds. What the men felt at the time is perhaps better reflected by a scene at the bridge as Doran watched the evacuation. At the tail of the column came a group of spectral creatures, unkempt and bleary-eyed. These were the Anglo-Americans who had stormed Reservoir Hill and had watched and cursed as Fascist steel cut down every second man. Spotting Doran, they crowded around. They were not at all like the Praetorian Guard with Caesar or the National Guard with Napoleon. They screamed in his face, "You dirty, filthy, fucking murderer! You butcher!" A burly Briton squared off in front of him and unleashed a torrent of obscenities, begging Doran to lift his fists or to reply. But Doran only turned his back and walked away. He was a zealot. He saw what others lower on the Party food chain did not see; he did not feel what others felt. Whatever Caspe was or became, it would be his.

After taking Caspe and Alcañiz, General Yagüe paused for two weeks to reorganize before resuming his offensive through Gandesa to the Mediterranean. His force had advanced more than one hundred kilometers, occupied seven thousand square kilometers containing a hundred small villages, and captured ten thousand prisoners along with a hundred machine guns, in addition to supplies and arms too immense to be counted.* What was left of Walter's 35th Division fell back to Maella and Batea without further molestation. The retreat had turned them into agoraphobes unnerved by open spaces and seeking cover of trees and ditches. After two days without food, the survivors began to coalesce at Batea.

Casualties in the XVth Brigade between March 10 and 17 were staggering. The number of Lincolns certified as killed during the seven-day retreat stood at 113—nearly half of the 230 that marched out toward El Santuario del Pueyo in the early morning of March 10.* This number includes forty-one Americans known to have been captured and executed on the spot by the Nationalists, but it does not take into account twenty-eight additional men taken as prisoners of war, an unknown count of men wounded in action, or an unspecified number of Americans who fell through the rosters because they lay somewhere dead on the battlefield or chose desertion.* The Mac-Paps fared better than the Lincolns. At the March 20 muster outside Batea, they numbered 250 men, half their original strength, although only half of these still carried rifles.*

Doran and other IB hierarchs blamed the catastrophe on internal weaknesses, particularly the failure of volunteers to adhere to Party doctrine and discipline. At Batea Harry Fisher worried about the health of his mentor, Pat Reid, a World War veteran and father figure to the rest of the communications team. Reid's politics lay somewhere between the Socialists and the Wobblies (he wore an IWW button in his cap), and in argument he was as tough as teakwood, even daring to endorse the dangerous POUM, warning that the Republic might win the war but lose the revolution.* "If all Communists were like me," he would say, "I'd be a Communist."* In a hard campaign he had kept up with men half his age, but now he was coughing up blood and refused to see a doctor because he might be forced to leave his comrades in the battalion. When Fisher reported the case to Doran, he was pleased to hear that Reid would be sent to the rear immediately. "That's great," said Fisher. "That guy is really sick, always coughing up blood. He needs attention." Doran cut him off, "That's not why I'm sending him to the rear. He's doing a lot of harm, always talking against the Communist Party."* (A pariah among the Party clique, Reid died of tuberculosis in 1949.)

In the early morning hours of March 17, while the XVth Brigade was trudging through oak forests to Batea, two prisoners were ushered to the headquarters of the First Bandera of the Falange of Navarre. They had been found among defenders of the Caspe railroad station, abandoned by Doran. Both were badly wounded. One was a fifty-year-old American oozing blood in the chest; the other a redheaded Scotsman hit in the leg. Since neither spoke any Spanish, an Argentine doctor attached to the Bandera interpreted for them. "I came to Spain," said the elderly American, "because I was told that I could spend a few agreeable months without any danger. As the trip was free and would give me an opportunity to see a beautiful country like Spain, I enrolled in the Red Army. I took this trip just like a tourist would take a Cook's tour." The speaker was a frightened, broken old man. He wanted only to live, and to live meant to please his captors, and to please them he had to lie with finesse. His interpreter was moved to pity. No one else was. . . . Both Americans were shot.*

14

THE ROUT AT GANDESA

When news of the Aragon disaster reached Albacete, commissars swept the IB training-camps and hospitals clean of recruits in a frantic attempt to plug gaps. It was pitch-black in the morning of March 14 when the barracks lights went on in Tarazona de la Mancha and the trainees were ordered to stand by. "Yow! We're moving!" somebody yelled. "So's your bowels," chimed in another. "Bring us Franco's balls!" shouted a stay-behind. "He ain't got no bloody balls," came the reply.* Night maneuvers or the real thing? One by one the men were summoned into the office of Major Allan Johnson and asked a perfunctory question, "Are you fit to go to the front!" There is no record of anyone saying no. Their names were checked—and the entire camp cleaned out—even base personnel. Before they boarded boxcars in Albacete, the major came down to see them off. "What you lack in training," he said, "you make up in enthusiasm and anti-Fascist commitment. The first Internationals who helped to save Madrid had no training at all." After letting this sink in, he added, "I wish I could be with you. Good luck."* (This from the officer famous at Jarama for his bunker mentality.) They picked up rations—packs of French cigarettes, loaves of bread, cans of Argentine beef. As they pulled away from the platform, a band blared out "Himno de Riego." Then as the train crept down the track to Valencia, they sang old favorites like "Just a Song at Twilight." No marching songs. The last American recruits had left Albacete, which soon shut down for good. If the Nationalists really reached the sea, Madrid, Valencia, and Albacete would be cut off from France entirely. En route others boarded the train—goldbricks from Valencia offices, truck drivers without trucks, along with jailbirds and political pariahs from the Camp Lukács prison, who were offered one last chance. If any of them had ever received military training, it had been forgotten long ago. The most experienced among the newcomers was a handful of convalescents from the brigade hospitals.

Though dispatched to the front with all speed, it took four days to get there. Reports from the front were so contradictory that no one could be blamed for the delay. At one point the train dropped them off at a deserted railroad siding in

the high tundra of Teruel province. They marveled at the bomb craters that pockmarked the place, which, as one rookie, said, "put the fear of God into us."*
Here they whiled away half a day without sign of friend or foe except a few distant shepherds—who seemed neither. Then Russian trucks picked them up and carried them, so crammed together that a man could not sit down or reach into his own pockets, down to the coast at Sagunto—through which they had passed the previous night—and up the coast to Tortosa, where hundreds of vehicles jammed the Ebro bridge as they moved through yellow fog toward the front—or where it was imagined to be. They were making a long detour to avoid the enemy blitzkrieg in Aragon. At dawn of their third day they bivouacked in an olive grove near Gandesa, each squad assigned to a tree. Commissars warned them not to start fires for fear of attracting enemy bombers and lectured them not to pay heed to any "weak and demoralized elements" that strayed in. They also posted guards on the periphery—even though they had no weapons—not to watch for Fascists but "to prevent pilfering" from deserters on the run. In the afternoon, fragments of a whipped army straggled past, "ragged, unarmed soldiers, their faces streaked with dirt, their beards long, a look of desperation in their eyes."* These were among the jumble of fugitives from countless Republican units that had retreated from Hijar, Alcañiz, Caspe, and dozens of other strange-sounding places unknown to the replacements. They met a Finnish-American fugitive and asked where they could find the Lincolns. His reply bordered on natural eloquence, "No more Fifteen Brigada; all killed; all dead; you got to smoke? . . . Hell up there; we no do anything, no can. You got to smoke? Everybody blow to pieces; everybody kill." With the "superiority of ignorance," the newcomers chided him for running away. "Sure I run; you run too; all over; all gone, no use no more, Brigada gone, only a couple get away. Me."*

News of the Aragon breakthrough electrified Marty into a frenzy of activity, less because the war might be lost than because Internationals had deserted en masse. He set up a prison at Horta, a suburb of Barcelona, exclusively to punish deserters. Living conditions quickly became so foul that the prisoners, who had run away to escape certain capture or death, pounded the walls and mutinied. Marty responded by having fifty men executed and another hundred sent to the regular IB prison at Casteldefels. The remainder were sent back to labor battalions in home units. (Later, when the Central Committee of the CPF asked Marty how he could explain his reputation as "The Butcher of Albacete," he was not the least contrite. "I ordered to be executed not more than 500—all of authentic criminals masking as defenders of liberty."*

While André Marty fumed over desertions, Ernest Hemingway worried about what would happen to the wounded. (The Moors had slaughtered men in their hospital beds when the Nationalist captured Toledo in 1936.) On March 30 he gave the U.S. ambassador a head count of Americans in IB hospitals: 30 in Barcelona, 328 in Benicasim and Villa Paz (southeast of Madrid), and 125 in Murcia, all of whom had to be protected and evacuated.* He sensed that the end had come; he was wrong—but the worst had just begun.

Shortly after midnight of March 18, the newcomers from Tarazona and the sweepings from hospital and office cadres marched fifteen kilometers to the XVth Brigade camp in an olive grove near Batea. Along the way they were shocked to see campfires by the hundreds in the valleys—egregious violations of security as taught by Major Johnson and dunned into their heads by their commissars. When split up among the remnants of the four battalions, they marveled that they outnumbered the survivors of the retreat. The Lincolns, for example, counted at this time perhaps two hundred ragged down-and-outers who greeted the newcomers with sarcasm or ignored them altogether. Eager questions elicited only reluctant grunts or lashing curses about rearguard yellow bellies at last forced to have a dose of real war. The veterans heaped mountains of verbal excrement upon Merriman, Doran, and especially Copic (who had at last returned to his command and was taking some heat from Soviet advisers because his brigade had fallen apart). Some of the heaviest vitriol came from a veteran who confessed, as though he were ashamed of it, that he had been commander pro tem of the Lincolns during the long retreat. This was Al Kaufman, a New York longshoreman who had begun the retreat as a low-ranking machine gunner and had inherited the battalion by default, after all the other officers had been killed, wounded, or captured, or had deserted.[1] A newcomer from Brooklyn, a zealot who had carried YCL placards during the 1936 East Coast seamen's strike, was aghast at what he overheard. "They criticized their command mercilessly; it sounded like treason to us. . . . They were good guys, scrappers, tough as nails. But these men seemed to be licked. . . . They barked at each other and at us; they cursed continuously, making accusations that horrified the new replacements."* When the new men inquired when food would arrive, they got jeering laughter. Food?—there was no food. There had been no food for days. They pointed to Spaniards in their outfit stripping leaves from some crazy-looking tree and eating them. Anything to fill their bellies. Some of the Americans tried it—it just made their diarrhea worse. (Mule stew

---

1. According to Sandor Voros of the XVth Brigade Historical Commission, Major "Nicolai," a "Russian" adviser, acted as commander of the XVth during the retreat from Belchite with John Gerlach, known as "Ivan," as his assistant. Whether "Nicolai" ever had personal contact with the scattered men remains to be substantiated.*

these days was cooked in old petrol drums and tasted like it.) When food finally did come up, men fought to get a chunk of bread or spoonful of rice and ate it from a tin can—if you could find one—or off leaves with their fingers.* The hard cases admitted—one might even say bragged—that they had been running since Belchite and were ready to run to Barcelona at first opportunity.

A smug youth, identified only as Irving Somebody, protested these defeatist mutterings. "But comrades," he said, "that's cowardice. . . . Don't you realize it's impossible to retreat from fascism; that unless we lick fascism all over the world it won't be long before . . ." "Shit!" broke in a voice. Haggard men glowered at this squirt, doubtless chockful of crap from the *Daily Worker.* They gritted their teeth and looked like they wanted to tear him apart. A vet, whose dirty face was streaked with perspiration, said, "Comrade, we've been through hell the last few days, and do I understand you're accusing us of being cowards?" Irving backed off. "Well," he said apologetically, "I don't want to be misunderstood." "Haul your ashes," broke in Joe Bianca. He spat and ended the discussion.*

Adding to their misery, a spring deluge drove them from the olive groves into the little theater in Batea, where they smashed chairs and benches to build fires on the concrete floor and dry out. The men had been "reduced to a truly animal level." Commissars blamed the Belchite disaster on saboteurs, tried and true scapegoats. "One major (Spanish) and two lieutenants and one sergeant were shot yesterday for cowardice," an awed rookie wrote in his diary.* The despairing mood was not helped when Merriman, after citing ten men for bravery and giving them wristwatches, concluded the ceremony with a warning that the sacrifice of all their lives might be asked in the coming battles. Since the rains dampened enemy pursuit, there grew a dim hope among the Lincolns—at least those at staff level—that the battalion might be able to recover and return to the line. This overlooked the condition of the rank and file. They were apprehensive and distrustful. They could not forget how they had been reduced to animals seeking burrows or any hiding place, pursued by a relentless enemy eager to trap and kill them. They could not forget that the bodies of friends lay out there somewhere, never recovered.

In the Batea cinema, Commissar Doran was starring in his very own melodrama. Billed as "Reorganization and Reeducation," a worn-out scenario in the best of times, it featured courts-martial, sentences, denunciations, and admonitions. Doran, who served both as prosecutor and judge, sentenced "a number of our comrades," as one witness later put it, to death for desertion and cowardice. There were vivid recollections of how he rolled his verdict through his twisted jaw as he proclaimed each sentence, "You are condemned to *die* before a firing squad!" It happened that one of the prisoners was a prominent member of the YCL from Cleveland named Jack Cooper. His offense was not greater than anyone else's: during the retreat—he had abandoned his machine gun. Doran pressed the point that his weapon was more valuable to the Republic than those of riflemen. At this stage a junior commissar testified that he had encountered Cooper during the retreat and remembered him as "nothing but a walking corpse intent on saving the few survivors of his company."* Others pitched in until the court-martial became a debating society. Ultimately, Copic's deep-toned baritone entered the dispute on the side of the prisoners. He said he feared that news of executions would leak out and alienate journalists like Ernest Hemingway and Herbert L. Matthews, regular visitors whose dispatches had always supported the Republic. He prevailed, despite Doran's grumbling that the decision smacked of "rotten bourgeois degeneracy." Doran issued a warning—"Any man mistreating a rifle or machine gun or throwing it away is to be shot on sight."* Too late. At that moment only fifteen rifles existed in the whole battalion.

All this while trucks with armed guards rolled into the camp bringing back comrades who had been caught trying to cross into France. (Those few who made it besieged U.S. consulates in Toulouse and Marseilles for assistance in getting home—a difficult task without passports.) When accused of desertion, they told fantastic lies that they had "heard" somewhere that the brigade was being reorganized in the frontier region.* These were the "demoralized elements" that brigade commissars had been warning the newcomers to avoid, at all costs. Twenty-one of them had made it as far as Barcelona, where some tried to stow away on ships, while others sought help from the U.S. consulate—always unsuccessfully.[2] Tony DeMaio, the brigade SIM hammer, knew this dodge; his military policemen kept the consulate under surveillance around the clock to intercept American strays. These were dropped into the dry cistern at Casteldefels castle on the Tarragona road, which had replaced Camp Lukács as the major IB prison, before they were moved to Batea. In a downpour the prisoners slept in an olive grove under armed guard without blankets or fire and received a daily ration of weak lentil soup and two pieces of bread. Always their

---

2. On March 29, Vice Consul Flood cabled Washington, suggesting that his office be authorized to issue emergency travel documents to France for American fugitives from the International Brigades, but two days later Secretary Cordell Hull replied that no assistance should be given to American volunteers "unless they are able to obtain discharge from military service of the Spanish government and permission of Spanish authorities to leave Spain." Public opinion had softened Hull's earlier ultralegal position that Americans who enlisted in the armies of foreign countries had lost their citizenship, but personally he seems too have felt that if these men did not return home—good riddance.*

hands were tied—even when they were eating. The plan was to put them between the lines when the brigade next went into action.

Among these prisoners, Vernon Selby and John G. Honeycombe had fine records at Teruel as observers in Jim Cody's team. Then as stretcher-bearers for David Reiss, they had been among the last Americans to leave the hermitage. Selby, a West Point dropout (1926), had been badly wounded in the leg and arm. Honeycombe, a former field organizer for the CP in California, assisted him on the road until they reached Barcelona, where Selby entered a hospital. Honeycombe, also wounded, applied to the War Ministry for a repatriation permit only to learn that the Republican Army did not handle IB affairs. The ministry official, disgusted by the Comintern network in his country, added, "Frankly, I would like to see all of you get out of Spain." Honeycombe turned himself in at the IB headquarters and was imprisoned for his pains. Thrown into the dungeon at Casteldefels, he found Selby, and both were trucked to Batea under guard.*

Meanwhile, on March 26, the XVth Brigade marched twenty-six kilometers to a new camp near Corbera for reorganization. Major Edward Cecil-Smith suffered a singular accident: while cleaning his pistol, it fired and blew a hole in his foot. (Men wondered whether it was self-inflicted to forestall a charge pending for his momentary lapse at Alcañiz.)[3] As a reluctant concession to the overwhelming majority of Spaniards now in the brigade, Hector Garcia took command of the Mac-Paps, and Carl Geiser, formerly the Lincoln commissar at Fuentes de Ebro, replaced Wellman, who went on medical leave. (In official parlance "chargé" was beginning to replace "commissar," as having a less political connotation.)

The Lincoln Battalion was also overhauled. Captain Milton Wolff became the commander. He had worked through the ranks as a machine gunner in the Washingtons beginning at Brunete. The Volunteer for Liberty billed him as "the young Lincoln," a comparison with surface merit, for Wolff's prominent cheekbones, aquiline nose, and shock of unruly black hair did bring Lincoln to mind. Politically and ethnically they had nothing whatever in common. Unmistakably from Brooklyn, the twenty-two-year-old Wolff was a shipping clerk by trade, but before coming to Spain he had toughened himself by a six-month stint in the CCC (U.S. Civilian Conservation Corps). In later years he resolutely denied before congressional committees that he had ever been a member of either the CP or the YCL (although battalion archives contain a vita in his own handwriting claiming membership in the YCL in America and the CP

---

3. The hierarchy assumed it was deliberate. A confidential report gives these details. "Was arrested once for deserting his Battalion during Caspe fight, then improved. Shot himself in leg when Battalion called to fill break in line. Began cleaning gun when at standby order. When commissar out of room he shot himself. No Proof." Gates refused to have him back in the brigade.*

in Spain).* Largely self-educated, Wolff was nevertheless a natural intellectual. In his knapsack he carried Thomas Mann's *Joseph in Egypt*, which he read during lulls in campaigns. In love letters from Spain he enjoyed juxtaposing romantic imagery with acerbic irony: "Stood guard shrouded in a warm Moorish coat-robe, and watched a misty moon melt away—watched the stars from hard pinpoints, become large and soft, luminous, phosphorous globes before departing. It was a beautiful night—for an air raid."*

Wolff detested elegant uniforms and patrician mannerisms, preferring baggy trousers, a stained leather jacket, no hat whatever, and rarely an insignia other than the three-pointed star of the International Brigades. In rainy weather he donned a wool poncho, not a silk-lined opera cape. One might visualize him as the leader of an Old Testament host. He was intelligent, blunt, and stubborn. In battle he had proved his mettle, but the CP, disturbed by his political inexperience, assigned Joe Brandt, head of the Party organization within the battalion, as his ideological watchdog. Ostensibly Brandt, a know-nothing in military affairs, served as a kind of crypto-commander with authority to veto decisions if he so chose.* On the other hand, most men admired and trusted Wolff, while Spaniards boasted about their commander, *el lobo*—the wolf. (By strange coincidence, Wolff's adjutant was a lamb—Leonard Lamb, a New York social worker.)

One morning three hundred Spanish *quintos* from the 1929 draft (aged twenty-six and up) joined the brigade. They came from agricultural districts in Valencia province, most of them exempted thus far from military service because they had families. A Spaniard among the Lincolns described them, "Virtually all the recruits arriving have paunches, and they resemble not so much soldiers-to-be as a bunch of old men who are not going to be up to fighting." They wore uniforms but few had ever fired a rifle. Spanish veterans of the brigade dubbed them "the grandpa draftees."* Within two days they would face their first battle.

To raise morale, Edwin Rolfe, a poetaster who edited the *Volunteer for Liberty* (precipitously transplanted from Madrid to Barcelona), bombarded the front with two-page broadsides exhorting the International Brigades to hold their ground. Immense headlines fairly shrieked:

ATRAS LOS INVASORES DE ESPAÑA!
(Drive out the invaders of Spain!)
NO CEDER UN SOLO PALMO DE TERRENO AL ENEMIGO
(Don't yield an inch of ground to the enemy!!)
FORTIFICAR ES VENCER!
(To fortify is to win!)

Skeptics in the ranks said that the ruling junta must be really alarmed, or else they would not suggest that the war could be won merely by holding ground.

Rolfe's news sheet started carrying articles of the how-to-do-it genre, recipes introduced by the phrase, "If time allows . . . ," as though taken from a Fannie Farmer cookbook. For example, "If time allows . . . ," a good soldier can defend himself against a tank even without armor-piercing weapons. First, one digs a pit (80 centimeters deep and 60 centimeters wide). Place into it two well-seasoned men armed with grenades and liquid explosives—preferably phosphorous bombs, but if these are not handy and cannot be borrowed from a neighbor, gasoline bottles will do. When the tank approaches within eight or ten meters, the men should rise up suddenly and throw their bombs at either the caterpillar treads or the fuel tank. One thing must be borne in mind: one must not panic and run away from a tank "because it has guns." If it is not possible to knock out the tank as it passes over the men in the pit, one should not lose heart, because tanks usually return by the same route and an opportunity will arise to destroy it on its way back. One can imagine the hoots and hollers of Lincoln vets on reading this screed.*

What should men do when support on their flanks melts away and the enemy infiltrates behind their position? Newcomers found the answer in an article written for the *Volunteer for Liberty* by "El Gallo" (Luigi Longo), inspector general of the International Brigades. At the alarm "Our flanks are broken!" soldiers tend to panic unnecessarily. Cooler reflection will tell you that if the enemy has outflanked you, your position might be improved. For while he has gotten behind you, you in turn are behind him!* (Logically, the next step might be for the respective adversaries to push past each other so rapidly that they miss each other completely.) At first, the men fumed at what they called "à la Pasionaria bullshit" prepared by scribblers fighting the good fight from behind their desks in Barcelona. But in time the newspaper did, in fact, help morale by providing a weekly target for derisive laughter. It became a kind of gag bag, cheering them up by what Sandor Voros called "back-ass propaganda."

Fausto Villar rejoined the brigade at this time and reported to his mentor, Jim Cody, to explain how he had escaped capture at Belchite. He said he had gone home to Valencia, had a tearful reunion with his mother and *novia*, who begged him to go into hiding until the end of the war, but had found transportation back to the battalion. Since Cody did not speak Spanish, he got Commissar John Gates to translate. After Gates learned that Villar had fled all the way to Valencia, he "erupted into a welter of curses in English before telling me in Spanish that he was going to have me shot."* Cody intervened, and after an argument, Gates apologized for cursing him, adding "that there have been a lot of runaways from the brigades, and that, on Merriman's orders, a goodly number of brigaders had been shot." Later Litween, the battalion interpreter, took Villar aside and mentioned "the spies in the Brigade whom Merriman had shot." Considerably agitated, he warned Villar not to speak the Valencia dialect to other Spaniards because none of the official translators understood it and might assume he is fomenting a secret conspiracy.

To perk up his men, Doran organized a grand fiesta at the camp on March 29. Around a huge bonfire they were treated to bottles of cheap champagne tasting like sour cider, baskets of almonds, and Colonel Copic's baritone. Female representatives from the United Social Youth, imported from Barcelona, delivered what the men did not want—patriotic harangues under the eagle eyes of suspicious chaperones. Copic mounted a wooden crate; and as flashbulbs popped, he assured the brigade there would be no repetition of a calamity on the order of the March retreat. He said that General Walter himself had promised that only units of the 35th Division would anchor their flanks. Henceforth, brigade officers would know what forces were on the left and right. The rookies warmly applauded Copic's harangue, but the veterans had heard all this stuff before. "It was merely words to send us once more into the breach." Copic surrendered his crate to Merriman, who spoke directly to the Spaniards of the brigade. If this war was lost, they would have to endure the crushing burden of defeat. Brutal Moors, depraved legionnaires, and other foreign opportunists in Franco's army would be turned loose to violate their wives and sweethearts and to turn the common people into slaves. The veterans were startled. They had never heard Merriman resort to this sort of jingoistic demagoguery before. He seemed to be losing control of his emotions. Such talk made them uneasy. It was as though Merriman, in not calmly and precisely outlining the task ahead, as was his way, had lost his confidence.

Speeches over, Catalan musicians struck up "The International" while the men stood at attention with right fists clutched to their hearts. Assistant commissars doled out chocolate bars and caramels, and a few men like Joe Bianca received wristwatches for their heroism during the retreat. There were no boxing matches or softball games, features of raucous fiestas at Albares in the old days. Life had become much too serious. The veterans were subdued and gloomy, scenting trouble to come. "We must be moving," said one. "When they throw a *fiesta* for you, it never fails."*

Even Commissar Doran, never one for sentimentality or defeatism, seemed unsettled by gloomy forebodings, for on this day he wrote his wife what for him was an extraordinary letter. Gone were his rabid boasts about "filling Fascist bellies with lead" along with the committee-report tone he usually employed, even with his wife:

> Please do not worry, darling, some day I am coming home to you, nes-
> tle close, and let nothing else take me away from you. I have fashioned
> a real lifelike picture of yourself in my mind and somehow even in the
> most difficult moments I feel your presence close by. I hope you have
> not changed much. I want you to be nearly exactly as you were. You
> must know, darling, that at moments just thinking of you, as you were,
> serves to fire and inspire me ever so much. Nothing can ever rob me or
> make me forget memories of the two of us, or ever impel me to blot
> out the burning desire within me to once more be at your side. I
> believe the entire Brigade knows about us, dear. Do you mind if I tell?*

Tell what? That he, the commissar of the XVth International Brigade, was ashamed of loving a woman like weaker men? Underneath the soap-opera phraseology of the letter is the voice of a man faced with thoughts of his own death. Marxism had given him a tough shell, but inside, perhaps Doran was as sentimental as the bourgeois culture that he professed to despise. On the other hand, since the tone and substance of this letter differ so markedly from the progress reports that Doran usually passed along to his wife, it may be a forgery—composed to "humanize" the "Hero of Caspe."

Robert Merriman also took pen in hand for a letter to his "Dearest Girl," who was in Hollywood with Dorothy Parker raising money for Spain. For her sake he put a bold face on the disasters of the preceding weeks—"When the roads were cut behind us and when it looked like we were being surrounded, the real stuff in men came out. . . . Now we know our people better since they received the roughest testing possible." After describing the misery of civilian refugees with bundles fleeing from the Fascists and the awesome wrecks of bombed villages, he concluded, "I am working hard so as we can have that vaca-tion together when you return. . . . I think of you always—love you more and more and hope that we are together again soon. Love and then some. Bob."*

That night at two o'clock the brigade moved out to confront the juggernaut.

The restiveness within the brigade, although founded upon intuition rather than information, nevertheless accurately mirrored concurrent developments at the front, for at that very moment, as they resumed their drive to the Mediterranean, the Nationalists were converting the Republican lines to soggy paper. While the 1st Navarre Division swept down from Caspe through Maella toward Batea and Gandesa, the Italian CTV moved along a converging road from Alcañiz. At Gandesa the two armies were to link up before driving through a gap in the Sierra de Pandols to Tortosa and the sea. Although the Lincolns were told that they occupied a reserve position well to the rear, events would shortly prove that the XVth Brigade had been thrust directly into the path of the enemy advance. And once again, despite Copic's assurances of shielded flanks, liaison and reconnaissance would prove to be so haphazard that the brigade staff never knew the identity, strength, or location of other Republican units to right or left. If, indeed, that would have mattered.

In the wee hours of March 30, 1938, the brigade lined up in the dark and received new Russian rifles, still packed in grease, which they wiped off with their shirttails. The metalwork bore the sign of the Russian imperial eagle, partially obliterated by another stamp, the hammer and sickle. Little paper packs of cartridges they stuffed into their pockets or blanket rolls. From a box they helped themselves to hand grenades. None of the new American replacements had ever tossed a live grenade; few of the new Spanish conscripts had ever seen one. In two files, one on each side of the road, they moved out toward the front from their camp outside Corbera.

Six kilometers beyond Gandesa, at the junction of the Batea road, Copic set up his headquarters. The brigade was responsible for a large fan of terrain between the Alcañiz and Caspe roads. The Lincolns moved north toward Batea, the British continued west toward Alcañiz, while the Mac-Paps and the 24th advanced cross-country to secure the terrain in between. Copic and Doran took charge of the right flank; Merriman, the left. General Walter had overall command of the 35th Division, which included the XIth and XVth Brigades. No immediate danger was anticipated—they were still officially in reserve behind the units of Modesto and Lister—the best fighting men in the Army. They spent the day digging defensive positions on rocky hilltops and among the scattered pine woods. Enemy airplanes swarmed overhead but dropped no bombs. They were seeking bigger game in the rear—convoys, depots, armor. As the day wore on, the rumble of artillery grew louder, reminding new rookies of a summer storm.

Daybreak of March 31 (Thursday) found the brigade, flanked on its right by its "sister" brigade, the German XIth (now reduced to about three hundred men, most of them Spaniards), feeling its way through their five-mile sector near Batea. With each kilometer of advance, the front line of the Lincolns became thinner. Miles away to the west, the British followed the Alcañiz road, while in the center the Mac-Paps and the 24th groped through a maze of orchards, vineyards, and pine barrens. By this time Gandesa lay six to nine miles behind them.

For the British, first contact with the Nationalist vanguard came with a galvanic shock when they single-filed through Calaceite at dawn. Since Merriman's information held that the nearest enemy troops were twelve miles farther west, the battalion straggled, their heavy weapons—machine guns and an antitank gun—bringing up the rear. They felt perfectly secure, for ahead were Enrique Lister's three Communist divisions, celebrated for their death-defying courage wherever they engaged the Fascists. What the British did not know was the Italian CTV had slipped through a gap in the mountains to the north and, without firing a shot, now straddled the Alcañiz road between the British and the Listers. Lining up their whippet tanks and machine guns in the neck of a horseshoe curve, with observers concealed in the hills, they waited patiently for their first victims. They had not long to wait.

The British had deployed scouts out front, but these assumed that the tanks belonged to the Listers and blithely walked past them. The head of the column thus passed into the jaws of the trap with Commissar Wally Tapsell at their head. As the light improved, a voice in the second company split the quiet air, "Tanks!" which, in effect, provided the signal for the Italians to open fire. Among the first to fall was Tapsell, who had approached a tank to chat with the driver. The commander yelled, "Head for the ridge!" pointing to the south side of the road. The tanks cross-stitched the road with point-blank fire that dropped the drowsy Britons where they stood in dumb surprise or propelled them in a clawing flight up the rocky cliffside. The slaughter was prodigious. Tanks throttled up and rumbled back and forth along the road, "their guns rattling like motor bikes." Some of their motorcycles had machine guns fitted on the handle bars.* One tank tried to run down a squad of Britons paralyzed with indecision; they dodged in time, but the tank crushed wounded men writhing in its path.

Within half an hour the British Battalion as functional entity had ceased to exist. A cluster of perhaps thirty men briefly rallied on a promontory above the road and pecked at the Italians below them, but they quicky melted away when CTV soldiers deployed to surround them. In tiny bands, the survivors of the Calaceite massacre, probably none of whom had maps, fell back through the barren Sierra de Pesells. In this brief fight the British lost 140 captured and about 150 killed or wounded.* Some escaped by following the Ebro River down to Tortosa. As the POWs trudged west on the Alcañiz road, they passed Italian Black Arrows who spat in their faces and threatened to set them on fire with gasoline.* Calaceite became notorious as the most humiliating defeat an English force ever suffered at the hands of Italians.

Back at the brigade command post, Sandor Voros spotted a group of men cutting across a field, avoiding the road and heading for the rear. He shouted, and they reluctantly stopped and explained what had happened to their battalion. They still had their rifles and had not lost their grit. On Voros's instruction they spread out and corralled other Britons drifting back. "They were tough about it. . . . They meant business, they fired after two men who refused to stop, which quickly brought them around." After collecting a group of stragglers, Voros led them back up the Alcañiz road, where they found General Walter, his forehead furrowed by a deep scowl, pacing up and down. Thinking they were the vanguard of reinforcements, his face brightened until he learned that they were the remnants of the British Battalion. He put José Maria Sastre, the division commissar, in charge of the division, ordered him to hold at all cost, and climbed into his staff car, saying that he would personally demand reinforcements from 5th Corps headquarters. Sastre was stunned. He was not a military officer, and corps headquarters lay far across the Ebro River, ninety kilometers in the rear. Merriman was the most reliable officer in the sector, but runners sent to find him did not return. He was said to be somewhere over in the right flank placing the Lincolns into defensive positions. The pressure was too much for Sastre: after uttering some clichés about "holding the line at all costs," he jumped into a staff car and declared he would bring Walter back.*

Meanwhile the Mac-Paps were engaged in a series of rearguard retreats that were a paradigm of Republican resistance in the region. Repeatedly, they fell back to hilltops, where no sooner had they set up a firing line than they found their flanks exposed. Throughout the morning they withdrew with textbook precision, contesting each hilltop; but by early afternoon they began losing cohesion. Stretcher-bearers, runners, and ammo carriers dispatched to the rear failed to return. Companies dissolved, squads carried on. Wooded valleys and ridges crackled and popped like a forest fire. "It was like playing cowboys and Indians," reported a Mac-Pap, "except there were too many Indians." They dribbled across the Alcañiz road into the rough mountain terrain on the south side.*

A few determined pockets of Mac-Paps north of the road held on. Sergeant Lawrence Cane remained on one hilltop until he ran out of ammunition and had to fall back along the road, where his group met Copic waving a Dichterev and yelling, "Who give you orders to retreat? Where are you coming from?" When Cane reported the battalion was no longer in front of him, Copic yelled, "What do you mean! No one has been given an order to withdraw—who gave the order!" "What are you asking me for?" Cane snapped. "All I know is that we got out with a whole ass!" As Copic was shouting, "Why didn't you stay there and fight?" an Italian tank rumbled down the road and opened fire. Copic had his answer. He "jumped fifteen feet" and had a fine running start on the others. "Then it was every man for himself."* Most of the Mac-Paps and the 24th succeeded in avoiding entrapment by fleeing into the mountains south of the road or by falling back into Gandesa and retreating down the deep canyon of the Ebro toward Tortosa.

Disaster overtook the Lincoln Battalion but slowly. On Thursday (March 31), they found not the expected rear guard of the Republican defense but potent signs of the enemy advancing toward them along the Caspe road. In the ragged hill country a mile or so northwest of Batea, they began to exchange shots. Scouts reporting to Captain Wolff found no evidence at all of support on their flanks, as Copic had promised. Directions from Brigade were "completely screwy. . . . Ordered to stand fast, we found the whole fucking fascist army!" Wolff wrote, adding parenthetically, "Intelligence was not one of our strong points."*

Twigs and leaves drifted down as Nationalist machine gunners opened fire. But the only casualty was a Spanish recruit who crawled across exposed ground toward a Lincoln gun crew. They tried to wave him back but he came on, shouting, "I want to see the machine gun working." Seconds later he was hit in the groin and thrashed about, shrieking, "Mama mia! Ai! Mama mia!" He was beyond the reach of stretcher-bearers. Some of the new recruits clucked like chickens with a fox in the barnyard. They were useless deadweight. When under attack, they froze and, ignoring encouragement or curses, often refused to fire a shot—assuming they knew how to use their new rifles. Meanwhile, experienced men fanned out and opened fire, easily beating off advancing skirmishers. "You see—it's not so bad" was the implicit message to the newcomers. The woods turned blue-gray from the fumes of discharged cartridges; hot gun barrels blistered hands. For the new men this should have been a soft initiation into war—less like a battle than a target shoot, except there was rarely a visible target. A mongrel dog, yapping now and then, tagged along behind some Americans. Fearing that his barking would give away their position, they resolved to kill it, but no one had the guts to bayonet it. The best they could come up with was "He's probably just lonesome, but what the hell."*

A second-echelon commissar led the twenty-odd prisoners of the labor battalion into a vacated artillery post well in advance of the Lincoln position. They had received a little rice but no wine or water in seventy-two hours. After untying their hands, he told them they had been sentenced to six months' hard labor—without trial—but could redeem themselves by holding back the Fascist advance. He then hustled back to the main body, without leaving them any weapons. They had had enough. As soon as a bombardment began, they scattered to the four winds. Honeycombe hitchhiked around Barcelona and reached Port Bou at the French frontier. Although he had turned in his passport at

Albacete, he did have an American union card, which he used to support a drunken sailor tale and walked through the tunnel to France.* Another prisoner, Henry Baskowski (also Basko and Baszczowksy in other rosters), formerly commander of First Company, crossed the Pyrenees south of Toulouse, where he cheerfully went to jail in France.* Because of his West Point training and military experience in Central America, Vernon Selby—still under close surveillance—rejoined the Lincolns as a scout. But the others in the labor battalion were gobbled up in the Nationalist advance.

Refugees streamed eastward. Their two-wheeled carts were heaped high with furniture, bed ticks, frying pans as large as shields, and always the family dog, tied with a piece of twine, running along between the wheels. There were many confusing movements and countermovements as staff tried to sort out the wobbly defense segments. Merriman found a hole in the line and moved some men along the rutted lane leading northeast to Villalba de los Arcos. As the afternoon wore on, the Nationalists cut loose with a brief artillery barrage. Men here and there tried to flee, but guards leveled rifles and forced them back. A boyish-looking American, husky and athletic, walked slowly to the rear, open-mouthed, his eyes bulging and unblinking. He refused to go back and mumbled, like a broken record, "I wanttogohome. I wanttogohome." To save him from being shot for desertion, a staff officer ordered him to lie down and rest. He collapsed like a stringless puppet, but slipped away unnoticed as soon as the barrage crept closer.*

Friday morning (April 1) was so quiet that most of the Lincolns slept off their exhaustion after a restless night of waiting and watching for a major attack that never came. During this lull they lay on pine-scented hillsides, studied local insect life, and wondered what the folks were doing back in the States. Food trucks came up, like morning milk trucks back in Allentown. "The war seemed very far away," mused one American, who also recalled that artillery rumbles were so distant that they sounded "musical and harmless."* They had not been told that the British Battalion had been nearly annihilated the day before, or that the Mac-Paps and the 24th were even then fighting for their lives just five miles south of their own arcadian knolls. What was worse, as events proved, was that they were totally ignorant of enemy movements in their right flank. The bulk of the Navarrese division, mainly Requetés (extreme Catholics from the Basque Country, who often fought with a sacred-heart emblem sewn on their blouses to ward off bullets), had spilled through holes in the defensive line and were at that moment pushing east toward Villalba de los Arcos to connect with a minor road leading into Gandesa from the north. In other words, by Friday afternoon the Lincoln Battalion had been almost surrounded. Not even chronic pessimists among them had any inkling of just how bad their situation really was. They lay in the quiet eye of a hurricane.

Scales fell from their eyes in late afternoon when Merriman's bullet-spattered staff car arrived with news that the left flank had been smashed and that it was just a matter of time before the Italians took Gandesa. Even as he was driving up to Batea, he came under fire from enemy snipers. Mouths went dry when men heard this report. Hovering over his map with Doran and Wolff, his professorial glasses drooped far down his nose, Merriman explained that they had to move cross-country to hills north of Gandesa, then down to the main highway leading to the Ebro bridge at Mora de Ebro. Doran, who is said to have been death-oriented at this point, wanted to fortify and fight to the last man. Wolff thought he had gone to pieces and had lost his capacity for command. At Caspe he had been outstanding, but now "an almost visible sense of doom emanated from him."* According to strict Comintern regulations, as brigade commissar Doran could overrule Merriman, but the others in the gathering just ignored him—commissar or no commissar. There was not a minute to waste on politics. Captain Wolff, looking like an opera star in his long black poncho, shouted, "Batallon! A formar! Let's go!" It was getting dark. In their haste to get away, a Lincoln company with machine guns far out on the left never got the message. They vanished from history.*

Men poured off the hillsides in frantic haste and formed a column as though preparing for a military parade. Some naively assumed that they were to make a night attack, but when they began marching away from the sunset, they sensed something terrible had happened. "No one said anything, no one asked any questions, but we knew we were moving, moving fast." Their nerves were frayed, still under control though fearing the worst. "The same old story," remembered one man, "no trace of Copic or of Walter, no one guarding our right or left flanks." They were famished—no food since a bite in the morning. Armorers stood in the trail trying to hand out extra rounds of ammunition and grenades, but got few takers. Sensing another disaster, men wanted to travel light. One man muttered over and over, "Never again! Never again!" Everyone knew exactly what he meant, but they did not want to hear it. The best argument was "Shut the fuck up!" This was no time for cranks, jokers, or cynics. Suddenly there was a gigantic explosion nearby, sending men sprawling facedown in the dirt. It was as though enemy artillery had zeroed in on their valley with a Big Bertha, but the battalion armorers had just blown up a munitions dump.*

That night the western sky glowed as hundreds of headlights bounced off clouds; Nationalist trucks were carrying men and matériel up to the front in total disregard of convoy security. With their immense resources of manpower and firepower, and the absence for weeks of Republican aircraft, they had no need of secrecy. "We knew," remarked one marcher, "that daylight would be a bitch."

On Merriman's chart the route of their anabasis seemed clear enough: follow a road labeled "*camino viejo de Gandesa*" until it intersected another marked "*camino viejo*" (old road) passing east of Corbera. But on a Spanish chart an "old road" might mean that it had been a bustling thoroughfare at the time of the Visigoths but nowadays was likely to be a gulley intersected by cart roads and mule paths, none charted. Road signs did not exist in this hinterland, and even during the daytime an experienced map reader would have had difficulty picking the correct route out of the profusion of intersecting lanes.[4] The advance guard moved out so rapidly that it soon outpaced those following and vanished altogether. In the darkness the long Indian file broke apart and men separated. Others, who had never been notified of the retreat and had been left behind, had to fend for themselves—whether fighting rearguard duels, seeking burrows in which to hide, or taking a chance that surrender might not necessarily mean execution—as they had been told. Whenever the file stopped, men fell asleep on the road, and when it resumed, the others plunged ahead and abandoned them. Under such conditions it was easy to imagine the enemy was everywhere. The night was filled with whispers, rising to angry shouts, from all directions, "Contact . . . CONTACT! Goddamn it to hell, where ARE you?" In this maze of terraces men groped down cul-de-sacs only to bump into walls. To be left alone within enemy lines was a terrifying sensation; a tic in the brain brought one nearer to the brink of panic. Piece by piece, men began throwing equipment away. Those behind stumbled over machine-gun belts, blanket rolls, mess tins, knapsacks. Cursing the waste and symptoms of panic, then seeing the logic of it, they began dropping equipment of their own.

Within minutes of their departure, the Lincolns had fragmented into countless clusters of hapless men, all bent upon getting as far east as possible before sunup brought discovery. Except for the staff, no one had compass or map. Nearly all survivors told of blundering through Nationalist camps that night. One band of perhaps eighty men, braced by a powerful old black named Edward Johnson, who refused to abandon his Dichterev, and a New York novelist named Alvah Bessie, strayed off northeast. A line from a song drummed monotonously in Bessie's brain—"Be it ever so humble, there's no place like home." In this stupefying, exhausting night march, he became aware that his

---

4. My daytime search of this sector in 1967, and again in 2000, revealed no trace of a road, only rutted lanes winding about in all directions. The 1:50,000 map from the Spanish Cartographical Institute that I used was printed in Germany in the 1920s. Both the Republican and Nationalist armies used this series during the war.

tongue was hanging out, like a dog's; he clamped his mouth shut, plodded on, and found it hanging out again. Just before dawn they spotted the lights of a village but hurried on—little caring what place it was or who held it. On the outskirts of this unknown place (it was Villalba de los Arcos) they passed silhouetted figures on the road. Wrapped in blankets and holding rifles, they stood fast and failed to challenge the Americans slipping across the cordon to the fields beyond. Suddenly Bessie's squad leader dropped his rifle and began to sprint. "Tabb!" shouted Bessie in alarm. "Where are you? I can't see you!" They were in a field humped with bundles of sleeping men. Bessie tripped over a soft obstruction on the ground—a man rose up and cursed, "Coño!" They were stumbling through an enemy bivouac! The darkness came alive with a din of noise—horses whinnying, pots and pans clanking, pounding footsteps in all directions. The Americans dashed blindly through the encampment, tripping over panicked creatures as frightened as themselves, and scaled a series of terrace walls on the far side of the field. From behind came hysterical shouts, "Alto! Los Rojos! Alto los Rojos!" Bullets snapped over their heads. Moaning with exhaustion Bessie and three others reached the top of the ridge at first light. They were alone—the others had been shot, captured, or dispersed. Ripping off the red-star emblems on their caps, they hurried toward the rising sun.

As it happened, Bessie's group had stumbled through a camp of the Nationalist 1st Division, for a Requeté officer included the incident in his report. He was among an advance guard of his division, which after a hard up-and-down march across rough country had camped half a mile from Villalba de los Arcos. They were awakened by exploding grenades in a nearby camp. "Not knowing what it was, we jumped to our feet and then realized we had camped with an enemy international battalion and took 124 prisoners, the rest of them running away."* (Among the captives was forty-seven-year-old Edward Johnson of Lynchburg, Virginia, who narrowly escaped execution but returned home safely after a year as a POW.)

Late that day this handful of fugitives reached Mora de Ebro and fell in with some Mac-Paps. "Where's the Lincoln?" asked a Canadian on the road. "We're the Lincolns," one of the four replied. "Pleased to know you," said the Canadian. Far to the west they could hear the thunder at Gandesa and the whine of diving airplanes. Somewhere in the middle of that noise was the main body of the Lincoln Battalion—assuming any were still alive.*

Elsewhere on the right flank, it was the same story. Enemy campsites seemed to cover the ground between the Lincolns and Corbera. As fugitives stumbled blindly through them, from all directions came cries, "Manos arriba! Rojo! Rojo!" followed by volleys of wild shots, the sounds of men thrashing through underbrush, voices whispering "Por acá! Por acá!" Not daring to strike a match, men wandered blindly in the dark, fragmenting even more.

At one point Harry Fisher found himself among eleven *transmisiones*, hiking along a road with a file of soldiers assumed to be friendlies until they noticed officers on horseback. Then it dawned on them—Republican officers did not ride horses. These had to be Fascists! Breaking ranks, they sat down beside the road until the column passed by. An officer, his suspicions aroused, stopped as if trying to decide whether to ride back and confront them. But evidently fearing an ambush, he changed his mind and galloped after his men. The *transmisiones* carried only switchboards, telephone wire, and a single rifle. Led by John Cookson, a University of Wisconsin instructor—regarded until that night as "a hysterical old lady"—they wormed through enemy nets and after three days were ferried across the river with telephone wire still hanging around their necks.*

Just after daybreak on Saturday morning (April 2), the main body under Merriman, Doran, and Wolff, reduced to perhaps two hundred men, reached a scrub-pine ridge about a mile above Gandesa. In eight hours they had covered less than seven miles of rough hill country, and—worse luck—they had failed to reach and to cross the Gandesa-Corbera highway before first light. Now, with sinking hopes, they watched the landscape below them unfold in the incandescent dawn like a print in a photographer's tray. A series of terraced vineyards and almond groves descended like a broad staircase to a wide valley, beyond which lay the peaks and folds of the Sierra de Cavalls—a perfect place to fortify or to hide, if they could just reach it. About a mile south lay Gandesa, a slate-colored town like neatly piled rocks in the green plain. They watched an enemy force—the Italian CTV—on the Alcañiz highway launch their morning attack on the town from the west. To their consternation, they could see a scattering of enemy troops moving toward Gandesa along the Mora de Ebro highway. (This was the fierce 1st Navarre Division, which, after engaging the Lincolns on the previous day, had marched all night to Villalba and by dawn were nearing Gandesa.) The Lincolns were bagged, with the drawstring being pulled tight even as they watched. Black smoke hung over Gandesa, which was being shelled to drive out the remnants of the Republican rear guard. Observation planes hung over the band radioing positions, and for several hours they were "sniped at by artillery," tearing apart what was left of their unity and confidence.

Below them lay a shallow valley, the remnant of a watercourse, sloping down through terraced almond trees to a wide swatch of vineyards with green shoots just nosing out of stumpy vines. Descending terrace walls would offer no cover, for they faced in the wrong direction. Merriman figured that their best chance was to make a dash through the vineyard, blast a gap across the Corbera road—only lightly held thus far—and strike out for the Sierra de Pandols on the far side. Since there were no signs of forces moving up toward them, possibly the enemy did not yet know they were there. The leadership split into two quarreling factions: Merriman arguing that they must move at once, in daylight, to take the enemy by surprise; others, including Wolff and Gates, wanted to hole up and cross in darkness. Brandt endorsed Gates, but Merriman collected men who chose to follow him and prepared to leave. After all, he was the senior officer in rank and in experience, while Wolff and Gates were Johnny-come-latelies.[5] Doran presumably joined the assault team, for years later Wolff wrote to Gates, "Why did you and me surrender the Battalion to Merriman and Doran?"

The "truth" about what happened next is no better known than what songs the sirens sang. However, all parties agree that a sizable band did follow Merriman down toward the road, while others remained concealed in the pine scrub on two hilltops, the Lincolns on one and the Spanish battalion on the other. (Probably a majority never arrived at all, having been permanently lost, or abandoned en route.) Villar, who stayed close to his mentor, Jim Cody, provides the only consistent eyewitness account of events among the Merriman group. "With a voice trembling with emotion, Merriman told us all that, sad to say, the enemy had us surrounded, but that the Lincolns would break out of the noose by a frontal assault on a single point and that he would lead us into this attack."[*]

A smattering of Germans from the XIth Brigade, which had been overrun the night before, had joined Merriman's escape party. Conrad Schmidt, a Swiss stretcher-bearer, left a brief record of that morning. Without knowing his name, he described Merriman—a leader, who looked like a university professor, who gave the order. Leaving their cover in the pine scrub, they scrambled down laddering terraces into a wide ravine and hustled across a vineyard. The vanguard entered a slight trough between two knolls, each several hundred yards distant. When they were about halfway across, enemy machine guns, concealed on flanking knolls, opened fire. From the tail end of the detachment, Schmidt described what he saw. The guns mowed down the Lincolns: "It was terrible." In a few minutes there were "hills of bodies." They sought the only protection they could find, flattening themselves in shallow furrows of the exposed vineyards. The slightest movement drew ferocious fire from the enemy gunners, who

5. Wolff felt like an alien around Merriman, who looked to him "like a college professor from an Ivy League College . . . all good clean-cut stock, like . . . Detro." Against these, he felt out of place and sensed that "he did not measure up."[*] He needed the support of Gates and Brandt in deciding to remain on the hilltop and attempt to cross at night.

seemed bent upon extermination, for they did not cease firing or demand surrender. With their guns raking the vineyard up and down, from side to side, it was less battle than slaughter. No Lincolns dared fire a shot in return.* Some men near the rear of the column, including Schmidt, succeeded in regaining the hill and joining the group who had decided to wait until nightfall.

Villar had not been hit. Paralyzed with terror and pretending to be dead, he lay next to Merriman and Cody. He described the scene:

> In a furrow higher up the slope and a little ahead was Cody. In the next furrow, higher still was Merriman. Higher up no one else was in sight. Doran I could not see. I called out to Cody, in my awful English, "Cody, we must move because they will kill us off in this place." There was no response. I called out again and again, but he did not answer. Cody was flat like the rest of us. I addressed them both, in Spanish, "Por favor, contestarme!" Then in my flawed English I pleaded with them, "Please, tell me something, Cody. Please, Merriman, Please!" By my reckoning their silence meant that both were dead, and the battalion was facing horrific slaughter. Beside myself with worry, I called out again, but there was no response. The thought flashed into my mind that I had to get out of this deadly rat-trap; otherwise I was going to end up like them. "Farewell, Cody! Farewell, Merriman!" This was our final leave-taking.*

Waiting for a lull in the murderous fire, Villar sprinted toward a wooded patch, bullets kicking up dirt at his heels, and plunged headfirst into the shrubbery. As a Lincoln scout, he had studied maps and knew exactly where he was. To escape he had to steer to the northeast and wait for a chance to cross the Villalba road.

It is alleged that a few Americans ran the gauntlet of fire unscathed and escaped into the mountains beyond the Gandesa-Corbera road, but if so, no survivors ever chronicled this dubious exploit. The experience of George Watt (Kvatt), an assistant battalion commissar, was probably more typical. Trailing behind the main body, he took refuge with half a dozen men in a *barranca* when the firing began. Watt figured they lay in a death trap, for this ditch would be a natural pathway up to the Lincoln hilltop whenever the Nationalists pressed their attack. He stripped himself of all equipment and identification papers. For a fleeting moment he wondered what to do with a packet of his wife's letters—then threw them away. When the firing died down, he made a break for the rear. The men with him were too frightened to budge. Watt got safely back, but he never saw those men again. Others farther back in Merriman's column, including Schmidt, also managed to rejoin the group back on Wolff's hilltop.*

Soon Nationalist cavalry galloped across the vineyard, sabering men who had played possum or, if wounded, were trying to get back to the hilltop. When trapped men tried to surrender, they were chopped down with sweeping saber strokes. Among those who died in this manner was Al Kaufman, who had led the battalion briefly during the long retreat from Belchite. Witnessing this butchery, the Americans above realized the futility of surrender and resolved to break out at whatever cost as soon as darkness fell. On their hilltops Lincolns frantically used bayonets to scratch out rifle pits in earth the color of blood. Since further retreat was out of the question, they set up their few remaining Dichterevs along a circular outer rim and waited, like Custer's men, to fight the last battle of their lives. A few shells ranged overhead, but for the most part, the enemy showed more interest in taking Gandesa than in mopping up an insignificant force in their rear, one they could overrun whenever they chose. There was a long period of agonized calm, raising hopes that they might be forgotten until sundown, when it might be possible to escape into the Sierra de Cavalls. They followed the path of the sun across the sky with empathic absorption. It was the longest day of their lives. Fear was palpable.

According to Commissar Fred Keller, later in the afternoon a line of enemy horsemen gathered in the valley below and trotted, as though on parade, up the slope toward the Lincoln ring, weaving in and out among the maze of terrace walls. With guidons fluttering gaily, they launched a beautiful charge-of-the-light-brigade assault upon the hilltop, but were beaten back after a crackle of fire from the ridge dropped perhaps a dozen riders off their horses in fine Hollywood style. Then with disbelief the Lincolns watched as the cavalry unit—said to be Italian, not Moorish or Spanish—assembled again and charged the adjacent hilltop held by remnants of the 24th Battalion.* Again the cavalry were cut to pieces.[6] Thereafter, the Nationalists subjected the two hilltops to sporadic artillery fire but abstained from further attacks. They knew that the Lincolns were in a box and had to surrender or try to break out.

At dusk, battalion scouts searched for a feasible route across the Corbera road to the mountains, and it was Vernon Selby, the despised deserter, who reported he had found one. (Other sources claim they intended to escape by

6. This story has improved with age. The first history of the Lincoln Battalion (Rolfe's *Lincoln Battalion,* published in 1939) says "it took no more than a few minutes to convince the attackers that their charge was futile" and mentions no casualties whatever. The next history of the "Lincoln Brigade" [sic] based primarily upon an interview with Fred Keller in 1965 (Landis's *Abraham Lincoln Brigade*), talks about "four or five hundred cavalry" led by an Italian officer who "shouted to the Americans to surrender in the name of Il Duce," before being cut down by the Lincolns' guns until "the slope of the hill was covered with dead and dying." Herbert L. Matthews interviewed Keller on April 11, 1938, and received a detailed account of the attempt to break out of the Gandesa

crossing the Villalba-Corbera road and veer northeast toward Fatarella and Asco.) Wolff moved his men out at once, so rapidly indeed that many men never learned of the withdrawal until the staff had disappeared in the gloom. Clement Markert, a new arrival from the University of Colorado, recalled with shame how they abandoned wounded comrades: "Some of them were cursing us for deserting them, and yet, what could you do? You could only barely manage yourself if you weren't wounded."* (The Lincolns left their Spanish comrades of the 24th to fend for themselves.)

A scout known as "Ivan" (John Gerlach) took the lead. (Selby's name disappears from the record.) The night was pitch-black under a new moon. The men were told to maintain contact by touch, but those in the rear quickly lost contact and dispersed into smaller groups. They thought they were bound for Gandesa, but few had ever seen a map of the area or had any idea where they were. Joe Young, ex-seaman, preparing for the worst, taught his squad how to navigate by the North Star. That seemed easy. One man faced the North Star and extending arms, said "That's east, that's west, and south is behind us. But where the hell is Gandesa?" After meandering in the dark they heard voices calling, "Brigada Americana!" Yelling back, "Aquí! Aquí!" fugitives rushed ahead and ran into a Requeté ambush. When they were being lined up to be shot, a soldier who had taken Young prisoner found a St. Christopher's medal in his clothes and showed it to an officer. A Catholic among these Reds? This saved Young's group from execution, for as they were led away they passed the bodies of two Americans, "boots missing and faces shot off."*

It was nearly midnight (April 2–3) when Wolff's group of about thirty men emerged from a sunken road and crept toward the Corbera highway. Two days later Ernest Hemingway published Ivan Gerlach's account of what happened next.

> I was ahead going through an orchard north of Corbera when someone in the dark challenged. I covered him with my pistol and he called for the corporal of the guard. As the guard came I shouted to those behind, "This way, this way!" and ran through the orchard *to pass*

---

pocket, yet Keller said nothing to him about a cavalry charge. Fact or fiction? I opt for fiction. Gates himself explicitly said the cavalry was too far away: "We didn't even touch them."* And for the record—Spanish cavalry, not Italian, sabered the trapped Americans. The Italian CVT was nowhere near that field of action.

Villar, who had no political agenda to defend and who had read the "official" histories of the Lincoln Battalion, absolutely denied (1) there was an organized retreat back up the hill from the vineyard—"it was a disaster"; (2) that Nationalist cavalry attacked the Lincoln group on the hilltop; and (3) that enemy artillery shelled Wolff's group on the hilltop.*

north of the town [my emphasis]. But no one followed. I could hear them running toward the town. Then I heard the commands, "Hands up! Hands up!" and it sounded as though they had been surrounded. Perhaps they got away, but it sounded as if some were captured.*

Some survivors reported that a blinding light lit up the whole column and they were attacked by cavalry—most unlikely over wooded terrain at midnight.* In any case, they scattered. In this instant of freezing confrontation, every semblance of order vanished. No one gave a command to return the fire. Every man had to satisfy the demon of his own reflexes, and these commanded him to flee. Afterward none of the survivors told exactly the same story—because the threads of memory were so different. Gerlach himself contradicted his own story, recounting that he ran across the Corbera-Gandesa highway and jumped down an embankment on the south side of the road, followed by Joe Brandt. As though blackjacked unexpectedly in a dark alley, no one ever was sure what had happened or when. Some insisted that the headlights of a car or a tank suddenly floodlit them; others said the crossing occurred in total darkness. Both may have been right because men perhaps crossed at different places at different times. A few dashed after Gerlach, but most probably fell back and fled through the vineyards and orchards from which they had come. Those who did, found themselves in enemy encampments where in most cases they were killed outright.

At this time the Lincoln Battalion as a military organization ceased to exist. It was every man jack for himself as they recoiled from the clamor and shots on the Corbera road. Most of them were city dwellers, trade-union men ill-prepared to strike out alone through open fields marked only by sinuous cow-lanes. Few had ever seen a map of the region. Rifles were anchors dragging them back—better throw them away. If captured, they could claim they were non-combatants. Darkness was an enemy, for it confused and separated them; yet they knew that when daylight came they would be hunted like wild animals. Captain Wolff had jumped off an embankment on the Corbera road and found himself alone. His sole thought was survival. "The collective impulse disappeared. Only in aloneness was there safety. . . . There was no exchange of news, of directions. Each man was intent to become invisible, or at least too insignificant to be noticed. Each had a secret plan for escape and survival. This was the way that the lost, the defeated and the demoralized traveled. Not together, not in mutual support, but privately, furtively, each man's fate his own."*

Commissar John Gates, who had been bringing up the rear, collected a few men and led a man-killing hike through hill country toward the Ebro. Just as they filed through a narrow valley before dawn, they spotted uniformed men on a ridge above them, one of whom shouted, "Alto!" A Spaniard named Copernico shouted back, "Alto!" The voice above called, "Quién es?" And Copernico echoed back, "Quién es?" Faint shapes collected on the brow of the hill. While others in Gates's group hurried through the valley, Copernico remained behind, playing echo to the voices on the ridge. Then he hoisted a white handkerchief and wound up the hill to surrender. He had parleyed with the enemy long enough to allow the others to escape. By the time the Nationalists had brought up a machine gun to rake the valley, Gates's band was gone. (A few months later Copernico sent a letter to the battalion, explaining that he had been taken prisoner but had managed to escape. The purpose of his letter—to collect his back pay.)* A few miles farther on they overtook a group of Lincolns led by Lieutenant Melvin Offsink, commander of First Company. He was in a bad way: his legs had given out. He lay like a beached fish while they cajoled, threatened, and cursed him to get up. But he refused. They left him where he lay. A used-up CCNY student named Ralph Wardlaw remained behind with him. Neither was ever seen again. Entirely alone, Elman Service, a University of Michigan student, wandered for many hours. About daybreak he found himself nearing a village that he assumed was many miles northeast of Corbera. On a wall he found a road sign. His heart jumped when he read CORBERA! He escaped by dashing south into the Sierra de Cavalls.

Beginning at dawn on Sunday (April 3) enemy patrols stalked remnants of the Republican Army squeezed into the ten-mile neck of land lying between Gandesa and the river. The hunted men slept in patches of prickly gorse by day and sought to find the river by night. They had no food. Sometimes local *campesinos* fed them and guided them over obscure trails to the river; but at other times, fearing reprisals, they turned them over to Nationalist patrols. The safest course was to approach a quiet farmhouse, take food at gunpoint, and depart quickly. After three days without food some men caught a rabbit but had no idea of how to eat it. "It's kicking and has fur on it. How to get it into a pot? Butchering made a hell of a mess." They ate grass and roots in an olive grove and became violently sick.* Some, guided by gut instinct, made the Ebro easily without seeing an enemy patrol, while others narrowly escaped traps many times. Another Michigan student, Robert Cummins, wandered alone and was completely lost when he spotted a Moorish cavalry patrol regarding him from a hilltop. He knew it would be death to run. He had lost his army cap in the melee and with a blanket over his shoulders, poncho-style, he prayed that the Moors would mistake him for a local *campesino*. When he covered enough distance to look back, the Moors had disappeared. Some Nationalist soldiers spotted Sydney Harris, a Chicagoan, badly wounded, lying in a hole They chambered

337

rounds into their rifles, shouting, "Russo! Russo Rojo!" Harris shouted back, "No! Americano! Dammit! Yo vivo en Chicago!" The soldiers began grinning, "Chicago? Chicago! Al Caponay!" as they mimicked gangsters shooting tommy guns. "We're tougher than you, Chicago!" Harris nodded vigorously, thinking that if he had come from Detroit, he would be dead."* If they had been Moors, Chicago would not have saved him.

On Sunday morning the Republican command prepared to blow up the bridge connecting Mora de Ebro and Mora la Nueva. What the villagers did not take across the great iron bridge, hordes of starving fugitives carried off for themselves. Newsreel cameramen had a field day. They caught on film the grubby pathos of retreat. Soldiers without rifles hugged live chickens, rabbits, and pigeons as they jogged over the bridge. A tattered man wearing captain's bars slung a ewe over his shoulder and tottered across. Boxes of dynamite lay stacked along the steel girders. Then at night there was a detonation that shook the earth, a black cloud spumed up, and the bridge toppled on its side into the yellow waters of the river. In this way the Republic prevented further enemy penetration east of the Ebro. Catalonia was safe—for the moment. But the Lincolns fleeing from the Corbera disaster found themselves stranded on the west bank. There was no other bridge within thirty miles. Luck had run out for nonswimmers.

Sandor Voros, who had crossed the river with a truck to carry ammunition back to the brigade, had been hamstrung by lethargy and red tape. Despite his pleas, cajolery, and curses, the armorers would only smile and say "Sí—Sí!" but refused to load the truck until they had completed a leisurely supper at a well-laid table. Then at the bridge a major had a fit when he learned that the truck was full of explosives. He called out the guard, who turned back Voros at rifle-point and forced him to drive back a good distance. As he watched, "impotent with rage, shame, and guilt," the bridge was blown and he was cut off from the brigade. Later in a huge high-domed dugout lit by kerosene lamps he unexpectedly met Colonel Copic striding up and down fretfully, talking to some Soviet officers in Russian. On seeing Voros he ran over. "Where is the brigade?" he demanded. "That's what I want to know," Voros replied angrily. Copic knew that the men on the far side would be hunted down like mad dogs. "We know we have lost the brigade," Voros wrote. "We glare at each other without uttering a word. Copic resents seeing me alive, my eyes full of accusation. I resent seeing him alive in his pressed uniform and shiny black puttees. It was his duty as military commander to stay with the troops. . . . I turn my back on him without a word and stride outside."* The Russian advisers with Copic had obviously exacerbated his attack of nerves. Most certainly he knew they would report his flight to the Kremlin. This time Copic would not be saved by a minor flesh wound.

On April 3 the Nationalists counted among their booty twenty truckloads of munitions and armament, a gasoline tanker, three tanks, and three motorcars. Republican prisoners numbered twenty-five hundred, including two chiefs of staff and ten staff officers.* Franco's statisticians did not publicize another stunning figure: ninety-nine Americans summarily shot *after* being taken prisoner, bringing the total of American dead in the Gandesa operation to 183. (These figures do not take into account the number of Spaniards, English, and Canadians of the XVth Brigade, nor those of the French, German, and Italian brigades also killed—in battle or as prisoners—during the three-day rout.)

Twelve days later Nationalist soldiers were filmed cavorting in the Mediterranean at Vinaroz. The Republic had been cut in two.

With enemy patrols dogging their heels, survivors stood in canebrakes along the wrong bank of the Ebro and peered at the turbulent, flooded river carrying stumps, bloated animals, and tons of yellow mud to the sea. At a few places engineers were setting up cable ferries to haul small groups across; elsewhere a man had to brave the river as best he could. The flooded condition of the river gave even strong swimmers pause—but seldom for long. They plunged in and swam, or failed to swim, across. But the Lincoln Battalion contained an unusually large number of nonswimmers (how many swimming holes existed in working-class neighborhoods?), and these men gaped helplessly at the swirling water and roamed the shore vainly seeking some way across. Many who had survived the fatigue and terror of the retreat were gunned down by patrols combing the river bank with the sporting zeal of duck hunters. (A favorite sport was chasing unarmed men into the river in order to target shoot them like bottles or tin cans as they floated downstream.)

When Commissar Gates reached the Ebro late Sunday night, his band had been reduced to a few exhausted comrades. He decided to swim over at first light. As they approached a small hut to catch some sleep, a voice inside cried out in alarm. Out came George Watt and six other Lincolns. Here all of them slept for the first time in over forty-eight hours. On Monday morning they ripped the wooden door off the hut and dragged it to the water. After stripping naked—in the excitement Gates kept his hat on—they pushed off, the four nonswimmers holding on to the door. When the current caught them, the nonswimmers panicked and furiously tried to climb onto the door, which sank. They drowned. Only Gates, Watt, and two others gained the far shore. On bare feet they crossed a field of cockleburrs and dropped, naked and exhausted, along a roadside "too beat to care." A short time later three war correspondents got out of a car—Ernest Hemingway, Herbert L. Matthews, and Sefton Delmer of the *Daily Mail*. They had rushed down from Barcelona after hearing that the XVth Brigade had been annihilated. Concluding their interview, Hemingway, who had a penchant for histrionics, shook his fist at the far shore and shouted, "You Fascist bastards haven't won yet. We'll show you!"[*7] Hemingway reported 30 wounded in Barcelona, 328 in Benicasim and Villa Paz, and 125 in Murcia. He feared massacre of the wounded and perhaps the medical staff. He, along with the Republican ambassador (in St. Jean), sensed the end had come.[*]

With countless variations the saga of Commissar Gates was repeated up and down along miles of riverbank. Lieutenant Leonard Lamb, a nonswimmer, attempted to crawl across the partially submerged skeleton of the bridge at Mora but had to turn back when he reached a yawning gap in the middle. Farther downstream he was ferried across by Spanish guerrillas. Commissar Fred Keller swam the Ebro not once but three times to show timid men how easy it was. (He had already been captured once but had knocked out his guard and run for it.) Easy for him, not them—they could not swim. Later he saw them machine-gunned on the far bank. One small group lucked upon a small skiff and pushed off. Once afloat they found the oars were missing. Paddling with their arms, they reached the other side after a five-mile ride downriver. A Midwestern student constructed a raft for his clothes and equipment and pushed off into the current. On reaching terra firma he noted with satisfaction that his gear was perfectly dry. After dressing, he let the raft drift downstream and moved "inland." A few steps later, he found himself on an island. He swam the remaining distance in full regalia.[*] Most members of the battalion, however, never reached the left bank of the Ebro.

The official count of American dead during the three weeks between March 10 and April 2, 1938, is 288, of which 55 were killed at Belchite, 50 on the retreat to Caspe, and 183 at Gandesa.[*] This includes 140 known to have been killed after being captured (41 during the retreat and 99 at Gandesa). Moreover, another 87 became POWs and were incarcerated in Franco's prisons until near the end of the war.[*] This brings the total number of American casualties to 375, but it does not include other categories such as missing in action—mainly deserters—and those wounded or hospitalized for illness during the campaign. However you tabulate it, the percentage of loss for this three-week campaign was not only the highest

---

7. A short time later, according to Delmer, Hemingway hailed an American black on the Tortosa road and gave him a sermon on how good soldiers returned to battle: "Look, Comrade. We all of us got to die once. So we may as well die clean as shitty." Temporarily inspired, the "Boogy comrade," as Hemingway called him, did turn back toward the front, but a short time later Delmer spotted him in Tortosa.[*]

suffered by the Americans fighting in Spain but also must rank as the most dev-astating defeat of an American military unit in history.

The most precarious moment for a soldier captured in battle is usually his first confrontation with an enemy angered or crazed by adrenalin during the fighting. Once securely caged, however, his chances for survival—not necessarily humane treatment—increase exponentially. The most comprehensive account of an American POW was written by Carl Geiser, a Mac-Pap commissar captured by the Italian CTV. After narrowly missing execution on the spot, he spent a year in a Nationalist prison. Internationals taken prisoner by the Italians had the best chance for survival; those by the Tercios de Extranjeros or Moors, the least, because the Nationalist tradition of executing Internationals was scrapped tem-porarily in early April 1938 so that they could be swapped for Italian prisoners held by the Republic. Spaniards serving in the International Brigades were in less danger of execution if captured. (In most instances they defended themselves by claiming they had been drafted into the International Brigades against their will and by denying any Bolshevik commitment.) For them prison terms at hard labor, not forgiveness, became their destiny—but at least they survived.

Carl Geiser's saga began on April 1, when Merriman, who had lost his run-ners, asked him to collect a light-machine-gun squad and make contact with the British or the Listers on the Alcañiz road. In a clearing Geiser found several hundred men hunched over campfires cooking breakfast. "Come on over. We're your friends," came a voice in perfect Brooklynese. Holstering his Luger (he had never been able to find cartridges for it), he led his squad over. Up close he noticed unfamiliar uniforms, then spotted shoulder patches designating the 23 di Marzo Division. Three machine guns were trained on him. The voice belonged to an Italian soldier who had once spent a year in New York as a short-order cook.

An Italian captain greeted them, "Welcome, men of the 15th! Glad to see you. You won't be needing your guns, so we will take care of them." He was astonished when he broke open Geiser's Luger. "Where's the ammo?" "Sorry, I don't have any." "Oh, that's all right," he joked. "I'll be able to get some." His eyes lit up when he saw Geiser's commissar card. He put a pistol against Geiser's spine and walked him over to the brow of a hill overlooking a Mac-Pap platoon. "This one's got ammo in it. Call those men up here." "I can't do that," Geiser said. As a hated Red commissar, he did not doubt that he would be exe-cuted: it might as well be then as later. Across the valley some Mac-Paps, sens-ing something was wrong, opened fire, and the captain pulled Geiser back.

Escorted to the rear with other brigaders, they passed masses of Italian troops in close-order formation, whippet tanks, batteries of antitank guns, and machine-gun companies, their gun carriages strapped on mules, a luxury that the Lincolns had never enjoyed. Briefly held in a walled farm enclosure, the men agreed that when interrogated they should call themselves "anti-Fascists," not Communists. All were interrogated, Geiser by a friendly Italian lieutenant, who shared his breakfast while his prisoner explained the duties of commissars. They were the equivalent of chaplains in other armies, he said. "Our main concern is with the soldiers' morale. Not only the reasons why they are fighting but also matters such as food, cigarettes, mail, and news." They had a polite debate about Fascism, which the lieutenant championed as preferable to World Communism. "Democracy leads always to Communism. Communism is the bastard stepson of democracy. . . . The Spaniards do not have an understanding that we do. We Italians must help them organize their society." He explained that ninety thousand men would be in Gandesa by noon and at the Mediterranean in two days. (In the latter prediction he was off by twelve days.) "The war will be finished very soon. It has dragged on too long already." He then expressed his appreciation for Geiser's conversation and personally conducted him back to the other prisoners. At no time had his interrogator asked any questions Geiser should not answer, nor at any time expressed any personal animosity.

A runner came from the farmhouse and called out, "Bring the Internationals!" An officer picked out sixteen of the prisoners and ordered them to stand against a wall facing a dozen soldiers with rifles, a hospital corpsman, and a priest in black gown. Edward Hodge, a Kentuckian, standing beside Geiser whispered, "This doesn't look so good." As an officer conferred with the sergeant of the firing squad, a black sedan passed by, then backed into view again. Officers ran over and saluted. After a brief parley, they returned to the firing squad, which shouldered arms and marched off. Hodge drawled, "Well, I'll be doggoned!" Back in the courtyard their guards seemed as pleased as the prisoners. They explained that the officers in the car had passed on an order that from April 1 to April 9 all Internationals would be accepted as prisoners. Late in the afternoon they heard the doomsday voice again, "Bring the Internationals!" But this time they climbed into an empty truck, which carried them under guard to the collegiate church at Alcañiz, the first leg of their journey to prison in remote Burgos province.

Spaniards serving in the Lincoln Battalion—or in the International Brigades generally—are the forgotten men of the Spanish civil war. Their histories, even the basic statistics—names, rosters, service, deaths—have never been collected. If the statistics are ever compiled, they will show that Spaniards in the Lincoln Battalion outnumbered the North Americans many times over, yet none has ever been included in the roster of the VALB (Veterans of the Abraham Lincoln Brigade). And, of course, no such veterans' group would have been tolerated in Franco's Spain, for after the war it was politically dangerous to advertise one's service with any unit of the Comintern army and even more unthinkable to seek out former comrades in arms. Franco's tribunals dealt harshly with that sort of subversion.

Very rarely do the personal narratives of American volunteers mention what befell their Spanish comrades cut off and chopped up during the melee above Gandesa. It remains for the Spaniards serving with the Lincoln and Mac-Pap battalions to chronicle their particular tragedies, but to date only Fausto Villar has done so. We left him as he plunged into a copse to escape the massacre that killed Merriman and Jim Cody. After catching his breath, he met another Valenciano and four Murcians who had also escaped the slaughter pit in the vineyard. Because Villar had been a Lincoln observer, he carried maps and told them they must bear northwest to strike the Ebro at Asco. The Murcians, "grandpa draftees" from the 1929 draft, were eager to follow any leader, but they warned him that if they met any enemy patrols, they would surrender without making any resistance. They had no quarrel with the Nationalists and merely wanted to live. In the woods the band came upon a small hut, and Villar told them they would have to rest there until nightfall. Burrowing in the straw Fausto hid his hand grenades, his maps, his fiancée's letters, and his binoculars. If captured, his best chance was to pass himself as an anonymous *quinto*. They all fell asleep immediately.*

At dusk they heard shouts outside. "Come out with your rifles over your right shoulder, but with the firing pin in your left hand, and both hands above your heads!" A squadron of enemy cavalry surrounded the hut, their carbines pointed and ready to fire. A reeducation course for the Reds began at once. A lieutenant on horseback ordered them to shout the Nationalist slogans "Arriba España" and "Viva Franco!" The officer asked whether there were officers among them. Villar feared that the Murcians, already terribly shaken, would ingratiate themselves by pointing at him, but they said nothing. Villar replied, "No, lieutenant, we are all draftees." A friendly trooper approached him and offered him a vile Spanish cigarette, a "Mataquinto" (recruit-killer), which he accepted with profuse thanks, even though he had a pack of Lucky Strikes in his pocket.

Suddenly bursts from a light machine gun concealed in the woods interrupted this parley, wounding two of the troopers. The lieutenant barked out commands to guard the prisoners and galloped off with a detachment to find the bushwhacker. One of the wounded men cursed them, "Red sons of bitches! Wait till our lieutenant gets back. Just last night you killed his brother and now

343

you ambush us." A corporal hustled them over to a sand bank and told them to pray, because after the lieutenant killed the sniper he would surely shoot them. The Murcians pleaded for mercy, enumerating their helpless children and declaring the sniper must be an American, not a Spaniard.

They heard volleys of shots in the woods, and minutes later the cavalry galloped back. The lieutenant furiously showered the prisoners with obscenities and called for volunteers to shoot "these sons of bitches." Only one of the wounded men—hit lightly in the leg—volunteered, so the lieutenant drafted others. The Murcians quit blubbering. "All that can be heard," writes Fausto, "is our terror-stricken silence." They prayed for a miracle, which came in the corporeal form of a major who rode in and demanded to know what was going on. He congratulated the lieutenant for trapping these Reds and killing the bushwhacker but admonished him for presuming to shoot prisoners without interrogating them first.

At the end of a short march they joined about a hundred other prisoners lined up in a field. Nearly all were Internationals. A captain shouted, "All Spaniards, one step forward." The entire line stepped forward as one man. He then shouted, "All Americans one step forward." No one moved. Although Villar knew that anyone could pick out most of the Americans by their size and complexion, the captain patiently went up and down the lines firing questions in Spanish at every man whom he suspected was an American: "*¿Cómo te llamas?*" Many opened their mouths and uttered Spanish names in atrocious accents and were taken aside. Those passing the first test got another, in quick time, "*¿Dónde naciste? Cuál es el pueblo más importante de la provincia donde has nacido?*" Villar noted that only a half dozen survived this test.[8] The failures were then marshaled together and taken away by soldiers carrying light machine guns. The captain assured the prisoners remaining that nothing would happen to them, unless found guilty of bushwhacking or other crimes.[9] A short time later they heard the rattle of machine guns.

For Villar, a worse scene followed. A Valencian prisoner denounced two of the remaining Americans who had passed the inquisition. The treachery of this Judas from his home province infuriated him, and he was sickened by the behavior of one of the Americans who threw himself at the feet of the captain,

8. In a letter sixty years later Villar estimated that the American captives numbered between twenty and thirty. Five or six of these survived the language test because he met them later at Orduña prison without other Spanish POWs. The remainder were shot.*

9. This captain was a Valencian nobleman, Puig de Carcer. Sixty years later, Villar, then a mechanic in Valencia, screwed up his courage and called upon the captain's family. The officer had died, but there was a touching ceremony with family members.*

begging for mercy, before being dragged away to be shot. "I nurse a repugnance toward them all," Villar wrote. "Any belief in human kindness deserts me. Evil is in the ascendancy and it might have been better had I been cut down in the morning. Cody and Merriman were lucky, for they were spared this evil time."

In the morning the prisoners underwent further interrogations by a high-ranking intelligence officer, believed to be German. He asked routine questions about the International Brigades, wanted to know whether German soldiers were in the 35th Division, and paid close attention to Villar's account of Merriman's death. Because the new recruits had only ponchos and Villar wore a greatcoat of earlier issue, the officer scrutinized the pockets, lining, and fabric for signs that an officer's patches might have been removed. Finding nothing, he returned the coat and ripped off the tripointed star from his shirt. He also confiscated a pencil bearing the three colors—red, yellow, purple—of the Republican flag, and remarked, "You can forget about the colors of that flag, for you are going to be completely defeated." Villar promised to scrape off the purple so long as he could retain the pencil, but the officer replied, "I'll hold on to it, by way of a memento of my conversation with you, for you are, like your countrymen, a proud Spaniard."

The prisoners were hustled promptly to the rear along a road jammed with Italian tanks, horses, trucks, and soldiers. Some blackshirts leveled rifles at them, pretending to shoot, as they called out, "Any Italian Reds among you?" But they smiled when guards identified the prisoners as Spaniards. They passed a field with more than a hundred cannon neatly aligned like vines in a vineyard, firing salvos at invisible targets in the Sierra de Cavalls, which smoked like a forest fire. This barrage was not returned. Villar was staggered to see all these guns arrayed in the open, without camouflage—unheard of in his army where gunners always nervously scrutinized the sky for enemy bombers. During all his service with the XVth Brigade, he had never seen more than twenty large guns at one time. An Italian lieutenant of the 23 di Marzo Division halted his cavalry squadron to talk with Fausto, who headed the line of prisoners. In a friendly way, he expressed surprise that the prisoners were either very young or very old. In pidgin Italian-Spanish he said that compared with Abyssinia, his division found the war in Spain "really heavy going." Now with the end near, they were all eager to return to Italy, and he predicted that the prisoners would also soon be freed. Before leaving he ordered his troops to fetch some full canteens for them and gave Villar a pack of Italian cigarettes—Virginia tobacco. The chat had been like "a couple of pals swapping stories, instead of the enemies we are—he the victor and I and my comrades the vanquished."

On the eastern edge of Gandesa, Villar's group was penned in the yard of an olive oil factory already filled with three or four hundred other prisoners as haggard as himself. Had he gone a few yards further toward the town center he would have seen something more horrible: something mistaken as neatly stacked sandbags forming an odd sort of palisade beside the road. These were the bodies of dozens of IB prisoners who had been marched into Gandesa and executed by firing squads. For four days they served as a putrescent reminder of how the Nationalists regarded the Army of the Comintern.* Left to himself, Villar found a rock for pillow, gathered his greatcoat around him, and dropped off to sleep. The war was no longer his affair. Flickering through his mind were recollections of the "starry-eyed American brigaders, devoted to the fine ideals of Peace and Social Justice for the dispossessed, fine men like Detro, Reiss, Merriman, Cody—all dead." Thus began his first day as a prisoner of Franco's victory. He would not sleep again as a free man until paroled, on good behavior, twenty-six months later.*

15

POSTMORTEM

On the sunny hillsides around Darmos, three miles east of the Mora bridge-head, survivors of the Lincoln Battalion set up a dreary little camp. The men had no more baggage than a band of hoboes, and during the first weeks of April their camp looked—and smelled—more like a Hooverville than a military bivouac. They had no shelter from pelting rain and pummeling sun, no fresh clothes, soap, or razors. Needing essentials, they cursed when a canteen truck from the *intendencia* came up to peddle leather wallets, shaving brushes, shoelaces, and toilet water. As though to compensate them for what they had endured (and he had avoided by deft footwork and a staff car), Colonel Copic sent the men at Darmos bottles of bad *coñac* and bad champagne. They drank Copic's "blood liquor" out of tin cans—not to celebrate but to forget. (Most certainly there would have been toasts had they foreseen that Colonel Copic, like General Gal, would soon vanish in a Moscow purge.) During the first week in April, Harry Hakim arrived with mail sacks bulging with letters and packages from home. He reeled off hundreds of names but only fifteen claimed mail. It took him half an hour to read the names, "and after the first few times nobody would say, 'Dead' or 'Missing'—we just kept silent."* Hakim's piercing cries sounded like a roll call for the dead.

Searching for stragglers, brigade trucks scoured the river roads of the east bank questioning Republican soldiers, "Quince brigada? Ha visto la quince?" For about ten days additional survivors, having just crossed the Ebro or fallen in with other units down or up the river, drifted into the Darmos campsite. No one seemed to know where the Fascists were, and few cared—so long as they were far from Darmos. "The bastards are driving to the sea," opined an American truck driver, a man with a road map and the leisure to study such matters. "If France don't come in now, we're fucked ducks. Mucho mal. Mucho fuckin' malo."* (France did briefly open its frontier for a shipment of war matériel—bought and paid for in Spanish gold—then clamped it shut again. Smelling salts to revive a dying neighbor.)

On the same day that Franco's army cut the Republic in two at Vinaroz, the Lincoln Battalion abandoned expectations that additional stragglers might drift in. A roll call netted 120 men (including Spaniards) of the approximately 400 who had gone into action at Batea two weeks before. It was the same old story, but no less tragic for that—the Lincolns had gone into battle and had been destroyed. Yet the consequences were probably worse than past disasters. Jarama, for example, had slaughtered the innocents in a legitimate battle, whereas the recent disaster had turned rational beings into frenzied animals, had broken their collective identity, and had forced them to confront the death rattle of the Republic. No survivor of that horror, that nightmare-come-true, would ever forget his utter helplessness as his world smashed to bits around him; nor would there be, as there was after the Jarama massacre, a supply of fresh replacements to repair deep psychic and physical wounds. From this time on, with few exceptions, the war in Spain was less a war to win than a disaster to avoid. John Bassett, one of the very few young Britons to join the XVth Brigade during this period, found only sick and wounded men returning to the line. A stranger greeted him, "I hear there's somebody just out from London!" Bassett snapped to and gave him the clenched fist salute, but the man "simply called me a bloody idiot and moved on without another word."* A Spanish commissar collected them for an *hora política*. When no one expressed any interest, he drew his pistol and forced them downstairs, where another commissar read an article explaining how the Republic was winning on all fronts—even when retreating. After tedious and incoherent translations into five languages, the commissar invited questions. The Britons asked in one angry roar, "When are we going home?" A lone Canadian asked for a pair of socks.*

All in all they were, as one confessed later, "a crummy bunch." Soldierly demeanor seemed washed away as completely as military discipline in the bitter waters of the Ebro. They resembled a paramilitary force badly whipped in a border incident. Gaunt, ragged, and unshaven, they might have served as models for cartoon Bolsheviks featured in the Hearst press. There was a Puerto Rican who, whenever planes came over (friend or foe made no difference), had to clamp a stick between his teeth to keep from biting his tongue in half. There was an eighteen-year-old who invariably prefaced his comments with "I'm dumb, yellow, and worthless." There was a Tennessee hillbilly who deserted every chance he got and when threatened by officers replied with head hanging, "You're sho' right, Cap' Sir. Ah'm no good. You ought to shoot me and git it over with."* There was an old miner, broken in mind and body, who sat for hours engaged in furious argument with some invisible antagonist locked in his own brain. And there was another who ran amuck, bleating hysterical wisdom, "They kill all the good guys. They're all dead and gone with their guts hanging out. I seen guys died had more room between the eyes than they got across the shoulders." With defiant impunity they debated whether they could steal a truck and hightail it to the French frontier or whether they could make North Africa in a small sailing craft. "I can sail a boat" or "I can swim" went the refrain.*

None of the three company commanders had made it back. And nobody was quite sure who commanded the battalion, or much cared. Probably it was Aaron Lopoff, a twenty-four-year-old New York writer of pulp fiction. At Batea, one short week before, Lopoff had been only an adjutant company commander; but at Darmos he found himself the highest-ranking officer. He was short, dark, and swarthy—looking like the kind of bayou chieftain who had rallied around Jean Lafitte. The men respected him—he had no truck with high-flown theories or utopian nonsense. Instead of giving them "Dear Comrade" lectures, he encouraged them to emulate the British, who were constructing *chavolas* out of cane and pine boughs to ward off the sun and rain. A spirited competition ensued—prizes of *coñac* and cigarettes went to those demonstrating the greatest architectural skill and aesthetic garnishment. "You'd have thought they were a crowd of undergraduate architects and artists that had designed them."* Otherwise "reeducation" was out of the question: men who had escaped by a hair and swum the Ebro had earned the equivalent of postdoctoral degrees in survival. They were in no mood for Marxist harangues from "comic-stars." They responded to orders like packs of snapping curs. Lopoff let them snap. The prevailing mood recalled that at Jarama after the February 27 massacre. Or worse.

The high-sounding trumpery that heralded the first volunteers in Spain had been replaced by choric jeremiads from ghosts who had narrowly escaped from Belchite, then from Caspe, then from Batea, and finally Corbera. Something had to be done to break the mood of desolation and mutterings of desertion—but what? Captain Sam Wild of the British Battalion, who had always opposed executions within the International Brigades, now warned that any man retreating without orders or arriving without weapons would be "instantly shot."* "Without weapons" was laughable. For rifles had been thrown away wholesale on the retreat and were now in such short supply at Darmos that men assigned to sentry duty had to sign one out from headquarters at the beginning of their shifts to be armed at all. A section leader of the Lincolns promenaded with a cavalry sword tucked into his belt.

There were diversions. Comrade John Little (Picallo), the New York executive secretary of the YCL, a busy man with a busier title, brought a million cigarettes for the brigade. The comrade had planned to turn over his smokes at a ceremony honoring Dave Doran, the most illustrious YCLeaguer in Spain. He had trouble finding the raw campsite of American survivors and was jarred to learn that Dave Doran had been swallowed up somewhere in the Fascist juggernaut. But even the dead could serve the Party. On returning to New York, his office produced, with astonishing speed, a forty-five-page memorial titled *The Life and Death of an American Hero*. In it Doran was canonized as a Marxist martyr. (The author, one Joseph Starobin, admired Doran enormously—but had no urge to emulate him.) Soon at rallies of the Party, the League, and the Pioneers, crowds were singing:

> Oh, we have come together
> From the forest and the plain.
> We're marching for our future—
> Hand in hand,
> With the banner—
> Of Dave Do-ran.

Not great lyrics, but what the hell!—it brought in a few bucks for the Party. This paean was never sung at Darmos. Oblivious to all the hagiolatry back home, the men enjoyed the smokes. This time, there were more than enough to go around.

Within a few days of their escape across the Ebro, Vincent Sheean of the *Herald Tribune* hitchhiked from Barcelona to see them. The arid, rolling landscape spotted with spiny plants, reminded him of New Mexico, except that it was jammed with people, refugees largely, whose overloaded carts clattered eastward. Near Falset he found brigade headquarters in a ditch equipped with telephone and met Copic, touchy about the retreat. He explained that of the 650 Lincolns at Batea, only 100 were known survivors. Everywhere Sheean found an army of shreds and tatters, subsisting on implausible hopes germinating in dry soil. Anxiety was the watchword among the Lincolns. Prospects seemed to be prefaced with "Maybe . . ." or "If only . . ." Those with a penchant for *weltpolitik* grasped at the Czechoslovakian crisis, hoping for a world war that would compel the democracies to aid Spain. They would break off personal narratives in mid-passage to ask eagerly, "What's Chamberlain going to do?" Sheean knew that Czechoslovakia was raw meat for Hitler, but not wishing to compound their despair, he said nothing about it.*

The Lincoln headquarters consisted of a smaller hole (without telephone). Nearby a few oblivious *campesinos* worked in the fields among almond trees in pink blossom. Periodically, the pastoral landscape was darkened by the wings of

Italian bombers, blunt-nosed Savoia-Marchettis, which scattered bombs nearby. During one raid someone counted fifty enemy planes—and not a single Republican fighter in the sky. An American lieutenant, who had quit law school to come to Spain, said, "When I start to make laws, I'm going to make a law abolishing airplanes. Anybody who makes an airplane or sells one or flies one will be put in jail." All concurred. Each man had a hair-raising narrative about his own encounter with a Fascist plane during the past months. A tall Tennesseean who wore, without clowning, a clown's costume so ragged that even his patches were patched, spoke for everyone when he said: "All airplanes are Fascist—until you know the difference." After the Belchite fiasco, Lincolns always looked upward like agoraphobics. "But you don't have very good view from a ditch."*

Moving on to the auto-park, Sheean found a strange assortment of vehicles, half of them belonging in junkyards and the other half in automotive museums. Because of their uncanny knack for cannibalizing abandoned vehicles or "organizing" parts from unwary outfits, the XVth Brigade normally rolled when others walked. (Mechanics used to boast that some of their rolling stock consisted of the same trucks that had carried the first Americans up to Jarama, even though no individual part, nut, or bolt was still the same.) But that period had passed. Almost everything had disappeared during the retreats. Lieutenant Louis Secundy chewed a piece of grass and grinned at squawks coming out of his telephone, demands for transport that did not exist. What he now had were "old rattletraps held together with safety pins and string." A Jewish lad of seventeen working on an engine told Sheean, "I promised my mother I would be home for Passover, but I guess I won't get there now." Brigade ambulances were no better. Both sides regularly used them as staff cars and ammo vans; therefore, they were regularly shelled and strafed. They cluttered the courtyards, punctured with bullet holes and broken glass. There was one exception—a brand-new ambulance in green-yellow camouflage stenciled, "From Workers in Barre and Montpelier, Vermont."*

A few days later Sheean revisited the Lincolns and found a semblance of order gradually returning. On the highway a sign, painted in neat red letters, read "LINCOLN BATTALION." Food had improved, for Comrade Amos Archer, a black cook, was back in the kitchen magically turning dried salt cod into crabmeat salad—or so went the story. Sheean was sitting in the command post when shouts came up from the *chavolas* as an angular figure, all legs and beard, jogged up the hill. Spanish voices shouted, "El Lobo!" The wolf had come back. He had to bend double to enter the shelter. "You built this thing plenty low," gruffed Captain Milton Wolff. "I guess you guys didn't think I was coming back."* He shook hands with the men brusquely, as though trying to ignore how glad they were to see him. He had wandered alone for four days before swimming the Ebro far downstream. He never forgave himself for burying his Party card and military carnet under rotting wood on the riverbank. The honorable course, he said, would have been to preserve his Party identity even among executioners. He regarded this "as a test he had failed."*

A few days later the Lincolns improvised a new campsite at Marsa, a village near Falset, where wounds and scars began to heal. Much of the credit for the resurrection goes to John Gates (Regenstreif), who replaced Doran as commissar of the XVth Brigade. The twenty-four-year-old son of a candy-store proprietor on Fordham Road, the Bronx, had surrendered his Regents Scholarship at City College to join the YCL as a Party organizer in the steel industry. The mayor of Warren, Ohio, once had him arrested on the courthouse steps for "making loud noise without permit" and publicly denounced him as a "young snotnose." If Wolff was wolf, Gates was terrier. He was pint-sized, wiry, and spunky. In 1933 he led a hunger march to Columbus at a time when nervous deputies with shotguns met the marchers at each county line. Eastern Ohio was Joe Dallet country, and for a time Gates, along with Gus Hall (many years later the quadrennial candidate for the U.S. presidency on the CP ticket), lived with Joe and his wife in a quasi-slum until Kitty kicked them out. In Spain, Dallet had regarded Gates as "insignificant" yet worried about his growing prestige in the Party. In particular he envied Gates's outstanding work as a battle commissar. Gates, on the other hand, wasted little thought on Dallet, whom he regarded as a poseur: "He always wore a flannel shirt, never a suit or tie—this was not the way proletarians dressed, only the way Dallet thought they dressed."*

On hearing about the Lincoln Battalion, Gates volunteered and was accepted with the proviso that he recruit four unmarried men from his district. This done, he made news as "the first volunteer from the State of Ohio." To prepare himself he took pistol lessons at the Youngstown YMCA. In transit to Spain he found ten thousand French francs in a Paris taxicab, whereby some anonymous capitalist had inadvertently made a donation to the fight against Fascism in Spain. At a time when most American volunteers went up to Jarama, Gates went to Córdoba with the 20th (International) Battalion, an experimental group composed of men from twenty different nationalities. The idea was to see whether chauvinism, always a problem in the International Brigades, could be rooted out by a melting-pot technique. It failed in much the same way that the Tower of Babel failed, but Gates, who became fluent in Spanish, soared to acting brigade commissar with the temporary rank of lieutenant colonel. So within a few months in Spain, he had catapulted higher in the International Brigades than all other Americans except Steve Nelson. (In a letter to Kitty, Dallet wrote unhappily of their former tenant's metamorphosis. "This is a funny place. Some of the most prominent people back home . . . turn out badly here, while some insignificant people like Johnny Gates rise to the top.")* When Bill Lawrence, the American CP representative at Albacete base, returned home in early autumn of 1937, Gates took his job. But he hated such piddling work—fending off disgruntled veterans who whined to the same tune, "When is it my turn to go home? Bill Lawrence promised me . . ." He denied all requests for repatriation except for physical disability. In his book a man served the Party, the Party did not serve the man. The men disliked, but did not despise him.

Gates abhorred desk work. In February 1938, he sloughed off his rank and privileges and joined the XVth Brigade during the Segura de los Baños campaign. Doran assigned him to drive a mule—its pannier filled with explosives—up a hillside under shellfire. (It is uncertain whether Doran was trying to test his rival or to kill him.) During the retreat from Belchite, Gates took charge of stragglers along the Azaila road. Later, during the final hours at Caspe, Doran ordered a group under Gates to block the enemy advance until instructed to withdraw. For twelve hours Gates waged a back-to-the-river fight. No retirement order ever came from Doran. In the nick of time he retreated on his own authority, purportedly in charge of the last American unit to leave Caspe. Later, when the Lincolns at Gandesa debated whether to break out of the trap in daylight or wait until dark, Gates sided with Wolff, whom he respected as a military leader even though he regarded him as "a greenhorn in politics."*

For all reporters converging on Marsa, the big question—what happened to Merriman and Doran?—met strained silence. No one seemed to know or wanted to talk about it. John Gates canvassed the survivors in order to piece together a logical sequence of events during that traumatic night of April 2–3 but found that while everyone had a personal story of panic and survival, none had a clear memory of time and place. "If there was any eyewitness of what happened it would have been described by those people. It never has been," he wrote.* And Doran appears to have completely vanished. Villar, who had endured the crossfire with Merriman in the vineyard, was not on hand to tell his story. If he had been, perhaps he would have been silenced: after all, it was ignominious to conceive that the two most famous American officers in Spain had not perished heroically but had been gunned down like terrified animals without firing a shot in return. In battalion records both are listed as "missing in action," a rubric meaning killed or captured. If the latter, they must have been executed, because Franco press officers would surely have publicized such a prestigious catch. "We felt the enemy did not know whom they had killed."*

Without any evidence, the Department of State wrote to Marion Merriman about a rumor that her husband had been seen in the Jesuit Commercial College of Bilbao, although Burgos officialdom would neither confirm nor deny this.* Theories proliferated—including a fantastic tale, circulating among the men, that they had run away to Albacete—but the truth is that their fate is as deep a mystery today as it was seven decades ago. Four Spanish historians have written books about the International Brigades, but despite their access to official records and archives, they have found nothing.

The "official" account by ALB historians—published in *The Lincoln Battalion* (1939) by Edwin Rolfe, a Lincoln veteran, and canonized by repetition— narrates that Merriman and Doran were leading Wolff's group as they groped their way toward the Corbera road about midnight of April 2–3. This would have occurred about fourteen hours after Villar's account of being pinned down by a murderous crossfire with Merriman and Cody. As we have seen, after the machine gunners quit, enemy cavalry ranged across the vineyard sabering anyone found alive. Some men at the rear of Merriman's assault team like George Watt and Konrad Schmidt fled back up the hill to join Wolff's group. While it seems unlikely that Merriman could have survived that slaughter and joined Wolff, it is not impossible. Although Schmidt had seen Merriman only once and was quite far away in the column, he does add a puzzling detail. Watching the slaughter from above, he saw the "battalion commander" with an adjutant rise up and race toward a hut, chased by bullets from the machine gunners but both reaching the hut. (Could this have been Villar?) Later he "heard" that both were captured in the hut.[*1] As for Cody, we know that his body was found and identified because his name appears with those of other Internationals on a nearby commemorative marker.[2]

Unaccountably, Rolfe minimized the devastation of the morning attack. We learn only that "the Americans swept forward in a broad front" until "stopped dead by batteries of machine guns on all sides," when they "retired section by section to a small hill farther north."* Retiring section by section bespeaks control, not collapse. Since Rolfe was not with the Lincolns during this period, where did he obtain his information? As an editor of the brigade magazine, the

---

1. After regaining the hilltop, Schmidt joined the one of the desperate bands of Lincolns trying to snake through enemy encampments in order to reach the Ebro. Captured on April 4, he was incarcerated with other American prisoners, who may have had knowledge of Merriman's capture at the hut, but unfortunately he gave no particulars.

2. Erected by XVth Brigade sappers in August 1938, this small monolith, which escaped destruction by Franco adherents, bears the names of six Americans of the XVth, including Merriman, Doran, and Cody.*

Volunteer for Liberty, he interviewed the survivors of Wolff's cohort who had watched the slaughter in the vineyard below them. Among these was an intelligence officer identified only as "Ivan," whose version of the attempted breakout became canonized by repetition. After nightfall Ivan led a group of "about thirty-five men," including Merriman and Doran, single-file on a path toward Corbera. At about midnight they reached either the Corbera-Villalba or the Corbera-Gandesa road—and prepared to go across. Rolfe writes, "What happened was so sudden and startling that *few of the survivors' stories afterward jibed*" (my emphasis). Unwittingly they "marched into a force of German and Spanish troops." (For the record, neither at Gandesa nor anywhere else in Spain did the Lincolns ever encounter German "troops.") In "a weird hysterical voice" a sentry yelled "Rojos! Rojos!" and fired into the group. Ivan and Brandt, the Party representative, "made a mad break for the hill opposite," while Merriman and Doran rushed "whether they knew it or not, toward the insurgents." Ivan heard "a series of shots ring out of the darkness" and finally "Manos arriba!"* At that point Merriman and Doran disappear from Republican and Nationalist records. There exists only an intriguing note in the daily operations log of the 1st Navarre Division for April 2–3, which reports many Republican dead and prisoners, including the chiefs of the XIth and XIIIth International Brigades. The XVth may have been mistaken for the XIIIth, which was not on the ground.*

In 1983, at the request of Marion Merriman, a University of Nevada researcher interviewed "Ivan," or John Gerlach (Rajcovic), a Yugoslav who had immigrated as a child to Detroit and settled in California. His story differed somewhat from the one he told half a century before. In the later account when the guard yelled, "Reds! Reds!" Gerlach ran back twenty-five yards to where Merriman and Doran waited with the column. Gerlach cried out "Bob, Dave, come this way, follow me. I know the way!" Looking over his shoulder he saw them "beginning to follow." Reaching a high drop-off on the far side of the road Gerlach grabbed a branch and eased himself down with Joe Brandt, "a young private on the brigade staff," right behind him. (Both Rolfe and Gerlach pretend that Brandt was only a minor player, whereas as the CP representative in the battalion he possessed the power of overriding any command. Or as Gates put it, "He was a runner for Wolff but he was Wolff's boss.")* They heard rifle fire but saw no sign of Merriman or Doran. Then Gerlach *thought* he heard the Spanish cry, "Manos arriba!"*

Rolfe was an honest man, but as a loyal Communist he presumably reported what had been authorized by Brandt and others, eager to downplay the Gandesa catastrophe. On the other hand, Gerlach's credibility as an objective witness

leaves much to be desired. A protégé of Markovicz, he attended KUNMZ (the indoctrination school for foreigners) in Moscow in preparation for a major role in the CP. With Stalin he shared a view that historical "truth" must necessarily serve the ends of political utility. History was not a record of what had happened but a script for what ought to have happened and what would happen after editorial surgery. In an undated letter after the war Gerlach argued that veterans ought to "embellish" their stories because "all history is embellished. All literature is total embellishment and wholly a figment of the writer's imagination." He went on to give examples of how military reports in the Spanish war could have been improved by embellishment. For instance, during a stalemate in the first battle of Belchite, Copic ordered him to inform Captain Amlie that "if he doesn't move, I'll have him shot, the S.O.B." Gerlach delivered the message, but writes of it, "Now today I have no recollection of what he said to me or what I said [to him]. Posterity shall have to *embellish*" (my emphasis).*
Perhaps his masterstroke of "embellishment" was a tale cooked up with Brandt.³ (There are other reasons why Gerlach would have been eager to please his superiors in the Party. During the Caspe retreat he lost some valuable records and told Jim Bourne, the personnel commissar, of his fear "that he might be shot for it. Seemed rather serious and worried about it." Adding to his troubles, at this time an order came down from Corps level to investigate him as a Trotskyite.)*

The rank and file remembered the whole campaign as a botch and wasted little time on the loss of higher-ups like Merriman and Doran. A group of half-naked survivors who reached the safe bank of the Ebro put together jigsaw scraps of memory. "Cut off and surrounded again. . . . Went to sleep only to wake up to fire from three sides. . . . Merriman decided to pull out and move down toward Gandesa. That's the last I saw of *him*." "Or Doran, for that matter," added a rookie, "I only saw Doran once. He made us a short speech. Said any man who lost a rifle would be shot." They laughed.* To date, Fausto Villar's account of Merriman's death is the most objective.

The Ebro front, except for random bombing and artillery fire, was dead. The Nationalist offensive had swerved south toward Valencia. The Republicans north of the river were far too weak to attempt anything beyond counting their blessing—the presence of a wide river as a moat keeping the enemy at bay. Several times every day a preposterously huge railroad gun poked its snout out of a

---

3. Hemingway interviewed "Ivan" a few days after the breakout, and his report in *New Republic* (April 27, 1938) perhaps served as an endorsement of Gerlach's tale.

railway tunnel near Marsa. It fired an angry salvo at some target miles beyond the river and then ducked back into its hole again. The gun, which fired a missile about the heft of a small Ford, was a blustering museum piece, but its aimless belch signaled, however crazily, that the old Republic still had a bang or two left in her. Even after hospitals and labor camps had been swept clean of convalescents and skulkers, the Lincoln Battalion numbered only two hundred Americans. "Maybe we'll be sent home," went the latest refrain. To bring the battalion up to paper strength, 250 more Spanish *quintos*—all between sixteen and eighteen years old—arrived in Marsa. With zealous illogic George Watt, the new Lincoln commissar, explained to the Americans that they had to realize the goal envisioned by Comrade Dimitrov—the foreign soldiers were to act as instructors and models for Spanish volunteers. (The men were supposed to ignore the obvious—that *quintos* were replacing Internationals only because the pool of foreign volunteers had dried up.) The recruits, Watt warned, might lack "political conviction," but only because they had been denied "an opportunity for education." Old-timers must assist them in understanding what it means to be an anti-Fascist crusader. "We will be their comrades, their brothers, their teachers, and their friends." They might as well have added mothers because "many are so young they cry when reprimanded."* Nothing much came of it. The Americans remained aloof while the *quintos* retained a "residue of distrust."* This was the rainy season, and the only training they got was how to hide from airplanes. At the sound of any airplane they dived into their holes like little prairie dogs. What all this came to, when purged of propaganda, was that Americans were expected to explain to Spaniards why Spaniards should fight for their own country. (No doubt at that very moment, on the far shore of the Ebro, Nationalist officers were explaining to moon-faced peasant boys why *they* had to fight for their country.) The Lincolns would have agreed with George Orwell's observation a year before that the Spanish conscripts were "so ignorant that they did not know to which party they belonged."*

The *quintos* were mainly soft adolescents of the late-acne phase who had been dragooned into manhood and stuffed into uniforms. (They arrived with neither weapons nor training in their use.) They were shorter in stature than many American children half their age. Along with their regulation kit, they brought cardboard suitcases and gunnysacks stuffed with the sundries thrust upon them at going-away festivities: cheap eau de cologne, handknit sweaters, wads of writing paper, little bottles of multicolored ink, bags of nuts, and even live rabbits. For them the ongoing crusade was little more than a homeless interlude made bearable by playing *fútbol* with bundles of rags, singing doleful songs of lost love, and—among those who could write—sending countless letters home. They enjoyed feeling and firing weapons—Hollywood B's had taught them that much—but in the style of kids in noisy sham battles. Even though officially absorbed into squads and *pelotones* (platoons) with the Americans, they kept to themselves in xenophobic enclaves, no more interested in crossing cultural or linguistic gaps than the Americans themselves were. What, really, did either group have to say to the other? What link could be forged that would connect the worlds of Youngstown and Xativa? Unlike Republican militia earlier in the war, the best of which had been products of rigorous indoctrination by trade-union organizations in urban centers, the present crop of *quintos* were mainly *rurales,* uprooted from uncomplicated environments and transplanted into a politically convoluted war. What did they care about the Czechoslovakian crisis, the theories of Carlos Marx, the dangers of Trotskyite deviationism, or the role of the Spanish monarchy? Why should they be grateful to the *extranjeros* who had come to Spain in order to teach them how to kill other Spaniards? They made no trouble, they listened politely while commissars tried to teach them the ABC's of dialectical materialism, and they raised no disturbing questions, probably because the issues were not important enough in their minds to justify any. Given time and a few battles, some—if they lived—would acquire the usual willingness to kill an "enemy" in the timeless way of soldiers in any army or epoch. What they actually were (though no one liked to talk about it) was *carne de cañón.* Behind fatalistic masks, the *quintos* sensed this. Meanwhile, like obedient sons they sent their money and tobacco home to their parents. Of battle, killing, and death they had no inkling. An American father of two preadolescents back in Brooklyn remarked, "It is shit that such babies should have to know this sort of thing."*

Back in the States the CP had stopped recruiting for Spain, and U.S. consuls at French ports no longer bothered to ferret out Americans bound for Spain. On March 2, 1938, for instance, only four men arrived on the *Manhattan,* compared with 101 who had debarked from the *Paris* eleven months earlier. In fact, the FALB was now trying to raise funds to bring home the wounded.[4] It was no coincidence that the CPUSA stopped recruiting just when the USSR began withdrawing its aircraft, tanks, and munitions. In order to send the Lincolns home, the New York organizations would need every dollar they could raise, unless

---

4. Wounded men had been returning home since Jarama, usually with the financial aid of an independent Paris group chaired by Louis Bromfield called the Emergency Committee for American Wounded from Spain. When this source dried up, the FALB openly solicited funds for wounded veterans. On July 3, 1938, the first publicized group of wounded Lincolns, eighteen men, arrived in New York.

the U.S. government could somehow be finagled into picking up the tab.[5] They did send, for booster purposes, six Jarama vets back to Spain, including one-eyed Joe Gordon. These were widely photographed drinking wine from a *purrón*, smoking foul "antitanks," and bucking up the home front. Asked how he thought the war would turn out—a tabooed, defeatist query—Gordon gruffed, "We're here, aren't we? And we certainly don't think we'll be on the losing side." He went on to say that he got sick and tired of playing war games with salt cellars and toothpicks in a beanery behind the FALB office and he would've come back even if it meant stowing away on a garbage scow.* But these six Jarama veterans were the last sere leaves of a dead branch.[6] The truth was that Spain no longer pricked the guilty conscience of the American Left. The avant-garde of the Party had started talking about the possibility of forming an international brigade to fight the Germans in Czechoslovakia or the Japanese in China. Fortunately for a fresh crop of college idealists, the Soviet Union never evinced the slightest interest in such ventures. In fact, the Comintern was itself soon dissolved.

The "last volunteer"—to use the tag of battalion publicists—stands out as perhaps the most atypical of all American volunteers. At twenty-three, he wore horn-rimmed glasses, had diplomas from Andover and Harvard, and was a son of author Ring Lardner. With press credentials from the *Herald Tribune*, James Lardner traveled to Spain as a junior war correspondent. He toured the Ebro front and interviewed General Lister, but when his dispatch was edited to the bone, he sought more meaningful commitment. Within a week he showed his friends Ernest Hemingway and Vincent Sheean a list of nineteen reasons for joining the International Brigades, methodically divided into two headings: first, why he wished to aid the Republic, and second, what this experience would do for him. Sheean figured that the brigade would accept him in order to cash in on the Lardner connections and would then put him in some safe spot

---

5. Not as far-fetched as it sounds. In April 1938, when it appeared that the Republic was on the verge of collapse, Secretary Hull, fearing that several thousand Americans would be imprisoned and/or executed by the Nationalists, notified his *chargé* at Paris that the cruiser *Raleigh* was standing by at Villefranche and would evacuate *all* Americans from Spain, even the troublesome Lincolns, in the event of a sudden Nationalist victory. When the Republic held, the *Raleigh* went elsewhere.*

6. Although the FALB sent no more volunteers, a few individuals continued to trickle into the Lincoln Battalion, making their own arrangements. Probably the last to try were seven Americans (four from Brooklyn) who were jailed at Le Havre on August 23, 1938, for having stowed away on the *Normandie*. Their pooled resources included US$17.85 American, 3 Spanish pesetas (Republican), 30 French centimes, and 5 Estonian kroons. After jail terms, they were deported back to the United States.*

in the rear. Hemingway, on the other hand, tried to dissuade him, arguing that enlistment at such a late period seemed wholly useless. "You can't get a story there. The only story you could get would be to get killed, and that'll do you no good. I'll write that." "Not half as good a story as if you get killed," countered Lardner, "and *I'll* write that!"*[7] (Privately Hemingway said of Lardner, "a nice kid but he is awfully gloomy to make a soldier.")* Even Martin Hourihan, on his way home after nine months in the hospital, tried to talk him out of it. Laughing at these objections, Lardner bought khaki trousers and a leather windbreaker (the Republic was short on uniforms and he felt guilty about taking one) and signed on. He left Sheean his traveling library—*Fighting Planes of the World,* a stack of Lenin's pamphlets, an oversize Shakespeare, and a sheaf of Republican songs. Sheean detected no symptoms of false heroics. Apparently Lardner distrusted the emotionalism of the Republic even as he shared its emotions. To his mother he wrote, "This is a most exclusive army. It has taken me twelve days of going from person to person and office to be where I am." He included a lopsided list of reasons for enlisting—the first was "fascism is wrong and must be exterminated." A secondary one was "there is a girl in Paris who will have to learn that my presence is not necessary to her existence."*

Opting for the artillery, Lardner was sent to an old factory building in Badalona housing many *inutiles de guerra,* men unfit for frontline service because of thievery, chronic demoralization, or habitual cowardice. An English veteran waiting reassignment to the front recalled it as "a filthy bloody place, minus mattresses or blankets, just boards," and jammed with "a collection of real lousy, useless hopeless bastards." Old tin cans served as eating utensils for the two servings of garbanzos and a tiny hunk of bread per diem. The mood of this hellhole was so defeatist that "the government would be better off shipping the whole lot home."*

For four days Lardner lay on a dirty straw pallet listening to them cursing Doran, Merriman, and Wolff. He learned that only one artillery unit existed, the John Brown Battery, but no one seemed to know where it was.[8] He

---

7. After the disastrous retreat from Belchite, Hemingway knew the Republic was through. On March 30—two days before the Gandesa massacre—he called on Ambassador Claude Bowers to urge the immediate evacuation of all American volunteers in hospitals. According to his canvass, these numbered 30 in Barcelona, 382 in Benicasim and Saelices (Villa Paz), and 125 in Murcia, all of whom could be evacuated from Alicante in six days. He feared that if the Nationalists won a rapid victory, Moors would slaughter these men in their hospital beds.*

8. The John Brown Battery, trained at Almansa, saw limited action on the Toledo front but never was attached to the Lincoln Battalion. Its ordnance consisted of a Krupp gun (vintage 1870) that absorbed its recoil by backing up an inclined track. At first spurned by volunteers, it later became a sought-after assignment, regarded as a safe berth.*

deserted—to the front. Stopping off at the Hotel Majestic for a bath in Sheean's tub, he left his tinned food and cigarettes. When Sheean suggested that these might be more welcome among the Lincolns, Lardner said, "I don't want to go bearing gifts."* Purging his old self, he departed for Marsa, where he asked no favors and got none. A very impressed George Watt, the Lincoln commissar, told Wolff, "You know who he is—Ring Lardner's son." But Wolff, egalitarian to the bone, retorted, "Yeah, I know! What d'you expect me to do about it? Put him in Company Three." For a time he was an odd fish: he did not swear, he blanched at obscene marching songs, he kept his nose in a book, and he lacked the common touch. Another intellectual, John Murra, a Romanian American, took him aside and gave him a crash course in proletarian mores. Soon Lardner was singing with the others, and the men realized his shyness was not snob-bery.* To Sheean's surprise, for there were "some prize roughnecks in the brigade," the men accepted him. Though more accustomed to lawn parties than to bivouacs, he never complained, behaved like a model soldier, and made corporal on his own merits. Party publicists capitalized on Lardner's presence in the battalion, for here was an all-American youth from a famous and wealthy family—a perfect Popular Front feature story.[9] They would later discover that while a wounded Lardner merited a notice in Big-City dailies, a dead Lardner could fetch a column.

The four months following the Gandesa tragedy were as quiet and uneventful as the four months after the Jarama massacre. On May Day the Mac-Paps tried to stir up apathetic Fascists on the far bank of the river by floating little rafts downstream bearing signs like "LOS ESPAGNOLES NUNCA SERA ESCLAVOS DE FASCISMO!" But they got a better result by shouting obscenities across the river, punctuated with great farting sounds from a bugle.* In the open fields outside Marsa, May Day took on a county-fair atmosphere as the *quintos* won most of the contests in grenade-throwing, infiltration (crawling without using knees), and wheelbarrow races (of questionable utility in combat). The winners carried away boxes of Sunshine crackers and Hershey bars. When a trade-union delegation arrived to meet International soldiers, it expressed surprise that most of the XVth Brigade were Spaniards. With the visitors came a busload of *Mujeres Libres* (Free Women)—but none lived up to their name. "All they

---

9. The *Volunteer for Liberty*, for example, twice featured stores about James Lardner, once when he enlisted and again when he was promoted—heady stuff for a mere corporal. Asked why he had joined the Lincoln Battalion, Lardner replied, "The cause is so plainly a worthy one that the question which the young men of the world should be putting to themselves is what justification they have for staying out of the struggle."*

wanted was to talk politics," grumbled a disappointed American. (A bathing-suit snapshot of one of these maidens, a little on the meaty side, later appeared in the *Volunteer for Liberty,* the closest thing to a pinup ever to appear in its chaste proletarian pages. Yet even this photograph served a political purpose, for the young girl was "defying enemy aviation as she takes a dip in the blue Mediterranean.")

Late in May the brigade was suddenly called up, issued rifles (still not enough to go round), and trucked north to the Balaguer sector near Lerida, where the Republic had launched a campaign to secure a hydroelectric station supplying Barcelona with power and to relieve the pressure on the Valencia front. They were held in reserve to mop up enemy pockets of resistance after the enemy line had caved in. For a time they camped in a fine forest of pines, where two platoons of *quintos* tried out their new 7.65 mm rifles on a solitary squirrel, which escaped unharmed. When rains came, they moved into big cattle barns on the outskirts of Fonderella, where they had a good time horse-laughing and singing bawdy songs like "The Ball of Kerrimuir" taught them by Scots of the British Battalion. Their bitterness began to seep away. Artillery rumbled at the front, but it was twelve miles away, and they moved no closer. Things seemed to be looking up. It was said that the French were going to open their frontier for war matériel, and they were cheered by the report of a Falangist radio announcer who argued that it would be better to join the Reds than to submit to Italian or German domination.* Abruptly the offensive quit, and they returned to Marsa. Odds went higher that the Lincolns would never again be pitched headlong into battle. But John Gates, brigade commissar, scotched that rumor. "I hear men say that the XVth Brigade will never go into action again. But I am here to tell you that it will . . . and when it does, it will maintain its tradition of sacrifice and courage."* Gates's arm was as long as Doran's, but the fist was gloved.

June and July were torrid, long months of monotonous waiting—whether for battle or repatriation no one knew. Replacements continued to trickle in, a less-than-happy crew leached from the dregs of noncombatant units—quartermasters, truck drivers, clerks, hospital orderlies. Among them came two prominent Jarama veterans: Arthur Madden, once Lincoln co-commissar-elect with Stember after the mutiny, and Ed Royce, formerly a company commander during the February 27 fiasco. Madden had been safely squirreled away in the auto-park detachment and let no one forget his heavyweight status in battalion politics. Angered by his demotion to foot soldier, he "complained all the time" because his applications for repatriation had been repeatedly turned down. Scooping up Royce as a last-ditch replacement was a great mistake, for he had never recovered from a mental breakdown after the battle. He blamed himself for the loss of his men. Given a desk job at Albacete, he had been jailed many times for alcohol and drug abuse.*

Not a breath of air stirred in Chavola valley, where volunteers stripped down and lay baking in their reed huts, fighting a losing battle against flies. Dysentery reached epidemic proportions, and the perennial jokes—"I could hit a dime at ten meters"—lost their humorous edge.* Mail was irregular, men wrote insulting marginal notes for the censor, food worsened (there was little bread in those days—most wheat grew in Nationalist zones), and tobacco substitutes ranged from almond leaves to asthma cigarettes. Folks at home were instructed to send cigarettes in their letters, some of which carried caustic messages like "Censor, please put these cigarettes back in the envelope after you have read the letter."

The brothels along the beach at Tarragona did a booming business now that the front was so near, but only hard-liners got passes, for too often these became one-way tickets for deserters. Trusted Party cadres, however, easily arranged for Barcelona leaves (often under the blanket of "official business"), even though most brought back unsettling stories about how far the city had departed from the revolutionary paradise of a year before, when even bootblacks had their union with their boxes painted in the Anarchist colors—red and black. Now Barcelona edged toward starvation. The city was living on chickpeas and dried cod. An ambulance driver remembered how "enormous cakes of dried cod dropped on the pavement from lorries in a cloud of mixed dust and cod-powder was enough to destroy the appetite of anyone not on the verge of starvation."* In working-class districts queues for bread and olive oil stretched hundreds of yards, although in private restaurants and hotels wealthy refugees and black marketeers could stuff themselves with delicacies at fantastic prices. Tipping, that dependable index of class demarcation, had returned to Barcelona, along with pastry shops with shocking prices. Bankers no longer had to play proletarian with open-neck shirts and blue boiler suits. The Revolution, having paid a brief visit, was long gone.

Harold Smith, a veteran Lincoln officer and dedicated Communist, had a meal at a restaurant catering to Jewish refugees from Germany, and became enraged at the clientele. Spain had given them refuge, he wrote, "But do you think those bastards would do what one would expect any man to do—join in the fight? The majority I have seen are too busy with their speculating, with their jewelry trading, with their black market transactions, to care. . . . If I had my way I'd run this whole kit and caboodle out—and if you did they would probably squawk to high heaven that they were persecuted. They won't become Spanish citizens because that would make them liable to the draft, and some I know definitely are gypping the Associated Jewish charities."* At the same establishment, Jim Lardner reported the price of a meal was thirty pesetas—three days' pay for an International—and "way over the heads of the wage-earners, and I think, only semi-legal." That was still a bargain, for another volunteer paid sixty pesetas for a poor meal in a cheap hotel.* When four wounded veterans homeward bound tried to enter a crowded upscale restaurant, the maître d' examined them from head to toe before repeating, "No hay pan" as they tried to push inside. The veterans remembered when the city shone in the ambiance of revolution and equality. "Barcelona had changed," wrote one of them bitterly. "The Party had done its work well. Down with the ragged and the hungry! Up with the bourgeoisie."*

Each day from battalion headquarters near Marsa, a red-stucco villa with an imposing fifteenth-century cow barn, the orders of the day came down relentlessly—target practice, maneuvers across hot terraces, scaling devilish mountains. But in the stifling heat of midsummer Catalonia, it was difficult to carry out such orders. Herbert L. Matthews of the *Times* came down from Barcelona in mid-June to watch three companies attacking a fourth, which was holed up in the Falset railroad tunnel. While the men sweated up terraces, he stayed below with Wolff and the battalion staff, who guessed that the tunnel would be captured, but not before chow time—which would mean cold mule and potatoes. All agreed it would be a Pyrrhic victory, at best.* For Pandit Nehru's visit the brigade put on a gunnery show: a Welshman firing a Maxim cut down a fig tree three hundred yards away.* Such Maxim demonstrations could be lethal. In the British Battalion, one veteran reported, "One poor bastard got a bullet at point-blank range right through his guts and another one through an arm and a leg." The first man bled to death.*

On June 7, Colonel Vladimir Copic surrendered his command and departed suddenly. (On May 8, General Walter had turned his 35th Division over to a Spanish successor and returned to the USSR.) Earlier, in a speech commemorating Doran, Copic had taken a swipe at the Lincolns for "refusing to obey military procedures as to saluting and discipline." Although he complimented Doran, insiders claimed that Copic had never forgiven him for breaking into his private hoard of edibles to feed the rank and file at Caspe. He vanished into the maw of the USSR as though he had never existed. The new brigade commander, Major José Antonio Valledor, was a veteran of the bitter Asturias fighting, where he had been captured and subsequently imprisoned in Pamplona. There he helped to engineer a massive prison-break and escaped to France. Quietly efficient and unhistrionic, he was "less an opera star" than Copic, although most Americans were barely aware of his existence. Since the baton of command had passed to a Spaniard, the title "International" became even more a misnomer.

Relations between Americans and Spaniards had worsened. Men groused that funds sent by the FALB for provisions were now distributed among the entire Republican Army, while private parcels from home were often broken open and looted. On lucky days they got only two cigarettes per man; on other days they smoked dried hazelnut leaves. News seeping down that all Internationals in Spain—including Germans and Italians serving with Franco—might be withdrawn nourished both hope and despair. How could men go into battle if withdrawal was imminent? Looking around him, Alvah Bessie, usually a resolute optimist, found "low morale, constant griping, expressed homesickness and disgust with all things military and Spanish. . . . We have only the worst of the International volunteers left, with few exceptions—guys who have been sent up from labor battalions, hospitals, misfits, and inutiles. Their presence widens the breach between us and the Spanish kids, who seem to have lost their early respect and enthusiastic friendliness for us." Among their leaders Gates was too hard-boiled, Watt hopelessly young and naive, and Joe Brandt, the Party representative, at best "an ungracious personality, a petty bureaucrat." Once the International Brigades had been a beacon shining all over the world, but now "we are a spent force, actively disliked in certain quarters, distrusted in others, considered indifferently in others." Only the German units commanded respect—for their discipline.*

To restore the revolutionary mission of the Lincoln Battalion, Commissar George Watt (a wiry towhead who had "got politics" in the way that other people "got religion") threw his support behind an elitist military movement in the Army known as "Activism." Its purpose was to sex-up political and military commitment through pep rallies and an Activist Congress through which "the military and political work of our brigade may reach new high levels of combat efficiency." To become a full-fledged Activist, one went through a Tom Sawyer-ish ceremony in which he vowed to obey ten commandments, including "Not to rest as long as there remains a soldier who is not an activist" and "To struggle without rest against pessimists and provocateurs."* Some of the *quintos* rallied to the standard of *el activismo* with the hebetic zeal of pledges to a college fraternity, but most Americans referred to the movement as "scoutmasterish." While the men respected Watt as a brave soldier, as commissar they thought his political tic bordered on mysticism. They dubbed him "Kilowatt" and made up a rhyme about Watt not knowing "what's what." Some men needled him by pretending they had formed an anti-activist order known as FONIC (Friends of the Non-Intervention Committee)—the brainstorm of Morris Mickenberg—

dedicated to the immediate withdrawal of all foreigners from Spanish soil, beginning with themselves. Scribbled on walls and etched on trees, FONIC came to resemble the eponymous KILROY of World War II. Yet all this was less subversive than good-humored. Their favorite song of this period had nothing to do with proletarian fervor, laments for dead comrades, or allusions to the wretched of the earth. Curt and nasty, it was sung with mingled curses and laughter.

> March-ing, march-ing, march-ing,
> Always fucking well march-ing.
> God send the day—
> When we will—
> Fucking well march no more!

On their good days they could be a battalion of Falstaffs.

16

IN THE PENAL COLONIES

After the Aragon offensive, which had reached the sea and cut the Republic in half, the Nationalists were rightly optimistic and exultant. On April 20, 1938, from his administrative headquarters in Burgos, General Franco announced that "the war is won." (El Caudillo had made the same announcement when the Alcázar at Toledo was relieved, when Malaga was captured, when Bilbao fell, and when his army retook Teruel. This time he was closer to the mark.) Two days later, under a press release titled "A Tower of Babel," Burgos released a count of XVth Brigade prisoners captured during their recent offensive. These included 141 British, 49 Americans, 21 Canadians, 18 Cubans, 12 Argentines, 4 Filipinos, 1 Mexican, 1 Icelander, and 1 Chinese. No names posted. The announcement came as a surprise. In the past, the Nationalists had usually denied the presence of Internationals in their prisons, because admitting it was tantamount to assuming some sort of responsibility for their lives. However, since the generalissimo considered the war practically over, he doubtless planned to barter these captives for diplomatic recognition by their native countries. The prisoners had become commodities whose market value would be tallied only after long periods of diplomatic haggling.

Meanwhile, in the United States, news of the Nationalist communiqué concerning American boys in Spanish jails attracted headlines. The *Daily Worker*, with no specific information to go on, ran its customary lurid exposés of "Fascist atrocities in the concentration camps of Franco's Spain." These made provocative reading, though barren of relevant details—such as how many men were there, who they were, and how they might be released. Months passed, but Burgos remained close-mouthed. Since no diplomats or war correspondents had seen the men, no hard evidence existed. Whenever the subject came up, the Nationalists hedged, probably because they had not decided what their commodities were worth. As ever, the U.S. Department of State refused to enter the imbroglio, because it would only further entangle the gossamer threads of

Non-Intervention. Charles S. Bay, a U.S. consul who was negotiating with Franco about the purchase of American school buses to transport tourists to lukewarm battlefields, did come to San Pedro de Cardeña on June 24 to speak with twenty American prisoners hand-picked by the warden. He reported that the captives were in "good condition," their food was "plain and nutritive," their hospital facilities were "adequate" even though latrines and lavatories were "distinctly insufficient." According to him "the only criticism [from the men] was about permission to write letters for money."* Based on his report, conditions at the prison, while not comfortable, were far from wretched. While the presence of Americans serving in a Spanish army had been a minor headache for the Department, the presence of Americans in a Spanish prison had the makings of a major migraine. If the captives were repatriated, the federal courts might be forced to prosecute them under the law forbidding American citizens from serving in a foreign army. On the other hand, if the authorities refused to prosecute, then the American Right, allied with the Catholic Church, would raise a storm. Better to ignore the problem.

The person most responsible for publicizing the plight of the prisoners and for oiling the machinery of repatriation proved to be William B. Carney, the *New York Times* correspondent in Nationalist Spain. It was ironic that "General Bill," as he was called by his detractors—and there were many—was regarded by most Lincolns as a Fascist mouthpiece.[1] In truth, he did favor the Nationalist side, especially because of its support of the Catholic Church in Spanish affairs. Not only did Carney have an inside track with Franco's press officers, but he had also enlisted a variety of "unofficial but usually dependable" sources of information. Whatever his faults, he was foremost an enterprising journalist with a keen nose for a story.

As early as March 14, Carney had spoken briefly to four Americans captured at Alcañiz and had subsequently learned that they had been executed, without trial, by an officer of the Tercios de Extranjeros. Then, on April 3, he interviewed six Americans picked up in the Gandesa area and deposited in the San Gregorio Military Academy at Zaragoza. They expressed great surprise, not only at being taken alive, but also in having been transported in the comparative comfort of trucks and boxcars. Five of them fervently denied that they had ever been combatants—the customary ploy to avoid execution—but John Logan, a thirty-three-year-old sailor from Boston, defiantly swore that he

---

1. It was alleged that Carney, who had covered the Republican zone for the *New York Times* before Herbert L. Matthews took that beat, had once written a dispatch revealing the sites of Republican batteries in the Madrid sector. I have not been able to find this dispatch in the *Times* file and doubt that it ever existed.

would "fight to the end in this war against World Fascism." (Logan survived the war and was exchanged with others a year later.) Later Carney learned that these men were sent to a monastery near Burgos, but he assumed the claim of fifty-nine American prisoners was bogus. His private sources put the figure at eighteen. For weeks he badgered Burgos for visitation privileges, without success. Finally, early in July, he received permission, collected eighteen cartons of cigarettes, and drove over to see his fellow countrymen.

The abandoned monastery of San Pedro de Cardeña rears its squat limestone bulk out of a remote hollow in the hill country six miles southeast of Burgos. Exclusive of subterranean dungeons along the northern side, the main building consisted of vast, empty naves and three stories of monastic cells. Tiny windows with broken panes and rotting sills looked out over a medieval enclosure of tool sheds, crumbling stables, chicken coops, and dung heaps. A low wall of bleached stone surrounded the establishment, taking in a fine stand of walnut trees on the hill behind the monastery. Beyond the low wall stood ramshackle hostelries—once lodgings for pilgrims bound for Santiago de Compostela—now serving as guard barracks. San Pedro had sometimes rated a small-print note in travel guides as the burial place of El Cid Campeador even though his bones had been carried off to the Burgos city hall long ago. An equestrian statue of the famous Moor-Killer—how *he* would have been surprised by General Franco's entente with Spain's traditional enemies!—still remained over the main gate, although the hand and sword of his outstretched arm had been broken off by anticlerical protesters in the 1830s.

Carney was met by a doleful commandant, a major well past the age of retirement, who had a long list of grievances against the Americans. They were "rebellious against all discipline," they objected to compulsory mass because they were not Catholics, and they discussed "political and social doctrines almost to the exclusion of every other topic." Even worse, they used what bad Spanish they knew to make disrespectful gibes at Nationalist leaders, politics, and religion. (Among other sins, they baited their guards by claiming that the stubby arm on the El Cid statue replicated the clenched-fist salute of the Communists.) The major's guards perforce had beaten some of them for saluting the Nationalist flag "with upraised fist rather than open palm." In sum, the Americans, lamented the major, were shameless incorrigibles who failed to understand the criminal nature of their professed politics. Because three thousand Spanish prisoners also incarcerated at San Pedro might be contaminated, the Internationals lived in isolation.*

A succession of massive wooden doors opened and banged shut before Carney reached the inner courtyard of the monastery. Here the major left him alone, surrounded by tiers of seemingly empty windows. A ground-level door swung open, and Americans shuffled out into the morning sunshine. As though on parade they formed silent lines facing him, glowering with sullen hostility. Carney could scarcely believe his eyes. Having expected only eighteen, he counted eighty. But their appearance shocked him even more than their number. He was no stranger to the misery and grubbiness of men in war, but as he later wrote, "I was not prepared for the rough aspect of the ragged, dirty, mostly unshaven crew confronting me." It was like a harbinger of Dachau or Buchenwald. Grimy flesh lay visible through rents in grimier rags. To obtain tobacco and extra morsels of food, they had long since sold every decent stitch of apparel they possessed. Most went barefoot because the guards had forced them to trade shoes—Nationalist leather being worthless stuff. Some men were mere skin and bones, barely able to stand. Knowing that the power of publicity might be able to pry open the doors of San Pedro, Carney asked them to write their names and hometowns in his notebook. Five prisoners, who made no secret of their contempt for "General Bill," refused. All but three had been picked up within a two-week period of the Aragon retreats, four months before. No one knew the fate of Major Merriman other than a story that he had been "cut off while defending a hopeless position." (There had been rumors that Merriman had been imprisoned in the Jesuit Commercial College of Bilbao.) Carney did not ask about Doran.

The men clustered around Carney wanted to learn whether any effort was being made to free them. They complained that the short visit of the U.S. consul had ignored their grievances, including, among others, their protest that American citizens were forced to salute the flag of a foreign country. (Probably the consul knew that they had had no such scruples about saluting the flags of Republican Spain or the Soviet Union.) They spoke to Carney of their urgent need for decent food, medicine, and surgical services. Since their arrival they said that one American had died of dysentery, one of pleurisy, and two of appendicitis. Many still carried bullets and pieces of shrapnel in their limbs and bodies. Among the other Internationals were several surgeons who had requested instruments and anesthesia, only to be turned down on the ground that the front took priority. The only medication available was aspirin, which had to be requested five hours in advance. One of the worst cases was Charles Barr, of Steubenville, Ohio. His left eye had been blown away by shrapnel at Belchite, while next to his right eye lay a tiny piece of metal that should be removed, lest a jolt sever the optic nerve and leave him permanently blind. The men were bitter about the way guards had buried one of their comrades: "just dumped him in a hole in the field by the river," even though they had collected money to buy him a wooden coffin.

When Carney asked who would pay their fare back to the United States if they were released, their spokesman said money should be paid by the same agencies that sent them over. (Only five men in the group said that they had paid their own way.) At first, no one would say who supplied these funds, for they understood that such persons or agencies would be liable to prosecution and they had sworn not to divulge the source. But when Carney explained that prosecution depended upon proof by written contract, they told him they had been sent by the CP or by "one of the organizations working with the Party such as the North American Committee or the Friends of the Abraham Lincoln Brigade." Carney found the five men he had met previously at Zaragoza. They had changed their story about coming to Spain seeking jobs; they now claimed that political reasons were the sole factor.

Before the interview ended, Robert Steck of Davenport, Iowa, pulled up his shirt to show red welts on his back—punishment for not kneeling in church. Among their last questions: Who would Joe Louis meet next, and had John L. Lewis formed a third party? "Anything else?" Carney asked. "Yes," said Charles Barr, "why aren't you wearing your Fascist uniform?" Carney laughed. "Do you really believe I am a Fascist or have ever worn any Fascist uniform?"[2] Most of them grinned. One man said, "Skip it." When the reporter turned to leave, he wished them good luck. A stalwart among the unregistered five spoke for the first and only time, "I don't want any of your luck!" (After the war Carney received a decoration from the Knights of Columbus but nothing from the Franco government or any other "Fascist" group.)

On July 11, 1938, the *New York Times* ran on its first page "WRITER SEES 80 AMERICANS HELD IN SPANISH REBEL CAMP." Carney's article listed seventy-five names with hometowns. There was an immediate outcry on behalf of the prisoners. A sympathetic *Times* editorial the next day declared that these men were "more American than International." Far from matching the stereotype of bomb-throwing Bolsheviks, they sounded "like homesick and stranded Americans, concerned about what's going on back home and how to get there." Because of Carney's dispatch, six hundred telegrams and one hundred letters flooded Secretary Cordell Hull's office, urging intervention to ensure the safety of the San Pedro prisoners.* Meanwhile, on another page of the *Times,* David McKelvey White, a former Brooklyn College professor who had briefly fought at Brunete before taking charge of the FALB, denied flatly that his organization

2. According to Norman Dorland, Carney's response to Barr's question was, "What do you want to do—lose your other eye." This appeared in *New Masses* (November 22, 1938). Dorland was one of a small group released from prison early and wrote a sensationalist account for *New Masses*.

had at any time recruited for Spain. But he did go on to say that the FALB was prepared to post funds with the Department of State to finance their return. And within two weeks, prodded by Carney's dispatch, State announced that negotiations were in progress to obtain their release.

Even though these negotiations dragged slowly, without the initiative of the much-abused Carney they might have commenced too late or not at all. Now the prisoners were named, and Burgos was responsible for them. (Responsible morally, not legally, because the Franco government regarded them as political prisoners, not prisoners of war.) In any case, it was likely that these men would not "disappear" like other Internationals captured by the Nationalists.

The doyen of the Americans at San Pedro was Louis Ornitz, a twenty-seven-year-old organizer for the Amalgamated Clothing Workers Union of New York. As one of nine children in a destitute immigrant family, he had mastered elementary survival skills in an East Side slum, but in Spain he had escaped death only through downright good luck. Way back at Brunete (July 1937), he had driven a salvage truck collecting shell fragments. When the front collapsed, he was ordered to haul away two artillery pieces from a threatened sector, but no sooner had he loaded them than a company of Moors surrounded his truck. One grabbed his head and forced his mouth open while another examined his teeth. Ornitz had no gold fillings. As they marched him to the rear, he watched them straddling the bodies of dead and wounded, using little rocks to peck at teeth. The sergeant in charge, a Spaniard, edged near and pointed to his prisoner's gold ring, enameled with a red star. Ornitz promptly passed it over: he had heard that Moors cut off fingers to get rings. The sergeant warned Ornitz never to admit that he had been a combatant—just to insist that he was an ambulance driver assigned to drive a truck against his will. Otherwise—the Spaniard pointed to a ditch, where human feet protruded from a shallow covering of earth.*

A Spanish officer with an English accent asked him how many Americans were fighting in Spain.[3] "Fifty thousand," replied Ornitz, "with tanks and planes arriving every day." The Oxford voice said, "We know all you fellows who believe in communism are Jews." Yet unaccountably he did not contest the ambulance-driver story. While other Internationals were pulled out of cells and

<hr>

3. This officer was probably Alfonso Merry del Val, a Spanish nobleman assigned to interrogate Internationals. At Jarama he questioned a small band of British captives, who were given paroles and allowed to return to England. One of them, James Rutherford, soon returned to the British Battalion. Captured again, during the Belchite retreat, he was recognized by del Val and summarily executed.

shot, Ornitz, though beaten repeatedly, escaped execution. After a series of provincial prisons near the Portuguese frontier, he was sent up to Santander with fifteen other Internationals and jailed with twelve hundred Spanish Republicans. Once each week the prisoners were turned out into a large pen and allowed to receive visitors. On their first Sunday the Internationals collected four gunnysacks of tobacco, sausage, chocolate, and bread from local people, after which the guards broke up this trafficking.

In the spring of 1938, Ornitz ended at San Pedro de Cardeña, which housed about two thousand Spanish prisoners being force-fed a course in political purification. Graduates could be freed if they agreed to serve in the Nationalist Army. (Internationals need not apply.) Since the *commandante* of San Pedro spent most of his time in the Burgos casino, a small sergeant known as El Palo (The Stick—or "Sticky," his American nickname), with his sidekick "Froggy"— bulbous eyes behind thick spectacles—ruled the premises. He carried a thin stick that he used to lash every man passing through the door to the parade ground. His Spanish was so rapid and idiomatic that few Internationals could understand it, yet failure to respond instantly meant a drubbing across the head or shoulders. Sticky harbored no particular grudge toward the prisoners. He beat his own men the same way, a hallowed custom in the Spanish army.

During his nine months of internment in twelve different prisons, Ornitz met no other Americans until mid-April of 1938, when he was awakened by a commotion in his cellblock. "What's going on?" he shouted. The answer, in English, startled him, "What the hell do you think is going on!" It was the voice of an old comrade, Matthew Dykstra of Los Angeles, a truck driver picked up with the British at Calaceite. There were so many new arrivals that Ornitz at first thought the whole XVth Brigade had been captured at one swoop. In all, there were 450 Internationals from twenty-five countries, most of them taken during the Aragon retreats.

They were bitter, debilitated, demoralized, and apprehensive. Erratically fed, endlessly photographed, repeatedly threatened with execution, they had been paraded like Roman slaves through streets of a dozen towns in their bloodstained rags and had been forced to salute with flat palm the Nationalist flag. Through fear and despair, some captives had already tried to curry favor with their captors to win a morsel of extra food or to skip a beating. A hierarchy of "rats," as the stalwarts called them, worked as go-betweens and informers. A Portuguese volunteer named Lieutenant Fuentes, once of the Mac-Paps, who knew that execution awaited him in Portugal, had divulged the number and location of XVth Brigade units when he was captured on April 1. And a German known as "Rin Tin Tin" sought to placate his captors with his tale of riding a white horse through the lines to escape Communist oppressors in the International Brigades. Military discipline faded in the shadow of jungle law, and hyenas were king.

Among the new arrivals at San Pedro, Commissar Carl Geiser was in grave danger. When the Italians confiscated his *carnet militaire* west of Batea, he assumed that execution was inevitable. But as the days passed and the prisoners were shuttled from one Aragon town to another, it dawned upon him that his papers must have been lost or misplaced and that his captors assumed he was an ordinary soldier. At Alcañiz, where they remained briefly in the parish church, the men pledged to conceal that he was a commissar. But shortly after their arrival at San Pedro, Lieutenant Fuentes and a Cuban prisoner were overheard talking about the advantages that might accrue if they turned Geiser in. Such divisive poison required a harsh antidote before it infected everyone. The medicine came in the form of an ad hoc committee who backed the "rats" into a corner and warned that if Geiser disappeared, neither of them would leave San Pedro alive. Next they cast out the go-betweens and instituted a tough line of resistance to the regimen of the prison. If a man was beaten, they clamored in chorus, which seemed to unsettle the guards. Years of Party discipline and warfare with armed goons on the picket line had taught them that timidity in the face of wrongs only served to increase them. Thievery of *churros,* their daily bread ration, was rife among the prisoners until Geiser and other commissars established constables to spot the thieves and a tribunal to judge them. To build *esprit de corps* rather than to destroy it, punishment of offenders consisted of nothing more than a public apology and forfeiting a portion of their daily ration for a few days.*

Each day the Internationals lined up outside facing a fenced-off plot containing an immense map of Spain created from growing plants—the Republican zone in weedy vegetation and the Nationalist in brilliant, multicolored flowers. Here they had to earn their breakfast by engaging in an exchange of patriotic shouts with a prison officer.

"España!" shrilled the officer, his palm shooting into the air.

"Una!" intoned the Internationals, barely audible.

"España!"

"Grande!" mumbled the chorus.

"España!"

"Libre!" came the thunderous response, while the Spanish prisoners watching this exercise from their windows took up the battle cry with defiant shouts of "Libre! Libre!"* It was a grand moment—tattered men in poor health, without legal protection or even human rights, breaking out in revolutionary chants against a hated ideology.

One day Sticky led them outside, lined them up three abreast and ordered them to run through an opening in a hedge with their hands held high in the air. On the other side a newsreel cameraman caught them as they came through. To magnify the number, they had to circle around and repeat the Keystone Cops sequence three times, culminating in an officer beside an orange crate handing an orange to each man as he passed by. But the camera did not film the finale—a soldier retrieving each orange and returning it to the crate. This was the closest the prisoners got to fresh fruit in their year at San Pedro.*

Daily existence came to resemble recurrent images of a feverish dream. Breakfast was unvarying—a *gazpacho* of hot water, vinegar, garlic, olive oil, and bread crumbs. Some men refused it because it aggravated dysentery, but on cold mornings there was no other choice. Then came a course in elementary Christianity conducted by a priest who treated Marx as the devil incarnate. A map covered the wall with a hand-lettered inscription "ABOVE SPAIN, ONLY GOD." To bait the priest with unanswerables was dangerous, because he invoked the secular arm of Sticky—wielded to save a soul. At the end of each six-week period the course ended; then at the beginning of every seventh week it resumed with the same scholars, all of whom were slow learners. Like God, the course was eternal. Jesus, however, had apparently enlisted on Franco's side, for it was not uncommon to see images of Christ on the cross wearing a loincloth painted in red and yellow stripes, the colors of the Nationalist flag.*

Lunch meant a bowl of lentils, which passed through the gut like liquid gravel, with an occasional topping of a single sardine per man. "Those sardines saved us from starving," recalled one prisoner. "The oil was so rich." Afterward there was free time—too much of it. In the whole prison only one book in English existed, *Lawrence of Arabia.* Since everyone wanted to read it, the pages were torn out and distributed among section leaders to be read aloud to their men. When Geiser requested reading matter in English, he received reams of anti-Communist propaganda. The men ripped them apart and fashioned packs of cards. This enraged a lieutenant known as "Tanky." (It was said that he had been wounded in a tank by a shell fired from a XVth Brigade antitank gun and hated Anglo-Americans.) He demanded that someone read aloud from an English homiletic pamphlet. There were no volunteers until a Welshman, encouraged by the bull-pizzle in Tanky's hand, was prodded to the front, where he struck a lyceum pose and began to read. "Mary had a little lamb, its fleece was white as snow, and everywhere that Mary went, the lamb was sure to go." The priest and Tanky nodded happily.*

Afternoon was an endless period in which the men were aware of their own rotting. Five hundred shared five cold-water taps and five "Egyptian" toilets—

noisome holes in a sunken room. Once it flooded five feet deep, and three volunteers dived under urine and excrement to clear the drain. For this they were rewarded with an extra eight-ounce loaf of bread, but two of the men died of typhoid within a week. Looking back on it, the lone survivor thought the dirty job was worth the loaf of bread. "It tasted beautiful—I can still recall the taste of that bread after forty years."* It was never possible to bathe or to wash their clothes, which stiffened on them like suits of cardboard. Twice during their long residence at San Pedro, they were marched to splash in a distant icy stream. Although their heads had been shaved to the skull, they were never deloused. Optimists rolled up their blankets in the morning to trap the lice, then employed afternoons unrolling the blankets slowly and crushing the lice with their fingernails. A one-armed Welshman could not pick his lice, so comrades teamed up to do the job for him. "Now it's bad enough killing one's *own* lice, but to kill someone else's . . . at least, I suppose they might have been one's own lice, but you didn't know."* There was infinite time to contemplate their wretchedness. San Pedro was worse than the prison at Bilbao, where inmates learned simple trades like crutch making, or Belchite, where they trucked away rubble. Yet it was better than the camp at nearby Lerma, which was filled with cripples, faceless creatures, and ghastly relics neither fully alive nor wholly dead.

Dinner consisted of a plate of beans and piece of bread—although sometimes they got a stew made of bones, sausages, and beans. During their entire period of imprisonment they received lettuce only twice and other green vegetables not at all. In summer they could buy, if they had money, braided strings of onions from *campesinos* in the vicinity. Teeth loosened and fell out, gums became pulpy, and sores festered. A rheumatic pain in ankles, shins, and knees was dubbed "San Pedroitis." Often it was unbearable and affected about forty percent of the prisoners. Four men died from appendicitis even though five IB doctors had volunteered to operate with pocket knives if allowed anesthesia. None was provided. Five hundred Internationals lived in two long halls and slept on straw pallets placed on the flagstone floor. In summer they nearly suffocated in the rank, foul air. In winter they stuffed rags and paper into broken windowpanes and bedded down in groups of two or three to keep warm. "*Nueve meses de invierno—tres meses de inferno*" ("Nine months of winter—three months of hell"), so went the famous line about Burgos weather.

The infirmary consisted of a raised wooden dais at the far end of the hall. Elsewhere in the prison there was a fifty-bed hospital run by nuns, but this was regarded as a dying place. The nuns had good intentions but were without training or medicine. Six out of every ten patients never recovered. One prisoner remembered how he lusted after the blanket on a dead-end case being carried to the hospital. "It was absolutely filthy . . . vomit on it and all kinds of things, but I whipped it and took it back. . . . The sort of blanket that if you saw it now it would make you heave just to look at it."* An American with lung cancer begged his comrades not to send him to the hospital. He wanted to die among friends. So they kept him, carrying him around like a child, until he became a husk and died.

To combat ennui and demoralization, Geiser and others organized SPIHL, an acronym for San Pedro Institute of Higher Learning. At first they provided courses in contemporary history, heavily imbued with Marxist interpretations (probably the only such courses in all of Nationalist Spain). But the men were sick and tired of polemics and propaganda, and most of them boycotted the courses. Beginning in September, SPIHL offered a revamped curriculum billed as "free— nonsectarian" in which the "unpopular courses have been dropped" in favor of nonpartisan offerings. The Institute began its fall semester in the black, with 169 pesetas in cold cash, a dictionary, a six-book reference library, and a ream of paper. Eventually there were twenty-one courses in eleven languages taught by instructors ranging from a member of the British Zoological Society to an Indian fakir specializing in palm reading. Each class was assigned a section of white-washed wall as blackboard; students sat cross-legged on the stone floor. A Welsh miner wrote an essay for his English class: "I am in San Pedro. The sergeants are all wicked fascists. I can do verbs. I have no tobacco, thou hast no tobacco, he has no tobacco, we have no tobacco, they have plenty bloody tobacco."*

The commissars had other projects for keeping spirits up. Robert Steck founded a newspaper called the *Jaily News,* and a short time later an opposition sheet called *Undercrust* appeared. They made chess pieces out of soap, masticated paper, and bits of wood carved with sharpened spoons. Even Tanky developed grudging admiration for the prisoners when Hy Wallach, a New Yorker, defeated thirty men simultaneously in a chess tournament.

But as weeks turned into months, temporary diversions palled. No news came concerning their release, and the war dragged on and on.

During their first months at San Pedro, the Americans feared they might be executed before the outside world even learned of their existence; later they feared they would all perish of debilitation and disease before anything would be done. The story got about that Franco demanded that five Italian prisoners held by the Republic be traded for each American. While there was a certain triumph in considering that one American Communist was worth five Italian Fascisti, it got them no closer to release. When Red Cross or diplomatic delegations came, guards issued knee-length smocks to cover their nakedness. Some of the British tucked the smocks into their ragged trousers when Sir Robert Hodgson of the British Mission came to San Pedro. Sir Robert had the surface mannerisms of a Colonel Blimp, but he was genuinely horrified to find fellow Englishmen treated so shabbily by Spaniards—of all people. After stopping in front of a tattered Scotsman and eyeing him up and down, he blurted out, "Rather ghastly—wot?" To which, in his best English accent, the Scotsman replied, "Raaw-therr!" During this visit each man received three small lettuce leaves, their first fresh vegetable in three months.*

All Internationals were privately examined by a plainclothesman rumored to be the Gestapo agent-in-residence. He took their head measurements to prove that they were of degraded, non-Aryan stock, and his photographer took pictures, many of which were passed on to Nationalist Front periodicals in neutral countries.[4] While the agent had only a perfunctory interest in the Americans, he spent a full day with each German prisoner and boasted that his organization had assembled a file of two million "Reds" in Spain. His Spanish photographer, however, had no stomach for this work: he sometimes slipped peseta notes to prisoners.* German prisoners suffered the worst harassment because as anti-Fascists they were enemies of their own government, an ally of Franco. Alone among the Internationals, they did not seek repatriation. Prison authorities also took motion pictures. Sid Rosenblatt had been captured while carrying Reiss from the hermitage. At San Pedro a Spanish officer ordered him to strip. When the camera rolled, the officer pointed a stick at his penis, noting the circumcision. All in the room grinned—here was visual proof that the Internationals were Jews.*

Late in September the prison was stirred with rumors that release was in the offing. Hopes soared but drooped again when only fourteen Americans were selected for repatriation. These included long-termers like Louis Ornitz, some dangerously ill like Charles Barr, or family men like Sam Romer. The ratio of exchange with Italians proved to be one to one.

On October 9, 1938, the fortunate fourteen, dressed in warm but seedy clothing, filed across the international bridge at Irun. Warned that their behavior must be impeccable so that those left behind would not be jeopardized, they did not say anything or look behind them. On the French side waited a swarm of cameramen, reporters, minor diplomats, and spectators. Receipts had to be signed and countersigned before the gaunt men were turned over to David Ameriglio (alias Leeds), the FALB agent in France, who had arranged for their

---

4. Usually these were pictures of black or Jewish prisoners labeled "typical International prisoners taken by the Nationalist Army." Their propaganda organ in the United States was *Spain*, a magazine published by the National Spanish Relief Association, which also sponsored a propaganda broadcast, *The Hour of Spain*, over WHN (New York) every evening except Wednesday at 11 p.m.

passage home. In the washroom of the Hendaye station, Ameriglio had the men don brand-new Republican Army uniforms, but when they came out, gendarmes drove them back inside again: in France, there were told, wearing the military uniform of another power was forbidden. (A variant account claims that the French objected to their tattered prison uniforms and that Amariglio bought blue overalls to cover them.)* For a time, French medical authorities threatened to quarantine them, but after a short hassle the men were vaccinated there and then for smallpox. Finding no other legal obstructions, the French allowed them to continue to Le Havre.

Disembarking from the *Queen Mary* in New York on October 18, the Americans found two hundred sympathizers with a band. They were not free men—not yet. FALB hierarchs escorted them across town to a dinner at the Commodore Hotel, which kicked off a new fund-drive for $150,000 to bring home all members of the Abraham Lincoln "Brigade." An ex-commissar, Norman Dorland, made a speech so impassioned that it was amplified and published with great éclat in *New Masses*. In it, he told how the Fascists collaborated with the Gestapo, shot and beat prisoners, and deprived sick men of medical attention. Perhaps angered by this lurid account of their war crimes, the Nationalists broke off negotiations for releasing other Americans from San Pedro.[5]

As compensation for being left behind, the FALB sent 54.10 pesetas to each of the remaining Americans at San Pedro—their first money in over six months. The major commanding the camp authorized a truck to purchase supplies in Burgos—tobacco, chocolate, milk, fruit, and sausage. Proving that capitalism was not incompatible with Communism, Ed Hodges of Kentucky opened a small store.*

In November the first snows fell upon San Pedro de Cardeña. Men had to wear blankets day and night. Those without shoes learned how to unravel burlap sacks, weave the fibers into cloth and fasten it to tire casings.* The weather turned brutal. Wind howled through broken windowpanes into unheated galleries. Yet despite the terrible cold, their health seemed to improve. Was it too cold for bacteria and viruses? In any case, lice and fleas burrowed deeper. Spaniards explained how to "cure" diarrhea—wrap your scarf around your midsection instead of your neck. On Christmas Day each man received a

---

5. Part of the delay resulted from the refusal of the State Department to accept financial responsibility for the Americans. At one point in the negotiations all prisoners could have been released at one stroke had the U.S. government agreed to supply a warship for returning an equal number of CTV prisoners waiting at Alicante. Washington was horrified by the thought that a U.S. naval vessel might be used to transport Italian combatants from Spain. Thus American POWs were held back long after other IB prisoners were released.

small can of fruit. All had dented ends and when opened spewed out a geyser of rotten fruit. Men converted the tins into ingenious stoves fueled by sardine oil. More successful was a Christmas Eve concert directed by Robert Steck, once on the staff of *New Theatre Magazine* in New York. The commandant with thirty of his men (including Tanky and Sticky—neither with batons) were greeted by Geiser and escorted to straw sack seats. There were humorous skits and folk songs from a dozen countries, a juggler, acrobatic Russian dances, a parody of *The Barber of Seville,* culminating in an eighty-voice chorale conducted by a graduate of the Heidelberg Conservatory of Music. At the conclusion the entire audience rose to its feet, clapping and shouting "Olé! Olé!"—"the distinction between prisoner and jailer lost in the wild applause."* At the major's request there was a repeat performance on New Year's Eve for his fellow officers from Burgos.*

Not until April 22, 1939, did the next group of seventy-one men cross into France. One man carried a copy of *Jaily News* stuffed in his shoe. On August 25, eleven more passed over. Franco's prisons were finally emptied of Americans when eight men were released in March of 1940, eleven months after the war's end. With them was Lawrence Doran of Los Angeles, who had been captured near Gandesa just two weeks after his arrival in Spain, accused of spying, and sentenced to death. One suspects that he spent two years in prison not because he was a deeper hue of Red than the others but because Nationalist authorities wanted to be absolutely sure that he was not really that notorious Bolshevik, Commissar Dave Doran, who had seemingly vanished into thin air.

THEIR COMRADES

Upset by the failures of the International Brigades during the Aragon disasters of March and April, Moscow mandated a full reckoning. The result was an illuminating array of statistical reports on manpower and morale. As of March 31, 1938, the grand total of all men who had served in the International Brigades stood at 31,969, of which 15,992 (50.0 percent) were currently in Spain. Of the grand total 5,062 (15.8 percent) had been badly wounded, and 4,575 (14.3 percent) killed or missing. This meant that 5,740 (17.9 percent) fell into a general category that included repatriated, deserted, prisoners of war, or jailed by the International Brigades. The tally of brigaders by country of origin revealed that the largest number had come from France with 8,778, and then in descending order Poland 3,034, Italy 2,908, the United States 2,274, Germany 2,180, the Balkans 2,056, England 1,896, and twenty other countries. These figures reveal that despite complaints by André Marty, the Americans were more than holding their own in providing manpower for the war. Moreover, their percentage of fatalities (14.8 percent) was exceeded only by the Baltic countries (20.5 percent), Switzerland (19.2 percent), Italy (18.0 percent), and Poland (16.0 percent). (Both Germany [14.1 percent] and France [10.7 percent] had lower percentages of deaths.)*[6]

After the disastrous collapse of the International Brigades during the March retreats, Moscow required that each brigade compile a list of its troublesome members, spelling out exactly the nature of their derelictions. This huge personnel file archived in Moscow includes a "List of Suspicious Individuals and Deserters from the XVth Brigade" based upon a survey conducted sometime between July and August 1938.[7] Out of approximately twelve hundred men on the rolls of the brigade at that time, 544 (about 37 percent) are listed with a short description of their crimes, misdemeanors, and/or "attitudes." Of this number 239 (about 20 percent) are listed as "deserters," a category that also included nuances like "deserted several times," "tried to desert," "accused of intent to desert," and "seems like he wants to desert." The remaining 305 malefactors not accused of desertion (about 25 percent) were listed by name and unit with a brief note about the problem area observed by a commissar—or reported to him by a mole. These range from nearly criminal to merely comical. Allowing readers to judge for themselves, a sampler follows: Argued with a sergeant—Trotskyist, being watched—Possible agent on a small scale—Tried to rape woman in Darmos—Spoke in defeatist manner—Friend of [Paul] White—Abnormal, illiterate—Very provoking—Spoke of deserting—Signaled the Fascists—Defeatist—Hates Spanish—Threatened chief of the SIM and anyone reporting him—Scorns officers—Coward—Idiot playboy—Very provoking—Imprisoned, left without permission—Repeated protest over food—Politically suspicious—and on and on.[8] Sometimes the commissars' obsession with ferreting out picayunish minor complaints as evidence of political deviation backfired. At Teruel, when a commissar went down the trench asking, "How is the

6. What raised the fatality percentage among the Americans was the Aragon retreat of March and April, when the XVth Brigade bore the brunt of the Franco blitzkrieg with its indiscriminate massacre of POWs.

7. For a detailed discussion of personalized reports on deserters, defeatists, and deviationists among the Americans, see Romerstein, *Heroic Victims*, 30–50. The full list of volunteers under close surveillance has been published in Harvey Klehr et al., *The Secret World of American Communism*, 164–84.

8. I have compiled a list of forty-eight men who deserted successfully (that is to say, who reached the United States) between April and July 1938. Until recently it was pro forma for the VALB to deny the existence of all but a small number of "crypto-Fascists."

coffee?" a canny veteran replied, "It depends. If I'm politically reliable, then it tastes great. If I'm politically unreliable, it tastes like horse piss."*

Following the chaotic March retreats, suspicion spread like an uncontrollable virus in all directions. In order to absolve himself of any blame for the fiasco, on August 2, 1938, General Walter sent a special report to Comrade Kliment Voroshilov (the people's commissar of defense of the USSR) titled "Espionage work by Fascist agents in the Republican Army." In it he stormed like a wild man against "the most stinking, fetid, treacherous activity by all the bastards of all shades and colors" who were undermining the International Brigades. The report consists of a thirty-point, scatter-shot invective attacking agents of the Gestapo, the Fascists, the Anarchists, the Trotskyists, Fifth Columnists, and the Polish Defensiv [sic]. The enemy had attempted a "mass poisoning of soldiers" through toxic chocolates sent to the front. Then after a typhoid epidemic "carried away" a thousand soldiers in two Spanish brigades, the Spanish officers refused to accept chemical disinfectant tablets offered by Soviet advisers until the advisers swallowed them to prove they were not poison. Blame for the March retreats fell upon the "intensive activity and work of defeatist elements and agents of the fifth column in the Republican Army," for "at the first shots, hysterical shouts about us being surrounded by the enemy would ring out," resulting in soldiers throwing away their rifles and fleeing in panic. So thoroughly had the Fascists infiltrated the Republican communication network that secret orders would sometimes be broadcast over Nationalist radio before the message reached its proper destination. The enemy even stooped to mailing him false news that his two children in Paris were dangerously ill, and later, that his daughter had died. (There were twenty-five more complaints in his report, all in great detail.)*

To combat these activities General Walter had requested help from Alexander Orlov's NKVD unit, but because they were preoccupied elsewhere he had to improvise a "crude, special department" within his own division. (No doubt Orlov's major preoccupation at this time was arranging for his successful defection to the West.) After the retreat from Caspe, Walter "organized a purge in [his] division" in order to drive out the hostile and defeatist elements, beginning with his division staff in which a French major was shot for "repeated organization of rabbitlike panics." He then "cleaned out the brigades," and after withdrawing to the left bank of the Ebro, "set up special brigade and division tribunals for another purge of the units." In effect, Walter was ordering purges in a desperate effort to negate his own. It was a great pity, for he had always been one of the most levelheaded and successful IB commanders in Spain.

There can be no doubt that in the aftermath of the Corbera disaster, some-where between fifty and ninety American volunteers, taking advantage of the widespread dispersion of Republican forces in the Ebro zone, deserted the front altogether. Mingling with the thousands of refugees who choked roads south to Valencia or north to Barcelona, the deserters sought not only to evade Fascist patrols but also to escape hawkish pursuit by sim policemen, whose job it was to compel others to keep up the good fight. They fled on foot, rode freight cars, hitched rides on trucks, hoping to find a haven in France, in Gibraltar, in North Africa. Every nerve and muscle told them that they had been outmanned, out-gunned, and outgeneraled. Wherever they looked they faced—doom, disaster, defeat. As the Fifth Column consisted of Nationalist sympathizers among the civilian population and army, so these fugitives might be called a Sixth Column—Republican soldiers who added to the pandemic disaster syndrome by attempting to escape from it altogether. From Le Havre to Casablanca they stormed or slunk into U.S. consulates seeking passports and passage home. The consulates at Valencia and Barcelona were now regularly under surveillance by sim agents, who intercepted deserters virtually beneath the American flags drooping from exterior windows. Although it was against iB policy to publicize to the world at large that deserters existed, much less that they received draco-nian punishment, sometimes the sim officers themselves openly boasted of their roles. One such, Lieutenant Alvin Cohen, told a reporter just after the March/April disasters, "When soldiers desert twice, they get shot."* Vessels departing from French ports carried stowaways. When the *Normandie* docked in New York on May 30, 1938, its passengers included Ernest Hemingway (who told reporters that the war in Spain was becoming a bore) along with four Lincoln stowaways, who were hustled off to Ellis Island. Elsewhere, two Americans somehow reached Cork, Ireland, where they were jailed for vagrancy. French frontier guards estimated that six hundred Internationals of all nations had crossed into France in the aftermath of the Aragon debacle.

Evan Shipman, an old crony of Hemingway from their Latin Quarter days, had gone to Spain to drive an ambulance but also had a brief stint in the Lin-coln Battalion. Well beyond the normal age, in poor health, and from a distin-guished American family, he was given a discharge and arrived in France, with Martin Hourihan as traveling companion, shortly after the Gandesa disaster. On June 21, 1938, he wrote Hemingway from Paris:

> Things down below were not going well at all when I left. I mean with the Americans. I am not talking about up at the front. That I don't know. But in Barcelona, Badalona, and back it was very bad. There

were desertions, and I mean on a fairly big scale, all the time. The morale was terrible and I felt that there was no adequate political work being done.*

Without a *salvo conducto,* escaping from Spain often required more cool nerve—not to mention ingenuity—than meeting the Fascists head-on. A Milwaukee volunteer stole a small launch in Valencia harbor and rowed it far out to sea one night in order to elude the patrol boats. Just before sunrise, he opened the engine hatch and found nothing inside except a pile of moldering ropes. He hailed a passing French ship, the crew of which gaily waved back. On the second night he rowed back into the harbor, moored the launch where it belonged, and got away by train to Cartagena, where he found a British ship that dropped him in Gibraltar. A brash Californian bought an elegant but secondhand tweed suit in Barcelona and rode up to Port Bou in style, where he bluffed his way through the frontier tunnel with a seaman's card and a tale that he had been left behind by his ship while on a toot in Barcelona. A deserter from Frederick, Maryland, walked across the Pyrenees, moving at night and holing up in culverts by day. It took him eleven days to cover the final twenty-five miles. Another American, run to ground in the Pyrenees, clung stubbornly to a patently phony story that he had been told the Lincoln Battalion was somewhere close by being "reorganized." George Orwell was right on the money when he told a friend after his own precarious escape from Spain: "It was a queer business. We started off by being heroic defenders of democracy and ended by slipping over the border with the police panting on our heels."*

Most of the deserters who escaped to the United States slipped inconspicuously into the anonymity of American life. Only a few were willing to play into the hands of Franco apologists and Red baiters by criticizing the Lincoln Battalion or Republican Spain. Not proud of having quit the good fight, for the most part they sat tight and kept their mouths shut. Yet there were a handful so embittered by their experiences in Spain, specifically by the role of the Communist Party in a *soi-disant* "People's Army," that they agreed to testify before the House Un-American Activities Committee (HUAC), chaired by Martin Dies of Texas. The tenor of their denunciations was that the leaders of the International Brigades were, as one witness put it, "political Capones" who "paraded under the guise of an ideal appealing to the highest social and moral feelings of men."* They did not denigrate Republican Spain, only the cynicism and opportunism of the CP policies.

Typical of the testimonies heard by the Dies Committee was the tale of Alvin I. Halpern, an ice-cream worker from Boston. (It is not recorded whether he earned his nickname "Hot-Air Hal" before or after his defection from the Lincoln Battalion.) Recruited by one Mannie Blanke at the CP headquarters on Essex Street, Halpern left for Spain in June 1937, under the impression that he could return home after six months' service. His passport was confiscated at Albacete and never seen again. At Tarazona some of the scales dropped from his eyes when the Dallet regime banned the *New York Times* because of its "Fascist tendencies." That autumn he served as a runner for Major Merriman— "Murderman we called him." He told the committee that any volunteer protesting against IB policies was branded a "Fascist provocateur" and sent to a detention camp where "they would shoot you down." He had never witnessed an execution, but he had seen undesirables assigned to labor battalions and sent into no-man's-land for the enemy to pick off. After battalion authorities refused to repatriate him after six months' service, he resolved to escape. When the Nationalists broke through to the sea, Halpern was in a Sagunto hospital recovering from a wound and found himself cut off from France. He slipped across the Mediterranean to Oran only to learn that the U.S. consul had died two weeks before and the French planned to extradite him to Spain. In desperation he clung to the British consul, who arranged for his passage to the States. Still wearing his Republican uniform, Halpern confronted Mannie Blanke on Essex Street. Blanke called him a deserter. Halpern asked why Blanke had never gone to Spain. Blanke said that he had flat feet. Halpern told him, "I saw guys going over the mountains into Spain with wooden legs, and other men aiming rifles who couldn't see ten feet beyond the barrel." The upshot was that Blanke promised him fifty dollars for a suit of clothes and money to have his wound treated, but when he bought the suit, Blanke refused to pay. Irate, he avenged himself by selling his story to the Hearst press. A few days later he was blacklisted by his union, an affiliate of the CIO.*

Less spectacular was the testimony of Abraham Sobel, another protégé of Mannie Blanke. A twenty-three-year-old nightschooler at Northeastern University in Boston, Sobel had met Blanke at the Ukrainian Workers' Club and, like many Jewish college men, had been intrigued by the prospect of "taking a crack at Hitler"—Blanke's best pitch. In applying for a passport, he was instructed to claim that he was bound for Austria while a companion posed as a theological student destined for Palestine. Before leaving Boston, Blanke told him, "You can leave Spain whenever you like." But Sobel was stalked by misfortune. He was aboard the *Ciudad de Barcelona* when it was torpedoed off the coast of Catalonia. After a near brush with drowning, Sobel listed himself as a truck driver on grounds that the survival rate was higher. But at Brunete his ammunition truck blew up under him. At Teruel he went into the line, much against his will, and was wounded on his first day in action. While a patient at the hospital at Mataró, a coastal town north of Barcelona, he heard of the Aragon debacle. Patients were being asked to volunteer to brace the crumbling front. Sobel was having none of that. He dressed quickly and hobbled over the Pyrenees to France. Once home, he vowed to make the Communist Party "pay through the nose" for his sufferings. Americans in Spain, he claimed, were virtually prisoners, and most of them would return at once if they could.*

Other testimonials like the foregoing were given, briefly publicized, and largely forgotten. But these case histories serve as a reminder that service in Spain was not always participation in a holy cause. Idealism masked methods as cynical and as tyrannical as the evils that good men and true went to Spain to destroy. The misfortune is that in responding to attacks from deserters like Halpern and Sobel, all too many "stalwarts" in the Lincoln Battalion overreacted. Details that clouded the bright mirror of that Holy Cause—whether of the Party or the Republic—they denied with burning hatred or else embalmed in their memory. For these, loyalty became the supreme virtue. Truth was expendable. The pity is that many men were willing to accept outrageous distortions only because, in so doing, they reaffirmed that loyalty. In the words of one veteran: "Of course, we all knew of bad things which happened in Spain, but I would not defile the memory of good things by telling you these."

Just after the stragglers of the Lincoln Battalion set up their camp at Marsa in April 1938, an order came down to Commissar John Gates from Division: court-martial all deserters and execute some as examples. Massive desertion must never be allowed again. Accordingly, Gates improvised a tribunal consisting only of brigade commissars and Party cadres. Three deserters received death sentences: an Algerian, a Spaniard, and an American named Paul White. White, a seaman with a splendid record in the Party, had deserted at least once before. (Merriman had complimented him for "doing a good job" in rounding up and provisioning the men scattered all over Madrid at the time of the Aragon offensive.) Executions followed that night. According to the later testimony of Major Umberto Galleani,[9] the firing squad was commanded by a "very excitable" New Yorker known as "Ivan."*

Some Lincolns bivouacked at Marsa heard isolated shots fired that night. Then four men were shaken out of their blanket rolls by one of Tony DeMaio's

---

9. Galleani, an officer in the Italian Army during the World War, was a naturalized American citizen who arrived in Spain in October 1936. As an officer of the Garibaldi (Italian) Battalion, he had participated in the defense of Madrid that autumn. During the spring of 1937 he made a propaganda tour throughout the United States and was tagged by *Newsweek* "the first American volunteer." On his return to Spain in September 1937, he served on the staff of the XVth Brigade and

henchmen, who handed them shovels and said, "Follow me, and don't ask questions." They dug a trench in the hillside and dumped in a body. By morning everyone in the battalion knew that someone had been shot without being told the details. Later in the day they were told that Paul White had been executed as a deserter "by the unanimous [sic] decision of the battalion." They, the men of the battalion, had decided nothing—certainly not unanimously. Joe Bianca, a friend from the New York waterfront, who knew that White's wife had just had a baby, vented his anger by shouting over and over, for all to hear, "Those sons of bitches!"* Having just been publicized as "the best soldier in the Battalion," Bianca had passed beyond the range of commissariat retaliation.[10] (According to John Gates, many years later, on the next day an order come down from Division countermanding the executions. It arrived too late for Paul White.)*[11] At this time Gates and Wolff conducted the trial of Bernard Abramofsky, accused of multiple desertions and black marketeering. This was held in a darkened room with a single light shining on his face. Like White, he was executed by a nocturnal firing squad.*

Just before the Nationalists cut the Republic in two, André Marty had moved his imperium into Catalonia. He closed down the IB prison at Camp Lukács and opened a new one in a castle on a crag above Casteldefels, a resort town south of Barcelona. From April 1938 to January 1939, the warden was Tony DeMaio, whose goon squads ransacked Barcelona and points as far north as the French frontier, picking up suspected deserters. Since fugitives usually headed for either the American consulate on the Plaza de Cataluña or the Hotel Majestic, headquarters of the press corps, these places were under surveillance around the clock. On one occasion the German poet Ernst Toller, mistaken for a deserter, was pulled over by one of DeMaio's guards, a hulking American black, who backed him against a wall with the muzzle of his gun and demanded proof of his identity. "Let's hear your fuckin' poems!" Toller obliged and proved his case. It was probably the most earnest reading he ever gave.* Even

---

became increasingly disaffected by the Communist domination of the International Brigades. After the war, to counter the Moscow orientation of the VALB, Galleani tried to found an opposition veterans' organization, but this quickly collapsed. Subsequently he was a major witness in the HUAC investigation of the Lincoln Battalion.

10. There is an inexplicable contradiction here. In a letter to Gates, Wolff clearly faults Bianca for not intervening to save White's life. "Bianca could have sent him to the rear for rest instead of setting him up on a rock to have his guts ripped out. That bothers me."*

11. When I researched the Lincolns during the 1960s, most veterans denied any knowledge of the White affair or of any other execution. Yet a poll of three hundred veterans, published in 1940, under the title *Fear in Battle*, reveals that 70 percent of them agreed that a two-time deserter deserved to be executed.*

DeMaio himself was often seen prowling the halls of the Majestic, looking for men who might wish to spill the beans to American journalists. A Lincoln who had watched DeMaio rise from a nobody at Villanueva de la Jara characterized him as "as chief ferret, finger man, and executioner as a Mafia bandit carries out a contract."* Once, during his absence, his second-in-command at Casteldefels, a rummy from Texas, wrote a *salvo conducto* for everyone, including himself, and led an abortive prison break.

Most Americans at Marsa viewed SIM agents with a mixture of fear and loathing. One time DeMaio came down from Barcelona and pushed his way to the front of the chow line, his spiffy tailored uniform and boots contrasting sharply with the un-uniforms of the Lincolns. Jack Shafran shouted, "Hey, you bastard, get your fucking ass to the end of the line." In a rage, DeMaio accosted Shafran, "Can't you see that I am a captain." "I don't give a shit if you're a general. Get to the end of the line, or go fuck yourself." DeMaio drew his pistol and placed Shafran under arrest for insubordination. Wolff, the battalion commander, not wanting to tangle with the SIM passed the problem down to the company commander, who was Spanish and had to have the translator explain the word "fucking." His conclusion was, "You Americans are very strange . . . sometimes fucking is good, other times bad. From now on there is to be no more fucking in this company." Shafran was assigned to dig a septic pit with two of his buddies posted as "guards"—both with good humor and empty rifles.[12]*

Early in April there was a brutal execution outside Tarragona (not Tarazona). Several hundred stragglers from the International Brigades had been herded into a minimum-security corral north of town while commissars graded them into three categories: (1) those to be returned to their units, (2) those to be placed into labor battalions, and (3) those to be imprisoned at Casteldefels. Bored with this rigmarole, three Finns—Paul Oskar, George Niemin, and George Kulksinem—broke out at night and went on a drunk in Tarragona. Jailed by civil authorities, they promptly escaped and returned to their compound in the morning. A court-martial followed, but few men took it very seriously. At dusk all the inmates of the stockade were marched down to the beach and lined up facing the sea. An ambulance arrived, and when the Finns stepped out, they were cheered like celebrities. Commissars thrust rifles in the hands of eighteen prisoners and ordered them to serve as firing squads. Everyone seemed to enjoy this spectacle enormously and waited for the finale—

12. When members of the Lincoln Battalion revisited Spain on excursion buses after Franco's death, they observed that DeMaio seemed mainly interested in finding sites and prisons where he had made police history. To his chagrin these places were not on the itinerary. The other vets tried to avoid sharing a seat with him on the buses.*

a commissar dashing in from the wings with a last-minute reprieve. Even the Finns regarded the affair as comic melodrama in which they had starring roles. But suddenly shots rang out—the crackle of rifles not synchronized. Somebody yelled, "My God! They're killing them!" Two of the Finns writhed on the sand, but Niemin had only been nicked. He stood upright like a bewildered animal as bolts rattled in rifles. Even after a second volley, Niemin, who looked as though he had been splashed with red varnish, still stood upright. Then he lifted his right fist, shook it, and toppled over.* Was that fist the Popular Front salute or a gesture of defiance? A stillness fell over the watchers as a Boston Irishman went forward to deliver the coup de grâce. Three Finns had come to Spain in the name of Liberty and had perished in the name of Discipline.[13]

How was international solidarity, precarious in the best of times, to be maintained in this growing atmosphere of despair and suspicion? As though the Fascist army in their front were not menace enough, the Lincolns had to endure police agents in their rear. They were caught, in Orwell's phrase, "Between the bullet and the lie." Under some circumstances a sacred word could become a monstrous oath. Consider the case of a wounded American volunteer passing through Barcelona on his way home who was hailed by an old friend from training days, "Hello, comrade." He grabbed the speaker by the lapels and hissed, "If you ever call me *that* again, I'll *kill* you!"*

13. This may be the same execution witnessed by John Penrod, who mistakenly identified them as Poles who had been on a drunk and broke up a bar in Tarragona (not Tarazona) and were executed at dawn as fifth columnists.*

17

THE FAR SHORE

One night in early July the battalion went out on an ominous night maneuver that left them "breathless and somewhat terrified." They carried full equipment, marched nine miles across rough country, and at dawn reached a dry riverbed. There they split into squads, paddled across the pebbled bottom in imaginary boats, and assaulted a mountain from which came harrowingly realistic rifle and machine-gun fire. Every day thereafter they crossed imaginary rivers and attacked deeply entrenched "enemy" positions. There was no explanation given for these training exercises—none was required. "Aha! We're going to cross a river," exclaimed one American, with mock puzzlement. "Now what river do you suppose *that* could be?"*

Concurrently came a fresh rumor "straight from the horse's ass" that the Internationals were to be separated from the Spanish troops in order to be counted and withdrawn from Spain. It was already common knowledge that wounded men in hospitals were being repatriated without reporting back to Brigade—a signal, perhaps, that this time the news they longed for might be true. Gates and Wolff repeatedly denied it, but they had to take a negative line so that morale would not collapse when the rumor was scotched. Question-answer skits made the rounds like vaudeville routines: "You heard the news?" "Sure, they're withdrawing the volunteers from Spain." "No crap, and here I was planning to get married and grow up with the country."

Competing with this loomed a more overwhelming question: Which would they cross first—the Ebro River or the French frontier? They desperately wanted to believe that the International Brigades would be withdrawn. "The world knows we're all washed up," exclaimed one man; "Not the *Daily Worker*," sneered his companion.*

In the third week of July 1938, the XVth Brigade began a two-day march that led them into a thick canebrake near the Ebro river-town of Asco. The men could not see the river, but they could smell it through the canebrake. The brigade photographer, whose duties usually kept him in Barcelona, stood nearby with bags of equipment. This might be the real thing. On July 24, Captain Wolff assembled his battalion and outlined the plan of attack. With a force of eighty thousand men they would cross the river and, traveling light and rapidly, over-run weak Nationalist positions between the Ebro and Gandesa. Only green troops held the line, for Franco's major attention had wheeled south toward Valencia. The first waves would cross in small fishing skiffs that had been hauled overland from the Mediterranean; later waves would cross on pontoon bridges. Until these bridges could be constructed, no tanks or artillery would be available for support. The inevitable question arose: If the enemy air force knocked out the bridges, then what? In that extremity they would live for a few days on iron rations carried on their backs or on captured enemy *intendencias*. If successful, this offensive would force Franco to abort his Valencia attack in order to meet this new threat against his rear. The Republic put up a few hap-less and hopeless planes, most of them aviation relics, dubbed by the Americans "Coxey's Army of the Air."*

It was an audacious plan. In effect, they would be breaking the enemy line with nothing more formidable than infantry, a tiny segment of a major offensive that would stretch north for sixty miles. But few of the Americans gathered around Milton Wolff in the twilight cared anything about becoming a footnote in the history of Spanish military heroics, for they remembered how the best-laid plans seemed always to turn into bloody catastrophes. There was a deep pause. Thousands of frogs drummed in the marshes. Then Morris Mickenberg, a Jarama survivor and currently ringleader of FONIC, voiced Everyman's question: How were they to get back across the Ebro? This drew some sardonic laughs, but Wolff replied brusquely, "We're not coming back!" and men cheered. Of course, that was exactly what troubled Mickenberg and other skeptics.*

In the remaining hours, veterans threw away all nonessentials. Even the raw *quintos* understood that wherever they were going was no place for guitars and suitcases. When the canteen came up on the supper truck, veterans bought overalls with big, roomy pockets (sixty *pesetas*—three days' pay—but worth it) and filled them with chocolate bars, packs of cigarettes, and extra ammo clips. Only the officers wore leather footgear. The men were shod in rope-soled *alpar-gatas* that laced up the ankles like ballet slippers and resembled, with trouser cuffs down, sneakers. The future was not a bright beacon, but at least their agony of suspense had ended. Men exchanged fatalistic grins and grimaces. Long ago they had abandoned hope of winning the war, and while they doubted that winning a battle was in the cards, they gamely roused themselves for another bitter round. They passed each other slips of paper with jotted names, streets, towns—just in case. (The battalion secretary rarely notified wives or parents when a man was killed or wounded, because casualties demoralized folks back home.)

Before first light they moved through the canebrake toward the riverbank, sensing rather than seeing the raw muscle of mule trains, columns of men, and trucks pulling skiffs and scows to crossing points. Just at dawn the coffee truck bumped down the streambed, bringing a last delivery of mail. A few shells shrieked overhead and exploded in the hills far behind them. The first wave had already crossed the Ebro. The wide river was spotted with colorful little rowboats that looked like they had been borrowed from a Catalonian tunnel-of-love. "It's Prospect Park in the summertime!" shouted the usually prosaic Lieutenant Lopoff. Upriver the Republicans were shelling Asco. Climbing into the bow of a craft named "Muy Bien," Lieutenant Lamb struck a mock-heroic pose like Washington crossing the Delaware as his men shoved off.* Other Lincolns remained less euphoric. "Why in the hell didn't they get guys who could row boats? It was a bloody mess . . . with us sitting in the middle of the Ebro going round and round." In another boat a Spanish commissar halted in midstream to give them a pep talk, "to tell us all about the great part we were about to play in the struggle. Eventually we made it to the other side."* There was a great logjam—the mules balked noisily at swimming across behind the boats.* Herbert Matthews of the *Times* wrote of the crossing, "If anyone believed that the spirit of Don Quixote was dead, here was proof to the contrary."*

Even as the first boats pushed off, an Italian trimotor, painted a nearly invisible pale blue, droned down the river at one hundred feet and scattered a load of bombs, creating great mud statues along the shore. Minutes later it returned, strafing the canebrake. On its third pass, nearly every man had a rifle or Dichterev ready and opened fire. The plane surged upward like a flushed quail as the men cheered and cursed. "That's the way to treat those bastards! Let him come back, the son of a bitch, and we'll put some lead in his ass!" A volunteer picked up a jagged hunk of shrapnel and examined it soberly. "Boy, that could make a hole in you. *Hombre!* That could do a thing or two." But they crossed the unlucky river without casualties. Exultant, they pushed through red hill country toward Gandesa, just twenty miles southwest.* Before the crossing, Ed Royce, the Jarama commander who had just come up as a replacement rifleman, begged an old New York friend, "Please get me out of here. I can't take it. I'm sick." When a guard fired his rifle to warn of approaching planes, Royce screamed and ran into the open. Men jumped him and held him down until his ear-splitting screams subsided. On the same day, he was sent to the rear and soon repatriated. (For the next thirty years, still obsessed with Jarama, he wrote and talked to anybody who would listen about the massacre on February 27, 1937.)*

Although for days the Barcelona highway had been crowded with fishing boats being trucked south, easily visible from the air, the crossing came as a surprise for the Nationalists, who had ruled out the possibility of a Republican offensive with the Ebro River at their back.[1] Within hours, Republicans were pouring through holes in the Nationalist defenses, the swath of their advance signaled by billowing clouds of yellow dust. The Lincolns pushed warily through a wooded terrain, which some recalled from their flight four months before. Behind them enemy bombers began pounding away at the pontoon bridges while observation planes buzzed over them but dropped no bombs. Some men waved mockingly to the pilots—others took potshots at them. As at Brunete, their worse enemy on this first day was dirt, sweat, and heat. Canteens quickly dried up. Enervated by the torrid heat, weaker men dropped behind. Recollections of the trap that had been sprung upon them at Corbera lurked in their minds even though they found no enemy patrols. Dusk found them camping in an open field slightly east of Fatarella, about halfway to Gandesa. Gunfire roused them wide awake at night. Men began firing in all directions. "Seems that a guard thought a tree was advancing on him, opened fire. Hot fire—our men firing on each other. Couple wounded."*

Before first light of July 26, Lieutenant Leonard Lamb led First Company into Fatarella and flushed out the garrison, which surrendered en masse. The Lincolns got shoes and helped themselves to captured chocolate, cookies, tinned octopus in tomato sauce, and Italian cigars. When they learned that their captors were Internationals, the prisoners were petrified. Huddling together, dirty and dejected, they refused to raise their hands when ordered, assuming this was an excuse for their captors to shoot them. Always they had been told that the Internationals killed their prisoners: that had always been given them to explain why they did the same. (When an IB captain asked a prisoner, "Suppose we were to shoot you?" he retorted, "That would be the first truth that Franco ever told.") Instead of impounding 240 prisoners with a few guards, Captain Wolff dispatched the whole lot to the rear, escorted by two entire sections of Third Company, men shortly to be direly needed. Few of the escort returned promptly, for on their way back they walked into an ambush—and strayed.

Meanwhile, Wolff continued the advance toward Villalba de los Arcos, seven kilometers southwest, without making contact with the enemy, which had

1. When General Franco heard the news, he said he was tempted to allow the Republicans to penetrate as far as they liked, then destroy them. A short time later, however, he became deeply despondent when his forces were unable to push the enemy out of the Gandesa salient. One of the translators on his staff recalls that he overheard Franco weeping, late at night, behind the walls of the Pullman compartment serving as his headquarters.*

fallen back in apparent rout or else was never there at all. Had liaison between battalions been better, they would have learned that the Mac-Paps and British were then being engaged against Hill 481—soon to be ever remembered as "The Pimple"—which overlooked Gandesa two kilometers east of town and which had to be secured before Gandesa could be taken. But the Lincolns were in a byway of the developing battle. Never entirely sure where the enemy was, they moved warily. By dusk of the second day they were short of Villalba. Although their sunburnt skin scaled off in layers, the night turned so cold that the men slept dovetailed in an olive grove.

Earlier that day Lieutenant Jack Cooper of the brigade headquarters company set up his Maxims on a ridge near Venta de Camposines, the main cross-road between Mora de Ebro and Gandesa. He knew that large pockets of Nationalists had been bypassed by the rapid Republican advance: when they tried to break out, the odds were that they would appear at this intersection. Surrounded by jagged knolls overgrown in pine scrub, it was a poor position to hold with a small force. Late in the afternoon Cooper heard yells of "Viva Franco!" and sporadic rifle shots nearby. Before he could withdraw his guns, he was overrun by swarms of Nationalists. With seven *quintos* he was taken prisoner and interrogated. "Where are your forces?" asked an officer. "Way ahead." "How many?" "Five army corps," lied Cooper. The Nationalist officer seemed visibly unnerved. His men had been bedeviled by Republican patrols while they subsisted on nuts and fruit picked off trees. Collecting their prisoners, the Nationalists hid in a thicket. In the morning an officer deferentially approached Cooper and said, "We surrender." At midday Lieutenant Cooper, who had once been sentenced to a firing squad by Dave Doran because he lost some guns on the retreat from Belchite, turned up at brigade headquarters with 208 prisoners. "I didn't know until that minute that we had taken so many," he said. Earlier, he had been stripped of his pistol, bullet clips, and fountain pen. The most lethal object in his pocket was a soiled handkerchief.*

On the third day, July 27, in the wooded hills near Villalba, the Lincolns met their first resistance. Moors eager to fight had thrown up a line blocking the Villalba-Gandesa road. This region was studded with scruffy hummocks rearing up like small islands above patchy fields planted in olives and vines. It was country made for defense. The Lincolns could not attack without exposing themselves to murderous enemy fire, and they had no tanks or artillery to knock out the opposing machine-gun nests and mortar positions. Bullets whipped overhead as the men deployed on lee slopes and crawled to the brows of hills to locate enemy fire. To the north, in the direction of Villalba a flash battle raged; while from Gandesa, seven miles south, came thunderous detonations.

Spearheaded by Lamb's First Company, the Lincolns drove off enemy snipers from the nearest hummocks and approached a valley several hundred yards wide. Fig trees and stony terraces separated them from an array of enemy machine guns on the next ridge, a clean hump like an Indian mound. Officers in front, the Lincolns attacked, dodging downhill and using warped fig trees for cover. Once in the valley, officers picked out possible approaches only to learn that whole sections of the *quintos* refused to budge. Mortar shells ranged along terrace walls where they crouched. The companies of the battalion lost their cohesion and dissolved into autonomous fragments. Men were falling, and almost inevitably these were the best men—the ones who had obeyed the attack order. Lieutenant Lamb, the most experienced company commander, was shot in the hip. Pinned down in the valley, they could do nothing but wait until those behind them turned the enemy's flank. But this was not done.

With each passing hour the firepower arrayed against them perceptively increased. Their three-day hike had ended, for the enemy had established a viable front. Not until nightfall was Captain Wolff able to unify his command. In three days they had covered about twelve miles. Casualties soared. Nearby on an unnumbered hill lay the corpse of Arthur Madden. Also dead was Arnold Reid, killed while directing his machine-gun section with the 24th Battalion.

The mortar fire was ferocious. Of the 126 men (40 of them Internationals) in Lopoff's Second Company only 66 remained, while in Lamb's First Company of about the same number only 36 were accounted for. (Many of the absentees had decided that assisting wounded to the rear was healthier than staying on the line.) That night Lopoff chose a small stone hut for his staff, admiring its heavy walls. When a nail-biter shrilled, "But they can drop them [mortar shells] through the roof!" Lopoff retorted, "What'ya want for a nickel?"*

Beginning at dawn of July 28, the Lincolns made three attacks upon the ridge, all beaten back. The new *quintos* remained oblivious to orders, pleas, threats. Only a handful could be driven past the crest of their hill. They had no cover, but lay down in vines and refused to budge. "The leaders urged, threatened, kicked and shot (a couple) of the Spanish kids, but couldn't get them to advance in the face of the machine-gun fire. Their heart was not in it."* Shooting two of them in front of the others just frightened them more, but they were far too traumatized by aerial bombs, mortar shells, and machine-gun fire to focus on an angry officer flourishing a little pistol. Taking that ridge was of absolutely no importance to them. The Americans gamely tried to advance, but all too many delayed, lagged behind, or escaped to the rear as ammo or food carriers. During a mortar barrage Frank Stout, battalion scout, dropped down wearily beside Alvah Bessie, adjutant of Second Company. "I'm hoping to get hit," he said. "I've been wanting a nice little blighty for some time." A shell exploded almost on top of them, heaping them with dirt as though heaved from a shovel. "I'm hit!" he yelled. Eagerly groping his side, he found only dirt, not blood. "Shucks, I guess it was a stone."* (Four days later he was disemboweled by shellfire.)

Explosions rent the brittle fig trees, showering them with green fruit warm from the sun. Figs passed through intestines like bits of sharp glass, but there was no other food. In the middle of the afternoon shouts went up and down the line, "They're coming!" During the enemy counterattack they crunched behind knolls and frantically lobbed grenades over the crests, awaiting the shock of long bayonets on the skyline. Men without grenades emptied clips into the smoke and dust without picking out targets. The object was to fence their positions with a cordon of lacerating metal. As the sun declined, the firing died out. In the past thirty-six hours the battalion had not advanced one foot. The element of surprise had been forever lost. With Lieutenant Lamb out, the two Lincoln companies merged with Lopoff as commander.

Elsewhere conditions were the same, or worse. The Mac-Paps had been stopped cold within sight of the soccer field on the eastern edge of Gandesa and had had to withdraw because they received no support on their flanks,* while the British had been cut to pieces in a vain attempt to seize Hill 481 ("The Pimple"). "Suicide really," recalled a survivor. The enemy had plenty of time to fortify it— "you could hear them working at night."* In desperation the British attacked in daylight, reached the bottom of the hill, and lay there trapped until nightfall. Seriously wounded men were left behind and listed as dead; Moors finished them off in their counterattack. Somewhere in this shell-pickled landscape some Anglo-Americans found a Moor with shattered leg holding on to a parcel like grim death. Medics pried it away as they pulled off his clothes to treat his wound and found German marks of World War issue. They were worthless, but the Moor believed they assured his way to wealth. Days later when the Mac-Paps moved over to assist the British, a Polish staff officer arrived and criticized Gunnar Ebb, the Mac-Pap acting commander for "not trying hard enough." Ebb picked up a light machine gun and said, through clenched teeth, "Come with me. I'll take you with us to attack the hill." The officer returned at once to Division.*

The underlying fallacy of the offensive had been laid bare: soldiers could be transported across wide rivers more readily than the heavy equipment necessary to supply and support them. The Nationalists dominated the air, and far upstream they opened floodgates, allowing the waters of the Ebro to sweep away the rickety pontoon bridges. At times the line of Republican trucks waiting their turn to cross stretched back three miles. Enemy aircraft attacked them with impunity, for their antiaircraft guns were not effective.* Ambulances were so far down on priority lists that none was allowed to cross the river until the third day of the offensive. Those wounded in the first days had to be evacuated by manpower, which pulled infantry from the line, hauled on supply trucks, or dragged by mules on *artolas* (crude litters). The wounded piled up on the western bank awaiting transportation in rowboats, while their wounds clogged with the fine dust raised by hundreds of vehicles bumper to bumper on the roads. Survivors told depressing tales of how wounded men were robbed openly as they lay helpless on the riverbank and how stretcher-bearers picked through the piles of wounded, taking men belonging to their outfit but ignoring others.

Among the Lincolns, July 29 was a day marked by little activity. A diarist recorded: "Other attacks. None successful. Quiet day." The best the men could do was to snipe at the now-familiar ridge that had blocked them for three days. There were thousands of hills in Spain that looked exactly like that one. It had no special name—not even an elevation number to distinguish it from others on a topographical chart. If they took it, there would be another just like it on the other side. It was a wart, a nodule, a bump—hardly worth making all this fuss about. Was it really worth a man's life? Yet in the evening Wolff was told that it was the only point holding up the advance upon Gandesa from the northeast. It had to be taken.

July 30 was memorable for breakfast—coffee, marmalade, ham, corned beef, and plums—the sort of rich fare given to condemned men before their last mile. Two Spanish battalions attacked through cover fire from the Lincoln and were slaughtered in the pale mist of first light. After this, handfuls of Americans ran down into the valley and took cover behind lumps of dead and wounded. Wolff came over and demanded that the ridge be taken. Lopoff said it was impossible. "The kids won't go over. They're scared stiff." "What'ya mean they *won't* go over?" demanded Wolff in an ugly voice. "We've *got* to take that hill—Brigade's orders." The phrase "Brigade's orders" seemed to impress no one. Were they to race into the jaws of death because some military pundit running his eyes across the contour lines of his chart two miles behind the line had concluded that the failure to occupy this crest would deprive the Republic of victory? Adolescent readers of Tennyson might have been thrilled by the prospect—but they were not. Ordered to fire his Maxim over the heads of attacking Americans, Nick Stamos, a top-notch gunner, refused, for he remembered too well how at Brunete gunners had shot their own men by accident. Now the Maxims were worn out. "You know what the cone of fire is on these old guns? I'm not killing any of our guys."* Wolff's instinct told him his men were right. For a long time he talked on the phone to Brigade; for a longer time he hunched over his maps. In the end he convinced Valledor to call it off. . . .

After nightfall they dragged their wounded from the blood-soaked valley. Then they were relieved.*

For another week the Lincolns shuttled about the sector between Villalba and Corbera in a "reserve" status. To be in reserve during the developing battle of the Ebro meant being shelled at long range instead of being machine-gunned at short. The Nationalists had begun to pull their artillery from the Valencia front. Lining up their guns almost hub to hub, they built a wall of shrapnel between the Republican forces and Gandesa. This technique was known as *aplastamiento,* or "plastering." The shells shrieked through the air like ban-shees. When they hit, the explosions raised towers of dirt in the air and rained down like vomit, shook the earth like jelly, and blew out craters six feet wide and four feet deep. The concussions alone were colossal and stupefying, and the whinnying of the nose caps from exploded shells added to the terror: "If they hit you, you'd be cut up into pieces." Amid such carnage and clatter the cries of wounded men seemed strangely distant, annoying, picayune, irrelevant to the more important business of holding on to one's own head, or arm, or mind. As the earth exploded about them, one's own fate was tragic, the fates of others merely pathetic. The men huddled together like sheep in a blizzard, each vaguely hoping that the flesh of others might somehow cushion their own. Some men made useful necklaces out of pieces of wood on a string so they could bite on it whenever it got really bad.*

They named this place "Death Valley." (The ancient name was Venta de Fusil—"rifle market.") It was a *barranca* leading up toward "The Pimple," which they were supposed to storm as soon as the barrage slacked off. Bad as it was, they were probably better off with the barrage than without it, for the slopes were cluttered with bodies minced by shellfire. As it happened, the bar-rage never slacked off.

Thirteen days after crossing the Ebro, the Lincolns were ordered back to the vicinity of Mora de Ebro for rest and reorganization. They were so overjoyed at leaving "Death Valley" that many men jogged the five-kilometer stretch to the Corbera road. Everyone knew that the offensive had been stopped cold; their own losses stood at fifty percent. The battle of the Ebro was conforming to the pattern of all other Republican offensives—Brunete, Aragon, Teruel—in which a sharp spear point was filed away by attrition. Only the scenery differed—but not by much.

In the moonlight the XVth Brigade marched through Corbera, a deserted village of cardboard fragility except for the church, which still loomed enor-mous on the hill. Most of the buildings, where they stood at all, had been reduced to two-dimensional walls like the false props of a Hollywood cow town plastered with Nationalist (yoke-and-arrow) graffiti. Festering carcasses of mules and horses lay scattered in the streets, but the solitary trace of humanity was the rotten-sweet smell of the dead hidden under the debris. It had taken centuries to build Corbera and less than two weeks to bring it down.

For about a week the Lincolns rested in terraced olive groves near Mora de Ebro. They received threadbare but clean clothes, although the delousing machine had broken down. At night, safe from strafing airplanes, they bathed in the lukewarm water, where it was easy to fantasize about Indiana rivers or Massachusetts ponds on summer evenings with sounds of thunderstorms far far away. During the day they lazed on their backs watching the hawklike descent of enemy bombers attacking the pontoon bridge. (They finally destroyed it, but others up and down the river were kept in repair so that traffic to the front was never entirely cut.) An airplane dropped leaflets with a polite invitation to surrender: "COME OVER TO US, with your officers or alone. Nothing will happen to you if you surrender; if not, you will all die, for you have no more bridges. In Franco's Spain, justice reigns; there is abundance, peace, and liberty. Come over to your brothers. Come over to us."*

The *quintos* read them reflectively—too reflectively to suit the staff—but the Americans chuckled. "Ain't got no union label—scab printing," said one. "Good ass-paper," said another. "We've run out of the *Worker*."* A rumor swept the brigade that Fifth Columnists planned an attack upon the Internationals, and Lincoln officers were instructed to carry pistols at all times. The men jeered at this, for they knew the real reason for the pistols was to abort any wholesale desertion scheme. (There were many such schemes investigated by brigade commissars, followed by punishments for the conspirators, although specific details, if recorded, have not survived.)*

Petitions to leave Spain inundated the brigade commissar, but Gates assembled the battalion and reiterated that all Americans would leave Spain together, or not at all. His language got rough, and the men resented it. "Not until we're through, and any cocksucker who says otherwise is an agent provocateur."* Time was when any volunteer worth his Party salt had spurned work on the staff of the *Volunteer for Liberty*, but now men who had written a line or two in a high school yearbook or prepared leaflets for a rally flaunted their literary credentials. The battle of the Ebro was taking a bad turn—the Nationalists were now counterattacking furiously—and men knew that soon they would be jammed into another leaking sector somewhere. (Nationalist historians record that after August 2 a second phase, "The Battle of Attrition," began, after which the final issue was no longer in doubt.)* The battalion doctor, John Simon, fortified himself with comic fatalism. In his high squeaky voice, he told a veteran complaining about scabies, "It won't make any difference if you cure 'em—you're gonna get bumped off anyhow, and no one will look at you then and say, 'Why how disgusting—he's got a skin disease.'" Though absent-minded most of the time, Simon had a reputation for outrageous courage. Men never decided whether he had enormous willpower or just "didn't know enough to come in out of the rain."* To buttress sagging morale, staff officers reported that the nature of casualties had changed radically—fewer men were getting killed, more were getting wounded. Here was grist for optimists.

They waited, bored but still grateful for boredom rather than what lay ahead. The July 29, 1938, *New York Times* reported that James Lardner had been wounded in the back by shrapnel. (Actually he had been wounded in the rear end after climbing an apple tree for fruit.) There were other bits of news. A prominent New York plastic surgeon, preparing to sail for Spain, waxed enthusiastic about the opportunities lying ahead for his profession, for he estimated that there would be twenty-five thousand cases requiring plastic surgery in the Nationalist zone. And when Joe Louis knocked out Max Schmeling, some of the guys chipped in to cable congratulations for "kayoing the myth of Aryan Racial Superiority. You have joined us in dealing a blow against the enemies of democracy." Limbo ended on August 14, when an order came to fill in latrine pits, turn in picks and shovels, and to stand by with battle kits.

Moving downstream by a back road to the hamlet of Pinell de Bray, they picked up a macadam road winding into the Sierra de Pandols, six miles northwest of Gandesa. After nightfall they turned off along a goat path that scaled upward toward peaks out of sight above them. How, they wondered, were food and water—not to mention ammunition—to reach them on this isolated cliff? At daybreak of August 15 they found themselves on the spine of a saddleback hump identified on charts as Hill 666. It was a windswept and treeless expanse of bare rock the color of bleached bone. The mountain gorse and stunted holly had been burned off by incendiaries dropped from Nationalist bombers to roast the living and the dead among the troops the brigade had relieved. The Lincolns faced west, straddling the backbone of a razorback ridge that looked like the spine of a scaly dinosaur. They were literally hanging on the edge of an escarpment with their fingernails. Fear of falling over the edge infected even men who were strangers to vertigo. Yet when a mule went over, men climbed down to cut off slabs of meat.* From higher elevations enemy machine guns raked their position. To their right there was a perpendicular drop three hundred feet to a mountain valley. Tourists would have loved it. From the cliff edge one had a bird's-eye panorama of Gandesa only two miles away and a thousand feet below. The whole battle zone looked like a scale model on a sand table. The Nationalists desperately wanted this mountain strip, for if they held it their artillery could pinpoint any object in the battle for Gandesa, including the bridgehead at Mora de Ebro.

The area was strewn with unburied dead. For the past two weeks the fighting had been ferocious, and the stench of semi-baked, putrescent flesh gagged and choked the living. *Sanidad* sent up camphor bags, which the men hung around their necks to deaden olfactory nerves. No burial was possible: the men could not dig even shallow rifle pits.[2] Picks and shovels made no more dents than spoons and helmets. "Nothing but rock. You'd ruin a diamond drill trying to dig a hole," recalled a miner.* But when shells or bombs exploded they split off lethal slivers of calcite bedrock. The only recourse was to find a crevice and build barricades of loose rocks and shards of exploded shells. Hill 666 was a geological nightmare, as hostile to human life as the surface of the moon. During the day the barren rock reflected the heat of the sun, and they broiled; at night they shivered as cold winds whipped over the crest. There was, however, one major consolation—the position favored the defense. If the enemy attacked in force, they would have to cross exposed rock slides in full view. Moreover, the volunteers' right flank was secure. Enemy troops attacking from that direction would have to come on goat legs or wings.

On their second day in the Pandols, the Lincolns, who held the right flank next to the cliff edge, were ordered to attack a Moorish outpost several hundred yards across the ridge. Brigade promised artillery and air support for the two hundred men scrounged together for the attack. At three in the afternoon Republican shells whistled over and exploded among the enemy parapets. Then five *Chatos*—one with a picture of Mickey Mouse on the fuselage—screamed down and strafed for five minutes. They left, but no order came to attack. An enemy observation plane circled high above, buzzing like a sluggish fly. Then enemy artillery opened up from far down in the Gandesa valley, their shells exploding among the British reserve positions in a bowl below the Americans. Gradually the shellbursts crept up the hillside to the Lincolns. Shrapnel clattered on the rocks, ricocheting crazily. "This is a hell of a way from Wall Street,"

2. The dead were never buried. When I visited 666 in 1968, the slopes were still littered with heaps of human bone and studded with rusty mortar fins, green cartridges, and scraps of leather. Evidently the only denizens up there since the war had been shepherds. Today it has become a scavenger heaven.

muttered a volunteer. Another claimed he counted 128 shells per minute. One landed squarely on two men coming up the hill, erasing them. Because of the barrage, the attack was postponed.

After dark, two halved companies filed out under Lopoff, who said cheerily, "It'll be a cinch. A handful of men could do it."* For half an hour those men left behind heard and saw nothing. Then, in the distance, there was sudden yelling and firing, followed by pink grenade explosions backlighted by tiny figures scrambling up a slope toward the Moorish outpost. As though a fuse had blown, silence and blackness fell again. There was one more flurry of distant gunfire. Then half an hour later the survivors dribbled back. Their faces were smeared with soot, out of which they peered with enormous white eyes. Some were sobbing—others were gasping.

"Christ! It was hell up there," blurted one man. "They had machine guns—they had barbed wire. Why didn't they tell us they had barbed wire? How were we to know they had barbed wire?" No one had given them wire cutters, and they learned of the wire by getting caught in it. Large numbers of men refused to attack: hidden by the darkness, they held back. A Spaniard handed an officer at the Lincoln command post a bloody automatic and announced theatrically, "La pistola del comandante." Lopoff had been hit in the eye while leading the assault. Since he walked part of the way to the dressing station, everyone thought he would live. (They were wrong—he died six weeks later.) Brigade sent in the British to take the outpost. They attacked before dawn and were beaten back with heavy losses. Only then did Brigade decide that the best tactic might be to hold, not to advance, their positions. The Mac-Paps had no better luck in attacking heights held by the enemy beyond a saucer-shaped valley carpeted with bodies. In the charge up the terrace, Ivor Anderson, a Canadian, lost both legs. He told a companion trying to comfort him, "When we get back home from here, boy, there's no pension, no nothing." He then shot himself with his rifle.*

On the days that followed, the initiative passed to the Nationalists. It was not uncommon to see overhead a squadron of twenty Junkers bombers escorted by sixty fighters—without a single friendly in the sky. They sowed their bombs up and down the Sierra. On one rare day the Lincolns spotted six Republican bombers hovering over the sector looking for enemy artillery to bomb. "They found it—in the form of antiaircraft—Of the six, only four returned."* And on the ground, Moorish antitank guns and mortars systematically demolished IB parapets. Mules brought up loads of empty sandbags, but on Hill 666 there was no sand to fill them with. (A company commander phoned Captain Wolff and suggested that pocket handkerchiefs might be more useful. "I got a bad case of sinus.") High-velocity shells caromed across outcroppings, spraying men with rock splinters. Sometimes one could see a shell bounce a couple of times before coming to rest. Commissar Watt named their position "The Ping Pong Hills." Yet sometimes men found a mysterious beauty in this fearful place. At sunset Harry Fisher enjoyed watching shells "flying through the sunshine, floating like slow motion. Graceful silvery objects."*

August 19 was "the worst day, so far, of this life."* A seven-and-a-half-hour shelling covered nearly every inch of their parapets, shells falling in three-second intervals. "You lie and insanely cover your face with your leather jacket—as though it offered any protection." After the barrage the Moors attacked and were beaten back by grenades. Then for an hour the enemy tried to scale the escarpment beside Hill 666. In the middle of the fighting, Lieutenant Donald Thayer, an erstwhile student at the University of Wisconsin, absorbed by his own problems, when asked what support his company could give to a company on his flank, replied, "Well, I can give you my heartfelt sympathy."* In the end the Moors took a bad drubbing and fled back to their lines. After the barrage, wrote a survivor, "It is almost impossible to walk—you lift your feet like a cat in paper boots—you feel weak and light as a feather. . . . But how much of this is it possible to stand? For myself, I am afraid of breaking."*

The Nationalists repeated their bombings, shellings, and assaults on succeeding days. Emanuel Lanser, commander of Fourth Company, was literally blown out of his clothes by a mortar shell but was not seriously hurt. But his best machine gunner, Joe Bianca, came back "slung in a blanket, gutted like a fish, green and slimy, white, dying."* Hit in the groin by shrapnel, "he lay cursing the enemy with every curse picked up in seven seas till out of breath, when he muttered to a scared man beside him, 'Well, I'll be seeing you in Sunday school.'"* Unable to dig, they buried him under a pile of rocks. After one attack had been repulsed, the commissar of First Company led his men singing "The Star-Spangled Banner." (Others claimed it was "The International.")* Though badly rendered by parched throats, they croaked it to a conclusion before the next barrage began. They did not advance. They did not retreat. They held.

On this same day, in Washington, HUAC voted to submit to the attorney general evidence accumulated that the Lincoln Battalion was a subsidiary of the Red Army. While the men in the Sierra de Pandols hurled back fresh attacks, a new series of battles, to be fought for thirty years behind barricades of lawyers' notes, obscure laws, and the Fifth Amendment, was beginning at home.

After eleven days in the Pandols, the XVth came down and the 43rd Division, including tough mountaineers from the Pyrenees, went up. They cheered each other as they passed in the dusk. The brigade was cited for its "magnificent defense of hill 666," but so far as the men were concerned, the greatest reward was leaving behind that damned mountain. "We came down," wrote one man, "a whole lot faster than we had gone up." Near Pinell de Bray, now reduced to ruins, they camped in a bower not far from the Ebro. For a "crummy bunch" they had done pretty well. There was plenty of grit left.

18

LA DESPEDIDA

September was a month of brutal fighting during which the XVth Brigade was hurled into breaches and plugged gaps in a continually breaking line around the road intersection at Venta de Camposines, about midway between Corbera and Mora de Ebro. Men were squeezed like putty into the leaking seams of a moribund "offensive" whose revised slogan was a phrase in doublespeak, "To Resist Is to Win." A handful of useless reinforcements came up from Badalona, the ramshackle and improvised IB base that replaced Albacete, "a scurvy lot, ex-prisoners, ex-deserters, and unreliable elements."* Often surrounded on three sides, the XVth fought on hilltops and they waited in holes. At times the massed rows of enemy troops, pushing like a city mob down the Corbera road, were close enough to read the divisional emblems stitched on their tunics. On one occasion "they were marching on us with banners flying—can you imagine it? Flags!" Some *quintos* tried to run up a white flag until an American commissar (name withheld) shot a couple of them. But the momentum for retreat could not be denied. "A lot got wounded and the rest of us ran. . . . Fifteen of [our] company got back." In two days of fighting about forty Lincolns—fourteen of them Americans—became prisoners of war. On their march to the rear an officer heard English voices, stopped the column, and called them aside. Without warning, machine guns opened fire at five meters. Among the captives all the Americans were killed, but the Spaniards were unharmed.* Yet in all this confusion, the Lincolns somehow captured an abject prisoner, who pleaded, "I know that I will die; but please shoot me; don't feed me to the lions in the Barcelona zoo."*

More often than not, the enemy barrage, that cursed *aplastimiento*, was so awesome that even Nationalist infantry feared to budge. The air became heavy with thick sulfurous fumes, as acrid as a city smog. The sun shone but looked like the moon. Whenever the Republic retook a hundred yards of lost territory, Barcelona papers cried victory and proclaimed a turning of the tide. The progress of the war was measured in lies and inches.

On September 21, 1938, in Geneva, Juan Negrin, prime minister of the Republic, announced to the League of Nations that all International volunteers would be withdrawn from the front immediately in order to be counted, labeled by nationality, and repatriated to their countries of origin. The underlying idea was to persuade, by example, foreign powers assisting the Nationalists to withdraw their support. Even as Negrin spoke, the XVth Brigade was being rushed, once again, into a ruptured sector a few hundred yards west of the Crossroads.

Only 280 men were at this time listed on the combatant rolls of the Lincoln Battalion, of which about 80 were Americans. News of the imminent withdrawal leaked to the brigade staff early in the morning of September 22. Since these men had already been committed to battle, nothing could be done until Division ordered them back. Commissar Gates confiscated all newspapers to keep the news from the men. Who would fight well if he knew that he would be permanently withdrawn within a few hours? On the day before "an intense barrage [had] put them in state of shock and numbness." However, Gates wanted the Lincolns to leave Spain with, as he put it, "the taste of victory on our lips."*

The Lincolns were deployed in a thin line on hill 376, about half a mile north of the Corbera road, with the British on the south side of the road. Beginning at dawn, artillery pounded their sector so unmercifully that individual shell-bursts could not be distinguished. "This sounds like the World War," remarked an American who had fought in it. An observer behind the lines claimed that he counted three hundred enemy planes in the sky at one time. Late in the afternoon Captain Wolff got an urgent appeal from a Polish battalion on a small knoll on his right flank—the enemy was breaking through.

It was growing dark when the Lincolns went over to help, and visibility was obscured. Wolff sent out patrols to reconnoiter the wooded hillsides, all of which looked exactly alike. Corporal James Lardner with two men went out to determine whether a knoll farther to the northwest was occupied. From the top came down the noise of spades and shovels. Lardner went up alone. Those below heard a shout of alarm and Lardner's reply in Spanish. Then came yells, popping grenades, and the clatter of machine guns. Lardner never returned. The next day the war ended for the Lincolns. Ironically only a few days before, Alvah Bessie, newly appointed to the staff of the *Volunteer for Liberty,* had come down to the Lincolns with a request that Lardner be sent to Barcelona to work on the paper. Commissar Watt turned it down, "I don't think he's a very good writer yet. He's learning things now that will mature him." "If he lives," said Bessie. Watt laughed.*

Meanwhile Wolff posted his men on hills behind the Poles. Gates had told him that they had to hold for just one more day. "Get it? One more day? And we can pack up and go home." When the food truck came up without the usual newspapers, the men smelled withdrawal but did not know what to believe. One thing was certain: no one was willing to be shot or killed during the final hours. "The last day was psychologically very bad," remembered one American. "Everybody wanted to live."*

On that last day, they had to endure what many recalled as the heaviest artillery barrage in Spain. On September 23 the brigade formed a thin line across hills 365 and 361, four kilometers southwest of Venta de Composines. Some companies never reached their assigned positions at the front. Scores of *quintos* had vanished overnight, deserting to the enemy or skulking far to the rear. Labor battalions were herded to the front lines, armed with cigars and bottles of gasoline, and ordered to repel enemy attacks.* Over on the far right Bill Wheeler reported that he had only seventeen men in his section left from seventy on the day before. The dead in his "barranca del muerto" were "thicker per square foot" than in any other battle he had seen in the war.* It was the last day on earth for many. After the barrage on the extreme right "only a handful of men were left amid dozens of smashed rifles."*

After a five-hour barrage, the Nationalists walked through the Lincolns as though parading in high grass. The whole battalion rolled back to the Corbera road. A hundred yards to the left, running parallel to the road, a deep *barranca* wound downhill toward the road intersection. The temptation to use it as an escape passage was irresistible. Men jumped into it and fled to the rear. The breakthrough happened so suddenly that Wolff did not hear of it until too late. He and Watt climbed out of their command post and gazed out upon a network of trenches filled with impedimenta but emptied of men. Looking to the north they saw swarms of enemy soldiers flooding into the abandoned trenches, advancing behind waving banners and trumpet blasts. In a daze Wolff found himself "unable to believe what we were seeing—the Fascists were all along the ridge dancing and jigging around, waving their arms, calling us to come back, but not shooting at us, just jeering."* Then the shelling began again, and everybody ran, the enemy moving laterally along the defensive line and rolling up the British flank. It was a heartbreaking denouement to the Lincoln Battalion saga. It had been a strong defensive position. "That goddamned ditch swallowed them up, funneled them out of the lines straight to the rear, and if Brigade HQ hadn't been in the ditch, Christ knows where they would have gone." To the end, wherever that was, Wolff later wrote that that last day was "the most painful of my period in Spain."*

The nearby British Battalion had also rotted away. A newcomer, John Bassett, perhaps the last Briton to reach the XVth Brigade, found no trace of the

much-publicized crusade against Fascism. Hope and comradeship had disappeared, replaced by fears of the mutilation and torture that was the lot of any
International captured by Moors. Nothing was ever explained to him, and he
never saw a map. With others he scrambled up hills from terrace to terrace supported only by the gun of a single tank below and the screams of a commissar,
"Death to the Fascist bastards!"* Of his original company he only saw one or
two again—and they had run away. Yet sometimes heroism bloomed in strange
soil. An exhausted Spanish conscript told a Scotsman, "'This is no life for me. I
am going to get away across the frontier as soon as I can.' Yet he stayed—and
saved the flank by beating back the enemy with short bursts of his machine gun.
Probably he was killed. I never saw him again."* When the enemy attack
petered out, the survivors thought the worst was over. With the Mac-Paps, an
unidentified American sergeant acting as adjutant of First Company called over
to Bill Matthews, his commander. "Bill, we made it!" He spoke too soon. A
squadron of bombers unloaded on them, and the American had his leg and arm
blown off. Looking around, Matthews saw men putting a bandage around the
head of the Third Company commander. "A chunk of the bomb was sticking
out of his head. In a moment he keeled over. We got blown to hell. It still bothers me."* Fortunately the enemy had had enough for the moment and pressed
no farther. The ragtags of the XVth Brigade waited in bitterness until midnight,
when the order came that they had been relieved. Most agree that this was the
heaviest barrage they had endured in Spain. Gates had no illusions about continuing, for the battalions "were no longer fit for combat."*[1]

At about two in the morning of September 24, some Spanish regulars filed
into their trenches and relieved the XVth Brigade permanently.[2] Among the
Lincolns there were no signs of jubilation on their hike to the Ebro. "It was a
silent and sad march—no joy in anyone on that last forced march."* Dawn had
come when on September 24 the last Americans tramped across the wooden
planks of the pontoon ridge at Mora de Ebro and climbed up the long hill on
the far shore. The sound of their marching feet was "a low shuffle, there were
no voices; there was no singing."* From the summit above the left bank they
looked back at the wide yellow river and the ruffled landscape beyond,

---

1. There were exceptions to the defeated majority. Although wounded five times, Sam Wild,
the British commander, spoke for a few, "Right until the end I never thought the fascists would
win. It sounds crazy."*

2. While the Spaniards in the XVth Brigade—sixty percent of the total—returned with the foreigners to rest areas, their obligations for further service had not ended. They shortly returned to the
Ebro battle, still members of the XVth Brigade but not under Comintern authority. All foreigners
were supposed to surrender their arms when officially relieved.* Presumably, the Lincolns did so.

obscured by the dirty haze of war. They were now spectators. It was possible to want to leave and, at the same time, want not to have left what was being thrashed out over there. Men wept, without shame. For them the war was over.

The Lincoln Battalion had a final rest in Marsa. Billeted in houses, stables, and farms nearby, the men luxuriated in the creature comforts of an almost forgotten civilization, for the village contained not only a cinema and soccer field but also a splendid café with a terrace looking out across a valley of almond trees to barren peaks shaped like big scoops of ice cream. Brigade established a hospital in an arcaded barn a mile from town, and men fatally wounded were buried in unused common land beside the small creek that ran through the valley. (A gravestone engraved with his name, rank, and brigade marks the burial site of John Cookson of Cobb, Wisconsin—the only known grave of an American volunteer killed in the war.)[3] Now that the worst was over and they were alive, humor resurfaced, and in a favorite song they fused their trauma of yesterday with anticipations of tomorrow:

> Send me over the sea
> Where the Fascists can't get at me—
> Oh, my, I'm too young to die,
> I want to go ho-OME!*

On October 5 Milton Wolff—now a major—drew up his old battalion on the Marsa soccer field for the last time. He ordered the Americans to fall out and to form in a far corner of the field. As an "International" brigade the XVth was thereby dissolved, but the number was retained for the Spaniards remaining. While the Spaniards marched away to fresh killing fields of the Ebro, the Americans had their pictures taken.[4] The demobilized Lincolns, standing or sitting cross-legged like a varsity club in a high school yearbook, smiled into the

---

3. Villagers of Marsa first located the grave for me in 1968. The site is now frequently visited by Lincoln veterans, who since the death of Franco have been publicly welcomed in Spanish communities. The barn used as a hospital contained many names of patients etched in glass or carved on wooden beams along with patriotic graffiti.

4. Absorbed into the Republican Army, the XVth Brigade, consisting of Spaniards, participated in the final battles of Catalonia, where the entire brigade was commanded by a lieutenant. On February 7, carrying satchels and knapsacks instead of rifles, they crossed into France at Le Perthus, singing revolutionary songs until silenced by French gendarmes, "Over here is peace and quiet—no songs, no noise." After helping themselves to "military equipment" like binoculars and personal watches, the guards conducted them to a heavily fenced barrens on the sands near Argelés, without huts, firewood, or sanitary facilities, where they dug holes and tried to make the best of it.*

lens. Not counting a villager who hurriedly scaled the wall behind them to get into the picture, one counts fifty-nine faces. (Hospital cases and Barcelona cadres slowly added to that number.) In the banquet following, Robert Minor as main speaker congratulated the Lincoln remnant as "the hard core upon which American revolution could be built." For the past year Minor had lauded the Spanish war a "godsend" to the CPUSA for creating "real Bolsheviks, men who had learned to fight."*

Then on October 17 the Germans of the XIth Brigade joined the XVth for a farewell fiesta at Marsa. A truck parked in a field outside the village provided a reviewing stand for Luigi Longo, inspector general of the International Brigades, and other worthies as the Internationals marched past. André Marty, who missed the parade, arrived in time for a banquet spread out on planks mounted on sawhorses at a farmhouse nearby. The walls were garnished with Republican streamers and a photograph of Lenin. Longo spoke of the International Brigades, which on this day, the eve of their disbandment, celebrated their second anniversary. Stirred into action, Marty delivered a fist-shaking tirade concluding with the words, "With a mad dog we cannot fool. We must annihilate it. Fascism is a mad dog, and we shall kill it."* There were no allusions to Trotsky, his bête noir, in the speech. After two years of war, André Marty may have learned, at last, who the real enemy was, or at least the dignity of silence.

Some members of the brigade traveled to Barcelona on October 29 for the grand parade of the International Brigades down the sycamore-lined Diagonal (shortly to be renamed Avenida del Generalissimo Franco). This was La Despedida (The Farewell), but it resonated like a victory march as well. Groups representing twenty-six nations from Algeria to Yugoslavia—but no Russians—tramped down the broad avenue as thousands of spectators lined the curbs, climbed lampposts and trees, and waved from balconies. Plaques listing the names of outstanding Internationals lined the route. (The only North Americans so honored were Dave Doran and Niilo Makela; as a non-Communist, Robert Merriman was left out.) The marchers carried no weapons. Their uniforms ranged from spit-and-polish to business suits. Compared with the Rákosi and the André Marty battalions, decked out in new uniforms with stiffly wired garrison hats, the Lincolns resembled a band of border marauders. With blanket rolls slung over their right shoulders, with nearly every kind of footgear known to man, and with patched uniforms bronzed with age, they swept past, some grinning and others dead-serious, eight abreast and trying to stay in step. Wolff remembered, "We've never been what you call very good at parade marching, and when we got on those streets with flowers up to our ankles I guess we did a kind of shag."* "These men had learned to fight before they had learned to parade," wrote Herbert L. Matthews, who was present that day. "They were not clad in spic-and-span uniforms; their garb was nondescript; they had no arms, and they could not seem to keep in step or in line. But everyone who saw them knew that these were true soldiers."* Near the end of the parade, girls broke through the cordon and doused them with flowers and clung to their necks. A New Yorker captured the moment: "The women and children were jumping into our arms, kissing us, calling us sons, brothers, calling 'Come back,' weeping. I never had such an experience because these men, such tough fighters, every last one of them was crying."*

In a farewell speech, Premier Negrin, with tears in his eyes, promised citizenship to any of them who returned to Spain after the war. Finally La Pasionaria delivered a speech no Lincoln veteran ever forgot:

> Comrades of the International Brigade! Political reasons, reasons of State, the welfare of that same cause for which you offered your blood with boundless generosity, are sending you back, some of you to your own countries and others to forced exile. You can go proudly. You are history. You are legend. You are the heroic example of democracy's solidarity and universality. We shall not forget you, and when the olive tree of peace puts forth its leaves again, mingled with the laurels of the Spanish Republic's victory—come back!*5

Through La Pasionaria, a volunteer could recover the vanished innocence of Communism. A military band burst forth with "Himno de Riego." Few Internationals knew the words, but they sang lustily. No man caught up in the collective pageantry of *La Despedida* could doubt, at that moment, that their sacrifice had been in vain.

At only one other time during the war did the populace of Barcelona flood the avenues to watch an army of strangers. That was on January 26, 1939, the day the Nationalist troops under General Yagüe took the city and knelt in prayer in the Plaza de Cataluña.

In late October during a cold downpour, the Anglo-Americans moved to Ripoll, a piedmont town thirty-five kilometers from France, where they occupied billets

---

5. La Pasionaria's invitation to "come back" was only a rhetorical pleasantry, because by this time the Republic was so eager to rid itself of the Internationals that once a brigader left Spain it was illegal for him to return.*

in a theater, a nasty place where men shook their lice-ridden blankets over the balcony to howls of rage from those bedding down in the stalls.* It was a grim and boring place, always short of firewood, where food reached an all-time low. Catalonia was near starvation. Brigade cooks boiled bones until they were white and then split them to remove the marrow. The bones were then dumped behind the cookhouse, where the locals foraged and took them home to concoct a meal.* After *La Despedida* there were no more parades, no more grand fiestas. As winter closed in, men swaddled themselves in blankets against the biting winds. It was dark when they marched to breakfast, and it was dark again by mid-afternoon.*

On November 2 commissioners from the League of Nations, consisting of a British general, Danish and Swedish colonels, and an American civilian, arrived to authenticate them. They sat at tables while the men filed past giving basic details, each receiving a lone cigarette from a commissioner. "Paste-white worms full of pomp and self-importance,"* Milton Wolff called them, for some tried to pump men about their political affiliation. The Lincolns bristled, particularly when invited for a longer confidential chat. "We showed our resentment to these well-fed, well-dressed questioners, who represented the callousness and unconcern of the European countries. In our rags we felt superior."*[6]

Initially the French government had insisted that disbanded Internationals embark at Spanish ports on vessels that would carry them directly to countries other than France, because rightists had expressed alarm that twelve thousand Red warriors would overrun their country. But finally France agreed to issue transit visas, provided that tickets were paid for in advance, that the ex-soldiers traveled on sealed trains, and that each of them carried documentation certifying that his respective country would accept him. For the Americans that meant that the Department of State had to certify each man's citizenship.

As to financial arrangements, the FALB, which had never had difficulty raising money to ship men over, claimed insolvency when the time came to bring them back. Special funds were solicited from such private donors as Bernard Baruch, who contributed ten thousand dollars to the cause. In November, however, the FALB succumbed to public pressure and deposited the required funds for repatriation with French authorities without publicizing the fact that the Spanish Republic had defrayed nearly all expenses.[7] Great Britain assessed each

6. The total number of all who served in Spain as tallied by the League commissioners, stood at 32,109, of whom 12,144 were present at the time.*

7. In December the Republican chargé in Washington called upon Pierrepont Moffitt, chief of the Division of European Affairs at the Department of State, to inquire whether the United States would agree to reimburse the Republic for its expenditures in bringing home the American volunteers. Secretary Cordell Hull's answer to this can be imagined.

repatriated volunteer two pounds, five shillings, to cover his homeward fare, but most never paid. (One former brigader wrote that he would pay his when all the British soldiers evacuated from Dunkirk in 1940 paid theirs.)*

The men waiting at Ripoll had originally been scheduled to cross into France on November 11, but they were delayed for three more weeks because Lincoln officers and the Department of State were each trying to outmaneuver the other in the matter of the "lost" passports. On November 6 the Republican official in charge of evacuating the Internationals was informed that 272 Americans waited at Ripoll with valid passports. The U.S. consulate at Barcelona accordingly sent three officers up to Ripoll on November 10 with instructions to stamp each passport: "Valid only for direct return to the United States." But on reaching the Lincoln camp, the consuls found 420 Americans and only 40 passports. Battalion officers claimed all the others had been lost between Albacete and Barcelona. The result was that information about each volunteer had to be cabled to Washington, innumerable affidavits had to be sworn to, innumerable forms had to be filled out, and the Lincolns lost their opportunity to cross the frontier on November 11, for which they blamed the State Department. State, however, feared that volunteers from other countries would take advantage of the confusion in order to enter the United States illegally. Moreover, it was widely believed (with good cause) that the missing passports would be used in Soviet espionage activities throughout the world.[8] (To make such use more difficult for forgers, the United States soon changed the passport binding from blue to green and redesigned the pages.) Canada made no such change and its bootlegged passports were more suitable for espionage. When it became clear that volunteers might be held back for months, some 201 passports miraculously turned up and were submitted to the Barcelona consulate ten days later. The "mystery" of what happened to the others will doubtless be solved when all the archives of the Soviet Union have been opened, unless such records have been destroyed.

Even as they prepared for their trip home, the commissariat compiled secret personnel reports on the Americans at Ripoll. Their purpose was to evaluate the performance of each man in relation to his future usefulness in Party activities. (These documents ended up in Moscow with the bulk of other IB archives.) Nor were forty-eight non-Party men overlooked. These received ratings according to

---

8. Passports belonging to members of the International Brigades were "prized at OGPU headquarters," reported W. G. Krivitsky. While he was visiting Lubianka prison in Moscow during the spring of 1937, one hundred passports arrived, half of them American. "Nearly every diplomatic pouch from Spain that arrived at the Lubianka contained a batch of passports from members of the International Brigades."*

five categories: Good (11 men), Mediocre (12), Drunks (5), Bad (12), and Very Bad (8). For instance, the major Lincoln armorer rated a "Good" but was marked down for "lacks political understanding"; George Peters earned a "Bad" because he was a "coward, deserter, and degenerate"; and James Murphy bottomed out as "Very Bad" because he was a "deserter and anti-Communist."*

On December 2, the first group of 327 Americans left Ripoll at eight in the morning aboard a special train festooned with evergreen wreaths—whether for decoration or camouflage they never were told. (Fifteen men missed the train because it left on time.) The townspeople gathered to see them off, and some gave the Popular Front salute. When a Spanish officer on the platform dabbed his eyes with a handkerchief, an American leaning out of a broken window shouted, "Hey, guys, pipe that captain going tragic on us!" The train crossed a barren waste to Puigcerda, the Spanish frontier town. At the station posters featured a helmeted aviator, goggles thrown back, watching a flight of planes in V-formation and labeled "1938—AÑO DE LA VICTORIA."* But the year was about to run out.[9]

The men sang their way into France, at La Tour de Carol, and from the station they looked back to see five Junkers on the Spanish side of the border unload twenty bombs on the tracks they had just passed over. "They were looking for us," Wolff said to Herbert L. Matthews, who had come from Barcelona to chronicle their departure. "I hope they won't still be looking for you when I drive back down," replied the reporter.* The Americans trooped through the station, whooping like schoolboys on holiday. They gorged on a simple meal of butter, bread, and ham (too rich—most men threw up at once); they chain-smoked their way through packs of French cigarettes. Matthews noted that by habit they nipped off the ends and dropped the butts into their pockets. The Republic had provided each man with a cheap pin-stripe suit but no overcoats, so they shivered in the thin wintry air. Fifty men still wore *alpargatas,* leather shoes being hard to find in Spain. Battalion officers told Matthews that probably 350 Americans still remained in Catalonia, including hospital cases, perhaps 100 cut off in Valencia, and about 15 men missing, probably AWOL in Barcelona. An additional 50 were questionables—they had lived in the United States but had never taken out citizenship papers. Even though some had wives or children in the States, they had been told that they must await openings on quotas.

9. The Canadians had to wait another month for clearance. In late January they moved to a cork factory at Casa de la Selva, where they received a call to volunteer again, this time for the defense of Barcelona. Although they had turned in their uniforms and received passports, they called a meeting and after heated debate decided that individuals could return. Many signed on, but the government remained committed to repatriation, so on February 4 the full complement arrived at Saint John, New Brunswick, via Great Britain.*

Perhaps the most pathetic case was Joe Morrison, a middle-aged American Indian who had no passport, no registration of birth, and no friends or relatives at home able to identify him.*

When Franco cut the Republic in two, an unknown number of Americans, including members of the John Brown Battery at Almansa, were trapped in the Valencia sector.* Billed as "Lost Legion" by American newspapers, they managed in January to escape by boarding a vessel jammed with crying children bound for Barcelona, where they found billets in a whorehouse. Marty intercepted them and demanded that they enlist for a last-stand defense of Barcelona. When the Americans excused themselves by explaining they had nothing to fight with, Marty lambasted them with his set speech as "cowards and dead-beats," adding that "the road to France does not represent peace and liberty—it is the road to slavery!"* The men opted for slavery over peace and liberty as they joined the mass of refugees trudging on foot toward the frontier. (After rounding up some scattered Internationals in northern Catalonia, Marty created a ghost brigade and, having no trust in senior officers, placed in command a very surprised young second lieutenant. The unit soon fell apart.) In late January, numbering one hundred and sixty-four, the Americans passed through the railway tunnel at Port Bou and crossed into France. They were safe at last, but with "no cheering, no elation."*

On December 2, 1938, at 4:44 p.m., the train carrying the main body of the demobilized Lincolns pulled out of La Tour de Carol station, ending their Spanish adventure. The sealed train immediately turned into a joyous bedlam of singing and drinking as it rolled northward through the night. *Gardes mobiles* guarded all platforms, but one contributed a bottle of cognac to the party. Lincoln officers traveled in first class, the men in third. Dawn found compartments of dozing men and empty bottles wobbling from side to side as though in a storm at sea. Fearing a recurrence of the tumultuous demonstrations that had marked the entry of the French volunteers a month earlier, the government shuttled subsequent trainloads of Internationals around Paris on a wide detour. But at each switch and station in the drab outer *arrondissements,* small groups of Frenchmen stood and lifted arms with clenched fist. How they identified their train among hundreds of others they never found out, but anti-Fascism was still alive in France.* Once the train made an unscheduled stop. Marion Noble looked out and saw it surrounded by cops, every three feet. Workmen on the tracks refused to let the train pass. They wanted to hand in food parcels "but the French officials were scared half to death there was going to be a revolution."*

At Le Havre, the main body of Lincolns was met by a small army of gendarmes and an official from the Compagnie Generale Transatlantique who
explained that the *Normandie* would not sail as scheduled because of a seamen's
strike. "Faut marcher au Parc de la Heve," he told them. "Park?" shouted an
American. "Who the hell wants to go to the goddamn *park?*"* The local prefect
had buses on hand to transport them to a dingy compound four kilometers
outside town, the Le Havre counterpart of Ellis Island. It consisted of brick hut-
ments enclosed by a chain-link fence, topped with barbed wire. "They give us
the bum's rush around Paris, and now a concentration camp," complained a
volunteer. The mattresses were filthy, there were no bathing facilities. The
director warned them that he expected order in his camp: if they made trouble,
he would call in the gendarmes patrolling outside the eight-foot fence. Le Havre
was already on the verge of a civil insurrection because of the bitter strike; the
authorities feared that the presence of *les voluntaires d'Espagne* might act as a
catalyst for the working class of the city. Wolff called a meeting. They had to set
an example of discipline "in the face of the hostility of the French government."
Then, echoing La Pasionaria's farewell speech, he added, "We have a history
and a tradition and will maintain it till we reach New York and disband."*

News of the strike came as a hard blow. They eagerly yearned for home, but if
they sailed on a ship manned by scabs, they would mock the basic principles of
working-class solidarity that had sent them to Spain. In the evening a delegation
from the seamen's union came out to the park for a meeting in the communal
mess hall. They had proposed to the company that they would crew the *Normandie* for the express purpose of carrying the American volunteers home, provided that all other passengers were excluded. This proposal had, of course, been
rejected. The union was distressed about the plight of the Americans, but it could
not cancel a strike solely for their benefit. Therefore they arranged with the
authorities for the Lincolns to ship out on the *Paris,* due to depart on December
6, manned by a crew from the French Navy. The only scabs aboard would be in
the stewards' department. "Then we won't sail," interrupted Wolff. But the union
spokesman explained that they had no choice: their transit visas would otherwise
expire, and they might then return home, not in honor but under arrest. He went
on to say that his union had "granted permission" for the anti-Fascist fighters to
embark on the *Paris;* indeed, they requested them to do so. Lifting his clenched
fist, the delegate shouted "Salud!" and the hall exploded with excited approval. A
college boy shouted, "Vive la France et les pommes de terre frites!" Two men
began singing "Le Marseillaise," and another called out, "Anybody we catch tipping the fink stewards goes over the side!"* On the spot, the Americans took up a
collection, in the currency of a dozen countries, for the strike fund.

Conditions in Le Havre became so volatile that the *Paris* had to move over to Cherbourg, where passengers and stewards could be taken aboard in a calmer atmosphere. Because of a backlog of passengers stranded in France by canceled sailings, only 148 Lincolns went aboard. They traveled to Cherbourg by train, where they embarked behind a thick cordon of gendarmes. Looking out at the Atlantic, a gloomy American said, "Just like them, once we get on a boat, to send a Nazi submarine after us and knock us off." It was the old story: "Nothing is too good for the working class, and nothing is what we get."* An American reporter needled Milton Wolff about his collaboration with the ship owners. Although Wolff tried to explain that the men really had no choice about it, the compromise left a bad taste in their mouths. The crossing was stormy the whole way, but much to their delight most of the scab stewards were seasick from shore to shore. Sheldon Jones, who had gone to Spain from Antioch College (Ohio), met a German-Jewish couple in first-class who argued with him that Hitler had done a lot for Germany by controlling labor unrest. It was pointless to reply to this.*

The wartime rule for good commissars—"First to advance and last to retreat"—continued to the last minute on the *Paris,* when Commissars Gates and Wellman met and expelled from the Party Mickey Mickenberg, the sarcastic naysayer who had forced them to look at each other through a comic mirror. (In New York, Mickenberg, who had been a Lincoln since the Jarama massacre, was denied medical assistance and not allowed to join VALB until protests from other veterans, who appreciated his cranky humor, overruled the policy.)*

On December 15, 1938, the *Paris* docked at its 48th Street pier in New York, bringing back the first discharged band of IB veterans from the Spanish civil war. Immigration officers held them back until all other passengers had gone ashore. Some men unable to prove American citizenship were transferred to Ellis Island to await help from CP attorneys. Among these were Mirko Markovicz, the Lincoln-Washington commander at Brunete, and Bob Gladnick, the Jarama "mutineer" who had joined the Soviet tank corps.[10] (Bill Lawrence admonished Gladnick because he had admitted his membership in the YCL to immigration officers: "No Communist ever admits anything.")*

Photographs on passports were scrutinized and matched with faces in the flesh, the men were fingerprinted, and their travel documents confiscated. "When will I get my passport back?" asked one veteran. "Never—I hope," came

---

10. Markovicz was released from Ellis Island on payment of $1,000 bail. Deported to Cuba a short time later, he returned to Yugoslavia in 1945 as dean of economics at Belgrade University. In 1949 he was jailed in the notorious prison on Goli Island for support of Stalin. Released after five years he continued to be harassed by Yugoslav authorities.*

the reply. The customs shed was nearly empty when they came down the gang-plank, passing through a cordon of policemen mumbling about goddam com-mie bastards, "Why don't you fight for *your* country?" Outside, they found massed policemen, mounted and on foot, keeping a welcoming crowd of two or three thousand on the far side of Twelfth Avenue. Cheering and clapping broke out as the Lincolns stepped out of the pier building and crossed over. The Brighton Beach Community Center Drum and Bugle Corps played in special honor of George Watt, native son (who had been left behind at Le Havre to per-form his last duties as IB commissar).

The FALB had arranged a parade. Led by Milton Wolff, the Americans, once again in the uniform of the Spanish Republic, marched across town. At their head waved the flags of the United States, the Republic, and the Lincoln Battalion. There were no red banners, no hammers and sickles, no portraits of Lenin. On their flanks mounted policemen rode like a cavalry escort. Trailing behind came the great throng of sympathizers and well-wishers carrying banners that read

LIFT, LIFT THE EMBARGO ON SPAIN

and

DOWN WITH DALADIER DECREES*

As in Barcelona, people dashed from the curb to embrace them or applaud as they passed. Many bystanders, however, stared in puzzlement, no doubt wondering who these men were and perhaps reflecting that they looked terribly young to be veterans of the Spanish-American War. At random points along the line of march, somber figures—mothers, fathers, wives, and lovers—held up crudely fashioned signs that begged the men for a word:

WHAT HAPPENED TO——?

ANYONE KNOW——? LOST AT JARAMA

PLEASE TELL ME ANYTHING ABOUT——

A wet-eyed woman of middle age held up an enlarged photograph with her query. The picture might have been of Paul White, but no one stopped to see.

By the time the procession reached Madison Square, many Lincolns had dropped out and slipped away forever. Milton Wolff remained with a hard core of disciples. An FALB sound truck boomed out a speech of welcome. Four veterans stepped forward carrying a wreath labeled "In Memory of Those Who Died for Democracy" and tried to lay it at the base of the Eternal Light in the park. But their way was barred by Lieutenant Charles Maura of the NYPD, who informed them that they needed a permit to place the wreath. Some Lincolns lurched forward angrily but were pulled back. The police bristled and closed ranks. For a moment it seemed as if the homecoming might turn into a free-for-all in the faint penumbra of the Eternal Light. But an FALB official trotted over to say that the Lincoln Battalion did not wish to make a scene. In the end the wreath was dropped outside the railing of the light. No permit was required for that. They did not sing "The International." Somebody played "Taps."*

Just two weeks later, on January 27, President Franklin D. Roosevelt at a cabinet meeting admitted that the embargo enforced against the Republic of Spain had been "a grave mistake" because it "controverted old American principles and invalidated international law."* And just two days before that, Barcelona had surrendered unconditionally, without a fight, to the armies of General Francisco Franco.

19

"PREMATURE ANTI-FASCISTS" AND ALL THAT

It was a war without pension and without medals. The only decorations most of them brought back were their wounds, although these were abundant enough. There was no mustering-out pay, no disability insurance, no military hospitals. They had gone fifteen rounds with a merciless foe who had cheated at the weigh-in, but they had climbed out of the ring groggy but under their own power. Ninety percent of them needed jobs, and seventy percent required some form of medical attention. Even those in perfect health required an estimated $75 to return them home, but for those who had lost an eye or a leg and perhaps had to learn a new vocation and receive convalescent care or prosthetic devices, the estimated cost was $300, while of the five percent totally blind, paralyzed, or permanently disabled the cost might run to $50 per week indefinitely.[*1]

The hard-wires, of course, could fall back upon the resources of the Party, but for most of the twelve hundred (estimated) veterans, nothing stood between their homeless homecoming and the wintry air except the FALB, with national headquarters at 124 West 45th Street. Their equivalent of a Veterans Administration—not much but all they had. The men flocked to this eternally poor-mouth organization that had collected money in the name of all the Americans who fought in Spain and disbursed it in favor of a privileged minority. (No malcontents, demoralized element, or FONICS were welcome.) If a vet had a beef, he could go downtown to Party headquarters on 12th Street and file a complaint in triplicate.

Assuming that a man had had a good political record in Spain and showed promise of good work within, or on the fringes of the Party, the FALB could arrange for expensive medical treatment, free housing and board, and night courses for the crippled. There were introductions to well-connected power-brokers in trade unions, and social outings to meet zealous young women prepared to give their all to "the conquering heroes of the revolutionary class

---

1. A blind veteran in 1939 protested to the Party and to whoever would listen that he had been swindled. During the war he had raised a lot of money for the battalion; now he was destitute and forgotten. As a bonus, or as hush-money, a wife was found for him and he was given funds to purchase a small shop in New York City.

who slew the ugly beast of Fascism," as one FALB handout described them. (An upper-class female who combined revolutionary fervor with sexual favors was yclept "Party Pussy.") But if a vet showed "political immaturity," that is, if he articulated dissenting attitudes toward the leadership of the VALB, the CPUSA, or the USSR, then he would probably be brushed off with a ten-dollar bill and a Greyhound ticket to Bartlesville, Oklahoma, or wherever he had come from. And any veteran who "ratted" was likely to find his name in the *Daily Worker* as an "enemy of the working class," which could mean a blackball by his old union.[2] Veterans who registered at the FALB headquarters knew at once how they stood in the eyes of the leadership. If important, they got money to buy a suit; if insignificant, they had to root through piles of hand-me-downs in a back room. One Boston veteran with twenty months' service in Spain who had never learned to echo the everlasting yea emerged from the storeroom clad in an oversized, double-breasted, pale-pink "zoot suit," but he took it in good humor. An Ohio veteran received the loan of an apartment in far-off Brooklyn until an FALB minion learned that he had once written for the *Daily Worker,* which netted him an apartment for two weeks in the Village.* As in all organizations, the hierarchy excelled in looking after the hierarchy, and the FALB had to answer not to the public or to the law, but only to itself.

Wounded men were not necessarily a liability or an embarrassment, for they could be used as persuasive exhibits in fund campaigns. Bill Harvey, who had been cut down at Jarama by a bullet that lodged in his neck next to the spinal cord, regularly solicited money from Uptown college groupies and Long Island ladies' societies. The publicity brochure that preceded him featured the profile of a handsome youth whose head was braced by a Rube Goldberg contraption of metal rods and leather straps. The FALB photographer, however, had airbrushed his nose, because he thought it "too Jewish"—the emphasis, in those days of the Popular Front being to sell the "American-ness" of the boys from Spain.* Back in 1938 Harvey had joined some twenty other Lincolns in a *Life* photo-article, "Americans Have Died Fighting for Democracy in Spain." Though he was a proud Communist and eager to proclaim it, he had been instructed by the FALB to say nothing about his Soviet proclivities. Instead he was quoted as explaining that he had gone to Spain only because "I am a Jew and I know what Hitler is doing to my people."*

2. When Marty Hourihan, once a Lincoln battalion commander, defected from the CP, his harassment by Party diehards was so relentless that he had to go underground. When I found him in 1967, he was manager of a country club in Terra Haute, Indiana, and made me promise never to divulge his whereabouts because he feared as a former Communist he would lose his job. To my surprise, he was not afraid of being denounced by the FBI but by the CP or VALB, as punishment for straying from the faith.

Even the dead could be resurrected and put to work. Friends and relatives of "missing" veterans received letters in which the opening paragraphs contained sentimental recollections and the concluding parts requests for funds. The usual pitch was to suggest that there was no concrete evidence that the veteran had been killed: perhaps he was very much alive but languishing somewhere in a Fascist prison. Efforts were under way . . . etc. The mother of Vernon Selby was strung along for three years in a wholly fictitious rigmarole. Sometimes the scheme backfired. Maxwell Wallach, whose son Albert had been executed in Spain, collected letters from FALB officials and turned his collection over to the HUAC in an effort to discover how his son had died and who was responsible.* This was the closest to a "war-crimes" trail that ever occurred in connection with the Lincoln Battalion. Nothing was ever proved, but the evidence published in the HUAC report pointed a steady finger at Tony DeMaio, the XVth Brigade SIM policeman.* In his grilling by the Committee, DeMaio rated near zero in conveying information about his activities or comrades in Spain. When shown a photo of Albert Wallach, last seen in the black hole at Casteldefels, DeMaio departed from his usual "Never saw him," when he replied, "It looks like Cary Grant, the actor."

In another shell game, FALB officials descended upon Elman Service, who had been James Lardner's closest friend in Spain, and urged him to seek out the wealthy Lardner family in order to dun them for money. Upset by this blood-money plot, Service stalked out as first step in putting his Lincoln experience behind him and returned to the University of Michigan.* But others plunged willingly into this work.

Probably a majority of veterans, disaffected with the Lincoln oligarchy even before they arrived in the States, slipped away as soon as their ship docked and vanished permanently. For them there was the bitter joke—"Q. What happened to Lincoln? A. Shot dead in cold blood for his ideals." But for others, disenchantment grew more slowly. During the early spring of 1939, for example, when thousands of Internationals from Fascist-controlled countries were stranded in French concentration camps near Argeles-sur-Mer, certain veterans begged the FALB to help them. With some justification, the FALB officials declared that their funds were small and their obligations large. Then— continued the appellants—would not the FALB be willing to petition the USSR to offer asylum to all "exiled victims of Franco"? After all, many key Spanish Communists like La Pasionaria and military leaders like Modesto and Lister had found sanctuary in the Soviet Union. But officialdom lashed out at this heresy—how could the FALB ask for the admission of these erstwhile Interbrigaders into the promised land when it was possible that among them were spies, saboteurs, deserters, dissidents, and counterrevolutionaries? Worse, many had already been hopelessly corrupted by residence in the bourgeois West. Indeed, why should such *lumpenproletariat* be allowed to worm their way into the Soviet Union when others far more worthy had no such opportunity? For many Lincolns, such black ingratitude came as an insult to former comrades-in-arms. In the end, the FALB did nothing tangible for the German volunteers who had twice saved Madrid.[3]

The burnish was wearing off the blade. It was becoming clear that the FALB was more sensitive to the moods of the Kremlin than to those who had fought the good fight in Spain. Political disenchantment affected certain Lincolns whose records in Spain had been outstanding. Leonard Lamb, several times adjutant or temporary commander of the battalion, bristled at the autocratic orientation of the CPUSA and finally defected: "Unless you agreed with the Soviet Union you were a son of a bitch. So I realized that for all the courage of rank-and-file Communists in Spain and in the union movement, the Party as such was absolutely useless." Even in Spain, "The faith I had was like the crap shooter with his last buck."*

On August 22, 1939, came the Hitler-Stalin Pact, which for so many American Communists, particularly the Jews, marked the beginning of their long retreat from Moscow. With Stalin's unilateral decision to abandon his crusade against Fascism, the Popular Front and the Comintern foundered and died. Stalin had always considered the Comintern as nothing more than fancy window dressing for the West—among Kremlin intimates he contemptuously called it his *lavochka* ("market stall").* A few days later Hitler launched his war against the Western democracies, and without blinking an eye, the CPUSA called for its members to rally round the slogan, "Keep America Out of an Imperialist War." This brazen turn about mocked all those who had signed "anti-Fascist" in their military passbooks at Albacete. Here was a dizzying zigzag in Soviet policy that many Lincolns refused to accept. Bill Harvey, a worker in a Communist-dominated New York union (and himself a red-diaper baby) was fired when he refused to sign a Communist "loyalty oath"—that is, a pledge to support the new line. It made no sense—"We fought Fascism in Spain and were fired for fighting Fascism." Henceforth, he was stigmatized as an "enemy of the people." As a Jew he believed that making deals with Hitler was not only unwise but immoral. In open rebellion he carried a hand-lettered sign with two other veterans through the Garment District:

---

3. Some of these men were evacuated to North Africa prior to Hitler's blitzkrieg through France in the spring of 1940. The French Foreign Legion recruited from this cadre. Those who remained in France but failed to melt into the population were handed over to the Nazis by the Vichy government. Jews among them were doubly damned.

LAST WEEK A HERO OF THE SPANISH CIVIL WAR
THIS WEEK A VICTIM OF THE HITLER-STALIN PACT

A female "spit brigade" gathered around him to insult and spit on him. Behind them males of the Furriers Union waited with long knives for Harvey to strike a woman. Then they could move en masse to protect their womenfolk.* Regarding Hitler as the enemy of all humanity, Harvey and a few others tried to organize another veterans' group called the Anti-Totalitarian Friends of Spain, which supported Great Britain and France, but Party hard-wires joined it, took it over from within, and then crushed it.*

Other veterans fully within the Party orbit found themselves in a psychic limbo on returning home. Pretty women flocked about Harry Fisher at get-togethers sponsored by the Party and the VALB. They eagerly questioned him about how many Fascists he had killed and how it had felt to kill one. He said he had no idea, but they didn't want to hear that, for they were steeped in *Daily Worker* stories about how happy Lincolns were to die for a holy cause, many with smiles on their faces. This brought to Fisher's mind his first sight of dead bodies the day after Villanueva de la Cañada—"Fascist" dead on one side of the road and "Loyalist" dead on the other. "They all looked alike, no matter which side of the road they were on." He had taken a family photo from the pocket of a "Fascist"—a young man and family posing with their pet dog. "And so I became depressed." From morning till evening he walked the streets. Eating became nearly impossible. "I would be careless crossing streets and would even hope that a car would hit me and end it all."*

Late in 1939 the FALB faded and died because the alliance against Fascism, which had germinated it and fostered it, was in disrepute in the USSR. By this time events in Spain were becoming as irrelevant to the world situation as earlier outrages in Ethiopia. David McKelvey White, the national chairman of the FALB, acquiesced in the dissolution of his organization in favor of a smaller cadre, comprising only veterans, known as the VALB (Veterans of the Abraham Lincoln Brigade). In December the VALB held its first national convention in New York, installing Milton Wolff as its national commander.[4] Its medallion of silvered alloy featured the profile of a volunteer in tasseled cap on the Liberty Bell (crack visible) with the words "For Liberty in Spain." In emulation of

---

4. The VALB had existed as a kind of shadow association prior to this. As early as December 1937, fifty veterans had attempted an organizational meeting and had agreed upon a slate of officers, but it did not intrude upon the domain of the FALB—which had established an efficient fund-raising system based upon a list of fifty thousand donors—until the Politburo moved to dissolve the earlier organization. Not until January 1940 did the VALB incorporate in New York State.

Stalin's loyalty trials, the VALB conducted its own mini-purges. Twenty members in Wisconsin were chastised for "opposition" remarks, and four were expelled from the organization. These outcasts were called deserters, which implied they had shameful war records in Spain, wholly false. (In order to maximize the membership roster, the executive committee, consisting solely of hard-liners like Steve Nelson, declared that the term "deserter" would no longer be used to libel men who had actually deserted in Spain but only applied to those who maligned or betrayed the VALB at home.)* A CP heavy when asked about VALB expulsion policies revealed more about his group than he intended when he replied, "We can't expel anybody, but if somebody is a rat, *like some of them have turned out to be,* they wouldn't be allowed to join" (my italics).* The committee wanted to issue membership cards but met with a poor response— too many vets had endured the long arms of commissars quite enough. *

Meanwhile, the CP campaign of the 1930s to enlist blacks en masse in the movement collapsed. Gone forever were such prewar plans as creating a separate black soviet somewhere in the American South. Oscar Hunter, a commissar in Spain admired by both blacks and whites, who had been groomed for a major role in the Party, faced expulsion because he refused to acknowledge that racial equality was as important as class warfare. At a Chicago meeting when he referred to blacks as "my people" while arguing that the Party should do more to combat black illiteracy, he was attacked by the speaker, "What's all this shit MY PEOPLE? There's no such a goddam thing."* Hunter was disgusted by white leaders who insisted they knew more about blacks than he did.* Later, during a secret session with Party hierophants, Hunter recalled, "A guy takes out a book and starts to read from Stalin. So I get up and say, 'When you read Stalin, you know what you're getting ready to do. I'm on trial. You're not going to do that to me, baby.' So I walked out." He was sickened by "all the cloak-and-dagger stuff—men spying upon one another and snitching—all the secret shit." Admiral Kilpatrick, another black veteran, who in 1931 had been trained in Moscow, was expelled from the Party for rejecting the reigning doctrine that you could build a viable movement with all classes. He called the agitprop that grouped together Lincoln, Washington, and Douglass as protocommunists "a lot of bull."* Disenchantment struck James Yates even earlier. On his first night home, buoyed by kisses and handshakes at the dock, he tried to book a hotel room with other Spanish vets only to be told by the clerk, "No vacancy." He had forgotten he was back in America. "Inwardly I winced. 'So soon?' The pain went as deeply as any bullet. But this was another front. I was home."*

In accordance with the Kremlin line, the VALB was rigorously pacifist during the brief period Hitler and Stalin pretended to patch up their ideological disagreements. In 1941 the VALB disseminated its "Seven Planks to Defend America," the first and foremost demanding that the United States "Get out and Stay out of World War II." This opposed military alignment with Great Britain and any agreement that would send U.S. forces to a foreign shore. On May 30 of that year Milton Wolff delivered the keynote speech at the VALB convention in Chicago, in which he attacked the policies of Franklin "Demagogue" Roosevelt, who "under the dishonest slogan of anti-fascism, prepares the red-baiting, union-busting, alien-hunting, anti-Negro, anti-Semitic, jingoistic road to fascism in America."* Only a few years before, American Communists vilified Washington for failing to oppose Hitler; now, because Hitler and Stalin were in cahoots, the VALB vilified Washington for failing to oppose the war against him. The new "Yanks Are Not Coming" antiwar policy came down as a commandment from Party bosses—a further example of "democratic centralism"—without being voted on, and VALB members who rejected it were not welcome at future meetings.*

Wolff had to eat his manifesto less than one month later, when Hitler invaded the Soviet Union, and the CPUSA resurrected "anti-Fascism" in full panoply. The VALB participated in the "Smash Hitler Rally" at Madison Square Garden in July 1941 and called for opening a second front aganst Hitler immediately. Then a few months later Wolff authored a pamphlet titled "Western Front Now," which demanded American intervention. The *Volunteer for Liberty* gave great attention to the "major phase" of the Allied war effort—in other words the Soviet effort—and urged veterans to participate actively in a war that miraculously had lost its "imperialistic" taint.

An estimated six hundred Lincolns joined the U.S. armed services or the merchant marine during World War II, or roughly half of those who had survived the Spanish civil war. Enlisting was not always easy. Asked about prior experience, John Gates mentioned his service in Spain. His recruiter was puzzled, "How old did you say you were?" "Twenty-eight." "Heck, you couldn't have fought in the Spanish American War." Gates had to write a personal letter to Roosevelt—covered by Drew Pearson—to be allowed to fight Fascists.* Sixty-five Lincoln veterans are alleged to have become commissioned officers. Twenty-five vets were killed—including Joe Gordon of Jarama fame, who perished as a seaman on the Murmansk run. A handful, including Milton Wolff, served with General William Donovan's O.S.S. in northern Italy, in association with anti-Mussolini partisans.[5] George Watt, the last Lincoln commissar, who was among an Air Force bomber

---

5. After joining Donovan's organization, Wolff sought permission from the CP to recruit Party members for English and American intelligence activity. Donovan had no objections to this—winning the war was his sole priority. But George Dimitrov saw this as a "political mistake." "This would give the [Allied] services a chance to penetrate the American and other communist

crew shot down in France, climbed the Pyrenees for a second time, and was interned temporarily in Franco's Spain. Yet because the HUAC hearings and nationwide publicity had publicized the relationship between the International Brigades and the Comintern, some Lincoln veterans claimed that U.S. service records had been marked S.D. ("suspected of disloyalty").*

Until recently it was accepted as gospel truth that the U.S. armed services routinely branded Lincoln veterans as "Premature Anti-Fascist" and confined them to bases as security risks. No evidence has ever been uncovered that any service record bears this pejorative label. John Haynes and Harvey Klehr examined thousands of documents without finding any trace of its use by a government agency. Evidence does exist, however, to show that Lincoln vets themselves used the term in a proudly sardonic vein to make fun of the government and that others picked it up under the assumption that it truly existed in service records.[6] Peter Carroll, in a recent book about the Lincoln Battalion, cited a letter of 1942 written by Milton Wolff that stated that one night he and a fellow brigader named Cook had sneaked into an office at Fort Dix and seen PA ("Premature Anti-Fascist") on their service records.* Carroll's footnote specified that the letter was archived at the University of Illinois, but after Haynes and Klehr requested a copy from Illinois, they learned that no such letter existed. When they asked Carroll for an explanation, he replied that he had read the letter in the original and "assumed" it had been deposited at Illinois. Then he changed his story—his source was not a letter but an interview with Wolff himself. However, when reinterviewed by Carroll, Wolff changed his story. Only Cook had broken into the office and seen their records, so he could not verify anything. It was the old CP defensive technique—verify nothing, deny everything. The upshot was that Haynes and Klehr charged Carroll with "scholarly malpractice" for asserting as fact that U.S. security agencies commonly stamped "Premature Anti-Fascist" on records of Americans who had fought in Spain.* This compulsion on the part of revisionist American historians to distort or to conceal truth when writing about Communist subjects came as no surprise to Haynes and Klehr, who had found that the *Journal of American History* contains not a single article about the CPUSA, but twenty-two articles portraying American Communism in a positive light or demonizing domestic anti-Communism.

---

parties." He demanded that expedient measures be taken for "stopping this recruitment and all contact with the indicated services. Warn the Spanish and Italian comrades about this also."*

6. It has passed into Lincoln folklore as though chiseled in granite. When doing research for my book *Between the Bullet and the Lie* (1969), I heard the label used so many times that I never questioned its authenticity. It was just "common knowledge," which in that instance was a pesky canard.

Two Lincoln veterans—Robert Thompson and Herman Bottcher—earned the Distinguished Service Cross for heroism in jungle fighting in the Pacific. Thompson, who had commanded the Mac-Paps at Fuentes de Ebro, enlisted early in the U.S. Army and served as a noncommissioned officer in the 32nd Division in New Guinea. When a UP reporter attending his DSC ceremony in the 32nd Division asked what he had done before the war, he replied, "Maybe you won't believe me but I'm a Young Communist League organizer in Ohio."* After the war the Veterans Administration canceled his disability pension because of his conviction under the Smith Act. Worse followed. When he died in 1966, his widow's request that he be buried in Arlington National Cemetery was denied until a legal fight forced a reversal.*

Herman Bottcher, an immigrant from Germany in 1931, was working his way through San Francisco State College as a gardener when he quit to go to Spain. A socialist, he went as a member of the ill-starred Debs "Battalion," which folded in Paris. With Pat Reid and Hans Amlie he joined the Lincoln Battalion, where he was remembered as being quiet, reclusive, and a stickler for military (not political) discipline. Because he had never taken out his final citizenship papers he was held on his return for some months on Ellis Island, but the day after Pearl Harbor he joined the U.S. Army. He served in the New Guinea campaign and wrote a friend, "I love the jungle . . . beautiful butterflies . . . the gorgeous plumage of birds . . . exquisitely fragrant flowers." A short time later he wiped out a line of Japanese pillboxes, for which he received a battlefield promotion to captain and the Distinguished Service Cross. To Army publicists he was "The One-Man Army of Buna," while his men called him "The Jungle Killer." During the Leyte campaign he spent forty-eight days behind Japanese lines, specializing in terror attacks on outposts. He died on Janaury 1, 1945, after a mortar shell blew off his leg.*

Three hundred veterans participated in John Dollard's pioneer study, *Fear in Battle*, an exploration of the effects of modern war upon riflemen. The results, buttressed by statistics from questionnaires, served as a guide for introducing recruits into World War II combat. Among Dollard's observations: while 70 percent had experienced fear before their first battle, 64 percent became less afraid in subsequent battles. During periods of panic 70 percent thought chronic deserters should be shot as against 21 percent recommending their removal from the line; on the importance of discussion of war aims, 93 percent believed it made better soldiers, as opposed to 6 percent, somewhat better; on the question whether hating the enemy made better soldiers, 83 percent said it did, while 15 percent said it did not.*

The VALB never had a democratic base. Decisions came down from above, and in its first quarter-century there is no record of a policy adopted which *opposed* the prevailing Moscow line. Arthur Landis, the "official" biographer, protested in 1979 that when he and others wrote a constitution and by-laws, their document was shelved by Moe Fishman, the executive secretary, without explanation. Landis used the word "Neanderthals" for those members who had rigidly adhered to "forty years of bullshit" disseminated under the blanket of "internal democracy."* The VALB has only rarely been much more than a protest organization with an ambitious mailing list.[7] Its newspaper, the *Volunteer for Liberty* (later renamed the *Volunteer*), averages about three issues a year. In moments of financial crisis, the part-time executive secretary makes personal appeals for men to chip in, although most financial support comes from well-connected and well-endowed patrons of the comic breed later satirized in Tom Wolfe's "Radical Chic." Except for the early years, it is unlikely that its active membership has ever consisted of more than one-tenth of surviving veterans.* At the 1967 convention, for example, attendance amounted to three hundred people, of whom only forty had actually fought in Spain, as against the estimated six hundred said to be still living. At this meeting Steve Nelson succeeded Milton Wolff as national commander, the latter having held the post for twenty-eight years.[8] A major order of business was condemnation of the U.S. role in Vietnam. Copies of Mao's quotations were peddled at the door—a refreshing departure from the monolithic Moscow orientation of the previous three decades.

The mood of exultation following the final defeat of the Axis Powers was short-lived among the Lincolns, for the Cold War brought anti-Communism in the United States to near paranoid heights and with it an unconscionable harassment of all too many veterans of Spain. This was an epoch of suits, subpoenas, and hearings during which Party stalwarts barricaded themselves behind the

---

7. A notable exception is ALBA (the Abraham Lincoln Brigade Archive), first established in the library of Brandeis University in Waltham, Massachusetts, and recently moved to New York University. This serves as a repository for records and materials pertaining to the American volunteers in the Spanish civil war. ALBA has acquired copies of most records found in the various Moscow archives, the most important body of information about the inner workings of the battalion. Originally the Moscow files were available only to veterans and their families, but have now been opened to the public.

8. Through his close association with Joe Dallet's wife, Kitty, Nelson gained access to Kitty's fourth and final husband Robert Oppenheimer, who supported various VALB appeals on the West Coast at a time when Nelson was the major CP representative in the area and was attempting to gather data about the atomic bomb of the Los Alamos project.

Fifth Amendment and bid defiance to what they dubbed "The Federal Bureau of Intimidation—Department of Injustice." Ostensibly the authorities wanted to root out Communists, not to punish men for service in Spain; it was just that in certain cases the two were symbiotically fused. Under the Smith Act, which made it illegal to conspire to overthrow the U.S. government, half a dozen veterans went to jail. No one was ever jailed simply for having fought in the Lincoln Battalion, although the broadsides issued by the VALB made it appear so. (And certainly no one in the United States was ever shot out of hand—like men at Marsa or Casteldefels—for voicing minority opinions.)

Finally in 1953, under the McCarran Act, which required registration of Communist-front organizations, the attorney general filed a petition with the Subversive Activities Control Board for an order requiring the VALB to register. The case dragged on for two years and devoured 4,576 pages of transcripts and 306 supporting documents before the attorney general's petition was granted. The evidence is convincing: it demonstrates that the VALB faithfully parroted the Kremlin line for fifteen years and that most of its leaders were members of the CPUSA. Yet reading the transcripts today, one feels an overwhelming outrage, less because of sympathy for the VALB than for the senselessness of spending so much time and money and accumulating such an enormous amount of data just to substantiate such an inconsequential point. The logic of proof was subverted by the illogic of effort. One might as well destroy a field of cornborers with an artillery barrage. And by unleashing such a flood of sympathy for the VALB, the government indirectly undid its own purpose. People and factions that had virtually forgotten the existence of the VALB now rushed to its defense, whether in courtrooms or cocktail parties. Such organizations grow fat upon their wounds, the bloodier the better, and the VALB had long experience in handling blood donors. The concluding remarks of the Subversive Activities Control Board have unfortunately been ignored by both patriots of the Right and partisans of the Left. "This report and the findings herein relate to the VALB as an organization and should not be considered as embracing all veterans of the war in Spain. *The record shows that some Americans fought there on behalf of the Republic out of motivations completely alien to Communist purposes* [italics added]. Further, it is clear that many veterans of the Spanish War are not members of the Respondent or in any way represented by it." The impact of placing the VALB on the attorney general's blacklist, however, may be readily imagined. Ignoring the fine print, rightists used the decision to bludgeon former members of the Lincoln Battalion who had nothing whatever to do with the VALB, while leftists rallied strength to annul the decision, which they erroneously claimed had impugned all men who had fought in Spain. That said, the veterans endured another crossfire, this one between fanatics of Left and Right. A columnist who knew many of them well wrote, "I can think of very few who survived as they were and are not somehow aliens in their own country."*

The high-level histrionics were by no means over. In 1962 the Emergency Civil Liberties Committee (ECLC) offered its services to carry the VALB counterpetition to the United States Supreme Court. The occasion was the twenty-fifth anniversary meeting of the Lincoln Battalion, a "fight-back rally" held at Palm Gardens in New York. (Palm Gardens was no Ukrainian Workers Hall, where the first Lincolns drilled—but a bourgeois watering hole.) On the stage were two three-pointed stars cut out of pasteboard and flanked by the American flag. Red-lettered signs read, "REPEAL THE MCCARRAN ACT" and "AMNESTY FOR FRANCO'S POLITICAL PRISONERS." Bosses came and went, platforms went up and came down, but the rhetoric never changed. Metaphors knocked heads just as they had in the old days, twenty-five years before. The featured speaker got this one off: "We have traveled a hard road seeing our liberties whittled away, our own tradition of freedom trampled upon. . . . Heroes and patriots, yes patriots, are today hounded as victims of the hateful McCarran Act. . . . The warmongers in order to achieve their goal of world holocaust must have conformity of the so-called mass mind. . . . Political prisoners rot in medieval Spanish dungeons." And so on. Stalin and Joe McCarthy were both dead by this time, but you would never have known it from the speeches. The ACLU spokesman called for a follow-up meeting at the New Yorker Hotel on April 13 to celebrate Thomas Jefferson's birthday and to call for the repeal of the McCarran Act. (First Lincoln, then Washington, now Jefferson—all crypto-Popular Fronters, it would seem.) Pete Seeger sang old Lincoln "Brigade" songs (omitting the gamier ones). The lights went off, and scenes of the Spanish civil war flickered on a screen. The hall was hot and stuffy, the atmosphere prickly and paranoid. But there was more sanity indoors than outside, where fifteen pickets from the Nationalist Party carried signs that read:

RED ANIMALS INSIDE

ABE LINCOLN BRIGADE MURDERED NUNS

The upshot was that on April 26, 1965, the Supreme Court vacated orders that had required registration of the VALB as a Communist-front organization on ground that the evidence was "too stale," most of it derived from moldering dossiers of two decades before. The date was memorable: it was one of the few times in its history that the Lincoln Battalion had won a battle—even though the political issues underlying it were long dead.

Meanwhile the VALB continued to picket and to protest. They demonstrated in front of Spanish consulates, carried placards on wharves overlooked by Spanish ships, boycotted Spanish dance and song troupes. Like skillful protesters anywhere, they could inflict a neutral bystander with a nagging but indefinite sense of guilt that something somewhere might be wrong and that he should do something about it.

Perhaps their most successful international demonstration occurred at the Spanish pavilion of the New York World's Fair in 1964. Since placards were prohibited on the grounds, the demonstrators wore four-inch, blue and white buttons labeled "AMNESTY FOR ALL POLITICAL PRISONERS IN SPAIN." The Fair security guards were stumped. There seemed to be no rule against wearing buttons. As soon as the protesters reached the pavilion, Spanish employees inside rushed out to wage verbal battle. As the two contingents shouted "Fascists!" or "Communists!" at each other, it brought back the glory days of yore— but without the obscenities. "We don't tell you what's wrong with the United States," cried a Spanish lady. "We read about it in the newspapers every day, but we just keep our mouths shut." Strolling players, the *tunas* from the University of Madrid, came out to soothe the demonstration by playing guitars and singing student songs. Passersby seemed perplexed. "What's going on?" one asked. "Must have something to do with integration," replied another. Led by Robert Raven, the blind vet, a group from the VALB attempted to hand a petition to the manager of the pavilion, who said he would receive it as a courtesy but not as an official intermediary. In the end, tempers cooled and cameras were busy. A *New York Times* reporter noted that many pavilion employees quietly pocketed amnesty buttons as *recuerdos* of their meeting with *el batallón Lincoln.* The button gambit was widely used by other protest groups who had failed to make a dent in the placard ban.*

In her farewell speech at Barcelona, La Pasionaria had said to the Internationals, "You are history. You are legend." So far as the Lincolns were concerned, she was only half right, for they have passed beyond history and are embalmed in legend. For the new generations temporarily radicalized and activated in the 1960s, the Lincolns became for a time spiritual godfathers who fought the good fight three decades before. Historical documentation labors hopelessly in restricting the growth of mythic accretions. Symbolically, the Lincolns became bigger-than-life figures, roughly sketched but instantly recognizable Hectors of a far-off but recognizable war. During the march on the Pentagon in the fall of 1967, for example, a small band of Lincoln veterans materialized among the vast throng and received cheers and applause. Joining hands with the other marchers, they surged across the green fields of Arlington

County just as they had climbed the black hill at Jarama or dropped into the parched valley of Brunete in *their* war three decades before. But Spain was far behind them, Franco only an old man like themselves. Ahead was the Pentagon, a refurbished Yoke and Arrows—a Kafkaesque metaphor of a new war. (Not too far away was the national headquarters of George Lincoln Rockwell's American Nazi Party, which fringed their line of march, hooked-cross arm-bands displayed aggressively.) Even though the Lincolns were all men of fifty-plus, the New Left, who knew only the legend, not the history, found them representatives of an ancient cause vitalized by their Marxist ideology. It was like an apostolic succession—a laying on of hands.

Of all the Americans who fought in Spain, John Gates, along with Steve Nelson, soared highest in the CPUSA hierarchy. After serving five years (1949–54) in Atlanta Federal Penitentiary for conviction under the Smith Act, Gates emerged as a charismatic Party martyr and took over the *Daily Worker* as editor-in-chief. It soon became clear that he was no bullhorn for Communism, Kremlin style, when at his direction the *Daily Worker* printed the full text of Khrushchev's speech denouncing Stalin (the only CP paper in the world to do this). Then at a meeting of the Party's National Committee in 1956 he condemned the Soviet invasion of Hungary. As colleagues sat with frozen faces, he delivered an apologia, "For the first time in all my years in the Party I felt ashamed of the name 'Communist.'" As if this were not enough, he incensed them further by arguing that "there was more liberty under Franco's fascism than there is any communist country." And how did he evaluate the historical role of the Lincoln Battalion (in which he was the last XVth Brigade Commissar)? "I don't think the International Brigades were that decisive." Men were not needed—it was matériel from the USSR that prolonged the war, but there was never enough to win it. Why did the VALB hold on so tenaciously to a long-past historical artifact like the Popular Front? "Because to do otherwise would be to admit that 'they got shot up for nothing.'"* When Arthur Landis, a former veteran, began collecting material for his "official" history of the Lincoln "Brigade" in the 1960s, he did not interview Gates, who had left the Party. After a VALB official told him that Landis had written the "definitive" book about the Lincolns, Gates shot back, "How could it be definitive when nobody even told me about it?" When it was explained that they had not known where to find him, he made a quicksilver reply that no one else had ever had trouble finding him—including U.S. marshals. Disliking its propagandistic bias, Gates characterized the Landis book as "thoroughly dishonest—some of it true, some imagined."* For him "Marxism was left behind by the changes in American life," and he quoted statistics to prove it: The CPUSA counted seventy-five thousand members in 1945 versus only seven thousand in 1957.* (One year later the membership dropped to three thousand.)*

Relations with Hemingway peaked in Spain, where most Lincolns respected him and were flattered by his attention. They awaited impatiently his novel in progress, which they assumed would stand as the definitive account of their war. After all, in a speech before the Writers' Congress at Carnegie Hall in 1937 he had issued his clarion call, "A writer who will not lie cannot live and work under fascism." Two years later, however, he apparently was beginning to feel the same way about Communism. He had no intention of trading in his genuine anti-Fascist sensibility for a blanket endorsement of another ruthless autocracy. Even before the Spanish civil war, he had opposed military alignments with European powers of any stripe. In his "Notes on the Next War," dating from September 1936, he declared: "The only way to combat the murder that is war is to show the dirty combinations that make it and the criminals and swine that hope for it and the idiotic way they run it, so that an honest man will distrust it as he would a racket."* (In the same year, he wrote about Mussolini, "the cleverest opportunist in modern history.")* As if this were not enough, he added, "No European country is our friend, and no country but one's own is worth fighting for." Although he went to Spain four separate times during the war and wrote extensively about it, his skepticism remained. In his "Program for U.S. Realism"—written in August 1938, more than two years after the war had begun—he staked out a noninterventionist credo that might have been penned by Secretary Cordell Hull himself: stay out of war in Europe; sell to both sides—for cash; and maintain strict neutrality.*

Publication of *For Whom the Bell Tolls* (1940) at first disappointed—then infuriated—those Lincoln veterans who expected the author to write something akin to socialist realism. Alvah Bessie, himself a veteran and the author of *Men in Battle,* a fine memoir of the war, wrote a review for *New Masses* that excoriated Hemingway's novel for betraying the Spanish people. Like others of the militant Left, Bessie had been encouraged by the conclusion of *To Have and Have Not* (1937), when Harry Morgan, the out-of-luck supreme individualist, recites his epitaph at the end, "A man alone ain't got no bloody——ing chance." For Bessie and others it was axiomatic that the "chance" consisted of moving one's political axis far, far to the Left. The great novel about the Spanish civil war should bring front and center the collective struggle of the People, not resort to "a morbid concentration upon the meaning of *individual* death, *personal* happiness, *personal* misery, *personal* significance" (italics in original).* Hemingway's degenerate mishmash was paradoxically "a book about Spain that is not about Spain at all!" Moreover, Bessie expressed shock and anger at the author's personal assault on André Marty, depicting him as "part of the incompetence, the red tape, and outright treachery that strangled Spain." Looking closely, Hemingway saw only a "fool, madman, and murderer" whose face looked "as though modeled from the waste you find under the claws of a very old lion."[*9] Nor did the Russian advisers escape Hemingway's acidic pen, for Robert Jordan in ruminating about the war wonders what the Russians are getting out of "the whole business," suggesting that the USSR is somehow "sinister and reprehensible." In sum, Bessie found *Bell* no more important than "a *Cosmopolitan* love story against a background in the Spanish Civil War." On the heels of the review a VALB resolution condemned the book.[*]

The VALB should not have been surprised by Hemingway's acerb treatment of Marty and company, for *Bell* was comparatively gentle in its treatment of the International Brigades when compared to "Below the Ridge," his short story of a year earlier. An American camera crew has been invited to film a major attack (presumably on the Jarama front) by a French International Brigade. It fails miserably: the artillery is inaccurate and inadequate, the tanks are driven by cowards, and casualties are heavy. In the midst of the battle the narrator—a persona for Hemingway—watches a middle-aged Frenchman walking "alone down out of the war." Two men in leather coats with wooden-holstered Mausers strapped to their legs pursue and shoot him. These are SIM, policemen who speak a foreign language—presumably Slavic. With the narrator sit a silent group of Spanish soldiers, one of whom, an Estremaduran, announces, "I hate all foreigners. . . . I hate the Moors, the English, the Italians, the Germans, the North Americans, and the Russians. . . . Perhaps I hate the Russians the most." He then tells the narrator of a boy named Paco in his unit who became so frightened during a bombardment that he shot himself in the hand, damaging it so badly that it had to be amputated. The same two policemen who had shot the Frenchman brought Paco back to his countrymen, who welcomed him joyfully. He confesses that he did a cowardly and foolish thing but tells them he will "do what I can with one hand for the Cause." The policemen insist on seeing the exact place where he shot himself. At that spot one holds his arm and the other shoots him in the back of the head. "He had no warning and no chance to prepare himself," says the commander. "It was very brutal." The Estremaduran says, "It is for this that I now hate Russians as well as all other foreigners. . . . You understand my hatred?" he asks. "I understand," replies the American. The camera crew learns

9. Twenty-five years later Steve Nelson said, "Hemingway was right on Marty but wrong on La Pasionaria."[*]

that the IB general failed to employ all his troops in the attack, that the French tank commander had gotten drunk to be brave "and was to be shot when he sobered up," that "the swine, the cowards" in the tanks had refused to advance, and that the tankers had slaughtered some prisoners captured in the attack. This story stands as one of the strongest indictments of the International Brigades ever written. Bessie's charge that Hemingway had betrayed the Spanish people neatly sidesteps the callous betrayal by the USSR, which used the war in Spain not as a "war against Fascism," but as a cynical—and very lucrative—cover for its own political machinations.

The Bessie review marked the beginning of a cooldown between Hemingway and the VALB cadre, who were acting as though Hemingway were somehow under Party discipline. Some years later Bessie went further when he lampooned *Bell* as a book "where the shattering struggle of 28 million people for survival and decency was subordinated to an endless episode in a sleeping bag, and the phrase 'the earth moved' was quoted by bohemians and bourgeoisie with a leer on their faces: 'How come the earth didn't move, only the bedsprings?'"* Hemingway held on to Marty Hourihan as a lifelong friend, but began to drift away from others like Milton Wolff, who parroted the Moscow line. In 1941 Wolff wrote to borrow money for a chicken farm and complained of harassment by the American government. Hemingway wrote back, "Milt, my feeling is that you guys sort of bought this anyway. You hired out to be tough and then somebody got hurt and says they can't do this to me." He said he had liked Wolff as a kid in Spain but hadn't seen him in a long time. (He enclosed a check for $425—at 2 percent interest—but explained that he himself had to pay 6 percent for his money.)* In 1946 Wolff tried to get Hemingway to chair a VALB convention commemorating the tenth anniversary of the Lincoln Battalion, but he refused. When the VALB published an anthology of poetry and prose about Spain (*The Heart of Spain*, 1952), they included nothing by Hemingway. It was as though the selection committee had forgotten—or never read—his fine elegy "On the American Dead in Spain," written in the last months of the war.* (A VALB officer lamented after Hemingway's death, "Everyone in the outfit now agrees that exclusion of EH was the goof of a lifetime.")*

As private tourists, Lincoln veterans had traveled to Spain as early as the 1960s, but after Franco's death in 1975 they arrived collectively, defining themselves openly as former Internationals. In November 1986 about a hundred Lincoln vets, joined by several hundred more brigaders from other countries, went to Spain to memorialize the fiftieth anniversary of the civil war. They visited the Jarama and Brunete battlefields, and met La Pasionaria, age 91, who had returned home from her exile in the Soviet Union. When a stray American reporter asked if the CP had organized the International Brigades, Charles Nusser replied that he would have volunteered "even if the czar of Russia directed recruiting." And in another setting he shouted, "The Republic we fought for was betrayed by the U.S. government, which enforced the arms embargo and sold oil and trucks to Franco. With guns, damn it, we would have won."* Other veterans took nostalgia trails. Jack Shafran of New York fulfilled a long-standing ambition, for he had boasted that if he ever returned to Spain he would urinate on Franco's grave. On arriving at the site he found the place so open that an intimate ceremony was out of the question. In default he returned to his hotel, urinated in a glass, and, waiting an opportunity, splashed a little on the generalissimo's grave.* By contrast, Tony DeMaio, the brigade SIM officer, found only disappointment when the tour bypassed the IB prison at Casteldefels, where he had served as commandant.* A special treat for former POWs was a night at San Pedro de Cardeña, purchased by Cistercian monks and completely restored. Instead of sleeping on stone floors with rats running over their bodies, they received clean, warm rooms with baths. The monks even arranged a visitation with one of their guards, a seventy-three-year-old farmer who embraced them and pulled them into his simple stone house for wine and cheese.*

By all odds the most excited Lincoln vet in Spain at this moment was Fausto Villar, who waited in the Valencia railroad station for the arrival of the Americans. For forty-nine years—including two years at hard labor in a Nationalist prison—he had mulled over his experiences with the Lincoln Battalion but had not met or spoken with any of them. However, he had read books about the battalion (including mine), which conformed to the tale woven by "Ivan" about how Merriman and Doran survived the massacre in the vineyard north of Gandesa and joined the remnant on the hilltop who tried to escape at night. To Villar it seemed impossible that Merriman could have survived that pummeling machine-gun fire, but he wanted to learn the truth, whatever it was. Could it be possible that Jim Cody, his mentor and protector, had survived the war and might even now be somewhere in the mob of weeping and laughing people at the station? But from great expectations he fell into bleak depression as he wandered among the groups without finding anyone who had even heard of Merriman—much less Cody. Why did Merriman's name fail to register among the Americans? Were memories really so short, or were they hiding something when they looked Villar over before saying, "Was he that West Point guy?"

Villar worked through the crowd to Milton Wolff, the only face he recognized from that late afternoon in 1938, when he had watched officers arguing about how to escape from the trap. But Wolff brushed him aside and continued to sign autographs. Villar's fifty-year wait to rejoin the members of his battalion came to nothing. His disenchantment cries out from a letter he wrote from the hospital shortly before his death. "The high chiefs and staff crept across to safety through the Fascist camps, succeeding in saving themselves and escaping. . . . What to think of all this?"*

In 1996, Lincoln vets converged again in Spain with former comrades from many countries. The occasion was King Juan Carlos's signing of Royal Decree no. 39, which awarded all IB survivors with Spanish citizenship.* Since the organizers had failed to consider that certain countries, like the United States, do not recognize dual citizenship, those attending received a certificate entitling them to future citizenship if they exercised that option. "A peculiar document," explained an organizer, "but at least they'll get a bit of paper with colors."* In the narrow halls of the Palacio del Congreso, the octogenarians, many of them in wheelchairs, waited three hours in a crush of media before being admitted into the great Chamber of Deputies, where they tottered along rows of empty seats and leaned on railings. A Lincoln vet recalled the ceremony, "Someone said some unintelligible words, and we were told to leave. It was a nonevent. There were a bunch of deputies who had their pictures taken. That was the only noteworthy thing." Only two of the 150 or so conservative deputies chose to attend, as a demonstration of their opposition to the citizenship gambit forged by left-of-center parliamentarians.

The most moving occasion came in the evening at the Palacio de los Deportes from packed galleries of young people cheering every allusion to the ancient war against Fascism. For them 1936 was 1996—platform speeches and flamenco laments renewed the call to battle for equality and justice. Then when a singer started his "Canción de la Libertad," the crowd joined in, thousands of young fists pumping the air and shouts bringing back the past, "España! Mañana! Republicana!" On every side people were weeping, and down in front rows of old warriors dabbed their eyes with handkerchiefs, their shoulders shaking and their faces buried in wrinkled hands. Tony Hendre, an American journalist, responded to the mood, "I'm having trouble not weeping myself, though for what I'm not quite sure. . . . But here it's impossible not to be swept away, as these old men must once have been, by the justness of this cause and the inevitability of its triumph. If there were something to volunteer for tonight, I'd volunteer for it."

The VALB continues to meet every year, although the number of survivors shrinks and shrinks. In 2003, at their sixty-seventh reunion in New York, a final tally enumerated that of the twenty-eight hundred Americans who had fought in Spain, eight hundred had been killed in action (28.5 percent). Ninety veterans were still living, although only seventeen attended the reunion. The obviously bourgeois audience reflected economic prosperity, very far from the slogans "Wretched of the Earth" or "Prisoners of Starvation" of revolutionary years. In the major speech of the evening, the actor Richard Dreyfus proclaimed, "No label is nobler than 'premature anti-Fascist.'" A veteran, Charles Kailin, said that he had left Wisconsin in 1937 to help defeat Fascism, concluding, "It wasn't the phony kind of fight for democracy that Bush talks about." Someone reminded them that at the 2001 reunion, Moe Fishman, long-standing executive secretary of VALB, had tried to denounce "globalization" but stumbled over the word. He received a chorus of laughter when he corrected himself, "It was much easier to say when we called it imperialism." At the end of the evening "The International" brought everyone, except the wheelchair cases, to their feet—many testifying to the memory and the moment with raised clenched fists. That revolution was over.

BATTLE MAPS

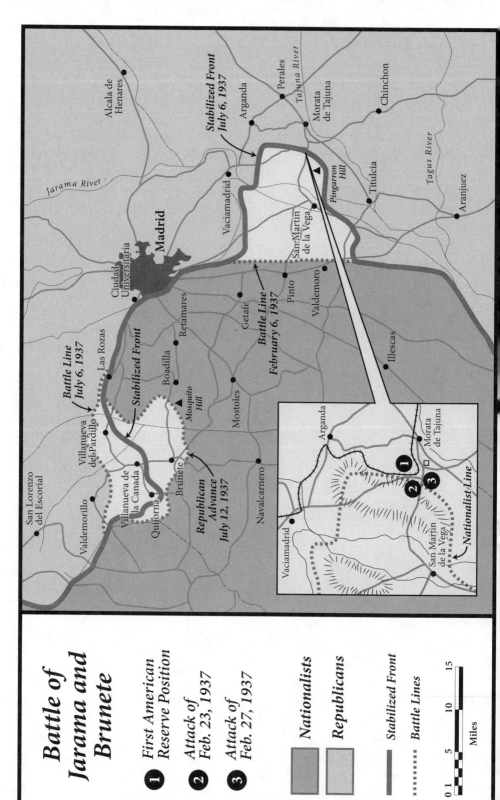

Battle of
Jarama and
Brunete

1 First American
Reserve Position

2 Attack of
Feb. 23, 1937

3 Attack of
Feb. 27, 1937

Nationalists

Republicans

Stabilized Front

Battle Lines

0 1   5   10   15
Miles

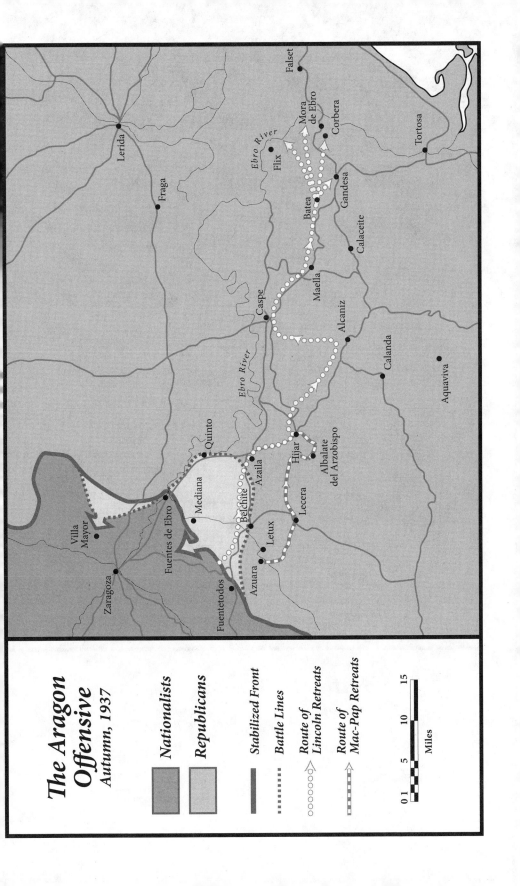

The Aragon Offensive
Autumn, 1937

Nationalists

Republicans

Stabilized Front

Battle Lines

Route of Lincoln Retreats

Route of Mac-Pap Retreats

0 1   5   10   15

Miles

Falset

Tortosa

Mora de Ebro

Corbera

Flix

Batea

Gandesa

Ebro River

Calaceite

Maella

Caspe

Alcaniz

Calanda

Aquaviva

Ebro River

Lerida

Fraga

Quinto

Mediana

Hijar

Albalate del Arzobispo

Villa Mayor

Fuentes de Ebro

Belchite

Azaila

Lecera

Zaragoza

Letux

Azuara

Fuentetodos

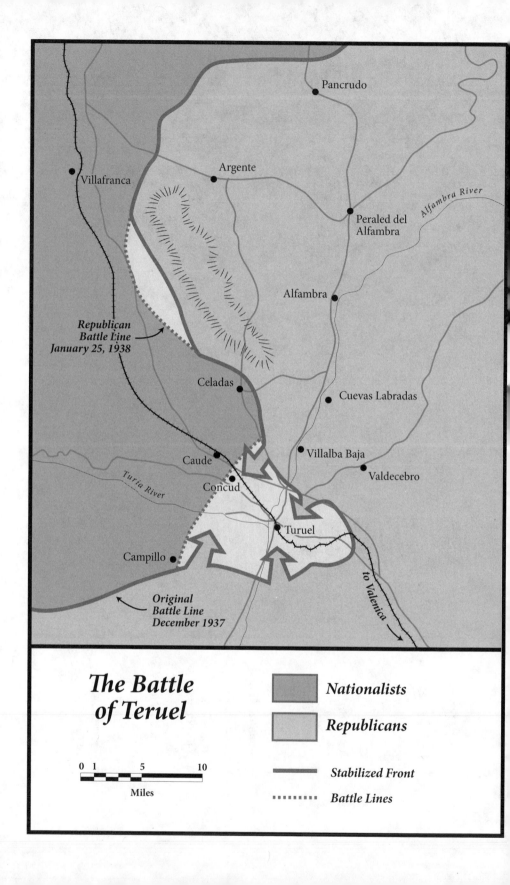

Pancrudo

Villafranca

Argente

Peraled del
Alfambra

Alfambra River

Alfambra

Republican
Battle Line
January 25, 1938

Celadas

Cuevas Labradas

Caude

Villalba Baja

Turia River

Concud

Valdecebro

Turuel

Campillo

to Valenica

Original
Battle Line
December 1937

The Battle of Teruel

Nationalists

Republicans

0 1   5   10

Miles

Stabilized Front

·········· Battle Lines

BIBLIOGRAPHICAL ESSAY—BASIC SOURCES

"Some day after we are all dead, some history professor will write
the definitive history of the war and get it all wrong."
—William Herrick, Jumping the Line, *110*

For more than forty years Hugh Thomas's *The Spanish Civil War* (1961, revised 2001) has offered the best bird's-eye view of the war, especially its campaigns and captains. Two sound studies focused upon the International Brigades are Verle Johnston's *Legions of Babel* (1967) and R. Dan Richardson's *Comintern Army* (1982). Among the half-dozen Spanish accounts of the International Brigades, perhaps the most useful is *Las Brigadas Internacionales* (1974), by Andreu Castells, himself an International Brigade veteran.

The Lincoln Battalion has been the exclusive subject of five historical books, two of them written by former volunteers: Edwin Rolfe's *The Lincoln Battalion* (1939) and Arthur H. Landis's *The Abraham Lincoln Brigade* (1967). Although both are imbued with partisan—that is to say CP—perspectives, if one acquiesces in a marriage of convenience between history and apologia and is prepared to recognize that certain subjects will be not be discussed at all, then both become indispensable books. Studies by noncombatants include my *Between the Bullet and the Lie* (1969), Robert A. Rosenstone's *Crusade of the Left* (1969), and Peter Carroll's *The Odyssey of the Abraham Lincoln Brigade* (1994). "Crusades" and "Odysseys"? (Why this uplift provided by dredging up ancient Christian wars or the itinerary of a half-lost Greek wanderer after the Trojan War?) Both Rosenstone and Carroll reflect the long-standing effort of the VALB to ignore my book in the hope that it will eventually disappear. Rosenstone charges that my "hostility to the CP is so blatant that it interferes with *any* [emphasis added] understanding of the Americans who went to Spain," while in his preface Carroll faults my "political bias and innumerable errors" without declaring what these are. Presumably I have not tried to curry favor by nuzzling the Party line. (Carroll's book has a picture of the author beaming happily as he embraces Morris Cohen, a former Lincoln veteran who later found permanent sanctuary in Moscow to avoid prosecution for transmitting atom bomb secrets to the Soviet Union.) On the positive side there are Hugh Thomas, who found that "the most rational account of the ALB is that of Cecil Eby" (691), and Dan

Richardson, who wrote, "By far the best and most penetrating study of the American battalion is *Between the Bullet and the Lie*" (222).

Despite its obvious one-sidedness, *Book of the XV Brigade* (1938), cast in a "yearbook" mold, is a major quasi-official document for the period from Jarama to Fuentes de Ebro, containing short accounts of battles by combatants and hundreds of photographs. Issued in Spain, the sixty-three issues of the *Volunteer for Liberty*, official news organ of the XVth Brigade, were published in facsimile by the VALB in 1949, making an invaluable record of battalion activities readily accessible. Often overlooked is K. E. Heikkinen's Finnish omnibus published in 1939 and translated in 2002 as *Our Boys in Spain*. Since the Finns preferred waging war to playing politics, their accounts are extremely accurate.

Although less objective and extensive than their counterparts in the British Battalion, all the memoirs of Lincoln veterans are indispensable. Perhaps the best of these is Alvah Bessie's *Men in Battle* (1939). Unfortunately his classic account of frontline service covers only events between late March and August of 1938. His papers have been published by his son, Dan Bessie, *Spanish Civil War Notebooks* (2002). Sandor Voros's *American Commissar* (1961) has been keelhauled by certain veterans, but this animus owes more to his defection from the CP than to misstatements of fact. As a commissar in the Historical Section of the XVth International Brigade, he had unlimited access to information of all sorts, now archived at Adelphi University. John Tisa, also serving in the Historical Section, used his personal diary to shape his useful memoir, *Recalling the Good Fight* (1981). Steve Nelson's *The Volunteers* (1953) is valuable for the period between Brunete and Belchite, when he served as commissar of the Lincoln Battalion (and later the XVth Brigade). Although it contains some fictionalization, his portraits are reliable and often hilarious. One cannot praise too highly Carl Geiser's *Prisoners of the Good Fight* (1986), a painstaking account of Lincoln volunteers captured by the Nationalists. A leading commissar in the XVth Brigade, Geiser was himself taken prisoner, narrowly escaped execution, and then years later returned to Spain as a private researcher. He lists the names and hometowns of 167 Americans believed to have been executed after their capture. Other important memoirs include Harry Fisher's *Comrades* (1997); D. P. Stephens's *A Memoir of the Spanish Civil War* (2000); and Warren Lerude and Marion Merriman's *American Commander in Spain* (1986). She was the wife of Robert Merriman, battalion commander and later chief of staff of the XVth Brigade. William Herrick's *Jumping the Line* (1998) contains a long segment about his service as a machine gunner and his later repudiation of the Party "line." Although cast as fiction, Milt Wolff's *Another Hill* (1994) is a memoir in disguise by the Lincoln commander during the Ebro campaign of late summer, 1938.

Other primary material includes Cary Nelson and Jefferson Hendricks's edition of letters from Spain, *Madrid 1937* (1996); Ronald Radosh's *Spain Betrayed* (2002), which prints documents and reports from Moscow archives including lists of American deserters, suspected Trotskyist spies, and political deviants; John Gerassi's *The Premature Antifascists* (1986), which is a valuable oral history of Lincoln veterans; and Danny Collum's *African Americans in the Spanish Civil War* (1992), which explores the contribution of ninety black Americans in the Lincoln Battalion. Herbert Romerstein's *Heroic Victims* (1994) makes convincing use of the Moscow archives to demonstrate how the USSR permeated the XVth Brigade.

A major source of information about the Lincoln Battalion can be found in studies of its brother battalions in the XVth Brigade. The best British source is James K. Hopkins's *Into the Heart of the Fire: The British in the Spanish Civil War* (1998). Two fine studies of the Canadians are Victor Hoar's *The Mackenzie-Papineau Battalion* (1969) and William C. Beeching's *Canadian Volunteers: Spain, 1936–1939* (1989). For the French, see Jacques Delperrié de Bayoc, *Les Brigades Internationales* (1978).

APPENDIX 2

INTERVIEW SUBJECTS FROM THE XVTH BRIGADE

PERSONAL INTERVIEWS (BY AUTHOR)

Fishman, Moe

Gates, John

Harvey, Bill

Hourihan, Martin

Jones, Sheldon

Mates, Dave

Nelson, Steve

Rowlson, Lester

Service, Elman

Smith, Harold

Taylor, Robert

Wellman, Saul

Wesson, Neil

TELEPHONE INTERVIEWS (BY AUTHOR)

Fisher, Harry

Gladnick, Robert

Shafran, Jack

Steck, Robert

Wolff, Milton

CORRESPONDENCE (WITH AUTHOR)

Amery, Alfred

Bessie, Alvah

Gibbons, Joseph

Gladnick, Robert

Grunblatt, Jacques

Harvey, William

Horan, Edward

Merriman, Marion

Shaker, Kenneth

Smith, David

Villar, Fausto

PERSONAL INTERVIEWS (ROBERT COWLEY)

Hunter, Oscar

Watt, George

TAPED AUDIO INTERVIEWS (VICTOR HOAR)

Cane, Lawrence

Geiser, Carl

ABBREVIATIONS

ALB	Abraham Lincoln Brigade, UI
ALBA	Abraham Lincoln Brigade Archive, NYU
AU	Voros collection, Adelphi University
BU	Brandeis University
CBC	Canadian Broadcast Company
DW	*Daily Worker* (New York)
Moscow	Russian Center for the Preservation and Study of Recent Historical Documents (Rossiskii Tsentr Khraneniia i Izucheniia Dokumentov Noveishei Istorii)
NA	National Archives
NANA	North American Newspaper Archive
NM	*New Masses*
NR	*New Republic*
NYT	*New York Times*
NYU	New York University
SACB	Subversive Activities Control Board
UI	University of Illinois
UM	University of Michigan

PREFACE

Page x. " . . . an earlier assertion by a like-minded author." Jackson, 30.

CHAPTER 1: GETTING THERE

Page 1. " . . . slipped into Spain." *FRUS, 1937,* January 8, 1937ff. (and other diplomatic notes).

Page 1. " . . . ABRAHAM LINCOLN BATTALION." *FRUS, 1937,* Perkins to Hull, Barcelona, January 18 and 21, 1937.

Page 2. " . . . NOT VALID FOR TRAVEL TO SPAIN." Ibid., Wiley to Hull, Le Havre, January 20, 1937.

Page 2. " . . . Bronx cheer." *NYT,* January 24, 1937.

Page 2. " . . . his tonsils." Landis, 16.

Page 2. " . . . Loyalist armies." *FRUS, 1937,* Perkins to Hull, Barcelona, January 8, 1937.

Page 3, note 2. *NYT,* September 30, 1937.

Page 4, note 3. Herrick to author.

Page 5. " . . . go *further*." Quoted in Radosh et al., 8; emphasis added.

Page 5. " . . . had been shelved." Richardson, 9.

Page 5. " . . . Marxist opposition." Radosh et al., 106.

Page 5, note 4. *NYT,* December 21, 1936.

Page 5, note 5. Ibid., July 4, 1938.

Page 6. " . . . inspector general." Longo, 52ff.

Page 6. " . . . until the Internationals arrived." Radosh et al., 110.

Page 7. " . . . political orientation." Longo, 52ff.

Page 7. " . . . gibbering madhouse." Nelson, *Volunteers,* 88.

Page 7. " . . . tailor from Lyon." Delperrié de Bayoc, 88.

Page 7. " . . . sent back." Ibid., 73.

Page 7. " . . . proud liberators." Gillain, 8.

Page 7. " . . . Spanish sun." Delperrié de Bayoc, 92.

Page 7. " . . . sabotage and sedition." Radosh et al., 54ff.

Page 7. " . . . democratic discipline." Ibid., 57.

Page 8. " . . . *enemy spies.*" Ibid., 60; emphasis added.

Page 8, note 6. Richardson, 135.

Page 8. " . . . Communists or Socialists." Ibid., 104.

Page 8. " . . . strong army." Ibid., 45.

Page 10. " . . . been accepted." Harvey interview.

Page 10. " . . . professional military experience." Carroll, 65.

Page 10. " . . . *proclaim* it." Gladnick to author.

Page 11, note 8. Morris Mickenberg (Maken), in SACB, 42.

Page 12, note 10. Ross, "American Volunteers."

Page 12. " . . . identical black suitcases." Quoted in Richardson, 41.

Page 12. " . . . with the other." Tisa, *Recalling the Good Fight*, 17.

Page 12, note 11. NA, Department of State, LM 74, reel 48.

Page 13. " . . . afoul of the law." Beeching, 11.

Page 14, note 12. Lizón Gadea, 11.

Page 14. " . . . This ain't Ethiopia, but it'll do." Oscar Hunter, in Bessie, *Heart of Spain,* 29.

Page 14, note 14. Gladnick to author, January 6, 1968.

Page 15. " . . . as natural as eating." Herrick interview.

Page 15. " . . . drinks for American soldiers." Gladnick to author.

Page 16. " . . . drill in the room." Joe Whelan, in Katz, 19.

Page 16. " . . . thought it was hilarious." Gladnick to author.

Page 16. " . . . a foreign war." Rolfe, 10.

Page 16, note 15. *NYT,* January 24, 1937.

Page 16. " . . . nothing else on." Rolfe, 22.

Page 17. " . . . from side to side." Herrick to author.

Page 18. " . . . my name on one of those trees." Stephens, 30.

Page 19. " . . . never held a gun." Herrick, *Jumping the Line,* 139.

Page 19. " . . . real men." Gladnick to author, November 24, 1937.

Page 20. " . . . dared not enter." Herrick to author.

Page 20. " . . . went the joke." Bessie, *Men in Battle,* 39.

Page 20. " . . . on top of a mountain." Corkill and Rawnsley, 310.

Page 21. " . . . to fight for it." Herrick, *Jumping the Line,* 140.

Page 21. " . . . like Hollywood villages." Bessie, *Men in Battle,* 38.

Page 22. " . . . THEY SHALL NOT PASS!" *NM,* April 20, 1937, 19.

Page 23. " . . . to their stamping feet." Herrick, *Jumping the Line,* 143.

Page 23. " . . . in dripping pushcarts." MacDougall, 127.

Page 23. " . . . latecomers on the floor." Monks, 3.

Page 24. " . . . along with some of the civilians." Cierva y Hoces, 149–54.

Page 24. " . . . even more money." Stephens, 33.

Page 24. " . . . soggy black flapjack." Hourihan interview.

Page 24. " . . . a bunch of *Huns?*" Gladnick to author.

Page 25. " . . . a revolutionary who knew him well." Regler, 293.

Page 25, note 19. Richardson, 175.

Page 26. " . . . into the infantry." Beeching, 30.

Page 26. " . . . amid cheers." *NM,* April 6, 1937.

Page 26. " . . . smoke 'em." *Volunteer for Liberty,* March 7, 1938.

Page 26. " . . . a starved-looking string orchestra in tails." Stephens, 37.

Page 27. " . . . wolves in sheep's clothing." Regler, 279ff.

CHAPTER 2: MEN OF LA MANCHA

Page 29. " . . . with a knife." Zuehlke, 84.

Page 29. " . . . whole place was flooded." Herrick interview.

Page 29. " . . . titillated each other." Herrick, *Jumping the Line,* 147.

Page 29. " . . . poison in the well." Villagers interviews, Villanueva de la Jara, 2000.

Page 29, note 2. Martin archive, box 19, BU.

Page 30. " . . . were built." Quoted in Richardson, 123.

Page 30. " . . . hard-core something-or-other." Oscar Hunter, interview by Robert Cowley, in Eby, notes.

Page 31. " . . . naughty children." Carroll, 97.

Page 31. " . . . their discipline stiffened." Voros, 349.

Page 31. " . . . Harry's Bolshies." Alexander, 73.

Page 31. " . . . less than two weeks away." Wintringham, passim.

Page 32. " . . . creep out like a mouse." Acier, 98.

Page 32. " . . . a bullet through [his] head." Cook, 65–66.

Page 32. " . . . poetic justice." Acier, 99.

Page 32. " . . . experience in handling them." Copeman, 85.

Page 34. " . . . rank and privilege." Cronin, 92.

Page 34. " . . . peeking in at the windows." Acier, 101.

Page 35. " . . . summed up the fracas." Stradling, *Irish,* 157.

Page 35, note 8. Cronin, 91.

Page 35. " . . . fighting amongst themselves." Lerude and Merriman, 86.

Page 35. " . . . Villanueva O'Hara." Gladnick to author, January 30, 1968.

Page 35. " . . . your own line of fire." Cronin, 90.

Page 36. " . . . never adopted it." Taylor interview.

Page 36. " . . . the boy scouts cheered." Herrick, *Jumping the Line,* 14.

Page 36. " . . . echoed by countless others." Hourihan interview.

Page 37. " . . . home in disgrace." Lerude and Merriman, 86.

Page 37. " . . . everyone played it differently." Tisa, *Recalling the Good Fight,* 25.

Page 37. " . . . a rather cruel sport." [Tisa], *Story,* 9.

Page 37. " . . . until the commissars caught on.)" Gladnick to author, 1967.

Page 37. " . . . You can masturbate." Herrick interview.

Page 37. " . . . the first free clinic in Villanueva history." Pike, letter to Tisa, ALB, UI.

Page 38, note 10. Mayor of Villanueva, interview, 1967.

Page 38. " . . . with the family in between." Fisher, *Comrades,* 137.

Page 38. " . . . On the peek-it, peek-it line." [Tisa], *Story,* 8.

Page 39. " . . . 'none of them inhibited.'" Tisa, *Recalling the Good Fight,* 28.

Page 39. " . . . Others called him 'The Jello.'" Gladnick to author, 1967.

Page 40. " . . . the Anacostia Flats." U.S. Archives, Dept. of State, 852.2221/794.

Page 40. " . . . your goddamn head broken?'" Herrick interview.

Page 40. " . . . back in January!)" *Foreign Affairs* 1 (1937): 236ff.

Page 40, note 12. Herrick to author.

Page 41. " . . . were easy." Lerude and Merriman, 10.

Page 42. " . . . to the United States." Ibid., 60.

Page 42. " . . . a separate black republic in the United States." SACB, 46.

Page 43. " . . . he never *stopped* smiling." Gladnick to author, 1967.

Page 43. " . . . the real McCoy." Herrick to author, March 16, 1968.

Page 43. " . . . recorded a volunteer." Voros, 349.

Page 43. " . . . Joe's ideal habitat." Swarthmore College Alumni Association.

CHAPTER 3: THE YANKS ARE COMING

Page 46. " . . . 'Best nourishment in the world,' he said." Hunter interview with Robert Cowley, 1965, in Eby, notes.

Page 46. " . . . they never knew us, really." Herrick interview.

Page 46. " . . . to face a firing squad." Tisa, *Recalling the Good Fight*, 35.

Page 47. " . . . menaced the brigade commander with clubs." Copeman, quoted in Cook, 70.

Page 47. " . . . food and water for two days." Copic diary, February 12, 1937.

Page 47. " . . . only flimsy linen ones." Rust, 15.

Page 47. " . . . to dress their men well." Cook, 75.

Page 48. " . . . a 'luster-bluster.'" Gladnick to author, March 8, 1968.

Page 49. " . . . we loved that man." Herrick interview.

Page 49. " . . . a defense of Madrid." Taylor interview.

Page 49. " . . . tons of machinery and comrades-at-arms." [Tisa], *Story*, 11.

Page 49. " . . . followed them all night." Ibid., 36.

Page 49. " . . . the drone overhead of bombers." Acier, 176.

Page 50. " . . . ever used a rifle before." Rolfe, 4.

Page 51. " . . . shouting '¡*Nuestros!*' (Ours!)." Taylor interview.

Page 51. " . . . fired shots at the empty sky." Rolfe, 32.

Page 51. " . . . we knew no better." Gladnick, "To the Battlefield."

Page 52, note 5. " . . . February 16, 1937." Clemente Garcia to author, September 10, 1971.

Page 52. " . . . swallowed up." Dr. William Pike, Brandeis-Nelson Papers, box 51, BU.

Page 52. " . . . blaming it on a 'Trotskyite spy.'" Herrick, *Jumping the Line*, 55.

Page 52. " . . . safe at the base?" Herrick to author.

Page 52. " . . . Das Fleisch kommt noch." Gladnick to author.

Page 53. " . . . the best shelter you can dig!" Tisa, *Recalling the Good Fight*, 39.

Page 53. " . . . my lung capacity." Herrick to author.

Page 54. " . . . kill us?" [Tisa], *Story*, 20.

Page 54, note 8. F. Thomas, *Brother Against Brother*, 94.

Page 54. " . . . 'Fuck you! I'm the observer,' he replied." Merriman interview, AU.

Page 54. " . . . a seaman and former teacher from Alabama." Hourihan interview.

Page 54. " . . . They're dropping leaflets!" Carroll, 99.

Page 54, note 9. Ibid.

Page 55. " . . . The next day he was gone." Taylor interview.

Page 55. " . . . nearer than 200 meters." Sundstrom, quoted in Heikkinen, 14.

Page 55, note 10. Herrick to author, February 2, 2002.

Page 55. " . . . to be evacuated." Herrick, *Jumping the Line*, 161.

Page 55. " . . . 'That was stupid.'" Gladnick to author.

Page 56. " . . . coward—a favorite word of his." Gladnick, telephonic interview with author, February 18, 2002.

Page 56. " . . . thirty dead bodies (not Americans) along the road." Heikkinen, 14.

Page 56. " . . . even when juiced he walked ramrod straight." Herrick to author, February 26, 1968.

Page 56. " . . . killed while fighting in the Dombrowski (Polish) Battalion." Ross, "American Volunteers."

Page 56. " . . . I've been hit." Copeman, 99.

Page 57. " . . . 'It'll look good on your hip.'" Herrick interview.

Page 57. " . . . and dashed down the hill toward them." Herrick, *Jumping the Line*, 170.

Page 59. " . . . blundered into the Fascist lines." Gurney, 127.

Page 59. " . . . looking for his lost sheep." Landis, 64.

Page 60. " . . . he returned to driving a cab." Gladnick to author.

Page 60. " . . . complications from an old wound." Voros notes.

Page 60. "... a coast-to-coast fund drive." *DW*, May 11, 1937.

Page 60. "... 'a nest of Maxims in her hair. Tsk. Tsk'" Acier, 137.

Page 60. "... He lived—but never fought again." Herrick interview.

Page 61. "... like some gigantic machine." *Book of the XV Brigade*, 110.

Page 61. "... like wild rabbits in every direction." Tisa, *Recalling the Good Fight*, 41.

Page 62. "... he must have either deserted or been executed." "Report of Comrade Dewitt," February 26, 1937, AU.

Page 62. "... the men disappeared." Moscow 545/2/2024.

Page 62. "... now look at the mess!" *Book of the XV Brigade*, 76–77.

Page 63. "... Scott had bled to death." Ibid.

Page 63. "... 'they'd have walked right through us.'" Hourihan interview.

Page 63. "... confronting an abstraction." Taylor interview.

Page 63. "... threw his cup away, and retched." Ibid.

Page 64. "... scraped off the red part and devoured the rest." Hourihan interview.

Page 64. "... twenty were dead and forty wounded." Lerude and Merriman, 105.

Page 64. "... To us it was a shaft." Hourihan interview.

Page 64. "... New York Gutter, my very own tongue." Herrick, *Jumping the Line*, 177.

CHAPTER 4: THE JARAMA MASSACRE

Page 66. "... 'a fetish of position.'" Matthews, *Two Wars*, 223.

Page 68, note 4. Wesson interview, 1966.

Page 68. "... dug on their knees all night." Heikkinen, 15.

Page 69. "... how easy it all was." Acier, 150.

Page 69. "... 150 rounds of ammunition." Stephens, 36.

Page 69. "... 'didn't know a butt from a barrel.'" Tisa, *Recalling the Good Fight*, 56.

Page 69. "... concentrated into one day." Cook, 66.

Page 70. "... safety of the cookhouse." Stephens, 39.

Page 70. "... and organizing groceries." Gladnick to author.

Page 70. "... established a front." Corona testimony, Wattis court-martial, AU.

Page 70. "... winding stems." Gladnick to author.

Page 73. "... Hell's angels of the World War." Ibid.

Page 73. "... a riveting machine." Tisa, in *Book of the XV Brigade*, 74.

Page 74, note 10. Box 20, AU.

Page 74. "... before breaking down." Stephens, 44.

Page 74. "... denied that *any* machine gun worked." Hourihan to author.

Page 74. "... belonging to men killed." Collum, 160.

Page 74. "... recent arrivals suffered tremendous casualties." *Volunteer*, March 2002, 13.

Page 74. "... found them all dead." Gladnick to author.

Page 75. "... to hide behind trees and rocks until nightfall." Stephens, 39.

Page 75. "... it had to be hacksawed off." Taylor interview.

Page 75. "... from forty-two men to ten." Acier, 150.

Page 75. "... and crawled back at night." Jack Kallenborn, in Acier, 170.

Page 76. "... to steal back after dark." Wattis court-martial, AU.

Page 76. "... glaring back at him." Graham, 30.

Page 76. "... It smelled like burning hair." *Book of the XV Brigade*, 105.

Page 76. "... 'nobody—but nobody—got near that wire.'" Gladnick to author.

Page 77. "... his comrades at Jarama." Moscow 545/2/2024.

Page 77. "... no food, no medicine, no doctors." Moscow 545/2/297.

Page 77. "... 'with puppy-like eyes.'" Gladnick to author, January 6, 1968.

Page 78. " . . . not with you." Corona testimony, Wattis court-martial, AU.

Page 79. " . . . to cover up his own mistakes." Merriman diary, in Nelson and Hendricks, 87.

Page 79. " . . . the positions of the enemy." Copic diary, February 27, 1937.

Page 79. " . . . 'a mess—full of mud.'" Wheeler letter, Landis file, BU.

Page 79. " . . . 'bent out of shape from firing.'" Heikkinen, 15.

Page 79. " . . . Like broken dolls." Graham, 48.

Page 79. " . . . pleading with the men to go back." Stephens, 41.

Page 80. " . . . who had a chance at all." Lerude and Merriman, 111.

Page 80. " . . . to wheelbarrow him off." Wesson interview.

Page 80. " . . . fifty miles to the south." Lerude and Merriman, 112.

Page 81. " . . . performed 'works of art' with eight flashlights." Mildred Rackley, in Acier, 13.

Page 81. " . . . danced with on our way to Spain." Carroll, 104.

Page 81. " . . . two hundred from the fight on the twenty-seventh." Martin, box 10, BU.

Page 81. " . . . Wounded. Come at once." Lerude and Merriman, 112.

Page 81. " . . . a countryman among the Americanskis." Gladnick to author.

Page 82, note 16. " . . . where asylum was denied." *FRUS, 1937*, March 9, 1937.

Page 82, note 17. " . . . under Gal, then Copic." *Book of the XV Brigade*, 182.

Page 82. " . . . a hopeless fight." Cook, 69.

Page 82. " . . . it would be 'catastrophic for enlistments.'" Ibid., 69 and 82.

Page 83. " . . . may have saved some Americans from summary execution." Gladnick to author.

Page 83. " . . . digging trenches in no-man's-land." Cook, 82.

Page 83. " . . . 35,000 rounds of ammunition." Van den Berghe memoir, AU.

Page 84. " . . . no one was willing to accept the job." "Lincoln Battalion Officers," n.d., AU.

Page 84. " . . . transferred into other units." Copic diary, March 1, 1937.

Page 84. " . . . would be in hell." Ibid.

Page 84. " . . . to stop the meeting." Mickenberg, in Carroll, 113.

Page 84. " . . . learning the ropes." Hourihan interview, AU.

Page 85. " . . . a child crying for its mother." Carroll, 113.

Page 85, note 21. " . . . returned home with the Lincolns in early 1939." Harry Fisher, in Nelson and Hendricks, *Madrid 1937*, 107.

Page 85. " . . . and phenobarbital for those with seizures." Nelson and Hendricks, 91–92.

Page 86. " . . . or we'll show you a war!" Hunter, interviewed by Cowley.

Page 86. " . . . *at a recent trial.* (emphasis added)" *Our Fight*, March 3, 1937.

Page 86. " . . . in the official newsletter." *Notre Combat*, March, 15, 1937, 1.

Page 87. " . . . in the heat of the day." Regler, 252.

Page 87. " . . . He's got to be a Nazi." Tisa, *Recalling the Good Fight*, 55.

Page 87. " . . . in which he is very skilled." Moscow 545/3/453.

Page 87. " . . . 'many years experience as a truck driver.'" Madden letter, AU.

Page 88. " . . . fighting amongst themselves." Quoted in Wattis court-martial, AU.

Page 89. " . . . casualties were to be expected." Stephens, 45.

Page 89. " . . . I was also terrified of being terrified." Gerassi, 128.

Page 89. " . . . an 'attempt to shut up the whole business.'" Landis interview, BU.

Page 89. " . . . roars of enthusiasm." Fisher, *Comrades*, 30.

Page 89. " . . . 2,800 of them in the International Brigades." Cortada, 277.

CHAPTER 5: WAITING . . . WAITING

Page 91, note 1. " . . . the XVth Brigade papers." Moscow 545/3/453.

Page 92. note 2. Hourihan interview.

Page 92. " . . . It was just a book." Hourihan interview, 1967.

Page 92. " . . . 'Go fuck yourself!'" Hourihan interview by Voros, August 6, 1937, AU.

Page 92. " . . . a road for ambulances." Katz, 21.

Page 93, note 3. " . . . but not in Belfast." Riordan, 76.

Page 93. " . . . were short and fat." Gillain, 39ff.

Page 93. " . . . the personal limousine of the 19th Corps political commissar." Ibid., 46.

Page 93. " . . . They're bums." Hourihan interview.

Page 93. " . . . just uncontrollable when drunk." Gillain, 42.

Page 94. " . . . had three troublemakers shot." Copeman, 108.

Page 94, note 6. Steve Nelson interview, 1967.

Page 94. " . . . than go over the top." Moscow 545/2/67.

Page 94. " . . . and led a flight to the rear." Copeman, 113.

Page 95. " . . . through the back of his head." Hourihan report.

Page 95. " . . . His forehead felt like pulp." Simon diary, in Nelson and Hendricks, 94.

Page 95. " . . . in the lurch!" Gladnick to author, January 20, 1987.

Page 95. " . . . in shock, could not function." Graham, 54–60.

Page 96. " . . . calling 'Comrade, Comrade.'" Quoted in Rolfe, 60–61.

Page 96. " . . . My toes! Damn you!" Rees, 96.

Page 96. " . . . He's going to get well." Hemingway, By-Line, 263–67.

Page 96. " . . . rose eyeless to address them." Kempton, 311.

Page 97. " . . . in this 'pacific manner.'" Copic diary, March 14, 1937.

Page 97. " . . . us in our trenches.'" Wendorf, in Book of the XV Brigade, 78.

Page 98. " . . . a growing cairn of rocks." Simon diary, in Nelson and Hendricks, 92.

Page 98, note 9. Hourihan to author, 1967.

Page 98. " . . . one of those slow, lazy slaves from down South." Stephens, 46–47.

Page 98, note 10. Frankson letter, in Nelson and Hendricks, 60.

Page 98. " . . . neither sing nor dance." Herrick, Jumping the Line, 207.

Page 98. " . . . undisciplined troublemakers." Stephens, 47–48.

Page 99. " . . . his notoriety as a folk rebel." Moscow 545/3/451.

Page 100. " . . . one if you were black." Katz, 8.

Page 100. " . . . a Yellow Cab in Chicago." DW, April 17, 1937.

Page 100. " . . . the whole human race!" Book of the XV Brigade, 99.

Page 101. " . . . 'ridiculously helpless and childish.'" Simon diary, in Nelson and Hendricks, 95.

Page 101. " . . . ran riot through [our] intestines." Alexander, 72.

Page 101. " . . . More laughter." Stephens, 43.

Page 101. " . . . both fully clothed." Our Fight, March 3, 1937.

Page 102. " . . . and promoted Spaniards only under duress." Radosh et al., 450ff.

Page 102. " . . . against the Capitalist class." Our Fight, March 3, 1937.

Page 102. " . . . BRIGADE can get it for us." Ibid., March 10, 1937.

Page 102. " . . . because men are buried under them." Ibid., March 26 and March 31, 1937.

Page 102. " . . . the triumph of democracy." Ibid., April 7, 1937.

Page 102. " . . . strolling off chuckling." Tisa, Recalling the Good Fight, 65.

Page 102, note 12. Simon diary, in Nelson and Hendricks, 93.

Page 103. " . . . to treat typhoid cases." Gerassi, 154.

Page 103. " . . . first contracted in the trenches of Jarama." MacDougall, 109.

Page 103. " . . . had docked at Albacete." Book of the XV Brigade, 121.

Page 103. " . . . Spring had come to Jarama." Ibid., 98.

Page 104. " . . . THEY SUFFER WHEN YOU HIT THEM." NYT, May 24, 1937.

Page 104. " . . . A Zeiss sight." Nelson, Volunteers, 104.

Page 104. " . . . doesn't seem like a fair fight." Fisher, Comrades, 49–50.

Page 104. " . . . a scissor-like maneuver." Copic diary, March 1, 1937.

Page 105. " . . . ever compiled." Hourihan file, AU.

Page 106. " . . . the Lincolns crawled back." Ibid.
Page 106. " . . . did not correspond to the truth." Copic diary, April 5, 1937.
Page 106. " . . . dugouts in Battery Park." *NYT*, May 24, 1937.
Page 106. " . . . played 'Night and Day.'" Nelson, *Volunteers,* 102ff.
Page 107. " . . . lightly wounding the inventor and his chums." *Book of the XV Brigade,* 86.
Page 107. " . . . hundreds of letters." Acier, 138ff.
Page 107. " . . . a Sunday afternoon in Machiasport, Maine." Ibid., 143.
Page 108. " . . . his cabin was bulletproof." Paul Burns, *NM,* July 20, 1937.
Page 109. " . . . a few more puffs." Rust, 127.
Page 109. " . . . as far as Barcelona." Copeman, 112.
Page 109. " . . . the death penalty." Ibid., 108.
Page 109. " . . . the death penalty for those responsible." Ibid., 109–12.
Page 109. " . . . in a labor battalion, where life was cheap." MacDougall, 60.
Page 110. " . . . runnin' after it with a lasso." Nelson, *Volunteers,* 106.
Page 110. " . . . away from the Jarama Front." Gurney, 148.
Page 110. " . . . not attached to his command." Copic diary, May 1, 1937.
Page 110. " . . . blind, paralytic drunk." Gurney, 148.
Page 110. " . . . their officers lost all control of them." Copic diary, April 30, 1937.
Page 111, note 14. Carroll, 129.
Page 111. " . . . Not so draughty." Nelson, *Volunteers,* 101.
Page 111. " . . . a pleasant change." Gurney, 149.
Page 111. " . . . you began to wonder what was taking place." Corkill and Rawnsley, 11.
Page 111. " . . . deserters intercepted at the French frontier." Gerassi, 155.
Page 111. " . . . they would play with a bomb-a." Battalion folklore.
Page 112. " . . . in the discard trench we used as a latrine." Fred Thomas, 29.
Page 112. " . . . Speaking of 'loss of manhood.'" Lerude and Merriman, 156.

CHAPTER 6: TOURISTS AND TRIPPERS

Page 113. " . . . massacre or mutiny." *NM,* April 4, 1937, 8–9.
Page 114. " . . . reliability of party leaders." Leonard Lamb, in Gerassi, 125.
Page 114. " . . . like 'ungathered wax fruit.'" Spender, 194ff.
Page 116, note 2. Davenport-Hines, 162.
Page 116. " . . . with his illusions intact." Ibid., 164.
Page 116. " . . . who don't even know that fire is hot." Orwell, "Inside the Whale," 185.
Page 116. " . . . are beginning to ogle each other." Nelson and Hendricks, 146.
Page 117. " . . . the wine was excellent." Cook, 79.
Page 117. " . . . He is also a man." Corkill and Rawnsley, 53.
Page 117. " . . . few men accepted this tale as gospel." Taylor interview.
Page 117. " . . . her mama in the other." Malcolm Cowley, *NR,* October 6, 1937, 29.
Page 117. " . . . a few 'monsters.'" Fisher, *Comrades,* 51.
Page 118. " . . . sunny days bad." Cox, 158.
Page 118. " . . . on two wheels much of the time." Nelson, *Volunteers,* 79.
Page 119. " . . . his fingers still locked around the Flit can." Delmer, 302.
Page 119. " . . . best known for coining the term 'Fifth Column.'" Ibid., 334.
Page 119. " . . . a faded blue background." Cox, 158.
Page 119. " . . . date of exit blank." Delmer, 315.
Page 120. " . . . wounded on the Madrid front." *NYT*, April 5, 1937.
Page 120. " . . . only very very average off." Moorhead, 121.

Page 120. "... like cassocks." Quoted in North, 145ff.

Page 120. "... has printed in two years." Wolff, 355.

Page 120. "... against the New York Giants." Hemingway to Rolfe, January 1940, Rolfe archive, UI.

Page 121. "... with a final 'crash of dust and granite.'" *NR,* April 11, 1937.

Page 121. "... a lie, and Hemingway knew it." Hemingway to Rolfe, January 1940, Rolfe archive, UI.

Page 121. "... 'Sure, Pop. Which side we on?'" Franklin, 216ff.

Page 122. "... a scientific fallacy, as they learned." Delmer, 318.

Page 122. "... to see exactly how a condom worked." Pike to Tisa, Tisa file, UI.

Page 122. "... We can't even get out of the hotel." *NYT,* April 23, 1937.

Page 123. "... good fellowship and excellent meals." Ibid.

Page 123. "... in a vigorous salute." Matthews, *Two Wars,* 229.

Page 123. "... ten miles off." Gellhorn, 23ff.

Page 123. "... treachery on both sides." Quoted in Moorhead, 126.

Page 124. "... grateful for the privilege." Cowles, 23.

Page 127. "... a chance against the new weapons." Herbst, 78–89.

Page 127. "... introduce me to the bitch." Taylor interview.

Page 127. "... He beamed." Fisher, *Comrades,* 51.

Page 127. "... lacked a 'heroic scale.'" Herbst, 89.

Page 128. "... only twelve remained?" Ibid.

Page 129. "... a country at war invites tourist travel." *NYT,* April 28, 1938.

Page 129. "... much more fun on the Franco side." Carroll, 77.

Page 129. "... beaten up by Nazis in a *Bierstube.*" Wolfe, 753–54.

Page 129. "... photographed at Irun." *NYT,* July 4, 1938.

Page 129. "... Tops required for men." *Spain,* April 1, 1939, 18.

Page 129. "... sandblasting later fails to clean it." Beeching, 176–77.

Page 130. "... was hungry, as everyone else is in Madrid." Ibid.

CHAPTER 7: THE TORRENTS OF SPRING

Page 131. "... everything he wrote in the *Daily Worker.*" Wolff, 382.

Page 131. "... rubbing up to respectable housewives." Voros, 434.

Page 132, note 2. Lincoln roster, ALBA.

Page 132, note 3. "... and the House by 406 to 1." Guttman, 88–89.

Page 133, note 6. *NM,* March 16, 1937.

Page 134. "... on price of your ticket." Ibid., April 27, 1937.

Page 134. "... helps buy smokes for our boys in Spain." Ibid., April 20, 1937.

Page 135. "... They shall not pass!" *DW,* February 21, 1937.

Page 135. "... love which Lenin had for Russia." Ibid., February 22, 1937.

Page 136. "... The unspent residue remained in the USSR." Howson, 121–51.

Page 137. "... overlooked by a large resort hotel." *NYT,* May 26, 1937.

Page 138. "... international law." Harold Ickes, quoted in Geiser, 194.

Page 139, note 11. Haywood, 311.

Page 140. "... to fuel the new commissar into Spain." Haywood, 471ff.

Page 140. "... the command was in error." Ibid., 475–76.

Page 140. "... he had lost the confidence of the Americans." Ibid., 474ff.

Page 141. "... the comic folklore of the Lincoln Battalion." Fisher, *Comrades,* 57.

Page 141. "... not each other." Steve Nelson interview with author, 1967.

Page 142. "... were heaving dirt." *Book of the XV Brigade,* 191ff.

Page 143. "... The worms had turned." Landis, 166–67.

Page 143. "... many of them are deserting." Voros, 271.

Page 144, note 14. Haldane, 97.

Page 144. "... the entire transit operation." Ibid., 96ff.

Page 144. "... thicker'n rats in a sewer." Nelson, *Volunteers,* 26.

Page 145, note 16. NA, Department of State, *Spain: Internal Affairs, 1930–39,* LM 74.

Page 145. "... quipped the consul." Fisher, *Comrades,* 190.

Page 146. "... 'got laid' three times." Toab diary, Moscow 545/3/468.

Page 146. "... gyrating on stage with three men." Nelson and Hendricks, 67.

Page 146. "... their morals were puritan." MacDougall, 119.

Page 147. "... cheered the Soviet statuary." Nelson and Hendricks, 68.

Page 147. "... forgot his instructions and smoked it." MacDougall, 58.

Page 147. "... more suckers." Bessie, *Men in Battle,* 8.

Page 147, note 17. Edward Pelaga (Moran) to HUAC, HUAC, 7733ff.

Page 148. "... how to perjure yourself." Herrick, *Jumping the Line,* 222.

Page 148. "... some months later on the Ebro front." Moscow 453/3.

Page 148. "... and he added the name of Bob Minor." Haldane, 127.

Page 149. "... demoralize the people back home?" Voros, 308.

Page 149. "... vegetables for hungry Spain." *NYT,* June 1, 1937.

Page 149. "... even before their arrival in Spain." Ibid., March 28, 1937.

Page 149. "... Vive le front populaire!" Nelson, *Volunteers,* 34–64; Dallet, passim.

Page 151. "... it just never occurred to me." Nelson, *Volunteers,* 60.

Page 151. "... to keep people from seeing it." Gates interview, Gates file, UI.

Page 152. "... mailed Joe a snapshot every week." Bird and Sherwin, 155ff.

Page 153. "... 'Then deport us to Spain!'" *Book of the XV Brigade,* 295.

CHAPTER 8: THE WASHINGTON BATTALION

Page 155. "... a thousand years ago and forgotten." Wolff, 11.

Page 156. "... certainly to that of Franco." Fred Thomas, 19.

Page 156. "... real soldiers." Fisher, *Comrades,* 32.

Page 157. "... what to reject." Markovicz interview, AU.

Page 157. "... good time till after midnight." Koblick memo, AU.

Page 157. "... even if they have too little." Fisher, *Comrades,* 33.

Page 157. "... a large knife to use against the hated enemy." Ibid., 34.

Page 158, note 1. Fisher, in Nelson and Hendricks, 51.

Page 158. "... put to decent use." Francis, 274.

Page 158. "... accept hardships like the British." MacDougall, 95.

Page 158. "... not enough to go round." *Our Fight,* April 15, 1937.

Page 159. "... With soap, you could buy anything." Bessie, *Men in Battle,* 59.

Page 159. "... were replaced with wooden mock-ups." MacDougall, 266.

Page 159. "... to italicize an order." Moscow 545/2/202.

Page 160. "... in the United States, too." Battalion folklore.

Page 160. "... when he went to Jarama." Fisher, *Comrades,* 38.

Page 160. "... spent any time with the boys in the trenches." Ibid., 45.

Page 161. "... the clenched fist." Baxell, 144.

Page 161. "... except his spoon." Nelson, *Volunteers,* 111.

Page 161. "... a lot of guts." Koblick memo, AU.

Page 161. "... Captain Johnson was a pushover." Fisher, *Comrades,* 88.

Page 161. " . . . as he heroically covered their flight." Landis, 420.

Page 162. " . . . to step on the line." Fisher, *Comrades*, 58.

Page 162. " . . . to do anything wrong!" Voros notes, box 43, AU.

Page 162. " . . . we'll shoot him." Fisher, *Comrades*, 44.

Page 162. " . . . with nary a word about 'babies.'" DW, May 11, 1937.

Page 162. " . . . dressing while there." Markovicz interview, AU.

Page 162. " . . . in disrepute." Moscow 453/Bourne report/file.

Page 162. " . . . transfers for volunteers." Moscow 545/6/945.

Page 163. " . . . scattered from hell to breakfast." Nelson, *Volunteers*, 88.

Page 163, note 4. Ibid., 87.

Page 163. " . . . insurance companies requiring evidence." Lerude and Merriman, 173.

Page 163. " . . . a clown with pom-poms." Ibid., 129.

Page 163. " . . . just wasn't up to it." Ibid., 143.

Page 163. " . . . She never divulged the man's name." Ibid., 147–49.

Page 164. " . . . continued his harangue." Herrick, *Jumping the Line*, 237.

Page 165. " . . . and responded accordingly." Moscow, Usera file.

Page 165. " . . . gripped Barcelona in May." Wellman interview, 2001.

Page 166. " . . . the scouts got lost." Markovicz interview, AU.

Page 166. " . . . knowledge of the labor movement." Wendorf report, Usera file, ALBA.

Page 167. " . . . an intellectual policeman." Maken, in SACB, 42.

Page 168. " . . . as the Fascistic 'señor.'" Lerude and Merriman, 142.

Page 168. " . . . while drunk in Albacete station." Moscow 545/3/963.

Page 168. " . . . the notorious swindler Max Eastman." DW, April 9, 1937.

Page 169. " . . . *Let us out!*" Spender, 216.

Page 169. " . . . I never understood." Hourihan interview.

Page 170. " . . . corresponding to that of general." Spender, 111.

Page 170. " . . . agreed with the Canadians." Zuehlke, 158.

Page 171. " . . . in Brigade interior matters." Copic diary, June 15, 1937.

Page 172. " . . . the next two weeks." Markovicz interview, AU.

Page 172. " . . . It was just plain slaughter." Fisher, *Comrades*, 41–42.

Page 172. " . . . never see 'em. It ain't bad at all." Bessie, *Men in Battle*, 9.

Page 173. " . . . transferred to the kitchen." Markovicz interview, AU.

Page 174. " . . . and sent to Albacete." Copic diary, June 18, 1937.

Page 175. " . . . singing revolutionary songs." Dashevsky memo, BU.

CHAPTER 9: STALEMATE AT BRUNETE

Page 176. " . . . left the trenches at Jarama." Copic diary, June 13, 1937.

Page 176. " . . . this number entered the canon." Nelson, *Volunteers*, 121.

Page 176, note 1. Sundstrom, in Heikkinen, 20.

Page 176. " . . . wept with shame." Nelson, *Volunteers*, 122–24.

Page 177. " . . . not to be too hard on those *pobres*." Ibid., 124.

Page 177. " . . . to cries of the youngsters' '¡Olé!'" Fisher, *Comrades*, 77.

Page 177. " . . . would not mind retiring there,' wrote a veteran." Stephens, 58.

Page 177. " . . . men in gas masks." Paul Wendorf memo, AU.

Page 178. " . . . four companies instead of three." Merriman interview, AU.

Page 178. " . . . at home once in a while!" Nelson, *Volunteers*, 126.

Page 178. " . . . always kept a few inches apart." Harry Fisher, in Nelson and Hendricks, 106.

Page 178. " . . . the neighboring village of Almoguerra." Stephens, 58.

Page 179. " . . . any time with them." Quoted in Hopkins, 172.

Page 179, note 3. " . . . about twenty were killed." Collum, 63–100.

Page 179, note 3. " . . . Jewish boy from New York." Hopkins, 227.

Page 179. " . . . within the black population." Carroll, 137.

Page 179. " . . . made him a figurehead." Hunter interview with Robert Cowley.

Page 179. " . . . most certainly not Law's." Hourihan to author.

Page 179. " . . . behind gigantic wine vats." Gladnick to author.

Page 180. " . . . our national independence." Matthews, *Two Wars*, 217.

Page 181. " . . . a dozen Welsh miners." Copeman, 123.

Page 181. " . . . shooting out the bulbs." Ibid., 122.

Page 181. " . . . neither forward nor backward." Copic diary, July 1, 1937.

Page 182. " . . . restricted to only one passenger." Brigade Auto-Park folder, AU.

Page 182. " . . . but we have to walk, etc." Detro file, AU.

Page 182. " . . . 'the Americanism of the 20th Century.'" *DW*, July 4, 1937.

Page 182. " . . . only trampled juniper." Taylor interview.

Page 182. " . . . he passed the note to Steve Nelson." Nelson, *Volunteers*, 144.

Page 182. " . . . like a day at the cinema." *Book of the XV Brigade*, 139.

Page 183. " . . . Pretty sight, eh?" Nelson, *Volunteers*, 145.

Page 183. " . . . the Lincolns had a short reprieve." *Book of the XV Brigade*, 140.

Page 183, note 6. Gladnick to author, January 6, 1968.

Page 184. " . . . along the Brunete road." Copeman, 126.

Page 184. " . . . they could carry in their gas-mask tins." Anonymous Brunete report—British Battalion, AU.

Page 184. " . . . You'll get killed and expose us." Moscow 545/2/2024.

Page 184, note 7. Moscow 545/3/453.

Page 184. " . . . completely inexperienced." Carroll, 138.

Page 184. " . . . 'grazed his ear, his prick and nuts.'" Moscow 545/3/453ff.

Page 185. " . . . The guys are tired." Nelson, *Volunteers*, 148.

Page 185. " . . . 'never go back,' wrote an awed Briton." *Book of the XV Brigade*, 140.

Page 185. " . . . did not enter until morning." Wendorf memo, AU.

Page 186. " . . . died screaming." *Book of the XV Brigade*, 141.

Page 186. " . . . found the place unoccupied." Alexander, 122.

Page 187. " . . . of them left. They were massacred in seconds." Cook, 90.

Page 187. " . . . a curious black." Copeman, 133ff.

Page 187. " . . . running wildly without orders." Anonymous diary, AU.

Page 187. " . . . and pinched our stuff." Fred Thomas, 36.

Page 187. " . . . behind him at full throttle." Wesson interview.

Page 187. " . . . rolling hills all around." *Book of the XV Brigade*, 153.

Page 187. " . . . in bas-relief like a Greek frieze." Wolff, 44.

Page 187. " . . . like a Goddamn roller-coaster." Wesson interview.

Page 187. " . . . a jolly affair." Brunete text, Nelson file, BU.

Page 187. " . . . gaping wounds in their backs." Sundrom, in Heikkinen, 20.

Page 188. " . . . lamented a Briton." Cook, 87.

Page 188. " . . . 'It was a fox hunt,' recalled a veteran." Nelson, *Volunteers*, 150.

Page 188. " . . . mortar men preparing a surprise." *Book of the XV Brigade*, 168.

Page 188. " . . . jotted in his diary." Moscow 445/2/204.

Page 188. " . . . and all the guys followed." Harold Smith report, BU.

Page 188. " . . . bulged eyes, and pissed pants." Harold Smith interview.

Page 189. " . . . in case it got shot off." Cook, 75.

Page 190. " . . . We can chase them off that hill." Fisher interview, BU.

Page 190. " . . . they were moving him." Wesson to Landis, May 4, 1966, BU.

Page 190. " . . . It was ridiculous." MacDougall, 32.

Page 191. " . . . to do much about it." Copic diary, July 11, 1937.

Page 191. " . . . were too weary to do anything but curse him." Fred Thomas, 40.

Page 191. " . . . and laid bets on whether they could get through." *Book of the XV Brigade*, 142.

Page 192. " . . . Socratic dialogues." MacDougall, 235.

Page 192. " . . . salute and faded away." Nelson, *Volunteers*, 153.

Page 192, note 12. " . . . to observe and report." Fisher, *Comrades*, 182.

Page 193. " . . . conspiracy and discrimination." Haywood, 480, passim.

Page 193. " . . . moved on without looking back." Ibid., 482ff.

Page 193. " . . . because he was a Negro." Moscow 495/14/109.

Page 193. " . . . lazy, ostentatious bastard." Rolfe diary, August 27, 1937, UI.

Page 194. " . . . dragging it out." Wesson interview.

Page 194. " . . . without a mark on his body." Nelson, *Volunteers*, 156.

Page 194. " . . . Copic apologized." Corkill and Rawnsley, 52.

Page 194. " . . . He has only got his neck." Quoted in Hopkins, 241.

Page 194. " . . . let alone a People's Army." Ibid., 242.

Page 195. " . . . cannibalized by other units." Gillain, 69–71.

Page 195. " . . . implying more than he said." MacDougall, 208.

Page 195. " . . . The men were promptly moved." Ibid., 211.

Page 196. " . . . I'll mucho malo you, you bastard." Ibid., 209.

Page 196, note 13. Cook, 97.

Page 196. " . . . the Russian got the message." Hugh Sloan, in MacDougall, 213.

Page 196. " . . . showers and underwear." *Book of the XV Brigade*, 158.

Page 196. " . . . targets for ranging bombers." Ibid., 262.

Page 196, note 14. " . . . according to order." Copic diary.

Page 196. " . . . which could mean anything." Ibid., 182.

Page 197. " . . . we won't do it anymore." Nelson, *American Radical*, 220.

Page 197. " . . . had in dear old Spain,' remembered one volunteer." *Book of the XV Brigade*, 167.

Page 197. " . . . to blast any truck from her path." Leland Stowe, *Harpers*, February 1939, 278ff.

Page 197. " . . . bore directly upon this problem." Nelson, *Volunteers*, 161.

Page 198. " . . . In the heat, everybody felt punchy and drained." Mickenberg, in *Book of the XV Brigade*, 145ff.

Page 198. " . . . into a million pieces." Ibid., 145.

Page 198. " . . . McQuarrie's body was thrown upon mine." Anonymous diary, BU.

Page 198. " . . . not a single one hurt. *Book of the XV Brigade*, 147.

Page 198. " . . . and five wounded by a bomb ten feet away." Ibid., 158.

Page 199. " . . . endangered the entire defensive line." Heikkinen, 24.

Page 199. " . . . their feet were raw." Peter O'Connor diary, in Stradling, *Irish*, 88.

Page 199. " . . . reported a Finnish-American officer." Heikkinen, 25.

Page 199. " . . . Markovicz had to back down." Ibid., 26.

Page 199. " . . . canceled the attack." Carroll, 144.

Page 200. " . . . blew up the Casa de Mange." Moscow 545/2/200.

Page 200. " . . . in case they strayed into enemy pockets." Heikkinen, 26.

Page 200. " . . . some anonymous Republican gunner." Ibid.

Page 201. " . . . only death, heat, and exhaustion." Anonymous diary, AU.

Page 201. " . . . not going to tell us to go back!" Nelson, *Volunteers*, 171–72.

Page 201. " . . . when they agreed to return to the battle." Ibid., 172, passim.

Page 201. " . . . denounced as 'traitors and Fascists.'" Brigade Auto-Park folder, AU.

Page 202. " . . . he kissed and fondled openly." Stephens, 66.

Page 202. " . . . only seventeen thousand." Radosh et al., 341.

CHAPTER 10: THE ROAD TO ZARAGOZA

Page 203. "... red and black kerchiefs." Gerassi, 145.

Page 203. "... a comic opera with an occasional death." Orwell, *Homage to Catalonia.*

Page 203. "... soldiers from each side." Official report on Aragon, "Aragon," AU.

Page 204. "... our casualties were light." Leslie Preger, quoted in Corkill and Rawnsley, 32.

Page 204. "... he fell out of bed, I suppose." Matthews, *Two Wars,* 295.

Page 204. "... to the fascists and the reactionary military." Delmer, 302.

Page 204. "... to one-twentieth or less." Nelson, *Volunteers,* 177.

Page 206. "... for the owners got to know me." Matthews, *Two Wars,* 216.

Page 207. "... a bottle of vodka in the other." Lerude and Merriman, 54.

Page 207. "... I'll smack you in the tits." Ibid., 151.

Page 207. "... rank-and-file tendencies." Moscow 453/Bourne file.

Page 207. "... privately called him 'The Hick.'" Nelson, *Volunteers,* 182.

Page 208. "... he was always 'Robbie.'" *Book of the XV Brigade,* 195.

Page 208. "... and 165 who 'disappeared.'" Radosh et al., 238.

Page 208. "... even officers are contributing to this demoralization." Ibid., 246.

Page 208. "... went down to reason with them." Alexander, 80.

Page 209. "... and nervous,' recorded a member of Merriman's staff." Shostek memoir, August 10, AU.

Page 209, note 2. "... a minor scandal." Johnson interview, Landis file, BU.

Page 210. "... back to active duty in the brigade." "Veterans' Company," folder 43, AU.

Page 210. "... had been shot,' recorded a newly arrived American." John Penrod, in Gerassi, 142.

Page 210. "... to ferret out the absentees." R1/133, UI notepad.

Page 210. "... dirty trick if you ask me." Lerude and Merriman, 159.

Page 211. "... a new unit formed around the old Dimitrov Battalion." Kraljic, 98.

Page 211. "... only three hours from Paris?" Koltzov, 454ff.

Page 211. "... whole damned front is that way,' he lamented." Nelson, *Volunteers,* 175ff.

Page 212. "... let us alone, and we let them alone." Ibid., 175–76.

Page 212. "... daylight found us in old location." Merriman, in Lerude and Merriman, 163.

Page 212. "..., every man fresh and ready for the attack." Anonymous, "Riding to Quinto," AU.

Page 213. "... that the Internationals were virtually on top of them." Martínez Bande, *La Gran Ofensiva,* 101.

Page 213. "... So much for protection." Gerassi, 88.

Page 214. "... Go ahead and take the hill." Beeching, 63.

Page 214. "... 'Pin? What pin d-ya mean?'" *Our Fight,* September 15, 1937.

Page 215. "... must have supposed us crazy." Anonymous, "Ringing the Bell," AU.

Page 215. "... opened fire into the murky interior." *Book of the XV Brigade,* 247ff.

Page 215. "... which 'finished the job.'" Ibid., 247.

Page 215. "... drainage hole barely a foot and a half wide." Geiser, 30.

Page 216. "... a good union worker and also loyal to Spain." Anonymous, untitled report, AU.

Page 216. "... We mingled—but not with the officers." Landis file, BU.

Page 216. "... as though it had never happened." Wolff, 76.

Page 216. "... thought the planes were ours." *Book of the XV Brigade,* 254.

Page 217. "... they had sworn to kill to the last man." Ibid., 253.

Page 217. "... broke out among the POWs over the canteens offered." Heikkinen, 31.

Page 217. "... and extremely happy to be safely in our hands." Geiser file, BU.

Page 217. "... lying around, covered with dust and dirt." Landis, 280.

Page 217. "... they took a Cyrillic Bible and a czarist sword." Ibid.; Gerassi, 130.

Page 217. "... officers were lined up." Anonymous report, AU.

Page 217. "... killed by a sniper." Geiser file, BU.

Page 217. " . . . I would not shoot someone in cold blood." Mugarza Gil, note 670.

Page 217. " . . . stepped up and shot him in the head." Geiser, 31.

Page 218, note 5. Anonymous note, box 2, AU.

Page 218. " . . . 'I intentionally forgot them.'" Fisher, *Comrades,* 77.

Page 218. " . . . felt that nothing could stop us now." Anonymous report, AU.

Page 219. " . . . the Fascist key-fortress." *Book of the XV Brigade,* 257.

Page 220. " . . . crammed with people of all ages." Martínez Bande, *La Gran Ofensiva,* 137–53.

Page 222. " . . . poured twenty-seven hundred shells into the town." *Book of the XV Brigade,* 280.

Page 222. " . . . them to come down here and we'll follow *them!*" Landis, 288.

Page 222. " . . . slaughter the whole damn battalion?" *Book of the XV Brigade,* 261.

Page 222. " . . . not received their morning coffee." Copic diary, September 1, 1937.

Page 222. " . . . him shot, the S.O.B." Gerlack letter, undated, ALBA, BU.

Page 223, note 10. " . . . occupied the factory." *Book of the XV Brigade,* 265.

Page 223. " . . . I await orders." Casper de Aguilar, quoted in Copic diary.

Page 224. " . . . place 'Dead Man's Point' to commemorate him." *Book of the XV Brigade,* 270.

Page 224. " . . . the owner doubtless sensitive to noise and vibration." 1967 visit to site by author.

Page 224. " . . . dedicating themselves to pillage." Martínez Bande, *La Gran Ofensiva,* 149.

Page 224. " . . . ghastly realism 'no Hollywood film could ever give.'" *Book of the XV Brigade,* 281.

Page 225. " . . . the grove north of town." Beeching, 69.

Page 225. " . . . was left behind." Lerude and Merriman.

Page 225. " . . . his monologue about seven children." Gerassi, 115.

Page 226. " . . . you will all be killed in the morning." *Book of the Brigade,* 278.

Page 226, note 11. Martínez Bande, *La Gran Ofensiva,* 139.

Page 226. " . . . they burst into tears." Fisher, *Comrades,* 82ff.

Page 226. " . . . on the Communist side." Ibid., 86.

Page 226. " . . . he did not mean prison terms." *Book of the XV Brigade,* 283.

Page 226, note 12. Martínez Bande, *La Gran Ofensiva,* 100.

Page 226. " . . . reinforcements from Madrid." Ibid.

Page 227. " . . . a gap of thirty kilometers with very few enemy." Lister, 297.

Page 227. " . . . the remains of humans, pigs, and goats." MacDougall, 219.

Page 227. " . . . Belchite had been captured." Gerassi, 125.

Page 228. " . . . they know their trade." *NR,* January 12, 1938, 273.

Page 228. " . . . in the subway, on any campus." Moorhead, 135.

Page 228. " . . . useful in propaganda,' a commissar wrote to Moscow." Moscow 545/6/857.

Page 228, note 15. Thomas Amlie to author, 1967.

Page 229. " . . . reporting on the Americans' performance in Spain." SACB, 52.

Page 229. " . . . culminating in a complete Franco victory." Vidal, 222.

CHAPTER 11: FUENTES DE EBRO

Page 232. " . . . and English was not one of them." Katz, 20.

Page 232. " . . . Enjoy the smoke." Wellman interview, December 2001.

Page 233. " . . . at finally being on the business end of one." Dallet, 45ff.

Page 234. " . . . a few of these had been executed." Bird and Sherwin, 159.

Page 235. " . . . coming true in steel." Dallet, passim.

Page 236. " . . . nothing more than cannon fodder." Radosh et al., 492.

Page 236. " . . . subdued by brigade security officers." Gillain, 107.

Page 237. " . . . his dislike of the Americans." Hopkins, 413.

Page 237. " . . . Wild was no diplomat." Corkill and Rawnsley, 7.

Page 237. " . . . disrespect toward their own country." Delperrié de Bayoc, 76.

Page 238. " . . . on the brink of mutiny." Ibid., 337–41.

Page 239. " . . . the same rank and pay as military commanders." Nelson and Hendricks, 320.

Page 239. " . . . 3,349 ensconced at Albacete." Luigi Longo report, in Radosh et al., section 47.

Page 240. " . . . the incompetence and featherbedding of the Albacete claque." Reports 60 and 70, in Radosh et al., 295 and 456ff.

Page 241. " . . . the 'cozy atmosphere of a Quaker society.'" Walter, report 70, in Radosh et al.

Page 241. " . . . given the plans for the attack to the enemy." Copic diary, October 1, 1937.

Page 241, note 5. Radosh et al., 449ff.

Page 242, note 6. HUAC, 7733ff.

Page 242. " . . . geography class and Joseph Conrad." Starobin, 10ff.

Page 244. " . . . a functionary of the League a number of years." Ibid., 37ff.

Page 245. " . . . every hour on the hour." Wolff, 119.

Page 245. " . . . to force their governments to lift the blockade." Beeching, 71.

Page 245. " . . . stamped it flat, and flung it back." Shafran, Brandeis interview, BU.

Page 246. " . . . to move Dallet to a less important position." Moscow 545/3/441.

Page 246. " . . . he claimed to be a spiritual Mississippian." Wolff, 104.

Page 247. " . . . I didn't like getting pushed around." *Book of the XV Brigade.*

Page 248. " . . . him the word 'comrade' did not come easily." Wolff, 104.

Page 249. " . . . and near-swamp, terrain." Gladnick to author, December 17, 1967.

Page 249. " . . . hoarding tobacco for his Stalinesque pipe." Carroll, 161.

Page 250. " . . . the way of the fire,' recalled a survivor." Larry Cane, CBC broadcast interview.

Page 250, note 13. Amery, 57ff.

Page 250. " . . . proved to be the Lincoln battalion on their right." Beeching, 72.

Page 251. " . . . say 'The celebration begins at noon.'" Amery, 57–58.

Page 251. " . . . one time all through the war." Ron Liversedge, in Beeching, 72.

Page 252. " . . . but I don't know where they went." Amery, 60–61.

Page 252. " . . . a Czech staff officer screaming, 'Advance!'" MacDougall, 217.

Page 254. " . . . quartermasters and cooks." Duarte report (see footnote 14).

Page 254. " . . . was no cover," remembered a Mac-Pap." Beeching, 73ff.

Page 254. " . . . to get them moving again." Thompson interview, BU.

Page 255. " . . . blasted the life out of him." Voros, 343.

Page 255. " . . . but a machine-gun is a good persuader." Ronald Liversedge, in Hoar, 145.

Page 255. " . . . were out of sight behind them." Makela, in *Book of the Brigade*, 290–92.

Page 256. " . . . some sort of diatribe." Hoar, 151.

Page 256. " . . . too far away to cover the attack." Keller interview with Landis, BU.

Page 257. " . . . their first comeback experience." Copic diary, October 13, 1937.

Page 257. " . . . get them used to used to attacking under fire!" Amery.

Page 257. " . . . their transit had already been arranged." Howson, 142.

Page 257. " . . . one of the most stupid operations of the war." Lister, 299.

Page 257. " . . . I don't think anyone else ever did." Wolff, 119.

Page 258. " . . . Joe had guts." Quoted in Hoar, 149.

Page 258. " . . . much-prized can of Prince Albert tobacco." Wolff, 130.

Page 258, note 20. Newspaper clipping, BU.

CHAPTER 12: TERUEL—THE BIG CHILL

Page 259, note 1. " . . . with the Americans of the International Brigade." Landis, 324.

Page 260. " . . . frozen in our tracks." Villar.

Page 262. " . . . admiration for these troops." *DW*, November 26, 1938.

Page 262. " . . . jacket he had supposedly worn during the World War." Radosh et al., 484ff.

Page 264. " . . . cried silently as we drove away through the trees." Lerude and Merriman, 179.

Page 265. " . . . armies of illiterate peasants." Elman Service interview.

Page 265. " . . . a precise instrument for eliminating Fascists." Stradling, *Irish*, 109.

Page 265. " . . . pausing to admire himself in the glass panes." Wolff, 137.

Page 266. " . . . an office that turns out twenty a day." Lee, 10.

Page 266. " . . . You are now in the Republican Army." Ibid., 24.

Page 266. " . . . the skimmed milk of the middle-Thirties." Ibid., 45.

Page 266. " . . . a succession of tubercular blasts." Ibid., 59.

Page 266. " . . . cigarettes of dried oak leaves." Ibid., 73.

Page 266. " . . . I can't do owt about that." Ibid., 103.

Page 267. " . . . a brigader who knew even rudimentary Spanish." Radosh et al., 448ff.

Page 267. " . . . These [guys] could not read anything." Wolff, 128.

Page 267. " . . . one of the editors, confessed years later." Voros, 372ff.

Page 268. " . . . to medical services 195 (7.8 percent)." Report, December 1, 1937, Moscow 545/6/5.

Page 269. " . . . to Moscow but were not available to the public." Ibid.

Page 269. " . . . lined up along the road in the winterish gloom." Gates, *Story*, 57.

Page 269. " . . . a bicycle designed for a six-footer." MacDougall, 214.

Page 269. " . . . I could have any of these men shot." Quoted in Voros, 340.

Page 269. " . . . and shot us from the church towers." Unknown.

Page 269. " . . . (*We* shall not pass!)." Delmer, 308.

Page 269, note 4. " . . . Communists, or Anarchists." Atlee, 134.

Page 269, note 4. " . . . British Labour Party of that day." Landis, 343.

Page 271. " . . . ran up and down the road flailing themselves." Fisher, *Comrades*, 91.

Page 271. " . . . and boiled it with onions." MacDougall, 160.

Page 272. " . . . a sergeant in the Canadian Army." Hoar, 162.

Page 273. " . . . a serpentine column ten miles long." Matthews, *Education*, 109.

Page 274. " . . . when hobnail boots ran out." *NM*, February 14, 1939.

Page 275. " . . . before collapsing into the ground again." Lee, 157.

Page 276. " . . . but of course I couldn't see beyond my ridge." Unknown.

Page 277. " . . . blown up and hanging in the air." Nelson and Hendricks, 367.

Page 277. " . . . most of them workers or peasants." Wolff, 168.

Page 278. " . . . a refrain increasingly heard in the Republican armies." Villar.

Page 278. " . . . although other gunners refused to fire." Hoar, 169.

Page 278. " . . . the typist disappeared." Beeching, 87.

Page 279. " . . . At least you can shoot yourself." Lee, 159.

Page 279. " . . . a bad but not usually a fatal wound." Wolff, 198.

Page 279. " . . . a romance with an American nurse." Box 84, BU.

Page 279. " . . . Americans—very odd people." Wesson interview.

Page 280. " . . . She did not reveal its provenance." Haldane, 135–38.

Page 281. " . . . when do I go home?" Fisher, *Comrades*, 101.

Page 283. " . . . all the bathtubs under lock and key." Wolff, 183.

Page 283. " . . . none of them ever seen again." Cane, CBC broadcast interview.

Page 283. " . . . Surrender, you bastards!" Landis, 393.

Page 283. " . . . vermin, inhuman gorillas, liars, apes." Wolff, 253.

Page 283. " . . . world revolution back in the States." SACB, 44.

Page 283. " . . . killed during the Segura fight." Ross, "American Volunteers."

Page 284. " . . . into a valley on the other side." Bonetti interview, Landis, BU.

Page 285. " . . . at the cost of two British lives." Rust, 116.

CHAPTER 13: RETREAT FROM BELCHITE

Page 287. " . . . slow in speech, quick to anger." Wolff, 150.

Page 288. " . . . an enemy attack upon our lines." Martínez Bande, *La Llegada al Mar*, 38.

Page 289. " . . . Republican double-barrel French guns." Toynbee, 100.

Page 289. " . . . a whole month without any pocket money?" Villar.

Page 289. " . . . dive-bombing by experimental Stukas." Fisher, *Comrades*, 103.

Page 290. " . . . Create a line of defense. Proceed immediately." Frank Rogers, in Heikkinen, 37.

Page 290. " . . . a nightmare,' remembered one American." Fisher, *Comrades*, 104.

Page 290. " . . . Crazy!" Ibid., 105.

Page 291. " . . . that they passed over them at head-level." Rogers, in Heikkinen, 37.

Page 291. " . . . a reserve post in the olive grove behind them." Stuart interview by Landis, BU.

Page 293. " . . . and others were seriously wounded." Rogers, in Heikkinen, 38.

Page 294. " . . . , oh please, come back to me soon." Kemp, 108ff.

Page 295. " . . . of Belchite at 4:30 p.m." Martínez Bande, *La Llegada al Mar*, 38.

Page 296. " . . . sweating, cursing, angry." Rogers, in Heikkinen, 38.

Page 296. " . . . I crossed the river and headed for the rear." Landis, 421.

Page 296. " . . . The British evacuated Belchite last." Castells, 312.

Page 296. " . . . evacuated by the populace." Rust, 132.

Page 297. " . . . period, most of them by the feared Moors." Geiser, 263–64.

Page 297. " . . . he does not say—but it was likely." Colmegna, 44.

Page 298. " . . . as if a maniac had torn them to shreds." Rolfe, 189.

Page 298. " . . . unable to stop the retreat." Cecil-Smith report, in Beeching, 96–108.

Page 298. " . . . inexplicably saved by an enemy officer." Hoar, 189.

Page 299. " . . . a wounded elephant limping in." *Volunteer for Liberty*, June 30, 1938.

Page 299. " . . . and kissed him." Lerude and Merriman, 206.

Page 300. " . . . They're International Brigades." Kemp 107–14.

Page 300. " . . . I had not come to Spain for this." Ibid., 110.

Page 300. " . . . he most certainly would have been shot." Ibid., 113.

Page 300. " . . . obligingly shot the prisoner for him." Ibid., 114–16.

Page 300. " . . . his rifle still over his shoulder." Quoted in Amery.

Page 300. " . . . not to the front, but to the rear." Ibid., 74.

Page 302. " . . . on a French ship and escaped to Marseilles." Amery, 85.

Page 302. " . . . were gone just as some of us started to fire." Matthews, in Beeching, 110.

Page 302. " . . . but the flanks and rear as well." Rolfe, 193–97.

Page 303. " . . . who had deserted to the enemy." Ibid., 193.

Page 303. " . . . nothing between us and the Fascists except those scouts." Voros, 390.

Page 304. " . . . he finally met friendlies at Maella." *Volunteer for Liberty*, April 25, 1938.

Page 304. " . . . credited with downing a plane with a lucky shot." Beeching, 133.

Page 305. " . . . after a five-day cross-country trek." Quoted in Hoar, 183.

Page 305. " . . . as alarmed as the tankers." Voros, 391.

Page 305. " . . . stampeded men into roadside ditches." Voros, 405.

Page 305. " . . . arms fire along the road, followed by silence." Beeching, 112.

Page 305. " . . . he rejoined them several days later." Ross, "American Volunteers."

Page 306. " . . . The gear arrived on time." Voros, 401.

Page 308. " . . . that five International Brigades held Caspe." Martínez Bande, *La Llegada al Mar*, 56.

Page 308. " . . . was to throw rocks and yell at them." Landis, 433.

Page 309. " . . . an unknown hill somewhere on Doran's map." Fisher, 114–16.

Page 309. " . . . maintaining that the tanks were Russian." Wolff, 242.

Page 310. " . . . Just look at *my* battle." Battalion folklore.

Page 310. " . . . on the verge of bursting into action." Avery to Beeching, in Beeching, 116.

Page 311. " . . . too immense to be counted." Martínez Bande, *La Llegada al Mar*, 63.

Page 311. " . . . del Pueyo in the early morning of March 10." Ross, "American Volunteers."

Page 311. " . . . or chose desertion." Geiser, 260–64.

Page 311. " . . . only half of these still carried rifles." Beeching, 115.

Page 311. " . . . Republic might win the war but lose the revolution." Nelson, *Volunteers*, 116.

Page 311. " . . . I'd be a Communist." Fisher, telephone interview.

Page 311. " . . . always talking against the Communist Party." Fisher, *Comrades*, 118–19.

Page 312. " . . . Both Americans were shot." Colmegna, 44.

CHAPTER 14: THE ROUT AT GANDESA

Page 312. " . . . ain't got no bloody balls,' came the reply." Bessie, *Men in Battle*, 63.

Page 312. " . . . wish I could be with you. Good luck." Ibid., 76.

Page 314. " . . . 'put the fear of God into us.'" Ibid., 77.

Page 314. " . . . long, a look of desperation in their eyes." Ibid., 81.

Page 314. " . . . gone, only a couple get away. Me." Ibid., 80.

Page 314. " . . . masking as defenders of liberty." Cierva y Hoces, 158.

Page 315. " . . . all of whom had to be protected and evacuated." *FRUS, 1938*, March 30, 1938.

Page 315, note 1. Voros, 388.

Page 315. " . . . accusations that horrified the new replacements." Bessie, *Men in Battle*, 83.

Page 316. " . . . find one—or off leaves with their fingers." Ibid., 86.

Page 316. " . . . He spat and ended the discussion." Ibid., 94–95.

Page 316. " . . . an awed rookie wrote in his diary." Dan Bessie, 17.

Page 317. " . . . intent on saving the few survivors of his company." Voros, 411ff.

Page 317. " . . . throwing it away is to be shot on sight." Bessie, *Men in Battle*, 85.

Page 317. " . . . reorganized in the frontier region." Ibid., 86.

Page 317, note 2. *FRUS, 1938*, 277.

Page 318. " . . . trucked to Batea under guard." Honeycombe testimony, *NYT*, April 4, 1938.

Page 318, note 3. Bourne personnel file, Moscow 543.

Page 319. " . . . the YCL in America and the CP in Spain)." CP Roster, BU.

Page 319. " . . . was a beautiful night—for an air raid." Nelson and Hendricks, 142.

Page 319. " . . . with authority to veto decisions if he so chose." Gates letter, UI.

Page 319. " . . . the grandpa draftees." Villar.

Page 320. " . . . reading this screed." *Volunteer*, May 25, 1998.

Page 320. " . . . behind you, you in turn are behind him!" *Volunteer for Liberty*, June 30, 1938.

Page 320. " . . . he was going to have me shot." Villar.

Page 321. " . . . throw a *fiesta* for you, it never fails." Bessie, *Men in Battle*, 93.

Page 322. " . . . , dear, Do you mind if I tell?" Starobin, 45.

Page 322. " . . . again soon. Love and then some. Bob." Lerude and Merriman, 208.

Page 324. " . . . machine guns fitted on the handle bars." Corkhill and Rawnsley, 118.

Page 324. " . . . and about 150 killed or wounded." Rust, 153.

Page 324. " . . . to set them on fire with gasoline." Corkhill and Rawnsley, 153.

Page 325. " . . . and declared he would bring Walter back." Voros, 413.

Page 325. " . . . the rough mountain terrain on the south side." Cane, CBC interview.

Page 325. " . . . every man for himself." Ibid.

Page 326. " . . . not one of our strong points." Wolff to Gates, December 28, 1970, UI.

Page 326. " . . . probably just lonesome, but what the hell." Bessie, *Men in Battle*, 104.

Page 327. " . . . walked through the tunnel to France." *NYT*, April 8, 1938.

Page 327. " . . . he cheerfully went to jail in France." NA, State Department.

Page 327. " . . . as soon as the barrage crept closer." Voros, 403.

Page 328. " . . . they sounded 'musical and harmless.'" Bessie, *Men in Battle,* 109.

Page 328. " . . . an almost visible sense of doom emanated from him." Wolff to Gates, December 28, 1970, UI.

Page 328. " . . . They vanished from history." Heikkinen, 42.

Page 328. " . . . had just blown up a munitions dump." Villar.

Page 330. " . . . the rest of them running away." Martínez Bande, *La Llegada al Mar,* 158.

Page 330. " . . . assuming any were still alive." Bessie, *Men in Battle,* 116–23.

Page 331. " . . . wire still hanging around their necks." *Volunteer for Liberty,* October 6, 1938.

Page 332. " . . . and that he would lead us into this attack." Villar.

Page 333. " . . . No Lincolns dared fire a shot in return." Schmidt, in Wullschleger, 288.

Page 333. " . . . This was our final leave-taking." Villar.

Page 333. " . . . to rejoin the group back on Wolff's hilltop." Watt interview, CBC.

Page 334. " . . . held by remnants of the 24th Battalion." Landis, 462–63.

Page 334, note 6. " . . . We didn't even touch them." Gates interview, UI.

Page 335. " . . . if you weren't wounded." Carroll, 174.

Page 335. " . . . boots missing and faces shot off." Geiser, 77.

Page 336. " . . . as if some were captured." NANA dispatch (April 4, 1938), in Lerude and Merriman, 217.

Page 336. " . . . most unlikely over wooded terrain at midnight." *NYT,* April 12, 1938.

Page 336. " . . . privately, furtively, each man's fate his own." Wolff, 300.

Page 337. " . . . of his letter—to collect his back pay." Beeching, 131.

Page 337. " . . . and became violently sick." MacDougall, 270.

Page 338. " . . . he would be dead." *Chicago Tribune Magazine,* December 4, 1983.

Page 338. " . . . and stride outside." Voros, 420ff.

Page 339. " . . . and ten staff officers." Martínez Bande, *La Llegada al Mar,* 158.

Page 340. " . . . Fascist bastards haven't won yet. We'll show you!" Gates, *Story,* 60.

Page 340, note 7. Delmer, 33.

Page 340. " . . . sensed the end had come." *FRUS, 1938,* March 30, 1938.

Page 340. " . . . swam the remaining distance in full regalia." Elman Service interview.

Page 340. " . . . 50 on the retreat to Caspe, and 183 at Gandesa." Ross, "American Volunteers."

Page 340. " . . . Franco's prisons until near the end of the war." Geiser, 260–66.

Page 343. " . . . They all fell asleep immediately." Villar.

Page 344, note 8. Villar to author, January 15, 1997.

Page 344, note 9. Villar to author, November 12, 1995.

Page 346. " . . . the Army of the Comintern." Schmidt, in Wullschleger, 291.

Page 346. " . . . on good behavior, twenty-six months later." Villar.

CHAPTER 15: POSTMORTEM

Page 347. " . . . we just kept silent." Bessie, *Men in Battle,* 140.

Page 347. " . . . Mucho mal. Mucho fuckin' malo." Ibid., 133.

Page 348. " . . . and moved on without another word." Toynbee, 135.

Page 348. " . . . A lone Canadian asked for a pair of socks." Ibid.

Page 348. " . . . ought to shoot me and git it over with." Bessie, *Un-Americans,* 75.

Page 349. " . . . 'I can swim' went the refrain." Bessie, *Men in Battle,* 142.

Page 349. " . . . artists that had designed them." Corkill and Rawnsley, 21.

Page 349. " . . . arriving without weapons would be 'instantly shot.'" Hopkins, 295.

Page 350. " . . . he said nothing about it." Sheean, 53–65.

Page 351. " . . . you don't have very good view from a ditch." Ibid., 58.

Page 351. " . . . 'From Workers in Barre and Montpelier, Vermont.'" Ibid., 59.

Page 351. " . . . you guys didn't think I was coming back." Ibid., 65.

Page 352. " . . . as a test he had failed." Wolff, 307.

Page 352. " . . . only the way Dallet thought they dressed." Gates, *Story*, 49ff.

Page 353. " . . . insignificant people like Johnny Gates rise to the top." Ibid.

Page 353. " . . . a greenhorn in politics." Gates interview, UI.

Page 353. " . . . It never has been,' he wrote." Ibid.

Page 353. " . . . the enemy did not know whom they had killed." Ibid.

Page 354. " . . . would neither confirm nor deny this." *NYT*, May 21, 1938.

Page 354. " . . . both were captured in the hut." Wullschleger, 289.

Page 354, note 2. *Volunteer*, fall 2000, 14–16.

Page 354. " . . . section by section to a small hill farther north." Rolfe, 211.

Page 355. " . . . and finally 'Manos arriba!'" Ibid., 213–14.

Page 355. " . . . the XIIIth, which was not on the ground." Landis, 448.

Page 355. " . . . but he was Wolff's boss." Gates interview, UI.

Page 355. " . . . *thought* he heard the Spanish cry, 'Manos arriba!'" Lerude and Merriman, 214.

Page 356. " . . . Posterity shall have to *embellish*." Gerlach letter, miscellaneous letters, ALBA, BU.

Page 356. " . . . to investigate him as a Trotskyite." Bourne file, Moscow 453.

Page 356. " . . . lost a rifle would be shot.' They laughed." Bessie, *Un-Americans*, 22.

Page 357. " . . . they cry when reprimanded." Dan Bessie, 38.

Page 357. " . . . while the *quintos* retained a 'residue of distrust.'" Bessie, *Men in Battle*, 154.

Page 357. " . . . they did not know to which party they belonged." Orwell, *Homage to Catalonia*, 101.

Page 358. " . . . babies should have to know this sort of thing." Dan Bessie, 49.

Page 359, note 5. *FRUS, 1938*, 281.

Page 359. " . . . stowing away on a garbage scow." *Volunteer for Liberty*, June 30, 1938.

Page 359, note 6. *NYT*, August 23, 1938.

Page 360. " . . . and *I'll* write that!" Sheean, 238.

Page 360, note 7. *FRUS, 1938*, 279.

Page 360. " . . . awfully gloomy to make a soldier." Moorhead, 133.

Page 360. " . . . not necessary to her existence." Lardner to mother, May 3, 1938, in Nelson and Hendricks, 45.

Page 360. " . . . shipping the whole lot home." Fred Thomas, 100.

Page 360, note 8. Sheldon Jones interview with author, 1968.

Page 361. " . . . I don't want to go bearing gifts." Sheean, 254.

Page 361. " . . . his shyness was not snobbery." Bessie and Prago, 280.

Page 361, note 9. *Volunteer for Liberty*, May 25, 1938.

Page 361. " . . . great farting sounds from a bugle." MacDougall, 272.

Page 362. " . . . Italian or German domination." Dan Bessie, 47.

Page 362. " . . . its tradition of sacrifice and courage." Gates, *Story*, 193.

Page 363. " . . . alcohol and drug abuse." Fisher, *Comrades*, 187.

Page 363. " . . . lost their humorous edge." Bessie, *Men in Battle*, 176.

Page 363. " . . . on the verge of starvation." Rees, 106.

Page 364. " . . . gypping the Associated Jewish charities." Nelson and Hendricks, 435.

Page 364. " . . . a poor meal in a cheap hotel." Fred Thomas, 112.

Page 364. " . . . Up with the bourgeoisie." Herrick, *Jumping the Line*, 218.

Page 364. " . . . a Pyrrhic victory, at best." *NYT*, June 14, 1938.

Page 364. " . . . a fig tree three hundred yards away." Corkhill and Rawnsley, 106.

Page 364. " . . . The first man bled to death." Fred Thomas, 112.

Page 365. " . . . for their discipline." Dan Bessie, 63.

Page 365. " . . . pessimists and provocateurs." Beeching, 124.

CHAPTER 16: IN THE PENAL COLONIES

Page 368. " . . . to write letters for money." *FRUS, 1938*, June 27, 1938.

Page 369. " . . . the Internationals lived in isolation." *NYT*, July 11, 1938.

Page 371. " . . . the safety of the San Pedro prisoners." Geiser, 58.

Page 372. " . . . a shallow covering of earth." Ornitz, 12.

Page 374. " . . . a portion of their daily ration for a few days." Gerassi, 116ff.

Page 374. " . . . defiant shouts of 'Libre! Libre!'" Dorland, 16.

Page 375. " . . . to fresh fruit in their year at San Pedro." Geiser, 108.

Page 375. " . . . the colors of the Nationalist flag." Gregory, 140.

Page 375. " . . . The priest and Tanky nodded happily." Geiser, CBC interview.

Page 376. " . . . recall the taste of that bread after forty years." Cook, 120.

Page 376. " . . . been one's own lice, but you didn't know." Ibid., 124.

Page 377. " . . . would make you heave just to look at it." Ibid.

Page 377. " . . . they have plenty bloody tobacco." Francis, 243.

Page 378. " . . . their first fresh vegetable in three months." Geiser, 159.

Page 378. " . . . slipped peseta notes to prisoners." Ibid.

Page 378. " . . . visual proof that the Internationals were Jews." Fisher, *Comrades*, 185.

Page 379. " . . . blue overalls to cover them." Geiser, 172.

Page 379. " . . . opened a small store." Ibid., 162.

Page 379. " . . . fibers into cloth and fasten it to tire casings." Ibid., 182.

Page 380. " . . . lost in the wild applause." Ibid., 190.

Page 380. " . . . his fellow officers from Burgos." Ibid., 162ff.

Page 381. " . . . had lower percentages of deaths." Radosh et al., 467–68.

Page 382. " . . . it tastes like horse piss." Hoar, 122–23.

Page 382. " . . . complaints in his report, all in great detail." Document 76, in Radosh et al., 477–87.

Page 383. " . . . desert twice, they get shot." *NYT*, April 10, 1938.

Page 384. " . . . no adequate political work being done." Nelson and Hendricks, 465.

Page 384. " . . . with the police panting on our heels." Quoted in Hopkins, 208.

Page 384. " . . . to the highest social and moral feelings of men." HUAC (1940), 7736ff.

Page 385. " . . . by his union, an affiliate of the CIO." HUAC (1938), 7747ff.

Page 386. " . . . would return at once if they could." Ibid., 7727ff.

Page 386. " . . . New Yorker known as 'Ivan.'" HUAC (1940), 7818ff.

Page 387. " . . . all to hear, 'Those sons of bitches!'" Bailey, in Gerassi, 110.

Page 387, note 10. Wolff to Gates, December 28, 1970, UI.

Page 387. " . . . executions. It arrived too late for Paul White." Fisher, in Nelson and Hendricks.

Page 387, note 11. Dollard, 49.

Page 387. " . . . executed by a nocturnal firing squad." Wolff to Gates, December 28, 1970, UI.

Page 388. " . . . the most earnest reading he ever gave." Payne, 290.

Page 388. " . . . as a Mafia bandit carries out a contract." Gladnick to C. Stewart, AU.

Page 388. " . . . good humor and empty rifles." Fisher, 135–36.

Page 388, note 12. Tom Entwhistle interview, 1984.

Page 389. " . . . and toppled over." HUAC, 7829ff.

Page 389, note 13. Gerassi, 142.

Page 389. " . . . ever call me *that* again, I'll *kill* you!" Herrick interview.

CHAPTER 17: THE FAR SHORE

Page 390. " . . . Now what river do you suppose *that* could be?" Bessie, *Men in Battle*, 195.

Page 390. " . . . 'Not the *Daily Worker*,' sneered his companion." Ibid., 198.

Page 391. " . . . Coxey's Army of the Air." H. Smith interview, BU.

Page 391. " . . . troubled Mickenberg and other skeptics." Wolff, 320.

Page 392. " . . . crossing the Delaware as his men shoved off." Rolfe diary, July 25, 1938, UI.

Page 392. " . . . Eventually we made it to the other side." Beeching, 127.

Page 392. " . . . swimming across behind the boats." Heikkinen, 46.

Page 392. " . . . proof to the contrary." Matthews, *Education*, 139.

Page 392. " . . . just twenty miles southwest." Bessie, *Men in Battle*, 214.

Page 392. " . . . the massacre on February 27, 1937." Fisher, *Comrades*, 187.

Page 393, note 1. Antonio Tovar, interview with author, 1963.

Page 393. " . . . Couple wounded." Dan Bessie, 70.

Page 394. " . . . a soiled handkerchief." Landis, 535–36.

Page 395. " . . . What'ya want for a nickel?" Bessie, *Men in Battle*, 238.

Page 395. " . . . Their heart was not in it." Dan Bessie, 82.

Page 396. " . . . Shucks, I guess it was a stone." Bessie, *Men in Battle*, 237.

Page 396. " . . . no support on their flanks." Beeching, 130.

Page 396. " . . . 'you could hear them working at night.'" MacDougall, 298.

Page 396. " . . . The officer returned at once to Division." Beeching, 151.

Page 396. " . . . for their antiaircraft guns were not effective." Ibid., 130.

Page 397. " . . . I'm not killing any of our guys." Wolff, 349.

Page 398. " . . . Then they were relieved." Fisher to author.

Page 398. " . . . bite on it whenever it got really bad." Cook, 139.

Page 399. " . . . Come over to us." Bessie, *Men in Battle*, 264.

Page 399. " . . . We've run out of the *Worker*." Ibid., 263–64.

Page 399. " . . . details, if recorded, have not survived." Klehr et al., 164–83.

Page 399. " . . . an agent provocateur." Wolff, 324.

Page 399. " . . . the final issue was no longer in doubt." Martínez Bande, *La Llegada al Mar,* passim.

Page 400. " . . . know enough to come in out of the rain." Bessie, *Men in Battle*, 274.

Page 400. " . . . men climbed down to cut off slabs of meat." MacDougall, 321.

Page 401. " . . . trying to dig a hole,' recalled a miner." Beeching, 152.

Page 402. " . . . A handful of men could do it." Bessie, *Men in Battle*, 274.

Page 402. " . . . He then shot himself with his rifle." Hoar, 219.

Page 402. " . . . Of the six, only four returned." Dan Bessie, 95.

Page 403. " . . . Graceful silvery objects." Fisher, *Comrades*, 150.

Page 403. " . . . worst day, so far, of this life." Dan Bessie, 91.

Page 403. " . . . Well, I can give you my heartfelt sympathy." *Volunteer for Liberty,* August 26, 1938.

Page 403. " . . . For myself, I am afraid of breaking." Dan Bessie, 92.

Page 403. " . . . fish, green and slimy, white, dying." Wolff, 357.

Page 403. " . . . I'll be seeing you in Sunday school." Joe North, *NM,* August 15, 1939.

Page 403. " . . . Others claimed it was 'The International.'" Wolff, 359.

CHAPTER 18: LA DESPEDIDA

Page 405. " . . . unreliable elements." Bessie, *Men in Battle*, 334ff.

Page 405. " . . . Americans were killed, but the Spaniards were unharmed." Geiser to Landis, BU.

Page 405. " . . . feed me to the lions in the Barcelona zoo." Bessie, *Men in Battle*, 322.

Page 406. " . . . the taste of victory on our lips." Gates, *Story*, 66.

Page 406. " . . . 'If he lives,'" said Bessie. Watt laughed." Bessie, *Men in Battle*, 325.

Page 407. " . . . Everybody wanted to live." Landis, 582.

Page 407. " . . . ordered to repel enemy attacks." Martínez Bande, *La Batalla de Ebro,* 229.

Page 407. " . . . any other battle he had seen in the war." Wheeler memo, box 84, BU.

Page 407. " . . . amid dozens of smashed rifles." Cook to Landis, April 15, 1966, BU.
Page 407. " . . . not shooting at us, just jeering." Wolff, 385.
Page 407. " . . . the most painful of my period in Spain." Wolff to Landis, BU.
Page 408. " . . . Death to the Fascist bastards!" Toynbee, 137.
Page 408. " . . . I never saw him again." MacDougall, 167.
Page 408. " . . . It still bothers me." Beeching, 139.
Page 408. " . . . no longer fit for combat." Gates, *Story*, 6.
Page 408, note 1. Cook, 139.
Page 408, note 2. " . . . when officially relieved." Delperrié de Bayoc, 313.
Page 408. " . . . that last forced march." Cook to Landis, April 15, 1966, BU.
Page 408. " . . . there was no singing." Bessie, *Men in Battle*, 345.
Page 409. " . . . I want to go ho-OME!" Battalion folklore.
Page 409, note 4. Lopez Silveira. Fugitive pamphlet.
Page 410. " . . . men who had learned to fight." SACB, 85–86.
Page 410. " . . . and we shall kill it." *Volunteer for Liberty*, October 17, 1938.
Page 411. " . . . I guess we did a kind of shag." Sheean, 266.
Page 411. " . . . these were true soldiers." Matthews, *Education*, 141.
Page 411. " . . . every last one of them was crying." Maury Cohen, in Katz, 61.
Page 411. " . . . laurels of the Spanish Republic's victory—come back!" Carroll, 205.
Page 411, note 5. Moscow 548/61/844.
Page 412. " . . . bedding down in the stalls." Toynbee, 104.
Page 412. " . . . took them home to concoct a meal." Beeching, 190.
Page 412. " . . . dark again by mid-afternoon." Fred Thomas, 165.
Page 412. " . . . full of pomp and self-importance." Wolff, 392.
Page 412. " . . . In our rags we felt superior." Ben Iceland file, BU.
Page 412, note 6. Alexander, 241.
Page 413. " . . . when British soldiers evacuated from Dunkirk in 1940 paid theirs." Ibid., 241.
Page 413, note 8. Krivitsky, 80.
Page 414. " . . . deserter and anti-Communist." Moscow 345/6/855.
Page 414. " . . . 1938—AÑO DE LA VICTORIA." Bessie, *Un-Americans*, 178ff.
Page 414, note 9. Beeching, 192.
Page 414. " . . . when I drive back down,' replied the reporter." Bessie, *Un-Americans*, 136.
Page 415. " . . . no friends or relatives at home able to identify him." *NYT*, December 3, 1938.
Page 415. " . . . trapped in the Valencia sector." Ben Iceland ms, BU.
Page 415. " . . . the road to slavery!" de Cunha.
Page 415. " . . . no cheering, no elation." *NYT*, January 25, 1939.
Page 415. " . . . still alive in France." Bessie, *Un-Americans*, 138.
Page 415. " . . . going to be a revolution." Katz, 62.
Page 415. " . . . to the goddamn *park?*" Bessie, *Un-Americans*, 139.
Page 416. " . . . till we reach New York and disband." Ibid., 140.
Page 416. " . . . catch tipping the fink stewards goes over the side!" Ibid., 142.
Page 417. " . . . and nothing is what we get." Ibid., 148.
Page 417. " . . . It was pointless to reply to this." Sheldon Jones interview, 1968.
Page 417. " . . . overruled the policy." SACB, 87, 97.
Page 417, note 10. Kraljic, 124.
Page 417. " . . . No Communist ever admits anything." Gladnick to author.
Page 418. " . . . DOWN WITH DALADIER DECREES." Bessie, *Un-Americans*, 184.
Page 419. " . . . Somebody played 'Taps.'" *NYT*, December 16, 1938.
Page 419. " . . . invalidated international law." Ickes diary, quoted in Geiser, 194.

CHAPTER 19: "PREMATURE ANTI-FASCISTS" AND ALL THAT

Page 421. " . . . an apartment for two weeks in the Village." Voros, 449.

Page 421. " . . . the boys from Spain." SACB, 92.

Page 421. " . . . I know what Hitler is doing to my people." *Life*, March 28, 1938.

Page 422. " . . . who was responsible." HUAC (1938), 7730–36.

Page 422. " . . . the XVth Brigade SIM policeman." Ibid., 7795–7811.

Page 422. " . . . returned to the University of Michigan." Elman Service interview.

Page 423. " . . . the crap shooter with his last buck." Gerassi, 126, 222.

Page 423. " . . . his *lavochka* ('market stall')." Howson, 241.

Page 424. " . . . to protect their womenfolk." Herrick to author.

Page 424. " . . . and then crushed it." Gladnick to author, August 8, 1968.

Page 424. " . . . a car would hit me and end it all." Fisher, *Comrades,* 166–67.

Page 425. " . . . betrayed the VALB at home." Steve Nelson papers, BU.

Page 425. " . . . wouldn't be allowed to join." SACB, 123.

Page 425. " . . . the long arms of commissars quite enough." Brome, 290.

Page 425. " . . . There's no such a goddam thing." Collum, 14.

Page 425. " . . . knew more about blacks than he did." Gerassi, 67.

Page 425. " . . . a lot of bull." Collum, 37.

Page 425. " . . . But this was another front. I was home." Ibid., 37.

Page 426. " . . . road to fascism in America." Quoted in Romerstein, 79.

Page 426. " . . . not be welcome at future meetings." SACB, 144.

Page 426. " . . . to be allowed to fight Fascists." Gates, *Story,* 84.

Page 427, note 5. Dimitrov to "Comrade Fitin," May 13, 1942 (original in Moscow 495/73/188).

Page 427. " . . . marked S.D. ('suspected of disloyalty')." Gates, *Story,* 84.

Page 427. " . . . on their service records." Carroll, 259.

Page 27. " . . . Americans who had fought in Spain." Haynes and Klehr, 123–27.

Page 428. " . . . a Young Communist League organizer in Ohio." Kempton, 317.

Page 428. " . . . until a legal fight forced a reversal." Carroll, 310, 348.

Page 428. " . . . a mortar shell blew off his leg." *Yank,* March 2, 1945; "Fire and Blood in the Jungle," *Liberty,* July 3, 1943.

Page 428. " . . . while 15 percent said it did not." Dollard, passim.

Page 429. " . . . under the blanket of 'internal democracy.'" Landis to Ben Iceland, BU.

Page 429. " . . . more than one-tenth of surviving veterans." Wellman interview, 2001.

Page 430. " . . . not somehow aliens in their own country." Kempton, 315.

Page 432. " . . . failed to make a dent in the placard ban." *NYT,* July 19, 1964.

Page 433. " . . . shot up for nothing." Gates notes, UI.

Page 433. " . . . some of it true, some imagined." Ibid.

Page 434. " . . . versus only seven thousand in 1957." Gates, *Evolution,* 6.

Page 434. " . . . dropped to three thousand." Haynes and Klehr, 39.

Page 434. " . . . distrust it as he would a racket." Hemingway, "Notes on the Next War," in *By-Line,* 205-17.

Page 434. " . . . the cleverest opportunist in modern history." Hemingway, "Wings over Africa," in *By-Line,* 229–35.

Page 434. " " . . . and maintain strict neutrality." Hemingway, "Program for U.S. Realism," in *By-Line,* 290–93.

Page 434. " . . . misery, *personal* significance." *NM,* November 5, 1940, 28.

Page 435. " . . . of a very old lion." Hemingway, *For Whom the Bell Tolls,* chap. 42.

Page 435, note 10. Nelson interview with author.

Page 436. " . . . a VALB resolution condemned the book."

Page 436. " . . . earth didn't move, only the bedsprings?" Bessie, *Un-Americans,* 212.

Page 436. " . . . himself had to pay 6 percent for his money." *American Dialogue,* October, 1964, 13.

Page 436. " . . . written in the last months of the war." *NM,* February 14, 1939.

Page 436. " . . . the goof of a lifetime." Fred Keller to Carlos Baker, May 12, 1966, Illinois Archive GI-107.

Page 437. " . . . we would have won." Katz, 77.

Page 437. " . . . splashed a little on the generalissimo's grave." *Volunteer,* September 2003, 3.

Page 437. " . . . where he had served as commandant." Herrick, *Jumping the Line,* 212.

Page 437. " . . . for wine and cheese." *Chicago Tribune Magazine,* December 2, 1983, 51.

Page 438. " . . . What to think of all this?" Villar to author.

Page 438. " . . . with Spanish citizenship." Cierva y Hoces, 368.

Page 438. " . . . a bit of paper with colors." Tony Hendra, "Old Soldiers," *Harper's,* July 1997, 4.

BIBLIOGRAPHY

PUBLISHED SOURCES

Acier, Marcel, ed. *From Spanish Trenches: Recent Letters from Spain.* New York: Modern Age, 1937.

Alexander, Bill. *British Volunteers for Liberty, Spain 1936–1939.* London: Lawrence and Wishart, 1982.

Angus, John. *With the International Brigade in Spain.* Loughborough: Loughborough University, 1983.

Atlee, C. R. *As It Happened.* New York: Viking Press, 1954.

Aznar, Manuel. *Historia Militar de la Guerra de España.* Madrid: Ediciones Idea, 1940.

Baxell, Richard. *British Volunteers in the Spanish Civil War.* London: Routledge, 2004.

Beeching, William C. *Canadian Volunteers: Spain, 1936–1939.* Regina: University of Regina, 1989.

Bessie, Alvah. *Men in Battle: A Story of Americans in Spain.* New York: Charles Scribner and Sons, 1939. Reprinted in 1954 under the title *Veterans of the Abraham Lincoln Brigade.*

——. *The Un-Americans.* New York: Cameron Associates, 1957.

——, ed. *The Heart of Spain.* New York: Veterans of the Abraham Lincoln Brigade, 1952.

Bessie, Alvah, and Albert Prago, eds. *Our Fight: Writings by Veterans of the Abraham Lincoln Brigade.* New York: Monthly Review Press, 1987.

Bessie, Dan. *Alvah Bessie's Spanish Civil War Notebooks.* Lexington: University Press of Kentucky, 2002.

Bird, Kai, and Martin Sherwin. *American Prometheus: The Triumph and Tragedy of J. Robert Oppenheimer.* New York: Alfred A. Knopf, 2005.

Bolleten, Burnett. *The Spanish Civil War: Revolution and Counterrevolution.* Chapel Hill: University of North Carolina Press, 1991.

Book of the XV Brigade. Madrid: Commissariat of War, 1938.

Brome, Vincent. *The International Brigades.* New York: William Morrow, 1966.

Calmer, Alan, ed. *Salud!* New York: International Publishers, 1938.

Cane, Lawrence. *Fighting Fascism in Europe: The World War II Letters of an American Veteran of the Spanish Civil War.* New York: Fordham University Press, 2003.

Carpenter, Humphrey. *W. H. Auden: A Biography.* London: George Allen and Unwin, 1981.

Carroll, Peter H. *The Odyssey of the Abraham Lincoln Brigade.* Stanford: Stanford University Press, 1994.

Castells, Andreu. *Las Brigadas Internacionales de la Guerra de España.* Barcelona: Ariel, 1974.

Cierva y Hoces, Ricardo de la. *Brigadas Internacionales, 1936–1996.* Madrid: Fenix, 1997.

Collum, Danny Duncan, ed. *African Americans in the Spanish Civil War.* New York: G. K. Hall, 1992.

Colmegna, Hector. *Diario de un Médico Argentino en la Guerra de España.* Buenos Aires: Espasa-Calpe, 1941.

Colodny, Robert. *The Struggle for Madrid.* New York: Paine-Whitman, 1958.

Cook, Judith. *Apprentices of Freedom.* London: Quartet Books, 1979.

Copeman, Fred. *Reason in Revolt*. London: Blandford Books, 1948.

Corkhill, David, and Stuart Rawnsley, eds. *The Road to Spain: Anti-Fascists at War, 1936–39*. Dunfermline: Borderline Press, 1981.

Cortada, James W., ed. *Historical Dictionary of the Spanish Civil War*. Westport, Conn.: Greenwood Press, 1982.

Cowles, Virginia. *Looking for Trouble*. New York: Harper and Brothers, 1941.

Cox, Geoffrey. *Defence of Madrid*. London: Victor Gollancz, 1937.

Cronin, Sean. *Frank Ryan: The Search for a Republic*. Dublin: Repsol Publishers, 1980.

Dallet, Joe. *Letters from Spain*. New York: Workers Library Publishers, 1938.

Davenport-Hines, Richard. *Auden*. New York: Vintage, 1999.

Delmer, Sefton. *Trail Sinister: An Autobiography, Vol. 1*. London: Secker and Warburg, 1961.

Delperrié de Bayoc, Jacques. *Las Brigadas Internacionales*. Madrid: Ediciones Jucar, 1978.

Dollard, John. *Fear in Battle*. New Haven: Yale University Institute of Human Relations, 1943.

Dorland, Norman. "In Franco's Prison Camp." *New Masses*, November 22, 1938.

Eby, Cecil. *Between the Bullet and the Lie: American Volunteers in the Spanish Civil War*. New York: Holt, Rinehart and Winston, 1969.

Elstob, Peter. *Spanish Prisoner*. London: Macmillan, 1939.

Felsen, Milt. *The Anti-Warrior: A Memoir*. Iowa City: University of Iowa Press, 1989.

Fischer, Louis. *Men and Politics*. New York: Duell, Sloan and Pearce, 1941.

Fisher, Harry. *Comrades: Tales of a Brigadista in the Spanish Civil War*. Lincoln: University of Nebraska Press, 1997.

Francis, Hywel. *Miners Against Fascism: Wales and the Spanish Civil War*. London: Lawrence and Wishart, 1984.

Franklin, Sidney. *Bullfighter from Brooklyn*. Englewood Cliffs, N.J.: Prentice-Hall, 1952.

Gates, John. *The Evolution of an American Communist*. N.p.: Published by author, 1957.

———. *The Story of an American Communist*. New York: Nelson and Sons, 1958.

Geiser, Carl. *Prisoners of the Good Fight*. Westport, Conn.: Lawrence Hill, 1986.

Gellhorn, Martha. *The Face of War*. London: Hart-Davis, 1959.

Gerassi, John. *The Premature Antifascists: North American Volunteers in the Spanish Civil War*. New York: Praeger, 1986.

Gillain, Nick. *El Mercenario: Diario de un Combatante Rojo*. Tangier: Editorial Tanger, 1939.

Graham, Frank, ed. *The Battle of Jarama, 1937*. Gateshead: Howe Brothers, 1987.

Gregory, Walter. *The Shallow Grave: A Memoir of the Spanish Civil War*. London: Gollancz, 1986.

Gurney, Jason. *Crusade in Spain*. London: Faber and Faber, 1974.

Guttman, Allen. *The Wound in the Heart: America and the Spanish Civil War*. New York: Free Press of Glencoe, 1962.

Haldane, Charlotte. *Truth Will Out*. New York: Vanguard, 1950.

Haynes, John Earl, and Harvey Klehr. *In Denial: Historians, Communism, and Espionage*. San Francisco: Encounter, 2003.

Haywood, Harry. *Black Bolshevik: Autobiography of an Afro-American Communist*. Chicago: Liberator Press, 1978.

Heikkinen, K. E., ed. *Meidan Poikamme Espanjassa [Our Boys in Spain]*. Finnish Workers Federation, 1939. Translated by Matti Mattson, 2002.

Hemingway, Ernest. *For Whom the Bell Tolls*. New York: Charles Scribner's Sons, 1941.

———. *By-Line: Ernest Hemingway*. Edited by William White. New York: Charles Scribner's Sons, 1967.

Herbst, Josephine. "The Starched Blue Sky of Spain." *The Noble Savage* 1 (1960): 76–117.

Herrick, William. *Hermanos!* New York: Simon and Schuster, 1969.

———. *Jumping the Line: The Adventures and Misadventures of an American Radical*. Madison: University of Wisconsin Press, 1998.

Hoar, Victor. *The Mackenzie-Papineau Battalion*. Vancouver: Copp Clark, 1969.

Hopkins, James K. *Into the Heart of the Fire: The British in the Spanish Civil War*. Stanford: Stanford University Press, 1998.

Howson, Gerald. *Arms for Spain: The Untold Story of the Spanish Civil War*. London: John Murray, 1998.

The International Brigades: Foreign Assistants of the Spanish Reds. Madrid: Spanish Office of Information, 1948.

Jackson, Michael. *Fallen Sparrows: The International Brigades in the Spanish Civil War*. Philadelphia: American Philosophical Society, 1996.

Johnston, Verle B. *Legions of Babel: The International Brigades in the Spanish Civil War*. University Park: Pennsylvania State University Press, 1967.

Katz, William L. *The Lincoln Brigade: A Picture History*. New York: Atheneum, 1989.

Kemp, Peter. *The Thorns of Memory: Memoirs*. London: Sinclair-Stevenson, 1990.

Kempton, Murray. *Part of Our Time: Some Ruins and Monuments of the Thirties*. New York: Simon and Schuster, 1955.

Klehr, Harvey, John Earl Haynes, and Fridrikh Igorevich Firsove. *The Secret World of American Communism*. New Haven: Yale University Press, 1994.

Koltsov, Mikail. *Diario de la Guerra de España*. Madrid: Ruedo Ibérico, n.d.

Kraljic, John Peter. "The Croatian Community in North America and the Spanish Civil War." Master's thesis, Hunter College, 2002.

Krivitsky, W. C. *In Stalin's Secret Service*. New York: Harper and Brothers, 1939.

Landis, Arthur H. *The Abraham Lincoln Brigade*. New York: Citadel Press, 1967.

Langer, Elinor. *Josephine Herbst*. Boston: Little Brown, 1983.

Lee, Laurie. *A Moment of War*. New York: New Press, 1991.

Lerude, Warren, and Marion Merriman, eds. *American Commander in Spain: Robert Hale Merriman and the Abraham Lincoln Brigade*. Reno: University of Nevada Press, 1986.

Lister, Enrique. *Memorias de un Luchador*. Madrid: G. del Toro, 1977.

Lizón Gadea, Adolfo. *Brigadas Internacionales en España*. Madrid: Editora Nacional, 1940.

Lojendio, Luís María de. *Operaciones Militares de la Guerra de España*. Barcelona: Montaner y Simon, 1940.

Longo, Luigi. *Las Brigadas Internaciones en España*. Mexico City: Ediciones Era, 1966.

MacDougall, Ian, ed. *Voices from the Spanish Civil War*. Edinburgh: Polygon, 1986.

Martínez Bande, José Manuel. *Brigadas Internacionales*. Barcelona: Luís de Caralt, n.d.

———. *La Gran Ofensiva sobre Zaragoza*. Madrid: Editorial San Martín, 1973.

———. *La Llegada al Mar*. Madrid: Editorial San Martín, 1975.

———. *La Lucha en Torno a Madrid en el Invierno de 1936–37*. Madrid: Editorial San Martín, 1968.

Matthews, Herbert. *Education of a Correspondent*. New York: Harcourt, Brace, 1946.

———. *Two Wars and More to Come*. New York: Carrick Evans, 1938.

Monks, Joe. *With the Reds in Andalusia.* London: John Cornford Poetry Group, 1985.

Moorhead, Caroline. *Gellhorn: A Twentieth-Century Life.* New York: Henry Holt, 2003.

Mugarza Gil, Bernardo. *España en Llamas.* Barcelona: N.p., 1988.

Nelson, Cary. *The Aura of the Cause: A Photo Album for North American Volunteers.* Urbana: University of Illinois Press, 1997.

Nelson, Cary, and Jefferson Hendricks. *Madrid 1937: Letters of the Abraham Lincoln Brigade from the Spanish War.* London: Routledge, 1996.

Nelson, Steve, et al. *American Radical.* Pittsburgh: University of Pittsburgh Press, 1981.

———. *The Volunteers.* New York: Masses and Mainstream, 1953.

North, Joseph. *No Men Are Strangers.* New York: International Publishers, 1958.

Ornitz, Lou. *Captured by Franco.* New York: Friends of the Abraham Lincoln Brigade, 1939.

Orwell, George. *Homage to Catalonia.* London: Secker and Warburg, 1938.

———. "Inside the Whale." In *Such, Such Were the Joys.* New York: Harcourt, Brace, 1952.

Payne, Robert. *The Civil War in Spain.* New York: G. P. Putnam's Sons, 1962.

Payne, Stanley. *The Spanish Civil War, the Soviet Union, and Communism.* New Haven: Yale University Press, 2004.

Radosh, Ronald, Mary R. Habeck, and Grigory Sevostianov. *Spain Betrayed: The Soviet Union in the Spanish Civil War.* New Haven: Yale University Press, 2002.

Rees, Richlard. *A Theory of My Time.* London: Secker and Warburg, 1963.

Regler, Gustav. *The Owl of Minerva.* New York: Farrar, Straus and Cudahy, 1959.

Richardson, R. Dan. *Comintern Army: The International Brigades and the Spanish Civil War.* Lexington: University Press of Kentucky, 1982.

Riordan, Michael. *Connolly Column.* Dublin: New Books, 1979.

Rolfe, Edwin. *The Lincoln Battalion.* New York: Random House, 1939.

Romerstein, Herbert. *Heroic Victims: Stalin's Foreign Legion in the Spanish Civil War.* Washington: Council for the Defense of Freedom, 1994.

Rosenstone, Robert A. *Crusade of the Left: The Lincoln Battalion in the Spanish Civil War.* New York: Pegasus, 1969.

Rubin, Hank. *Spain's Cause Was Mine: A Memoir of an American Medic in the Spanish Civil War.* Carbondale: Southern Illinois University Press, 1997.

Rust, W. *Britons in Spain.* London: Lawrence and Wishart, 1939.

Salus Larrazabal, Ramón. *Historia del Ejercito Popular de la República.* Vols. 1–3. Madrid: Editora Nacional, 1973.

Sheean, Vincent. *Not Peace but a Sword.* Garden City, N.Y.: Doubleday, Doran, 1939.

Smith, W.H.B. *Small Arms of the World.* New York, 1962.

Spender, Stephen. *World Within World.* NewYork: Harcourt, Brace, 1951.

Starobin, Joseph. *The Life and Death of an American Hero.* New York: Young Communist League, 1938.

Stephens, D. P. *A Memoir of the Spanish Civil War: An Armenian-Canadian in the Lincoln Battalion.* St. John's: Memorial University of Newfoundland, 2000.

Stradling, Robert. *History and Legend: Writing the International Brigades.* Cardiff: University of Wales Press, 2003.

———. *The Irish and the Spanish Civil War.* Manchester: Manchester University Press, 1999.

Thomas, Frank. *Brother Against Brother: Experiences of a British Volunteer in the Spanish Civil War.* Bridgend: Sutton, 1998. Includes "Diary of Sid Hamm," 155–71.

Thomas, Fred A. *To Tilt at Windmills: A Memoir of the Spanish Civil War*. East Lansing: Michigan State University Press, 1996.

Thomas, Hugh. *The Spanish Civil War*. New York: Harper and Brothers, 1961; rev. ed. Modern Library, 2001.

Tisa, John. *Recalling the Good Fight: An Autobiography of the Spanish Civil War*. South Hadley, Mass.: Bergin and Garvey, 1981.

[Tisa, John]. *Story of the Abraham Lincoln Battalion*. New York: Sheridan Square Press, 1937.

Toynbee, Philip, ed. *The Distant Drum: Reflections on the Spanish Civil War*. London: Sedgwick and Jackson, 1976.

U.S. Congress, House. *Hearings Before a Special Committee on Un-American Activities*. Washington, D.C., 1938 and 1940.

U.S. Department of State. *Foreign Relations of the United States*. Washington, D.C.: Government Printing Office, 1937–39.

United States, Subversive Activities Control, docket No. 108-53. *Report and Order of the Board*. Washington, D.C., December 1955.

Vidal, César. *Las Brigadas Internacionales*. Madrid: Editorial Espasa, 1998.

Volunteer for Liberty (facsimile of Spanish issues). New York: Veterans of the Abraham Lincoln Battalion, 1949.

Voros, Sandor. *American Commissar*. Philadelphia: Chilton, 1961.

Weintraub, Stanley. *The Last Great Cause: Intellectuals and the Spanish Civil War*. New York: Weybright and Talley, 1968.

Williams, Colin, et al., eds. *Memorial of the Spanish Civil War*. Stroud: Alan Sutton, 1996.

Wintringham, Tom. *English Captain*. London: Faber and Faber, 1939.

Wolfe, Thomas. *The Letters of Thomas Wolfe*. Edited by Elizabeth Nowell. New York: Charles Scribner's Sons, 1956.

Wolff, Milton. *Another Hill*. Urbana: University of Illinois Press, 1994.

Wullschleger, Max. *Schweizer Kampfen in Spanien*. Zurich, 1939. Contains Konrad Schmidt, "In Francos Kriegsgefangenschaft."

Zuehlke. *The Gallant Cause*. Vancouver: Whitecap Books, 1996.

UNPUBLISHED SOURCES

Amery, Al. "Something More." Labadie collection, UM.

Copic, Vladimir. "Diary." ALBA, NYU.

Cunha, Jose Gay de. "La Bandera de la Brigada," Fugitive offprint.

Gladnick, Robert. "To the Battlefield." [Jarama.]

Lopez Silveira, Juan. "Última marca de lás brigadás internacionales." Fugitive offprint.

Ross, Adolph. "American Volunteers in the Spanish War." Typescript. 1993.

Villar, Fausto Esteban. "Un Valencianito en la Brigada Lincoln" Labadie Collection, UM. English translation by Paul Sharkey under the title "A Little Valencian in the Lincoln Brigade."

race. *See also* chauvinism
  Communist Party of the United States
    of America and, 99–100, 139, 178–79,
    193, 425
  in XVth International Brigade, 268
  in International Brigades, 179n3, 192–93
  in Lincoln Battalion, 98, 178–79
  veterans and, 425
Rackley, Mildred, 80
Radosh, Ronald, 447
Rahman, Evelyn Hutchins, 197
Rajcovic, John. *See* Gerlach, John
Rajk, Lajos, 79n13
Rappoport, Milton, 76
rations
  at Albares, 263
  at Belchite, 306
  for British Battalion, 33
  at Brunete, 197, 199, 201
  at Ebro River, 351, 391
  for XVth International Brigade, 282,
    286, 306, 315–16
  at Gandesa, 315–16, 397
  for International Brigades, 7, 109–10,
    240n4, 313
  at Jarama, 63–64, 107, 109–10
  at Madrid, 117
  for prisoners of war, 374, 375, 376, 378,
    379–80
  at Ripoll, 412
  at San Pedro de Cardeña, 374, 379–80
  at Tarazona de la Mancha, 313
  at Teruel, 276, 277, 282, 286
  in transit, 15, 17, 18, 19, 21
  at Villanueva de la Jara, 29, 36
  at Zaragoza, 211–12
Raven, Robert, 16, 96–97, 160, 432
Recalling the Good Fight (Tisa), 446
records, xii, xii–xiv, 11n9, 429n7
recruitment. *See also* muster; transit
  for British Battalion, 237, 266
  by Comintern, 4–9, 25n20
  by Communist Party of Spain, 6
  by Communist Party of the United
    States of America, xi, 4, 9–12, 131–32,
    133n5, 138–44, 164–65, 358, 371, 384–86

Fifth Regiment assists with, 6–7
for XVth International Brigade,
  100–101, 259–62, 287, 319, 405
by Friends of the Abraham Lincoln
  Brigade, 136
for International Brigades, 4–9, 25n20,
  208–9, 266–67, 313–14, 437
for Lincoln Battalion, xi, 9–12, 44, 69,
  89, 131–32, 133n5, 136, 138–44, 178, 352,
  357–61, 362–63, 384–86
for Mackenzie-Papineau Battalion,
  231–32, 237
by *Mundo Obrero*, 3
for Republican Army, 6
by Soviet Union, 4
for 24th Battalion, 100–101
U.S. government opposes, 1–3, 16, 136–37
for Washington Battalion, 143, 155, 164–65
by Young Communist League, 4
Red Cross, 377
Regan, Charlie, 104, 224
Regenstreif, John. *See* Gates, John
Regler, Gustav, 25, 27
Reid, Arnold, 144, 145–46, 147, 148, 234, 395
Reid, Pat, 311
Reilley, H. J., 253n14
Reisky, Arnold. *See* Reid, Arnold
Reiss, Dave, 263, 283, 287, 289–91, 292–93
relief
  at Brunete, 176–80
  of Dimitrov Battalion, 171
  at Ebro River, 347–53, 356–58, 361–62,
    362–66, 398–, 403–4, 408–9
  of XVth International Brigade, 280–81,
    286, 408–9
  at Jarama, 142–43
  of Mackenzie-Papineau Battalion, 361
  at Marsa, 352–53, 356–58, 361–62,
    362–66, 409–10
  at Mora de Rubielos, 286
  at Morata, 171, 172
  at Teruel, 280–81
  at Zaragoza, 241–42
repatriation. *See also* demobilization;
  veterans
  from British Battalion, 412–13